22nd Pacific Asia Conference on Language, Information and Computation 2008 (PACLIC 22)

Cebu City, Philippines
20 – 22 November 2008

ISBN: 978-1-5108-4021-8

Proceedings of

The 22nd Pacific Asia Conference on Language, Information and Computation

PACLIC 22

Dates
November 20-22, 2008

Venue
The University of the Philippines Visayas Cebu College
Cebu City, Philippines

Hosted By
De La Salle University – Manila

Sponsored by
Philippine Council for Advanced Science and Technology Research and Development, Department of Science and Technology

Commission on Higher Education, Philippines

Published by

De La Salle University – Manila (DLSU)

http://www.dlsu.edu.ph

(contact information)

Dr. Rachel Roxas

College of Computer Studies

De La Salle University – Manila

2401 Taft Avenue,

Manila, Philippines 1004

(roxasr@dlsu.edu.ph)

ACKNOWLEDGEMENTS

PACLIC 22 is financially supported by De La Salle University-Manila, the Philippine Council for Advanced Science and Technology Research and Development - Department of Science and Technology, and the Philippine Commission on Higher Education.

FOREWORD

It is my great pleasure and honor to present to you the proceedings for the 22nd Pacific Asia Conference on Language, Information and Computation which is held for the first time in the Philippines!

I have been eagerly anticipating the hosting of the 22nd PACLIC this year 2008 for it also marks the 12th year of our involvement in natural language processing (NLP) research in the country. Way back in 1996, Allan Borra and I started a funded project on IsaWika!, a machine translation (MT) system involving the Filipino language. We have come a long way in our NLP research since then. For the past years, we have considered not only MT, but also text summarization, text simplification, natural language generation, information extraction, information retrieval, and language documentation, to name a few.

Secondly, consistent with the vision of PACLIC, we are also happy with the growth of the collaboration between experts on linguistics and computational aspects of languages in the country. This is evidenced by this year's 5th National Natural Language Processing Research Symposium, which reflects the zeal and commitment of researchers from all over the country to get involved in this area of research and maximize the potential of bringing these two areas of knowledge together.

And last, but not the least, we have come to realize that our attempts to remain in our comfort zone of textual information had become futile, and we have consequently expanded on input data from pure text to audios (speech) and videos (Filipino sign language).

This growth of our activities and participation is consistently reflected in Pacific Asia researches as evidenced by the papers that are presented in this Conference, and by the topics of our invited and plenary speakers to this conference. We have received a wide variety of papers on linguistics, information, and computation projects of researchers from thirteen countries (namely: Brazil, Canada, China, France, Hong Kong, India, Indonesia, Japan, Philippines, South Korea, Taiwan, United Kingdom, and the United States). Our Program Committee members have done a difficult undertaking in examining the 71 papers submitted to us for evaluation. Through double-blind review, 41% were accepted as regular papers (or 29 papers) and another 20% as posters (or 14 papers), or an overall acceptance rate of 61%. PACLIC Conference proceedings are ISI indexed and is made possible through the coordination of Professor Yasunari Harada through the Waseda University Library Institutional Repository.

Our colleagues from all over the world have graciously accepted our invitation for them to speak at our Conference this year to share with us their expertise in various fields in linguistics, information and computation. We have the privilege of having Mr. Adam Pease as invited speaker, and Professors Danilo Dayag, Trevor Johnston, Chungmin Lee, Haizhou Li, Patrick Saint-Dizier, Sachiko Shudo and Gary Simons as plenary speakers.

I would also like to thank our partners in academe, government, and industry for the support that they have provided for the successful hosting of this Conference.

Gratitude is also expressed to our program committee co-chairs, Professors Hee-Rahk Chae and Tom Lai, and of course, to our local organizing committee headed by Professor Charibeth Cheng, with members Nathalie Rose Lim, and local Cebu partners, Professors Cherry Lyn Sta. Romana and Robert Roxas, and their institutions, the Cebu Institute of Technology and the University of the Philippines Visayas Cebu College (which generously hosted the venue for the conference), and to our staff and students.

I sincerely hope that we will all benefit and be refreshed by the ideas shared in the Conference, and enjoy the beautiful Cebu City, Philippines.

Rachel Edita O. Roxas
Program Committee Chair, PACLIC 22
Dean, College of Computer Studies
De La Salle University-Manila

CONFERENCE ORGANIZERS

Steering Committee of PACLIC

Jae-Woong Choe, Korea University, Seoul

Yasunari Harada, Waseda University, Tokyo

Chu-Ren Huang, Academia Sinica, Taipei

Kim Teng Lua, Chinese and Oriental Languages Information Processing Society, Singapore

Maosong Sun, Tsinghua University, Beijing

Benjamin T'sou, City University of Hong Kong, Hong Kong

Program Committee Chair

Rachel Edita Roxas, De La Salle University-Manila (Chair)

Program Committee Co-Chairs

Hee-Rahk Chae, Hankuk University of Foreign Studies (Co-Chair)

Tom Lai, City University of Hong Kong (Co-Chair)

Program Committee

Sae-Youn Cho (Kangwon National University)

Kazuhiko Fukushima (Kansai Gaidai University)

Takao Gunji (Kobe Shoin Women's University)

Yasunari Harada (Waseda University)

Shu-Kai Hsieh (National Taiwan Normal University

Kiyoshi Ishikawa (Hosei University)

Dong Hong Ji (Wuhan University, China)

Jong-Bok Kim (Kyung Hee University)

Hiroki Koga (Saga University)

Oi Yee Kwong (City University of Hong Kong)

Minhaeng Lee (Yonsei University)

Qin Lu (The Hong Kong Polytechnic University)

Laurent Prevot (CNRS, Université de Toulouse)

Byong-Rae Ryu (Chungnam National University)

Shu-chuan Tseng (Academia Sinica)

Jie Xu (Huazhong Normal University)

Eun-Jung Yoo (Seoul National University)

Ae-Sun Yoon (Pusan National University)

Quan Zhang (Chinese Academy of Sciences)

Jun Zhao (Chinese Academy of Sciences)

Reviewers

Winnie Cheng (Hong Kong Polytechnic University)

Kazuhiko Fukushima (Kansai Gaidai University)

Takao Gunji (Kobe Shoin Women's University)

Yasunari Harada (Waseda University)

Shu-Kai Hsieh (National Taiwan Normal University

Chu-Ren Huang (Academia Sinica)

Kiyoshi Ishikawa (Hosei University)

Dong Hong Ji (Wuhan University, China)

Jong-Bok Kim (Kyung Hee University)

Hiroki Koga (Saga University)

Oi Yee Kwong (City University of Hong Kong)

Minhaeng Lee (Yonsei University)

Qin Lu (The Hong Kong Polytechnic University)

Thi Minh Huyen Nguyen (Vietnam National University)

Laurent Prevot (CNRS, Université de Toulouse)

Byong-Rae Ryu (Chungnam National University)

Shu-chuan Tseng (Academia Sinica)

Doreen Wu (Hong Kong Polytechnic University)

Jie Xu (Huazhong Normal University)

Eun-Jung Yoo (Seoul National University)

Quan Zhang (Chinese Academy of Sciences)

Jun Zhao (Chinese Academy of Sciences)

PACLIC22 Local Organizing Committee

Charibeth Cheng, De La Salle University-Manila (Chair)

Nathalie Rose Lim, De La Salle University-Manila

Robert Roxas, University of the Philippines Visayas Cebu College

Cherry Lyn Sta. Romana, Cebu Institute of Technology

TABLE OF CONTENTS

The Discourse of Print Advertising in the Philippines: Generic Structures and Linguistic Features

Danilo T. Dayag
Department of English and Applied Linguistics
De La Salle University
Manila, The Philippines

This paper aims to examine the generic structures and linguistic properties of ads in Philippine magazines. Taken from the *Corpus of Asian Magazine Advertising: The Philippine Database*, the corpus consists of seventy-four ads for consumer nondurables such as medicines, vitamins and food supplements, and cosmetic/beauty/personal hygiene products. The study found that the ads demonstrated preference for certain generic structures and linguistic features, making them 'reason' (rather than 'tickle') ads which may be described as direct. The paper argues that the directness of these ads contributes to making them covert communication.

Key words: print ads, genre, generic structures, linguistic novelty, assertives, directives

1. Introduction

One of the most ubiquitous discourses is advertisements. When we watch TV in the comfort of our living rooms, we are bombarded with ads; when we read a newspaper or magazine, somehow our attention is distracted by one form of an ad or another. On our way to school or office, we come across ads in various shapes or colors. Indeed, advertising, whether print, broadcast, or any other type, is part of our everyday lives.

It is no wonder then that advertising discourse has attracted the attention of scholars in over two decades. Simpson (2001) acknowledges that there has been "an enormous upsurge of interest in the linguistic and discoursal characteristics of advertising" (p. 589), adding that the studies conducted have been anchored on different traditions and perspectives, such as cognitive, cultural and anthropological, genre and register analysis, critical discourse analysis, and linguistic pragmatics (Simpson, 2001, p. 590). In recent years, research has focused on reader effects of poetic and rhetorical elements in ads from a relevance-theoretic perspective. For instance, van Mulken, van Enschot-van Dijk, and Hoeken (2005) aimed to find out whether slogans in ads are appreciated more than slogans without a pun, and whether puns containing two relevant interpretations are appreciated more than puns containing only one relevant interpretation (p. 707). To do this, 68 participants rated their appreciation of 24 slogans. The results showed that the presence or absence of puns had a significant impact on the respondents' appreciation of the slogans. Furthermore, whether the pun contained two relevant interpretations or only one did not influence the extent to which they were considered funny, but the former were considered a better choice than the latter (van Mulken, van Enschot-van Dijk, and Hoeken, 2005).

Lagerwerf (2007), on the other hand, examined the effects on audiences of irony in ads and of sarcasm in public information announcements. Two studies were conducted. Sixty students took part in the first study, with stimuli consisting of 12 magazine ads, six of which were positively formulated and six negatively. In the second, there were 40 students who participated in the experiment, with stimuli consisting of ads that were partly based on the researcher's own designs and partly on actual ads. In advertisements for commercial products and services, irony was found in the use of negative captions where positive captions were expected. Sarcasm was used by placing a positive caption against a background displaying a harrowing picture. Such departures from common practice in the use of negative and positive wordings were regarded as inappropriate. It turned out that advertisements with ironic intent were appreciated more when the inappropriateness was re-interpreted correctly as irony (Study 1). Even so, irony and

22nd Pacific Asia Conference on Language, Information and Computation, pages 1–15

sarcasm may impede a proper understanding of the advertisements' informative intention. This has a negative impact on the assessment by an audience of the importance of the societal issues emphasized in sarcastic announcements (Study 2) (Lagerwerf, 2007).

Working within the pragmatic construct of metadiscourse, Fuertes-Olivera, *et al.* (2001) analyzed the metadiscourse devices typically used by ad copywriters to construct their slogans and/or headlines. The researchers' analysis proceeded from the assumption that advertising English should be represented as a continuum of text functions fluctuating between "informing" and "manipulating" in accordance with the idea that advertising is an example of covert communication. Based on an examination of ads from a women's magazine, they concluded that both textual and interpersonal metadiscourse devices help copywriters to convey a persuasive message under an informative mask (Fuertes-Olivera, *et al.*, 2001).

The present study seeks to contribute to the ongoing interest in describing the discourse of advertising. In particular, it aims to describe magazine ads in the Philippines in terms of their generic structures and linguistic properties, including speech acts performed by utterances. The study is anchored on Simpson's (2001) 'reason'-'tickle' binary distinction between types of advertising discourse, which expands Bernstein's (1974) proposal. In Simpson's view, 'reason' ads are those which suggest a motive or reason for purchase. Furthermore, these ads follow a basic discourse pattern and the corresponding conjunctive adjuncts – conditional, causal, and purposive – which realize the pattern. This pattern parallels the notion of generic structure) (see discussion of generic structure below). 'Tickle' ads, by contrast, are those which appeal to humor, emotion and mood. Unlike reason ads which are stable in terms of structure and whose language is straightforward, 'tickle' ads are indirect, and therefore need the reader's inferencing strategies to figure out what they convey (Simpson, 2001). Figure 1 locates the 'reason'-'tickle' construct within three well-known pragmatic models:

		Grice (1975)	*Brown & Levinson (1987)*	*Sperber & Wilson (2004)*
Reason	↑ Direct	'maximal' efficiency	bald-on-record	strong relevance
Tickle	↓ Oblique	implicature	off-record	weak relevance

Figure 1. 'Reason'-'tickle' distinction and pragmatic models (Simpson, 2001, p. 593)

In looking at the generic structure of print ads as texts, the study proceeds from the assumption that an ad is a genre, defined here as "a class of communicative events, the members of which share some set of communicative purposes. These purposes are recognized by the expert members of the parent discourse community, and thereby constitute the rationale for the genre" (Swales, 1990, pp. 45-58). The unit of genre analysis is *rhetorical move* (or simply *move*), a functional unit (Halleck and Connor, 2006, p. 72) or a semantic unit related to the writer's purpose (Hassan, 2008, p. 39), which has been used by several genre-analytic studies. These include research that has focused on academic texts like research article introductions (e.g. Swales, 1990) and on professional texts such as sales letters (e.g. Bhatia, 1993).

Taking its cue from Simpson (2001), the study uses modified generic structures consisting of the following moves: *Giving Reason/s for Buying + Citing Positive Benefits* (or *Cause + Effect*), and *Creating Need/Purpose + Recommending Course of Action*. In addition, five other structures have been used in the study. They are *Identifying Product Name/Features + Citing Positive Benefits, Creating Need + Identifying Product Name, Describing Company/Product + Identifying Product Name, Identifying Product Name + Slogan, Conditional Constructions*

(*Antecedent + Consequent*), and *Combination of structures* (e.g. Creating Need + Identifying Product Name + Citing Positive Benefits).

The linguistic properties used in this paper are based on features which were found by Lakoff (1982) and Geis (1982) to have been possessed by advertisements, which, in turn, were used by Schmidt and Kess (1986) in characterizing televangelism. Among these properties are linguistic novelty, repetition of names, adjectivalization processes, and imperative structures. In addition, the description of noun phrases, especially their pre-modification structures, has been influenced by Rush's (1998) characterization of the complexity of NPs in the ads. Finally, code-switching patterns in the ads are described in terms of Dayag (2002), which differentiates between inter-sentential code-switching, intra-sentential code-switching, and tag switching, using the terminology of Poplack (1980).

Drawing upon the works of Searle (1979), the present study also analyzes the speech acts performed by utterances in the ads. Specifically, it uses Searle's (1979) taxonomy of illocutionary acts consisting of five general types, namely, assertives (representatives), directives, commissives, declarations, and expressives. Huang (2007) defines assertives as "those kinds of speech act that commit the speaker to the truth of the expressed proposition, and thus carry a truth-value. They express the speaker's belief" (Huang, 2007, p. 106). Examples are "asserting, claiming, concluding, reporting, and stating" (Huang, 2007, p. 106). In this study, an assertive generally takes the form of a claim, which is "an assertion, statement or implication (as of value, effectiveness, qualification, eligibility) which predicates a past or present event and whose justification is not readily verifiable" (Schmidt and Kess, 1986, p. 49). Directives, on the other hand, are "those kinds of speech act that represent attempts by the speaker to get the addressee to do something," and they include "advice, commands, orders, questions, and requests" (Huang, 2007, p. 107). Commissives "commit the speaker to some future course of action," and "offers, pledges, promises, refusals, and threats" are some examples (Huang, 2007, p. 107). Declarations (or declaratives) "effect immediate changes in some current state of affairs" (Huang, 2007, p. 108). Also called institutionalized performatives, declarations include "bidding in bridge, declaring war, excommunicating, firing from employment, and nominating a candidate" (Huang, 2007, p. 108). Lastly, expressives "express a psychological attitude or state in the speaker such as joy, sorrow, and likes/dislikes" (Huang, 2007, p. 107). Examples include "apologizing, blaming, congratulating, praising, and thanking" (Huang, 2007, p. 107).

In Austin's (1962) view, certain conditions must be fulfilled for a speech act to be felicitous. Searle (1969) elaborated on this by proposing felicity conditions of speech acts, i.e. constitutive rules (or rules that create the activity itself) (Huang, 2007, 104). The felicity conditions for assertive and directives are shown below:

Propositional content	p
Preparatory condition	1. S has evidence (reasons etc.) for the truth of p 2. It is not obvious to both S and H that H knows (does not need to be reminded of, etc.) p
Sincerity condition	S believes p
Essential condition	The utterance of e counts as an undertaking to the effect that p represents an actual state of affairs

(Searle, 1969, p. 67, cited in Allan, 2008)

Figure 2. Felicity conditions for assertives

Propositional content   Future act *A* of *H*
Preparatory condition   (a) *S* believes *H* can do *A* (b) It is not obvious that *H* would do *A*
                          without being asked
Sincerity condition   *S* wants *H* to do *A*
Essential condition   The utterance of *e* counts as an attempt to get *H* to do *A*
                where: A = act
                        S = speaker
                        H = hearer
                        e = linguistic expression
                                        (Searle (1969) quoted in Huang, 2007, p. 105)

Figure 3. Felicity conditions for directives

2. Methodology

The corpus of the study consists of 74 ads for non-consumer durables, broken down as follows: 28 (medicines), 25 (vitamins and food supplements), and 21 (cosmetics/beauty/ personal hygiene products). They were taken from health and entertainment magazines published from 2005 to 2007, which were sub-components of the *Corpus of Asian Magazine Advertising (CAMA): The Philippine database* (Dayag, 2008). The CAMA corpus building project "seeks to compile a corpus of advertisements from various East and Southeast Asian magazines. The completed corpus as well as a catalogued database of the advertisements will be made available to each research team working to complete the corpus" ("CAMA sampling guidelines," p. 1).

For the purposes of this study, only the verbal elements of the headline and body text of each ad were considered for analysis. These were coded in terms of generic structures and linguistic features including speech acts, following the discussion above.

3. Generic Structures of Print Ads

In this section, I describe the preferred generic structures of print ads as well as speech acts performed by utterances in the ads.

Table 1 shows the preferred generic structures of the 74 magazine ads included in the corpus of the study.

Table 1. Preferred generic structures of print ads

Generic Structure	Medicines	Vitamins & Food Supplements	Cosmetics/Beauty/ Personal Hygiene Products	TOTAL
Conditional (Antecedent + Consequent)	1 (1.35%)	0	0	1 (1.35%)
Reason + Benefits (Cause +Effect)	1 (1.35%)	1 (1.35%)	4 (5.40%)	6 (8.11%)
Need/Purpose + Course of Action	6 (8.11%)	5 (6.76%)	3 (4.05%)	14 (18.92%)
Product Name/Features + Benefits	11 (14.86%)	12 (16.22%)	4 (5.40%)	27 (36.49%)
Need + Product Name	3 (4.05%)	4 (5.40%)	0	7 (9.46%)
Company/Product Description + Product Name	5 (6.76%)	1 (1.35%)	6 (8.11%)	12 (16.22%)
Product Name + Slogan	1 (1.35%)	2 (2.70%)	2 (2.70%)	5 (6.76%)
Combination (e.g. Need + Product Name + Benefits)	0	0	1 (1.35%)	1 (1.35%)
Unidentified	(1.35%)0	(1.35%)0	1 (1.35%)	1 (1.35%)
TOTAL	28 (37.84%)	25 ((33.78%)	21 (28.38%)	74 (100%)

The aggregate figures in Table 1 show that a little more than one-third of the ads follow the global structure *Product Name/Features + Positive Benefits*, followed by *Need/Purpose + Course of Action, Company/Product Description + Product Name, Need + Product Name*, and *Reason + Benefits (Cause +Effect)*. In terms of specific product types, it is vitamins and food supplements and medicines that use the first of these three structures more often than the other patterns. By contrast, cosmetics/beauty/personal hygiene products prefer the third structure to the other two. In the paragraphs that follow, the first five preferred generic structures are presented.

3.1 Identifying Product Name/Features + Citing Positive Benefits

The most preferred generic structure, though constituting less than 50% of the ads, consists of moves such as Identifying Product Name/Features and Citing Positive Benefits. Below are examples.

(1) *Introducing GARDASIL*
   The one and only quadrivalent vaccine that protects against
   CERVICAL CANCER
   VULVAR/VAGINAL CANCERS
   CERVICAL DYSPLASIA

GENITAL WARTS
Caused by Human Papillomavirus Types 6, 11, 16, and 18.
(Gardasil)

(2) *DNA TECHNOLOGY-DRIVEN...*
  Recombinant Human G-CSF (Filgrastim)
  MACROLEUCO
  (150 mcg/vial and 300 mcg/vial)
  Boosting Neutrophil Counts to New Highs!
(Macroleuco)

(3) *OMEGA – 3 P.U.F.A.*
    OMEGABLOC (1000 mg)
    Omegabloc helps reduce blood thickness thereby helping prevent heart attacks and strokes. Based on the world-renowned GISSI-Prevenzione Investigators' study, published in "THE LANCET" Vol. 354 No. 9177, Omega-3 PUFA reduces total deaths by 20%, heart related deaths by 30% and sudden deaths by 45%.
(Omegabloc)

Extracts (1), (2), and (3) are examples of ad copies where the moves Identifying Product Name/Features and Citing Positive Benefits are arranged in that order. In these ads the first move usually occurs in the headline segment, and the second move constitutes the body text. In some ad copies, however, the benefits are cited ahead of the product name or features, as exemplified by (4) and (5).

(4) *Overcoming anemia in patients on chemotherapy*
  EPOETIN ALFA
  EPOKINE
  Your Safe and Effective Choice!
(Epokine)

(5) *More Energy Everyday*
  Mas Happy Everyday (Happier Everyday)
  MULTIVITAMINS
  ENERVON
(Enervon)

It is interesting to note that, in terms of linguistic properties, all five ad copies above have one characteristic: the use of sentence fragments (e.g. *Boosting Neutrophil Counts to New Highs! More Energy Everyday*) brought about by the absence of subjects and verbal auxiliaries. The absence of subjects and auxiliaries has been described by Lakoff (1982) as one type of syntactic innovation found in her study of television advertising, which is a characteristic shared by televangelists (Schmidt and Kess, 1986). This is the same property of newspaper ads found by Dayag (1999). That these ads contain sentence fragments may be explained in relevance-theoretic terms. That is, the absence of subjects and auxiliaries may make these ads more relevant to the reader because less processing effort is expended when reading them (Wilson and Sperber, 2004).

3.2 Creating a Need/Purpose + Recommending Course of Action

The second preferred generic structure displayed by ads in the corpus is composed of two moves, namely, Creating a Need/Purpose and Recommending Course of Action. This has been identified by Simpson (2001) as one of three types of ads that appeal to reason. The following ad copies exemplify the second structure.

(6)   *Ordinaryong pangangasim?* (Ordinary hyperacidity?)
      Mag-Kremil Regular (Take Kremil Regular)
      O extra-tinding pangangasim at heartburn (Or serious hyperacidity and heartburn?)
      Mag-Kremil Extra Strength (Take Kremil Extra Strength)
                              (Kremil)

(7)   *Back and forth all night?*
      Frequent pit stops on the road?
      You've got prostate protest.
        The Urological Sciences Research Foundation used this unique blend of plant extracts in one of the longest, best-controlled botanical studies in the United States. The study confirms that saw palmetto with nettle root helps maintain a healthy prostate and normal urinary flow. Look after your health and your body with NUTRILITE Saw Palmetto and Nettle Root.
                              (Nutrilite)

(8)   *Experience Full Body Pleasures...*
      Ever Billena Body Butter
      Indulge your body in the pleasure of Ever Billena Body Butter.
        Among its natural ingredients is the internationally acclaimed skin wonder SHEA BUTTER as its base content.
        Shea Butter nourishes, moisturizes and rejuvenates skin naturally.
        Combined with Jojoba oil, Ever Billena Body Butter brings you healthy, smooth-textured younger-looking skin!
                      (Ever Billena Body Butter)

In (6) and (7) need/purpose is created and articulated through the use of rhetorical questions (*ordinaryong pangangasim, o extra-tinding pangangasim at heartburn, back and forth all night, frequent pit stops on the road*), whereas (8) does it through an imperative structure that performs the speech act of directive (see section 4.4.2 for discussion of directives). Recommending a course of action, on the other hand, is done through imperatives (*Mag-Kremil Regular, Mag-Kremil Extra Strength, Indulge your body in the pleasure of Ever Billena Body Butter*).

3.3 Describing Company/Product + Identifying Product Name

The third preferred generic structure consists of two moves, namely, Describing Company/Product and Identifying Product Name. Here are examples of ads that adopt this two-move structure.

(9)   *GENASIA*
      Biotech L.L.C.
      Blazing the trail
      Myelodysplastic Syndromes (MDS)
      Azacitidine
      Vidaza
                  (Vidaza)

(10) *Losartan*
      Lifezar 50 mg & 100 mg Tablet

...because endpoint matters!

Losartan + Hydrochloride
Combizar 50 mg/12.5 mg Tablet
When Endpoint Matters Most...
            (Lifezar and Combizar)

Because they refer to the company (*GenAsia*) or product (*Losartan*), (9) and (10) make use of NPs (e.g. *Biotech L.L.C., Myelodysplastic Syndromes (MDS), Azacitidine, Lifezar 50 mg & 100 mg Tablet*).

3.4 Creating a Need + Identifying Product Name

This generic structure starts with the move Creating a Need, followed by Identifying Product Name. This is similar to 3.2 except that in this structure, there is not much information about product features nor claims about the effectiveness of the product. The first move is couched in an imperative structure, a characteristic shared by some ads which adopt the two-move structure Creating a Need/Purpose + Recommending Course of Action.

(11) *Celebrate life's precious moments*
        Simvastatin Vidastat
            Now for Life!
                (Vidastat)

3.5 Giving Reason/s for Buying + Citing Positive Benefits (or Cause + Effect)

The last preferred generic structure begins with the reasons for buying, followed by positive benefits, which could roughly be deemed as equivalent to the Cause-Effect structure, the second of the three 'reason' ads identified by Simpson (2001). In (12) the first sentence describes the cause of the problem or the reason for buying the product, whereas the succeeding sentences give the solution and cite positive benefits from buying the product. Note the use of "that's why" in (12), which is used in cause-effect texts.

(12) *With all the many whitening products in the market, it's hard to choose which one really works. That's why there's Kojie-san Skin Lightening Soap.*
    Kojie-san Skin Lightening Soap is made of kojic acid, a by-product in making sake, the Japanese rice wine...
                (Kojie-san Sin Lightening Soap)

One way of looking at the above data is to treat the ads in this corpus as 'reason' ads. This is because, as Simpson (2001) puts it, the ads follow a stable discourse pattern, as borne out by Table 1. In addition, apart from the fact that all of them include the name of the product and/or company, mostly accompanied by a logo, their language is straightforward, with none of them appealing to the emotion and with all of them highlighting product features and positive benefits. In other words, none of them may be considered 'tickle' ads. This preference for reason-oriented campaign by copywriters when advertising medicines, vitamins and food supplements, and cosmetic/beauty/personal hygiene products, may be explained by several factors. Simpson (2001) posits that the most significant is the nature of the product advertised, thus:

> whereas 'healthy' commodities, such as nappies, sanitary protection and pain killers ...lend themselves easily to reason advertising, one would be hard pressed to extol the virtues of cigarettes or alcohol in similar terms. It may well

be…that in the marketing of 'luxury' commodities "the best route to take is an indirect one…" (p. 605).

In the case of the present study, the three product categories are all health-related, which probably explains why ads for them are highly structured and direct. As for nonessential products such as cigarettes and liquor, it may be good to conduct research to validate Simpson's (2001) claim.

4. Linguistic Features of Print Ads

In this section of the paper the linguistic features of print ads are described. These include the use of the expression "introducing," linguistic novelty, code-switching, and speech acts.

4.1 The Use of "introducing"

Of the 74 ads included in the corpus of the present study, only four used the expression "introducing." Three of the four ads are for medicines, and one for a shampoo/conditioner. Aside from (1) above (the ad for *Gardasil*), the following extracts show how this expression is used in the ads:

(13) *If you think Ibuprofen is only for adults, think again.*
Introducing KID-friendly IBUPROFEN DOLAN FP
The Ibuprofen specially made for children to beat fever.
(Dolan FP)

In (13), the ad starts with a conditional structure (introduced by "if") presumably to erase the popular perception that the product is exclusively for adults, which paves the way for introducing the new product for children.

(14) *Introducing a new, once-daily oral iron chelator*
New Deferasirox EXJADE…
(Exjade)

Like the ad for *Gardasil* (see (1) above), (14) is the first sentence in the ad for Exjade, which may be the canonical position of clauses that begin with the expression "introducing." However, this is not true for all ads that use the expression. (15) below, for example, is embedded within the body text of the ad for *Kolours*.

(15) *Introducing the shampoos and conditioners made for colored Asian Hair:*
Kolours Color Recharge Shampoos and Conditioners…
(Kolours)

Preceding (15) are the headline (*Your sun radiates again and again*) and product name (*KOLOURS Color Recharge Shampoos and Conditioners*).

4.2 Linguistic Novelty

Two types of linguistic novelty were found in the data: (1) lexical novelty and (2) lengthy noun phrases. Examples of novel terms and expressions are the following: *new highs* (*Macroleuco*), *pharmacoeconomically priced* (*Norizec*), *purrfectly healthy* (*Cetrinets Hello Kitty*), and *biovailable* (*Zimuvite*). It is interesting to note that, except for the first, all expressions are formed by the lexical process known as blending.

The second type of linguistic novelty is in the form of syntactic innovation mainly brought about by the use of lengthy noun phrases. Whereas Rush's (1998) study of ads found that "premodification in the noun phrase is characterized by the abundant use of comparative and superlative adjectives and of colourful compounds," the data of the present study show the use of lengthy NP postmodifiers. Below are examples:

(16) *Anastrozole*
> *Arimidex*
> *A "new standard" adjuvant treatment for Breast Cancer assuring better reduction in disease recurrence with long term safety.*
>> (Arimidex)

(17) *FiberMate*
> *A brand of natural dietary fiber supplement, made from psyllium, proven to cleanse your body of harmful elements...*
>> (Fiber Mate)

(18) *Zimuvite Drops*
> *A complete immune boosting formulation with zinc and antioxidant Vitamins A, C, E.*
>> (Zimuvite)

(19) *Z-Vita Syrup*
> *The growth-promoting Zinc with Vitamin B complex formulation*
>> (Z-Vita Syrup)

As (16)-(9) show, the postmodifiers are also NPs that describe the product being promoted and mention the positive benefits from using it.

4.3 Code-switching

Of the number of ads in the corpus, 12 used code-switching, a manifestation of the contact between languages (in this case, Tagalog and English) in the Philippines, a multilingual nation. Though this is a small percentage of the total, it is worthy to note that code-switching occurs across product types. Here is an example of code-switched ad for medicine:

(20*) Puyat na naman si Juan kaya lulugo-lugo siya sa umaga!*
> (Juan lacks sleep again, that's why he's lethargic in the morning!)
> *Para sa mahimbing na tulog sa hindi makatulog*
> (So that insomniacs can have a sound sleep)
> *Mag Trianon Melatonin-T ka kasi!*
> (Take Trianon Melatonin-T)
> *Other benefits reported in the scientific journals:*
>> • *Helps boost immune system to prevent diseases and fight cancer.*
>> • *Helps enhance sexual function.*
>> • *Shows anti-aging and life-extending properties in experimental animals.*
>> (Trianon)

The above extract is an example of intersentential code-switch since the shift is from a series of Tagalog sentences (lines 1-3) to a sentence which contains a list of benefits all couched in English (lines 4-7). Worth mentioning is the fact that the code-switch is in the headline and body text of the ad. (21) below comes from an ad for *Caltrate Plus*, which falls under the vitamins/food supplements category, and is also an example of inter-sentential code-switching.

(21) *...Take Caltrate Plus. It's calcium plus vitamin D and minerals that is essential for*
     bone formation.
               Ang mommy dapat matibay ang buto. (Mothers should have strong bones.)
                                        (Caltrate Plus)

Some cases of code-switching in the data occur at the intra-sentential level, such as the following:

(22) *Ordinaryong pangangasim?* (Ordinary hyperacidity?)
     Mag-Kremil Regular   (Take Kremil Regular)
     O extra-tinding pangangasim at heartburn? (Or extra-serious hyperacidity and heartburn?)
     Mag-Kremil Extra Strength... (Take Kremil Extra Strength)
       Kremil
       Expert sa pangangasim. (Expert against hyperacidity)
                                        (Kremil)

In (22) intra-sentential code switching occurs at the second line to the last line of the body text of the ad. *Mag-Kremil Regular* derives from combining Tagalog verbal prefix *-mag* and the product name *Kremil*, thus resulting in an intra-sentential code-switching. Other intra-sentential code-switches in the extract are *extra-tinding pangangasim at heartburn* and the last line *expert sa pangangasim*. It should be noted that the matrix language of (22) is Tagalog. (23) is another example of intra-sentential code-switching, but this time the base language is English.

(23) *More energy everyday. Mas* (more) *happy everyday. Multivitamins Enervon.*
                                        (Enervon)

In (23) the Tagalog comparative term "mas" (more) is used as a premodifier of the adjective "happy."

4.4 Speech Acts in Print Ads

4.4.1 Assertives

As stated earlier, assertives, especially with reference to advertisements, usually take the form of claims (Dayag, 2001). In the corpus of the present study, all but four of the ads contained at least one claim. This is usually found in the body text of the ads. (24) is an example from Neulastyl.

(24) *Simple once-per-cycle dosing*
     Powerful protection against neutropenic complications
     Freedom from daily injections
                                        (Neulastyl)

It is interesting to note that the assertives in (24) are all expressed in the form of NPs which outline the positive benefits derived from using the product. (25) below differs from (24) above in that the former includes details such as the scientific elements of the product that help bring about the positive effect.

(25) *Moisture Extreme UV Lipstick*
     Protects with SPF 15.

*The only lipstick that provides moisture, nourishment and UV protection with Jojoba
Oil, Vitamin E and Allantoin.
Lips feel softer, smoother.*
                                                    (Maybelline)

(26) is a long list of assertives designed to convince the reader about the effectiveness of the product being advertised. Using a more personal tone, the assertives directly involve the reader by using the second person pronoun "you."

(26) *The secret to a fairer skin is now in just one capsule.* **Met Tathione L-Glutathione
Dietary Supplement** *has a main ingredient, Glutathione – a master antioxidant that
gives you a fairer and even skin tone in just two weeks. It is the same type of
antioxidant that improves your immune system, keeping you from getting sick as it
helps fight diseases such as Alzheimer's, Parkinson's, HIV, AIDS, cystic fibrosis,
sickle cell anemia, strokes, asthma, allergies and infections. With Met Tathione,
you get fairer and healthier.*   (Met Tathione)

Notwithstanding the inclusion of scientific explanation in assertives, it is safe to say that the claims are not readily verifiable, and therefore do not carry much weight. But this probably is what makes ads persuasive in nature. That is, in order not to sound like direct selling which may be frowned upon by consumers, they include information to lend credibility to the claim.

4.4.2 Directives

The use of directives is somewhat pervasive in print ads. This is because 33 (out of 74 ads) contained at least one directive couched in imperative structures. In terms of their position in the ads, directives usually appear in the headlines, as shown by the following examples:

(27) *"You can't solve LACTOSE INTOLERANCE overnight.
        But you can fix it in 5 minutes."
        Chew 1 to 3 LACTEEZE tablets 5 minutes before taking milk or any dairy
        product!*   (Lacteeze)

(28) *Help your patients go on with good life…*
                                        (Casodex and Zoladex)

(29) *Give your child the IQ and Memory Advantage!*
                            (Memorx)

(30) *Drink your B's and C's with Active 8!*
                            (Nutrilite)

(31) *Build his strength with Nutren Fibre.*
                            (Nutren Fibre)

(32) *Discover herbal remedies from our alternative food supplement essential for
        greater fitness.*
                            (Ming's food supplement)

In the above examples because the directives are the headlines of the ads, they are used to attract the attention of the reader. However, not only do directives show up in the headlines, they also appear in the body text of the ads. Below are examples:

(33) *Give life to color-treated hair like never before.*
   A colored hair care system that gives more than just brilliant shine…
            (Kolours Color Recharge)

(34) *Experience soft, smooth cotton with Purity.*
            (Purity)

(35) *Get visibly whiter skin in one week!*
            (Ellen's whitening cream)

(36) *So say goodbye to dark spots with New Pond's Detox Spotless White Cream.*
            (Pond's)

In the above extracts, the directives either open the body text (such as (33) and (34)) or are interspersed with product features. In a few instances such as (35) and (36), however, directives are the last part of the body text, thereby providing a fitting closure to the ads.

5. Conclusion

In this paper I described the generic structure and linguistic properties of magazine ads in the Philippines. First, the study found that the ads follow certain generic structures and that these structures are realized linguistically. In other words, there are linguistic correlates with respect to the discourse structure of the print ads. For instance, we have seen that the move Creating a Need is minimally marked by imperative structures and/or rhetorical questions. Corollary to this is the idea that the ads adopt predictable and stable (rather than rigid or fixed) generic structures or discourse patterns, and that linguistic features are ascribed to them. That they share these properties appears to make them 'reason' (instead of 'tickle') ads, going by Simpson's (2001) typology of ads. According to Simpson (2001), 'reason' ads appeal to reason, and are distinguished from 'tickle' ads in that they are straightforward and direct.

But while it is straightforward and direct, advertising in Philippine magazines (at least based on the corpus of the present study) may still be what Tanaka (1994, 1999) calls "covert communication." In distinguishing between ostensive (or overt) communication and covert communication, she defines the latter as:

> a case of communication where the intention of the speaker [copywriter] is to alter the cognitive environment of the hearer [reader], i.e. to make a set of assumptions more manifest to her, **without making this intention mutually manifest** (Tanaka, 1994/1999, p. 41, emphasis supplied).

First of all, the relationship between copywriter and reader in print advertising is not always smooth, with the latter skeptical about the real intentions of ads. This is because in advertising in general, "communication takes place in a context where cooperation between sender and addressee is not at all guaranteed and this factor hinders the communicative process" (Duran Martinez, 2005, p. 85). Owing to their constant exposure to ads and their corresponding layout and textual elements (e.g. headline, slogan), they are immediately aware of the ads' aim, namely, "to persuade their audience to buy a certain product and not a similar one" (Duran Martinez, 2005, p. 85). Because of this particular cognitive environment on the part of the reader, advertisers resort to "discourse strategies" (Fuertes-Olivera, *et al.*, 2001, p. 1295) or "persuasive devices" (Duran Martinez, 2005, p. 85). As borne out by the present study, these include a preference for generic structures as well as linguistic features such as sentence fragments, code-switching, rhetorical questions, and imperatives. These strategies are necessary because advertisers know that a persuasive message needs to be under an "informative mask so that the receiver gets a delusive impression of a referential message" (Fuertes-Olivera, *et al.*, 2001, p. 1295). This is the bottom line of covert communication. As Duran Martinez (2005) puts it,

> as cooperation and trust are really low at the social level, the advertiser knows that revealing his informative intention – selling a product in order to make a profit – would have an adverse effect on its fulfillment. Covert communication also makes the audience become more involved in the process of communication, inviting them to spend a certain amount of time in processing the utterance of the [advertisement] (p. 87).

In the case of the present study, claims about product features and the effectiveness of the product being promoted, which are organized in terms of preferred generic structures and couched in carefully chosen linguistic features, take the form of covert communication, enabling advertisers to avoid "pushing consumers to buy," but rather persuading them, "thus reducing the psychological burden consumers suffer during their buying sprees" (Fuertes-Olivera, *et al.*, 2001, p. 1293). But whether print ads succeed in persuading consumers, which can be measured in terms of a positive change in buying behavior, is beyond the scope of this study and may be worth investigating.

References

Allan, K. (2008). Meaning and speech acts. Retrieved 6 October 2008 from http://www.arts.monash.edu/linguistics/staff/kallan-speech-acts.php

Austin, J. (1962). *How to do things with words*. Oxford: Oxford University Press.

Bernstein, D. (1974). *Creative advertising*. London: Longman.

Bhatia, V. (1993). *Analysing genre: Language use in professional settings*. London and New York: Longman.

Brown, P. & S. Levinson. (1987). Politeness: Some universals in language usage. (An abbreviated version of the book appears in Adam Jaworski and Nikolas Coupland (Eds.), *The discourse reader* (pp. 321-345). London and New York: Routledge, 1999.

Cialdini, R. B. (2001, February) The science of persuasion. *Scientific American* 284, 76-81.

Dayag, D. T. (2008). *Corpus of Asian Magazine Advertising (CAMA): The Philippine database.* [CD]. Manila, Philippines: De La Salle University.

Dayag, D. T. (2002). Code-switching in Philippine print ads: A syntactico-pragmatic description. *Philippine Journal of Linguistics, 33*(1), 34-52.

Dayag, D. T. (2001). Persuasion as a macro-speech act. *Philippine Journal of Linguistics, 32*(1), 53-74.

Dayag, D. T. (1999). *Pragmatics of Philippine print advertising discourse.* Unpublished Ph.D. dissertation, De La Salle University, Manila, Philippines.

Duran Martinez, R. (2005). Covert communication in the promotion of alcohol and tobacco in Spanish press advertisements. Retrieved 8 October 2008 from dialnet.unirioja.es/servlet/fichero_articulo?codigo.

Fuertes-Olivera, P., M. Velasco-Sacristan, A. Arribas-Bano, and E. Samaniego-Fernandez. (2001). *Journal of Pragmatics, 33*, 1291-1307.

Geis, M. L. (1982). *The language of television advertising*. New York: Academic Press.

Grice, H. P. (1975). Logic and conversation. In J. Cole and J. Morgan (Eds.), *Speech acts (Syntax and Semantics 3)* (pp. 41-58). New York: Academic Press.

Halleck, G. and U. Connor. (2006). Rhetorical moves in TESOL conference proposals. *Journal of English for Academic Purposes, 5*(1), 70-86.

Hassan, N. (2008). *The structure and linguistic features of industrial law reports.* Unpublished Ph.D. dissertation, University of Malaya.

Huang, Y. (2007). *Pragmatics.* New York: Oxford University Press.

Lagerwerf, L. (2007). Irony and sarcasm in advertisements: Effects of relevant inappropriateness. *Journal of Pragmatics, 39,* 1702-1721.

Lakoff, R. T. (1982). Persuasive discourse and conversation, with examples from advertising. In D. Tannen (Ed.), *Analyzing discourse: Text and talk.* Washington, D.C.: Georgetown University Press.

Poplack, S. (1980). Sometimes I'll start a sentence in Spanish y termino en español: Toward a typology of code-switching. *Linguistics, 18,* 581-618.

Rush, S. (1998). The noun phrase in advertising English. *Journal of Pragmatics, 29,* 155-179.

Searle, J. (1979). *Expression and meaning: Studies in the theory of speech acts.* Cambridge: Cambridge University Press.

Simpson, P. (2001). 'Reason' and 'tickle' as pragmatic constructs in the discourse of advertising. *Journal of Pragmatics, 33,* 589-607.

Schmidt, R. and J. Kess. (1986). *Television advertising and televangelism: Discourse analysis of persuasive language (Pragmatics & Beyond: An interdisciplinary series of language studies.* Amsterdam/Philadelphia: John Benjamins Publishing Company.

Searle, J. (1979). *Expression and meaning: Studies in the theory of speech acts.* Cambridge: Cambridge University Press.

Searle, J. (1969). *Speech acts: An essay in the philosophy of language.* Cambridge: Cambridge University Press.

Swales, J. (1990). *Genre analysis:English in academic and research settings.* Cambridge: Cambridge University Press.

Tanaka, K. (1994/1999). *Advertising language: A pragmatic approach to advertisements in Britain and Japan.* London: Routledge.

Van Dijk, T. A. (1977). *Text and context: Explorations in the semantics and pragmatics of discourse.* London: Longman.

Van Mulken, M., R. van Enschot-van Dijk, and H. Hoeken. (2005). Puns, relevance and appreciation in advertisements. *Journal of Pragmatics, 37,* 707-721.

Wilson, D. and D. Sperber. (2004). Relevance theory. In G. Ward and L. Horn (Eds.), *The handbook of pragmatics* (pp. 607-632). Oxford: Blackwell. Retrieved 19 July 2004 from http://www.dan.sperber.com/relevance_theory.htm

From archive to corpus: transcription and annotation in the creation of signed language corpora[*]

Trevor Johnston

Department of Linguistics, Macquarie University, Sydney, Australia

trevor.johnston@mq.edu.au

Abstract. The essential characteristic of a signed language corpus is that it has been annotated, and not, contrary to the practice of many signed language researchers, that it has been transcribed. Annotations are necessary for corpus-based investigations of signed or spoken languages. Multi-media annotation software can now be used to transform a recording into a machine-readable text without it first being necessary to transcribe the text, provided that linguistic units are uniquely identified and annotations subsequently appended to these units. These unique identifiers are here referred to as *ID-glosses*. The use of ID-glosses is only possible if a reference lexical database (i.e., dictionary) exists as the result of prior foundation research into the lexicon. In short, the creators of signed language corpora should prioritize annotation above transcription, and ensure that signs are identified using unique gloss-based annotations. Without this the whole rationale for corpus-creation is undermined.

Keywords: corpus linguistics, corpora, annotation, sign language, language documentation, Auslan (Australian Sign Language).

1 Introduction

A modern linguistic corpus is something more than just a reference dataset of written or transcribed texts of a particular language on which a description of a language is based. If anything, this is an old fashioned sense of *corpus*. Rather, a corpus in the modern sense is a collection of spoken and spoken texts *in a machine-readable form* that has been assembled for the purposes of studying the type and frequency of lexical items and grammatical structures and constructions in a language (McEnery and Wilson, 2001). A modern linguistic corpus contains linguistic annotations and appended sociolinguistic and sessional data (metadata) that describe the participants and the circumstances under which the data were collected. With the development of digitized video recording and multi-media annotation software, signed language corpora can now be described as sub-types of 'spoken' (i.e., 'face-to-face') language corpora.

Signed language corpora promise to vastly improve peer review of descriptions of signed languages and make possible, for the first time, a corpus-based approach to signed language analysis. Corpora are important for the testing of language hypotheses in all language research at all levels, from phonology, through lexis, morphology and syntax to discourse (Baker, 2006; Halliday *et al.*, 2004; Hoey *et al.*, 2007; McEnery *et al.*, 2006; Sampson and McCarthy, 2004; Sinclair 1991). There are several reasons why this is especially true of deaf signing communities. First, signed languages—inevitably young minority language communities—lack written forms

---

[*] Acknowledgments: research towards this paper was supported by a Hans Rausing Endangered Languages Documentation Project (University of London) grant #MDP0088 to Trevor Johnston. Additional archived corpus material was contributed through Australian Research Council (ARC) grant #LP09346973 to Adam Schembri and Trevor Johnston. Additional corpus annotation were partially supported by Australian Research Council grant #DP0665254 to Trevor Johnston and Louise de Beuzeville. I also wish acknowledge the support of the Australian deaf community native signer participants who have contributed to the Auslan archive and corpus and research assistants and annotators who contributed to the current body of annotations: Julia Allen, Donovan Cresdee, Karin Banna, Michael Gray, and Gerry Shearim.

22nd Pacific Asia Conference on Language, Information and Computation, pages 16–29

and well developed community-based standards of correctness. Second, they have interrupted generational transmission and few native speakers. Third, the representation of signed language examples using written gloss-based text has meant that these data have remained essentially inaccessible to other researchers for meaningful peer review. Thus, although introspection and observation can still be of valuable assistance to linguists developing hypotheses regarding signed language use and structure, one must also recognize that intuitions and researcher observations may fail in the absence of clear native signer consensus of phonological or grammatical typicality, markedness or acceptability. The previous reliance on the intuitions of small numbers of informants has thus been problematic in the field. Despite the fact that research into signed languages has grown dramatically over the past three to four decades, progress in the field has been hindered by these obstacles to data sharing and processing.

As with all modern linguistic corpora, signed language corpora should be representative, well-documented (i.e., with relevant metadata) and machine-readable (i.e., able to be annotated and tagged consistently and systematically) (McEnery and Wilson, 1996; Meyer, 2002; Teubert and Cermáková, 2007). This requires dedicated technology (e.g., ELAN), standards and protocols (e.g., IMDI metadata descriptors), and transparent and agreed grammatical tags (e.g., grammatical class labels) (Crasborn et al, 2007). One aim of this paper is to describe these resources and to identify the principles that need to be adhered to in the creation of signed language corpora such that the goals and practices of corpus linguistics, as now generally understood, can be achieved and implemented with respect to signed languages.

The guiding principle behind the annotations being created for the Auslan (Australian Sign Language) corpus is machine-readability, not transcription narrowly understood. The aim is to create an annotated signed language corpus, and not, contrary to the practice of many signed language researchers, a body of signed language texts which have been transcribed to a greater or lesser degree of detail. The reason is that one can now use multi-media annotation software to transform a video recording of signed language into a machine-readable text without it first being necessary to transcribe that text. Transcription is defined here as the encoding of face-to-face language (signed or spoken) using a recognized notation system that represents the phonetic or phonological form of the signal, or using a dedicated writing script that represents the conventional units of the language. This is an important consideration in building signed language corpora because there is no standard or widely accepted signed language transcription system. Using this type of multi-media annotation software it is thus now possible to gain instant and unambiguous access to the actual form of the signs being annotated—the video recording—because they are both time aligned. In saying this, it should be noted, however, that this type of multi-media annotation software can only profitably be used to create a machine-readable corpus if signed units are consistently and uniquely identified before more detailed linguistic annotations and tags are appended to them. A secondary aim of this paper is to describe how this can be achieved, using the example of the Auslan corpus.

The Auslan corpus annotations that have been created to date are intended primarily for investigations of grammar and discourse, rather than a basic phonological or lexical analysis of the language. The investigation centres on the modification of indicating verbs in terms of frequency of types/tokens, and their environments of occurrence (e.g., during periods of constructed action, with or without contiguous pointing signs, or with reference to the sequential order of related nominal arguments). The focus is on the analysis of the grammatical use of space in Auslan in terms of semantic roles and grammatical relations.[1]

---

[1] An Australian Research Council project grant awarded to Louise de Beuzeville and Trevor Johnston—#DP0665254 *The linguistic use of space in Auslan: semantic roles and grammatical relations in three dimensions.* For initial data on indicating verbs see Johnston *et al* (2007) and de Beuzeville *et al* (submitted). For details of the controlled vocabularies and codes (tags) used in these annotated texts the reader is referred to annotation guidelines produced as part of the above mentioned project (see Johnston and de Beuzeville, 2008.). The guidelines do not attempt to set specific annotation protocols for all signed language corpora. Provided each signed language corpus is internally consistent in its annotation conven-

What is being claimed in this paper is that there are two principles which all signed language corpora should adhere to in order to facilitate their optimal use: prioritise annotation above transcription, and identify signs uniquely using gloss-based annotations. Without this the whole rationale for corpus-creation is undermined.

2 The Auslan Corpus

The Auslan Corpus is a digital video archive of Australian Sign Language (Auslan). The archive is an Endangered Languages Documentation Project funded through the Hans Rausing Endangered Languages Documentation Programme at the School of Oriental and African Studies (SOAS), University of London (grant #MDP0088 awarded to Trevor Johnston). The corpus was deposited during 2008 at the Endangered Languages Archive (ELAR) at SOAS. Access will be initially limited for a period of three years from 2009 to 2011, after which it will be openly accessible, subject to the standard ELAR conditions of use.[2]

The corpus brings together into one digital archive a representative sample of Auslan in video recordings to which are appended annotation and metadata files. It consists of two sub-corpora: data collected through the Endangered Languages Documentation Project (ELDP), mentioned above, and data collected as part of the Sociolinguistic Variation in Auslan Project (SVIAP).[3] Both datasets are based on language recording sessions conducted with deaf native or early learner/near-native users of Auslan. A native signer is here defined as someone who has acquired Auslan from birth from a signing deaf parent or parents or an older deaf sibling, and an early learner/near-native as someone who has acquired or learned Auslan before the age of seven (Johnston and Schembri, 2006).

The ELDP corpus consists of approximately 300 hours of unedited footage taken from 100 participants from the same five cities. Each participant took part in three hours of language-based activity that involved an interview, the production of narratives, responses to survey questions, free conversation, and other elicited linguistic responses to various stimuli such as a picture-book story, a filmed cartoon, and a filmed story told in Auslan. This footage has been edited down to around 150 hours of usable language production which, in turn, has been edited into approximately 1,100 separate digital movie texts for annotation. To date approximately 130 of these texts have been annotated using ELAN (see below for more details).

The SVIAP corpus consists of films of 211 participants from the five major cities in Australia (Sydney, Melbourne, Brisbane, Adelaide and Perth). This yielded over 140 hours of unedited digital video footage of free conversation, structured interviews, and lexical sign elicitation tasks.[4]

3 Distinguishing between notation, transcription, annotation, tagging and metadata

In order to appreciate the different degree and levels of detail that may be encoded in a corpus—and importantly, to determine if all must of necessity be present for a corpus in the modern sense to be created—it is very useful to make distinction between *notation, transcription, annotation* and *tagging* (cf. Johnston, 1991a). In the creation of the Auslan corpus these distinctions

---

tions, second-order cross-linguistic comparisons can fruitfully be made after language-internal analyses have been conducted.

[2] Requests for access to the corpus before the end of the limited access period will be considered on a case by case basis and should be directed to ELAR: http://www.hrelp.org/archive/.

[3] Australian Research Council research grant awarded to Adam Schembri and Trevor Johnston — #LP0346973 *Sociolinguistic Variation in Auslan: Theoretical and applied dimensions.*

[4] Access to the SVIAP data to subject to separate access restrictions than the ELDP data and requests for access should be directed to either Trevor Johnston or Adam Schembri. Contact for Adam Schembri: Project Director, British Sign Language Corpus Project, Deafness, Cognition and Language (DCAL) Research Centre, University College London, 49 Gordon Square, London WC1H 0PD, United Kingdom.

have proved to be very relevant in guiding how and why the data is encoded in a machine-readable text.

3.1 Notation and transcription

Many scholars make no real distinction between notation and transcription, but it is often useful to do so. *Transcription* is defined here as the graphic representation of a text in face-to-face or 'oral' language, i.e., a text which has been signed or spoken. It uses some kind of dedicated script. *Notation* is more narrowly defined as either the writing down of individual words or signs (rather than text as such) or the actual system of symbols used for this purpose ('script' if a bona fide writing system). One of the major purposes of transcription and notation systems is to enable the reader of the graphic symbols to reproduce, with greater or lesser accuracy according to the degree of detail in the notation or transcription system, the original spoken or signed text. Figure 1 is an example of an Auslan sign represented in a dedicated signed language notations system (HamNoSys[5]).

Figure 1: The Auslan sign CENTRE represented in HamNoSys.

Generally speaking, transcriptions are usually created as reference points for, or stages in, linguistic analysis, such as in the creation of scripts for writing systems, for phonological analysis, or for grammatical analysis. They also serve as written forms of source texts which are in turn machine-readable and, therefore, able to be processed by computers. Once isolated, the transcribed and/or written words or signs of a text can then also be annotated for various linguistic features.

Transcription was an absolutely essential step in linguistic analysis before the invention of analogue sound recording in the early 20th century. Without it, the object of study was completely ephemeral. Indeed, the advent of recordings did not reduce the reliance on transcriptions of spoken texts in order to conduct linguistic analysis, as transcriptions could not be time aligned with recordings using the earlier analogue technology. The development of digital recording and multi-media annotation software in the late twentieth century changed the situation further, as it now enabled annotations to be directly time-aligned with recorded segments. This has become especially relevant in transforming the conduct of signed language research. Somewhat surprisingly, it is still often assumed by signed language researchers that transcribing a signed text is a first and necessary step in the creation of a signed language corpus. Given that this usually entail scores of hours of notation and transcription *per minute of video recording* without producing as output a useable, machine-readable text, this practice not only represents a significant waste of resources by failing to use appropriately the potential of the new technology, it also represents a fundamental misunderstanding of the nature of modern linguistic corpora.

3.2 Annotation and tagging

Initially, an annotation was any kind of 'additional commentary' added to an already existing written text, be it a transcription of a spoken text or a piece of conventional writing (i.e., a text

---

[5] HamNoSys = Hamburg Notation System for signed languages, developed at the Institute for German Sign Language, Hamburg University, Germany.

that did not necessarily previously exist as a spoken text or was never intended to become a spoken text by being written down). Annotations were often bilingual commentaries on 'difficult' foreign or ancient texts and were intended as aids to understanding.

For linguists, annotations have evolved into 'mini' linguistic commentaries that are appended to identified units in a language. Annotations add phonological, morphological, syntactic, semantic and discourse information about linguistic forms, depending on the purpose of the analysis. As such, annotations are an invaluable aid in helping linguists discern patterns in language at many different levels, with or without the aid of computers.

In principle, there is no clear cut distinction between an annotation and a tag—both append linguistically relevant information to a unit of language. However, what is now commonly called 'tagging' refers particularly to the kind of automatic annotations appended to written texts after they have been digitized and then processed using computers. For example, the addition of the tags to the written English sentence *Joanna stubbed out her cigarette with unnecessary fierceness* can in a large part be done automatically with reference to computerized dictionary of English in conjunction with the application of simple rules of word collocation and distribution.[6] The process is illustrated in example (1), below, taken from the Lancaster-Oslo/Bergen Corpus of English (cited in McEnery and Wilson, 2001 p. 47). It uses underscores and capitalization suffixed to lexical items as its linguistic tags (see Table 1).

(1) Joanna_NP stubbed_VBD out_RP her_PP$ cigarette_NN with_IN unnecessary_JJ fierceness_NN ._.

Table 1: Key to tags used in example (1)

Tag	Meaning	Tag	Meaning
_NP	singular proper noun	_NN	singular common noun
_VBD	past tense form of lexical verb	_IN	preposition
_RP	adverbial particle	_JJ	adjective
_PP$	possessive pronoun	_.	full stop

Most tags (or annotations) in the Auslan corpus are not appended to a gloss sequentially as in the above example; rather, they are inserted into annotation fields with are time-aligned to the ID-glosses that are located on separate tiers in the ELAN annotation file. As can be seen from Figure 2, they are vertical tags, rather than sequential ones.

3.3 Metadata

Metadata refers to any additional and relevant information about a text or dataset which is essentially data about that data as a whole, rather than individual linguistic units within that dataset. Within linguistics that information is essentially sociolinguistic and sessional in nature. Sociolinguistically, metadata appends information about characteristics of the participants such as age, sex, region, class, religion, education, ethnicity, race, dialect and so on. Sessional metadata appends information about where and when the data was collected, under what circumstances and by whom.

3.4 Coding overall

In summary, it should be noted that regardless of the type or degree of detail in the coding or analysis, only behaviours that are (or are assumed to be) linguistically meaningful are identified in transcription and annotation. This means ignoring all articulations and movements that are not (or appear not to be) related to language. With respect to signed languages, for example, a hand scratching a nose or someone leaning forward to pick something up would be ignored, unless these acts are (or are assumed to be) part of a period of role shift or constructed action. There are, of course, other behaviours which are not clearly extra-linguistic, especially in signed

---

[6] Using the large databases of the most well-described and documented languages, such as English, this process is able to yield accuracy rates of up to 98% (Garside and Smith, 1997).

languages which are perforce face-to-face languages. For example, some behaviours may or may not be aspects of the linguistic system (eye-gaze, facial expressions, movement modifications, etc.) and they will need to be encoded in the first instance *as part of investigations to determine their role within the language.* Coding for a particular feature of this type is usually based on a reasonable hypothesis about its grammatical role in the language. One must do this type of coding before extracting instances from the corpus to determine if a given hypothesis is correct. Only then could the coding for the feature be continued or discontinued on a principled basis.

4   ELAN

The corpus is being annotated digital video annotation software called ELAN (<u>E</u>UDICO – <u>E</u>uropean <u>D</u>istributed <u>C</u>orpus – <u>l</u>inguistic <u>a</u>nnotator) (Hellwig *et al.,* 2007). The software allows for the precise time-alignment of annotations with the corresponding video sources on multiple user-specifiable tiers. It allows one to create, edit, visualise and search annotations for video data. It supports display of video with its annotation; time linking of annotations to media streams; linking of annotation to other annotations; unlimited number of annotation tiers defined by users; different character sets; export of annotations as tab-delimited text files and a complementary ability to import text file annotations. Relevant metadata for the digital recordings is appended to media files. The following screen-shot of an opened ELAN annotation file shows an ID-gloss tier with several daughter tiers that exemplify the type of vertical tags, discussed above.

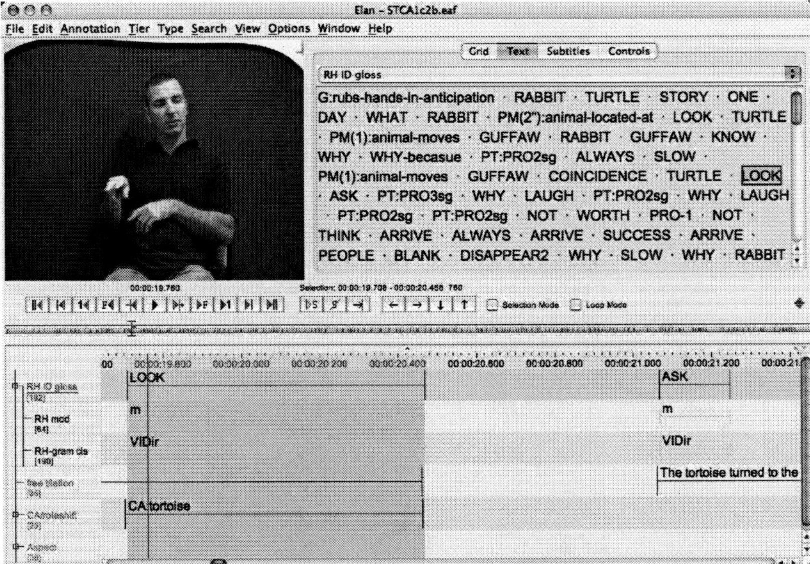

Figure 2: A screen grab from ELAN—the ID-gloss LOOK is tagged with 'm' (for 'modified') on the RH mod tier and 'VIDir' (for grammatical class 'Directional Indicating Verb') on the RH-gram cls tier.

4.1 The tiers in ELAN

The tiers currently available in the Auslan corpus ELAN template are shown in Figure 3. Since, the majority of tiers have yet to be used with a very large collection of texts, the number and type of tiers in a standard ELAN annotation file is yet to be fixed. This is partly due to the fact that a certain amount of trial and error will be needed to determine what should be the minimum core number and type of tiers for all files in the corpus. Cumulative experience from repeated annotation parses focussing on different aspects of grammar will be needed before this can be done.

Tier map	Expansion*
	RH ID gloss: retrieved from databases
	RH meaning: a temporary gloss for the meaning of a sign when ID-gloss is unknown
	RH-gram cls: the grammatical class of the sign
	RH mouthing: the word (or parts of a word) being mouthed during the sign
	RH mouth-gc: the grammatical class of the mouthed word (not the sign)
	RH brow: eyebrow behaviour
	RH mod: spatial modification
	RH aspect-form: movement modification which is assumed to be aspectual
	RH aspect-meaning: the meaning of an aspectual modification
	RH-loc: modified (non-citation) location or direction
	RH-h/s: the handshape(s) on the RH, for phonological analysis (cf transcription)
	RH-mov: the movement(s) of the RH, for phonological analysis (cf transcription)]
	RH-ar/ment: codes singling/doubling of hands (cf transcription) [now included in ID-gloss] see "Marked use of one or two hands" in guidelines).
	Ref rec RH: the recoverability of the referent related to a spatial modification [now discontinued]
	RH CA co-occ: codes co-occurrence of CA during the sign performance [now discontinued]
	RH-sem.roles: the semantic role being played by the sign
	LH ID-gloss: retrieved from databases
	LH meaning: a temporary gloss for the meaning of a sign when ID-gloss is unknown
	LH-gram cls: the grammatical class of the sign
	LH mouthing: the word (or parts of a word) being mouthed during the sign
	LH mouth-gc: the grammatical class of the mouthed word (not the sign)
	LH brow: eyebrow behaviour
	LH mod: codes for spatial modification
QuickTime™ and a TIFF (Uncompressed) decompressor are needed to see this picture.	LH aspect-form: a movement modification which is assumed to be aspectual
	LH aspect-meaning: the meaning of an aspectual modification
	LH-loc: modified (non-citation) location or direction
	LH-h/s: the orientation on the LH, for phonological analysis (cf transcription)
	LH-mov: the movement on the LH, for phonological analysis (cf transcription)
	LH-orient: the orientation on the LH, for phonological analysis (cf transcription)
	LH-ar/ment: codes singling/doubling of hands (cf transcription) [now included in ID-gloss]
	Ref rec LH: the recoverability of the referent related to a spatial modification [now discontinued]
	LH CA co-occ: codes co-occurrence of CA during the sign performance [now discontinued]
	LH-sem.roles: the semantic role being played by the sign
	CA/roleshift: the start and finish of a period of body shift (BS), role shift (RS), constructed action (CA) or constructed dialog (CD) (with character/role specified), as appropriate
	Body: body shift behaviour including 'swivelling'
	Head: head movements and facial expressions
	Gaze: direction of gaze and eyebrow movements
	transcription: transcription using dedicated fonts and systems (e.g. HamNoSys)
	clause: identifies a clause
	phrase: identifies a phrase
	part/situ: [to be deleted]
	affect-form: any facial expression features no elsewhere coded, especially spreading over more than one sign
	affect-meaning: the meaning of that facial expression
	aspect: tier replaced by equivalent RH and LH tiers [now discontinued]
	aspect meaning: tier replaced by equivalent RH and LH tiers [now discontinued]
	free t/lation: free translation in prosodic or meaning units
	lit t/lation: literal translation in prosodic or menaing units
	metadata: possible string of metadata codes
	annotator: possible annotator ID code
	notes: any notes or queries about the annotation (time aligned to queried annotation)

Figure 3: Current list of all tiers in the ELAN template used for the Auslan (under revision)
* RH = right hand; LH = left hand.

5   Annotation parses

The Auslan corpus is designed to be added to over time. Each ELAN annotation file (file extension *.eaf* for *Elan annotation file*) is intended to be expanded and enriched by various researchers through repeated annotation 'parses' of individual texts (digital movies). In grammar *to parse* means *to analyse a sentence into its parts and identify their syntactic roles*. Here we mean by annotation parse *a pass of the text which identifies sign units and/or attaches a particular type of linguistic annotation to identified units*. This information is placed on dedicated tiers using certain conventions, codes, or controlled vocabularies. Thus, during an annotation parse an annotator will be looking at (and annotating) different aspects of sign structure and grammar on different tiers within the file.

An annotation usually begins with information just on the tiers used to identify and name signs (the *ID-gloss* tier). Information can subsequently be added to the identified unit during a second annotation parse that looks at, and tags for, some particular linguistic feature. Over time repeated annotation parses makes each annotation file—and the whole Auslan corpus—very detailed and a rich source of data for research. The process is represented in Figure 4.

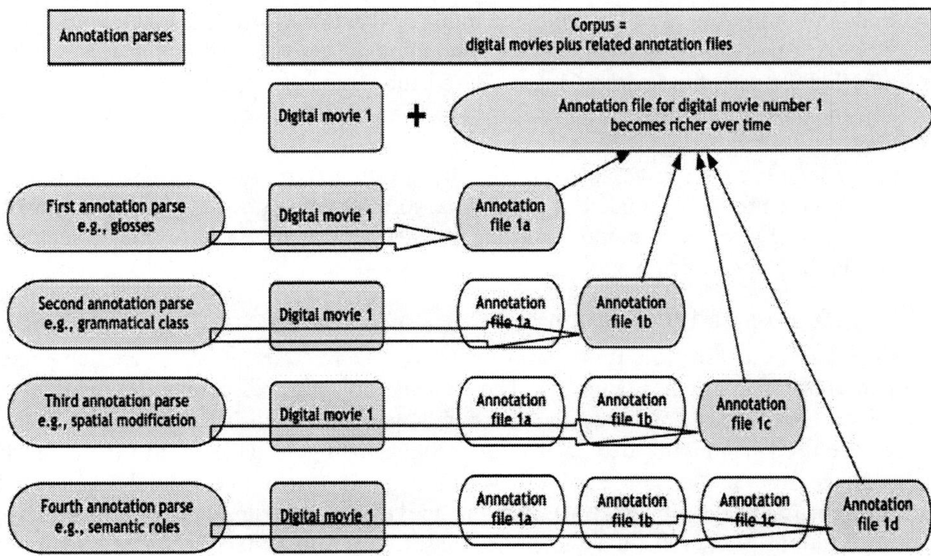

Figure 4: Repeated annotation parses in ELAN of a given video text
produces an ever richer annotation file.

5.1 From indeterminate to determinant in subsequent parses

One positive consequence of repeated annotation parses is that it encourages the use of tentative or generalized annotations (or tags) at times when fine-grained linguistic categorization may be difficult to make, if not premature, in the absence of extensive data from the corpus itself. For example, the tags *pred* (meaning 'a predicating element which may be a noun, verb, or adjective, but not any other grammatical class') or *norv* (meaning 'a noun or a verb, but not any other grammatical class including adjective') are available as 'interim' tags (for details of controlled vocabularies and tags, see Johnston and de Beuzeville, 2008). This avoids the need to make a more specific annotation which may force a premature choice between noun, verb or adjective—the final decision on the categorization may not be possible until hundreds of annotation files have been created and thousands of examples are available for comparison. The interim tag at least reduces the set of signs which must be revisited on a subsequent annotation parse for reconsideration.

6   Creating a machine-readable text with annotation glosses

In order for a corpus of recordings of face-to-face language in either spoken or signed modalities to be machine-readable, time-aligned annotations need to be appended to the source data using some form of multi-media annotation software. In the first instance, these annotations are simply glosses that identify the sign units in the text.

The identification of segments within a recording is precisely what modern digital multi-media annotation software makes possible. Prior to the existence of such technology, a transcription of the face-to-face text needed to be made in order to create a medium to which annotations and tags could be appended. In today's multi-media digital files, the time-aligned annotations appended to segments of the text are read by machine, not the text (i.e., source data) itself, nor, necessarily, a transcription of the source text, whether spoken or signed. Thus, despite what many signed language researchers continue to believe, a full written phonetic or phonological transcription of signed texts is no longer essential in order to conduct corpus-based research at various levels of linguistic analysis, even the phonological. Time aligned multi-media gloss-based annotations are adequate for this task because one need not transcribe all signs in their entirety—one could append a relevant phonetic or phonological tag for a feature under investigation. Of course, the use of a dedicated transcription tier(s) within ELAN would be necessary in order to carry out detailed phonetic or phonological research. Overall, however, there is little doubt that the use of time aligned gloss-based annotations is superior to transcription-based annotation in terms of the time it takes for a sizable amount of text to be make available for processing.

In order to segment the source data into sign units to which gloss-based or linguistic annotations can subsequently be appended, it is essential to integrate all *available* lexical information about the language into the common identifier for each lexical sign, and to follow standard protocols for glossing non-lexical signs.

6.1 Gloss, ID-gloss and translation

A gloss is a kind of annotation. It is a brief one or two word 'translation' in one language for a word or morpheme in another language. The 'translation' must, of course, be relatively crude and simplistic. In the Auslan Corpus, the glossing language is English.

Glosses are used in running text in the sign language linguistics literature (e.g., the British Sign Language sign SISTER is identical to Auslan sign SISTER but completely different to the American Sign Language sign SISTER). It is the convention to write glosses in upper case. Importantly, different glosses for the same sign may be used in different contexts to reflect the meaning of that sign in that context. Consequently, it is often very difficult to know with certainty which sign form is actually being referred to by a particular gloss because a gloss does not contain any information about sign form.[7]

By contrast, there needs to be a level in corpus annotation where signs ars identified uniquely and consistently because one cannot productively use ad-hoc glosses which may vary from context to context. In the Auslan Corpus project, this type of identifying gloss is referred to as the *ID-gloss* (Johnston, 2001).

An ID-gloss is the (English) word that is consistently used to label a sign within the corpus, regardless of the meaning of that sign in a particular context or whether it has been systematically modified in some way. For example, if a person signs HOUSE (a sign iconically related to the shape of a roof and walls) but actually means *home*, or performs a particularly large and exaggerated form of the sign HOUSE, implying *mansion*, (without that modified form itself being a recognized and distinctive lexeme of the language), the ID-gloss HOUSE is used in both instances to identify the sign in the gloss annotation. A consistently applied label of this type means it is possible to search through multiple annotation files and find all instances of a par-

---

[7] The additional use of a dedicated signed language notation/transcription system, such as the Hamburg Notation System, can overcome this.

ticular sign in order to determine the ways and environments in which it is used. We can only do this if all relevant signs have the same ID-gloss in the corpus. Of course, corpus-based evidence could itself lead to the re-analysis (and hence re-glossing) of certain signs (e.g., see the discussion of homonyms and pointing signs below).

With respect to distinguishing between glossing and translation, meaning is assigned to the text through glossing only indirectly through the unavoidable fact that the ID-gloss, which is primarily intended to identify a sign, actually uses an English word that bears a relationship to the meaning of the sign. In other words, the ID-gloss is not chosen arbitrarily or capriciously because the choice of the English word is highly motivated. However, the ID-gloss is still not intended as a translation. Translations are made on their own dedicated tiers in the ELAN annotation files. So if the signer produces SUCCESS but means 'achieve something', it is still annotated with the ID-gloss SUCCESS; and if a person signs IMPORTANT but means 'main' or 'importance', it is still labelled IMPORTANT.

6.2 Summary of ID-glossing

In assigning an ID-gloss to a sign form one is simply labelling a sign so that it can be uniquely and quickly identified or tagged (e.g., for grammatical class, sign modification potential, presence or absence of constructed action, semantic roles, and so on) during a later annotation parse, or searched for with or without these tags being taken into consideration (i.e., as search constraints). Apart from the obvious motivation of the English word used to gloss a sign, no serious attempt is being made in the assigning of an ID-gloss to translate a sign.

Failure to use ID-glosses and standardized glossing procedures in multi-media corpus annotation would create two problems. First, the consistency and commensurability of data that is annotated (i.e., glossed) by different researchers (or even by the same researcher on different occasions) can not be assured any other way. Second, the dataset would become effectively unbounded if there was no constraint on 'meaning-based glossing' because each sign articulation which may be distinctive in form could potentially have its own distinctive gloss reflecting its meaning in each context. The unique identification of sign types, which is one of the prime motivations for the creation of a linguistic corpus in the modern sense (e.g., for the purposes of searching and quantification of types and token), would thus not be achieved.

Without consistency in using the ID-gloss, it will be impossible to use the corpus productively and much of the time spent on annotation will be effectively wasted because the corpus will cease to be, or never become, machine-readable in any meaningful sense. It will not actually be the type of corpus that linguists aspire to today. Rather, it will just be a collection of reference texts—a 'corpus' in what is rapidly becoming a superseded sense in the literature.

7 The annotation glosses for lexical signs, non-lexical signs, and pointing signs

Not all of the signs produced when a signer is communicating in a signed language are of the same type. There are two major types of signs which have been described as *lexical* signs and *non-lexical* signs (Johnston and Schembri, 1999; Sandler and Lillo-Martin, 2006).[8]

A *lexical sign* is a signed form whose meaning in context is more than the conventionalised and/or iconic value of its components (handshape, location, etc.) within the inventory of meaning units of a given signed language in a given context; and that meaning is stable or consistent across contexts. A lexical sign is, essentially, equivalent to the commonsense notion of word (Sandler and Lillo-Martin, 2006) and should thus not be confused with *lexical word* (or *content*

---

[8] Another terminology should be developed for describing the conventional signs of signed languages with respect to form/meaning pairings at the level of individual sign parameters (and whether these parameters are each fully specifiable) and at the level of the sign itself and its degree of lexicalization. For example, it would appear that a construction grammar approach and terminology (Croft, 2001; Goldberg, 2006) would be more appropriate to describe this lexical cline in signed languages (i.e., as constructions that vary continuously along the two dimensions of the atomic-to-complex and the substantive-to-schematic).

word) and not opposed to *grammatical word* or *grammatical sign*. A *non-lexical sign* in this terminology is thus a signed form that has little or no conventionalised or language-specific meaning value beyond that of its components in a given context (e.g., depicting or 'classifier' signs). The annotation conventions for lexical and non-lexical signs are described below.

7.1 Lexical signs and ID-glosses

Lexical signs are identified using an ID-gloss. In the annotation fields created in ELAN that contain the ID-glosses, the lexical glosses are written in upper case, as is the norm for glossing in signed language linguistics. In mainstream linguistics, it is usually only glosses for grammatical morphemes or function words which are written in upper case, as in the following example. (In the example, the source and glossing language are both English. Commonly, when interlinear glossing is used, the source and glossing language are different.)

(2)   Source language: He   walked   home
        Glossing language: PRO3.MASC   walk-PAST   home

The use of uppercase for all glosses commonly found in signed language linguistics is partly due to the fact that doing so helps to distinguish the signed language gloss from the surrounding English text with which it could easily be confused. We maintain this convention in the ELAN annotation files. Thus the ID-gloss HOUSE appears on an ID-gloss tier as:

(3)   (As seen in Figure 2, the boxed annotation field delimits a period of time in the digital media during which a sign is articulated and to which the annotation within the field is time-aligned)

| HOUSE |

7.1.1   Choosing the appropriate ID-gloss

The standard ID-gloss for a sign is found by consulting the Auslan lexical database. The database contains over 7,000 individual sign entries in which short digital movie clips are headwords (i.e., headsigns). There are multiple fields coding information on the form, meaning and lexical status of each headsign. Meaning fields include several for definitions, semantic domains, and synonyms and antonyms. Lexical status fields include several for dialect, register, and stem/variant identification. The database lists a citation form of a lexical sign as a major stem entry, with common variant forms listed separately. A public view of the database can be accessed online through *Auslan Signbank* (www.auslan.org.au). Annotators log in to a special researchers' reference view which includes much more information than in the public view (including the ID-gloss), as well as many more additional signs (e.g., variant signs and newly identified signs).

Signs can be accessed by searching for any English word which may be commonly associated with a sign form (know as a *keyword*). For example, the sign IMPORTANT could be found by searching under the keywords *important, importance, main,* or *primary,* all of which are possible meanings or translations of the sign IMPORTANT in various contexts. In addition, entries for signs in the database are ordered formationally, i.e., they are sequenced according to major phonological features of signs, such as handshape and location, so that scrolling through the database records displays formationally similar signs one after the other. This is useful for an annotator who cannot find a particular sign because there is no gloss or keyword match to their initial enquiry (or at least one that is not expected and, hence, queried by the annotator). In other words, an annotator is able to locate a sign with a similar form whose gloss or keyword is known or matches, and then manually search around that sign to see if the form they have seen in a text is recorded in the database despite there having been no initial gloss or keyword match (i.e., it may be entered under an unexpected gloss or keyword).

A lexical database of this type is a necessary tool for ID-glossing. It is the result of linguistic research and organized according to linguistic principles (i.e., phonological formational features of signs). Without a lexical database the creation of a corpus using the annotation procedures described here are unlikely to succeed. Linguists need to be able to identify each sign form uniquely and this must be done by sorting sign forms phonologically. Otherwise, one could not locate and compare sign forms in order to determine if a new unique gloss is required for a particular sign form rather than just the association of an additional sense to an existing one. The lexical database and its representation in dictionaries in various forms, is thus an unavoidable prerequisite for creation of a viable corpus. However, it need not be exhaustive. After all, it is highly likely a corpus will actually reveal unrecorded lexical signs which need to be added to the reference lexical database.

7.1.2   ID-glosses and homonyms

A single sign form can have two entries and two separate ID-glosses if it has been determined that two separate signs exist which are homonyms. The only time an existing sign form will be assigned a different ID-gloss than what is recorded in the database is when corpus data justifies the identification of a completely distinct and unrelated meaning for the sign form in question. In such cases, the sign form receives its own distinctive ID-gloss and the two signs are treated as homonyms. The corpus and database managers then update the lexical database to create a new sign entry.

7.1.3   Annotation conventions for various other sub-types of lexical signs

In order to maximise the consistency and uniqueness of annotations of lexical signs it has been necessary to develop and implement conventions for the treatment of various lexical or morphological phenomena found in Auslan (and other signed languages). For example, the existence of negative incorporation in Auslan signs (in both suppletive and 'affixed' forms) needs consistent treatment when glossed using English words in order to avoid potential suppletive or opaque forms in English obscuring the relationship between certain signs. Details can be found in the guidelines for Auslan corpus annotators (Johnston and de Beuzeville, 2008). These comprehensive guidelines deal with phenomena such as negative incorporation, variant forms, the marked used of one or two hands in normally two-handed or one-handed signs respectively, numbers, sign names, and borrowings from Signed English and other signed languages.

7.2 Annotation conventions for non-lexical signs

As with ID-glosses, a relatively small set of annotation and glossing conventions need to be followed in order to ensure that similar types of non-lexical signs are glossed in similar ways. Without such conventions, these categories of signs cannot be easily extracted from the corpus for analysis and comparison. Non-lexical signs are primarily represented by depicting signs (also known as 'classifier signs' in the literature), but also included fingerspelled signs and buoys of various types: list, theme, fragment and pointer buoys (Liddell, 2003). Annotation conventions for non-lexical signs include prefixing all depicting sign glosses with the tag PM, and all fingerspelling strings with FS. By following these simple conventions one can incorporate consistent codes in annotations for these types of signs while at the same time using sign specific—and potentially 'inconsistent'—codes for individual signs, and yet create a set of annotations that can be easily read, sorted or otherwise processed by machine.

7.3 Annotation conventions for pointing signs

All ID-glosses for points begin with PT (for 'point') in upper case. By following this convention it is possible to search for all instances of pointing signs in the corpus and on this basis analyse (or re-analyse), categorize (or re-categorize), and label (or re-label) them, as appropriate. In other words, corpus evidence itself will assist in understanding the function of these types of signs. Generally speaking, it is not unusual for an annotator to be unable to make a detailed grammatical annotation, beyond identifying a PT, with any certainty during a first parse. It can be a difficult task. All points are thus coded with PT (followed by a colon) at minimum, with additional specification being made during later annotation parses.

8 Annotation conventions for gesture

Gestures can be culturally shared or idiosyncratic. Even if culturally shared, however, gestures which have not become lexical Auslan signs will not be found in the dictionary database and will thus not have an assignable ID-gloss. Gestures of both types occur commonly in speech and during signed discourse. When annotated the gloss for a gesture is prefixed with G: for 'gesture' followed by a brief description of the meaning of the gesture. One can see a sign's form from the associate movie clip in the annotation file, so it is not essential to have that information separately encoded in an annotation. By annotating the types of meanings encoded in gestures, it is possible to see both the types of meanings commonly expressed through gesture and the degree of conventionalization a gesture-meaning pairing may be undergoing by comparing annotations of similar meanings. When hundreds of annotation files have been created and a large number of examples are available for comparison, some of these 'gestures' may be identified has having subtly distinct forms and/or specific functions that may justify recategorisation and reglossing. This is one of the great advantages of using a corpus as part of empirical language description, but in order to do so, it requires that annotators are as consistent as possible in assigning ID-glosses or glossing conventions to various other types of non-lexical signs and gestures.

9 Conclusion

The Auslan corpus project was one of the first to attempt to compile a large machine-readable corpus of a signed language. It was begun in 2004. Since that time a number of other signed language corpus projects have begun (e.g., the NGT or Netherlands Sign Language corpus and the BSL or British Sign Language corpus), are about to begin (e.g., the DGS or German Sign Language corpus), or are planned (e.g., the ASL or American Sign Language corpus). Some, like the NGT corpus, have been completed, in the sense that the archived video recordings have been edited and catalogued and are now openly accessible through a digital video archive on the internet. A small percentage of these texts have also been transcribed using ELAN.

However, this paper has tried to show that the creation of signed language corpora as corpora in the modern sense involves more than recording, digitising, editing, cataloguing and archiving video texts. This is not to deny the importance of the creation of reference corpora for signed language researchers. After all, there have, to date, been very little publicly available reference texts of any signed language. Nonetheless, corpus creation must also involve the transformation of this archived material into a machine-readable corpus by the principled application of annotation procedures that make optimal use of the new digital technologies. Business-as-usual with these new digital archives—so-called enrichment through the addition of transcriptions—does not add value to the archive in ways that corpus linguists would assume and expect. Happily, the annotation and tagging of ID-glosses, as described in this paper, is not only less time consuming than detailed phonetic or phonological transcription, it is actually much more productive.

References

Baker, P. 2006. *Using Corpora in Discourse Analysis*. London: Continuum.

Crasborn, O., Mesch, J., Waters, D., Nonhebel, A., van der Kooij, E., Woll, B., et al. 2007. Sharing sign language data online: Experiences from the ECHO project. *International Journal of Corpus Linguistics, 12*(4), 535-562.

Cormier, Kearsy and Jordan Fenlon. To appear. Possession in British Sign Language. In *Expression of possession*, ed. by W. B. McGregor. Berlin: Mouton de Gruyter.

Croft, W. 2001). *Radical Construction Grammar*. Oxford: Oxford University Press.

de Beuzeville, L., Johnston, T., and Schembri, A. (submitted). The use of space with lexical verbs in Auslan: a corpus-based investigation. *Sign Language & Linguistics*.

Dudis, P. G. 2004). Body partitioning and real-space blends. *Cognitive Linguistics*, 15(2), 223-238

Garside, R., and Smith, N. 1997. A hybrid grammatical tagger: CLAWS4, in Garside, R., Leech, G., and McEnery, A. (eds.) *Corpus Annotation: Linguistic Information from Computer Text Corpora.* Longman, London, pp. 102-121.

Goldberg, A. E. 2006). *Constructions at Work: The Nature of Generalization in Language.* Oxford: Oxford University Press.

Halliday, M. A. K., Teubert, W., Yallop, C., and Cermakova, A. 2004. *Lexicology and Corpus Linguistics.* London: Continuum.

Hellwig, B., van Uytvanck, D., and Hulsbosch, M. 2007. EUDICO Linguistic Annotator (ELAN). http://www.lat-mpi.eu/tools/elan/

Hoey, M., Mahlberg, M., Stubbs, M., and Teubert, W. 2007. *Text, Discourse and Corpora: Theory and Analysis.* London: Continuum.

Hoting, N., and Slobin, D. I. 2002. Transcription as a tool for understanding: The Berkeley Transcription System for sign language research (BTS). In G. Morgan and B. Woll (Eds.) Directions in Sign Language Acquisition (pp. 55-75). Amsterdam/Philadelphia: John Benjamins.

Johnston, T. 1991b. Spatial syntax and spatial semantics in the inflection of signs for the marking of person and location in Auslan. *International Journal of Sign Linguistics, 2*(1), 29-62.

Johnston, T. 1991a. Transcription and glossing of sign language texts: examples from Auslan (Australian Sign Language). *International Journal of Sign Linguistics, 2*(1), 3-28.

Johnston, T. 2001. The lexical database of Auslan (Australian Sign Language). *Sign Language & Linguistics, 4*(1/2), 145-169.

Johnston, T., and de Beuzeville, L. 2008. *Researching the linguistic use of space in Auslan: guidelines for annotators using the Auslan corpus.* Manuscript, Department of Linguistics, Macquarie University, Sydney, Australia. Downloadable at www.auslan.org/about/corpus/.

Johnston, T., de Beuzeville, L., Schembri, A., and Goswell, D. 2007. *On not missing the point: Indicating verbs in Auslan.* Paper presented at the 10th International Cognitive Linguistics Conference, Kraków, Poland (15-20 July).

Johnston, T., and Schembri, A. 1999. On defining lexeme in a sign language. *Sign Language & Linguistics, 2*(1), 115-185.

Johnston, T., and Schembri, A. 2006. Issues in the creation of a digital archive of a signed language. In L. Barwick and N. Thieberger (Eds.), *Sustainable data from digital fieldwork: Proceedings of the conference held at the University of Sydney, 4-6 December 2006* (pp. 7-16). Sydney: Sydney University Press.

Johnston, T., and Schembri, A. 2006. *The use of ELAN annotation software in the Auslan Archive/Corpus Project.* Paper presented at the Ethnographic Eresearch Annotation Conference, University of Melbourne, Victoria, Australia (Feburary 15-16).

Kennedy, G. 1998. *An Introduction to Corpus Linguistics.* London and New York: Longman.

Liddell, S. K. 2003. *Grammar, gesture and meaning in American Sign Language.* Cambridge: Cambridge University Press.

McEnery, T., and Wilson, A. 2001. *Corpus linguistics.* Edinburgh: Edinburgh University Press.

McEnery, T., Xiao, R., and Tono, Y. (Eds.). 2006. *Corpus-Based Language Studies.* London and New York: Routledge.

Meyer, C. F. 2002. *English Corpus Linguistics: An introduction.* Cambridge: Cambridge University Press.

Sampson, G., and McCarthy, D. (Eds.). (2004). *Corpus Linguistics: Readings in a Widening Discipline.* London: Continuum.

Sinclair, J. 1991). *Corpus, concordance, collocation.* Oxford: Oxford University Press.

Teubert, W., and Cermáková, A. 2007. *Corpus Linguistics: A Short Introduction.* London: Continuum.

van der Hulst, H., Crasborn, O., and van der Kooij, E. 1998. *How SignPhon addresses the database paradox.* Paper presented at the Second Intersign Workshop, Leiden, The Netherlands, December, 1998.

Scalar Implicatures:
Pragmatic Inferences or Grammar? [*]

Chungmin Lee

Dept of Linguistics
Seoul National University
Seoul 151-742, Korea
clee@snu.ac.kr

Abstract. This talk discusses the nature of different kinds of scales and controversies over issues on the generation of scalar implicatures, particularly those in complex sentences involving disjunction and another operator in its scope, and so on. The pragmatic position based on Gricean reasoning in opposition to the grammatical position based on alternative semantics and LF syntax employing the exhaustivity (*Exh*) operator will be examined. The context-driven view and the default view largely still within the pragmatic position will also be discussed. In doing so, the talk will offer my position that scalar implicatures are motivated by Gricean pragmatic reasoning but that they are deeply and crucially rooted in the grammatical devices of Contrastive Topic (CT), overt or covert. CT requires PA (pero/aber) conjunction, *i.e.* 'concessive *But*' and that's why scalar implicatures begin with *but* and its equivalents cross-linguistically. The CT operator rather than the exhaustivity (*Exh*) operator must be represented to be related to the previous discourse and the forward concessive conjunction.

Keywords: scalar implicatures, Gricean reasoning, grammatical system, disjunction, context-driven vs. default, exhaustivity, Contrastive Topic, PA (concessive) conjunction.

1. Introduction

---

*I express my gratitude to the audiences of LELNS 2006 in Tokyo and of ICKL 2006 in Guadalajara. I also deeply thank Rachel Roxas for her gracious patience in editing the Proceed's with her team.

22nd Pacific Asia Conference on Language, Information and Computation, pages 30–45

1. 1 Scales

There are many gradable adjectives, to which different degrees of the state of an entity can be assigned such as *clean* and *dirty* (Kennedy 1999). The adjective *clean* shows the degree of no dirt on its subject entity (maximum standard, total-universal), as an <e, d> type function, taking an entity and returning a degree. Its antonym *dirty*, on the other hand, starts from the minimum degree of having dirt on an entity (minimum standard, partial-existential) (Yoon , Lee). These adjectives, but not un-gradable adjectives such as *alive* and *dead*, can easily be modified by degree adverbs such as *a little* and *very*, and intensifiers such as *terribly* and *awfully*. But the so-called un-gradable adjectives can also generate scalar implicatures, as will be discussed later. Gradable adjectives typically constitute scales with degree modification on the same single adjectives (intra-lexically).

In contrast, scales in connection with scalar implicatures may be different in the sense that they are typically formed by a set of scalar alternatives of different lexical items, mostly predicates. Horn's (1972) scalar predicates are related by entailment asymmetrically – a stronger one entails the weaker one in the scale but not vice versa. A sentence containing a scalar value or item can generate a scalar implicature when the scalar value is replaced with a stronger item from the scale, resulting in an alternative sentence. All such stronger alternative sentences are implicated to be negated (or false):

(1) *ScalAlt*(φ) = {φ': φ contains scalar value *s* and φ' is formed from φ by replacing only *s*
       with a value from the same Horn scale}

(2) Scalar Implicatures: $\forall$ φ' $\in$ *ScalAlt*(φ) . (φ' $\Rightarrow$ φ) ~> ~φ'

This is a standard neo-Gricean approach to scalar implicature generation mechanism with limited formally defined scalar alternatives from among all possible alternatives generated by Grice's informativeness Maxim of Quantity. Horn scales are as follows:

(3) a. Cardinals <1, 2, 3, --- >

    b. Quantifiers <some, half, most, all>

    c. Connectives <*p* or *q*, {*p*, *q*}, *p* and *q*> (Y. Lee 1995, Sauerland 2004)

    d. Modals <may (possible), must (necessary)>

    e. Adjectives <warm, hot>

    f. Verbs: <believe, know>; <like, love>

    f. Negatives <not all, few, none>; < ---, ~3, ~2, ~1>

If the values of a positive scale are negated, the scale is reversed, as in (3f). Hirschberg (1985=1991) extended the range of scales from entailment scales to non-entailment scales to generate similar scalar implicatures, as follows:

(4) a. Nominals of ranking <Harrison, Lennon>, <assistant professor, associate professor>, <porridge, (steamed) rice>
   b. Stages of events <dating, engaged, married>

So far all the scalar items or values discussed have been semantic predicates, but I propose that propositions also be scalar values, as follows:

(5) a. Propositions < Korea will beat Togo,   Japan will beat Brazil>.
   b. Korea will beat Togo ~> But it is not the case that Japan will beat Brazil.

Hirschberg (1985) and Matsumoto's (1995) further available scalar implicatures in specific contexts after entailment-based computation as in the exclusivity of disjunction should also be included in my propositional scales.[1]

1. 2 Issues

Chierchia (2004) and some other authors recently attacked Gricean and neo-Gricean theories of scalar implicature computation, claiming that these theories based on Gricean reasoning cannot account for the scalar implicatures of certain complex sentences involving disjunction etc.. Thus they proposed grammatical (semantic or syntactic) systems for computing scalar implicatures.

Russell (2006) and others, on the other hand, have defended a global, Gricean pragmatic framework, offering arguments against the critics' challenges.

What do experimental studies of processing and acquisition of scalar implicatures say? Initially Breheny et al (2006) largely supports the context-driven pragmatic approach as opposed to the default approach, which says implicatures are associated with scalar items by

---

[1] Sauerland's (2004) footnote 2 shows one such context: *Kai had peas or broccoli* is less rewarding than Kai's cleaning up his room. Then, the utterance implicates *Kai didn't clean up his room.* This implicature is context-specific or particularized, whereas *Kai didn't have both peas and broccoli* is generalized. It is interesting, however, to note that the relevant evaluative expression 'rewarding' is still a predicate. Such evaluative predicates, saying 'higher in what?' in the scale, must be underlyingly scalar, mediating propositions to scales. 'Tough and glorious' may underlie scale (5). The *even*-marked utterances are also propositional in likelihood implicature (as Horn, p.c., reminded me).

default as generalized conversational implicatures (GCIs). The context-driven approach claims that scalar implicatures arise only if there is some contextual reason, like Grice's particularized conversational implicatures. The default view has a long neo-Gricean tradition from Horn (1972), Gazdar (1979), and Horn 1984) to Levinson (2000) and, in a sense, the view is a precursor, with its formally-defined notion of scales, to the proposed view of grammatical (semantic or syntactic) computational systems (CS), although it is still pragmatic with its use-related communicative inferences.

This talk will take up some controversies over related issues between the different positions and try to address the big question of whether scalar implicatures are pragmatic inferences or grammar. Tentatively I can say that the generation of scalar implicatures is rooted in and motivated by pragmatic inferences and the interpretation of them is at least schematically and sometimes overtly triggered by grammatical devices of language-specific morphemes or intonation.

2. Debates

2.1 Disjunction Problem

In (3c), the Horn scale of connectives originally had *<or, and>*, with *p and q* entailing *p or q* and with *p or q* implicating *p and q*. But Chierchia (2004) indicated that a global approach in general fails to treat implicatures in complex sentences including cases with disjunction and another operator in its scope (also Schwarz 2000), as in (6), and proposed a local semantic system.

   (6) Kai had the broccoli or some of the peas last night.
   (7) (6) ~> Kai didn't have the broccoli and some of the peas last night.

Facing this problem of disjunction with another operator like *some* in its scope, Sauerland (2004) offered a solution by positing a pair of disjuncts {p, q} or {*L, R*} in between *<or, and>* in the scale, making it a partially ordered set. Otherwise, (7) is the only implicature generated and cannot handle (8), which Sauerland argues, is an intuitively adequate scalar implicature generated by (6).

   (8) (6) ~> Kai didn't have all of the peas last night.

Sauerland bases his claim on the intuition that if I happen to know that Kai ate all the peas last night and hear (6) I would say (9):

(9) No (#Yes), he had all of the peas last night.

Sauerland also discusses scalar items in the scope of negation, a logical operator, but negation reverses scales (Horn 1972, Atlas and Levinson 1981, Lee 2000 *CLS* 36) and scale reversal explains some past inadequacies in treatment. The assertion *Sam didn't have all of the peas* implicates *Sam   had some of the peas* via double negation. Sauerland uses the cross product of the two scales expressed in sentences for their implicatures as in (10):

(10) Kai ate peas or broccoli on Monday or Tuesday.
    ~>~[Kai ate peas and broccoli on Monday or Tuesday.]
    ~>~[Kai ate peas or broccoli on Monday and Tuesday.]
    (~> ~[Kai ate peas and broccoli on Monday and Tuesday.])

Saueland takes the position of Soames (1982) and Horn (1972, 1989) in viewing implicatures as epistemologically modalized. What follows from Grice's maxims of conversation is that a stronger statement ψ is uncertain (~$\mathbf{K}\psi$), a weak implicature, rather than that ψ is certainly false ($\mathbf{K}$~ψ). $\mathbf{K}$~ψ follows from ~$\mathbf{K}\psi$ only if some additional knowledge (such as that $\mathbf{K}\psi \vee \mathbf{K}$~$\psi$ holds). He arrives at the strong implicatures (7) and (8) of (6), the disjunctive utterance, using the distinction between weak and strong and moving from weak to strong, also using individual disjuncts p and q in (p or q). Sauerland criticizes Chierchia about his drastic departure from Gricean reasoning for a local semantic system on the grounds of the disjunction problem ("not valid") and other empirical facts that are "less than clear." Chierchia heavily relies on the conventional content for his "semantics."

2.2 Global vs Local Problem

Russell (2006) examines Chierchia's (2004) arguments on the following types of apparent embedded implicatures against Gricean analysis:

(11) a. Sam believes that some of his advisors are crooks.
    ~> l. Sam believes that not all of his advisors are crooks.
    ~> g. It is not the case that Sam believes that all of his advisors are crooks.
    . b. Sam knows that some of his advisors are crooks.
    ~>Not all of his advisors are crooks.

Chierchia claims that hearers can make conclusions about the negation of competing utterances as a whole a la Gricean reasoning in (11a.g.) and that implicatures are added to an expression's meaning by the compositional semantics at each type *t* meaning (extensionalizing). The embedded S in (11) is computed to give a strong meaning of *some of his advisors are crooks and not all of his advisors are crooks* for (11a.l.). Russell also argues that (11a.l.) follows (11a.g.) in every context where Sam has some belief about whether all of his advisors are crooks. Russell argues that (11b) is apparently equally felicitous whether or not all of his advisors are crooks – *in fact* is not needed to cancel that supposition, whereas it is needed to cancel an ordinary scalar implicature, as in (12). (13) shows a case of Contrastive Focus (CF)-marking on *some* and *all*, and a restricted meaning of *some but not all* for *some* (Carston's explicature).

(12) a. Sam knows that some of his advisors are crooks, and (in fact) they all are.

b. Some of his advisors are crooks, and #(in fact) they all are.

(13) It is better to eat *some* of the cake than it is to eat *all* of it.

Russell also treats DE contexts where their operators have a *reversed* pattern of implicatures.

(14) If Sam eats all his vegetables, he'll get dessert.

~> It is not the case that if Sam eats some of his vegetables, he'll get dessert.

This effect is predicted by Gricean reasoning, as Levinson (2001) notes, while Chierchia must stipulate a special rule for this, as Russell indicates. However, this place may be a meeting point between reasoning and semantics. Russell treats intervention as well. He strongly defends Gricean pragmatics of a very general global theory, looking for a better theory of competition for a wider range of implicarures resolution.

3. Grammar and Exhaustivity

After Chierchia's (2004) semantics for scalar implicatures, Fox (2005) developed his LF syntax, positing an Exhaustivity operator, which is an abstract lexical item largely equivalent to 'only', following the exhaustivity semantics tradition (Groenendijk and Stokhof (1984) and others, to treat scalar implicatures in syntax.

4. Conjunctive Discourse Markers, Contrastive Topic, Scales and Implicatures

There are two different types of contrastive or adversative sentence conjunctions and their corresponding discourse markers (DM), as in:

(1) Concessive (Cncssv) PA type: *pero/aber,   -ciman*;   DM: *haciman, kurehciman*
(2) Metalinguistic negation SN type: *sondern/sino* ; *-ka anira*; DM: *kukey anira.*

The Concessive (Cnsccv) PA type is fundamentally correlated with Contrastive Topic (CT) in the first conjunct and the SN type with Contrastive Focus (CF) construction, as I argued elsewhere (Lee 2006). The parallel applies even when an utterance with CT has no explicit second conjunct; its scalar implicature begins with the corresponding Cnsccv PA type DM 'But' in (1a). I will show how CT along with the PA type DM typically generates scalar implicatures and possibly implicatures by denial of 'generic entailment' (Koenig and Benndorf 1998), which I claim can be scalar, on one hand, and why CF along with the SN type fails to do so, on the other.

I go back to the discussion of scales extended and repeat the propositional type of scales from 1.1 (5a) as (3):

(3) propositions < [Korea will beat Togo], [Japan will beat Brazil]>.

Horn is certain about his entailment scales and Hirschberg (1991) takes up some non-entailment scales, arguing that they also show the same scale behavior. I added a scale of entire propositions (of likelihood/easiness), as in (3), and will discuss a wider range of processes scales Hirschberg does not seem to cover shortly. (3) is exemplified by (4) in Korean:

(4) na-nun [hankwuk-i Togo-rul   iki-l   kes-i-ra-ko]-NUN mit-nun-ta
        I –TOP Korea   -NOM T-ACC beat-PRE COMP-COP-CT   believe
        'I believe [that Korea will beat Togo]$_{CT}$ => (But not that Japan will beat Brazil.)

In (4), an overt CT marker *–nun* is used and if it occurs the implicature of the denial of a higher value is unavoidable. A CT-marked utterance is concessively admitted. If the marker does not occur, the implicature is evoked when the context licenses it, in which case I claim CT is overt. With the above scales, the principle in (5) applies:

(5) If p is uttered with overt (or covert) CT-marking in it, it is represented as '*CT*(p).' Then
        concessively (and contrastively) (with PA 'But') 'not q' is conveyed (the speaker
        believes so), with the *CT* operator being associated with a CT-marked element (focal and
        topical) in p. In this case, q has a relevant and comparable stronger/higher element in one
        and the same scale to be denied.

If the elements in a scale are negated, simply the scale is reversed and the **same principle** applies (with the effect: if not-q is uttered with CT-marking, its representation 'CT(not-q)' conveys concessively (and contrastively) 'p' (a weaker/lower positive element).

(6) Yumi-ka   notebook-ul   sa-ci-NUN anh –ass-ta   => (haciman ---)

    Y   -NOM   -ACC   buy-ci-CT   not-PAST-DEC

    'Yumi $_{CT}$ did not buy $_{CT}$ a notebook PC $_{CT}$.' => But (buy $_{CT}$) just browsed ones or

    But (a notebook PC $_{CT}$) Yumi bought just an organizer or But (Yumi $_{CT}$) Mia bought

    one.

In (6), the CT operator can be realized at the end of V-*ci* and can be associated with either with the verb, the object, the predicate, or the subject, depending on which one is focal. The verb and the object can be doubly CT-marked with doubly evoked implicatures and even the subject can be CT-marked at the same time but the triple CT-marking with triple implicatures is hard to compute and is rather avoided.

This talk makes the distinction between typical **conversational** scalar implicatures (contextual, optional) and **conventional** scalar implicatures. The latter, unlike in Buring (2001), are those evoked by a Contrastive Topic (CT) contour (fall-rise (L+H*LH%) B accent) intonation or CT markers –*nun* (Korean) or –*wa* (Japanese) with high tone, *shi* (with tone 4-Fall) (Chinese), *-thi* (with high tone) (Vietnamese), *i.e.*, a linguistic device. Unlike the former, the latter cannot be cancelled without roundabout epistemic hedges. Observe:

(7) A: You have many friends, don't you?

    B: ses-UN iss-e.   (K)

        3-CT exist-DEC 'I have THREE$_{CT}$' => (**conventionally** implicates)

                      [*haciman te-nun eps-e*] '***But*** not more than three.'

    B': I have THREE$_{CT}$. ?*((In fact, four.)) (the above implicature not cancelable)

    B'': san-nin-WA imasu.   (J) [**ga** san-nin yori oku-wa arimasen]

        3-CL-CTexist-DEC

        'I·have·THREE$_{CT}$'

(8)   A. manh-ci-NUN anh-e (K)   oku-WA nai-desu/arimasen (J)

    many -CT   not   [but a few]

    A': I don't have \MANY/$_{CT}$ friends. [but a few]

(9) A. manh-ci   anh-e (K)   oku   nai-desu/arimasen (J)

    many   not   [but a few, no]

    A': I don't have MANY friends. [but a few, no]

(10) A: How did she do on her exam?

B: She \PASSED/$_{CT}$ (L+H*LH% or Fall-Rise B Accent) =>(**conventionally**) [**But** she didn't ace the exam.] (?*In fact, she aced the exam.)

By the distinction between (8) and (9), the dispute between Horn (2005) and Chierchia (2004) about implicatures of negative scales seems to disappear; Chierchia's claim that they are 'somewhat weaker and flimsier' is one-sided, dealing with conversational ones, and lacks the notion of CT, which Horn also lacks. With CT, Horn is right but without it, Chierchia is right.

Let us consider further examples of CT with PA:

(11) a. watashi-wa kanozo-ga suki-deWA aru => [*ga ai-shi-te   -wa   inai*] (J)

I   -TOP her-NOM like - CT be   but love-do-CON-CT not

'I LIKE$_{CT}$ her' => 'But I don't LOVE$_{CT}$ her.

b. watashi-wa kanozo-o ai-shi-te-WA inai => [*ga* suki-de-wa aru]

(12) chim **thi** bay => [***nung*** ca **thi** lo] (Vietnamese) (a scalar implicature required by CT)

'Birds$_{CT}$ fly' => '**But** fish$_{CT}$ swim' (from a larger fixed set of animal kinds)

Let us turn to scales of processes with apparent 'non-entailment':

(13): <touch, push, beat, hurt, kill>

< S1,   S2,   S3,   S4,   S5>   Severity of attack

< 1,   2,   3,   4,   5>

Sm ← Sn for each $m<n$

The logical structure of all the relevant and comparable alternative predicates (processes or events) at a more "abstract" level (I owe Seligman for this kind of level via e-mail 5/2/06) is not different from that of Horn's "entailment" scales in generating scalar implicatures. Furthermore, this kind of process scales may be far more prevalent than Horn scales in every day language, as Potts hinted (in my talk at LELNS). Let's take S1,..., S5 to abbreviate the increasing different degrees of the severity of my attack from low to high (*less severe than*) like levels 1, 2, ... 5, where the severity of a mere *touch* is level 1 and that of killing is level 5, then Sn implies (=entails) Sm for each $m<n$. In other words, we get some sort of abstract level 'entailment' in general. The scalar implicature of the CT-marked sentence (14)

(14) I PUSHED$_{CT}$ her

in a suitable scalarity context, is that the (overall) severity of my attack was no higher than that of the *push*. If the severity of a push is at level 2, say, then this would entail S2, which in turn scalarly implicates that I didn't beat, hurt or kill her, with the aid of the PA connective/DM despite the fact that none of these processes in the scale literally entails pushing. No right side predicate literally asymmetrically entails the left side predicate for that matter. In severity the prototypical maximal element is killing, which behaves like universal quantifier, e.g.,

(15) a. ???I KILLED$_{CT}$ her.   Cf. b. ?*ALL$_{CT}$ came. (Lee 2000)

If, however, a context accommodates an extended scale including *decapitate/dismember*, S6, then (15a) can become appropriate with the implicature of [***But*** I didn't decapitate her]. This way, a scale of property degree ranking (along with information strength degree entailment) evokes scalar implicatures. Because scales are contextually (pragmatically) evoked, a positive scale in one context can be reversed in another context without polarity reversal marking, e.g.,

(16) a. <cwuk/kayu 'porridge,' 'gruel,' pap/gohan 'rice,' 'meal'>
     cwuk-UN mek-ess-e   'I ate PORRIDGE$_{CT}$.' haciman pap-un an mek-ess-e 'But not rice.'
   b. <pap, cwuk> (<gohan, kayu>) [scale of nutrition and specialty].
     pap-UN mek-ess-e 'I ate RICE$_{CT}$.' haciman cwuk-un an mek-ess-e 'But not porridge.'

This nature of context dependence of scales does not mean at all that there is no principle of scalarity we can rely on. It is a matter of choice between different gradable **properties** or **dimensions** in different contexts. In the ordinary scale of (16a), *cwuk* 'porridge' is weaker than *pap* 'rice,' in the dimension of meal status, generating a scalar implicature, unlike (16b), where the scale is reversed because of the new salient contrast in the context/world, which Hirschberg would see as a particularized conversational implicature (PCI), trying to unite these implicatures with Levinson's (2000) lexicon-based generalized conversational implicatures (GCI) in her broader theory. Levinson maintains a general theory of GCI, arguing that all the mutual scale knowledge is based on the lexicons speakers carry on their backs from context to context. But I further claim that overt CT-marked scale implicatures are **conventional**; CT-marking involves linguistic devices of CT morphemes and CT intonations. For some uses of common nouns, however, there may be no scalehood of property/dimensionality as such. Those nouns may denote a **list** of non-scalar entities. But if they are once CT-marked, they can be said to generate quantity-based scalar implicatures; the total list of items constitute a sum and a CT-marked item is less than the sum and if that item is asserted the sum minus the item is denied to be conveyed as a scalar implicature (Lee 1999). The CT-marked item's prior potential Topic is the sum. The item is typically a part/kind of the sum denotation but it may be one item of the sum of apparently arbitrarily grouped objects in a special context, e.g., *<monster, monster+beauty>*.[1]

5. Contrastive Topic vs *Only*-like Exhaustivity Operator

Groenendijk and Stokhof (1984) see the denotation of a question as a proposition which expresses the true (quality) and complete (quantity) answer, which is typically interpreted exhaustively, to that question in the same given world. They believe the answer *Mary* to the question *Who came* generally implies no one *else* came and stipulate a semantic exhaustivity operator that relates the answer to the abstract underlying the question. The exhaustivity operator is assumed to have the semantic effect of the word *only*, defined as *Exh*(A, P) = {w: w $\in$ A and there is no w' $\in$ A such that w'$<_p$w and w and w' give the same denotation to all predicates distinct from P}. (17A), then, would mean 'Mia and Sue came and no one else came.' But other non-exhaustive (19) and wondering (18) interpretations are possible for the same question-answer in addition to an exhaustive interpretation (17). Consider the following dialogues:

(17) Q: Who came?   A: Mia and Sue. Q': Why didn't Joe come?
(18) Q: Who came?   A: Mia and Sue. Q': But no one else?/Did anyone else come?
(19) Q: Who came?   A: Mia and Sue. Q': And who else? (modified from Sevi 2005)

The hearer has the option. But if the fragment answer has the CT contour (L+H*LH%) (e.g. in a situation where everyone is expected to come), a scalar implicature such as '*but not Joe and Mary*' (from the contextually evoked scale <Mia&Sue, Mia&Sue&Joe&Mary>) is required and the response to the answer in (19) and '*Did anyone else come?*' in (18) are odd. In Korean a fragment reply ending with the CT *–nun* is impossible (e.g. *Mia-hako Sue-**nun*** 'Mia-and Sue-CT') in all contexts including a post-verbal sentence final position (Lee 2001), although in English a CT intonation freely occurs S-finally and with fragments.

If, however, an answer is taken to have a semantic exhaustivity operator with the meaning of *only*, as in most adoptions of the operator (Zeevat ms, Sevi 2005, Spector 2003, Fox 2006), the denial of the entire alternatives except the prejacent of the *only* clause or the one in the utterance is already at least **entailed** or **asserted** (and the prejacent is not asserted – 'assertorically inert,' of which the status is controversial over whether it is presupposed or conventionally implicated or what not (Horn 2002)). If that is the case, there is no room for scalar **implicatures** to arise of the same propositional content that has been already asserted or entailed. Consequently, the following conjunctions/discourses with PA type conjunction/DM are not acceptable:

(20)   a. ?***Only** Mia and Sue came but Joe and Mary didn't come.

      b. ?*I **only** bought three books but not more than that.

      c. ???I **only** bought three books. But I did not buy more than that.

      d. ?*na   chayk sey kwon-**man** sa-ss-e. haciman ke isang-un an sa-ss-e

          I   book 3   CL-only   buy-PAST-DEC But that more than not bought

          (same as c)

Without *only* or *–man*, the sentences in (20) are perfect; the potential implicatures can be explicitly uttered. With *only*, the second conjuncts or utterances are redundant and *but*/*haciman* there is incoherent. The DMs *But* (20c) and *haciman* (20d), without *only*, are monologic but they can occur dialogically with the same intent, e.g. A: Mia hapkyekhaysse 'Mia passed' B: **haciman** swusek-un mot haysse 'But she didn't ace the exam'). With *only*, the negative alternatives are already so assertive that the concessive use of *but/(ha)ciman* is not applicable in the conjunction or discourse. The concessive meaning of *but* is not truth-conditional; *but* and *and* are identical truth-conditionally. But in a PA *but* conjunction/discourse, the first conjunct/utterance is concessively admitted and the second one is stronger in its argument, claim or conclusion (Lee 2001, Anscrombre and Ducrot 1977). The exact translation of (20c) is rather a negative S *na chayk sey kwon **pakkey** an sa-ss-e* '(Lit.) I didn't buy beyond three books,' which is not distinct from the second part of (20d) and cannot be followed by it. Therefore, the use of *only* or its equivalent *exh* operator for generating a scalar implicature is not well justified.

As a consequence, Sevi (2005) argues that scalar implicatures are not implicatures and that they are merely entailments of *exh (A, Q)*, where *A* is taken to be a complete and partial semantic answer to some question *Q*, which may be explicit or implicit. The effect of the stronger meaning of *A* is analyzed as an ambiguity – depending on the optionality of the applicability of *exh* (applied to (17A) but not to (18A, 19A)). His argument is based on Grice's maxim of quality – a **true** answer. As long as the stronger meaning of *no one/nothing else* (in the given domain) is entailed, there cannot be cancellation. But sentences with *only* and without it behave quite differently regarding their following conjunct/utterance, as we observed above, and the difference must be accounted for.

My claim is that the PA type conjunction/DM is adjusted to occur with a prior concessive conjunct or utterance for the following conjunct or utterance, which is argumentatively stronger, and that overt or covert CT is exactly concessive for coherence between CT and PA. If the second PA part is not uttered, it must be conveyed as a scalar implicature because of the CT in the prior utterance. I see this as a sort of semantic ellipsis. Although the conveyed meaning is motivated pragmatically by general inference (Levinson 2000), its working in grammar is already conventional and a way of representing it via CT as an operator, as shown in (5). In other words, *only* or *exh* is too strong. If a *wh*-word - information focus pair occurs in a question - answer pair, it is normally recast in an accommodated question - answer pair that contains a potential Topic - CT pair. A negative answer (if not metalinguistic) is typically associated with CT (see (6)). This explains why a CT utterance generates a scalar implicature and why a scalar implicature begins with a PA *but*. So far, conjunction types and information structure have been studied separately.

6. Metalinguistic Negation or SN (sino/sondern) Conjunction

Let's turn to the use of SN type conjunction/DM, shown in (2), that involves metalinguistic negation (MN). Typically a clause with MN is followed by the second (elliptical) clause led by an SN connective/DM (or connected by a comma/semicolon), distinct in form in most languages except in English (*but*) and French (*mais*). The MN clause may sometimes be implicit, as in (22) but rarely the other alternative offered.

(21)   a. I am not HAPPY $_{CF}$ (*unhappy) but ECSTATIC $_{CF}$.

      b. na-nun hayngpokha-n   kes-i ani-ra hwangholhay.

        I   TOP happy   -COMP-NOM not-CONJ ecstatic   (same as (a))

(22) Q. You read part of the mystery novel already, didn't you?

    A. I read the WHOLE $_{CF}$ novel.   (Not PART $_{CF}$ of it.)

(23) a. It's not eSOTeric; it's esoTERic. (due to Burton-Roburts and Carston)

    b. Is the correct pronunciation eSOTeric or esoTERic?

The pairs of alternatives above are known to get extra heavy stress and I claim all of them constitute Contrastive Focus (CF), which, I claim, comes from a prior alternative disjunctive question (such as (23b)), either explicit or accommodated (Lee 2003). Then, the metalinguistic or echoed (Carston 1996) alternative is refuted on 'whatever grounds' (Horn 1985), the target of negation being claimed to be scalar implicatures, aspects of linguistic forms, or even propositions (Horn p.c.). This is in sharp contrast with concessive admission of the first conjunct/ utterance in CT-PA. In typical MN utterances such as (21) and (22), in which the negation, if interpreted in descriptive negation, creates contradictions, therefore, the conclusive positive alternative must be **scalarly upward** and assertorial, showing a scalar implicature blocking effect, unlike in CT. Such blocking and garden-path effect in Horn may not be real except in written English. The informational CF frame and its correlated SN connection, including a pause, comma and semicolon (see Potts 2005 for the importance of such orthographic marks), are cross-linguistically required. The contrastiveness here is tightly restricted, typically to a pair. In correction type MN utterances, on the other hand, the refuted echoed alternative and the newly presented positive alternative do not constitute a scale – they are non-scalar in the sense of objectively recognized scale discussed above. A Contrastive Focus tone (L+)H* is generally higher in pitch than a presentational focus (Selkirk 2002) and a Corrective Focus is the highest in pitch (350 mh) among neutral focus, *wh*-Q/A information focus, and Corrective Focus,   being higher in this order (Kang 1997). The corrective (all MN has certain corrective force) alternative can also be uttered dialogically by a different speaker starting with an SN DM (then, the first speaker's utterance must be recast for CF in accommodation by the second speaker).

7. Contrastive Topic - Pero/Aber vs. Contrastive Focus – Sino/Sondern

Let's consider the following follow-up responses by B and C that look alike but differ in CT-PA and CF-SN inferences (adapted from Dascal and Katriel 1977):

> (24) A: Bill Gates is an economist.
>> B: He is not an economist, but/*aber/aval/-ciman* he is a businessman.
>> C: He is not an ECONOMIST$_{CF}$ but/*sondrn/ela/anira* a BUSINESSMAN$_{CF}$

Dascal and Katriel adopts and tries to improve Ducrot's (1976, later Anscrombre and Ducrot 1977) intuitive argumentative theory, based on the different conjunction types, but neither they nor he show any sign of their correlation with CT and CF and fail to give a fully adequate characterization of the constructions. In (24A&B), it is true that B's implicit conclusion may lead to "So, let's hear his opinion," regarding the goal/direction/force of argumentation in the context of discussing the economic situation and trying to get a specialist's opinion. But it starts with a covert CT, generating a scale of <businessman, economist> in the rank order of degree of knowledge of economic affairs). Although he is not an economist [concessive admission], he has certain degree of knowledge of economic affairs as a businessman, though lower than an economist. From here, the argumentative goals may vary from context to context. The utterance part led by PA may be implicit as a scalar implicature with a similar effect. In (24A&B), A's utterance is flatly refuted without concession by MN in CF and there is no room left for further consideration. The metalinguistically negated CF alternative is correlated with and requires SN connection. "So, there is no need to hear his opinion" is C's conclusion regarding the argumentative goal.

8. Further Inferences in Contrastive Topic – Pero/Aber Correlation

Consider the logical contrast of contradiction involving PA in (25a) and the compatibility between the negative pair of opposite gradable adjectives in (25b):

(25) a. *Yumi-nun khu-*ciman*   cak-e

   *'Yumi is tall but/*aber* she is short.'

   b. Yumi-nun khu-ci-to anh-ciman/ko cak-ci-to anh-e

   'Yumi is not tall but is not short either/is neither tall nor short.'

The adjective 'short' is a contrary of 'tall,' entailing 'not tall' and constituting a contradiction with 'tall.' If (25a) changes to 'Yumi is tall (with CT marking in Korean) but (she is) not very tall,' via Quantity-maxim it becomes an instance of CT – PA conjunction. (25b) shows that 'not tall' licenses an in-between range of 'neither tall nor short,' 'short' being a part located at the extreme end of 'not tall.'   In this case, the CT –*nun* cannot occur on both 'tall' and 'short' in Korean. It can occur on 'tall' but –*to* 'also' must occur on 'short' because of the repeated negation. The additive   –*to* 'also' can occur on both with PA but it must occur on both if the conjunction is –*ko* 'and.' Turning to a prevalent CT-PA inference like (26), it suppresses a generic entailment of 'tall persons play the basketball well,' which otherwise can occur as an R-inference. (27) shows that because of 'only' in the CT phrase, the potential implicature turns entailed or asserted. Consider:

(26) Yumi-nun khu-ki-NUN hay ~>   *haciman nongkwu-rul cal mot-hay*

   'Yumi is tall.'   'But cannot play the basketball well.'

(27) i pen –man –UN yongse-ha-n-ta → *taum pen –ey-nun   an hay*

   this time-only-TOP (I) forgive   next time-at-TOP   not (I) do

9. Concluding Remarks

PA and SN are respectively correlated with CT and CF, which are information structural and quantificationally domain-restricted. CT-PA and CF-SN suppress R- and Q-implicatures, respectively.

Scalar implicatures are motivated by Gricean pragmatic reasoning but they are deeply and crucially rooted in the grammatical devices of Contrastive Topic (CT), overt or covert. CT requires PA (pero/aber) conjunction, *i.e.* 'concessive *But*' and that's why scalar implicatures begin with *but* and its equivalents cross-linguistically.

References

Anscrombre, J.-C. and O. Ducrot. 1977.   Deux *mais* en francais? *Lingua* 43. 23-40.

Breheny, R., N. Katsos, J. Williams. 2006. Are Generalized Scalar Implicatures Generated by Default? *Cognition* 100, pp. 434 - 463.

Carston, R. 1996. Metalinguistic negation and echoic use. *Journal of Pragmatics* 25, 309-30.

Chierchia, G. 2004. Scalar Implicatures, Polarity Phenomena, and the Syntax/Pragmatics Interface.

Fox, Danny 2006. Free Choice and the Theory of Scalar Implicatures. Ms, MIT.

Horn, Laurence. 1989. *A Natural History of Negation.* Chicago University Press.

Horn, Laurence. 2002. Assertoric Inertia and NPI Licensing. *CLS* 38, II. 55-82.

Keshet, Ezra. 2006. Scalar Implicatures with Alternative Semantics, *SALT*, Tokyo.

Koenig, J.-P. and B. Benndorf 1998 'Meaning and Context: German *aber* and *sondern*,' in J.-P. Koenig (ed) *Discourse and Cognition*, CSLI, Stanford.

Lee, Chungmin. 2001. Acquisition of Topic and Subject Markers in Korean. In *Issues in East Asian Language Acquisition* 41-66, M. Nakayama(ed.) KLW Series Vol. 7, Kurosio Publishers, Tokyo, Japan.

Lee, Chungmin 2003 'Contrastive Topic and/or Contrastive Focus,' in Bill McClure (ed.) *Japanese/Korean Linguistics* 12. CSLI, Stanford

Lee, Chungmin 2006 'Contrastive (Predicate) Topic/Focus and Polarity in Discourse,' in von Heusinger and K. Turner (eds) *Where Semantics Meets Pragmatics* CRiSPI, Elsevier.

Potts, C. 2005. *The Logic of Conventional Implicatures.* Oxford Studies in Theoretical Linguistics. OUP.

Russell, B. 2006. Against Grammatical Computation of Scalr Implicatures, *Journal of Semantics* 23. 361-381. ,

Sauerland, Uli 2004 'On Embedded Implicatures,' *Journal of Cognitive Science* 5 (1).

Sevi, Aldo 2005 *Exhaustivity*, Tel Aviv University Dissertation.

Zeevat, H. 1994 'Applying an Exhaustifying Operator in Update Semantics.' In H. Kamp (ed.).

NIST 2007 Language Recognition Evaluation: From the Perspective of IIR[*]

Haizhou Li, Bin Ma, Kong-Aik Lee, Khe-Chai Sim, Hanwu Sun,
Rong Tong, Donglai Zhu, and Changhuai You

Institute for Infocomm Research,
Agency for Science, Technology and Research (A*STAR), Singapore
{hli,mabin,kalee,kcsim,hwsun,tongrong,dzhu,echyou}@i2r.a-star.edu.sg

Abstract. This paper describes the Institute for Infocomm Research (IIR) system for the 2007 Language Recognition Evaluation (LRE) conducted by the National Institute of Standards and Technology (NIST). The submitted system is a fusion of multiple state-of-the-art language classifiers using diversified discriminative language cues. We implemented several state-of-the-art algorithms using both phonotactic and acoustic features. We also investigated the system fusion and score calibration strategy to improve the performance of language recognition, and worked out a pseudo-key analysis approach to cross-validate the performance of the individual classifiers on the evaluation data. We achieve an equal-error-rate (EER) of 1.67 % on the close-set general language recognition test.

Keywords: Automatic spoken language recognition, NIST Language Recognition Evaluation, phonotactic features, acoustic features, fusion system, pseudo key.

1. Introduction

Automatic spoken language recognition (SLR) is a process of determining the identity of the language in a spoken document. As multilingual applications are demanded by the emerging need for globalization and the growing international business interflow, SLR has become an enabling technology in many applications such as multilingual conversational systems (Zue and Glass, 2000), multilingual speech recognition and translation (Waibel et al., 2000), and spoken document retrieval (Dai et al. 2003). It is also a topic of great importance in the areas of intelligence and security, where the language identities of recorded messages and archived materials need to be established before any information can be extracted. SLR technology also facilitates massive on-line language routing for voice surveillance over telephone network.

The National Institute of Standards and Technology (NIST) has conducted a series of evaluations of SLR technology in 1996, 2003, 2005 and 2007 (NIST, 2007). The language recognition evaluations (LREs) focus on language and dialect detection in the context of conversational telephony speech. They are conducted to foster research progress, with the goals of exploring promising new ideas in language recognition, developing advanced technology incorporating these ideas, and measuring the performance of this technology. The Institute for

---

Infocomm Research (IIR) team has participated in the 2005 and 2007 NIST LREs and demonstrated the state-of-the-art technologies.

One of the fundamental issues in SLR is to explore the discriminative cues for spoken languages. In the state-of-the-art language recognition systems, these cues mainly come from the acoustic features (Sugiyama, 1991; Torres-Carassquilo et al., 2002; Burget et al., 2006; Campbell et al., 2006) and phonotactic representations (Hazen and Zue, 1994; Zissman, 1996; Berkling and Barnard, 1994; Corredor-Ardoy et al., 1997; Li and Ma, 2005; Ma, Li, and Tong, 2007), which reflect different aspects of spoken language characteristics. Another issue is how to effectively organize and exploit these language cues obtained from multiple sources in the recognition system design for the best performance.

Significant improvements in automatic speech recognition (ASR) have been achieved through exploiting the acoustic features representing the temporal properties of speech spectrum. These acoustic features, such as Mel-frequency Cepstral Coefficients (MFCCs), are also good choices to be the front-ends in language recognition systems. Gaussian mixture model (GMM), which can be seen as a one-state hidden Markov model (HMM) (Rabiner, 1989), is a simple modeling method to provide a multimodal density and is reasonably accurate when speech data are generated from a set of Gaussian distributions. It has demonstrated a great success in text-independent speaker recognition (Reynolds, Quatieri, and Dunn, 2000). In language recognition, GMM is also an effective method to model the unique characteristics among languages (Torres-Carassquilo et al., 2002). The support vector machine (SVM) has proven to be a powerful classifier in many pattern classification tasks. It is a discriminative classifier to separate two classes with a hyperplane in a high-dimensional space. The generalized linear discriminant sequence kernel (GLDS) has been proposed to apply SVM for speaker and language recognition (Campbell et al., 2006). The cepstral feature vectors extracted from an utterance are expanded to a high-dimensional space by calculating all the monomials.

In recent years, phonotactic features have been shown to provide effective cues for language recognition. The phonotactic features are extracted from an utterance to represent phonetic constraints in a language. Although common sounds are shared considerably across spoken languages, the statistics of these sounds, such as phone n-gram, can differ considerably from one language to another. Parallel Phone Recognizers followed by Language Models (PPR-LM) (Zissman, 1996) uses multiple parallel phone recognizers to convert the input utterance into a phone token sequence. It is followed by a set of n-gram phone language models that imposes constraints on phone decoding and provides language scores. Instead of n-gram phone language models, vector space modeling (VSM) was proposed as the classifier (Li, Ma, and Lee, 2007), called PPR-VSM. For each phone sequence generated from the multiple phone recognizers, the occurrences of phone n-grams are counted. A phone sequence is then represented as a high-dimensional vector of n-gram occurrence. SVM is used as the classifier on the concatenated n-gram occurrence vectors.

It is generally agreed upon that the integration with different cues of discriminative information can improve the performance of language recognition (Adda-Decker et al., 2003). The information extraction and organization of multiple sources has been critical to a successful language recognition system (Singer et al., 2003; Tong et al., 2006). In this paper, we will report our language recognition system submitted to the 2007 NIST LRE. The system is based on the fusion of multiple classifiers, each providing unique discriminative cue for language classification. In order to avoid a spoiled classifier in the submitted fusion system, we have designed a pseudo key analysis approach to check the integrity of each individual classifier before the system fusion.

The remainder of this paper is organized as follows. The evaluation data and evaluation metric of the 2007 NIST LRE will be introduced in Section 2. The system structure together with the phonotactic and acoustic language classifiers will be presented in Section 3. The fusion of multiple language classifiers and language recognition results on the 2007 NIST LRE evaluation data will be described in Section 4. The pseudo key analysis will be shown in Section 5. Finally in Section 6, we summarize our findings in language recognition.

2. Data and Metric

2.1. Evaluation Data

There are six test categories in the 2007 NIST LRE involving 26 target languages and dialects:

- General Language Recognition (LR) including 14 languages, Arabic, Bengali, Chinese, English, Hindustani, Spanish, Farsi, German, Japanese, Korean, Russian, Tamil, Thai and Vietnamese.
- Chinese LR including four Chinese dialects, Cantonese, Mandarin, Min and Wu.
- Mandarin Dialect Recognition (DR) including Mainland Mandarin and Taiwan Mandarin.
- English DR including American English and India English.
- Hindustani DR including Hindi and Urdu.
- Spanish DR including Caribbean Spanish and non-Caribbean Spanish.

Both closed-set and open-set tests in the six categories were conducted. For the closed-set tests, the non-target languages will be limited to those languages and dialects known to the system. For the open-set test the non-target languages will also include all other unknown languages such as Italian, Punjabi, Tagalog, Indonesian, and French. These unknown languages were not disclosed to participants, and the training data for these languages were not made available.

There are three test conditions to evaluate the system performance under different test segment durations:

- 3 seconds of speech (2-4 seconds actual)
- 10 seconds of speech (7-13 seconds actual)
- 30 seconds of speech (25-35 seconds actual)

The silence was not removed from speech so a segment could be much longer. There are 2510 segments for each of the three durations.

2.2. Training and Development Data

All the phonotactic and acoustic classifiers were trained with the LDC CallFriend corpus[1] and the LRE 2007 development databases released by NIST to all the participants. The phone recognizers used for phonotactic features were trained with OGI Multilingual database (Muthusamy, Cole, and Oshika, 1992) and IIR-LID database (Tong et al., 2006). The weights of fusion system were tuned on the LRE 1996, 2003, 2005 databases as well as the LRE 2007 development database.

2.3. Evaluation Metric

The primary evaluation metric is taken as the average cost performance C_{avg} (NIST LRE, 2007), which indicates the pair-wise language recognition performance, represented in terms of detection miss and false alarm probabilities, for all target/non-target language pairs. For the case of closed-set test condition, the C_{avg} is given by

$$C_{avg} = \frac{1}{N_{tar}} \sum_{l \in L_{tar}} \left\{ 0.5 P_{miss}(l) + 0.5 \times \frac{1}{(N_{tar}-1)} \sum_{l' \in L_{non}} P_{FA}(l,l') \right\} \tag{1}$$

where L_{tar} is the set of N_{tar} target languages (e.g., $N_{tar}=14$ for general LR). Notice that the miss probability P_{miss} is computed separately for each target language. All other languages are treated as non-target languages to compute the false alarm probabilities P_{FA} for each target/non-target language pairs. A complete definition of C_{avg} can be found in (NIST LRE, 200). In addition to the C_{avg}, we also report the results in terms of the average equal-error-rate (EER). That is, we compute the EER for each of the target language and take their average as the performance measure.

---

[1] http://www.ldc.upenn.edu/

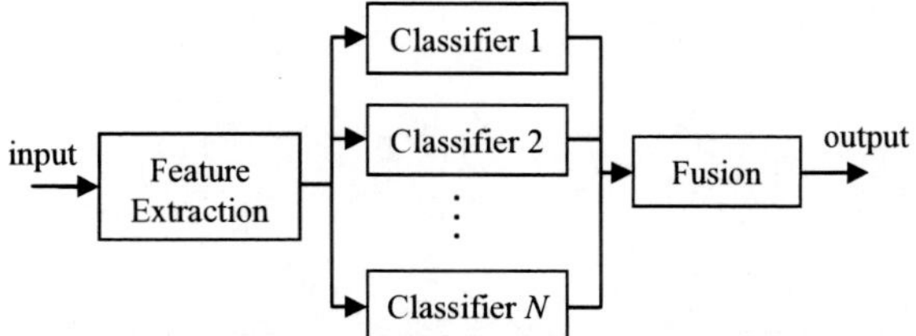

Figure 1: Fusion of multiple language classifiers.

3. System Description

The IIR system submitted to the 2007 NIST LRE is a fusion of multiple language classifiers. Figure 1 shows the overall framework.

3.1. Feature Extraction

The first stage of the feature extraction process is the Voice Activity Detection (VAD). Two types of VAD were used:

- Frame-based VAD

  For the acoustic classifiers, an energy based voice activity detector (VAD) is applied to remove silence frames and to retain only the high quality speech frames for language recognition. The frames whose energy level is more than 30dB below the maximum energy of the entire utterance are considered silence and therefore removed. Furthermore, if there are more than 40% of the frames are retained, only the top 40% of the frames with higher SNR are retained. The rest of the frames are discarded. There are approximately 30% of the frames which are actually selected for further processing.

- Segment-based VAD

  For phonotactic classifiers, segment-based VAD is used. Based on the VAD speech frame index obtained in the above, we first join continuous speech frames to form the speech segments. If the resulting segment is longer than 8 seconds, the segment is further split at the frame in that segment with the lowest energy. This is repeated until the resulting segment is less than 8 seconds in long. The final segments are padded with 200ms silence at both ends.

After VAD, two types of short time cepstral features, Mel Frequency Cepstral Coefficients (MFCCs) and Linear Prediction Cepstral Coefficients (LPCCs), are adopted as the basic features for acoustic classifiers. To capture temporal information across multiple frames, Shifted Delta Cepstral (SDC) coefficients (Torres-Carassquilo et al., 2002) are further applied to the frame-based MFCCs and LPCCs.

3.2. Phonotactic Classifiers

The phonotactic classifiers use multiple phone recognizers as the front-end to derive phonotactic statistics of a language. Since the individual phone recognizers are trained on different languages, they capture different acoustic characteristics from the speech data. Therefore, combining these recognizers together improves the overall language recognition performance.

The PPR front-end can be followed by both the phone n-gram language models (LM) (Zissman, 1996) and the vector space modeling (VSM) backend (Li, Ma, and Lee, 2007). The LM backend evaluates each token sequence using multiple language models, each of which describes a token sequence from the perspective of a target language. With VSM backend, the n-gram statistics from each token sequence form a high-dimensional feature vector, also known as a *bag-of-sounds* (BOS) vector (Li and Ma, 2005). A composite vector is constructed by stacking multiple *bag-of-sounds* vectors derived from multiple token sequences.

3.2.1. PPR-LM Classifier

With the PPR front-end, the backend of the language classifier can be language models for capturing the phonotactic constraints for each target language. PPR-LM approach (Zissman, 1996) uses the PPR front-end to convert a spoken utterance into multiple sequences of phones.

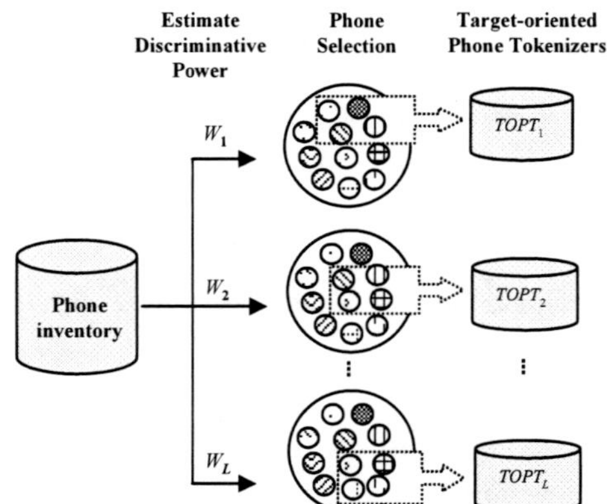

Figure 2: Construction of target oriented phone tokenizers.

Then a set of L n-gram phone language models estimates the likelihood phonotactic scores for the spoken documents in order to produce classification decisions.

3.2.2. PPR-VSM Classifier

Suppose that we have F phone recognizers with a phone inventory of $v=\{v_1,...,v_\tau, ...,v_F\}$ and the number of phones in v_τ is n_τ. An utterance is decoded by these phone recognizers into F independent sequences of phone tokens. Each of these token sequences can be expressed by a high dimensional phonotactic feature vector with the n-gram counts. The dimension of the feature vector is equal to the total number of n-gram patterns needed to highlight the overall behavior of the utterance. If unigram and bigram are the only concerns, we will have a vector of $n_\tau + n_\tau^2$ phonotactic features, to represent the utterance by the τth phone recognizer.

For each target language, an SVM is trained by using the composite feature vectors in the target language as the positive set and the composite feature vectors in all other languages as the negative set. With L target languages, we project the high dimensional composite feature vectors into a discriminative feature vector with a much lower dimension (Ma, Li, and Tong, 2007).

We formulate the language recognition as a hypothesis test. For each target language, we build a language detector which consists of two GMMs $\{\lambda^+,\lambda^-\}$. The GMM trained on the discriminative vectors of the target language is called the positive model λ^+, while the GMM trained on those of its competing languages is called the negative model λ^-. We define the confidence of a test sample O belonging to a target language as the posterior odds in a hypothesis test under the Bayesian interpretation. We have H_0, which hypothesizes that O is language λ^+, and H_1, which hypothesizes otherwise. The posterior odd is approximated by the likelihood ratio $\Lambda(O)$ that is used for the final language recognition decision.

$$\Lambda(O)=\log\left(\frac{p(O|m^+)}{p(O|m^-)}\right) \tag{2}$$

3.2.3. Target-Oriented Phone Tokenizer (TOPT)

In the PPR framework, the languages of parallel phone recognizers, also known as phone tokenizers, and target languages may not have to be the same languages. For example, an English phone recognizer functions as a human listener of English background, trying to extract the discriminative information from the spoken utterances of each target language from its perspective. The discriminative information is expressed in an English phone sequence. In general, the performance gain increases with a greater number of parallel recognizers.

We proposed to design the target-oriented phone tokenizers (TOPTs) (Tong et al., 2008) rather to use the same phone recognizer for all the target languages in the PPR practice. For example, Arabic-oriented English phone tokenizer, Mandarin-oriented English phone tokenizer, as Arabic and Mandarin each is believed to have its unique phonotactic features to an English listener.

Note that not all the phones and their phonotactics in the target language may not provide equally discriminative information to the listener, it is desirable that the phones in each of the TOPTs can be those extracted from the full phone set of a phone recognizer, and having highest discriminative ability in distinguishing the target language from other languages.

The target-oriented phone selection strategy is illustrated in Figure 2. Assuming we have a language recognition task of L target languages, given a phone recognizer with phone inventory $v=\{v_1,v_2\cdots,v_i,\cdots,v_n\}$ which contains n phones, we estimate the discriminative power of each phone v_i in distinguishing a target language l_k from other target languages: l_j with $j\in[1,L]$ and $j\neq k$. The discriminative power of phones in v for distinguishing language l_k from others can be denoted as $W_k=\{w_{v_1,k}w_{v_2,k}\cdots w_{v_m,k}\}$. We select a subset of phones that have highest discriminative power to construct a new target-oriented phone tokenizer, $TOPT_k$. In this way, we can construct L new target-oriented phone tokenizers, one for each target language.

3.2.4. *Phonetic and Acoustic Diversifications (PAD)*

Phonetic and acoustic diversifications may be applied to both PPR-LM and PPR-VSM systems. The conventional approach adopts phonetic diversification, where the parallel phone recognizers are trained on speech data from different languages with different phone sets. On the other hand, we proposed an alternative methodology where phone recognizers using different acoustic models trained on the same speech data with the same phone set (Sim and Li, 2007, 2008) are used to achieve acoustic diversification. Analogous to system combination for speech recognition in which merging outputs from multiple systems with different error patterns helps to improve the final performance, using multiple acoustic models aims to form the contractive parallel phone recognition systems using different modeling techniques and training paradigms, without requiring additional phonetically transcribed speech data.

3.3. Acoustic Classifiers

Acoustic classifiers exploit acoustic features directly. There are two main approaches, Gaussian mixture modeling (GMM) on short-time cepstral features, such as MFCCs, LPCCs, and the Shifted Delta Cepstral (SDC) coefficients, and support vector machine (SVM) modeling on high dimension acoustic features, such as the polynomial expansion of short-time cepstral features.

3.3.1. *MMI-GMM*

In the standard Maximum Likelihood (ML) training framework for GMM, the objective function is to maximize the total log likelihood of training data:

$$F_{ML}(\theta)=\sum_{r=1}^{R}\log p(O_r|s_r)\qquad(3)$$

where θ is the model parameter set and O_r is the rth observation sequence, R denotes the total number of training utterances, and s_r is the correct language identity of the rth utterance. The ML estimation maximizes the likelihood of each model generating the training data independently.

The discriminative training techniques have been successfully applied in large vocabulary continuous speech recognition (LVCSR) systems. One of the most popular discriminative training approaches, *maximum mutual information* (MMI) training, has been proved to efficient in the Gaussian mixture modeling for language recognition (Bueget, Matejka, and Cernocky, 2006). The objective function of MMI is posterior probability of correctly recognizing all training utterances. It estimates the GMM parameters in a discriminative manner by maximizing the following objective function:

$$F_{MMI}(\theta)=\sum_{r=1}^{R}\log\left(\frac{p_\theta(O_r|s_r)P(s_r)}{\sum_{\forall s}p_\theta(O_r|s)P(s)}\right)\qquad(4)$$

where $P(s_r)$ and $P(s)$ are the prior terms and we consider the prior probabilities of all languages equal. The denominator $\sum_{\forall s}p_\theta(O_r|s)P(s)$ is the likelihood of utterance O_r given the competing language models.

3.3.2. GLDS Kernel

SVM has been proven to be an effective two-class classifier for pattern classification problems. To adopt SVM for classification of speech utterances is not straightforward since speech utterances are often parameterized as variable-length sequences of cepstral feature vectors. A kernel function that can measure the similarity between two sequences of speech feature vectors has to be constructed. The *generalized linear discriminant sequence* (GLDS) kernel has been proposed for speaker and language recognition (Campbell et al., 2006) on acoustic feature vectors. Given two sequences, $X=\{\mathbf{x}_1, \mathbf{x}_2, ..., \mathbf{x}_m\}$ and $Y=\{\mathbf{y}_1, \mathbf{y}_2, ..., \mathbf{y}_n\}$, of feature vectors, the GLDS kernel is given by

$$K_{\mathrm{GLDS}}(X,Y)=\mathbf{b}_x^T\mathbf{R}^{-1}\mathbf{b}_y \tag{5}$$

where m and n denote the number of feature vectors in the sequences X and Y, respectively. In (5), the two sequences become comparable by mapping them to a high-dimensional vector space via

$$\mathbf{b}_x=\frac{1}{m}\sum_{\mathbf{x}\in X}\tilde{\mathbf{b}}(\mathbf{x}) \text{ and } \mathbf{b}_x=\frac{1}{n}\sum_{\mathbf{y}\in Y}\tilde{\mathbf{b}}(\mathbf{y}) \tag{6}$$

where $\tilde{\mathbf{b}}(\cdot)$ denotes the polynomial expansion function. For $\mathbf{x}=[x_1, x_2]^T$ and considering all monomials up to the second order, the expansion function is given by $\tilde{\mathbf{b}}(\mathbf{x})=[1,x_1,x_2,x_1^2, x_1x_2,x_2^2]^T$. In our final implementation, we used all monomials up to the third order. In (5), $\mathbf{R}=(\mathbf{U}^T\mathbf{U})/N_U$ is a correlation matrix calculated from a data matrix $\mathbf{U}$ that consists of the expansions of the entire set of N_U training feature vectors. For computational simplicity, it is customary to assume that the matrix $\mathbf{R}$ is diagonal. An SVM is then constructed as the sum of kernel functions in the following form

$$f(X)=\sum_l\alpha_l K_{\mathrm{GLDS}}(X_l,X)+\beta \tag{7}$$

Here, $\{X_l\}$ denotes the support vectors, β is the bias, and the term α_l, for $\sum_l\alpha_l=0$, $\alpha_l>0$, indicates the weight of the lth support vector in the expanded feature space.

3.3.3. Probabilistic Sequence Kernel (PSK)

The PPR (see Section 3.2) serves as a front-end decoder that extracts phonotactic information (i.e., phone sequences) from which the speech utterance can be characterized in terms of the occurrence and co-occurrence statistics of various phones. In (Lee, You, and Li, 2008), we explored the use of acoustically-defined units, instead of the linguistically-defined phones, in characterizing speech utterances and spoken languages. In particular, we train an ensemble of acoustic sound classes in a self-organized manner, each modeled with a Gaussian distribution, to form a speech sound inventory analogous to the phone inventory. We interpret the acoustic sound classes to represent some general vocal tract configurations in producing various speech sounds. The self-organized nature of these acoustic sound classes circumvents the need of laborious phonetic transcription. Furthermore, the structural simplicity of the Gaussian distributions allows us to train sufficient number of acoustic units to transcribe the sound of spoken languages in an effective manner.

We formulate the acoustic sound inventory in a form of sequence kernel, referred to as the *probabilistic sequence kernel* (PSK), for SVM. Similar to that of the GLDS kernel mentioned earlier, the PSK maps variable-length utterances into fixed- and high-dimensional vectors in order to transform a complex classification task into a linearly separable one in a higher-dimensional vector space. Let $p(\mathbf{x}|j)\sim N\left(\mathbf{x}; \boldsymbol{\mu}_j, \boldsymbol{\Sigma}_j\right)$, for $j=1,2,...,L$, denote the inventory of acoustic sound classes. Using these sound classes as bases, the feature expansion is defined as

$$\tilde{\mathbf{p}}(\mathbf{x})=[p(j=1|\mathbf{x}), p(j=2|\mathbf{x}), ..., p(j=L|\mathbf{x})]^T \tag{8}$$

where $p(j|\mathbf{x})$ denotes the posterior probability of the jth acoustic class (the prior probability of each acoustic class is determined during the training stage as noted below). Each element of the expansion $\tilde{\mathbf{p}}(\mathbf{x})$ gives the probability of occurrence of the jth acoustic class evaluated for a given feature vector $\mathbf{x}$. The average probabilistic count across the entire sequence X is given by

$$\mathbf{p}_x = \frac{1}{m}\sum_{\mathbf{x}\in X}\tilde{\mathbf{p}}(\mathbf{x}).\tag{9}$$

The vector $\mathbf{p}_x$ can be interpreted as an M-bin histogram indicating the probabilities of occurrence of various acoustic sound classes observed in the given speech utterance X. Given two sequences, the PSK measures their similarity as the inner product between their expanded vectors, $\mathbf{p}_l$ and $\mathbf{p}_x$, as follows

$$K_{\mathrm{PSK}}(X,Y)=\mathbf{p}_x^T \mathbf{R}^{-1}\mathbf{p}_y.\tag{10}$$

Compared to the GLDS kernel (5), the PSK hinges on the prior knowledge that the frequency of occurrence of speech sounds differs from one language to another in establishing the bases. This prior knowledge is not exploited in the GLDS kernel, leading to some performance deficiency.

4. Fusion of Classifiers

This section describes the fusion strategy for the IIR submission to the NIST 2007 Language Recognition Evaluation (LRE07). The final submitted system is a linear fusion of the scores contributed by ten individual classifiers. These classifiers are summarized in Table 1.

Half of the classifiers are phonotactic classifiers while the remaining halves are acoustic classifiers. Two novel PPR-VSM classifiers were introduced to the LRE07 submission, namely the TOPT and PAD classifiers (see Sections 3.2.3 and 3.2.4 respectively). In addition, our system also made use of the HMM/NN hybrid phone recognizers provided by the Brno University of Technology (BUT)[2]. On the other hand, PSK, a novel acoustic classifier with generative front-end was also used (see Section 3.3.3). Furthermore, two GLDS acoustic classifiers were built using the MFCC and LPCC features. Two GMM classifiers were also trained using the ML and MMI criteria.

The final system was obtained by means of linear fusion of the scores from the ten individual classifiers:

$$s_i = \sum_{c=1}^{C} w_c s(c,i)+b\tag{11}$$

where C is the total number of classifiers and $s(c,i)$ is the score of the ith trial from the cth classifier. The fusion parameters consist of the classifier specific weights w_c and the global bias b. Two objectives were used to tune the fusion parameters:

a. minEER:

$$(w_c,b)_{\mathrm{minEER}} =\min_{w_c,b}\left\|P_{miss} -P_{FA}\right\|\tag{12}$$

where the miss and false alarm probabilities are given by

$$P_{\mathrm{miss}} = \frac{\left|\{i:i\in\mathrm{True},s_i <b\}\right|}{\left|\{i:i\in\mathrm{True}\}\right|}$$

$$P_{\mathrm{FA}} = \frac{\left|\{i:i\in\mathrm{False},s_i \geq b\}\right|}{\left|\{i:i\in\mathrm{False}\}\right|}\tag{13}$$

and $\left|\{\ldots\}\right|$ denotes the cardinality of the set.

b. Logistic Linear Regression (LLR):

$$(w_c,b)_{\mathrm{LLR}} =\max_{w_c,b}\sum_{\forall i}\left(\frac{1}{1+\exp(-y_i s_i)}\right)\tag{14}$$

where

---

[2] http://www.fit.vutbr.cz/research/groups/speech/index_e.php?id=phnrec

Table 1: List of 10 individual classifiers used in the IIR NIST 2007 Language Recognition Evaluation submission.

Phonotactic Classifiers	Acoustic Classifiers
PPR-VSM	PSK
TOPT-PPR-VSM	MFCC-GLDS
PAD-PPR-VSM	LPCC-GLDS
BUT-PPR-LM	ML-GMM
BUT-PPR-VSM	MMI-GMM

Table 2: C_{avg} performance using the minEER+LLR fusion method for the General LR closed-test tasks.

Systems	C_{avg} (%)		
	30s	10s	3s
Worst individual	10.23	18.16	33.05
Best individual	3.54	9.22	20.59
Fusion	2.75	6.15	16.40

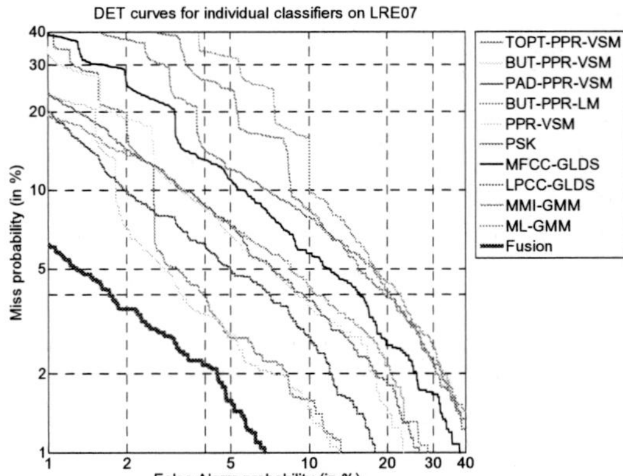

Figure 3: DET curves of individual classifiers and the final fusion system for the 30s General LR closed-test task.

$$y_i = \begin{cases} 1, & i \in \text{True} \\ 0, & i \in \text{False} \end{cases} \tag{15}$$

LLR attempts to transform the scores from multiple classifiers to the log likelihood ratios. The LLR is performed using the FoCal toolkit[3].

The final fusion parameters were obtained as the average of the parameters estimated using the above objectives, i.e.,

$$w_c = \frac{1}{2}\left[(w_c)_{\text{minEER}} + (w_c)_{\text{LLR}}\right]$$
$$b = \frac{1}{2}\left[(b)_{\text{minEER}} + (b)_{\text{LLR}}\right] \tag{16}$$

The fusion parameters were calibrated on the development data comprising the NIST 1996, 2003 and 2005 evaluation sets as well as the 2005 OHSU development data.

4.1.1. Fusion results

Figure 3 shows the Detection Error Trade-off (DET) curves for the 10 individual classifiers as well as the final fusion system for the 30s General LR closed-test task. The top 3 performing classifiers include the BUT-PPR-VSM, TOPT-PPR-VSM and PAD-PPR-VSM classifiers.

The C_{avg} performance of the best and worst individual classifiers as well as the fusion system for the 30s, 10s and 3s General LR closed-test tasks is summarized in Table 2. The relative improvements obtained from fusion over the best individual classifier were 22.3%, 33.3% and 20.3% for the 30s, 10s and 3s tasks respectively.

4.1.2. Open-test versus Closed-test

Table 3 shows the comparison of the *EER (%)* and C_{avg} *(%)* performance for the open-test and closed-test conditions on various tasks. In general, it was found that the General LR tasks are relatively easier compared to the Chinese LR and the other dialect recognition (DR) tasks. In particular, the Hindustani DR and Spanish DR tasks were the hardest, with C_{avg} performance greater than 30%. As expected, the performance of the closed-test tasks is generally better than that of the open-test tasks due to the presence of the out-of-set languages in the open-test

---

[3] http://www.dsp.sun.ac.za/~nbrummer/focal/index.htm

condition. Note that the C_{avg} performance depends on the decision threshold which may not coincide with the EER operating point. There are several cases (e.g. Hindustani DR and Spanish DR) where the C_{avg} performance for the open-test condition outperformed the closed-test condition due to the poor decision threshold in the later condition. The decision thresholds for the open-test conditions were estimated using development data that contains some out-of-language (OOL) languages to learn the appropriate trade-off between false acceptance (false alarm) and false rejection (miss). This has been found to yield improved performance compared to using data without OOL languages. For example, the C_{avg} performance for the 30s General LR open-test task would have been 5.71% instead of 4.28% if the decision threshold was tuned using development data without OOL languages.

Table 3: Comparison of EER and C_{avg} performance for the open-test and closed-test conditions on various tasks

Systems	Test Conditions	30s		10s		3s	
		EER	C_{avg}	EER	C_{avg}	EER	C_{avg}
General LR	Closed-test	1.67	2.75	5.87	6.15	15.38	16.40
	Open-test	2.34	4.28	6.79	8.20	15.92	17.88
Chinese LR	Closed-test	4.90	5.99	8.30	9.51	19.01	20.96
	Open-test	4.89	5.96	9.03	8.02	21.71	18.29
Mandarin DR	Closed-test	12.66	12.72	24.69	24.45	29.74	31.70
	Open-test	15.83	13.39	24.05	19.89	36.07	30.03
English DR	Closed-test	9.38	17.34	14.38	23.13	23.75	24.06
	Open-test	11.25	14.59	16.88	18.58	26.88	26.45
Hindustani DR	Closed-test	32.34	31.56	35.00	34.84	41.09	41.72
	Open-test	35.16	29.12	39.06	32.40	43.75	38.15
Spanish DR	Closed-test	27.97	34.38	33.12	40.00	42.50	44.06
	Open-test	32.66	30.28	40.00	33.50	42.50	37.88

5.
Pseudo Key Analysis

We apply a pseudo-key analysis scheme to cross validate the performances of individual classifiers. It is to find out the abnormal classifier and prevent the error in the final fusion system without knowing the true keys of evaluation data. Suppose that the ratio of genuine/imposter test trials is around $1:(L-1)$, where L is the number of the target languages. From the pool of scores of M trials from each classifier c, we choose M/L trials with the highest scores as genuine trials and the remaining trials as impostor trials, i.e.,

$$\tilde{k}(c,i) = \begin{cases} \text{True,} & \text{if } s(c,i) \geq \tilde{T}_c \\ \text{False,} & \text{if } s(c,i) < \tilde{T}_c \end{cases} \tag{17}$$

where $\tilde{k}(c,i)$ denotes the pseudo key for the ith trial of the cth classifier and the threshold $\tilde{T}_c$ is set such that there are M/L trials whose scores are above it. In the above equation, $s(c,i)$ represents the score of the ith trial from the cth classifiers. Using the pseudo keys from all classifiers, we compute the pseudo EER for the cth classifier as

$$EER_{Pseudo}(c) = \frac{1}{N-1} \sum_{g=1, g \neq c}^{N} EER(c|g) \tag{18}$$

where

$$EER(c|g) = \alpha(s(c,i)|\tilde{k}(g,i), i=1,M) \tag{19}$$

is the operator computing the EER of cth classifier using the psuedo keys obtained from the gth classifier, and N is the total number of classifiers.

We found that the genuine and imposter scores can be roughly expressed as two Gaussian distributions. The probability of error with the pseudo keys obtained from the cth classifier is given by

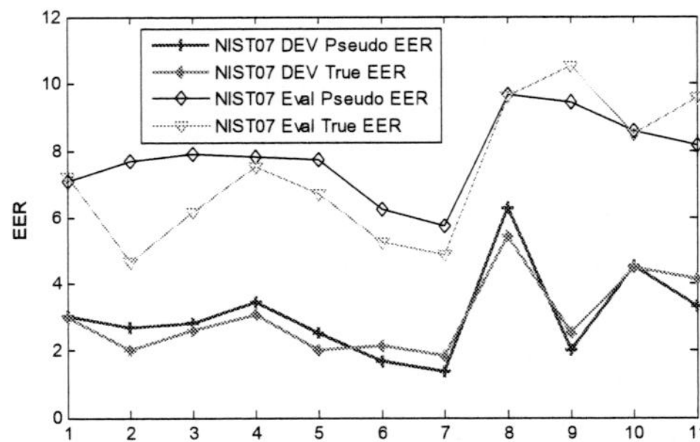

Figure 4: Pseudo and actual EERs evaluated on the development and evaluation sets of the NIST LRE 2007 (30s General LR close-test condition).

$$P(error,c)=P\left(s<\tilde{T}_c\,|\,m_1,\sigma_1\right)+P\left(s\geq\tilde{T}_c\,|\,m_0,\sigma_0\right) \tag{20}$$

where $\{m_1,\sigma_1\}$ and $\{m_0,\sigma_0\}$ are the mean and variance of the genuine and imposter score distributions, $N\left(s;m_1,\sigma_1\right)$ and $N\left(s;m_0,\sigma_0\right)$, and $\tilde{T}_c$ is the threshold defined in (17). Obviously, the error probability is the overlapped sections of the two distributions as indicated in (20). The performance of each classifier depends on the area of this overlapped section. The smaller the overlapped section, the better the classifier is. When this overlapped section is minimized, the classifier achieves desired performance. An outlier classifier will give a large overlap between the genuine and imposter distributions, resulting in high error rate with respect to pseudo keys.

We used the pseudo-key approach to analyze the performance of individual classifierson the LRE07 development and evaluation data sets. The pseudo EERs were computed using (17) and (18). Figure 4 compares the pseudo and actual EERs for all the classifiers. It is shoen that there exists a consistency between the pseudo and actual EERs on both the development and evaluation sets. The pseudo EERs can therefore provide a rough performance indication of the classifiers.

6. Discussion

A description of a language recognition system has been presented as it was developed for the 2007 NIST LRE. The submission was built upon multiple classifiers using generative and discriminative classification techniques, and was purposely designed to exploit the benefits of both phonotactic and acoustic features. Notably, we introduced three novel language classifiers, two phonotactic and one acoustic, in our LRE07 submission. The TOPT and PAD classifiers were shown to be successful refinements to the conventional phonotactic approach. On the other hand, the PSK bridges the gap between acoustic and token-based techniques. All the classifiers were combined at the score level with a simple linear fusion giving an EER of 1.67 % and a C_{avg} of 2.75 % under the general LR core test condition. The LRE results represent the state-of-the-art performance with an effective design and implementation.

7. References

Zue, V. W. and J. R. Glass, "Conversational interfaces: advances and challenges," Proc. IEEE, vol. 88, no. 8, pp. 1166-1180, 2000.

Waibel, A., P. Geutner, L. M. Tomokiyo, T. Schultz, and M. Woszczyna, "Multilinguality in speech and spoken language systems," *Proc. IEEE*, vol. 88, no. 8, pp. 1181-1190, 2000.

Dai P., U. Iurgel, and G. Rigoll, "A novel feature combination approach for spoken document classification with support vector machines," in *Proc. Multimedia Information Retrieval Workshop*, 2003.

National Institute of Standards and Technology. http://www.nist.gov/speech/tests/lang/2007/.

Sugiyama, M., "Automatic language recognition using acoustic features," in *Proc. ICASSP*, 1991.

Torres-Carassquilo, P. A., E. Singer, M. A. Kohler, R. J. Greene, D. A. Reynolds, and J. R. Deller, Jr., "Approaches to language identification using Gaussian mixture models and shifted delta cepstral features," in *Proc. ICSLP*, 2002.

Burget, L., P. Matejka, and J. Cernocky, "Discriminative training techniques for acoustic language identification," in *Proc. ICASSP*, 2006, pp. I-209-212

Campbell, W. M., J. P. Campbell, D. A. Reynolds, E. Singer and P. A. Torres-Carrasquillo "Support vector machines for speaker and language recognition," *Computer Speech and Language*, vol. 20, pp. 210-229, 2006.

Hazen, T. J. and V. W. Zue, "Recent improvements in an approach to segment-based automatic language identification," in *Proc. ICASSP*, 1994.

Zissman, M. A., "Comparison of four approaches to automatic language identification of telephone speech," *IEEE Trans. Speech and Audio Processing*, vol. 4, no. 1, pp. 31-44, 1996.

Berkling, K. M. and E. Barnard, "Analysis of phoneme-based features for language identification," in *Proc. ICASSP*, pp. 289-292, 1994.

Corredor-Ardoy, C., J. L. Gauvain, M. Adda-Decker, and L. Lamel, "Language identification with language-independent acoustic models," in *Proc. Eurospeech*, 1997.

Li, H. and B. Ma, "A phonotactic language model for spoken language identification," in *Proc. ACL*, 2005.

Ma, B., H. Li, and R. Tong, "Spoken Language Recognition Using Ensemble Classifiers", *IEEE Transactions on Audio, Speech and Language Processing*, vol. 15, no. 7, pp. 2053-2062, Sep. 2007.

Rabiner, L. R., "A tutorial on hidden Markov models and selected applications in speech recognition," *Proc. IEEE*, vol.77, no.2, pp. 257-286, 1989.

Reynolds, D. A., T. F. Quatieri, and R. B. Dunn, "Speaker Verification Using Adapted Gaussian Mixture Modeling," *Digital Signal Processing*, vol. 10, no. 1-3, pp. 19-41, 2000.

H. Li, B. Ma, and C.-H. Lee, "A vector space modeling approach to spoken language identification," *IEEE Trans. Audio, Speech and Language Processing*, vol. 15, no. 1, pp. 271-284, 2007.

Adda-Decker, M., et al., "Phonetic knowledge, phonotactics and perceptual validation for automatic language identification," in *Proc. ICPhS*, 2003.

Singer, E., P. A. Torres-Carrasquillo, T. P. Gleason, W. M. Campbell, and D. A. Reynolds, "Acoustic, phonetic and discriminative approaches to automatic language recognition," in *Proc. Eurospeech*, 2003.

Tong, R., B. Ma, D. Zhu, H. Li, and E. S. Chng, "Integrating acoustic, prosodic and phonotactic features for spoken language identification," in *Proc. ICASSP*, 2006.

Muthusamy, Y. K., R. A. Cole, and B. T. Oshika, "The OGI multi-language telephone speech corpus," in *Proc. ICSLP*, 1992.

The 2007 NIST Language Recognition Evaluation plan, http://www.nist.gov/speech/ tests/lang/2007/LRE07EvalPlan-v8b.pdf.

Tong, R., B. Ma, H. Li, and E. S. Chng, "Target-oriented phone tokenizers for spoken language recognition," in *Proc. ICASSP*, 2008, pp. 4221-4224.

Sim, K. C. and H. Li, "Fusion of contrastive acoustic models for parallel phonotactic spoken language identification", in *Proc. Interspeech*, 2007, pp. 170-173.

Sim, K. C. and H. Li, "On acoustic diversification front-end for spoken language recognition", to appear in *IEEE Trans. Audio, Speech and Language Processing*.

Bueget, L., P. Matejka, and J. Cernocky, "Discriminative training techniques for acoustic language identification", in *Proc. ICASSP*, 2006, pp. 209-212.

Lee, K. A., C. You, and H. Li, "Spoken language recognition using support vector machines with generative from-end," in *Proc. ICASSP*, 2008, pp. 4153-4156.

A Call for Executable Linguistics Research [*]

Adam Pease

Articulate Software,
420 College Ave
Angwin, CA 94508, USA
apease [at] articulatesoftware.com

Abstract. This paper mirrors my invited talk at PACLIC-22. It describes a call for a renewed emphasis in work on the logical semantics of languages. It lists some of the computational components needed for symbolic interpretations of language, and of automated reasoning within those semantics. It details existing components that meet those needs and provides short examples of how they might work. It also touches on how open source products can support collaboration, which is needed on a project that has the scope of creating a full semantics of language.

Keywords: ontology, natural language understanding, controlled languages, automated deduction, first order logic

1. Introduction

Talks that state the obvious, or review well-known research are boring and risk losing an audience. Talks that give controversial positions often have the same result. But I'd rather take the dangerous route, in hopes of spurring some new ideas and new research. A further risk is that I'm a computer scientist by training, not a linguist. I may have substantial blind spots in computational linguistics, and there are undoubtedly people I'm not aware of already working in the direction I will advocate, but that provides a big opportunity for me to learn from your feedback on this talk.

I'll focus on a broad goal of language understanding or language processing in Artificial Intelligence. I'll define this as a set of techniques for processing human language that show evidence of the same competencies or behaviors as human language processing. Fundamental to this is the ability to accept statements in language that affect future responses, and the ability to respond to questions that demonstrates prior assimilation of knowledge. I don't believe that a "tabula rasa" approach is feasible in this context; I will take it as a given that a great deal of knowledge must already reside in a practical language understanding system.

There has been considerable research in computational linguistics that takes particular linguistic features and subjects them to semantic analysis, with the goal of specifying a formal semantic interpretation derived from syntactic features. This entire area of research has waned however, in part because it was so difficult to combine these sorts of analyses into a single

---

[*] While this paper discusses nearly a decade of research, which preludes mentioning all the sponsors and collaborators who have contributed, we hope that we will not slight those not mentioned by listing some of the major supporters of this work, who include, US Army CECOM, Army Research Institute, ARDA and DARPA.

22nd Pacific Asia Conference on Language, Information and Computation, pages 58–64

semantic theory. The need for providing some interpretation of all text has moved the computational linguistics field to robust shallow interpretations, rather than brittle and deep ones. A contributing factor has been the need for some very large resources to make it possible to have non-toy implementations of deep linguistic semantic processing. Another issue is that because the scope of linguistic semantics is so large, it's hard to tell if different component theories result in a harmonious total interpretation. We're now at the threshold of being able to address these issues. This is why I call for a new direction of Executable Linguistics Research.

Note that I'm not proposing an exclusive alternative to statistical linguistic methods. There are portions of this general problem that benefit from the marriage of statistical and logical approaches, most notably, word sense disambiguation. I'm proposing a shift in emphasis, recommending that more people concentrate on an approach to linguistics that has been somewhat neglected – a shift to focusing on a more difficult and longer term approach, because the utility of current robust and arguably shallow approaches to understanding are yielding less substantial incremental improvements as time goes on.

I'll first sketch an outline of the products that I think are needed. Then I'll discuss existing resources that can meet some of those needs. Next I'll provide some concrete examples to show how this all might work.

2. What's Needed

A fundamental component of any practical and large scale language understanding system is a large vocabulary. Any system that understands language must be able to identify words. It should know basic relationships among words that form some of the building blocks of meaning – synonyms, antonyms, and which words subsume others' meanings or entail them, at a minimum. Harder to acquire, though no less necessary, is a corpus of groups of words that are "tokens", which have a single and collective meaning that is more than the sum of their component words, and which repeatedly appear in group form.

For English at least, polysemy is a significant issue in language understanding. While better models and algorithms are certainly needed to handle word sense disambiguation the foundation of most algorithms of this sort is the availability of data on which to train the algorithms. Specifically, there is a need for both balanced and domain specific corpora where words have been manually disambiguated with respect to a lexicon.

All this may be relatively uncontroversial so far. Now for the more controversial part. While word meanings change over time, the vast majority of meanings are constant. While meanings can't be legislated, they can be discovered and described, and will largely remain fixed. Linguists often study language at the margins, where there are changes and differences and scientifically interesting features, but much of language is certainly stable, at least over decades. If our goal is machine understanding, it's not enough to know that one word is more specific than another, we must know in what way it is more specific, and what knowledge logically follows from using the more specific word instead of the more general one.

If we agree that this sort of specific information is needed about word meanings, then the next question is in what form it should be represented. There are broadly two options: statistical representations that specify approximate relationships learned automatically, and logical ones that at least at the moment must largely be crafted by humans. Each general approach has advantages.

Statistical approaches require human effort to create a good algorithm, but then can be run automatically on large data sets without human intervention. Such approaches are robust in terms of coverage, but decidedly not robust in terms of the precision of the data. We may be able to learn entailment relationships one inference deep, but I would venture that truth-preserving inferences from automatically acquired data are a long way away. The combinatorics of inference dictate that even if only 10% of the entailments learned are wrong (and the state of art is more like >50% even for simple entailments (TAC 2008), even a simple five step deduction will usually be wrong.

Logical representations can be truth-preserving, and the consistency of any logical theory can be automatically tested (subject to time limitations of course). The main problem is that the effort to craft theories requires human effort, and that effort is specialized and often expensive. I'll return to the issue of open source development later, but for now, let me just state as a given that the scope of such an effort requires open collaboration with many entities and individuals involved.

One issue with logical representations is that words are not logical terms with mathematically precise definitions (at least in most cases). If we treat words as logical terms, or logical terms as though they were words, we'll have an inaccurate model. I'd suggest that we need both a lexicon and a logical model, and relations between them. It is not enough simply to classify words with a small number of formal terms. Knowing that "water" is a "substance" is not sufficient. Any system for understanding must know the implications, uses and properties of water. It must know that water dissolves some other substances, that people can both swim and drown in it, that it can become ice or steam, and many more facts. So, the logical model must ultimately be as large as a dictionary, and it must be subject to continuous evolution as language changes and expands.

Language does not just consist of isolated words. English has many standard phrases in which the meaning of a phrase is more than the sum of its constituent words. A simple case of this is light or "helper" verbs like "take" as in "take a walk" in which the noun functions to modify the mostly meaningless verb. Note that one cannot simply replace the verb with the verbal form of the noun, since "take a hit" is not the same as "hit". Other examples such as "pay attention" are pairs in which the word choices are specific to a given phrase. We cannot simply make these multi-word lexicon entries since we also have examples like "take a long walk" and "a walk was taken". So we must have a corpus of phrases that have logical templates that are filled in by the remaining context of a given sentence.[1]

Beyond a corpus of words and phrases we must have a way of interpreting the overall semantics of a sentence. The building block of a lexicon, phrase corpus, and logical definitions for each is not sufficient. We must be able to interpret the appearance of subject, object, negation, word morphology, conjunction and disjunction, conditionals, modals and many other features. We must handle a host of possibly more mundane linguistic elements like statements about metric time and numbers with units. There is a wealth of research in this area, but not to my knowledge much effort (with Fuch's ACE (Fuchs, 1999) and Kamp& Reyle's DRS work (Kamp&Reyle,1993) as notable exceptions) in systematizing interpretations of all of these different linguistic elements.

The next challenge once we have a system for converting language into logic is to do something useful with the logic. A key enabler is the availability of the same large logical theory that helped us to define individual words in the first place. Those definitions become the corpus of facts and rules that tie together individual logical assertions, and allow us to deduce new consequences. To cover a useful space of knowledge, this theory must be very large. The larger the theory however, the harder it is for a deductive system to process queries on that theory. We must have deductive theorem provers that use smart and adaptive techniques to order the relevance of knowledge, learn how to segment it, and process queries with great efficiency.

3. What We Have

The preceding discussion is not just an abstract exercise, but a guide to research that exists and research that is needed. For each proposed component we have a solution, but all components would benefit from significant focused, collaborative and open research and development.

---

[1] Examples taken from (Pease&Fellbaum, in press)

The foundation of my current work is the Suggested Upper Merged Ontology (Niles&Pease, 2001). It fulfills the need for the logical theory in my proposed model. Although large, it certainly is not large

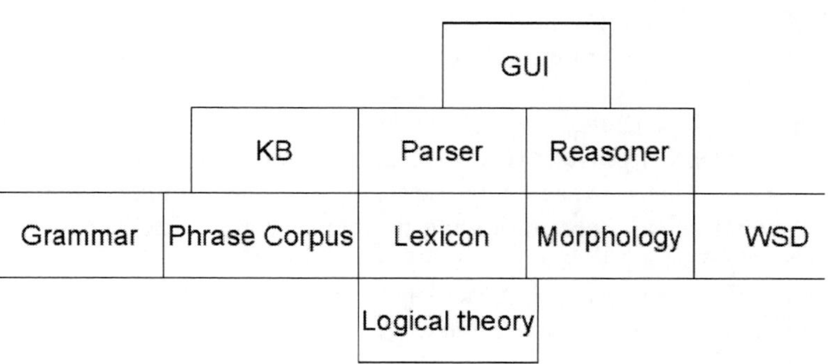

Figure 1: Proposed System Architecture

enough. It has some 20,000 terms, but that's much smaller than even a collegiate dictionary. It has 70,000 formal statements (axioms) but that's much smaller than the equivalent of all the definitions in a small dictionary. We use WordNet as our English lexicon (Fellbaum, 1991). SUMO has been mapped by hand (Niles&Pease 2003) to all of WordNet . This has been a massive effort, but much more is needed. There are 10946 mappings from WordNet instances to equivalent SUMO instances and 3774 mappings from synsets to equivalent SUMO classes. The remaining 100459 mappings are from specific WordNet synsets to more general SUMO terms. These mappings are the basis for future work, and are necessary but not sufficient. We need all mappings to be direct equivalences, but this requires a great effort in defining the remaining 100,000 synsets that lack a direct equivalent in SUMO. One might claim that this job is too big to be practical, but efforts of even greater size have happened once people realize a need (wikipedia for example), and join together on community projects. After all, what is the alternative? To persist with shallow understanding based on statistical similarities, and without the ability in computation to deduce logical conclusions from chains of facts as people do? Already, there are efforts such as the one to merge YAGO's 14 million facts (de Melo et al, 2008), which are derived from Wikipedia, into SUMO.

Word sense disambiguation is one of our biggest current challenges. We use WordNet SemCor (Landes et al, 1998), which is a corpus of manually disambiguated sentences from the Brown Corpus (Kucera&Francis, 1967). It is at least two orders of magnitude too small. Many synsets do not appear at all in the corpus, and those that do co-occur with even other common words so few times that there is rarely statistical significance for any given word sense pair. We have also not begun to use any particularly sophisticated methods for employing even the data that we have. There are larger corpora of manual disambiguations, but they are all proprietary. I'll return to that issue later in discussion of open source.

Although we've written in more detail proposing a corpus of phrases (Pease&Fellbaum,in press), the current implementation is a bit ad hoc, and an integral part of the overall English parsing and interpretation system called the Controlled English to Logic Translation system (CELT) (Pease&Murray 2003), (Pease&Li, 2008). Our parser relies on a simple definite clause grammar (Covington 1993) in Prolog augmented with Discourse Representation Theory (DRT) (Kamp & Reyle 1993) to handle anaphor and multiple sentence processing. We use WordNet's "Morphy" algorithm to handle morphology.

CELT takes a certain reductionist approach to handling English grammar. In particular, it does not attempt to handle all of English, as a full semantics of English is simply not possible at the moment. Instead, it is a constructed subset of English. We began with the simplest possible grammar of handling subjects and verbs, then added support for objects and indirect objects, then determiners and quantifiers, conjunction, prepositions etc. At each stage we looked at how we could add a given linguistic feature without creating ambiguity and breaking the understanding of the existing range of grammatical elements. After some five years of development, the scope of what CELT can handle is quite large, although a long way from the full complexity of English. We see CELT as an excellent testbed for theories of linguistic semantics, since any new theory can be tested computationally, and must necessarily interact with a range of theories about other linguistic constructions. As such, it is completely practical.

We use a suite of tools called Sigma (Pease, 2003) to handle processing the logical forms that CELT generates. For the past 6 years we have used the Vampire (Riazanov&Voronkov, 2002) theorem prover. However, as newer provers are now developed that are released open source, we have expanded the set of provers that Sigma includes. Recently, we sponsored a competition on theorem proving performance in SUMO (Pease et al 2008) that inspired the development of a new prover called SInE (Hoder, 2008). Theorem proving performance however remains a significant obstacle to practical implementations of question answering within a logical deductive framework.

4. Diversion: Open Source

While scientific achievement throughout history has often provided the potential for direct financial reward, that potential is great today, and is particular significant in computational linguistics. That profit potential unfortunately leads many researchers and their institutions to control the dissemination of their research, in the hopes of licensing it for profit, or creating a company that develops that research into a product. Profit can be a powerful motivator, but it can also prevent us from engaging in the sort of open collaboration that leads to large research projects and tangible products that engender significant research. Worse yet, the hope of a big financial return leads to much good research remaining unknown and unused, while the researchers also fail to turn the work into a profitable product.

I'll cite one major project I'm aware of in computational linguistics where after many years of US government funding, there is a significant body of work with great potential for reuse. It could result in even more great research, but it remains proprietary. Yet, after several years, the institution has only sold one license for a few thousand dollars. During that same time, they could have collaborated with others on grants, potentially resulting in hundreds of thousands of dollars in new funding, and research results that would have only enhanced the standing of the researchers and their work. This example can be contrasted with the example of WordNet, which having been free from its inception has resulted in near ubiquitous use in English-based computational linguistics, countless funded grants and collaborations for its developers and thousands of publications describing its use on a near unimaginable variety of topics.

5. Example: How it Works

Take the very simple example of "Robert has an orange." CELT interprets this as

<table>
<tr><td>

```
(exists (?orange)
   (and
      (attribute Robert-1 Male)
      (instance Robert-1 Human)
      (instance ?orange OrangeFruit)
      (possesses Robert-1 ?orange)))
```

</td><td>

```
o attribute(Robert-1,Male) ^
  Human(Robert1) ^
  OrangeFruit(o) ^
  possesses(Robert-1,o)
```

</td></tr>
</table>

Table 1: "Robert has an orange" in SUO-KIF (Pease, 2008) format (left) and conventional logical notation

CELT has a simple database of proper names so it interprets "Robert" correctly. The sense of "orange" as fruit is the most common, and in the absence of a longer sentence or set of sentences, CELT fortunately chooses the a priori most common sense and then retrieves the mapping to the SUMO term of **OrangeFruit**. Now we ask "Who has a fruit?" (note that the variable that gets the value for "who" is unbound).

```
(exists (?fruit)
  (and
    (instance ?fruit FruitOrVegetable)
    (instance ?who Human)
    (possesses ?who ?fruit)))
```

```
f FruitOrVegetable(f) ^
Human(w) ^
possesses(w,f)
```

Table 2: "Who has a fruit?" in SUO-KIF format (left) and conventional logical notation

Posing this query to the theorem prover, along with SUMO and the statement asserted above will result in a very simple proof. It relies on the SUMO subclass hierarchy that defines **OrangeFruit** as a **FruitOrVegetable**. In this simple example, one could certainly imagine a statistical information retrieval system that uses WordNet's hypernym taxonomy and some simple query relaxation to get the right answer. Pose a more complex query like "What country is between France and Austria" and unless that fact is already explicitly stated, no IR system will find the answer. Of course, for complex queries on large knowledge bases, the logical approach is not guaranteed to find an answer either, but at least it can in theory and there is a clear objective of improving the speed of automated deduction to make reality fulfill the promise.

6. Why Use a Logical Framework

I've explained why this general approach of logical formalization is useful for language understanding software systems. I also believe it's useful for research in language itself. Take for example work on a semantic theory of possession relations in English and the phrases "Robert's nose", "The car's color", "Tom's father". If one is required to state such an interpretation logically, and with recourse to a large theory, some mistakes are easily found and corrected. If we map all possessions to a general relation "owns" and then we ask questions like "What does a car own?" a theorem prover will find automatically that a car owns its color, which is nonsensical. While such mistakes may seem obvious and amenable to human inspection and discovery for an isolated theory of possession, the potential for errors on a much larger theory is much greater. A linguistic theory that is fully implemented with a non-trivial logical theory and lexicon can be tested on a variety of sentences not generated by the creators of the theory.

By collaborating on linguistic research with a common logical theory, linguistics researchers open up the possibility of doing work that directly builds on each others' progress, without the need to create a new harmonization their target representations or notation each time. Working together on a common target semantics enables large-scale executable and testable research in deep linguistic semantics.

Take for example Terence Parsons' excellent book (Parsons, 1990). How do we know that his theories fit with Kamp&Reyle's? While Parsons book has a tighter focus just on event semantics, Kamp&Reyle also cover that area in detail. In neither book is there a formalization (in logic) for relations like subject(x,y) or object(x,y), or the deictic "now". While these are common notions understood by all linguistics, there are undoubtedly different intuitions at the boundaries. Without a logical theory built on a common logical semantics, we are left to test their compatibility by inspection rather than automation. I cite these books because they are some of the best examples, in my view, of comprehensive linguistic theories with semantics in formal logic. For other work, even more is needed, in my view.

I look forward to hearing from you now about all the good research that I may have missed that meets these goals, and to working with you in the future to help drive linguistics research closer to the ideals that I have described.

References

Covington, M. (1993) Natural Language Processing for Prolog Programmers. Prentice Hall.

de Melo, G., Fabian Suchanek and Adam Pease (2008). Integrating YAGO into the Suggested Upper Merged Ontology. To appear.

Fellbaum, C. (ed.) (1998) WordNet: An Electronic Lexical Database. MIT Press.

Fuchs, N., U. Schwertel, R. Schwitter. (1999). Attempto Controlled English (ACE) Language Manual, Version 3.0, Technical Report 99.03, Department of Computer Science, University of Zurich, August 1999.

Hoder, K., (2008). SinE.0.3. Online description at
http://www.cs.miami.edu/~tptp/CASC/J4/SystemDescriptions.html#SInE---0.3

Kamp, H., Reyle, U. (1993). From Discourse to Logic. Kluwer Academic Publishers.

Kucera and Francis, W.N. (1967). Computational Analysis of Present-Day American English. Providence: Brown University Press.

Landes S., Leacock C., and Tengi, R.I. (1998) "Building semantic concordances". In Fellbaum, C. (ed.) (1998) WordNet: An Electronic Lexical Database. Cambridge (Mass.): The MIT Press.

Niles, I & Pease A., (2001). "Towards A Standard Upper Ontology." In Proceedings of Formal Ontology in Information Systems (FOIS 2001), October 17-19, Ogunquit, Maine, USA, pp 2-9.

Niles, I., and Pease, A. (2003) Linking Lexicons and Ontologies: Mapping WordNet to the Suggested Upper Merged Ontology, Proceedings of the IEEE International Conference on Information and Knowledge Engineering, pp 412- 416.

Parsons, T., (1990). Events in the Semantics of English: A Study in Subatomic Semantics, MIT Press.

Pease, A., and Fellbaum, C., (in press) Formal Ontology as Interlingua: The SUMO and WordNet Linking Project and GlobalWordNet, In: Huang, C. R. and Prevot, L. (Eds.) Ontologies and Lexical Resources. Cambridge: Cambridge University Press.

Pease, A., and Li, J. (2008) Controlled English to Logic Translation. In Theory and Applications of Ontology, ed. Michael Healy, Achilles Kameas, and Roberto Poli, to appear.

Pease, A., and Murray, W., (2003). An English to Logic Translator for Ontology-based Knowledge Representation Languages. In Proceedings of the 2003 IEEE International Conference on Natural Language Processing and Knowledge Engineering, Beijing, China, pp 777-783.

Pease, A., Sutcliffe, G., Siegel, N., and Trac, S., (2008) The Annual SUMO Reasoning Prizes at CASC. Proceedings of IJCAR '08 Workshop on Practical Aspects of Automated Reasoning (PAAR-2008). Volume 373 of the CEUR Workshop Proceedings.

Pease, A., (2003). The Sigma Ontology Development Environment, in Working Notes of the IJCAI-2003 Workshop on Ontology and Distributed Systems. Volume 71 of CEUR Workshop Proceeding series.

Pease, A., (2008). The Standard Upper Ontology Knowledge Interchange Format (SUO-KIF). Available at http://sigmakee.cvs.sourceforge.net/*checkout*/sigmakee/sigma/suo-kif.pdf

TAC (2008). Recognizing Textual Entailment.(RTE) Web site
http://www.nist.gov/tac/tracks/2008/rte/

Riazanov A., Voronkov A. (2002). The Design and Implementation of Vampire. AI Communications, 15(2-3), pp. 91—110.

Some Challenges of Advanced Question-Answering:
an Experiment with How-to Questions [*]

Patrick Saint-Dizier

IRIT-CNRS, 118, route de Narbonne

31062 Toulouse, France

stdizier@irit.fr

Abstract. This paper is a contribution to text semantics processing and its application to advanced question-answering where a significant portion of a well-formed text is required as a response. We focus on procedural texts of various domains, and show how titles, instructions, instructional compounds and arguments can be extracted.

Keywords: text semantics, question answering.

1. Introduction

Question answering (QA) is an area that operates on top of search engines (such as Google, Exalead, Yahoo, etc.) in order to provide users with more accurate and elaborated responses where search engine response outputs remain punctual, difficult to understand, and sometimes incoherent. QA builds on top of search engine responses via language processing tools, reasoning mechanisms and response production techniques. QA has been recognized as an essential component of man-machine communication since it greatly improves communication with the Web or textual databases, allowing users to communicate in their own language, in order to get much more precise, accurate and user-tailored responses.

Factoid questions (questions about facts, e.g.: *what is the capital of X ?)* have been largely investigated (witness, e.g. the TREC competition), but the other types of questions, frequently encountered such as : procedural (how to), causal (why), evaluative and comparative questions (*what is the cheapest air ticket to go to Cebu from Singapore ?*) have received little attention so far. However, they correspond to the majority of the 'real' questions asked either by the large public or by professionals to the web or to textual databases. Questions cover a large number of everyday life (health, employment, administrative life, tourism, etc.) as well as technical areas (investments, competitive intelligence, etc.).

Complex questions require language processing (to process the question and on the outputs of search engines), reasoning (e.g. data fusion, incoherence solving, summarizing, etc.) and response production in natural language (in a way accessible and user-friendly). These complex questions are in fact those users ask most of the time, these users being professionals or from the large public. Complex questions are traditionally classified according to the type of response which is induced, e.g.:

- definition questions,

---

[*] Acknowledgments: we are grateful to a number of MA students who contributed to this work, among which: Estelle DELPECH, Lionel FONTAN, Isabelle DAUTRICHE and Clementine ADAM. We also thank the ANR-RNTL French program for supporting part of this research.

- how-to questions for procedures,
- why questions for causes/consequence (possibly involving chains of events),
- evaluative and comparative questions (asking for comparisons between two or more elements such as fares).

Considering the technology which is required, it is clear that search engines will not be able in the near future or even in the mid-term future to correctly process these questions due to the complexity of the task, the need of some domain knowledge and the necessity to provide natural language responses, beyond text extracts.

The current trend in TREC Question Answering is towards the processing of large volumes of open-domain texts (e.g. documents extracted from the World Wide Web). Open domain QA is a hard task because no restriction is imposed either on the question type or on the user's vocabulary. This is why most of the efforts (in evaluation campaigns such as TREC) are focused on answering factoid style questions, and, to a little extend, definition questions, using shallow text processing which is roughly based on pattern extraction or information retrieval techniques. However, QA should integrate more complex techniques, in order to provide, for example, deep semantic analysis of NL questions such as anaphora resolution, context and ambiguity detection, complex question processing, better answer ranking and answer justification, responses to unanticipated questions, response fusion or integration, and response summarization to cite just the main topics. It is also important to be able to resolve situations in which no answer is found or when the answer is incomplete or fuzzy in the data sources. This can be resolved for example via dialogue or interactive QA scenarios.

In order to address these future challenges and to guide research in this field, a number of QA roadmaps have been proposed: in 2001, Advanced Question and Answering for Intelligence, the (AQUAINT) program initiative, was created by ARDA. It was then revised in 2002 by the participants of the LREC (Language Resources and Evaluation Conference) QA workshop and further refined at the AAAI (American Association of Artificial Intelligence) Spring Symposium in 2004 and by the KRAQ series 2004-2008. In these roadmaps, the research community states that QA systems should support the integration of deeper modes of language understanding as well as more elaborated reasoning schemas in order to boost the performances of current QA systems as well as the quality and the relevance of the produced answers. Advanced QA systems can be viewed as an enhancement, rather than a rival to retrieval based approaches.

In this paper, we present the main principles that we followed to identify titles, instructions, instructional compounds and arguments. From this point of view, our work is a contribution to the semantics of texts, including the recognition of some rhetorical relations, which is known to be a hard problem. This work is applied to French; we are developing a similar study for Thai. A priori, it should be possible to transpose it to a number of other languages. It is interesting to note how useful text semantics can be for question-answering.

2. How-To questions and the Structure of Procedural Texts

The main goal of the work presented here is to be able to answer procedural questions, which are questions whose induced response is typically a fragment, more or less large, of a procedure, i.e., a set of coherent instructions designed to reach a goal. Recent informal observations from queries to Web search engines show that procedural questions is the second largest set of queries after factoid questions (de Rijke, 2005). The current text emerges from (Delpech et al 2007, 2008).

Answering procedural questions thus requires being able to extract not simply a word in a text fragment, as for factoid questions, but a well-formed text structure which may be quite large. Analyzing a procedural text requires a dedicated discourse analysis, e.g. by means of a grammar. Such grammars (Webber 2004) are not very common yet due to the complex intertwining of lexical, syntactic, semantic and pragmatic factors they require to get a correct analysis. Discourse grammars have basically a top-down organization, they take discourse acts as their basic units, instead of just words, they account for the structure and for the interactions between these acts and they require a relatively elaborated conceptual representation as output. Such a grammar must capture the discourse cohesion, possibly the communicative intentions, as well as the discourse organization, e.g. in terms of plans.

Procedural texts are organized sets of instructions (Adam 2001); they may also be sets of advices, as in social behavior texts. In our perspective, procedural texts range from apparently simple cooking recipes to large maintenance manuals. They also include documents as diverse as teaching texts, medical notices, social behavior recommendations, directions for use, assembly notices, do-it-yourself notices, itinerary guides, advice texts, savoir-faire guides etc. Even if procedural texts adhere more or less to a number of structural criteria, which may depend on the author's writing abilities and on traditions associated with a given domain, we observed a very large variety of realizations, which makes identifying the structure of such texts quite challenging.

Procedural texts explain how to realize a certain goal by means of actions which may be temporally organized. Procedural texts can indeed be a simple, ordered list of instructions to reach a goal, but they can also be less linear, outlining different ways to realize something, with arguments, advices, conditions, hypothesis, and preferences. They also often contain a number of recommendations, warnings, and comments of various sorts. The organization of a procedural text is in general made visible by means of linguistic and typographic marks. Another feature is that procedural texts tend to minimize the distance between language and action. Plans to realize a goal are made as immediate and explicit as necessary, the objective being to reduce the inferences that the user will have to make before acting. Texts are thus oriented towards action; they therefore combine instructions with icons, images, graphics, summaries, warnings, advices, etc.

Research on procedural texts was initiated by works in psychology, cognitive ergonomics, and didactics. Several facets, such as temporal and argumentative structures have then been subject to general purpose investigations in linguistics, but they need to be customized to this type of text. There is however very little work done in Computational Linguistics circles. The present work is based on a preliminary experiment we carried out (Delpech et ali. 07), (Aouladomar 2005) where a preliminary structure was proposed. From a methodological point of view, our approach is based on (1) a conceptual and linguistic analysis of the notion of procedure and (2) a mainly manual corpus-based analysis, whose aim is to validate and enrich the former. Other works on this topic include (Delin et al. 1994), (Takechi et al. 2003) and (Yin, 2004).

In terms of research, analyzing procedural texts is of much interest. Indeed this is a 'genre' which is quite well restricted, but that is rich enough to allow investigations in semantics and pragmatics: rhetorical relations, temporal relations, illocutionary force, etc. It makes relatively feasible studies that would be impossible in the open language. However, results remain proper to those texts. In fact, our approach, at several levels is to try to focus on prototypical structures describing a phenomenon, and then to investigate the conditions its extension to other areas. For example, titles in procedural texts on the web are very diverse in form and contents; they nevertheless share some properties that make their tagging relatively possible. This would not be the case on open texts.

3. Basic Analysis: Recognizing Titles and Instructions

Let us now develop in more depth the different phases of our system. Preliminary steps include cleaning and labeling text objects. Then title and instructions can be recognized and tagged.

3.1. Cleaning Web texts and tagging

The inputs of our system are raw Web pages. From these pages, we need:
  (1) to extract relevant text, that is, any kind of text that is not navigation help, advertisements or comments posted by cybernauts

(2) to select and simplify the html tags so as to keep the main typo-dispositional information (paragraph breaks, subdivisions of paragraphs into lines, lists and their subdivision into elements, emphasis).

Although (2) was quite an easy task, we had some difficulties achieving (1). We designed an algorithm that returns, for each paragraph, if its text can be considered relevant or not. It mainly uses paragraph length and proportion of close-class words criteria. We evaluated it on 100 Web pages, coming from 12 different web sites. The results were: 0,95 precision and 0,76 recall. We evaluate the recognition of titles and instruction on a hand-cleaned corpus.

The next stage is to tag the different lexical objects of the text, so that the segmentation of titles and instructions can be done properly. For that purpose, we use the Treetagger that labels all the objects (syntactic category, morphological features). We also add some semantic considerations about action verbs. Of particular interest to us is the recognition of verbs, some nouns and adjectives, modals and connectors of various kinds.

3.2 Recognizing Titles

For answering How-to questions it is obviously of much importance to recognize titles and possibly hierarchies of titles in complex texts since, in general, titles express the main goals of procedures. However, for some domains (like health) additional information should be used to index a text, in addition to titles. A first observation is that html encodings are, by far, not homogeneous. Titles are coded with the tag <h$_i$> in only 20% of the cases over the 600 titles observed. In most cases the tag <b> is used, possibly also <emp>, <u> and a few others (macros...). Encodings may be quite homogeneous within a given web site, but heterogeneity prevails over different sites, even in the same domain.

We identify titles in two steps. First, an algorithm processes the paragraphs of the text one by one, and gives them one of these tags: title, text or ambiguous. This first step processes easy cases. For example, an easy case for a title is a paragraph composed of a unique sequence of words, less than 12 words long and bearing emphasis. The tag text will be given without doubt if the paragraph is subdivided into smaller units or is longer than 12 words. Ambiguous paragraphs are mainly short sequences of words (12 words or less) with no emphasis.

The second step disambiguates the ambiguous paragraphs one by one, using the tags given by the first step to its surrounding paragraphs. For example, an ambiguous paragraph between two paragraphs tagged as text will be considered a title. Similarly, an ambiguous paragraph followed by a title is labeled text. We have elaborated about 7 such rules that deal with ambiguities. This second step also operates some repairs on the tags yielded by the first step. For example, any sequence marked *title* at the end of the text will be repaired as *text*. Each disambiguation/repair rule is applied sequentially and in a specific order on the list of tags.

The title hierarchy is very difficult to identify without content analysis. However, standard procedural texts are not very long and tend to be relatively linear. This means that, besides the page title, we observed in 80% of our texts not more than 2 levels of titles (excluding the main title). We observed two regular types of titles that can be correlated to some form of hierarchy. Type 1 is a title separated from its following paragraph by a <p> tag. Type 2 is a title separated from its following paragraph by a <br> tag. Although we still have no means to tell the exact level titles, we can quite confidently say that a type 2 title will be at a lower level than a type 1 title, whatever the website or the domain. This information may be useful for question-title matching: type 2 titles are expected to introduce paragraphs that deal with more specific aspects of the procedure than paragraphs introduced by a type 1 title. Type 2 titles could help answering specific questions. One remaining difficulty for question-title matching is that titles have often a very elliptic structure.

3.3 Recognizing instructions and instructional compounds

While working on corpora, we noted that what is usually called an instruction ranges from clearly injunctive clauses to implicit prescriptions (Talmy 2001) (this complexity is reflected in the complexity of our manual annotation tasks). Instructions are recognized (Delpech et al. 2008) on the basis of two factors: contents, around action verbs in certain forms to identify an instruction and typographic factors for its delimitation (beginning and end) via html tags, punctuation marks or connectors. Currently, we use a set of only 14 lexico-morphological patterns that encompass the most prototypical ways of expressing instructions. We use lexical resources such as action verbs, incentive verbs, nouns and adjectives. They must have in French specific forms: imperative, infinitive, modal + infinitive, dummy pronoun 'on' + finite verb (this pattern has a semantic restriction: only action verbs are allowed), middle reflexive constructions, and gerundive forms. The frequency usage of each of these forms largely varies across domains (e.g. cooking recipes mainly use imperative while video game solutions make high usage of the dummy pronouns 'on' or even of finite forms in the first person singular). The segmenter is implemented in standard Perl. Note that English seems to have a simpler set of forms making instructions slightly more difficult to recognize.

Instructional compounds are composed of groups of instructions together with sentence fragments which are in a rhetorical relation with the instructions (advices, warnings, elaboration, etc.). They are delimited as follows: by means of typographic marks: ending of enumeration (e.g. <li> sequences) or by 'strong' marks in long paragraphs. These marks are in general temporal (Two hours later,...), conditional expressions or goal expressions.

Finally, a grammar, based on a simple transposition of a few Minimalist Theory principles allows us to bind all the parts of the text. The grammar runs in Prolog in our prototype. The output is an XML file that reflects the text structure. Here is an extract of what we get before the grammar application, where terminal elements are tagged:

```
<p> <b> <titre>Gâteau au chocolat gourmand</titre>
</b></p>
<prerequis><p><b>
<titre> Ingrédients</titre>
</b></p>
<li> 150 g de chocolat noir </li>
<li> 75 g de beurre doux  </li>
<li> 210 g de lait condensé  </li> ..........</prerequis>
<p>Utilisé depuis la nuit des temps, le chocolat .... si vous souhaitez l'inclure dans la composition de votre oeuvre .</p>
<p>temps: 2 heures, assez facile. </p>
<p><b><titre> la préparation :</titre></b></p>
<li> <compinstr> <instr> 1. Tapisser un petit moule rectangulaire de papier aluminium.</instr></compinstr> </li>
<li><compinstr> <instr> 2.    A l'aide d'un couteau tranchant, concasser les amandes. </instr></compinstr></li>
....
<compinstr> <instr> Dans une casserole à fond épais, placer le chocolat cassé en morceaux, le beurre, le lait et la cannelle.</instr>
<instr> Chauffer doucement à feu doux pendant 3 à 4 minutes en remuant avec 1 cuillère en bois.</instr>
<instr> Bien battre le mélange. <instr> Incorporer les amandes, les biscuits et les abricots en remuant bien. </instr> .... </compinstr>
<compinstr> <instr> Au bout d'une heure, .... </instr> ...... </compinstr> ........</p>
```

4. Explanation structure in procedural texts

First, in most types of texts, we do not find just sequences of simple instructions but much more complex compounds composed of clusters of instructions, that we call **instructional compounds**. These are organized around a few main instructions, to which a number of subordinate instructions, warnings, arguments, and explanations of various sorts may possibly be adjoined. All these elements are, in fact, essential in a compound for a good understanding of the procedure at stake. For example, explanations and arguments help the user understand why an instruction must be realized and what are the risks or the drawbacks if he does not do it properly. An example of an instructional compound is:

> **[*instructional compound* [*Goal* To clean leather armchairs,]**
> **[*instruction* choose specialized products dedicated to furniture,**
> **[*advice* [*instruction* and prefer them colorless],**
> **[*arguments* they will play a protection role, add beauty, and repair some small damages.]]]]**

Next, from our development corpus, we established a classification of the different forms explanations may take. Basically, the explanation structure is meant to help the user by making sure that he will effectively realize actions as they are specified, via e.g. advices and warnings. The main structures are facilitation and argumentation structures; they are either global (they are adjoined to goals, and have scope over the whole procedure) or local, included into instructional compounds, with a scope local to the instructional compound. These structures are summarized as follows:

– **facilitation structures**, which are rhetorical in essence (Kosseim et al 2000) (Van der Linden 1993), correspond to *How to do X ?* questions, these include two subcategories:

    (1) user help, with: hints, evaluations and encouragements and

    (2) controls on instructions realization, with two cases:

        (2.1) controls on actions: guidance, focusing, expected result and elaboration and

        (2.2) controls on user interpretations: definitions, reformulations, illustrations and also elaborations.

– **argumentation structures**, corresponding to *why do X ?* questions. These have either:

    (1) a positive or neutral orientation with the author's involvement (promises) or not (advices and justifications) or

    (2) a negative orientation with the author involvement (threats) or not (warnings). In what follows, we will mainly concentrate on this second point, and in particular on warnings which are the most frequently encountered, besides advices.

5. Identifying arguments in procedures

5.1 General structure of arguments

Roughly, argumentation is a process that allows speakers to construct statements for or against another statement called the conclusion (Amgoud et al. 2001, 2005). These statements are called supports. The general form for arguments is : **Conclusion 'because' Support** (noted as C *because S*). Arguments may be more or less strong, they are in general associated with a certain weight. (Anscombre et al. 1981) .In the case of procedural texts, the representation is as follows.

Let G be a goal which is realized via the sequence of instructions $Ai,\ i \in [1,\ n]$, whatever their

exact temporal structure is. A subset of those instructions are interpreted as arguments where the conclusion is the instruction (*Aj*), associated with a support *Sj* that stresses the importance of *Aj* (*Carefully plug in your mothercard vertically, otherwise you will damage the connectors*).

Their general form is: *Aj because Sj* (we use here the term 'because' which is vaguer than the implication symbol used in formal argumentation, because natural language is not so radical). Supports *S* which are negatively oriented are warnings whereas those which are positively oriented are advices. Similarly to the principles of argument theory, but within the framework of action theory, if *Aj* is associated with a support of type warning *Sj* then if *Aj* is not realized correctly, the warning *Sj* is 'active' and attacks the goal G, i.e. it makes its realization more difficult if not impossible. Conversely, if *Sj* is an advice, it supports the goal G, making its full realization easier if *Aj* is executed. As can be noted, our definition includes terms which are gradual: 'more difficult', 'easier', because in practice, failing to realize an instruction properly does not necessarily mean that the goal cannot be reached, but the user will just be less successful, for various reasons. In the natural language expressions of conclusions (the *Aj*) as well as of supports, there are many modals or classes of verbs (like risk verbs) that modulate the consequences on G, contrast:

use professional products to clean your leathers, they will give them a brighter aspect.
with:
carefully plug in your mothercard vertically, otherwise you will most likely damage its connectors..

In the latter case, the goal 'mounting your own PC' is likely to fail, whereas in the former, the goal 'cleaning your leathers' will just be less successful.

5.2 Processing arguments

From the above observations, we have defined a set of patterns that recognize instructions which are conclusions and their related supports. We defined those patterns from a development corpus of about 1700 texts of various domains (cooking, do it yourself, gardening, etc.). Let us focus here on warnings. The study is made on French; English glosses are given here for ease of reading. The recognition problem is twofold: identifying propositions as conclusions or supports by means of specific linguistic marks (Cruse 1986), (Rosner et al 1992) (sometimes we also found a few typographic marks), and then delimiting these elements. In general boundaries are either sentences or, by default, instructional compound boundaries. We have basically a unique structure composed of an 'avoid expression' combined with a proposition. The variations around the 'avoid expressions' capture the illocutionary force of the argument via several devices, here ordered by increasing force:

(1) 'prevention verbs like avoid' NP / to VP (*avoid hot water*)

(2) do not / never / ... VP(infinitive) ... (*never put this cloth in the sun*)

(3) it is essential, vital, ... to never VP(infinitive).

In cases where the conclusion is relatively weak in terms of consequences, it may not have any specific mark; its recognition is then based on the observation that it is the instruction that immediately precedes an already identified support.

Supports are propositions which are identified from various marks:

(1) via connectors such as: *sinon, car, sous peine de, au risque de* (otherwise, under the risk of), etc. or via verbs expressing consequence,

(2) via negative expressions of the form: *in order not to, in order to avoid, etc.*

(3) via specific verbs such as risk verbs introducing an event (*you risk to break*). In general the embedded verb has a negative polarity.

(4) via the presence of very negative nouns: *death, disease, etc.*

Some supports have a more neutral formulation: they may be a portion of a sentence where a conclusion has been identified. For example, a proposition in the future tense or conditional following a conclusion is identified as a support. However, as will be seen below, some supports may be empty, because they can easily be inferred by the reader. In that case, the argument is said to be truncated.

The same strategy applies for the recognition of advices, which mainly introduce optional actions. However, they are slightly more difficult to recognize due, precisely, to their 'optional' character: terms are less marked, less injunctive, and therefore more difficult to identity.

Patterns are implemented in Perl and are included into the TextCoop software. We do not have space here to discuss about algorithms, but so far these are quite straightforward. From the above observations, with some generalizations and the construction of lexicons of marks, we have summarized the extraction process in only 8 patterns for supports and 3 patterns for conclusions. Arguments are tagged by XML tags. We carried out an indicative evaluation (e.g. to get improvement directions) on a corpus of 66 texts over various domains, containing 262 arguments. We get 89% for the conclusion recognition, and 86% for the support. Correct delimitations are 84 and 81% respectively.

Besides identifying arguments (advices, warnings) in a text and other structure, a major application of this work is the acquisition of **domain know-how knowledge**, which is probably quite basic, but which could be subject to interesting generalizations. Obviously, to make this know-how operational, it is necessary to analyze it and transform it into a formal representation that supports inference.

5. Conclusion

In this paper, we have shown how titles, instructions and arguments of various sorts can be tagged in procedural texts. This work is designed to respond to how-to questions where a well-formed portion of a text is expected as a response. Besides this level, we investigated how titles can be indexed for response retrieval (given that titles are often incomplete). A last step we are investigating is the production of the response, involving data fusion techniques as well as the development of navigation tools among and within documents when there are several candidate responses.

References

Adam, J.M., Types de Textes ou genres de Discours? Comment Classer les Textes qui Disent De et Comment Faire, Langages, 141, pp. 10-27, 2001.

Amgoud, L., Bonnefon, J.F., Prade, H., An Argumentation based Approach to Multiple Criteria Decision, in 8th European Conference on Symbolic and Quantitative Approaches to Reasoning with Uncertainty, ECSQARU' 2005, Barcelona, 2005.

Amgoud, L., Parsons, S., Maudet, N., Arguments, Dialogue, and Negotiation, in: 14th European Conference on Artificial Intelligence, Berlin, 2001.

Anscombre, J.-Cl. Ducrot, O., Interrogation et Argumentation, in Langue francaise, no 52, L'interrogation, 5 - 22, 1981.

Aouladomar, F., Saint-Dizier, P., An Exploration of the Diversity of Natural Argumentation in Instructional Texts, 5th International Workshop on Computational Models of Natural Argument, IJCAI, Edinburgh, 2005.

Cruse, A., Lexical Semantics, Cambridge Univ. Press, 1986.

Delin, J., Hartley, A., Paris, C., Scott, D., Van der Linden, K., Expressing Procedural Relationships in Multilingual Instructions, Proceedings of the Seventh International Workshop on Natural Language Generation, pp. 61-70, Maine, USA, 1994.

Delpech, E., Saint-Dizier, P., A Two-Level Strategy for Parsing Procedural Texts, VSST'07, Marrakech, October 2007.

Delpech, E., Saint-Dizier, P., Anonymous, Investigating the Structure of Procedural Texts for Answering How-to Questions, LREC 2008, Marrakech.

Davidson, D., Actions, Reasons, and Causes, Journal of Philosophy, 60, 1963

Kosseim, L., Lapalme, G., Choosing Rhetorical Structures to Plan Instructional Texts, Computational Intelligence, Blackwell, Boston, 2000.

Rosner, D., Stede, M., Customizing RST for the Automatic Production of Technical Manuals, in R. Dale, E. Hovy, 2002.

D. Rosner and O. Stock eds., Aspects of Automated Natural Language Generation, Lecture Notes in Artificial Intelligence, pp. 199-214, Springler-Verlag, 1992.

Takechi, M., Tokunaga, T., Matsumoto, Y., Tanaka, H., Feature Selection in Categorizing Procedural Expressions, The Sixth InternationalWorkshop on Information Retrieval with Asian Languages (IRAL2003), pp.49-56, 2003.

Talmy, L., Towards a Cognitive Semantics, vol. 1 and 2, MIT Press, 2001.

Van der Linden, K., Speaking of Actions Choosing Rhetorical Status and Grammatical Form in Instructional Text Generation Thesis, University of Colorado, 1993.

Webber, B., D-LTAG: extending lexicalized TAGs to Discourse, Cognitive Science 28, pp. 751-779, Elsevier, 2004.

Yin, L., Topic Analysis and Answering Procedural Questions, Information Technology Research Institute Technical Report Series, ITRI-04-14, University of Brighton, UK, 2004.

How *Even* Revises Expectation in a Scalar Model:
Analogy with Japanese *Mo*[*]

Sachiko Shudo

Waseda University

shudo@waseda.jp

Abstract. This study, concentrating on multi-focus usages of scalar additive particles, such as English *even*, *mo* in Japanese and *to* in Korean, shows that they signal the survival of a correlational continuum in a scalar model despite the described unexpected event. This analysis, building upon the scalar model proposed by Fillmore, et al (1988) and Kay's (1990) analysis of *even*, extends Shudo's analysis (1998, 2002) of *mo* and claims that *even* behaves like scalar *mo* and *to*.

Keywords: scalar, additive, presupposition, *even*, *mo*, *to*, expectation

1. Introduction

The usages of some linguistic expressions and constructions are constrained such that certain conditions must be satisfied by the context. When such a linguistic item is used, the hearer simply assumes that the required condition has been satisfied. In other words, some information is delivered to the hearer because of the presence of the linguistic item. In this paper, the information that is delivered to the hearer in this process is referred as 'presupposition'. This notion of presupposition is closest to Stalnaker's (1973) notion of presupposition. The difference is that while Stalnaker's notion refers to the relation between a person and a proposition, I would like to think it as one between a sentence containing a presupposition-trigger and a presupposed proposition, following Karttunen (1974). Although the notion of presupposition is so ubiquitous, how to identify it has not been clear. The dominant approach to identify a presupposition is to try to isolate the non-truth-conditional meaning in a given sentence that includes the presupposition-trigger. In other words, what we often assume to be a presupposition triggered by a linguistic item is discussed rather subjectively.

In this study, following the approach employed in Shudo (1998, 2002) and Shudo and Harada (2008), I will try to identify a presupposition by reconstructing a condition that the context must satisfy in order for the speaker to use the presupposition-trigger. In particular, I will investigate the presupposition of *even*. The basic explanation for the assumed equation between the presupposition of a linguistic item and the contextual constraint on the usage of the item is simple: if a meaning is generated because of the usage of a presupposition-trigger, that is because the linguistic item is constrained such that it cannot be used unless the condition generating the meaning is satisfied.

Shudo (1998, 2002), following Kay's (1990) analysis on *even*, contended that the Japanese particle *mo*, which is equivalent to *too* or *also* and sometimes is used to generate the *even*-like meaning, is different from the English *even*. However, in this paper, I will argue that the meaning of *even* is indeed quite similar to the Japanese *mo*.

---

[*] An earlier version of this paper was presented at the Pragmatic Society of Japan's annual meeting in 2007. I would like to thank Yasunari Harada as well as Harumi Sawada for their comments.

2. Problem

While there are disagreements on details, most works on *even* agree that *even* triggers two types of presupposition, existential presupposition and scalar presupposition (Horn 1969, 1972, Karttunen and Karttunen (K&K) 1977, Karttunen and Peters (K&P) 1979, Rooth 1985, Kay 1990, Wilkinson 1996, Schwarz 2005, Nakanishi 2006, inter alia).[1] (1a) gives a rise to an existential presupposition, shown in (1b), and a scalar presupposition, shown in (1c).

(1) a. Even Emily smiled.
     b. Someone other than Emily smiled.
     c. Emily is a less likely (or the least likely) candidate to smile.[2]

In this paper, as mentioned earlier, whatever meaning is generated by the usage of *even* is assumed to be the result of the constraint on the usage such that it cannot be used unless the condition is satisfied. This paper contends that existing accounts for presupposition triggered by *even* are correct but not sufficient to explain the presupposition because *even* may not be used although the context satisfies the above mentioned two types of presupposition.

Let us start with a scenario. Amelia (A) teaches German in a college. Brenda (B) is her colleague who also teaches the same class. Harry is one of the least proficient students. One day Brenda gave students a quiz. When Brenda comes back from the class, the following conversation begins.

(2) a. A: Hi. How was the quiz?[3]
     b. B: I am afraid it was too easy.
     c.   Even Harry got seven right answers.

Now let us observe the following in which Amelia starts differently. She has been lately quite concerned with Harry's academic performance.

(3) a. A: Hi. How did Harry do on the quiz?
    b. B: #Even he got seven right answers.

(2c) and (3b) offer exactly the same semantic content. As for the performances of students on the quiz, not only Harry's but also those of others, the context of (2) and (3) should be identical. In other words, what applies to the usage of *even* in (2), the existential presupposition, the scalar presupposition, etc, is expected to be present in (3). However, the usage of *even* in (3b) is problematic. It is obvious that the inappropriateness of (3b) has something to do with Amelia's question. However, we can easily come up with a slightly different context in which (3b) is not problematic such as the following.

(4) a. A: Hi. How was the quiz?
    b. B: Everyone did very well.
    c. A: How did Harry do?
    d. B: Even he got seven right answers.

---

[1] K&K (1977), K&P (1979) and Wilkinson (2005) treat these non-truth-conditional propositions associated with even as conventional implicature.

[2] K&K (1977), K&P (1979), and Nakanishi (2006) take the end-point view.

[3] With 'Hi' in (1a), (2a) and (3a), I merely intend to indicate is that there is no prior conversation on the same subject.

How should we explain the difference in acceptability between (3b) and (4d)? What is the constraint on the usage of *even* that (3b) does not satisfy but (4d) does. (4) includes the exchange about the quiz in general. Why does the exchange in (4a)-(4b) make it appropriate to use *even* in (4d)? To answer these questions, I hypothesize that there is a contextual constraint on the usage of *even* that the existing accounts on its presupposition have not identified.

In the following, I will first examine Japanese and Korean additive particles, *mo* and *to* respectively, and show how they are contextually constrained. I will then show how they generate the *even*-like meaning. The difference between English *even* on one hand and Japanese *mo* and Korean *to* on the other hand is that the former inherently places the host proposition on a scale, the latter generate the scalar meaning when the scale becomes available with the context. I will show that the English *even* is indeed contextually constrained in a similar manner.

3. Additive *mo* and *to*

The Japanese *mo* and the Korean *to*, both roughly equivalent to the English *also*, are often used to generate scalar meanings similar to the English *even*, while *also* and *too* cannot generate such meanings. Before discussing *even*-like *mo* and *to*, I will first examine basic operations of *mo* and *to*, which I claim monosemously apply to usages including those with scalar meanings.

3.1 Traditional approaches

According to conventional grammars, the use of the Japanese particle *mo* is described with examples in which the *mo* sentence contains a property which has been evoked in the prior context as the following example shows:

(5) a. Boku wa Osaka ni ikimasu.
       I   TOP   to go
   'I am going to Osaka.'
  b. Watashi *mo*   Osaka ni ikimasu.
      I c   ADD   to go
   'I am going to Osaka, too.'

Defining the proposition of the *mo* sentence ((5b) above) as the HOST PROPOSITION or the hp and the proposition that the host proposition is responding to ((5a) above) as the ANTECEDENT PROPOSITION or the ap, the usage of *mo* in (5b) is summarized as follows:

(6)   MO (x, F) (x is the constituent marked by *mo*; F is the property held by x)
    hp: F(x)
    ap: F(y)
    Mo-presupposition: $\exists y\ [y \neq x\ \&\ F(y)]$

Kato (1985), Makino and Tsutsui (1986) and Noguchi and Harada (1994, 1996) share the analysis of *mo* in (6).[4]
    The Korean counterpart *to* receives similar traditional analyses (Lee 2006, An 2007).

(7)   TO (x, F) (x is the constituent marked by *to*; F is the property held by x)
    To-presupposition: $\exists y\ [y \neq x\ \&\ F(y)]$

The above analyses of both *mo* and *to* are basically the same as Karttunen's (1974) analysis of *too*. The difference between *mo* in (6) and *to* in (7) on one hand and *too* on the other hand is that the former syntactically mark x, while the latter phonologically marks x by focus.

---

[4] Noguchi and Harada (1994), indicating the meaning of a *mo* sentence as $F(x) \land \Box y\ [y \neq x\ \&\ F(y)]$, do not make a distinction between what is asserted and what is presupposed.

3.2 Bridge-building usages of *mo*

Shudo (1998, 2002) shows that the actual usages of the Japanese particle *mo* indicate that (6) is not sufficient to describe the relationship between the host proposition and the antecedent proposition. Examine the following, what Shudo describes as a "BRIDGE-BUILDING" usage:

(8) a. Boku wa   Tokyo ni ikimasu.
      I   TOP   to go
   'I am going to Tokyo.'
   b. Watashi *mo*   Osaka ni ikimasu.
      I   ADD   to go
   'I am going to Osaka, too.'

The usage of *mo* in (8b) is not strange if the above exchange happens outside Japan. It simply points out the similarity between the two events, the first speaker's going to Tokyo and the second speaker's going to Osaka, i.e., both speakers are going to Japanese cities. Numata (1984, 1986, 1995, inter alia) addresses such usages, pointing out that although there is no lexicologically synonymous relation between the properties, there is context-dependent similarity (1995: 136). Her discussion on this issue, however, rather abruptly ends with the remark that how the similarity occurs depends on the context or social common sense.

Shudo's (1998, 2002) solution is that the usage *mo* of is not constrained such that the properties are identical, but merely is constrained such that the properties are similar, treating the bridge-building usage of *mo* in (8) as the canonical usage of the particle, and leaving (5) as a special case in which the similarity between two events amounts to the extent that the two properties are identical. As the two properties present some similarity, the presence of a common property is necessary as the following

(9) MO (x, F)
   hp: F(x)
   ap: G(y)
   $\exists y \, \exists H \, [y \neq x \,\&\, H(y) \,\&\, F(x) \subseteq H(x) \,\&\, G(y) \subseteq H(y)]$

However, needless to say, (9) does not serve as a constraint unless the common property is lower-bounded. Otherwise, any property, such as going somewhere or doing something, can satisfy the common property requirement. The constraint could be intuitively represented as requiring that it is worthwhile for the speaker to signal the similarity.

To represent the 'worthy similarity' requirement, Shudo (1998, 2002), employs the notion of 'contextual effect' by Sperber and Wilson (S&W hereafter, 1986). The lower-boundary for the common property is represented as follows:

(10) $\exists y \, \exists H \, [y \neq x \,\&\, H(y) \,\&\, F(x) \subseteq H(x) \,\&\, G(y) \subseteq H(y) \,\&\, R\,(H(x), C)]$

The similarity is lower-bounded by the presence of a 'contextual effect' in the proposition with the common property (H(x)) in the context, C. S&W's notion of contextual effect is a central notion for their theory of relevance, but in this paper, I will simply apply the notion in order to identify whether a proposition contributes to a set of propositions in a certain way. The set of propositions that I am interested here is the context, the set of propositions that the speaker and the hearer share at the time of utterance.[5]

---

[5] Sperber and Wilson (1986) uses the term 'context' to refer to a set of assumption. Their claim is a 'context' is not determined but selected by the speaker to process information. Thus, I am not using the term in the way S & W use it.

According to S&W, a piece of information has a contextual effect in a set of assumptions if it has a contextual implication, strengthens the existing assumptions, or contradicts the existing assumptions. For the constraints of time and space, I will explain their account of how contextual implication occurs.

(11) Contextual implication [S&W 1986: 107-108]
   A set of assumptions P contextually implies an assumption Q in a context C if:
   (i) the union of P and C non-trivially implies Q,
   (ii) P does not non-trivially imply Q, and
   (iii) C does not non-trivially imply Q.

(12) Non-trivial implication [S&W 1986: 97]
   A set of assumptions P logically and non-trivially implies an assumption Q if and only if, when P is the set of initial theses in a derivation involving only elimination rules, Q belongs to the set of final theses.

I apply the above notion of contextual effect to determine whether a proposition has certain contribution to the context. When a proposition P has a contextual effect in context C, I represent it as $R(P, C)$. The requirement for the proposition with the common property, H(x), is expressed as R(H(x), C) in (10).

3.3 Bridge-building usages of *to*

The Korean additive *to* is also used when the ap and the hp do not share the same property, but merely share a common property (Shudo, 2008). It seems that the usage of Korean *to* receives exactly the same constraint as its Japanese counterpart.

(13) a. Na-nun Tokyo-ey kamnida .
         I-TOP   to go
       'I am going to Tokyo.'
     b. Na-*do*   Osaka-ey kamnida.
         I-ADD   to go
       'I am going to Osaka, too.'

(14) TO (x, F)
    hp: F(x)
    ap: G(y)
    $\exists y \, \exists H \, [y{\neq}x \, \& \, H(y) \, \& \, F(x) \subseteq H(x) \, \& \, G(y) \subseteq H(y) \, \& \, R(H(x), C)]$

Shudo (2008) claims that both Japanse *mo* and Korean *to* can generate the *even*-like scalar meaning because both particles are constrained such that they allow the bridge-building usages. This issue will be later discussed more in detail.

4. Analysis of *even*

Now we are back to the English *even*. The interpretation of a sentence including *even* requires the notion of scale. While the scale is usually assumed to be one-dimensional, a multi-dimensional scale may be needed if that is intended (Kay 1990).

4.1 Scalar model for *even*

Fillmore, Kay, and O'Connor (1988) (FKO hereafter) propose the notion of scalar model, which represents a set of propositions with internal structure of generalization to n dimensions, what is known as a Guttman scale. In a scalar model, there are entailment relations between propositions such that a propositional function P, whose domain is an argument space, is constrained as follows:

(15) For distinct d_i, d_j in D_x, $P(d_i)$ entails $P(d_j)$ iff d_j is lower (or equivalently closer to the origin) than d_i.

Kay (1990), noting that *even* sentences like the following require two-dimensional scale, applies the above model to his analysis of two-dimensional *even*:

(16) A: Can Stretch jump six feet?
   B: Sure. Dumpy can even jump seven feet.

(17) A: Can Dumpy jump seven feet?
   B: No. Stretch can't even jump six feet.

For the above examples, Kay proposes a scalar model with a dimension of a set of jumpers ordered with respect to jumping ability and another dimension of a set of obstacles ordered with respect to difficulty (see Figure 1 for (12) and Figure 2 for (13)).

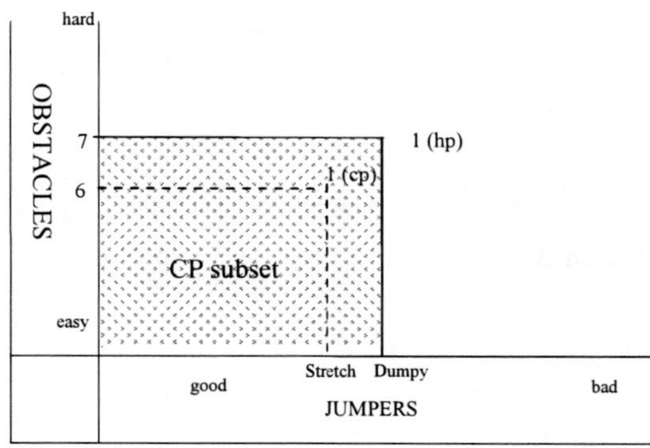

Figure 1(for (16) from Kay (1990))

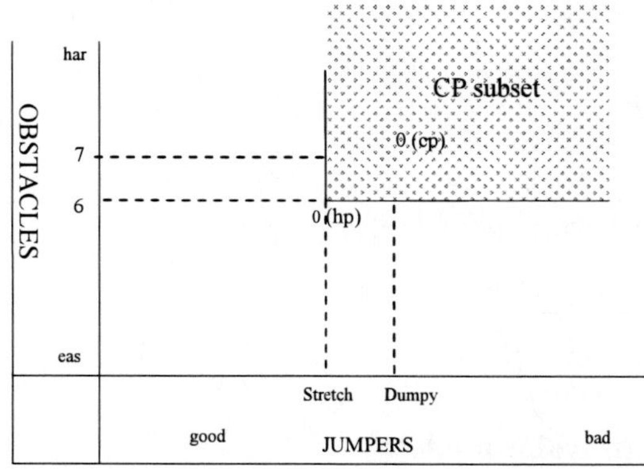

Figure 2 (for (17) from Kay (1990))

According to Kay, *even* indicates that the proposition of the *even* sentence (the hp in Figures 1 and 2) is more informative than some other proposition which is taken to be already present in the context (the context proposition or the cp in Figures 1 and 2) in the same scalar model. For example, as for (16), the truth condition of the proposition that *Dumpy can jump seven feet* (=the hp) entails the truth condition of the proposition that *Stretch can jump six feet* (=the cp). Kay points out that the cp is either explicitly present in the context as in examples (16) and (17) or generated through accommodation. Kay claims that the cp is a proposition less informative than the hp in the scalar model and that *even* signals what the Maxim of Quantity (Grice 1975) tells us to optimize.

Shudo (1998, 2002) accepts Kay's account on *even* and contends that the difference between the English *even* and the Japanese scalar *mo* is that, while the former relies on the informative relation in a scalar model between the hp and the cp, the latter relies on the similarity relation based on the monosemous account on *mo*. However, there are some usages that Kay's account of the informative relation between the hp and the cp cannot handle. For examples, observe the following proverb about a blind squirrel.

(18) Even a blind squirrel finds an acorn sometimes.

This proverb has several variations in which sometimes is replaced by expressions such as "now and then," "every now and then," "once in a while," "every once in a while," etc. Whatever the expression is, it is clear that a blind squirrel is one of the least likely candidates "to find an acorn," not "to find an acorn sometimes." In other words, "sometimes" in (18) should be an item on a second dimension, the dimension of frequency to find an acorn. Then, what would be the cp that is less informative than the hp? These expressions to indicate infrequent occurrences of finding an acorn are definitely selected for their least likelihood. We can intuitively infer that *even* in (18) indicates seeing squirrels find acorns far more frequently than sometimes. However, an argument space corresponding to such a proposition is outside the CP subset as Figure 3 shows. If the informativeness relation of the *even* sentence is within the CP subset, why does (18) have an item that is closest to the origin on the vertical dimension? In the following, I will show that the operations of Japanese *mo* and Korean *to* interact not only with the Maxim of Quantity but also with the Maxim of Relevance (Grice 1975) and claim that the same operation applies to *even*.

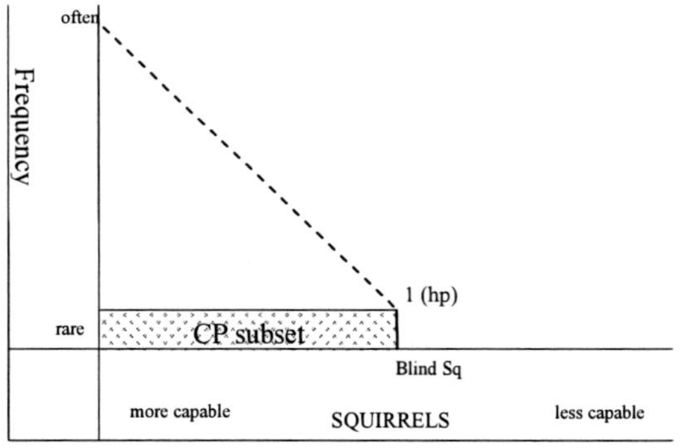

Figure 3(for (18))

4.2. *Even*-like *mo* and *to* in scalar models

Japanese *mo* generates scalar meanings similar to English *even* (Numata 1984, 1986, 1995, Sadanobu 1995, Noguchi and Harada 1994, 1996, Shudo 1998, 2002, inter alia). According to Noguchi and Harada (1994, 1996), the presence of scale is not semantically encoded in the particle, but is contextually provided. Shudo's (1998, 2002) also claims that *even*-like meaning is generated in the interaction between the monosemous account of *mo* and the context which places the hp on a scale. *Mo* requires the presence of an ap either already evoked in the context or implicated as a result of 'accommodation for presupposition' (Lewis 1979). When there is no ap already evoked and when the context places the hp on a scale, an ap is implicated by the interaction of the hp and the scale.

According to Shudo (1998, 2002), it is too much for the hearer to identify the ap from the Mo-presupposition represented in (10). While Shudo (1998, 2002) discusses in detail how the contextual effect of H(x) in (10) determines the property of G(y), for the constraints of space and time, I will only make a simpler claim here that the ap has to be the one that interacts with H(x) so that H(x) can have a contextual effect.

When the scale is one-dimensional, accommodation for presupposition is a rather straightforward process. Observe the following:

(19) [John is one of the least likely candidates to laugh.]
    John mo   waratta.
          even   laughed
    'Even John laughed.'

In (19), the scale consists of individuals ordered with respect to the likelihood of laughing. With such a one-dimensional scale, the ap implicated by the presence of *mo* is something like the following:

(20) Individuals who are more likely to laugh than John laughed.

In the above example, what is presupposed in the traditional approach applies to (20), which share exactly the same property as the hp.

Double-focus scalar *mo* sentences are not so simple. Observe the following:

(21) [Harry is one of the least proficient students. The speaker and the hearer are discussing
      how their students did on a recently administered quiz which had ten questions.]
    Harry de   mo nana-mon   seikai   datt-a.
           EMP even seven-questions right-answers COP-PAST
    'Even Harry got seven right answers.'

If we were to treat (21) the same way as (19)-(20), it would implicate the following:

(22) Students who are more proficient than Harry got seven right answers.

Our intuition tells us there is something strange about (22). There is of course nothing incorrect about the truth condition of (22). We do expect that students who are more proficient than Harry got *at least* seven right answers. However, what we infer from (21) is more like the following:

(23) Students who are more proficient than Harry got <u>more than</u> seven right answers.

The Korean equivalent sentence shown below generates the same inference as (23).

(24) Harry-do   ilgob-gae   majasseo-yo.
      -even seven-questions got-right-PAST
    'Even Harry got seven right answers.'

Let us observe the relationship between the argument spaces corresponding to the hp of (21)/(24) and (22) in a two-dimensional scalar model in Figure 4. The hp in Figure 4 shows the cell corresponding to (21)/(24). The argument spaces corresponding to (22) are at the upper boundary of the range covering cells in which the truth values are entailed by the truth value of the hp (the CP SUBSET).

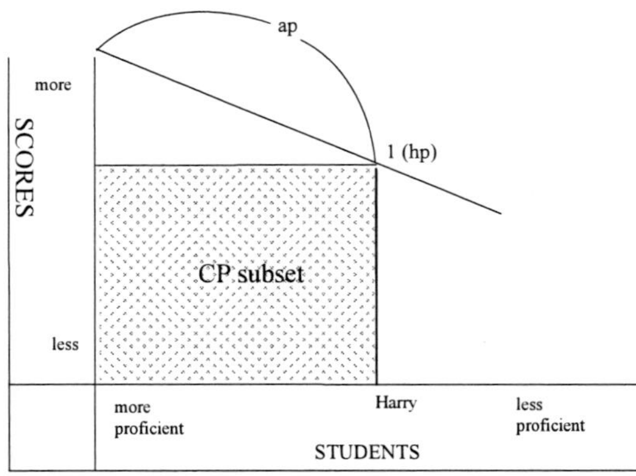

Figure 4

Now compare the above with what (23) expresses. The argument spaces corresponding to (23) are outside the cp subset. The process in which (23) is implicated is obviously quite different from what Kay (1990) defines as 'entailment' relation between the hp and the cp. Let us apply Shudo's (1998, 2002) analysis of *mo* mentioned earlier (presented in (10)) to the above example. The hp (=F(x)) that Harry got seven right answers requires that the ap (=G(y)) share a common property (=H) and that H(x) have a contextual effect in the context. What is the entailment of the hp which has a contextual effect in the context? To answer the question, we should note that (21) does not really mean to provide information about Harry's performance on the quiz. (21) is produced to indicate that the exam was easy and therefore students did better than expected.

(25) Harry did better than expected.
(26) Students more proficient than Harry did better than expected.

This property of having performed better than expected is held not only by Harry but also other students more proficient than Harry and thus (25) above is a good candidate for H(x). If we assume the property of having performed better than expected as H, (25) and (26) can serve as H(x) and H(y). Shudo (2008) claims that in order for the additive particles, such as Japanese *mo* and Korean *to*, to produce the scalar meaning, they must allow the relationship between the hp and the ap as propositions with 'similar' properties, not only identical properties as the traditional approach of these particles have put it.

4.4 Correlational expectation in a scalar model

It should be noted that the notion of scalar model with n dimensions, proposed by Fillmore, Kay and O'Connor (1988), explains an expectation of an event or a state from a set of expectations based on the n dimensions that are correlated. The items on a dimension and items on another dimension are arranged in particular orders so that there is a positive correlation between the two dimensions. In Kay's examples of (16) and (17), jumpers are supposed to be ordered with respect to jumping ability, not with respect to cooking ability.[6]

---

[6] To be rigid about the practical aspect of the scenario, it is rather unrealistic for the first speaker to ask the question: if s/he is expected to know the jumping ability of Stretch and Dumpy, why does s/he ask the question? We have to assume that s/he only knows their 'relative' jumping ability. To capture what Kay tries to represent in (16) and (17), it is better to assume that jumpers are ordered with respect to general physical ability, or something of the sort, that helps us make a prediction about jumping ability. Or, if the question were about the jumper's performance on a particular day ("Did Stretch jump six

What is crucial about the notion of scalar model is that a positive correlation between the items of the orthogonal dimensions is always expected. Shudo (1998, 2002) calls such expectation the CORRELATIONAL EXPECTATION in a scalar model. While the correlational expectation is quite ubiquitous (most of us rely on prejudgment to some extent), the expectation can be easily betrayed. Life is far more complicated. To recycle the scenario about the German quiz, it is possible that Harry finally decided to work hard. Needless to say, we cannot expect others to have done better than expected in this case. In other words, we can expect the correlational expectation to be preserved only when a factor affects everyone equally, such as the quiz was easy. The above argument can be summarized below.

(27) a. Harry did better than expected
b. because there is a factor that affects everyone equally such as an easy quiz.
OR
c. because Harry did something unexpected that caused him perform better on the quiz (such as he prepared harder, he cheated, Martians kidnapped and transformed him into someone smarter overnight, etc.).

The above reasoning may be generalized as follows:

(28) a. Something unexpected, event P, happened.
b. Event P happened because there was a factor S that affected the event. The factor S equally affected other comparable events. (=The correlational expectation is preserved.)
OR
c. Event P happened because there was a factor T that affected the event. Factor T did not affect other comparable events. (=P is an OUTLIER.)

Even indicates that it is (28b), not (28c). Needless to say, the correlational expectation needs to be revised to accommodate the unexpected event described in the *even* sentence. The following conditions provide a general representation of the unexpectedness of an event or a state in a two-dimensional *even* sentence.[7]

(29) Even (x_1, F_1)
a. The speaker and the hearer share a pre-existing correlational expectation between the members of D_x and D_F, where D_x is a set of elements comparable to x_1 and D_F is a set of elements comparable to F_1, and
b. the truth value of the cell of $<x_1, F_1>$ is expected to be false according to the pre-existing correlational expectation.

The pre-existing correlational expectation should be revised to accommodate the newly introduced information. However, the relative correlational expectation should not be revised. (see Figure 5.)

---

feet?" for example), the question may make sense since there are other conditions, the ground, the temperature, etc., that relatively equally influence jumping.

[7] There is an even sentence in which the unexpectedness does not come from direct contravention, but indirect contravention, such as Even Portia got 5 when Portia is one of the most proficient and 5 is less than expected for her. Here, $<x_1, F_1>$ is not expected to be false according to the pre-existing correlational expectation, but its scalar implicature contravenes the pre-existing correlational expectation. For further discussion on this, see Shudo (1998, 2002).

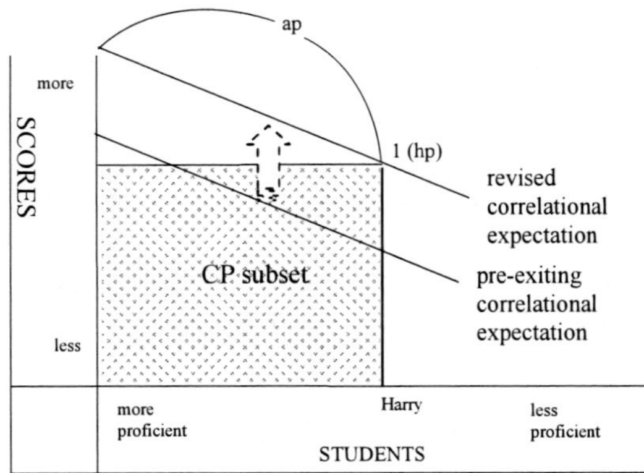

Figure 5

This point can be represented as follows:

(30) Even (x_1, F_1)
 a. The relative correlational expectation between the members of D_x and D_F is maintained, and
 b. the pre-existing correlational expectation is revised (shifted vertically, without changing the slope) to comply with the truth value of the cell of $<x_1, F_1>$

Now let us observe the following sentences in English, Japanese, and Korean, that present a proposition truth-conditionally identical to the *even* sentences but are not accompanied by a scalar operator.

(31) a. Harry got seven right answers.
    b. Harry wa nana-mon   seikai   datt-a.
       TOP seven-questions right-answers COP-PAST
      'Harry got seven right answers.'
    c. Harry-un ilgob-gae   majasseo-yo.
       -TOP seven-questions got-right-PAST
      'Harry got seven right answers.'

When the context is such that seven correct answers are more than expected of Harry's score, all of (31) should entail that *Harry did better than expected* (=(25)). In other words, without the presence of *even*, the unexpectedness should be recognized by the hearer anyway. On the other hand, neither of (24) seems to implicate that *students more proficient than Harry did better than expected* (=(22)). Thus, it seems fair to assume that when an unexpected event happens, unless it is marked with a scalar operator, the unexpected event is usually interpreted as an outlier. It should be noted that the presence of *even* semantically indicates what is represented in (29a)-(29b) and (30a)-(30b) while the absence of *even* pragmatically signals that the speaker's intention is most likely not the scalar interpretation. *Even* interacts with the Maxim of Relevance, which tells us to optimize the implicature so that the correlational expectation in the scalar model survives.

4.4 Correlational expectation as a contextual constraint

Now we are ready to go back to the problem that I mentioned in the beginning: Why is (3b), repeated below, inappropriate when (4d) is appropriate?

(3) a. A: Hi. How did Harry do on the quiz?

b. B: #Even he got seven right answers.
(4) a. A: Hi. How was the quiz?
    b. B: Everyone did very well.
    c. A: How did Harry do?
    d. B: Even he got seven right answers.

Although the context provided for (3) clearly shows that the hp of (3b) has a contextual effect by answering A's question, the presence of *even* makes the sentence pragmatically inappropriate. There seems to be a constraint that the contextual effect of an *even* sentence should not be obtained by the hp itself. Since *even* sentences necessarily require accommodation for presupposition, just like *mo/to* sentences with scalar readings, the contextual effect of an *even* sentence should be obtained through the interaction between the implicated ap and H(x). The problem of (3b) is that, while *even* indicates the contextual effect should be obtained through the interaction between the ap and H(x), (3a) forces the contextual effect of the answer sentence to be obtained by the hp alone.

On the other hand, (4d) can contribute to the contextual effect that has already been pointed out in (4b) by strengthening it. In other words, (4d) is doing two things. It answers B's question by offering the hp. It also provides a piece of information that strengthens the contextual implication that (4b) has already produced. (4b) interacts with (32a) below that is expected to be present in the prior context to contextually imply (32b).

(32) a. If everyone does well on a quiz, the quiz is probably easy.
    b. The quiz was probably easy.

It should be noted that (32b) is precisely what causes the revision of pre-existing correlational expectation since everyone's score is inflated because of the easy quiz.

5. Conclusion

While sentences containing *even*, as well as Japanese scalar *mo* and Korean scalar *to*, express some unexpectedness, the lexical items mark that the state or event describe in the hp is not an outlier in terms of the scalar expectations. Therefore, the correlational expectation is conserved, although the y-intercept has changed because of the unexpectedness. The usage of *even* interacts with correlational expectation in the scalar model and signals that the relative correlational expectation is conserved in order to accommodate the presupposition.

References

An, D. -H. 2007. On the distribution of NPI in Korean. *Natural Language Semantics* 15.

Fillmore, C., Kay, P. and O'Connor, M. 1988. Regularity and Idiomaticity in Grammatical Constructions: The Case of Let Alone. *Language* 64.

Grice, H. P. 1975. Logic and Conversation. In Cole, P. and Morgan, J. L. (eds.), *Syntax and Semantics* 9: Speech acts. New York: Academic Press.

Horn, L. 1969. A presuppositional analysis of *only* and *even*. In Papers from the fifth regional meeting of the Chicago Linguistic Society. Chicago: University of Chicago. 98-107.

Horn, L. R. 1972. *On the Semantic Properties of Logical Operators in English*. Ph.D. Dissertation, UCLA.

Karttunen, F. and L. Karttunen. 1977. *Even* Questions. *Proceedings fo the Seventh Annual Meeting of the North Eastern Linguistic Society*. 115-134.

Karttunen, L. 1974. Presupposition and linguistic context. *Theoretical Linguistics* 1. 181-194.

Karttunen, L. and S. Peters. 1979. Conventional implicature. In C.K. Oh and D. A. Dineen. (eds.), *Syntax and semantics 11: Presupposition*. New York: Academic Press. 1-56.

Kay, P. 1990. *Even. Linguistics and Philosophy* 13: 1.

Lee, C. 2006. Contrastive (Predicate) Topic, Intonation, and Scalar Meanings. In Lee, C, Gordon, M and Buring, D. (eds.), *Topic and Focus: Meaning and Intonation from a Crosslinguistic Perspective*. Kluwer Academic Publishers.

Lewis, D. 1979. Scorekeeping in a Language Game. *Journal of Philosophical Logic* 8.

Nakanishi, K. 2006. The Semantics of *Even* and Negative Polarity Items in Japanese. *Proceedings of the 25th West Coast Conference on Formal Linguistics*. 288-296.

Noguchi, N. and Harada, Y. 1994. Toritate joshi to ryouteki kaishaku. [Focus particles and quantitative interpretations]. *Proceedings of the 11th workshop Linguistics Society of Japan*.

Noguchi, N. and Harada, Y. 1996. Toritate joshi no kinou to kaishaku: ryouteki kaishaku wo chuushin ni. [Functions and interpretations of focus particles: on their scalar readings]. In Gunji, T. (ed.), Seiyaku ni motozuku nihongo no kozo no kenkyu. [Reports on constraint-based research on Japanese structures]. Tokyo: International Japanese Cultural Research Center.

Numata, Y. 1984. Toritateshi no imi to bunpou: mo, dake, sae wo chuushin ni. [The meaning and the grammar of focus particles: on examples of mo, dake and sae]. *Nihongogaku*. [Japanese Studies]. 3-4. Tokyo: Meiji Shoin.

Numata, Y. 1986. Toritateshi. [Focus particles]. In K. Okutsu, Y. Numata, and T. Sugimoto, (eds.) *Iwayuru nihongo joshi no kenkyuu* [Study of so-called Japanese particles]. Tokyo: Bonjinsha.

Numata, Y. and Jo, K. and 1995. Toritateshi mo no fokasu to sukopu. [Focus and scope of focus particles]. In Masuoka, T, et al. (eds.) *Nihongo no shudai to toritate*. [Japanese subjects and focus]. Tokyo: Kuroshio.

Rooth, M. 1985. *Association with Focus*. Ph.D. dissertation. University of Massachusetts, Amherst.

Sadanobu, T. 1995. Shinteki purosesu kara mita toritateshi mo/demo. [Cognitive processes and Japanese focus particles mo and demo.] In Masuoka, T, et al. (eds.) *Nihongo no shudai to toritate*. [Japanese subjects and focus]. Tokyo: Kuroshio.

Schwarz, B. 2005. Scalar Additive Particles in Negative Contexts. *Natural Language Semantics* 13. 125-168.

Shudo, S. in press. Japanese *mo* and Korean *to* in *even*-like usages: What Gricean Maxims tell us to optimize in a scalar model. *In Proceedings of the 10th Conference of Pragmatic Society of Japan*.

Shudo, S. 2002. *The Presupposition and Discourse Functions of the Japanese Particle mo*. London/New York: Routledge.

Shudo, S. 1998. *The Japanese Particle mo: Its Presupposition and Discourse Functions*. Ph.D. dissertation. Georgetown University.

Shudo, S. and Y. Harada. 2008. Bunmyakuteki seiyaku no saikochiku ni yoru zentei no tokutei: joshi mo to bunmyaku izonteki ruigisei. [Identifying a presupposition by reconstructing its contextual constraints: Context-dependent similarities in usages of the Japanese particle *Mo*.] *Proceedings of the 136th Conference of Linguistics Society of Japan*.

Sperber, D. and Wilson, D. 1986. *Relevance: Communication and Cognition*. Cambridge, MA: Harvard University Press.

Wilkinson, K. The Scope of *Even*. 1996. *Natural Language Semantics* 4. 193-215.

Toward a Global Infrastructure for the Sustainability of Language Resources [*]

Gary F. Simons[a] and Steven Bird[b]

[a]SIL International and Graduate Institute of Applied Linguistics
7500 W. Camp Wisdom Road, Dallas, TX 75236, USA
gary_simons@sil.org

[b]Dept of Computer Science and Software Engineering, University of Melbourne, Victoria 3010, Australia
and Linguistic Data Consortium, University of Pennsylvania, Philadelphia, PA 19104, USA
sb@csse.unimelb.edu.au

Abstract. This paper describes work the Open Language Archives Community (OLAC) is doing to contribute to a global infrastructure for the sustainability of language resources. After offering a definition of language resource, it addresses the issue of what makes language resources sustainable by defining six necessary and sufficient conditions for their sustained use, then discusses what it takes to make such sustainability a reality by describing the roles of four key sets of players—creators, archives, aggregators, users. With this background, the paper describes the community infrastructure OLAC has developed for allowing its members to express consensus about best practices for digital archiving, plus the technical infrastructure it has developed to provide aggregation and search for the language resources community. The concluding section probes the broader issue of sustainable development to consider the sustainability of language resources in the context of the sustainability of language development and of languages themselves.

Keywords: Language documentation, metadata, digital archives, sustainable development

1. Introduction

Sustainability has become a byword of our times. In fact, *The Global Language Monitor* recognized *sustainable* as the Top Word of 2006.[1] Behind all the buzz there is an important concept that has significance even for our language resources community. Focus on the sustainability of the planet in the news media is making us increasingly aware that unless we mend our wasteful ways, we could squander the world's natural resources along with the opportunity of future generations to enjoy the same quality of life that we do.

The language resources community is no stranger to waste. Waste happens when the resources resulting from prior work are no longer available due to the deterioration of the media

---

[*] This work is supported by the NSF Project *OLAC: Accessing the World's Language Resources*, awards 0723357 and 0723864 to the University of Pennsylvania and the Graduate Institute of Applied Linguistics. Components of the infrastructure have been developed with our research assistants Haejoong Lee and Debbie Chang and archiving consultant Joan Spanne. We are grateful to members of the OLAC community for their collaboration in developing and implementing OLAC's standards and recommendations.

[1] http://www.languagemonitor.com/top_word_lists

that store them or the obsolescence of the formats that encode them. Waste also happens when a new project redoes work that has already been done by someone else, because the new project does not know about the prior work or because the prior work was not made available in a form they could use. Even more pervasive is the waste that happens when ordinary users, who would have no ability to create the needed resources, miss out entirely on the opportunity to benefit from resources that already exist because they are not able to discover or access or use them. Rather, we should be seeking to create an environment in which language resources thrive through regular use by all who can benefit from them.

This paper describes the work the Open Language Archives Community (OLAC) is doing to address issues like these. First, the paper defines the scope of OLAC by offering a definition of language resource (§2). Next, it identifies the conditions that are necessary for the sustainable use of language resources (§3) and defines the roles of the four sets of players—creators, archives, aggregators, and users—that are involved in making such sustainability a reality (§4). With this background, the paper is then able to describe what OLAC is doing to contribute to a global infrastructure for supporting the sustainable use of language resources (§5). The concluding section probes the broader issue of sustainable development to consider the sustainability of language resources in the context of the sustainability of language development and of languages themselves (§6).

2. Defining Language Resource

The notion of "language resource" is something our community tends to take for granted and is something that OLAC has taken for granted since its inception. As the founding mission statement says, the primary goal of OLAC is "creating a worldwide virtual library of language resources."[2] OLAC recognizes that the language resources of interest to our community come not only from sources within our community but also from many sources that would not identify themselves as part of our community (e.g., libraries, national archives, book sellers). As OLAC has begun interacting with such institutions in order to bring their resources into a single global infrastructure, we have found it necessary to define exactly what we mean by a language resource. This is the latest version of our definition:

> A language resource is any physical or digital item that is a product of language documentation, description, or development or is a tool that specifically supports the creation and use of such products.

The following paragraphs elaborate the major concepts used in the definition.

Language resources are rooted in the study of language. More specifically, they arise from a series of activities that could be termed the "three D's": language documentation, language description, and language development.

The distinction between language documentation and language description is defined in Himmelmann's (1998) seminal work. Language *documentation* "aims at the record of the linguistic practices and traditions of a speech community." Documentation is concerned with the primary data of language study. It is done by compiling a sample of instances of language in actual use (whether spoken or written), commenting on those instances (such as through situational metadata, transcription, translation, annotation), and then archiving the whole collection. Language *description,* by contrast, is concerned with the secondary data of language study. It is done by analyzing the primary data and generalizing over it to produce works like a dictionary and grammar that describe how the language works as a system of signs.

Language *development* adds a third dimension involving resources that focus on acquiring language skills. The term "language development" is used in two ways by different subcommunities. It is most widely used to refer to the process by which humans learn language. Documentary corpora of individuals learning language and secondary descriptions based on those primary data are certainly within the scope of language resources. So are works that

---

[2] http://www.language-archives.org/

reflect a second sense of "language development," namely, in reference to the activities that result from language planning (Cooper, 1989). Under the heading of corpus planning, these include terminology development and the production of prescriptive dictionaries and grammars. Under the heading of acquisition planning, these include the development of materials that are designed to help people learn a language or learn language skills like reading and writing. A twenty-first century approach to language planning could also include "automation planning" which involves the development of processes that leverage new language technologies so as to amplify human productivity.

With these background definitions for documentation, description, and development, it is now possible to elaborate the other key terms in the definition. First, a language resource is defined as any resource that is a product of any of the three D's. The intention of *any* in the definition is to place no limit on the form of a resource; for instance, it may be physical or digital, textual or audiovisual, published or unpublished. The intention of *product* is to say that being the output of language documentation, description, or development is what identifies a resource as a language resource, not being the input. The input to description is typically documentation, and the input to development is typically documentation and description, so it is tempting to see the input role as being a defining characteristic. However, it is clear that this approach fails when we consider documentation. If the inputs to documentation were language resources, then every speech event in daily life and every article in a newspaper and every text page on the web would be a language resource. It is true that all of these are potential inputs to the study of language, but they wouldn't become language resources until somebody performed the documentation process of compiling them into a collection, providing metadata (and possibly other commentary) for the collection, and lodging the result in an institutional archive.

Secondly, the community that produces language resources is vitally interested in the tools that are used in that work; in fact, many in the community focus on the development of such tools. Thus, any resource that is a *tool* that supports the creation of language resources is also defined to be a language resource. Such tools can take a number of forms; for instance, a tool might be a textbook on theory or a software program that automates aspects of the work or a blog that gives methodological advice to practitioners. The definition limits the scope to tools that are *specifically* designed to support the creation or use of language resources. For instance, a general word processor or recording device might be used to create a language resource, but it is not itself a language resource. However, a document giving advice on how to use such general tools in creating language resources would be. Similarly, a software tool that automates a specific aspect of language description (like dictionary building) would be a language resource.

This definition of language resource, then, identifies the scope of the worldwide virtual library that OLAC seeks to build. It aims to encompass any resource that is the product of language documentation, description, or development, and any resource that is a tool for supporting these activities.

3. Necessary and Sufficient Conditions for Sustainability

Sustainability, in the general sense, refers to the ability to maintain indefinitely a given process or a desired state. (The richer sense implied by "sustainable development" is discussed below in §6.) In the case of language resources, we want to sustain their use. Thus the problem of sustaining language resources can be understood as the problem of maintaining the use of language resources over time. That problem can be summarized as follows:

> Given the relentless process of entropy that degrades digitally stored information, the relentless process of innovation that makes equipment and methodologies obsolete even while they are still in common use, and the relentless proliferation of information resources of all kinds that makes it ever harder to find language resources of interest, how do we keep our language resources from falling into disuse and wasting away as yet more detritus on a digital scrap heap?

To be sustainable, the results of our work must transcend computer environments, communities of practice, domains of application, and especially the passage of time (Bird and Simons, 2003). Ensuring availability to future generations is particularly crucial for resources that document languages that are themselves in danger of being lost (Simons, 2006).

If our goal is to sustain the use of language resources, then we must begin by asking, "What does it take to sustain the use of language resources?" By identifying the necessary conditions for the use of language resources, we can identify the objectives that an infrastructure for sustainability must meet. If the identified conditions are also sufficient to ensure use, then they would constitute a complete set of objectives. We propose that there are six necessary and sufficient conditions for the use of a language resource. That is, to sustain use, the community's infrastructure must establish and maintain the following characteristics of a language resource:

- The resource must be *extant.*
- The resource must be *discoverable.*
- The resource must be *available.*
- The resource must be *interpretable.*
- The resource must be *portable.*
- The resource must be *relevant.*

The middle four conditions form a group that defines the attributes that make a resource usable. Thus the model can be summarized as follows: A resource will be used if it still exists, if it is usable, and if a user finds it relevant.

The first necessary condition for the use of a language resource is that it be *extant.* Once a resource comes into existence, we cannot assume its ongoing existence, particularly in the case of digital resources which can be lost in an instant through an event like a disk crash or can be lost gradually as storage media degrade over time. Sustainability requires that the custodian of a resource follows procedures to ensure that the resources are preserved against all reasonable contingencies (e.g., via offsite backup), that the resources are periodically migrated to fresh and current media, and that all file copies are authenticated as exactly matching the source file.

Second, the resource must be *discoverable;* it cannot be used unless the prospective user is able to discover its existence and its whereabouts. The key to this is descriptive metadata. Metadata is "data about the data;" it is like the catalog card in a library that describes a book and tells where to find it. But it is not enough that descriptive metadata simply exists. The description of the resource must be published in such a way that the prospective user who knows nothing about the resource is able to discover its existence when searching. Furthermore, the description of the resource must be done in such a way that the prospective user is able to judge it as being relevant without having to first obtain the resource. If these conditions are met, then a resource is discoverable.

Third, once discovered, the resource must be *available;* it cannot be used unless it is truly available to the prospective user. Availability has two major facets. First, the user must have the right to access and use the resource. In order to guarantee sustainable use of a resource, it is essential that the rights of future users be established when the resource is created and clearly stated when it is archived. Where possible, distributing resources under the terms of Open Access[3] (such as under a Creative Commons[4] license) fosters the most widespread use. Second, the user must know the procedure for accessing the resource. In the case of physical resources, this involves knowing how to gain access to the single archived instance of a resource or how to order a copy of a published resource. In the case of digital resources, maximal availability is achieved through dissemination via links on the Internet, but sustainable long term access requires persistent URLs that will not break.

Fourth, once accessed, the resource must be *interpretable;* it cannot be used if the user is not able to make sense of the content. The *Reference Model for an Open Archival Information*

---

[3] http://www.eprints.org/openaccess/
[4] http://creativecommons.org/

System (CCSDS, 2002), the standard adopted as ISO 14721 in 2003, states that one of the fundamental functions of an archive is to ensure that the resources it archives are "independently understandable" by the designated user community. That is, the prospective user should be able to use the resource without needing to consult the creator to clarify any details of content. For a language resource, this means documenting things like the situational context, methodologies, terminologies, abbreviations, markup conventions, and character encodings.

Fifth, once accessed the resource must be *portable;* it cannot be used if it does not operate within the user's working environment. A resource must work with the user's hardware and operating system, and with the software tools that are available to the user. Maximizing portability means using formats that are open and transparent and thus supported by many software vendors (including open source projects), rather than using proprietary formats that force users to buy proprietary software that is not even likely to still be available to future generations. Another practice that promotes use in a wider variety of contexts is following the best practices (such as for markup or terminology) of the target community of practice.

Finally, the resource must be *relevant*. Maintaining the five conditions above makes it possible for a resource to be used well into the future, and unless these conditions are met, it cannot be used. But these conditions are not sufficient to guarantee that a resource will be used. The final condition is relevance; a resource will not be used unless it is relevant to the needs of the prospective user. In the case of endangered languages, the members of the language community themselves form a critical user group. The linguistics community has come to recognize that when we work with endangered languages, we have an ethical responsibility to create resources that are relevant to the language community and their aims for their language (e.g., Nathan, 2006). Funding agencies also play a role when they wield their perceptions of relevance as a factor for deciding which resource development efforts they will fund.

4. The Key Players and their Roles

No single person or institution can achieve the sustainable use of language resources; rather, it takes an infrastructure involving four key sets of players who have distinct roles:

- Creators — Persons who create language resources
- Archives — Institutions that curate language resources for long-term preservation and access
- Aggregators — Institutions that gather language resources from multiple archives and make them interoperate
- Users — Persons who want to use language resources

The basic model, illustrated in Figure 1, is as follows. Individuals (shown as ellipses on the left side of the diagram) create and use language resources, but they depend on institutions (shown as rectangles on the right side of the diagram) to bridge the gap between producer and consumer. Creators place the resources they create under the care of Archives that are committed to preserve the resources and provide access over the long term. It is impossible for an individual Creator to achieve sustainability since life is short; resources cannot be sustainable unless they are under the care of long-lived institutions. However, archival care itself is not enough to guarantee sustained use. This is because there are so many institutions curating language resources that the User who could truly benefit from using the resources cannot possibly know about all the Archives to look in. Aggregators are thus the key to linking the supply (in Archives) with the demand (by Users). Aggregators harvest resources from Archives (either full data or metadata) and provide services where Users can make a single search request to find and retrieve resources from all participating Archives.

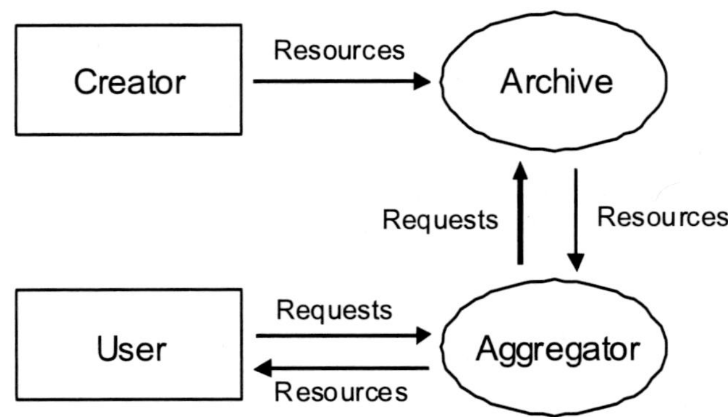

Figure 1: Key players in the infrastructure for sustainable language resource use.

The roles of the players can be further elucidated by considering the function each performs with respect to the six necessary and sufficient conditions introduced above. The results are summarized below in Table 1. The functions listed in the table identify best current practices (which are not always common practices). The following paragraphs explain the roles by considering one condition at a time.

Table 1: The roles of the key players in sustaining language resource use.

	Creator	Archive	Aggregator	User
Extant	Supplies complete and valid original	Follows preservation procedures	Harvests data or metadata of extant resources	Has potential to use any extant resource
Discoverable	Supplies descriptive metadata	Publishes interoperable metadata	Provides search service over all resources	Searches for resources of relevance
Available	Secures and documents access rights	Provides access consistent with access rights	Mediates access to resources in archives	Accesses resources that seem relevant
Interpretable	Supplies documentation of content	Ensures independent understandability for target group	Interprets resources to provide aggregation	Uses resources if they are understood
Portable	Supplies a portable original	Migrates resources as formats change	Interoperates over aggregated portable resources	Uses resources if they operate in user's context
Relevant	Prioritizes creation of resources deemed relevant	Prioritizes curation of resources deemed relevant	Provides services relevant to its target community	Determines if resource is actually relevant

Extant. It is the Creator who first brings a language resource into existence. In order to ensure sustained existence, the Creator must supply the complete original resource to an Archive. The Archive confirms that the submission is complete and valid as to formats on acceptance; it then follows "documented policies and procedures which ensure that the information is preserved against all reasonable contingencies, and which enable the information to be disseminated as authenticated copies of the original" (CCSDS, 2002:3-1). The Aggregator harvests information about all extant resources being preserved by Archives, which gives the User the potential to use any extant resource since it will be discoverable through the Aggregator.

Discoverable. The Creator's contribution to making resources discoverable is to provide the descriptive metadata that answers the basic questions of who, what, when, where, why, and how. The User's role is to search for resources that are relevant to the present need. The metadata in a catalog record is what makes it possible to match a User's search query with the resources that are likely to be relevant. The role of the Archive is to ensure that the descriptive metadata follow best practice guidelines and then to publish these descriptions in such a way that Aggregators can harvest them and build search services that interoperate over the resources in all known Archives.

Available. The Creator's contribution to making resources available is to secure the needed permissions for sharing the resources with others and to document any restrictions to access that the rights holders may stipulate. The User's role is to access resources that, upon discovery, seem relevant. The role of the Archive is to ensure that the access rights are clearly known and documented, and then to provide a means by which a User who meets any restrictions on access can obtain a copy of the resource. The role of the Aggregator is to link the User with resources in the Archive, either through a direct URL in the case of an openly accessible digital resource or through information on what to do next in the case of a restricted resource.

Interpretable. It is the role of the Creator to make the language resource understandable to its prospective users. For language documentation, this may involve augmenting a recording with things like transcription, translation, commentary, and a description of the situational context. For language description, this may involve adding definitions of terms, abbreviations, markup conventions, and character encodings. The role of the Archive is to ensure that the resource to be preserved "is Independently Understandable to the Designated Community" (CCSDS, 2002:3-1). In other words, the anticipated User should be able to understand the resource without needing the assistance of the Creator. When the resource is independently understandable, it is possible for an Aggregator to harvest the data itself and provide services that interoperate over aggregated data. It is also possible for a User to interpret and use the resource. In the case where the Creator has archived a resource that conforms to a community-wide standard for information encoding (such as a markup schema or an ontology), then the Aggregator can harvest such resources to provide services that interoperate over the shared semantics of the standard.

Portable. The Users can use a resource only if it operates in their working environment, including their hardware, operating system, and available software tools. Since different Users have different working environments and the environments of the future will be different yet, the Creator should prepare resources in such a way that they operate across the variety of environments that Users typically have. This means that the Creator must look beyond favorite working and presentation forms to produce archival forms that provide LOTS—lossless, open, transparent, and supported by multiple software suppliers (Simons, 2006). The role of the Archive is to ensure that the form of the resource is adequately portable to be an archival form, and then to provide a service that will migrate the resource to new forms in the future if the archived form ceases to be widely usable. The role of the Aggregator is to harvest portable resources from the Archives and create services (like search and conversion) that exploit their interoperability.

Relevant. The Creator has limited time and resources and thus prioritizes the creation of resources that are deemed relevant. Similarly the Archive cannot afford to preserve every item that has ever been created and thus prioritizes what it will accept for long-term curation to resources that are deemed relevant. An Aggregator has a particular target community and develops services that are relevant for that community; a specialized Aggregator will therefore selectively harvest and interoperate over resources that it deems relevant to its target community. Ultimately, it is the User who determines whether a resource is relevant when deciding whether or not to use it.

5. OLAC's Contribution to Global Infrastructure

As set out in its mission statement, the Open Language Archives Community is "an international partnership of institutions and individuals who are creating a worldwide virtual library of language resources by: (i) developing consensus on best current practice for the digital archiving of language resources, and (ii) developing a network of interoperating repositories and services for housing and accessing such resources." Thus, OLAC's mission has two facets, and these are reflected in two kinds of infrastructure that OLAC is building—a community infrastructure and a technical infrastructure.

Community Infrastructure. Language resource creators, archives, and users comprise a loose network involving scholars, language learners, archivists, and technologists, along with their associated institutions. As we have already discussed, the key players engage with language resources in various ways. There is no centralized coordination of activities among all these players, and innovations tend to spread virally as new standards and practices are supported by tools. OLAC has a special role in this community, namely, that of providing an agreed upon process for the community to develop and document its consensus on best practices in digital archiving. This is done by means of a standards process defined in *OLAC Process,* [5] the founding standard adopted by OLAC to define its governing ideas (i.e. the purpose, vision, and core values) and to describe how it is organized and how it operates.

The initial focus has been on discoverability as a necessary condition for language resource use. To this end OLAC has established a consensus standard on metadata for describing language resources (Bird and Simons, 2004). OLAC has extended Dublin Core metadata,[6] the dominant metadata standard in the digital library and World Wide Web communities, by providing the following additional descriptors that are tailored to language resources:

- Subject language: for identifying precisely (with a code from the ISO 639 standard[7]) which language(s) a resource is "about";
- Linguistic type: for classifying the structure of a resource as primary text, lexicon, or language description;
- Linguistic field: for specifying a relevant subfield of linguistics;
- Discourse type: for indicating the linguistic genre of the material; and
- Role: for documenting the parts played by specific individuals and institutions in creating a resource.

All of these vocabularies are formally defined on the OLAC site, along with best practice recommendations[8] and comprehensive usage guidelines.[9] This metadata infrastructure slots into the discoverability row of Table 1. The OLAC process has the potential for being used to develop infrastructure in other rows of the table, for example, defining consensus on best practices for preservation, for systematic description of access rights, for encoding specific data types, and more.

Technical Infrastructure. Aggregators are a key part of the global infrastructure set out in Table 1, since they permit users to discover and access relevant language resources without needing to know about all the individual archives and resource creators. In the early days of the web, manually constructed topical indexes played this role. However, such indexes go out of date quickly and do not scale up as the number of resources to index increases exponentially. Here, too, OLAC has a special role within the language resources community, namely, that of providing the primary aggregator dedicated to language resources. Participating language archives publish their catalogs in an XML format, and these records are "harvested" twice a day by OLAC services using the Open Archives Initiative (OAI) Protocol for Metadata

---

[5] http://www.language-archives.org/OLAC/process.html
[6] http://dublincore.org/documents/dcmi-terms/
[7] http://www.sil.org/iso639-3/
[8] http://www.language-archives.org/REC/bpr.html
[9] http://www.language-archives.org/NOTE/usage.html

Harvesting,[10] another standard of the digital library community (Simons and Bird, 2003). OLAC's technical infrastructure takes care of archive registration, metadata validation, crosswalks to Dublin Core and HTML for discovery in broader communities, together with search services and usage tracking.

The technical infrastructure for the OLAC aggregator is defined in two standards that have been adopted by the community. *OLAC Metadata*[11] defines the XML format used for the interchange of metadata records within the framework of the Open Archives Initiative OAI. *OLAC Repositories*[12] defines the standards OLAC archives must follow to implement a metadata repository that can be harvested by an aggregator using the OAI Protocol for Metadata Harvesting. The list of participating "archives" includes more than just archives. The metadata infrastructure works well to describe online services; thus, many participants are services that publish catalogs (indexed by language) of the language resources they provide.

Examples. The following listing shows a sample metadata record in the XML format prescribed by the *OLAC Metadata* standard. It is the description of a Shoebox[13]-format lexicon of the Ega language (Côte d'Ivoire) that is housed in the University of Bielefeld Language Archive.

```
<olac:olac xmlns:olac="http://www.language-archives.org/OLAC/1.0/"
    xmlns:dc="http://purl.org/dc/elements/1.1/">
  <dc:title>Ega lexicon (Gbery)</dc:title>
  <dc:creator>Gbery, Eddy Aime</dc:creator>
  <dc:creator>Baze, Lucien</dc:creator>
  <dc:contributor>Lindenlaub, Juliane</dc:contributor>
  <dc:description>Ega lexicon in Shoebox format</dc:description>
  <dc:date>2003-03</dc:date>
  <dc:type xsi:type="olac:linguistic-type" olac:code="lexicon"/>
  <dc:format>shoebox</dc:format>
  <dc:subject xsi:type="olac:language" olac:code="ega"/>
  <dc:language xsi:type="olac:language" olac:code="fra"/>
  <dc:language xsi:type="olac:language" olac:code="eng"/>
  <dc:language xsi:type="olac:language" olac:code="ega"/>
  <dc:language xsi:type="olac:language" olac:code="deu"/>
  <dc:coverage>Cote d'Ivoire</dc:coverage>
</olac:olac>
```

Note the use of domain-specific code values on the Type, Subject, and Language elements. These make it possible to support precise searching for languages and resource types within the aggregated catalog. The entire metadata repository in which this record can be found is openly available (in the format prescribed by the *OLAC Repositories* standard) at:

```
http://www.spectrum.uni-bielefeld.de/langdoc/olac.xml
```

In accordance with the OAI Protocol for Metadata Harvesting, the archive has assigned the above record a unique identifier of *oai:langdoc.uni-bielefeld.de:UBI-EGA-010*. The following URL is thus the *GetRecord* command (following the OAI protocol) for harvesting that single record from the repository at the University of Bielefeld in OLAC format:

```
http://www.language-archives.org/sr/
    www.spectrum.uni-bielefeld.de/langdoc/olac.xml?
    verb=GetRecord&
    identifier=oai:langdoc.uni-bielefeld.de:UBI-EGA-010&
    metadataPrefix=olac
```

Current Status. At present, OLAC has some 35 participating archives, and the OLAC search engine indexes a combined total of approximately 36,000 records. The larger participating archives include the Alaska Native Language Center (U Alaska), Archive of the Indigenous

---

Languages of Latin America (U Texas), Audio Archive of Linguistic Fieldwork (UC Berkeley), Oxford Text Archive, PARADISEC (Pacific And Regional Archive for Digital Sources in Endangered Cultures), SIL Language and Culture Archives, and the Linguistic Data Consortium (U Penn).

This is an excellent beginning, but in surveying the current status we have identified three significant shortcomings. First, the quality of metadata in the majority of participating archives does not meet the level of the best practice recommendations and this limits the quality of search. Second, many significant language archives are not yet participating in OLAC. Third, many of the participating "archives" are more accurately described as digitization projects and are not yet following best practices in digital archiving that will ensure long-term preservation (e.g., CCSDS, 2002).

Future Directions. In addition to these shortcomings, OLAC—and the language resources community more broadly—is confronted with three major challenges that need to be addressed before the promise of universal access to relevant resources is realized. First, due to the huge scale of the search space and the absence of precise indexing vocabularies, users of web search engines such as Google typically experience low precision and recall when searching for language resources. Searches for scarce resources are often swamped with irrelevant results (low precision). Furthermore, many resources are just not returned at all because search terms do not match the synonymous terms used in the desired documents (low recall). A second challenge is that library automation solutions are part of the deep web and remain hidden to the language resources community at large. This means that users searching for language resources need to visit other services like WorldCat and OAIster; it would be better for the language-resource content of these services to be fully integrated with OLAC. A third challenge is that users who try to find language resources using any of these non-OLAC services are unlikely to discover that OLAC can provide additional value, such as richer metadata and more focused result sets.

In order to address these shortcomings and challenges, OLAC has been awarded NSF sponsorship for a new project named "OLAC: Accessing the World's Language Resources"[14] which aims to greatly improve access to language resources by achieving an order-of-magnitude increase in the coverage of the OLAC catalog and in the use of OLAC search services. This involves improving access to language resources on two levels. First, to address the above-listed shortcomings and improve access to resources in language archives, the project includes activities aimed at achieving the following outcomes:

- All OLAC repositories should have up-to-date catalogs that contain metadata conforming to best practice.
- All major language archives should be participating in OLAC.
- All OLAC repositories should conform to current best practices for the long-term curation of their holdings.

Second, in order to address the above-listed challenges and improve access to language resources on the web, the project includes activities aimed at achieving the following outcomes:

- Low-density language materials identified by linguistic web mining should be reliably categorized with OLAC vocabularies.
- Language resources held in libraries and digital repositories should be indexed in OLAC through services that crosswalk and enrich existing catalog records.
- Web search engines should index all OLAC records, so that users who discover language resources using a conventional web search quickly find OLAC records and are drawn to the OLAC site for more precise searching.

The first phase of the project is drawing to a close. It has focused on developing documentation and services to improve the quality of metadata and search. The improved technology infrastructure is now ready to accept registrations from new participants; all interested projects

---

[14] http://olac.wiki.sourceforge.net/

or institutions which archive language resources or which offer language resources through online services are invited to contact the authors.

6. Toward Sustainable Language Development

The recent emphasis on sustainability in public discourse arises from the global concern over the deteriorating natural environment in many parts of the world. Damage to the environment is leading to what many refer to as "the extinction crisis."[15] For instance, noted biologist Edward O. Wilson (2002) warns that human activities, if left unchecked, could result in the extinction of half the world's plant and animal species by the end of this century.

The pressures of globalization are having a similar effect on the world's minority languages. Early in the last decade, linguist Michael Krauss extrapolated from what had already taken place in Australia and North America to warn that the twenty-first century "will see either the death or the doom of 90% of mankind's languages" (1992:7). His essay closes with a sobering challenge: "Obviously we must do some serious rethinking of our priorities, lest linguistics go down in history as the only science that presided obliviously over the disappearance of 90% of the very field to which it is dedicated" (1992:10). He advocates going beyond the scientific work of documenting and describing languages to also working with members of the language community to participate in language development and even working politically beyond the community to increase the language's chance of survival.

We are thus confronted with a challenge that is even greater than the sustainability of language resources, namely, the sustainability of languages themselves. Where languages are threatened because children are no longer learning them, acquisition planning becomes a priority and the sustained products of language documentation and description are key inputs to the language development activities that are needed. Thus, the sustainability of language depends in part on the sustainability of the language resources that contribute to language development, which will lead to the production of new language resources that can in turn enable further development, and so the cycle of sustainability continues.

In 1983, global concern over the world's deteriorating natural and social environment prompted the UN General Assembly to establish the World Commission on Environment and Development. The commission's final report (Brundtland, 1987) is what brought the term *sustainable development* to the world's attention. To this day, their definition of sustainable development is most often cited definition, namely, "development that meets the needs of the present without compromising the ability of future generations to meet their own needs." The commission recognized that the solution must simultaneously address interrelated environmental, economic, and social dimensions—the so-called "three pillars of sustainability." Elkington (1994) picked up this basic model and applied it to doing business in terms of the "triple bottom line"—later popularized as "People, Planet, Profit." The idea is that sustainability is achieved not by maximizing shareholder profit but by coordinating the interests in all three areas of all stakeholders (that is, of everyone affected by the business activities, whether directly or indirectly). Those interests are to simultaneously pursue the three bottom lines of economic prosperity, environmental quality, and social equity.

By analogy this threefold purpose can inform the broader agenda of the language resources community. (1) As for the economic agenda, doing linguistics can be likened to a quest for riches—the riches of knowledge about language in general and about thousands of languages in particular (Simons, 2007). Developing a central aggregator gives the language resources community a means of amassing its treasures into a single virtual storehouse and of being able to measure the size and scope of that treasury. Such an initiative is already underway through the efforts of OLAC. (2) As for the environmental agenda, the analog for the language resources community is improving the quality of the linguistic ecosphere. One piece of our global infrastructure is the *Ethnologue* (Gordon, 2005) which monitors factors like the population and vitality of all known languages. Where it is clear that a language is endangered, one goal of the

---

[15] http://www.well.com/~davidu/extinction.html

language resources community should be to at least ensure that good documentation and description of the language are preserved so that future generations (especially of the ethnic community) will still have access to the language in some form. (3) As for the social agenda, the language resources community should be looking to attain a form of social equity in which minority languages are not overlooked in the efforts of language resource development and in which the products that result include ones that are relevant to the needs and aspirations of the language communities themselves and not just ones that are relevant to outsiders.

The technical infrastructure of OLAC could be exploited to help the language resources community track the availability of documentation, description, and development resources for all the languages of the world. The community could thereby monitor the world situation with respect to the triple bottom line of sustainable development. Table 2 gives a taste of what is possible. It shows a breakdown of language resources currently known to the OLAC aggregator in terms of the size of the associated language. (Resources that are not cataloged with a specific ISO 639 language code are not included in the tabulation; nor are the 7,296 records for the language descriptions in *Ethnologue*.) The *Languages* column gives the number of known living languages in the world in the given population range as reported in the *Ethnologue* (Gordon, 2005). The *In OLAC* column gives the number of languages for which resources are cataloged in OLAC, first as an absolute number and then as a percentage of the known languages in that population range. These two columns give some indication of the quality of the linguistic environment, first in terms of the languages themselves and then in terms of the response of the language resources community. For instance, 99% of the languages with more than 10 million speakers have resources that are discoverable through OLAC, but only 37% of the languages with 100 to 999 speakers do.

Table 2: OLAC coverage in relation to language size. (as of 15 Sept 2008)

Population Range	Languages	In OLAC		Resources
10,000,000 or more	83	82	99%	3,341
1,000,000 to 9,999,999	264	223	84%	1,431
100,000 to 999,999	892	575	64%	2,607
1,000 to 99,999	3,746	1,797	48%	9,012
100 to 999	1,071	392	37%	2,305
1 to 99	548	271	49%	832
Unknown population	308	86	28%	307
Total living languages	*6,912*	*3,426*	*49%*	*19,835*
Extinct languages	602	130	22%	315

The *Resources* column in Table 2 is a count of the total number of OLAC resources for all languages in the given population range. Dividing *Resources* by *Languages* gives the average number of OLAC resources per language in the population range. That number is plotted for each population range as a bar graph in Figure 2. The graph gives some indication of how the language resources community is performing with respect to a goal of "social equity." We see that the largest languages have more resources by more than an order of magnitude and that the number of resources available declines steadily as language groups get smaller.

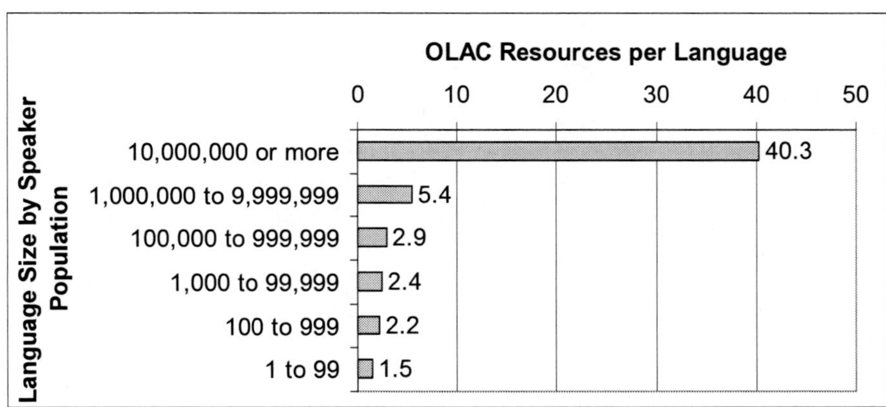

Figure 2: Average OLAC resources per language by language size.

These results are only suggestive since the coverage of OLAC is far from complete. However, they do give a glimpse of how the technical infrastructure offered by OLAC could help the language resources community to monitor the availability of documentation, description, and development resources for all the languages of the world. The simple counting of resources as employed in Table 2 is a rather crude metric since resources vary so widely in type and in their extent. The work of McConvell and Thieberger (2001, especially pp. 69–70) is instructive in pointing a way forward. They developed a 20-point index for assessing the level of documentation and description for the endangered languages of Australia. If OLAC were to adopt a standardized vocabulary for identifying the complete range of language resource types, as well as for quantifying their extent, it would be possible to use the aggregated catalog to automatically generate indices for the level of documentation, description, and development of languages as reflected in the total set of resources that are known to exist for each.

7. Conclusion

The development community has long recognized that achieving sustainable development requires coordinated efforts of many actors. This is equally true of sustainable language development. A recent World Development Report (World Bank, 2003:xiv) observes that sustainable development efforts fail when:

- The actors fail to take the long view. That is, they opt for the short-term solution which ends up creating a bigger problem in the long term.
- The actors fail to represent dispersed interests. That is, powerful actors are driven by self interest with the result that they benefit at the expense of the less powerful who are adversely affected.
- The actors fail to commit to allowing assets to thrive. That is, over consumption or hoarding of resources leads to their ultimate loss.

We must not make those same mistakes as a language resources community. Let us not fail to take the long view; rather, by embracing the six factors for sustainability of language resources, we should strive to ensure their long-term use. Let us not fail to represent dispersed interests; rather, by giving attention to disempowered minority languages that are under threat and by pursuing language development efforts that are relevant to their needs and aspirations, we can encourage their survival. And finally, let us not fail to commit to allow our assets to thrive; rather, by committing to both of the above we will help the language resources and the languages themselves to thrive through sustained use.

References

Bird, S. and G. Simons. 2003. Seven Dimensions of Portability for Language Documentation and Description. *Language,* 79, 557–582. <http://www.language-archives.org/documents/portability.pdf>

Bird, S. and G. Simons. 2004. Building an Open Language Archives Community on the DC Foundation. In D. I. Hillmann and E. L. Westbrooks, eds., *Metadata in Practice,* pp. 203–222. Chicago: American Library Association. <http://www.ldc.upenn.edu/sb/home/papers/mip.pdf>

Bruntland, G., ed. 1987. *Our Common Future: The World Commission on Environment and Development.* Oxford: Oxford University Press.

CCSDS. 2002. *Reference Model for an Open Archival Information System (OAIS).* CCSDS 650.0-B-1. Blue book, Issue 1. Consultative Committee for Space Data Systems. <http://public.ccsds.org/publications/archive/650x0b1.pdf>

Cooper, R. L. 1989. *Language Planning and Social Change.* Cambridge: Cambridge University Press.

Elkington, J. 1994. Towards the Sustainable Corporation: Win-win-win business strategies for sustainable development. *California Management Review*, 36(2), 90–100.

Gordon, R. G., Jr., ed. 2005. *Ethnologue: Languages of the World, Fifteenth Edition.* Dallas: SIL International. Online version: <http://www.ethnologue.com/>

Himmelmann, N. 1998. Documentary and Descriptive Linguistics. *Linguistics,* 36, 165–191.

Krauss, M. 1992. The World's Languages in Crisis. *Language,* 68(1), 4–10.

McConvell, P. and N. Thieberger. 2001. *State of Indigenous languages in Australia — 2001.* Australia State of the Environment Second Technical Paper Series (Natural and Cultural Heritage), Canberra: Department of the Environment and Heritage, <http://www.environment.gov.au/soe/2001/publications/technical/pubs/indigenous-languages.pdf>

Nathan, D. 2006. Proficient, Permanent, or Pertinent: Aiming for sustainability. In L. Barwick and N. Thieberger, eds., *Sustainable Data from Digital Fieldwork: From Creation to Archive and Back,* pp. 57–68. Sydney: Sydney Univ. Press. <http://ses.library.usyd.edu.au/bitstream/2123/1618/4/sddftoc.pdf>

Simons, G. 2006. Ensuring that Digital Data Last: The priority of archival form over working form and presentation form. *SIL Electronic Working Papers* 2006-003. <http://www.sil.org/silewp/abstract.asp?ref=2006-003>

Simons, G. 2007. Doing Linguistics in the 21st Century: Interoperation and the quest for the global riches of knowledge. *Proceedings of the E-MELD/DTS-L Workshop: Toward the Interoperability of Language Resources,* 13–15 July 2007, Palo Alto, CA. <http://linguistlist.org/tilr/papers/TILR%20Plenary.pdf>

Simons, G. and S. Bird. 2003. Building an Open Language Archives Community on the OAI Foundation. *Library Hi Tech,* 21(2), 210–218. <http://arxiv.org/abs/cs.CL/0302021>

Wilson, E. O. 2002. *The Future of Life.* New York: Alfred A. Knopf.

World Bank. 2003. *World Development Report 2003: Sustainable Development in a Dynamic World.* New York: World Bank and Oxford University Press.

A Rule-based Morpho-semantic Analyzer
of the Japanese Verb Phrases of Simple Sentences [*]

Yukiko Sasaki Alam

Hosei University, Department of Digital Media,
3-7-2 Kajino-cho, Koganei, Tokyo, 184-8584 Japan
sasaki@hosei.ac.jp

Abstract. This paper presents the design and algorithms of a morpho-semantic analyzer to parse the Japanese verb phrases of simple sentences. This parser aims to understand the whole semantics of verb phrases by parsing them into semantic units, and thus differs from existing morphological analyzers that primarily segment sentences into morpho-phonemes, labeled with the classifications. Unlike other statistically aided morphological parsers, the algorithms used are based on rules derived from linguistic analysis. The present system can identify the syntactic category of the head word of a verb phrase, and, if it is a verb, the conjugation group, even when not listed in the dictionaries of the system. This ability of the system enables quick access to the dictionary in the category of the head word. The design is object-oriented, modeling linguistic constructions and the components, and it is thus easy to grasp the structures and algorithms, enhancing scalability, maintainability and portability. The system can be embedded in a larger system, and be used when the larger system starts parsing verb phrases.

Keywords: Morpho-semantic analyzer, Japanese verb phrases, Morphological parser, Rule-based, Object-oriented, Parsing

1. Introduction

The purpose of the current morpho-semantic analyzer is to understand the semantic structures of Japanese verb phrases, and to contribute to the semantic understandings of sentences. At present the system understands the morpho-semantic structures of the verb phrases of simple sentences. It employs the algorithms based on linguistic analyses and several lists of carefully grouped verbs. Being able to understand verb phrases semantically, it differs from other Japanese morphological analyzers, notably *Juman* (Kurohashi and Nagao, 2003) and *Chasen* (Matsumoto et al., 2000), which focus primarily on the segmentation of sentences into morpho-phonemes such as prefixes, suffixes, inflections, Case particles and the components of compound words, and on labeling them with syntactic classifications. Another major difference from other morphological analyzers is that the current system is exclusively rule-based while most analyzers, whether morphological or syntactic, are based on statistics, such as Uchimoto et al. (2003) and Murata et al. (2005), to name a few. The third difference is that the present system is able to identify the syntactic category, such as the adjective and the verb, of the head word of a verb phrase, and, if it is a verb, the conjugation group, even when it is not listed in the dictionaries of the system.

The current system, unlike finite state models, is easy to trace the problems and extend itself according to needs, because each step in the algorithms is linguistically accountable and

---

22nd Pacific Asia Conference on Language, Information and Computation, pages 101–112

intuitively comprehensible. It parses the Japanese verb phrases of simple sentences, but not those with modal and honorific expressions and those in complex sentences. It can be embedded in a larger parsing system such as a sentence phrase analyzer (Alam, 2007).

The system is encoded in Java programming language on an object-oriented design, consisting of several packages including those named *phrases*, *words*, *suffixes*, *vp_parsers*, *verb_lists* and *utils*. In the following, I will explain the components of each suffix class and the algorithms of their main methods all called *check*, with the *Causative* class in most detail, and then discuss future work, together with concluding remarks.

2. The Package of Suffixes

The package of suffixes is composed of *Causative*, *Passive*, *Desiderative*, *Negative* and *Inflection* classes. Each class represents a verbal suffix having the same name. The suffixes appear in verb phrases in the fixed order in which the classes are listed above. Each class has a static method named *check*, and the *check* methods are called for in that order by the controller class of the system. In this section, I will explain each class, with the *Causative* class in more detail, because the ideas underlying many of the algorithmic steps in each class are similar.

2.1. The *Causative* Class and the *check* Method

Among the Japanese verbal suffixes, the causative suffix, if any contained in the verb phrase, is the first that follows the stem of a verb. Thus, the parser must check first if it immediately appears after the stem, and the checking is performed by the static method of the *Causative* class entitled *check*. This method is called for from the class that embodies the main algorithm of the parser. The *check* method takes as the argument an object of the *verb_phrase* class, the components of which are to be identified in the process of parsing. It checks if the *verb_phrase* object contains an input string that matches a causative suffix, instantiates, when a matching string is found, a causative suffix object in the *Suffix* class, and registers the suffix object as a component of the verb phrase object, before returning to the system the verb phrase object with the added information.

2.1.1.   The Causative Suffix and Regular Verbs

The most important function of the *check* method is to check if the initial portion of the unprocessed string of the verb phrase instance matches a string that forms a causative suffix. For that purpose, the class provides two sets of patterns which are in the form of *regular expressions*, one to identify a causative suffix following a consonant verb[1], and the other for a vowel verb, as illustrated below:

(1)   (a) Causative suffix pattern for a consonant verb
            static final String CAUSATIVE_CV = "[kgsmnbtwr]ase"[2];
        (b) Causative suffix pattern for a vowel verb
            static final String CAUSATIVE_VV = "[kgsmnbtwr][ei]sase";

Given the two sets of causative suffix patterns, the parser is able to find out if the head word of the verb phrase is a consonant verb or a vowel verb. As shown in (1a) and (1b), the instances in the *String* class used for matching are in the form of regular expressions.

Using the two string matching sets, the stem of the head verb of the verb phrase is determined in the following way. When one of the string sequences in the two sets matches the initial portion of the unprocessed string of the verb phrase, that means that a causative suffix is found, and that the stem of the head verb is ready to be determined. When the matched string is among the set for a consonant verb, the stem should be the one of a consonant verb, and it is

---

[1] Japanese verbs can be divided into two major groups: consonant verbs and vowel verbs, depending upon the final sounds of the stems. The stems of consonant verbs end in consonants, while those of vowel verbs end in either of the two vowels /e/ and /i/. This classification is due to Bloch, 1946.
[2] In the formalism of *regular expressions*, for instance, in (1a) any one letter in square brackets is a candidate that can precede the string "ase", which is the causative suffix for a consonant verb.

determined to be a combination of both the passed-on string that had been processed[3] and the initial consonant of the matched string in the set. For instance, when the argument verb phrase has as its attribute representing the processed string the String object "か" (pronounced as /ka/) and the matched string is "kase" (a string in the set for a causative verb in (1a)), the stem of the head verb is computed to be "かk", a combination of "か" and the initial consonant "k" of the matched string "kase", and the dictionary form of the verb is determined to be "かく" (/kaku/)[4], created by combining the stem "かk" and "u", the non-past inflection for a consonant verb.

When a match is found, on the other hand, among the set for a vowel verb, the stem of the vowel verb is computed to be a combination of both the preprocessed string and the initial one-*hiragana* or syllable equivalent portion of the matched string[5]. Specifically, the stem of the vowel verb is a combination of the preprocessed string and the first one *hiragana* character consisting of a consonant followed by "e" or "i" or the first one *hiragana* character representing one of the two vowels /e/ or /i/. For instance, the stem "たべ" (pronounced as /tabe/ and meaning eating) is a combination of the preprocessed string "た" (/ta/) and the string "べ" (/be/), which is composed of the initial consonant letter "b" and the next vowel letter "e" in the set for a vowel verb given in (1b).

2.1.2.   *Two Pitfalls in the Process of Checking for a Causative Suffix*

In the process of identification of the causative suffix following a consonant verb, there occur two types of pitfalls, if no measures are taken to prevent them. One potential pitfall is caused by vowel verbs with one-*hiragana*- (or one Japanese syllable-) long stems such as "み" (/mi/) meaning seeing and "え" (/e/) meaning getting. A sequence of the one-*hiragana* stem of a vowel verb, for instance, "mi", followed by the string "sase" (the causative suffix for a vowel verb) is falsely parsed as a sequence of the preprocessed portion "mi" followed by "s" (the stem-final consonant of a consonant verb followed by "ase" (the causative suffix for a consonant verb). In this system, the parser always starts reading one *hiragana* character by assuming that the very initial *hiragana* character or syllable of a verb phrase cannot be part of a suffix or an inflectional ending, because it should be part of the stem of the head verb or part of the word in the other category which is the head of the verb phrase. Under the same assumption, the matching pattern in (1b) begins with one of the stem-final *hiragana* characters or syllables of vowel verbs to find the causative suffix following the vowel verb, whereas the pattern in (1a) begins with one of the stem-final consonants of consonant verbs to find the causative suffix following a consonant verb. Once the stem-final *hiragana* of a vowel verb with a one-*hiragana*-long stem has been preprocessed, the sequence cannot be found in the pattern in (1b), and the following remaining causative suffix "sase" for a vowel verb is wrongly interpreted as the stem-final consonant "s", followed by "ase", the causative suffix for a consonant verb. This does not happen when the stem of a vowel verb is more than one *hiragana* as in "たべ" (/tabe/ meaning eating) and "おき" (/oki/ meaning getting up), because the stem-final *hiragana* or syllabue, for instance "べ" (/be/) and "き" (/ki/), can be the initial portion of the matching strings for the causative suffix for vowel verbs.

---

[3] The parser, before starting any suffix checking, always reads one *hiragana* character, because the verb phrase minimally must consist of the uninflected (or stem) portion and the inflected portion.
[4] This verb means writing.
[5] Phonologically, one *hiragana* character, which is composed of either a combination of a consonant followed by a vowel or a single vowel, represents a Japanese syllable.

The solution to avoiding this problem is to find out if the verb in question is a vowel verb with a one-*hiragana*-long stem by looking it up in the list of such short vowel verbs, and, if it is, to register it as a vowel verb, but otherwise to register it as a consonant verb with the stem-final consonant "s". This checking should not take time because the list of such verbs is very short, with nine registered at present. We call this problem the *one-hiragana-stem-vowel-verb pitfall*, because similar problems are caused in other suffix classes as well.

There is another trap found in the process of assigning the head word of the verb phrase as a consonant verb. Like the case discussed above, this solution also requires the use of a list of verbs, but unlike the previous one, this problem is specific to the Causative class. Given the causative suffix matching set for consonant verbs illustrated in (1a), a certain group of consonant verbs in their potential forms causes a false interpretation as the causative forms. The stems of the consonant verbs in this group all end in a consonant followed by "as", as exemplified in "ぼか s" (/bok**as**/ meaning shading off a color). Since the verbal suffix indicating potential is the vowel /e/ for consonant verbs, the potential forms of the verbs in this group generate a sequence of a consonant followed by "as+e", for instance, "kase", which is exactly the same sequence that can be found in the causative suffix matching set for consonant verbs. The parser must distinguish between the two strings of the same letter sequence, one created from C (consonant) + /as/ (stem-final string) + /e/ (potential), and the other resulting from C (stem-final consonant) + /ase/ (causative suffix for a consonant verb). To distinguish between the potential form of an "as"-ending consonant verb and the causative suffix for a consonant verb, the parser constructs the dictionary form of the verb in question[6], looks for it in the list of "as"-ending consonant verbs, and, when found, assigns the head verb as a consonant verb while registering the suffix as potential.

2.1.3.   Shorter Causative Suffix and the Treatment in the Current and Other Parsers

A word of caution is in order about preparing the list of verbs with the stems ending in "as", which has been discussed in the previous section. Not all such verbs belong in the same group. In fact, verbs ending in "as" are controversial, because they can be divided semantically into two subgroups: those with causative sense that have the corresponding (non-causative) intransitive verbs, and those without any implication of causation and without the counterparts. For instance, among verbs ending in "as", the verb "活か s" (/ikas/ with the meaning of utilizing) does not imply any causation and does not have the corresponding intransive verb, while "泣か s" (/nakas/ with the meaning of causing someone to cry)   does have the non-causative intransitive counterpart of "泣k" (/nak/ with the meaning of weeping). In the latter case, the parser should be able to identify the composition of the sequence of "nak" (meaning weeping) followed by "as" (the shorter causative suffix[7] for a consonant verb). Otherwise, the dictionary must contain both verbs independently when the two verbs are semantically related because one is derived from the other. Treating such related verbs individually would lead to the larger size of the dictionary.

With respect to verbs with the "as"-ending stems, an inconsistent treatment is observed in *Chasen*[8], a large-scale Japanese morphological analyzer that parses sentences (Matsumoto et al

---

[6] The dictionary form is generated from (a) the preprocessed string followed by (b) the string from the set followed by (c) the non-past form "u".

[7] The shorter causative suffix differs from the longer one presented in the causative suffix matching set for consonant verbs in (1a). It is kind of a lexicalized verbal suffix, and more restricted in use in that it only affixes to a consonant verb, and not as productive as the longer one, which can be affixed to both consonant and vowel verbs to create the causative forms.

[8] Having made an enormous contribution to the fields related to natural language processing, *Chasen* is used in this paper as a reference point.

2001). For instance, "書かした" (/kakasita/ with the meaning of having caused someone to write) is a combination of /kak/ meaning writing, /as/ indicating causation, and /ta/ representing the past inflection, but it is incorrectly parsed as illustrated below:

Surface form	Basic form
書か (/kaka/)	書く (/kaku/ 'write')[9]
し (/si/)	する (/suru/ 'do')
た (/ta/)	た (/ta/ auxiliary)

The meaning of causation contained by this string is not regognized in this analysis, and it would be difficult to obtain the real meaning of "書かした" (/kakasita/ with the meaning of having caused someone to write) from this analysis.

On the other hand, a similar string, "泣かした" (/nakasita/) should be analyzed as a combination of /nak/ (meaning weeping), /as/ (denoting causation), and /ta/ (the past inflection), but it is treated as a single verb, as given below:

Surface form	Basic form
泣かし (/nakasi/)	泣かす (/nakasu/)
た (/ta/)	た (/ta/ auxiliary)

These analyses suggest that *Chasen* is not equipped with treading such derived verbs, and lists them as single verbs in the dictionary, resulting in the larger size of the dictionary. The size of the dictionary would increase even more if the meanings of verbs are furnished with. The present system is able to identify a derived verb containing the shorter causative suffix by examining if the form without the suffix is found in the list of consonant verbs. When found, it is a derived verb containing the meaning of causation. This checking takes place not in the *Causative* class, but at the very end of the parsing for double checking by using the *Verb* class.

The above is a case in which the shorter causative was not parsed as such or wrongly parsed. There is another type of case involving verbs in the same group that would require careful handling, but is not properly dealt with. The potential form of an "as"-ending verb that does not have the implication of causation does not seem to be analyzed as such. "活かせた" (/ikaseta/ with the meaning of having being able to utilize) is a combination of /ikas/ meaning utilizing, /e/ indicating potential, and /ta/ representing the past inflection, but is analyzed as follows:

Surface form	Basic form
活 (/katu/)	活 (/katu/ NOUN)
かせ (/kase/)	かせる (/kaseru/)[10]
た (/ta/)	た (/ta/ auxiliary)

The part of speech of the head verb is analyzed as a noun, and thus the pronunciation is wrong with the one used for the noun, not for the verb. This suggests that the dictionary does not list the verb "活かす", thus resulting in a wrong analysis. The proposed model is able to parse most verbs correctly even when they are not listed in the dictionaries, because the decision relies on the forms of verbal suffixes. It is able to parse such verbs as "活かす" (/ikasu/ meaning utilizing) correctly even when they are not listed in the dictionaries.

---

[9] The meanings are inserted by the author because *Chasen* does not provide the meanings of verbs nor the functions of verbal suffixes. The pronunciations are transcribed there in Japanese orthography, but converted into roman letters for convenience sake in this paper.

[10] The verb "かせる" (/kaseru/) is not a modern word, and not listed in a modern Japanese dictionary.

2.1.4. The Irregular Verbs

The above treatments are for regular verbs, but Japanese has two irregular verbs, which require different treatments. Their non-past (dictionary) forms are "する" (/suru/) and "くる" (/kuru/), respectively meaning doing and coming. The causative form of "する" (/suru/) is "させる" (/saseru/)[11], and thus the string sequence of "se" that follows the preprocessed string "sa" must be identified as the causative suffix for this particular irregular verb. The minimum length required for parsing this string is four letters, because a shortest remaining string could be a combination of "se" followed by an inflection of a shortest string such as the past form "ta" and the non-past form "ru".

The stem of the other irregular verb is "来" (/ku/) when written in Chinese character or "く" (/ku/) in *hiragana*. The causative form of this verb is "来させ" (/kosase/) or "こさせ" (/kosase/). As the parser always reads the first character, "来" or "こ" in this instance, it must recognize the sequence of "させ" (/sase/) together with the preprocessed string "来" or "こ" (/ko/).

2.1.5. The Algorithm used in the check Method

Figure 1 in the Appendix illustrates the algorithm used in the *check* method in the *Causative* class. The algorithm proceeds in the descending order of maximum string length required to examine. As the checking for a sequence of a vowel verb followed by the causative suffix requires the longest string, it is performed first, and if the sequence looked for is found, the vowel verb is registered as the head word of the verb phrase instance, together with the causative suffix instance. Once the head word and the causative suffix have been registered, the other steps that follow are skipped.

2.2. The *Passive* Class and the *check* Method

A search for the passive suffix takes place in a similar way to that for the causative suffix. The parser examines if the initial letter sequence of the unprocessed string matches the string that forms the passive suffix. Similarly, two matching sets of strings are provided with: one to look for the passive suffix following a consonant verb, and the other for the passive suffix following a vowel verb, as below:

(2) (a) *static final String PASSIVE_CV = "[kgsmnbtwr]are";*
(b) *static final String PASSIVE_VV = "[kgsmnbtwr][ei]rare";*

As (2a) suggests, the identification of the passive suffix after a consonant verb is made by checking if the stem-final consonant of a consonant verb is followed by the passive suffix "are". As (2b) shows, on the other hand, the identification of the passive suffix after a vowel verb is made by examining if the stem-final syllable, for instance, "ke" or "ki" is followed by the passive suffix "rare" for a vowel verb[12].

The big difference in the looking for the causative and passive suffixes is that the passive suffix can follow either a verb or the causative suffix, whereas there is no suffix other than a

---

[11] The sound of the stem of this verb also changes according to a verbal suffix or inflection that follows. The stem "す" (/su/) of the irregular verb "する" (/suru/) in the non-past dictionary form changes to "さ" (/sa/) before the causative suffix, resulting in "させる" (/saseru/ meaning causing someone to do).

[12] In fact, the stem-final syllable of the stem of a vowel verb does not always consist of a consonant followed by a vowel, such as /ke/ and /ki/, but can consist of a single vowel such as /e/ and /i/ because a vowel can represent a Japanese syllable. However, as the length of such stem-final syllables is shorter by one letter than those consisting of a consonant and a vowel, and the algorithm of the system uses the length of the string for checking, they cannot be included in the pattern given in (2b).

verb that precedes the causative suffix. Therefore, the algorithm in the *check* method of the *Passive* class starts with a yes-no question. It begins by asking if the head word (or verb) has already been registered in the verb phrase instance, while there is no need for such a question in the search for the causative suffix. In the looking for a passive suffix, when the head verb has already been registered, then the decision about the verb group can be dispensed with, and the system skipps the verb group-finding procedure described in the previous paragraph, and only checks if the passive suffix follows the causative suffix. When the causative suffix precedes, since it conjugates like a vowel verb, the system examines if the unprocessed string passed on begins with "rare", the passive suffix for a vowel verb, and if it does, an instance of the *Passive* class is created, and registered in the verb phrase instance.

There is a similar problem in the process of checking for the passive suffix to that for the causative suffix, which has previously been termed the *one-hiragana-stem-vowel-verb pitfall*. The cause of the problem is that as the entire stem of such a vowel verb is always preprocessed, and the passive suffix "rare" that follows is falsely interpreted as a stem-final consonant ("r" in this case) followed by the passive suffix "are" for a consonant verb. As in the checking of the causative suffix, the parser must resort to the use of the same very short list of such vowel verbs to avoid the misinterpretation of a vowel verb as a consonant verb.

2.3. The *Desiderative* Class

The desiderative suffix "た" (/ta/), which means wanting, is transcribed in one *hiragana*. Unlike the causative and passive suffixes, which conjugate like a vowel verb, the desiderative suffix conjugates like an adjective. Table 1 shows that the desiderative suffix precedes the non-past inflection "i", the adverbial ending "ku" [13], the TE-form "kute", and the past inflection "katta".

Table 1: String sequences (consisting of the desiderative suffix "ta" followed by possible inflections) used to check if the desiderative suffix follows a causative or passive suffix or a vowel verb with one-*hiragana* long stem.

non-past	t	a	i				
adverbial	t	a	k	u			
TE-form	t	a	k	u	t	e	
past	t	a	k	a	t	t	a

The algorithm in the *check* method of the *Desiderative* class first asks if the head word of the verb phrase instance has already been registered, and if it has, that means the causative or passive suffix has also been found. If the desiderative suffix appears after one of the two suffixes, the unprocessed string of the verb phrase begins with the desiderative suffix "ta", followed by one of the four possible strings as listed in Table 1. Therefore, the algorithm, after finding out that the head word has been registered, examines four such possible sequences one after another until a match is found.

The above process is a simple one. The algorithm in the *check* method, however, must also deal with cases of the desiderative suffix immediately following a verb. The number of the sequences to examine is larger than when it follows another suffix that conjugates like a vowel verb, because the algorithm has to examine the varied contexts that precede the desiderative suffix. The desiderative suffix requires a particular context when it follows a consonant verb: it inserts the vowel "i" after the stem-final consonant of a consonant verb to avoid an unwelcome double consonant sequence that otherwise results from the stem-final consonant of a consonant verb followed by the initial consonant of the desiderative suffix. This insertion of "i" does not happen to a vowel verb, because the stem ends with a vowel. Possible string sequences to

---

[13] For instance, the negative suffix "na" requires the adverbial form of the desiderative, resulting in a sequence of "ta+ku+na+i" ("want-not-non-past" meaning not wanting to do something).

examine for the desiderative suffix immediately following a verb are listed in Table 2, in which the letter "C" stands for a consonant.

The larger circle in the first row of Table 2 denotes a sequence of a consonant followed by "i" or "e" followed by "tai", whereas the smaller circle, a sequence of a vowel "i" or "e" followed by "tai". The sequence in the larger circle handles (i-ii) a vowel verb with the stem ending in one *hiragana* or one syllable that consists of a C followed by "i" or "e", for instance, "たべ+た+い" (/tabe+ta+i/ meaning wanting to eat) or "おり+た+い" (/ori+ta+i/ meaning wanting to get off). The same sequence also deals with (iii) a consonant verb with the epenthetic "i" between the stem-final consonant and "ta", for instance, "かき+た+い" (/kak+i+ta+i/ meaning wanting to write). The sequence in the smaller circle handles (iv-v) a vowel verb with the stem ending in one *hiragana* transcribing a single vowel /i/ or /e/, for instance, "か+え+た+い" (/kae+ta+i/ meaning wanting to change). In fact, each row should contain two circles indicating such cases, resulting in 20 possible sequences to examine for the desiderative suffix immediately following a verb.

Table 2: String sequences consisting of the desiderative suffix "ta" followed by possible inflections which are used to check if the desiderative suffix follows a verb ("C" stands for a consonant).

non-past	C	i/e	t	a	i			
adver-bial	C	i/e	t	a	k	u		
TE-form	C	i/e	t	a	k	u	t	e
past	C	i/e	t	a	k	a	t	t	a

A problem that occurs in the process of looking for the desiderative suffix is caused by the insertion of "i" between the stem-final consonant of a consonant verb and the initial consonant of the desiderative suffix "ta", because a consonant verb stem followed by the epenthetic "i" may result in the same sequence as a vowel verb stem ending in "i". For instance, "おきたい" (/oki+ta+i/ with the vowel verb stem meaning getting up "oki" followed by the desiderative "ta" followed by the non-past "i") and "かきたい" (/kak+i+ta+i/ with the consonant verb meaning writing followed by the epenthetic "i" followed by the desiderative "ta" followed by the non-past "i") shares the same sequence of /kitai/, even though one is a vowel verb stem and the other, a consonant verb stem. After processing the initial *hiragana*, "お" (/o/) and "か" (/ka/) in these examples, the unprocessed strings are "kitai" in each example, and the only way the parser knows that one contains the epenthetic "i" is by reference to the list of vowel verbs with the stems ending in "i". Fortunately, the number of vowel verbs with the stems ending in "i" is much smaller, with 304 such verbs listed at present. To distinguish, the parser creates the dictionary form of the verb in question, and determines whether the verb is a vowel verb by referring to the list of such vowel verbs.

Lastly, there also occurs the *one-hiragana-stem-vowel-verb pitfall* in the *check* method of the *Desiderative* class. For vowel verbs with the one-*hiragana*-long stems, string sequences in Table 1 as well as the preprocessed string must be examined, and, when a match is found and the preprocessed string is one-*hiragana* long, the dictionary form must be created and validated by looking it up in the very short list of one-*hiragana* stem vowel verbs. Two irregular verbs that precede the desiderative suffix must be treated in a similar way as in the *check* method of the *Causative* class.

2.4. The *Negative* Class

The Negative suffix "na" can follow immediately a verb, the causative suffix, the passive suffix or the desiderative suffix. When it immediately follows the causative or the passive suffix, the unprocessed string of the verb phrase instance begins with "na". Since this suffx conjugates like an adjective, the string sequences to examine is similar to those for the desiderative suffix in Table 1, as indicated in the smaller circle in Table 3.

Table 3: String sequences consisting of the negative suffix "na" followed by possible inflections that are used to check if the negative suffix follows a causative or passive suffix or a vowel verb with the one-*hiragana* long stem.

non-past	k	u	n	a	i				
adverbial	k	u	n	a	k	u			
TE-form	k	u	n	a	k	u	t	e	
past	k	u	n	a	k	a	t	t	a

The difference from Table 1 for the desiderative suffix is that Table 3 has an extra set of the string "ku" preceding the negative suffix. Although omitted, the larger and smaller circles must be on each row of Table 3 as on the first row. The sequences in the larger circles are used to identify the sequence of the negative suffix immediately following an adjective or the suffix that conjugates like an adjective such as the desiderative. The negative suffix requires the adverbial inflection "ku" for an adjective or the equivalent in conjugation.

When the head verb (or word) has not been identified, the algorithm needs to find out the head word and its syntactic category, and, if it is a verb, its conjugation group. To identify these, the algorithm requires information on the contexts that precede the negative suffix. Unlike the vowel /i/ for the desiderative suffix, the vowel /a/ is inserted between the stem-final consonant of a consonant verb and the initial consonant of the negative suffix. Table 4 shows the vowels, /i/, /e/ and /a/ each of which can exist between a consonant and the initial consonant of the negative suffix. The former two vowels, /i/ and /e/, are the stem-final vowels of vowel verbs, and the last vowel /a/ is the epenthetic vowel used to avoid an unwelcome double consonant sequence resulting from the stem-final consonant of a consonant verb followed by the initial consonant of the negative suffix. Thus, the existence of "a" in that position implies a possible presence of a consonant verb, whereas the existence of "i" or "e" in that context, a plausible presence of a vowel verb, and the algorithm uses this information to determine the conjugation group of the verb in question.

Table 4: String sequences consisting of the negative suffix followed by possible inflections used when it follows a verb ("C" indicates a consonant).

non-past	C	a/e/i	n	a	i				
adverbial	C	a/e/i	n	a	k	u			
TE-form	C	a/e/i	n	a	k	u	t	e	
past	C	a/e/i	n	a	k	a	t	t	a

Like Table 2 for the desiderative suffix, the two circles on the first row on Table 4 indicate two sequences of strings, the longer of which deals with (i-ii) such vowel verb examples as "た べ+な+い" (/tabe+na+i/ meaning not eating) or "おり+な+い" (/ori+na+i/ meaning not geting off). The longer circle also includes the treatment of (iii) the negative form of a consonat verb with the epenthetic vowel /a/ such as "かか+な+い" (/kak+a+na+i/ meaning not writing). The shorter circle is to handle (iv-v) such an instance as "かえ+な+い" (/kae+na+i/ meaning not changing), involving a vowel verb the stem of which ends in a vowel /i/ or /e/ transcribed in one *hiragana*. Each row having two such circles and five strings to examine, thus altogether 20 strings are provided with for checking.

As in the case of the desiderative suffix, vowel verbs with the stems of one *hiragana* followed by the negative suffix are identified by referring to sequences listed in Table 3 as well as the very short list of one-*hiragana* stem vowel verbs.

2.5. The *Inflection* Class

The *check* method in the *Inflection* class also begins by asking whether the head word has been found or not. When it has been found and registered, that means a suffix that may appear before the inflection has also been recorded in the verb phrase instance. The verbal suffixes either conjugate like a vowel verb as the causative and passive suffixes do or like an adjective as the desiderative and negative suffixes do[14]. Table 5 shows the string sequences used to identify the inflections for verbal suffixes that conjugate like vowel verbs or adjectives.

Table 5: String sequences representing the inflections to examine when the head word has been found and the inflection immediately follows a verbal suffix ("ADJ" stands for an adjective or a suffix that conjugates like an adjective, and "VV", a vowel verb or a suffix that conjugates like a vowel verb).

non-past (after a VV stem)	r	u			
non-past (after an ADJ stem)	i				
past (after a VV stem)	t	a			
past (after a ADJ stem)	k	a	t	t	a
adverbial (after an ADJ stem)	k	u			
TE-form (after a VV stem or an ADJ adverbial form)	t	e			
TE-form (after an ADJ stem)	k	u	t	e	

When the head verb (or word) has not been identified yet in the process of checking for suffixes, it should be recognized by resorting to the strings listed in Table 6. A row containing "C" actually has two string sequences each, one beginning with a consonant indicated by "C" in the larger circle, and the other without it in the smaller circle.

Table 6: String sequences containing inflections used to identify a head verb and the conjugation group ("VV" indicates a vowel verb, and "CV", a consonant verb).

non-past (for a VV)	C	i/e	r	u
non-past (for a CV)	C	u[15]		
non-past (for a CV with the stem-final "w" appearing in the negative form)	C	a/u/o	u	
past (for a VV)	C	i/e	t	a
past (for a CV)	i/t	t	a	
past (for a CV)	i/n	d	a	
past (for a CV)	s	i	t	a
TE-form (for a VV)	C	i/e	t	e
TE-form (for a CV)	i/t	t	e	
TE-form (for a CV)	i/n	d	e	
TE-form (for a CV)	s	i	t	e

The Japanese consonant verbs undergo sound changes in the past forms as well as the TE-forms, and the parser must recover the stem-final consonants from the altered consonants found in the

---

[14] There are other suffixes that appear before inflections, and conjugate like consonant verbs. Among them are honorific suffixes such as /nasar/ and the suffix meaning appearing to want, /tagar/. The current system does not handle them. In addition, some words or modal suffixes are syntactically nouns, requiring inflections that follow nouns. When the current system is extended to handle more than simple sentences, Table 5 should include inflections for nouns as well as a certain group of consonant verbs.

[15] The second row also should have two string sequences, "C+u" and "u" alone. The string "u" is applied only after the unprocessed string has been exhaustively examined in vain. The string is used to identify such verbs as "いう" (/iu/ meaning saying) and "あう" (/au/ meaning meeting) when the unprocessed string consists of "う" (/u/) after the one-*hiragana*-long stem has been processed.

past forms or the TE-forms. Once the stems are identified, it is easy to form the dictionary (or non-past) forms, because they are combinations of the stems and the non-past form "u".

The current system has a class entitled *Verb*, which has a static method that computes the dictionary form of a consonant verb in reference to the past form or TE-form. It generates possible dictionary forms, looks them up in the lists of consonant verbs that are grouped accoding to conjugation types, and when found, it determines the dictionary forms. For that purpose, consonant verbs are divided into four groups, based on different sound changes occurring in the past and TE-forms.

3. Future Work and Conclusion

The current parser handles verb phrases of simple sentences, and still remains to be extended to handle complex verb phrases containing modal, honorific and polite expressions as well as verb phrases ending in the conjunctive and conditional forms. The system is designed to be object-oriented, simulating linguistic components, and the algorithms are easy to understand intuitively, because each step is linguistically accountable. Thus it offers high scalability, maintainability and portability. The current parser is powerful in that it is able to identify the syntactic category of the head word of the verb phrase, and, if it is a verb, the conjugation group via algorithmic inference even when it is an unknown word. The current system uniquely differs from other morphological analyzers in that its aim is to segment verb phrases into semantic units to understand the semantics of the verb phrases rather than to segment sentences into morpho-phonemes and label them with syntactic classification. The present system can easily be embedded in a larger parsing system. Much work remains to be done, but the objective of the proposed system and the methodology employed seem to be promising.

References

Alam, Sasaki Yukiko. 2007. Analyzer to Identify Phrases and the Functional Roles in Sentences: Its Architectural Aspects. *Proceedings of PACLIC 21*, pp. 67-75.

Bloch, Bernard. 1946. Studies in Colloquial Japanese–Inflection. In Roy Andrew Miller, ed., *Bernard Bloch on Japanese*, pp. 1-24. New Haven: Yale University Press.

Covington, Michael A. 1990. *A Dependency Parser for Variable Word-Order Languages. Research Report AI-1990-01*. Artificial Intelligence Programs University of Georgia.

Fuchi, Takeshi and Shinichiro Takagi. 1998. Japanese Morphological Analyzer using Word Co-occurrence. *Proceedings of the COLING*, pp. 409-413.

Kameda, Masayuki. 1996. A Portable & Quick Japanese Parser: QJP. *Proceedings of the COLING*, pp. 616-621.

Kashioka, Hideki, Yasuhiro Kawata and Yumiko Kinjo. 1998. Use of Mutual Information Based Character Clusters in Dictionary-less Morphological Analysis of Japanese. *Proceedings of the COLING*, pp. 658-662.

Kazama, Jun'ichi. 2001. *Adaptive Morphological Analysis with a Small Tagged Corpus*. Master Thesis: University of Tokyo.

Kurohashi, Sadao and Makoto Nagao. 2003. Building a Japanese Parsed corpus– while improving the parsing system. In Anne Abeille, ed., *Treebank Building Using Parsed Corpora*, pp. 249-260. Dordrecht: Kluwer Academic Publishers.

Matsumoto, Yuji, Akira Kitauchi, TatsuoYamashita, Yoshitaka Hirano, Hiroshi Matsuda, Kazuma Takaoka and Masayuki Asahara. 2001. *Morphological Analysis System ChaSen version 2.2.4 Manual*. Nara, Japan: Nara Institute of Science and Technology.

Murata, Masaki, Masao Utiyama, Hiroshi Isahara and Qing Ma. 2005. Correction of Errors in a Verb Modality Corpus for Machine Translation with a Machine-Learning Method. *ACM Transactions on Asian Language Information Processing*, 4 (1), 18-37.

Uchimoto, Kiyotaka, Chikashi Nobata, Atsushi Yamada, Satoshi Sekine and Hitoshi Isahara. 2003. Morphological Analysis of a Large Spontaneous Speech Corpus in Japanese.

Proceedings of the 41st Annual Meeting of the Association for Computational Linguistics,
pp. 479-488.

Appendix

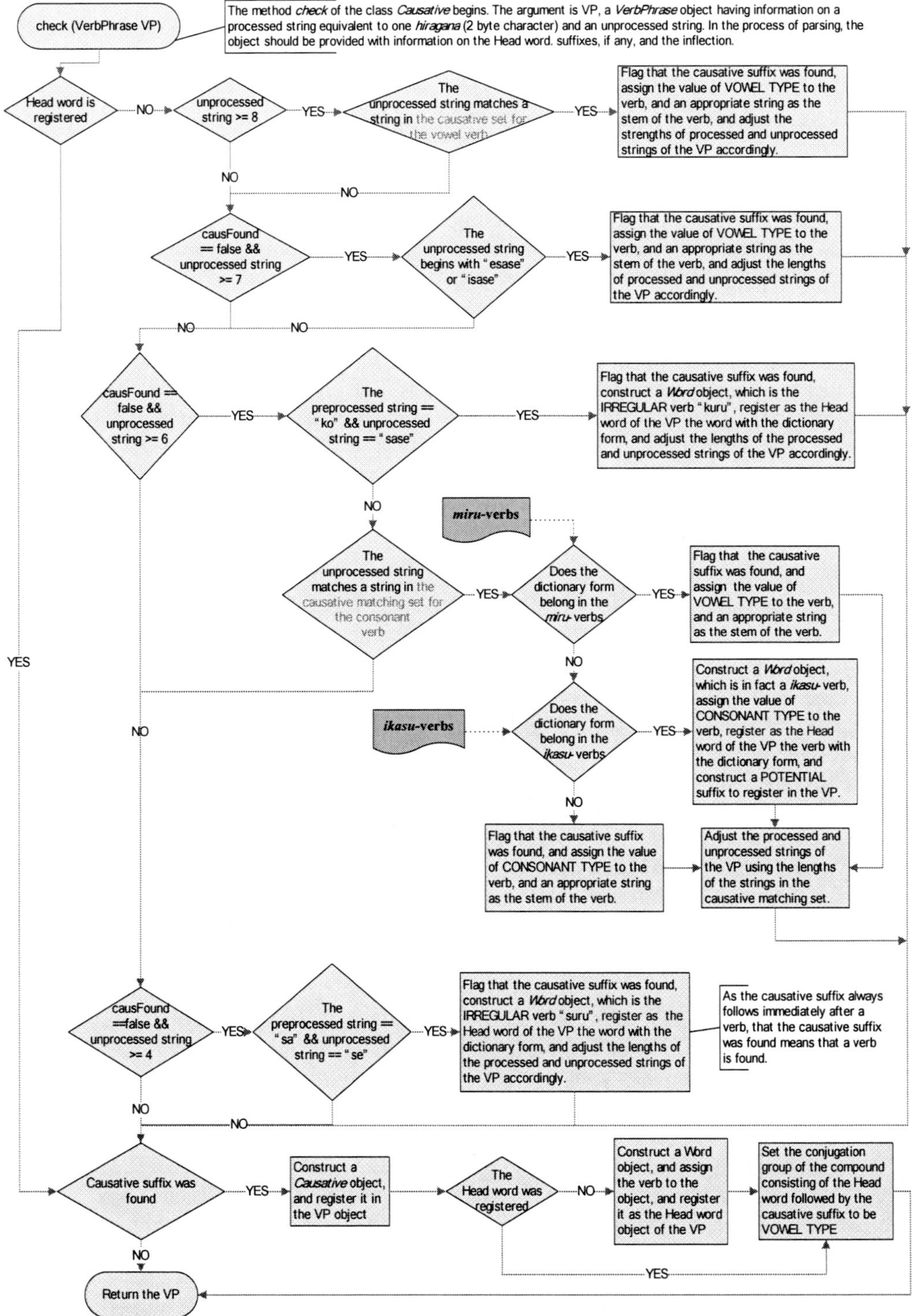

Figure 1: Algorithm used in the *check* method of the *Causative* class

112

Constituent Structure for Filipino: Induction through Probabilistic Approaches[*]

Danniel Alcantara and Allan Borra

College of Computer Studies, De La Salle University, 2401 Taft Avenue,
1004 Manila, Philippines
{alcantarad, borraa}@ dlsu.edu.ph

Abstract. The current state of Philippine linguistic resources, which includes formal grammars, electronic dictionaries and corpora are not yet significant to address industrial-strength language technologies. This paper discusses a computational approach in automatically estimating constituent structures from a corpus using unsupervised probabilistic approaches. Two models are presented and results show an F1 measure of greater than 69%. Issues and phenomena of the Filipino language are identified and discussed

Keywords: Computational Linguistics, Probabilistic Approach, Constituent Structure, Context Free Grammar, Grammar Induction

1. Introduction

This paper discusses the algorithms used for the automatic induction of grammar for the Filipino language.

The rationale for the study stems on the minimal work done on the development of a computational grammar for the Filipino language for the development of robust and industrial-strength natural language analysis and technologies. Existing Filipino grammars can only handle a subset of declarative type sentences. Considering the difficulty to manually construct a robust grammar capable of parsing a broad scope of sentences, automatic grammar induction is a consideration that can be used for learning language structure.

Automated grammar induction systems deals with the generation of a *grammar* based from input corpora. Existing work for grammar induction fall under two categories based on their input constraints: Supervised and Unsupervised. *Slightly supervised* systems generate grammar rules from bracketed corpora or tree banks. *Bracketed corpora* are text documents that have been bracketed by a linguist to represent the skeletal syntactic structure of the sentences. *Treebanks* are large corpora that have been annotated with the part of speech tags, syntactic structure, and other functional attributes necessary. *Unsupervised* systems make use of non-bracketed corpora while applying searching and clustering algorithms to attempt to learn the language rules.

Works on slightly supervised grammar induction, such as the works of Lari and Young(1991), Brill(1993), Sekine and Grishman(1995), and Charniak(1996), present different output formalisms to represent the grammar. However, Filipino is currently a resource-limited language and does not have the computational resources necessary for the algorithms presented. There are existing corpora available for the language, but these have not yet been bracketed.

---

[*] The authors wish to thank Dr. Shirley Dita for providing the initial gold standard.

22nd Pacific Asia Conference on Language, Information and Computation, pages 113–122

Osborne and Briscoe(1997), Clark(2001), Klein and Manning,(2001) attempt to learn the grammar formalism for the language through the use of statistical analysis methods applied to a tagged corpus. Klein and Manning(2002) applies a context-constituency model and achieved promising results, precision rate of 55% and recall rate of 48%. Existing systems are designed for the English language and have had modifications applied that are specific to the right-biased nature and Subject-Verb-Object structure. The Filipino language does not follow these structures; rather it has free word order patterns, and Predicate-Topic phenomena, wherein the focus of a sentence is referred to as Topic rather than as a Subject.

Klein(2005) experimented with a combination of the said context-constituency model and a dependency model Klein and Manning(2004), which was then applied to English, German, and Chinese. The English language reached recall of 88% and precision of 69%. The German language had a corresponding recall value of 90%, but a considerably lower precision of 50%, caused by relatively flat gold standard corpora. The flat structure of the German language is attributed to free word order, a phenomena also identified in Filipino.

The aim is to develop an automated grammar induction system using an unsupervised approach. The approach chosen is influenced by the limitation of computational grammar resources in Filipino. Existing induction algorithms, usually for the English language, are modified to handle Filipino language phenomena.

2. Unsupervised Grammar Induction Approaches

Unsupervised grammar induction systems apply statistical or probabilistic analysis to estimate the necessary grammar formalism. Most unsupervised approaches apply language specific heuristics to improve computational reliability.

2.1.Current Solutions in Other Languages

Clark(2001) developed an unsupervised approach for extracting the phrase-structure from an input English corpus. Contiguous tag subsequences are identified from an input tagged corpus, and are considered as constituent candidates. Tag sequences that occur at least 5000 times are clustered together based on their context, the part of speech tag immediately preceding and following.

The clustering process identified sequences with clear syntactic correspondence. Accordingly, the procedure identified clusters with poor syntactic quality. Mutual Information criterion is applied to justify the valid clusters and filter out spurious candidates. Mutual Information indicates the importance of a relationship between the prior and subsequent part of speech tags. This intuitively implies that a correct constituent structure is highly sensitive on the context of usage and can appear in different contexts.

The presented algorithm introduces the possibility to induce grammatical structure from an unsupervised approach. The initial results are filtered through Mutual Information heuristics to remove spurious candidates. The implementation of the algorithm minimizes the requirement on input corpora, but is computationally expensive and requires sufficient memory to handle clustering.

Klein and Manning(2001) describes two systems for learning linguistic constituency in natural language grammars. Radford's study, as cited in Klein and Manning(2001) discussed two linguistic criteria for constituency identified that serves as the primary basis for the work: 1. External distribution: A constituent is a sequence of words which appears in various structural positions with larger constituents; and 2. Substitutability: A constituent is a sequence of words with (simple) variants which can be substituted for that sequence.

Klein and Manning take a tagged corpus and apply statistical analysis to identify most commonly occurring contiguous tag sequences. The tag sequences that reach the target criteria, based on a combination of entropy and divergence, are identified as constituent structures.

Another work by Klein and Manning(2002) develops a "Constituent Context Model" describing contiguous subsequences within a sentence. Each sentence is described by a list of all possible subsequences, identified by their span, enclosed terminals, and context, terminals before and after.

Bracketing of the sentence is identified through probabilistic analysis of a class conditional independence model based on the input corpora. Subsequences are estimated as constituent structures or non-constituents, referred to as distituents.

Initial bracketing is approximated based on a random split mechanism that promotes generation of unbalanced binary trees. The conditional completion likelihood of the current state is computed based on the specified Expectation parameters. Bracketing is adjusted and Maximized to further improve the generated constituents.

This model focuses on identifying hidden bracketing structures, based on observable sentence and tag structures. A precision rate of 55% and recall rate of 48% was achieved through experimentation of the identified model, the best published unsupervised results at the time. The implementation of the EM algorithm maximizes the combinational likelihood of generating a correct bracket span.

Although currently beyond the scope of the study of grammar induction for Filipino, it is noteworthy to discuss the work by Klein and Manning(2004) which made use of dependency structure and extraction to model the language. Unlike standard approaches, where the tree or phrase structure is being identified, the work identifies dependencies between words. Each word is directly dependent on another word, and a single word dependent on the ROOT component of the sentence.

2.2. Probabilistic Induction for Filipino: Architectural Design

Figure 1 provides the overall architectural design for the system. The first module is the training module. In the process of training, the training corpora are tokenized into sentences. Quotations found within sentences, words enclosed within double quotes, are separated from their host sentence and are tokenized further. Tokenized sentences are then tagged through the use of an external part of speech tagger. The tagged sentences are passed through statistical analysis, in order to retrieve the necessary data used for probabilistic computations in rule generation.

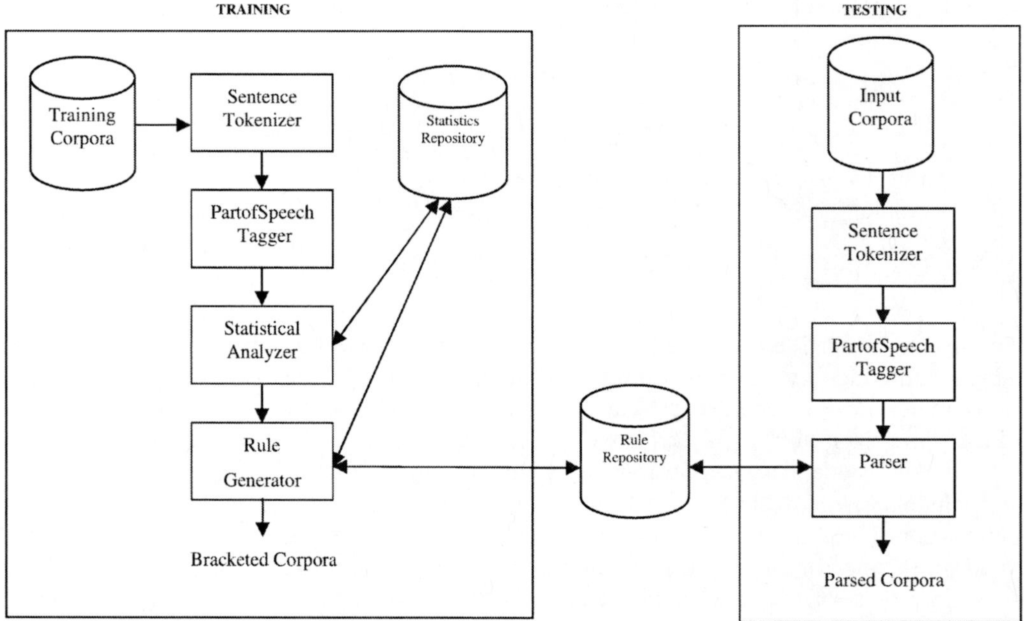

Figure 1: Overall Architectural Design of the Probabilistic Constituent Structure Induction System for Filipino

The statistical analyzer identifies all part of speech tag sequences that occurred in the training corpus. The symbol α will denote a specific part of speech tag sequence. The occurrence count of each α is scored and this value is one of the primary measurements used in rule generation.

All occurrences of α is identified within a context of two adjacent tags or sentence boundaries: x α y. x denotes the symbol directly before α, and y directly after. These two contexts may be merged together to form a local linear context, x-y. The distribution of contexts in relation to α will be denoted by $\sigma(\alpha, x)$, $\sigma(\alpha, y)$, and $\sigma(\alpha, x$-$y)$ for pre, post, and linear respectively.

According to Klein and Manning(2001), a study by Radford states that "a constituent is a sequence of words which appears in various structural positions within larger constituents". The phrase "various structural positions" suggests that the constituency of α can be identified by the entropy of its linear context, $H(\sigma(\alpha, x$-$y))$.

However, entropy alone is not enough to recognize a constituent. This is due to uncommon but possible linear contexts having little bearing on the entropy. A scaled entropy, (listing 1) takes into consideration the uniform distribution of contexts in relation to α, $\sigma u(\alpha, x$-$y)$, and the uniform distribution of all possible contexts u.

$$Hs(\sigma(\alpha, x\text{-}y)) = H(\sigma(\alpha, x\text{-}y)) \, [H(\sigma u(\alpha, x\text{-}y)) \, / \, H(u) \,] \; (1)$$

Clark(2001) discussed that if one were to consider the tag previous of a true constituent, one should be able to presume the tag directly after. However for non-constituents, possibly referred to as distituents, the two contexts form independent distributions. Therefore, one measure of constituency is identified by the Mutual Information between the pre and post contexts, $MI(\sigma(\alpha, x), \sigma(\alpha, y))$.

Towards the end of the training phase, the resulting probabilities are applied to the input sentences and an estimated parse is proposed. Two models are implemented for bracket estimation and rule generation. The first is a Greedy Selection approach that brackets the highest ranked sequence per iteration based on the measurement identified.

Algorithm Skeleton for the Greedy Selection Model.

```
Rules GreedySelection (Corpus corpus)
   apply statistical analysis of corpus
   while (at least one sequence meets filter criteria)
     maxSeq = filtered sequence with maximum measurement
     generate production rule based on maxSeq
     for (all sentences in Corpus)
       parse sentence with generated production rule
     apply statistical analysis based on new parse
   return Rules
end.
```

The selection and filtering criterion is based on available measurements of the sequence. The simplest filtering criterion is requiring the sequence size to be at least two. Different types of measurements can be applied for selection and filtering, such as requiring Mutual Information of 0.2 while obtaining the maxSeq based on occurrence.

The second model designed for training is a modification of the "Constituent Context Model" of Klein and Manning(2002). Sequences σ and linear contexts x-y are assigned probabilities of being a constituent or a distituent. Initial probabilities are derived from enumerating all possible valid bracketings of all sentences of the input corpora. Valid bracketing requires the bracket result in a binary tree. To minimize execution time, a three-dimensional dynamic matrix was implemented for said completions.

Overview of the Constituent Context Model Induction.

```
Rules CCMInduction (Corpus corpus)
   apply statistical analysis of corpus
   Collection inside = sequence probabilities
   Collection outside = context probabilities
   do
     for (all sentences in Corpus)
       bracketSentence =
         InsideOutside(sentence, inside, outside, 0, sentence.size-1)
     apply statistical analysis base on new parse
     inside = bracketed sequence probabilities
     outside = bracketed context probabilities
   while inside changes and outside changes
   combine inside and outside to generate Rules
   return Rules
end
```

The Inside Outside algorithm is utilized to dynamically estimate the optimum binary bracketing
of each sentence. Sequence probabilities σ represent the inside computations and linear
contexts x-y represent the outside. The process applies a divide and conquer approach to
identifying the bracketing that will maximize the resulting probability. The estimated
probabilities can also be weighted based on the previously identified measurements.

Skeleton of the Inside Outside Algorithm

```
[bracketSentence,prob] InsideOutside
    (Sentence sentence, Collection inside, Collection outside,
      int nStart, //starting index token or tag
      int nEnd)   //end index token or tag
  String yield = sentence[nStart..nEnd]
  String context = sentence[nStart-1] + sentence[nEnd+1]
  double probC = inside[yield] * outside[context]
  double probD = (1-inside[yield]) * (1-outside[context]
  double prob = weight(yield) * probC / (probC + probD)
  if(nStart != nEnd)
    for( k = nStart ; k < nEnd ; k++)
      left = InsideOutside(sentence,inside,outside,nStart,k)
      right = InsideOutside(sentence,inside,outside,k+1,end)
      maxProb = max( left.prob * right.prob )
    prob *= maxProb
    bSentence = merge left.bracket with right.bracket based on max
  return [bSentence, prob]
end
```

After initial bracketing of all sentences, probabilities are recomputed and the process iterates in
the form of an Expectation-Maximization algorithm. This will induce structure to the corpora
and create a globally higher score as compared to the previous model.

The second module parses the input sentences utilizing the rules estimated during training.
Prior to the actual parsing process, the input corpora is processed by the sentence tokenizer and
part of speech tagger, equivalent to the learning phase.

The architecture makes use of three data sources, the Training Corpora, the Statistics
Repository, and the Rule Repository. The Training Corpora is a non-bracketed data source that
contains sentences for Grammar generation. It is possible that the training corpora be pre-
tagged for correctness, but that is the only amount of preprocessing necessary for the
unsupervised approach. The Statistics Repository will contain data relating to the training
corpora, this includes the occurrence of tag sequences, the contexts of these sequences, and the
corresponding occurrence. The Rule Repository will be the storage facility for grammar rules in
the learning phase and the source of these rules for the testing phase.

3. Linguistic Data

The system presented takes as input a collection of sentences. The part of speech tags for each word are then identified and the algorithms only take into consideration the tags rather than their surface form. Sentences were manually verified, to minimize tagging error; however this is the only amount of preprocessing for both learning and parsing phases. A bracketed version of the corpus is available, and this is used for evaluation purposes only.

The part of speech tagset used contains 66 word classes, each falling into one of 9 supersets (noun, pronoun, determiner, conjunction, verb, adjective, adverb, cardinal, punctuation), and one added word class used to signify a quotation. The tagset is based on the updated tag set of TPOST. Punctuation marks are not removed from the input corpora, however statistical data is not gathered for sequences that contain punctuation marks. The punctuations are part of the final grammar rules, but they do not directly contribute to the estimation of constituents.

The corpus used for training was the Filipino translation of The Little Prince by Antoine de Saint – Exupéry. The selected corpus contains 1,685 sentences composed of approximately 15,000 words, and can be categorized under the domain of literature. The dataset contains a range of sentences, mostly simple and declarative sentences.

Due to the fictional narrative nature of the input corpora, a high percentage of the sentences serve a declarative purpose. There are blocks of dialogue found inside the story; this introduces the other types of sentence structures. "The Little Prince" is generally a children's book, the reason for the majority of simple sentences, but compound and complex sentences are also identified in the narration.

The experiments presented are done using sentence lengths of 1-10. Majority of the simple sentence structures can be found within this range. Compound and complex sentences are variations of the simple sentence construct and experimentation focused on simple sentences only is imperative.

4. Preliminary Results and Analysis

This section discusses the results and analysis from statistical data as well as evaluating proposed bracketings produced by the system against a linguistically verified gold standard.

4.1. Analysis of Statistical Data

Preliminary analysis is focused on the statistical analyzer, and identifies the appropriateness of the identified measurements. **Table 1** lists the top ten most frequently found constituents in the Gold corpus.

Table 1. Selected constituent sequences found in the gold corpus with corresponding statistics.

Sequence	Gold Probability	Gold Count	Occurrence	Raw Entropy	Scaled Entropy	Mutual Information
CCB NNC	87.16%	129	148	4.495	2.376	0.760
JJD NNC	94.16%	129	137	3.956	1.976	0.691
DTCP NNC	83.00%	83	100	4.670	2.381	0.839
CCB JJD NNC	100.00%	71	71	2.944	1.168	0.375
DTC NNC	52.46%	64	122	5.787	3.440	1.435
CCT PRSP	76.25%	61	80	4.908	2.534	1.132
NNC PRS	71.21%	47	66	4.875	2.452	1.696
PRSP NNC	86.79%	46	53	3.466	1.375	0.548
CCT NNC	67.74%	42	62	4.930	2.514	1.498
VBW CCB JJDNNC	93.18%	41	44	0.994	0.150	0.000
RBI PRS	3.57%	2	56	5.222	2.680	2.292
CCB JJD	2.63%	2	76	2.158	0.782	0.307
RBF PRS	1.43%	1	70	4.759	2.341	0.739

`DTC NNC` has a lower gold probability due to modifiers attached to the noun such as in the example `[ang [kopya [ng drowing] ] ]`. `Ang kopya` with no consideration of context can be considered as a constituent, however in this scenario the constituency should be primarily placed on `kopya ng drowing`, before the `ang` is included in the bracketing.

The occurrence count heuristic is the measurement that most closely resembles the gold count. However, as is the case with `CCB JJD` and `CCB JJD NNC`, sequences found inside constituents will have as high or possibly higher occurrence counts, but not be actual constituents.

The scaled entropy adjustment to the raw entropy measurement improves the criteria slightly. Both entropies appear to address the issue of occurrence concerning `CCB JJD` and `CCB JJD NNC`. However, both entropy measures rank noun phrases considerably lower, while considering conjunctive and prepositional phrases considerably high as is the case for `RBI PRS` and `RBF PRS` which ranked in the top ten of both entropies.

The mutual information measurement fares poorly in the listing, none of the high constituency sequences are correctly identified. This heuristic was originally proposed as a filter rather than a selection criterion.

Identifying a solid measurement to duplicate the actual rankings can potentially increase the quality of bracketing, especially when using the Greedy Selection Model.

4.2. Evaluation of Proposed Bracketing

Further discussion focuses on evaluating the output of the system. The system produces two output, the proposed bracketing and estimated rules. The estimated rules are the more representative output and may be compared to an existing formalism of the language. However when dealing with natural languages, especially resource limited languages, the grammar formalism is debatable and is not available for evaluation purposes. Furthermore, there are no predefined metrics useable for comparing two grammars, one can only state if the two grammars are the same or not.

The alternative output of grammar induction systems are the predicted structures the grammar rules produce. This is implemented through bracketing of input text and evaluated through comparison with a linguistically motivated gold-bracketed corpus. The gold standard represents the linguist's grammar, and equivalence to the gold-standard is equivalent to meeting the linguist's standard.

Precision, recall, and their harmonic mean, F1 measure are quantifiable statistical measures for identifying similarity, and in this case correctness, between the proposed and gold brackets.

Precision: the percentage of non-terminal bracketings in the predicted parse that also appeared in the tree bank parse

Recall: the percentage of non-empty non-terminal bracketings from the tree bank that also appeared in the predicted parse

F1 Measure: the combination of Precision and Recall

$$F1 = 2 * Precision * Recall / (Precision + Recall) \qquad (2)$$

Estimating entirely left-branching and right-branching bracketing of a structure is used to serve as a baseline for the resulting scores. The English language has been proven by both Brill(1993) and Klein(2005) to realize good results using a right-branching structure. This is illustrated with the example sentence "`[I [am [responsible [for [my [rose]]]]]]`". This can be translated into "`[Pananagutan ko [ang [rosas ko]]]`", which also implies a right biased heuristic for the Filipino language.

Each of the statistical measurements were used as the selection mechanism for the Greedy Selection Model and scored accordingly. As seen in Table 2, the occurrence measurement proves the better heuristic of the three, entropy was excluded in favor of scaled entropy. However, the difference between occurrence and scaled entropy is negligible. Mutual

Information produced significantly lower results, which can be stemmed back to the discrepancy identified in table 1.

Table 2. Precision, Recall and F1 Measures for various settings of Greedy Selection Model

	Precision	Recall	F1 Measure
Left branching	26.32%	37.69%	30.99%
Right branching	55.78%	62.17%	58.80%
Occurrence	70.91%	66.95%	68.87%
Raw Entropy	68.61%	62.05%	65.17%
Scaled Entropy	70.91%	66.40%	68.58%
Mutual Information	65.89%	55.32%	60.14%

The Greedy Selection Model emphasizes precision, a higher percentile of proposed constituents, but it identifies less bracketings thus a lower recall value. The precision of the Selection Model can be attributed to the accuracy of the selection metric in identifying the most likely constituent from the corpus.

The Greedy Selection Model identifies the locally optimum sequence to be bracketed per iteration. Once a sequence has been bracketed, this bracketing can not be undone, and results in the issues identified earlier with CCB JJD and CCB JJD NNC. To address this issue, the Constituent Context Model was designed that implements the Inside Outside algorithm.

Table 3. Precision, Recall and F1 Measures for various settings of Constituent Context Model

	Precision	Recall	F1 Measure
Left branching	26.32%	37.69%	30.99%
Right branching	55.78%	62.17%	58.80%
None	55.52%	60.38%	57.86%
Occurrence Weight	63.64%	69.20%	66.31%
Scaled Entropy Weight	66.73%	72.56%	69.52%
Mutual Information Weight	66.75%	72.58%	69.54%

Table 3 presents the results of the Constituent Context Model, with the inclusion of weighting system to increase bias towards sequences that are higher in the identified measurement.

The Constituent Context Model always results in a binary bracketing, increasing the amount of proposed constituents. This increases recall significantly, and the decrease in precision is not as significant, thus achieving the highest F1 measure, when weighted.

Without any additional heuristics, the output score of the Constituent Context Model is low. This is because, the model is highly reliant on a descriptive initial seed, and the probability generated from all possible binary trees is not sufficient to model the language. This produces lower results due to the lack of information concerning the actual sequences.

Occurrence count is an improvement to the basic model, but the commonly occurring sequences are given too high priority, and the high precision that was found in the Greedy Selection Model, is negated by the recall-oriented nature of the Constituent Context Model. Scaled entropy and mutual information produce the best overall results, because of the consideration for contextual information of each sequence.

The low precision is attributed to the fact that Filipino is relatively flatter than English. Consider the example sentence "[Pananagutan ko [ang [rosas ko]]]", translated to "[I [am [responsible [for [my [rose]]]]]]". The English translation produces a binary tree, while Filipino commonly produces a ternary tree, and it is even possible for a tree with 4 children to a single node.

The common problem identified with both models is handling nouns with describing phrases. Among the most frequently under proposed sequences is NNC CCB NNC. The CCB NNC serving as a phrase describing the primary NNC. In the example, ng tren describes the riles, and ng riles describes the tagapaglihis. Neither dependency is sufficiently identified by the models, rather CCB NNC is given priority on all occasions.

```
Gold:       QOT [sabi [ng [tagapaglihis [ng [riles [ng tren]]]]]]
Selection:  QOT [[[sabi [ng tagapaglihis]] [ng riles ]] [ng tren]]
CCM:        QOT [[[sabi [ng tagapaglihis]] [ng riles ]] [ng tren]]
English:    QOT [ said [ the [ railway signalman ] ] ]
```

5. Conclusion

Two models for the unsupervised constituent structure induction were presented. One of which is a Greedy Selection Model focused on maximizing the specified measurement on a local level. The other is a simplified Constituent Context Model modified to make use of identified heuristics in order to produce results taking into consideration the entire sentence structure. Both models are capable of estimating constituent structure rules from unbracketed corpora and producing promising scores.

The Greedy Selection Model was shown to achieve a precision rate of 70.9% and an overall performance of 68.9%. Analysis of the model shows that the occurrence of a sequence is currently the most effective measurement for identify constituency.

The Constituent Context Model estimates a globally optimized bracketing based on constituency probabilities placed on the sequences and contexts found. This model achieved a recall value of 72.6% and an overall performance of 69.5%, when applying either scaled entropy or mutual information as a weighting heuristic.

Experimentation identified that the Filipino language does not follow as strict a binary structure as English, but they are similar in the right-biased nature of the languages.

Future work include consideration of the dependency between words, incorporating the use of the right branching tree as a base case, improving on the statistical measurements identified, and implementing a slightly supervised approach to grammar induction.

References

Brill, E. 1993. Automatic grammar induction and parsing free text: A transformation based approach [online]. Proceedings of the 31st annual meeting on Association for Computational Linguistics: 1993, 259-265. Available: http://acl.ldc.upenn.edu/P/P93/P93-1035.pdf (April 1, 2008).

Charniak, E. 1996. Tree-bank grammars [online]. Proceedings of the Thirteenth National Conference on Artificial Intelligence: 1996, 1031-1036. Available: http://citeseer.comp.nus.edu.sg/cache/papers/cs/138/ftp:zSzzSzftp.cs.brown.eduzSzpubzS ztechreportszSz96zSzcs96-02.ps.gz/charniak96treebank.ps.gz (April 1, 2008).

Chomsky, N. 1965. Aspects of the theory of syntax. MIT Press, Cambridge, MA.

Clark, A. 2001. Unsupervised induction of stochastic context-free grammars using distributional clustering [online]. Proceedings of the 2001 workshop on Computational Natural Language Learning: 2001, 1-8. Available: http://wing.comp.nus.edu.sg/acl/W/W01/W01-0713.pdf (April 1, 2008).

Hopcroft, J., Motwani, R., & Ullman, J. 2001. Introduction to automata theory, languages, and computation. Addison-Wesley.

Lari, K. & Young, S. J. 1991. Applications of stochastic context-free grammars using the Inside-Outside algorithm [online]. Computer Speech and Language: 1991, 237-257. Available: http://64.233.179.104/scholar?hl=en&lr=&safe=off&q=cache:rVtjtefvq8J:staff.science.uva.nl/~jzuidema/temp/lariYoung90csl-insideOutside.pdf (April 1, 2008).

Klein, D. 2005. The unsupervised learning of natural language structure [online]. PhD thesis, Stanford University. Available: http://www.cs.berkeley.edu/~klein/papers/klein_thesis.pdf (April 1, 2008)

Klein, D. & Manning, C. D. 2001. Distributional phrase structure induction [online]. Proceedings of the Fifth Conference on Natural Language Learning: 2001, 113-120. Available: http://ucrel.lancs.ac.uk/acl/W/W01/W01-0714.pdf (April 1, 2008).

Klein, D. & Manning, C. D. 2002. A generative constituent-context model for improved grammar induction [online]. Proceedings of the 40th Annual Meeting of the Association for Computational Linguistics: 2002, 128-135. Available: http://www-nlp.stanford.edu/~manning/papers/KleinManningACL2002.pdf (April 1, 2008).

Klein, D. & Manning, C. D. 2004. Corpus-based induction of syntactic structure: Models of dependency and constituency [online]. Proceedings of the 42nd Annual Meeting of the Association for Computational Linguistics: 2004. Available: http://acl.ldc.upenn.edu/acl2004/main/pdf/341_pdf_2-col.pdf (April 1, 2008).

Kroeger, P. 1993. Phrase Structure and Grammatical Relations in Tagalog. Stanford: CSLI Publications.

Osborne, M. & Briscoe, T. 1997. Learning stochastic categorial grammar [online]. Proceedings of CoNLL97: Computational Natural Language Learning: 1997, 80-87. Available: http://acl.ldc.upenn.edu/W/W97/W97-1010.pdf (April 1, 2008).

Schachter, P. & Otanes, F. 1972. Tagalog reference grammar. Berkeley : University of California Press.

Sekine, S. & Grishman, R. 1995. A corpus-based probabilistic grammar with only two non-terminals [online]. Proceedings Fourth International Workshop on Parsing Technologies: 1995, 216-223. Available: http://www.cs.nyu.edu/~sekine/papers/iwpt95.pdf (April 1, 2008).

Steedman, M. 1993. Categorial Grammar. Lingua, 90: 221-258. Available: http://repository.upenn.edu/cgi/viewcontent.cgi?article=1490&context=cis_reports

Who's Missing in the Group?
Argument Sharing in Core Cosubordinate Construction in Filipino[*]

Aquiles P. Bazar III

De La Salle University
2401 Taft Avenue, Manila, Philippines 1004
bazara@dlsu.edu.ph

Abstract. This paper examines the relationship between two important arguments in core cosubordinate construction in Filipino: namely, controller found in the matrix core and the missing argument (controllee) in the linked core using the framework Role and Reference Grammar of Van Valin (2005). This paper has proved that there is really an argument sharing between two cores and each core plays a crucial role in the syntactic development of cosubordinate clauses. The first core assigns the juncture levels and nexus of relations of the units involved, whereas the second core determines the syntactic structure of the clause. The researcher also found out that regardless of the number of arguments found in the linked core, the matrix core argument which is also the controller is the same with the missing actor argument from the linked core.

Keywords: cosubordination, arguments, control construction, nexus, core.

1. Introduction

Cosubordination is defined as one type of nexus relation in which units of equivalent sizes are strung together in a coordinate-like relation with no marker of syntactic dependency is found between and among units (Olson, 1981). These units share some grammatical categories such as arguments, aspects, negation, and other operators. Argument sharing is a process in which one argument in the matrix core is the same with another argument found from the linked core. However, the problem lies in the syntactic representation of a cosubordinate clause in which there is a missing argument from the linked core. That seems to be a violation of a theory known as Completeness Constraint as it states that all arguments overtly expressed in the semantic representation of a clause must be realised in the syntax (Van Valin, 2005). Before we move on to our discussion of argument sharing, let us first clarify some terms in the literature. Control construction, as one theory applied in analysing argument sharing in cosubordination, refers to how the controller of the missing NP in the linked core is to be determined (Van Valin, 2005). In an ergative language like Filipino, subject control and object control cannot be used, for these terms will lead to some problems. Thus, non-subject actor, controller, or syntactic pivot will be used to avoid confusion. In sentence (1), the single argument of the matrix core realised by *ko* 'I' is in ergative case functioning as a non-subject actor in the construction and cannot be called either subject or object controller. The semantic role of the argument *ko* 'I' is assigned by its nucleus *pinilit* 'tried', a patient verb. The argument in the linked core, on the other hand, is missing but although this argument is not overtly expressed in the syntax, it is clear that this argument is the same with the syntactic argument in the matrix core making this non-subject actor the controller by default.

---

[*] Copyright 2008 - Aquiles P. Bazar III

22nd Pacific Asia Conference on Language, Information and Computation, pages 123–130

(1) *Pinilit kong matulog ng maaga*
    -in-pilit ko-ng ma-tulog ng ma-aga
    PAT.PERF-try.hard 1SG.ERG-LNK ACT-sleep OBL ADJ-early
    'I tried (hard) to sleep early.'

Even in transitive clauses like in sentence (2), the overt syntactic argument in the matrix core realised by *Nanay* 'mother' is the same with the missing argument from the linked core. It is apparent, however, that the matrix argument *Nanay* 'mother' is in ergative case and therefore functioning as a non-subject actor.

(2) *Iniisip ni Nanay na lutuin ang pansit*
    -in-iisip ni=Nanay na luto-in ang=pansit
    PAT-IMPRF-think ERG=mother LNK cook-PAT ABS=noodle
    'Mother is thinking of cooking the noodles'

On the other hand, in sentence (3), the second argument of the matrix core realised by *ako* 'I' is the controller of the construction, for the missing argument of the linked core is the same with this argument. Though this NP takes the role of a patient because of the semantic role of its verb, the term object control cannot be used, for this argument is in absolutive case and therefore functioning as a subject. The first argument, on the other hand, realised by *niya* 'he or she' is an ergative pronoun but not functioning as the subject of the construction.

(3) *Pinilit niya akong matulog ng maaga*
    -in-pilit niya ako-ng ma-tulog ng maga
    PAT.PERF-force 3SG.ERG 1SG.ABS ACT-sleep OBL ADJ-early
    'He/she forced me to sleep early.'

2. Discussion

In nonsubordinate constructions, the semantic role of the overt syntactic argument is determined by the nucleus of the first core which also assigns the nexus relations and levels of junctures of the units involved, whereas the nucleus of the second core assigns the syntactic structure of the sentence (attransitive, single argument, transitive) and the grammatical relations of its arguments. This is the case of a number of verbs in Filipino like *pinilit* 'tried or forced' that may be interpreted either as cosubordinate or coordinate depending on their function and meaning. In sentence (4), the verb *pinilit* 'tried' requires a single argument in the matrix core which is and must be the same with the missing argument from the linked core. This construction is interpreted as cosubordinate.

(4) *Pinilit niyang buksan ang pinto*
    in-pilit niya-ng bukas-an ang pinto
    PAT.PERF-try 3SG.ERG-LNK open-PAT ABS door
    'He/She tried to open the door.'

If the verb *pinilit* 'forced', on the other hand, functions as a causative verb requiring two arguments in the matrix core, one as an actor and the other as undergoer, the controller will therefore be realised by the undergoer and not by the actor. This is interpreted as coordinate construction, as shown in

    Pinilit niya akong ligawan ang kapatid niya
    -in-pilit niya ako-ng ligaw-an ang kapatid niya
    PAT.PERF-try 3SG.ERG 1SG.ABS-LNK court-PAT ABS sister 3SG.GEN
    'He/she forced me to court his/her sister.'

Having one overt syntactic argument in the matrix core is not an indication that this construction is cosubordinate. An example of this is the coordinate verb *gusto* 'want' in sentence (5) in which the matrix argument may be the same with the missing argument from the linked core, as shown in

(5)   *Gusto ni Lisang basahin ang libro*
        gusto ni=Lisa-ng basa-in ang=libro
        want ERG=Lisa-LNK read-PAT ABS=book
        'Lisa wants to read the book'

However, the same overt syntactic argument in the matrix core may not also be the same with the actor argument in the linked core, as shown in

(6)   *Gusto ni Lisang basahin ko ang libro*
        gusto ni=Lisa-ng basa-in=ko ang=libro
        want ERG=Lisa-LNK read-PAT=1SG.ERG ABS=book
        'Lisa wants me to read the book'

Levels of junctures are also assigned by the nucleus of the matrix core. This will be realised when the matrix core takes a *ma*-prefix. Sentence (7) is in core juncture, for the two cores have their own sets of arguments. The non-subject actor Marta is an argument of the matrix verb *sumubok* 'tried' as it assigns its semantic role, whereas the absolutive NP *puto* 'rice cake' is an argument of the linked verb *iluto* 'cook'. The missing argument from the linked core, however, is the same with the matrix core Marta.

(7)   *Sumubok si Martang iluto ang puto*
        -um-subok si=Marta-ng i-luto ang=puto
        ACT.PERF-try ABS=Marta-LNK PAT-cook ABS=rice.cake
        'Marta tried to cook (the) rice cake'

On the other hand, when the two verbs occur closer to each other, the argument Marta is no longer an overt sole argument of the verb *sumubok* 'tried' as seen in its morphosyntactic coding. In sentence (8), the role of the argument Marta which is in ergative case is no longer assigned by the actor verb *sumubok* 'tried' nor by the patient verb *iluto* 'cook' but these verbs merge as one requiring one set of arguments. There seems to be no argument sharing in this construction anymore because this sentence is in nuclear juncture.

(8)   *Sumubok iluto ni Marta ang puto*
        -um-subok i-luto ni=Marta ang=puto
        ACT.PERF-try PAT-cook ERG-Marta ABS=rice.cake
        'Marta tried to cook (the) rice cake'

One important thing to realise about single-argument cosubordinate constructions is that if there is any argument in the clause, it belongs to the matrix core and not to the linked core. Sentence (9) shows control construction where the single overt syntactic argument realised by Pedro found in the matrix core is the controller by default; that is, the missing core argument of the actor verb *tumakas* 'escape' is also the same with this core argument.

(9)   *Tinagka ni Pedrong tumakas*
        -in-tangka ni=Pedro-ng –um-takas
        PAT.PERF-try ERG=Pedro-LNK ACT-escape
        'Pedro tried to escape'

Even when the two nuclei or verbs occur closer to each other, the presence of one overt syntactic argument will suffice the need for the second one, as shown in

(10) *Sinubok umawit ni Lisa*
       -in-subok um-awit ni=Lisa
       PAT.PERF-try ACT-sing ERG=Lisa
       'Lisa tried to sing'

What is interesting about a single-argument clause is when the two verbs take two different focus affixes to assign two different morphosyntactic codes to one syntactic argument. In the sentence below, the verb *binalak* 'try' takes the semantic role of a patient or undergoer, whereas the verb *sumayaw* 'dance' takes the role of an actor. The pronominal *niya* 'he or she' which is in ergative case agrees with the verb *binalak* and not with the verb *sumayaw* which is apparent for this pronominal clitic is an argument of this matrix core, as shown in

(11) *Binalak niyang sumayaw sa plasa*
       -in-balak niya-ng –um-sayaw sa plasa
       PAT.PERF-plan 3SG.ABS-LNK ACT.AGT-dance DAT park
       'She was planning to dance in the park.'

In sentence (12), the first core *pinilit* 'try' takes the role of a patient, whereas the linked core realised by *kumalma* 'to be calm' takes the role of an actor. It is apparent, however, that the missing argument from the linked core is the same with the overt core argument in the matrix core whose semantic role is determined by its nucleus.

(12) *Pinilit niyang kumalma*
       -in-pilit=niyang um-kalma
       PAT.PERF-try=3SG.ERG-LNK ACT-calm
       'She tried to (be) calm'

Even when the two verbs occur closer to each, it is clear that the semantic role of the overt matrix argument is determined by the matrix core or verb and not of the verb closer to it. In sentence (13), the role of the non-subject actor Lisa is determined by the matrix verb *binalak* 'planned' although the actor verb *sumayaw* 'dance' occurs closer to this argument.

(13) *Binalak sumayaw ni Lisa sa plasa.*
       -in-balak –um-sayaw ni Lisa sa plasa
       PAT.PERF-plan ACT.AGT-dance ERG Lisa DAT park
       'Lisa was planning to dance in the park.'

When the verb of the matrix core takes the role of an actor, it is still apparent that the morphosyntactic coding of the overt syntactic argument is determined by the semantic role of the matrix core, as shown in

(14) *Nagbabalak siyang sumayaw*
       nag-babalak=siya-ng –um-sayaw
       ACT-IMPRF-plan=3SG.ABS-LNK ACT-dance
       'He/she is planning to dance.'

This is different from another structure very much closer to sentence (13) as discussed above. When the matrix verb takes the role of an actor and the second verb occurs closer to it, it is quite apparent that the argument Lisa is no longer determined by any single verb as seen in sentence (15), but the two verbs *nagbabalak* 'planning' and *isayaw* 'dance with' merge as one forming one semantically complex verb having one set of arguments. Having said that, this construction is interpreted as a serial verb construction in nuclear lever.

(15) *Nagbabalak isayaw ni Lisa ang bata*
     nag-ba-balak i-sayaw ni=Lisa ang=bata
     ACT-IMPRF-plan PAT-dance ERG=Lisa ABS=child
     'Lisa planned to dance with the child'

Looking into the missing syntactic argument of the linked core, on the other hand, will make us realise that although this argument is the same with the overt syntactic argument of the matrix core, it takes a different morphosyntactic coding assigned by its nucleus. As shown in sentence (16), the matrix core *binalak* 'planned' assigns a patient role to its syntactic argument *niya* 'he or she'. However, although the argument of the linked core *'sumayaw* 'dance' does not appear in the clause syntactically, we can conclude that the semantic role of this argument will be absolutive as assigned by its verb.

(16) *Binalak niyang sumayaw (siya)*
     -in-balak niya-ng –um-sayaw siya
     PAT.PERF-plan 3SG.ERG-LNK ACT-dance 3SG.ABS

If the argument of a single-argument cosubordinate clause takes the role of an actor in order to agree with the second verb, the result is ungrammaticality of the sentence, as shown in,

(17) **Binalak sumayaw si Lisa sa plasa.*
     -in-balak –um-sayaw si Lisa sa plasa
     PAT.PERF-plan ACT.AGT-dance ABS Lisa DAT park

Cosubordinate construction at core level becomes more complicated in transitive clauses. In a single-argument clause, the controller is the overt syntactic argument of the matrix core by default and there is no other overt syntactic core argument in the linked core. In transitive clauses, on the other hand, the controller in the construction is always realised by a non-subject actor as stated in La Polla and Van Valin (1997).
   Theory of obligatory control
         1.   Causative and jussive verbs have undergoer control.
         2.   All other (M-)transitive verbs have actor control.

In transitive cosubordinate clauses, the relationship between the controller in the matrix core and the controllee (missing argument) in the linked core, which are both actor arguments, is not affected by the number of arguments present in the linked core and the semantic role taken by the linked verb. Core chain illustrates control construction in which the overt core argument in the matrix core realised by Leo is the same with the missing argument from the linked core despite the presence of an absolutive argument *pinto* 'door'.

(18) *Pinilit ni Leong buksan ang pinto*
     -in-pilit ni=Leo-ng bukas-an ang=pinto
     PAT.PERF-try ERG=Leo-LNK open-PAT ABS=door
     'Leo tried to open the door.'

Even if the linked core takes different semantic roles- e.g. instrumental, benefactive, locative- the missing argument from the linked core will still be the same with the non-subject argument in the matrix core. In sentence (19), although the linked core realised by the verb *ipansayaw* 'dance with' takes the role of an instrument, the missing argument is still the same with the non-subject actor in the matrix core. The presence of an absolute argument *sapatos* 'shoes' does not affect the argument sharing of the two cores making the nonsubject actor *niya* 'he or she' the controller.

(19)   *Pinilit niyang ipansayaw ang bagong sapatos*
       -in-pilit=niya-ng ipan-sayaw ang=bagong=sapatos
       PAT.PERF-try=3SG.ERG-LNK INSTRM-dance ABS=new=shoe
       'He/she tried to dance with her new shoes'

In sentence (20), the linked core realised by the benefactive verb *iluto* 'cook' requires to have an absolutive argument realised by Ana. This does not affect the argument sharing of the two cores because the missing argument from the linked core is still the non-subject actor found in the matrix core. The semantic argument that is absent syntactically from the linked is recoverable from the matrix core.

(20)   *Sinubok ni Nanay na iluto si Ana ng paborito niyang meryenda*
       -in-subok ni=Nanay na i-luto si Ana ng paborito niya-ng meryenda
       PAT.PERF-try ERG=Nanay LNK BEN-cook ABS Ana OBL favourite 3SG.GEN snack
       'Mother tried to cook Ana her favourite snacks'

Even if the two nuclei or verbs occur closer to each, the controller in the matrix core is the same with the missing argument from the linked core which is also an actor argument. The presence of other arguments even the absolutive arguments does not affect the controller-controllee relationship of the two cores, as seen in

(21)   *Pinilit kunin ni Alex ang pera kay May*
       -in-pilit kuha-in ni=Alex ang=pera kay=May
       PAT.PERF-try get-PAT ERG=Alex ABS=money LOC=May
       'alex tried to get the money from May'

(22)   *Sinubok ipansayaw ng babae ang bago niyang sapatos*
       -in-subok ipan-sayaw ng=babae ang=bago=niya-ng=sapatos
       PAT.PERF-try INSTRM-dance ERG=woman ABS=new=3SG.GEN-LNK=shoe
       'The woman tried to dance with her new shoes'

(23)   *Iniisip niyang pagkulahan ng damit ang bubong namin*
       -in-i-isip=niya-ng pag-...-an-kula ng=damit ang=bubong=namin
       PAT-IMPRF-think=3SG.ERG-LNK LOC-bleach OBL=clothes
       ABS=roof=2PL.GEN.EXCL
       'He/she is thinking to bleach their clothes on our roof'

When a matrix verb takes a ma-prefix, the argument sharing of the two cores is not affected, because although the matrix core argument is in absolutive case, the missing argument from the linked core is still the same with it, as seen in

(24)   *Nagplano si Tatay na ibenta ang bukid*
       nag-plano si Tatay na i-benta ang bukid
       ACT.PERF-plan ABS Father LNK PAT-sell ABS farm
       'Father planned to sell the farm'

(25) *Nagsimula na si Lisang ipansayaw ang bagong damit*
      nag-simula=na si=Lisa-ng ipan-sayaw ang=bagong=damit
      ACT.PERF-start=already ABS=Lisa INSTRM-dance ABS=new=dress
      'Lisa has started to dance with her new dress'

In sentence (26), there seems to have two absolutive arguments: one realised by the matrix core argument Rodel and the other realised by the linked core argument *libro* 'book'. Although the linked verb *sulatin* 'write' has an absolutive verb, the fact remains that its missing argument is the same with the absolutive argument found in the matrix core and therefore making argument sharing possible in this construction.

(26) *Sumubok si Rodel na sulatin ang libro*
      -um-subok si Rodel na sulat-in ang libro
      ACT.PERF-try ABS Rodel LNK write-PAT ABS book
      'Rodel tried to write the book'

In the theory of obligatory control, it state that causative verbs should have undergoer control, whereas all other (M-)transitive verbs actor control. The verb *nahirapan* 'have a hard time' seems to be a violation of this theory. In control construction, only causative verbs must have undergoer control. But in sentence (27), the argument *estudyante* 'student' in absolutive case seems to be the controller. However, looking into structure will tell us that the verb *nahirapan* 'having a hard time' is uses a *ma*-prefix which predicts that its sole argument *estudyante* 'student' should be in absolutive case. And since *nahirapan* 'have a hard time' functions as an actor verb in the construction requiring only a single actor argument in the matrix core, its single argument will be its controller by default, and therefore not violating the theory.

(27) *Nahirapan ang mga estudyanteng sagutin ang test*
      na-...-an ang mga estudyante-ng sagot-in ang test
      ACT.PERF-have.a.hard.time ABS PL student-LNK answer-PAT ABS test
      'The students had a hard time answering the test.'

3. Conclusion

1. Non-subject actor is a better term to use in identifying the controller in cosubordinate construction. The use of subject control and object will lead the readers to confusion, because the language is interpreted to exhibit an ergative system.
2. In nonsubordinate constructions, the semantic role of the overt syntactic argument is determined by the nucleus of the first core which also assigns the nexus relations and levels of junctures of the units involved, whereas the nucleus of the second core assigns the syntactic structure of the sentence (attransitive, single argument, transitive) and the grammatical relations of its arguments.
3. In a single-argument clause, the overt syntactic argument found in the matrix core is the controller by default.
4. One important thing to realise about single-argument cosubordinate constructions is that if there is any argument overtly expressed in the clause, it belongs to the matrix core and not to the linked core.
5. In transitive cosubordinate clauses, the relationship between the controller in the matrix core and the controllee (missing argument) in the linked core, which are both actor arguments, is not affected by the number of arguments present in the linked core and the semantic role taken by the linked verb.

ABBREVIATIONS

1	first person
2	second person
3	third person
ABS	absolutive
ADJM	adjective marker
ACT	actor
AGT	agent
ARG	argument
DAT	dative
ERG	ergative
EXPRSV	Expressive particle
BEN	benefactive
GEN	genitive
HON	honorific particle
INCMP	Incompatibility particle
IMPRF	imperfective
INSTRM	instrumental
LNK	linker
LOC	locative
MOD	modality
NEG	negative marker
OBL	oblique
PAT	patient
PERF	perfective
PL	plural
PRED	predicate
S	subject
SG	singular
SVC	serial verb construction
TAM	tense/ aspect/ mood

References

Aikhenvald, Alexandra Y. 2003. 'Some Thoughts on Serial Verbs', Paper presented at International Workshop on Serial Verb Constructions, La Trobe University

Collins, Chris. 1997. Argument sharing in serial verb constructions. *Linguistic Inquiry* 28, 3: 461-497.

Hansell, M. 1993. Serial verbs and complement constructions in Mandarin: a clause linkage analysis. In Van Valin, ed., 197-233.

Kroeger, Paul. 2004. Analyzing syntax: a lexical-functional approach. London. Cambridge University Press.

Olson, M.L. 1981. Barai clause junctures: toward a functional theory of inter-clausal relations. PhD dissertation, Australian National University.

Schachter, P & Otanes F. (1972). *Tagalog reference grammar*. Berkeley: University of California Press.

Van Valin, R. & La Polla R. (1997). *Syntax*. London: Cambridge University Press.

Van Valin, R.(2005). *Introduction to role and reference grammar*. London: Cambridge University Press.

Whitman, John and Waltraud Paul. 2005. Reanalysis and conservancy of structure in Chinese. In: Batllori, M. et al. (eds.). *Grammaticalization and parametric change*. Oxford: OUP; pp. 82 - 94.

Towards a Model for the Prediction of Chinese Novel Verbs*

Paul You-Jun Chang[a] and Kathleen Ahrens[a, b]

[a] Graduate Institute of Linguistics, National Taiwan University, Taipei, Taiwan R. O. C.
r95142005@ntu.edu.tw
[b] Hong Kong Baptist University, Kowloon Tong, Hong Kong
ahrens@hkbu.edu.hk

Abstract. As previous word adoption models, though proposing potential factors that influence the survival of neologisms, receive little empirical examination, this corpus-based study compares the performance of two such models by providing clear operational criteria for each factor in the models and, consequently, proposes a hybrid model that improves the previous results. We focus on seventy-seven Chinese novel verbs that appeared about ten years ago, defining their survival/failure in the real world, and examine the accurate prediction ratio of the two models. Both models display an overall accuracy of about 60 percent. However, as certain factors, e.g., unobtrusiveness, appear to be invalid predictors for the Chinese data, we attempt to improve the results by deleting inappropriate factors and by adjusting the weightings. As the overall accuracy was improved to about 70 percent, we suggest that this study would shed light on the potential factors that influence the survival of Chinese novel verbs.

Keywords: Neologism, Word Adoption Model, Unobtrusiveness.

1. Introduction

One interesting aspect about the human cognition is its ability to create. And creativity in language has doubtlessly inspired numerous studies. Among others, one phenomenon that commonly occurs would be the emergence of neologisms. For one thing, all words, together with their senses, that exist in our current vocabulary were once new (Klein and Murphy, 2001) and must have undergone a certain developmental process to finally remain in the vocabulary. For another, we still see this process going on in everyday life as can be seen from the coinage of new words, such as *blog* or *Y2K*. Previous studies on neologisms, therefore, mostly focused on the collection of new words (e.g., Algeo and Algeo, 1991), the analysis of their inherent features (Hsu, 1999; Rey, 1995), or their relationship with the society (Hsu, 1999). Metcalf (2002; cf. Chang, 2008) and Kjellmer (2000), among the few, nevertheless attempted to observe the factors that influence the adoption of neologisms in a language and, respectively, proposed a scoring system to assess the possibility for novel words to survive or to fail.[1] Interestingly, these two models are similar regarding certain factors as important, e.g., morphological productivity,

---

* We appreciate comments from two anonymous reviewers and Siaw-Fong Chung, as well as comments from the audience in CLDC-2 for a previous, smaller-scale paper. We also appreciate Professor Janice Fon for her comments on the statistics and Yu-You Chen, Yao-Zhu Zhang, and Yi-Wei Lin for help in collecting the frequencies. The remaining errors are our own.
[1] Part of this paper (mainly 2.1 and parts of Sections 3 and 4, about Metcalf's model,) were presented at The Second Conference on Language, Discourse, and Cognition (CLDC-2). As an extension, this study contrasts Metcalf's model with Kjellmer's and proposes a hybrid model for improvement of the results.

22nd Pacific Asia Conference on Language, Information and Computation, pages 131–140

and yet are contrastive in their evaluation of linguistic gaps and borrowings. Following their studies, Sabino (2005) used the two models to evaluate the possibility of the word *gameday* to survive and found that both models yield a roughly 0.7 probability. While this interesting study displayed the possibility to test Metcalf's and Kjellmer's models empirically, the fact that the study looked at only one word, and that *gameday* itself was a new word in development, leaves the accuracy of prediction, i.e., the performance of the two models, unaddressed. Moreover, although Chang (2008) empirically examined Metcalf's model, no such study was done for Kjellmer's model or for the comparison of the two models. Therefore, for a more adequate evaluation, comparison, and improvement of the performance of both of the models, an empirical study with a set of clear criteria for each factor in the two models would seem necessary.

This study, therefore, attempts to examine the models proposed by Metcalf (2002) and Kjellmer (2000) by focusing on Chinese novel verbs that appeared around ten years ago. In doing so, we propose, for each factor in the models, a set of criteria for the scoring of the neologisms by using corpus tools. We ask the following questions: (1) Can we predict the survival of Chinese novel verbs from 1996 to 2006 according to Metcalf's and Kjellmer's models? (2) If yes, which provides better prediction? (3) If no, how can we better predict the survival of these words by modifying their conditions? And, as these two models contrast in their notion of linguistic gaps and borrowings, we hypothesize that (1) in Chinese, unlike the situation observed in English, borrowings and translated words take no disadvantage, while gap-filling is beneficial, if not essential, for the survival of novel verbs. We demonstrate, by setting up clear criteria, that although the two models perform similarly in predicting successful words, Metcalf's model performs better at predicting failure words. While the results suggest room for improvement of the models, we further analyze the factors, deleting inappropriate ones or adjusting the weightings; consequently, we improved the overall accuracy to about 70 percent.

2. Word Adoption Models

2.1. Metcalf's Fudge Scale

Metcalf (2002) proposed the FUDGE scale to measure the probability of a word's survival based on his observation of English neologisms. The crucial factors, as Metcalf stated, involve (1) frequency of the words; (2) unobtrusiveness, i.e., a successful word should not be exotic or too cleverly coined; (3) diversity of users and situations, i.e., the range of their usage; (4) generation of other forms and meanings, namely the productivity of the word; and (5) endurance of the concept, related to the concept's reference to a historical event. The method of assessing the probability is to rank the new words from level 0 to level 2 in each factor and sum up the total scores in the end. The higher the scores are, (7, as proposed,) the more likely the new words are to survive.

Metcalf downplays cleverness, exoticness, and linguistic gaps. He states that obtrusive new words cannot last long, and that words such as *skycap*, *scofflaw*, *agnostic*, etc., caught on because they do not look exotic, or they do root from a certain source language, which English has opened to all along. In addition, Metcalf claims that lexical gaps do not necessarily provoke new words. For example, although the Hebrew word *hesed* implies God's mercy, tenderness, and love, it was inadequately translated as *mercy* in English, thus losing certain original meanings. Metcalf states that gaps such as these do not seem likely to be filled in the near future; communication can be sustained without a proper word for everything. As will be noticed later, this model differs from Kjellmer's model in terms of humor, gap filling, and exoticness.

2.2. Kjellmer's Model

Kjellmer (2000) presents thirteen conditions to assess potential words, which can be divided into five categories: semantic, phonological, morphological, and graphematic conditions, and others, such as prestige.

Firstly, semantic conditions include the existence of a semantic parallel, namely a pre-existing semantic pattern in the language (e.g., *–able* for adjectives meaning "*capable of being V-ed*") as well as semantic transparency, the straightforwardness of the new word's meaning. Secondly, phonological parallels, i.e., well-established sound combinations in the language, and ease of pronunciation are considered influential factors. Thirdly, a word is more likely to survive if it has a morphological parallel, filling up a gap in a pre-existing morphological pattern in the language; e.g., the potential word *pensivity* would fill up a gap where the suffix pattern *–ive* would turn into its nominal form *–ivity*. In addition to this, Kjellmer states that a new word is also likely to survive if it does not fill up a morphological gap and yet follows the general morphological rules in the language. Besides, Kjellmer states that highly productive affixes (e.g., *-ness*) may facilitate the survival of new words. Furthermore, the more compatible the etymological roots of the new word and its affixes are, the more likely the word will be accepted. In terms of graphemes, a word following the graphematic customs in the language and a word whose spelling agrees with the pronunciation would possibly succeed. Finally, words that carry a prestigious, exotic, or humorous connotation, together with words that are concise, would also possibly survive.[2]

In the following sections, we therefore seek to evaluate the performance of the two models.

3. Methodology

3.1. Real World Cases: Evaluating the Words' Survival in UDN Database

3.1.1. Defining Neologisms and Narrowing Down the Scope

In this study, we gather our data from the collection of neologisms from July 1996 to December 1997 in Taiwan (National Languages Committee, 1998). Containing 5,711 new words, this collection selects new words according to their appearance in the Revised Dictionary of Mandarin Chinese based on a day-by-day examination of major newspapers. For our current study, we narrowed down our scope to the category of fashion words (cf. Hsu, 1999) and focused only on non-sense-neologism verbs (cf. Rey, 1995; Hsu, 1999), since we could not obtain accurate frequencies for sense-neologisms from our current corpus, and verbs and nouns may behave differently (Ahrens, 1999). Excluding inappropriate words, such as English acronyms, monosyllabic words, and foul language, we obtained seventy-seven verbs in the end.[3]

3.1.2. Normalizing the Frequencies and Defining Their Actual Success

As researchers working on LIVAC (Linguistic Variations in Chinese Speech Communities) synchronic corpus (http://www.livac.org/) and Fischer (1998) have conducted similar studies, we would currently collect the year-by-year frequencies of these neologisms in the UDN (a major newspaper in Taiwan) database[4] from 1996 to 2006, since newspapers might capture the emergence and fading away of new words. These frequencies were further normalized to the frequencies per 10,000 characters. Thus, we obtained the normalized ratios of the words.

We further set up criteria to define the words' actual survival or failure by looking into the words' normalized ratios in 2006. As the words' appearance in print would indicate a wide usage, we set the threshold at a low level, in this case 0.3 (about 10 tokens) and 3 (about 100 tokens). Namely, a word having a normalized ratio less than or equal to 0.3 in 2006 (e.g., 哈草, *ha1 cao3*, 'to smoke,' normalized ratio=0.11) would be counted as a failure, and a word having a normalized ratio greater than 3 (e.g., 抓包 *zhua1 bao1*, '(to be) caught doing something,' normalized ratio=4.24) would be counted as a survival. If a word has a normalized ratio greater than 0.3 but less than or equal to 3 (e.g., 哈啦, *ha1 la1*, 'to chat,' normalized ratio=2.67), we would further look at its slope of the normalized ratios throughout the years to observe its

---

[2] Kjellmer actually discusses three more factors: semantic needs, prompting of media, and fashion; however, since no actual scores are assigned to these factors, they are currently not included in the analysis. Please visit http://graftedlife.googlepages.com for details about the factors and scores in Metcalf's and Kjellmer's models (appendices I and II) as well as for all the other appendices of this paper.

[3] For the list of verbs and related data, please refer to appendix III.

[4] For a description of the corpus, please refer to appendix IV.

developmental tendency, since we cannot be sure whether such words would really survive; in this case, only words with a slope of less than -0.06 would be counted as failures. All of these criteria were set up through our observation and comparison in the data. The results of our definition are summarized as follows:

Table 1. Survival and Failure Thresholds

Failure		Survival	
NR$\leqq$0.3	0.3<NR $\leqq$3		NR>3
	Slope $\leqq$-0.06	Slope>-0.06	
23	1	29	24

3.2. Prediction of Metcalf's and Kjellmer's Models

3.2.1. Operational Definitions for Metcalf's Model

The five conditions in Metcalf's model will now be discussed in sequence. Firstly, for frequency, the method and rationale would be similar to what we did in the previous section for defining the words' actual survival or failure, except in this case we look at the normalized ratio in the year 1996 in order to simulate the prediction process. We score a word as zero if the normalized ratio is less than or equal to 0.3; as one if the normalized ratio is greater than 0.3 but less than or equal to 3; and as two if the normalized ratio is greater than 3.

Secondly, as unobtrusiveness, in fact, explains for various levels of factors, including phonology, morphology, semantics, and foreign borrowings, its operational criteria would also involve different levels of information in the hope that the scores would be close to the original model's prediction. As a score zero in the model denotes a conspicuous word, exotic, strange-looking, or cleverly invented, we would assign to it words that are borrowings, violate morphological/phonological rules, or lack a clear form-meaning relationship. To score one, noticeable obtrusiveness, we assign words whose meaning can only be (indirectly) inferable from the word form in Chinese, perhaps through certain metonymical/metaphorical links. And to score two, we assign words with a transparent relationship between form and meaning.

Thirdly, since diversity involves the variety of users and situations, we define a diversity score of zero for specialized terms, as Metcalf defined, and for words that never occurred in the database, since Metcalf states that score zero words would only appear in specialized documents and not newspapers; score one for words that need further explanations in the 1996 UDN data[5]; and score two for the remaining words.

Fourthly, generation of other forms and meanings in Metcalf's model refers to the word's ability for POS alternation, inflectional changes, or the word's ability to extend to other forms and meanings. For clear criteria, we would regard a word's productivity as reflected in the variety of the collocates they have. In this case, we look into the Chinese Word Sketch (http://wordsketch.ling.sinica.edu.tw/). If Chinese Word Sketch shows that a word can collocate with more than one type of words, perhaps not belonging to the same domain with its dominant meaning, than we consider the word able to be applied to various types of situations, thus having a greater productivity. Practically, and also through comparison, we set up the criteria that words having more than ten collocates would be scored as two; those with less than ten collocates but having more than three Word Sketch functions would be considered moderately productive and scored as one; and those with less than ten collocates and having less than or equal to three Word Sketch functions would be scored as zero.

---

[5] In our observation, we would also consider words that need a pair of quotation marks with their usage to be words that need further explanations.

Fifthly, for endurance of concept, we would simply follow Metcalf's definitions that score zero for nonce word forms, one for words pertaining to historical events, and two for words with long-enduring concepts.

3.2.2. *Operational Definitions for Kjellmer's Model*

The thirteen conditions will be listed briefly with the operational definitions we use to score the words. (1) S1: Since having semantic parallels means filling up semantic gaps, we look into the Chinese Word Sketch to look for the words' near synonyms; if there are no competing synonyms, then we consider the word filling up a semantic gap.[6] In this case, we set minimum similarity at zero, since neologisms usually have low frequencies.[7] (2) S2: For transparency to the layman, we adopt identical operational definitions as in Metcalf's model, i.e., the meanings of transparent words should not be specialized and must be clearly inferable from the form. (3) Ph1: To fill up phonological gaps, two operational criteria should be met. Firstly, a word should have parallel phonological patterns but have no homophones. Secondly, we compare the neologisms (with novel pronunciation) to a non-word list. Only legal non-words, i.e., possible pronunciation (Lin, 1999) that observe the Chinese phonological constraints can be regarded as filling up a phonological gap. (4) Ph2: For ease of pronunciation, as Kjellmer notes its overlapping with the previous condition, we would still compare the word to a non-word list; the criterion would require it not to be an illegal non-word in Chinese, i.e., its pronunciation is allowed in Chinese (whether it is currently existing or not). (5) M1: For morphological parallels, we check the words' morphemes in Souwenjiezi (搜文解字, http://words.sinica.edu.tw/) to look for patterns of a certain morpheme and decide if a word fills up a morphological gap in a certain pattern. (6) M2: For following the morphological principles, as also noted by Kjellmer for its overlapping with the previous condition, here the words do not have to fit into a certain pattern but have to observe the general morphological rules. (7) M3: For productive affixes, we check Souwenjiezi for words formed with a certain affix; if more than ten words are formed with the same morpheme, we consider the morpheme productive. For example, 打 *da3*, 'hit' is a productive morpheme as suggested in the database. (8) M4: To measure affix compatibility (i.e., the affixes deriving from the same root with the stem), we attempt to provide an operational definition that the words should not have morphemes of mixed origins, since in Chinese, often a Taiwanese morpheme combines with a Mandarin affix, e.g., 大 *da4*, 'big,' to form a word. (9) G1: For the filling of graphematic gaps, although rare in Chinese, we check the words in Soucixunzi (搜詞尋字), utilizing its radical searching function to decide whether a word fills up a graphematic gap. (10) G2: For agreement between spelling and pronunciation, we check if the word's pronunciation deviates from the usual case, i.e., the word should not be a homograph that has inconsistent pronunciations or needs to be pronounced in its original language, e.g., Taiwanese. (11) O1: We follow the original model, which recognizes the advantage of borrowings/foreign prestigious words. (12) O2: For conciseness, we examine whether a more concise word exists and can convey the same idea as the new word does. (13) O3: For humorous meanings, we follow basically two criteria proposed by previous scholars, namely incongruity (a discrepancy between the expression and the situation) and surprising meanings, the decision of which would be based on our intuition.

3.2.3. *Success Threshold at 0.5*

In order to compare the results of the two models, we transfer the scores on each scale into proportions; for example, score zero on Kjellmer's scale ranging from -16 to 14 would be

---

[6] Note, however, that sometimes the CWS lacks enough data for a thesaurus; then we make a decision on whether a synonym exists based on our world knowledge.

[7] Therefore, if under this setting the near synonym shown in the thesaurus is not likely to be a real synonym of the neologism, we look further into Word Sketch Difference to decide; if the two words do not have shared patterns, or only share certain common patterns, e.g., verbs like *become*, we consider it a sign for a lack of synonyms.

transferred as [0-(-16)]/30=0.53. In this work we adopt a threshold of 0.5 in defining success. Three reasons are provided for this threshold: (1) Metcalf, in his work, merely stated that words scored as 7 or higher are *more likely* to survive; however, in our observation this would lead to a bias where only a few words may be predicted as successful, while most words are predicted as failures in this model. (2) Kjellmer did not mention a threshold for success in his model, but score zero in his model would mean a neutral effect, the probability for which, as shown before, is 0.53. (3) As might be seen later, in a modified model, we find the lowest score for a word to survive would be 0.47 (and the score next to which would be 0.53, since there are only a fixed set of scores on this kind of scaling). Therefore, for consistency and for later comparison, we deem it proper to set the threshold at 0.5, which would be neither suspiciously high nor low.

4. Results and Discussion

4.1. Correct Prediction Ratio and Evaluation of the Two Models

The correct prediction ratio of the two models is summarized in Table 2.[8] It is shown that both models, especially Metcalf's model, perform better in predicting failures than survivals, while overall and in survival prediction the two generally do not differ much, with Metcalf's model slightly better than Kjellmer's model. However, as one might consider, the correctness ratio in both models can still be low.

Table 2. Predictions of the Two Models and Their Correct Prediction Ratio

	Real Case	Metcalf		Kjellmer	
Survival	53	29	54.72%	29	54.72%
Failure	24	20	83.33%	17	70.83%
Overall	77	49	63.64%	46	59.74%

We, therefore, propose that certain modification might be done to improve the results after the evaluation of the two models. In our observation, the advantage of Metcalf's model lies in its simplicity and his consideration of endurance of concept, which could provide explanations for certain data, while Kjellmer's model distinguishes the factors across different linguistic levels and takes conciseness into consideration. However, problems emerge when: (1) previous models, being designed for English, may not appropriately account for the Chinese data, where there might be a trend of accepting borrowed words (e.g., 變身 bian4 shen1, 'to transfigure,' a borrowing from Japanese), as contrary to our operational criteria for Metcalf's model (cf. Hsu, 1999); (2) vague definitions render establishing scoring criteria difficult, e.g., three levels of frequency in the FUDGE scale are vaguely defined from usages in family/among friends from 1,000~10,000 users to 'widely used'; (3) overlappings may lead to biased results, as in Kjellmer's M1-M2 (filling up a morphological gap and following the morphological rule) and Ph1-Ph2 (filling up a phonological gap and following the phonological rule); and (4) most importantly, in our observation, the scores in certain factors, such as G1or Ph2, appear almost the same across the seventy-seven items, which might indicate that these factors currently do not qualify as good predictors.[9] We, therefore, propose to examine the distribution of scores within each factor so as to determine the potentially important factors for our data. In addition, we would like to conduct statistical tests on Metcalf's/Kjellmer's models to see whether certain factors, as we hypothesized, would have an effect on the words' frequencies in 2006.

4.2. ANOVAs for Verification of Factors

Assigning scores to a word would, in effect, mean to categorize them; e.g., a word can obtain score one for generation and score two for endurance of concept, which would distinguish it

---

[8] For predicted scores of the two models, please see note 2 in appendix III for further information.
[9] Except for endurance of concept, since the items chosen mostly pertain to long-enduring concepts.

from other words with different scores. We, therefore, can draw distribution tables to see how many words fall in a certain category, conduct ANOVAs with factors in the models as independent variables, and log normalized ratios in 2006 as the dependent variables. Due to the limits of our number of tokens, we currently select factors in interest for analysis, examining whether Metcalf's/Kjellmer's concepts are correct. If Metcalf/Kjellmer are right in their hypotheses, that the factors they propose are influential for the words' survival, then we probably can detect certain main effects in ANOVAs that support their ideas. In this study, we select unobtrusiveness and generation from Metcalf's model and S1 (semantic gaps), M1 (morphological gaps), and O1 (prestige) from Kjellmer's model for analyses. These factors either reflect the conflicting concepts of the previous models (gaps and prestige), or represent certain general concepts that both models deem as important (productivity).[10]

The distribution tables of the factors in the two models, as given below, suggest three kinds of possible ANOVAs that we can conduct: (1) a one-way ANOVA for G0, G1, and G2 when all the words are under U0; (2) a one-way ANOVA for U0, U1, and U2 when all the words are under G0; (3) a 2×2 ANOVA between U (0 and 2), and G (0 and 2); and (4) a 2×2×2 ANOVA among S1, M1, and O1. Planned comparisons were designed to detect the source of effects.

Tables 3 and 4. Distribution Tables for Metcalf's Model (U and G) and Kjellmer's Model (S1, M1, and O1) (Numbers in the cells: the number of words in each category; numbers in parentheses: the scores of the conditions according to the models.)

	U(0)	U(1)	U(2)
G(0)	17	8	11
G(1)	13	4	4
G(2)	11	2	8

	S1(-1)		S1(1)	
	M1(-1)	M1(3)	M1(-1)	M1(3)
O1(0)	13	14	6	9
O1(2)	23	6	4	4

4.3. ANOVA Results and Discussion

(1) One-way ANOVA showed a significant difference between the 2006 log normalized ratios of G0, G1, and G2 [F(2, 38)=8.00, p<.01, α=0.05] when these words all belong to unobtrusiveness level zero. Planned comparisons suggest significant differences in G0-G2 and G1-G2 [t(38)=-4.00, p<0.001; t(38)=-2.24, p<0.05] but not in G0-G1 [t(38)=-1.708, p=0.10]. The results showed that words with different degrees of productivity, namely the ability of generating other forms and meaning, are different in their log normalized ratios in 2006 when all of these words are on unobtrusiveness level zero; generation, thus, would be a good predictor in Metcalf's model.

(2) One-way ANOVA showed no significant effect in the log normalized ratios of U0, U1, and U2 [F(2, 32)=0.43, p=0.66] when the words all belong to generation level zero, suggesting that putting prestigious (exotic, borrowed) words at a lower grade and non-conspicuous words at a higher grade may not lead to a good predictor of survival; as can be seen in the following Figures 1, 2, and 3, non-conspicuous words actually obtain lower log normalized ratios in the end, and U0 (prestigious) words got a little higher log normalized ratios than U2 words. This does not support Metcalf's hypothesis and implicates prestige may not take a disadvantage.

(3) Two-way ANOVA displayed a main effect in the log normalized ratios between G0 and G2 [F(1, 43)=47.47, p<0.001] but not between U0 and U2 [F(1, 43)=1.29, p=0.26]; no significant interaction was found [F(1, 43)=3.32, p=0.08]. This does not support Metcalf's idea concerning unobtrusiveness and reinforces our previous statement that generation (productivity) would serve as a good predictor, whereas putting prestigious words at a lower level may not be

---

[10] The reason for not having other selections is that the scores in frequency were themselves obtained by categorizing frequency levels, and the items chosen here mostly denote long-enduring concepts (in terms of endurance of concepts), and diversity of users is currently not of interest to us. For Kjellmer's model, we select gap/prestige-related factors as shown here; phonological and graphematic gaps are not selected, both due to limits of tokens and to the lack of discernment in their scores.

appropriate for Chinese data. Figure 3 shows a main effect in G0/G2 but not in U0/U2; the interaction was not significant.

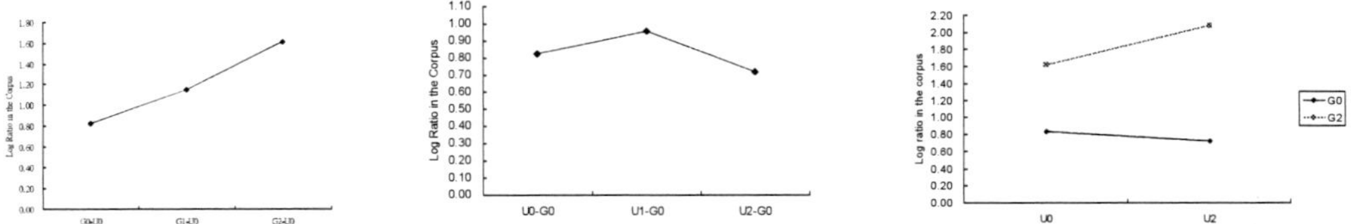

Figures 1, 2, and 3. 2006 Log Normalized Ratios: (3) G0, G1, and G2 (Left); (4) U0, U1, and U2 (middle); and (5) U0/U2 and G0/G2 (right).

(4) Three-way ANOVA showed a significant main effect in S1 [$F(1, 69)=5.29$, $p<0.05$], indicating that words filling up semantic gaps are different in their log normalized ratios from those not filling up a gap. However, no significant main effect was found either in M1, morphological gaps [$F(1, 69)=3.05$, $p=0.09$] or O1, prestige [$F(1, 69)=0.41$, $p=0.53$]. We also found no significant interaction in S1×M1, S1×O1, M1×O1, or S1×M1×O1 [S1×M1: $F(1, 69)=0.39$, $p=0.53$; S1×O1: $F(1, 69)=2.95$, $p=0.09$; M1×O1: $F(1, 69)=2.62$, $p=0.11$; S1×M1×O1: $F(1, 69)=0.10$, $p=0.75$]. Nevertheless, we suspect that the lack of significance would be due to our insufficient tokens, especially for words with score three in M1 and score two in O1. For one thing, the following figures suggest that semantic gap-filling words have higher log normalized ratios than those not filling up semantic gaps in non-borrowed words, but this is not obvious in borrowed words. Moreover, we further examined near-significant interaction effects and found a near-significant difference between O1, score two and O1, score zero, when the words are all scored as three for the M1 condition (i.e., when we do not take S1 into consideration) [$F(1, 30)=2.33$, $p=0.14$]. This would hint at the fact that words filling up morphological gaps (M1(3)) have higher log normalized ratios for borrowed words than for non-borrowed words:

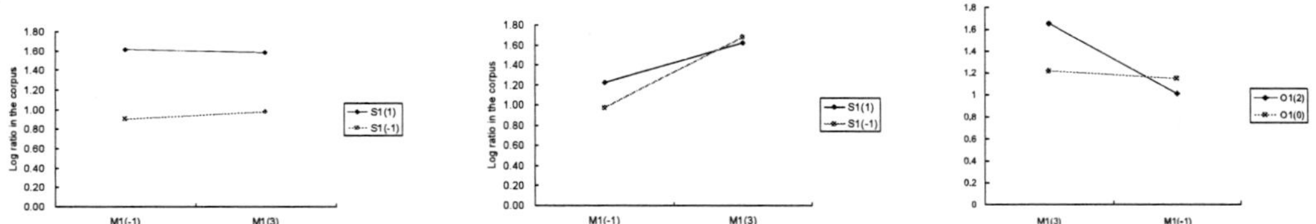

Figures 4a/4b and 5. 2006 Log Normalized Ratios: (4a) S1×M1 at O1, score zero (left, non-borrowed words); (4b) S1×M1 at O1, score two (middle, borrowed words); (5) M1×O1 (right).

In all, we have shown significant effects in both productivity and semantic gaps; there is no support for Metcalf's statement that prestigious words are at a disadvantage. We cannot be sure that morphological gaps and prestige have an effect on log normalized ratios; however, the effect for morphological gaps is marginal ($p<0.1$), and from the graphs and further examination of the data, we can see prestige and morphological gaps may still have some effects under certain conditions, though this is not significant.

5. Towards a Model for the Prediction of Chinese Novel Verbs

So far in our discussion, we find at least three ways to improve the results: (1) select important factors from the two models (or, to be more conservative, to delete inappropriate factors); (2) combine certain factors in order to avoid overlappings; and (3) adjust the direction and the magnitude of the weightings. Here we adopt Kjellmer's model as our basic design, since it distinguishes different levels of factors clearly, except that the conditions might be wrongly weighted. We believe that after deleting inappropriate factors, solving overlappings, and adjusting the weightings, we should be able to make some improvement.

Firstly, we want to select conditions and solve the overlappings. In Metcalf's model, this would mean deleting unobtrusiveness (as previously discussed) and diversity (D2 overlaps with F2, and D0, specialized terms, overlaps with our operational definition for Kjellmer's semantic transparency). Frequency and endurance of concepts are kept because the two are complementary for Kjellmer's model. In Kjellmer's model, this would mean deleting Ph1, Ph2, and G1 (these factors generally have the same scores across items, as discussed in 4.1), and M4 and O3 (currently not of interest).

Secondly, we combine M1 and M2 to solve its overlapping. As noted before, filling up a morphological gap would imply following the morphological rule, and not following the rule would mean not filling up a gap. We, thus, adopt a dichotomy: the word either does not follow the rule or it follows the rule (including filling up a gap). Now the following ten factors remain: frequency, productivity (generation), semantic gaps, transparency, endurance of concept, morphological rules and gaps, productive affixes, agreement between spelling and pronunciation, prestige, and conciseness.

Thirdly, while we adopt identical operational definitions with those used previously for Metcalf's and Kjellmer's models, we merely want to adjust the weightings. Throughout the factors, we observe the principle, similar to Kjellmer's idea, that zero is the neutral score for a word to survive, while positive scores mean a beneficial effect and negative scores mean a disadvantage. The weightings in the factors are discussed as following (except for the first two factors, the others are all yes/no questions): (1) Frequency: We adopt the three frequency levels as those in Metcalf's model, except that we change the weightings to -1, 0, and 1, the reason being that low frequency may be a disadvantage; (2) Productivity: We adopt the three levels as those in Metcalf's generation factor, except that we change the weightings to -1, 0, and 2. The weighting for high productivity is 2 because both Metcalf and Kjellmer take this concept into consideration and even assign high scores to related concepts (e.g., productive affixes); (3) Semantic Gaps: Instead of the original 1/-1 pair of scores, we change the weightings to 1/0, since we deem the filling up of a gap as beneficial but not being gap-filling should not be negative; (4) Transparency: We adopt the original 0/-1 pair of scores as in Kjellmer's model; (5) Endurance of Concept: Different from Metcalf's model, here we only adopt a dichotomy, i.e., a neutral zero for long-enduring concepts, and -1 for nonce forms or words pertaining to historical events; (6) Morphological Rule Observation/Gap Filling: The two factors are combined and assigned for a 1/0 pair of scores, the idea being consistent with that in semantic gaps; (7) Productive Affixes: The weightings are changed from 3/-1 to 2/-1, in consistency with the previous productivity condition's weightings and to maintain Kjellmer's original heavy weight for words with highly productive morphemes; (8) Agreement between Spelling and Pronunciation: The pair of scores is changed from Kjellmer's 0/-1 to 1/0, since in our observation, words pronounced differently from the norm (e.g., in Taiwanese pronunciation) would not take a disadvantage; (9) Prestige: Since, as noted before, prestige appears to have some effects on the words, we would currently adopt it but reduce the weightings from 2/0 to 1/0; and (10) Conciseness: Since we consider conciseness a normal situation, and not being concise a disadvantage, instead of the original 1/0, we adjust the weightings to 0/-1.[11]

The results of the modified model are shown following in Table 5. As can be seen in the table, we improved both the overall and survival prediction correctness to around 70 percent, although the correctness ratio of failure prediction is lower:

---

[11] For a summary of the ten factors, please refer to Appendix V.

Table 5. Correct Prediction Ratios in the Three Models

	Real Case	Metcalf		Kjellmer		Current Model	
Survival	53	29	54.72%	29	54.72%	39	73.58%
Failure	24	20	83.33%	17	70.83%	16	66.67%
Overall	77	49	63.64%	46	59.74%	55	71.43%

6. Concluding Remarks

By focusing on Chinese novel verbs that appeared around ten years ago, we evaluate two word adoption models in this study. In addition to the finding that the two perform similarly in predicting survival words and in overall accuracy, we suggest that borrowings may not take a disadvantage in Chinese, and that words that fill up semantic gaps would be potentially accepted into the vocabulary. We also propose a model that is specifically designed for the group of words, and by deleting inappropriate factors and adjusting the weighting in the factors, we attempt to elevate the ratio of accurate predictions. As the improved results would imply a need for re-evaluated factors and weightings for new words in different languages, we would suggest, for future study, a test for other combinations of factors and weightings as well as an investigation on novel nouns and sense-neologisms, which, as we hope, would facilitate our understanding of the underlying mechanism for sense-creating and extension as well the fascinating process of creation.

References

Ahrens, K. 1999. The Mutability of Noun and Verb Meaning. *Chinese Languages and Linguistics* V. Interactions in Language, Y. Yin, I. Yang, and H. Chan (eds.), pp. 335–548. Taipei. Academia Sinica.

Algeo, J., and Algeo, A. 1991. *Fifty Years among the New Words: A Dictionary of Neologisms, 1941–1991*. Cambridge: Cambridge University Press.

Chang, Y. J. 2008. On the Rise and Fall of Chinese Neologisms in the Last Decade. Paper presented at *The Second Conference on Language, Discourse, and Cognition* (CLDC-2). National Taiwan University, Taiwan. May 17–18.

Fischer, R. 1998. *Lexical Change in Present-Day English: A corpus-based study of the motivation, institutionalization, and productivity of creative neologisms*. Tübingen: Gunter Narr Verlag.

Hsu, F. h. 1999. 台灣當代國語新詞探微 *'Exploring the Contemporary Mandarin New Words in Taiwan.'* MA Thesis, National Taiwan Normal University.

Kjellmer, G. 2000. Potential Words. *Word* 51:205–28.

Klein, D. E., and Murphy, G. L. 2001. The representation of polysemous words. *Journal of Memory and Language* 45:259–82.

Metcalf, A. 2002. *Predicting New Words: the Mystery of Their Success.* Boston New York: Houghton Mifflin Company.

National Languages Committee, (國語會). 1998. 新詞語料彙編 *1 'Collection of Neologisms I.'* Taipei: Ministry of Education.

Rey, A. 1995. The Concept of neologism and the evolution of terminologies in individual languages. In *Essays on Terminology*. Amsterdam: John Benjamins.

Sabino, R. 2005. Survey Says . . . Gameday. *American Speech* 80:61–77.

Natural Language Generation of Museum Object Descriptions based on User Model

Hsiao Wei Chen, Mary Grace Lim, Patricia Bea Perez,
Joanna Patricia Reyes, and Nathalie Rose Lim

De La Salle University- Manila
{hsiao_wei_chen, mary_graces, lil_nawty_gurl13, snowdrop_106}@yahoo.com,
and limn@dlsu.edu.ph

Abstract. Natural Language Generation (NLG) techniques can be applied in generating virtual documents dynamically using information from a database (Dale et al, 1999). One of the applications of NLG techniques to generate documents dynamically is the web-based interactive virtual museum, VIGAN. NLG is used to generate the descriptions of the objects in a virtual museum dynamically based on the profile and interests of the visitor. The focus of the research is on incorporating user's interest, age group, and visit history in the generation of museum object descriptions. The descriptions do not vary only on user's profile but also in lexicalization. Facts are not only in describing the objects, but also in describing Ilocano personalities. User Acceptance Testing proved that object descriptions do vary based on age groups, category of interest, and lexicalization. They commented that the descriptions are easy to understand, the user interface is user friendly and the suggested objects are appropriate.

Keywords: Natural Language Generation, Dynamic User Modeling, Knowledge Representation, Virtual Museums

1. Introduction

With the emergence of the Internet, lack of information is no longer a major problem most users face. The vast amount of information available is overwhelming and it is important to hide information that is irrelevant to the users. One example that provides vast information to the people is museums. A museum is an institution providing services—acquiring, conserving, researching, communicating, and exhibiting objects for education and enjoyment (ICOM, 2001). Some museums are made available online through virtual museums so that more people can have access to the information provided by the museum.In order to improve the services that virtual museums provide, they should be able to determine which information is most relevant to a particular user and object information should be presented in such a way that the user can understand (Bandelli, 1999).

Similar to internet users, visitors of museums have different expectations, needs and behaviors, and it is important to address these differences. Ambeth Ocampo, a columnist at a notable Philippine newspaper, says that, "While I appreciate the educational task of museums, I would like to think that all our best efforts are still not enough to get the youth into museums and keep them returning... The problem lies not with a museum but a child's first encounter with it" (Ocampo, 2007). Ocampo also says that for many college students who had to endure a grade school trip to the museum, going there a second or third time is considered a cruel and unusual punishment. This mind-set is not the fault of the museum; it is the fault of the teacher or museum guide who did not infect the students with a sense of discovery and appreciation of our past. Thus, improving the encounter with a museum through a web-based interactive virtual museum that generates descriptions based on user profile is the motivation for this research.

The next section introduces the virtual museum we have created. Section 3 expounds more on the components of the virtual museum. In Section 4, we discuss how we modeled the user preference and how these are updated. Section 5 presents the rules created to generate the different types of description. Samples of generated descriptions based on user profile is also discussed in this section. In Section 6, we discuss the testing done for the system. Lastly, we give our conclusion and indicate some future work in Section 7.

2. Our Virtual Museum

We have chosen to create a virtual museum for three (3) well-known musuems in Vigan, Philippines, namely: Padre Jose Burgos Museum, Crisologo Museum and Syquia Museum. These musuems are quite small, but contain a substantial collection of objects that represent the culture of the Southern Ilocos Region. We call this interactive virtual museum VIGAN.

As VIGAN controls the amount of information generated depending on age group, the user is first asked to register upon first use of the virtual museum. Refer to Section 3 for a more detailed discussion on the information requested in the registration page. On succeeding sessions, the user is tasked to log in his user name and to choose which of the three-mentioned museums he wants to visit first. Once the user has chosen a particular museum, he has to choose a room from a list that is provided to him. After selecting a room, a 2D panoramic image of the actual museum is displayed. Hotspots in green represent another room to enter, while those in red represent objects. Clicking on the green hotspot will introduce the user to the next room with another 2D panoramic view consisting of one or more objects. On the other hand, clicking on the red hotspots indicates that the user wants to view the description for that particular object. Aside from generating the description of that object, each click on objects updates the user model. Updates in the user model involve increasing the weight of preference for that particular type of object, as well as storing the information that was already produced. Storing the information would allow the program to determine which new information can be given to the user, should he request for it. Moreover, storing the actual statements used will provide consistency in the generated text should the user choose to revisit the same object. The preference weight and the items that were visited is also used in producing a list of related objects that the user might be interested in viewing.

It should be noted that the 2D panoramic view is done via the Panorama Tool Viewer (PTViewer 2.8 of Senore, 2006). The pictures were personally taken by the researchers and the information stored in the database where from consultations with locals or the curators of the museums. The information stored in the database is called the Knowledge Base. The objects from the knowledge base are divided into four categories: customs, economic life, history and household items. Customs refer to rituals, practices, traditions and way of life of the Ilocanos, such as musical instruments used in traditional dances and way of life of the Syquia, Crisologo and Burgos families during the Spanish era. Economic life refers to how the Ilocanos made a living, such as cottage industries, farming, fishing, hunting. History refers to events and personalities that had happened in Ilocos that has historical importance. Household items refers to items that are seen at home, such as cooking and gardening equipments, paintings and antiques. The knowledge base is hand-constructed and contains keywords that will be used by the NLG to generate descriptions. The type and amount of information given to the user is analyzed from the information given by the curators and from the consultation with a psychologist. The generation of the descriptions in natural language is through SimpleNLG 3.5 (Reiter, 2007), but the various sentence structures for each type of description is defined by the researchers. The types of descriptions for the objects are in the form of messages. Aside from the name of the object, descriptions generated can be a combination of the following:

- `basicMsg(<noun>basic_name,<noun>basic_what-is,`
  `<adjective>basic_description)`
  The basicMsg includes the name of the object, what the object is and the description of the object. It is applicable to all object categories and subcategories.

- `purposeMsg(<verb>purpose_action,<noun>purpose_object)`
  The purposeMsg includes the name of the object, what the object is and the description of the object. It is applicable to all object categories and subcategories.

- `make-upMsg(<noun>make-up,<adjective>make-up_description,`
  `<noun>make-up_location,<noun>make-up_alternative-make-up)`
  The make-upMsg includes what the object is made up of, the description of the makeup of the object, where the makeup of the object is found, and alternative makeup of the object. It is applicable to the household item and economic item category. It is applicable to the some subcategories.

- `people-involvedMsg(<noun>people-involved_relation,<noun>people-`
  `involved)`
  The people-involvedMsg includes the people involved with the object and the relation of the people involved with the object. It is applicable to all categories and subcategories. For example, for the object bolo, the people-involvedMsg will be people-involvedMsg(<noun>owner, <noun>Elpidio Quirino).

- `akaMsg(<noun>aka)`
  The akaMsg includes what the object is also known as. It is applicable to all categories and subcategories.

- `used-inMsg(<noun>used-in)`
  The used-inMsg includes where the object is used in. It is applicable to household item, customs and economic item categories. It is also applicable to some subcategories.

- `consist-of(<noun>consist-of)`
  The consist-ofMsg includes what the object consists of, because some objects are made up of more than one parts. It is applicable to household item, customs and economic item categories. It is applicable to some subcategories:

- `personMsg(<noun>person_name,<noun>person_bdate,<noun>person_bplace`
  `,<noun>person_ddate,<noun>person_gender)`
  The personMsg includes the name of the person, his/her birth date birth place, death date and gender. It is applicable to the history category and the personality subcategory.

- `paintingMsg(<noun>painting_name,<noun>painting_theme,<adjective>`
  `painting_description, <noun>painting_age)`
  The paintingMsg includes the name, the theme, description and age of the painting. It is applicable to the household item category and art subcategory.

- `parentsMsg(<noun>parents_fathersName,<noun>parents_mothersName)`
  The parentsMsg includes the father's name and the mother's name. It is applicable to the history category and personality subcategory.

- `educationMsg(<noun>education_degree,<noun>education_year,`
  `<noun>education_school)`
  The educationMsg includes the degree, year and school. It is applicable to the history category and personality subcategory.

- `siblingMsg(<noun>sibling_siblingsName)`
  The siblingMsg includes the sibling's name. It is applicable to the history category and personality subcategory.

- `original-paintingMsg(<adjective>original-painting_description, <noun>original-painting_artist,<noun>original-painting_location)`
  The original-paintingMsg includes the description, artist and location of the original painting. It is applicable to the household item category and art subcategory.

- `sizeMsg(<noun>size_unit-of-measure, <noun>size_height, <noun>size_width)`
  The sizeMsg includes the unit of measure, height and width of the object. It is applicable to all categories and all subcategories.

- `award(<noun>award_ prize,<noun>award_ sponsor,<noun>award_ year)`
  The awardMsg includes the prize, sponsor and year of the award. It is applicable to the household item category and art and personality subcategory.

3. VIGAN's Architectural Design

The architecture of VIGAN can be seen in Figure 1. There are basically two (2) main processes in VIGAN: the Natural Language Generator (NLG) and the Virtual Environment (VE). These components access and update data from the databases User Model, Plan Library, Knowledge Base, Discourse History, Lexicon, and the text file Grammar.

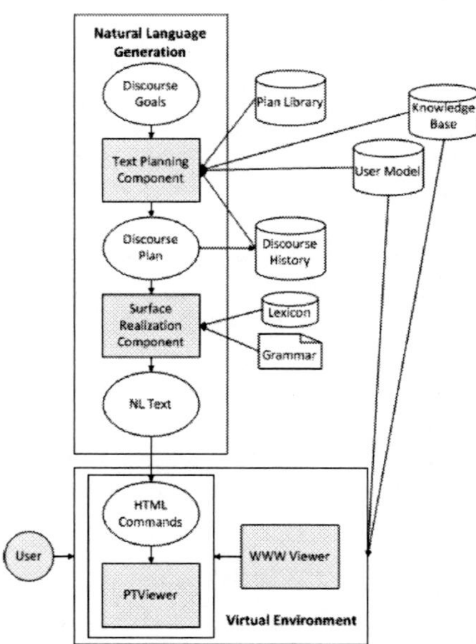

Figure 1: The Architecture of the VIGAN System

The user chooses an object from the 2D panoramic view of the museum in the Virtual Environment. The chosen object's identification number is then passed on to the NLG component where the object description will be generated.

The NLG component starts with the Discourse Goal, in order to provide a description for the selected object. The Discourse Goal is represented as the ID number of the object selected. Based on the Discourse Goal, the Text Planning component will decide which information will be included and how it will be ordered in text that will be generated. The Text Planning component will get the User Model (UM), which is used to tailor the description according to the user, Discourse History, a database that contains the facts about the objects that have been presented to the user, a message (1), which is a pre-configuration of domain elements grouped

```
basicMsg(name, what-is, description) (1)
```

in categories and arranged according to level of importance, from the Plan Library, and facts about the object stored in the database. The Text Planning component will decide based on the age group of the user (as obtained from the UM) how much information will be included. The UM is also used to make suggestion of objects more appropriate to the user. UM is a database which contains non-decision and decision properties. Non-decision properties about the user which includes username, password, name and gender are gathered from the user explicitly during registration. The user model is dynamic or always changing because new information about the user is gathered each time the user visits an object in the museum. The new information gathered as the session progresses are decision properties that will aid the system in generating descriptions for the objects in the museum. In VIGAN, decision properties are interest rating on each category of objects, importance rating on each available fact and age, because the amount of facts to be presented to the user for each description will depend on it.

The Text Planning component will fill in messages with information stored in the Knowledge Base, such as that message in (1) will be (2).

```
basicMsg(burnay, Ilocano earthen jar, null) (2)
```

Once the messages have been filled, it will include it in the Discourse Plan, which is an ordered and structured set of messages that will be included in the generated text. The Discourse Plan is passed to the Surface Realization component, and the facts used in the Discourse Plan are stored in the user's Discourse History so that the system will know which information has already been presented to the user to avoid redundancy for future presentation of object description.

VIGAN uses SimpleNLG (Reiter, 2007), a Java class library developed by the University of Aberdeen, which performs NLG lexicalisation and realisation, as its Surface Realization component. The Surface Realization component makes use of the Grammar and Lexicon to produce Natural Language expressions based on the Discourse Plan. For the Grammar, VIGAN uses a set of grammar rules used to form English sentences (see Example below).

Example of grammar rules for English language:

```
<Simple Sentence> = <Declarative Sentence>
<Declarative Sentence> = <subject> <predicate>
<subject> = <simple subject> | <compound subject>
<simple subject> = <noun phrase> | <nominative personal pronoun>
<noun phrase> = "the" <specific proper noun>
               | <proper noun>
               | <non-personal pronoun>
               | <article> [<adverb>* <adjective>] <noun>
               | [<adverb>* <adjective>] <noun-plural>
<noun> = <noun> [<prep phr>*]
```

The system reads the Grammar file using the bottom up approach, where it will start with filling the grammar rules at the bottom with facts, before working its way up. Grammar rules that have not been filled up will be removed, while grammar rules that have been filled will be used to generate the description. A message can be applied to more than one grammar rule. A message can result in more than one type of sentences. The selection of sentences to use for the description is done randomly.

VIGAN uses WordNet 2.0 (Miller, 2005) as its Lexicon, along with Java WordNet Library (JWNL), a Java API that is used to access WordNet. It will be used to map the messages in the Discourse Plan into words and phrases. Words and phrases that are used frequently in the sentence generation are stored in a Word Bank along with its senses, will be replaced with different lexicalizations, including incorporating synonyms, based on the senses automatically. The building of the Word Bank is done manually before runtime.

Natural Language (NL) Text will be the output of the Surface Realization component. The NL Text will be the description of the museum object selected by the user. The NL text will be passed to the WWW Viewer.

The WWW Viewer is the website which also links the user to the VE. It is in the VE that user can explore the virtual museum, select objects from the rooms in the virtual museum, and view descriptions of an object. Every time the user selects a uniqueobject, the user model is updated by increasing the interest rating of the user based on which category the object belongs to, refer to Section 4 for a more detailed discussion. For example, the user selects burnay which belongs to Household Items category, therefore the system will increase the percentage of the user's interest on household items. While exploring the virtual museum, WWW Viewer also suggest objects that might be of interest to the user by determining which category the user is most interested with and getting random objects with that category from the database.

4. User Modeling

User's preferences are modeled in the UM. Each user will have a rating of interest per category of object and rating of importance per facts. Interest rating is the rate of how interested the user is to each category of object (i.e., history, economic life, customs, household items). Interest rating of each category of object will initially be 0.0. During the sign-up phase, the users will be asked to select the categories of object that they are interested in. The rating of the categories is computed using (3). So when the user selects Household Items and Customs as his interests, then his initial interest rating will be 50.0/50.0/0.0/0.0 where the rating corresponds to Household Items, Customs, History, and Economics, respectively.

$$100/number\_of\_selected\_category \quad (3)$$

UM will also be updated whenever the user clicks on a new object and whenever the user clicks on "more information". The interest rating of each category will be updated using (4)

$$(number\_of\_clicks\_per\_category/total\_clicks) \ \text{x} \ 100 \quad (4)$$

where `total_clicks` is non-unique because it represent the total number of objects that the user clicks to view.

Importance rating per fact is the assumed rate of how important for the user to know the facts of objects. Facts of objects are the properties of objectives like description of the object, creator of the object, and the like. The text planning component will decide the information that will be included in the generated description through the rate of importance. The rating will be from 1 (lowest) to 5 (highest). The rating of a description will depend on the age group of the user where in a child is 6-16 years old and an adult is 17 years old and above. The facts that have higher rating will be presented to the user. For example, it is assumed that a twelve-year old user is not so interested in the creator of the painting therefore the fact creator will have a lower rating compared to other facts so that the generated description will not include the creator of the painting.

The database design of the user model is divided into two types, namely, user profile and user model. User profile stores the non-decision properties (i.e., name, password, etc.) while user model stores the decision properties (interest rating, importance rating, and age group) for each user.

5. Generation of Natural Language Descriptions based on Message Type

The Natural Language Generation will generate descriptions based on messages. Messages, as discussed in Section 3, are pre-configuration of domain elements grouped in categories and arranged according to level of importance. Messages are classified per category, similar to the category of objects, can have more than one category per message. For example, basic message, which include the name, brief description and what the object is, has 4 categories, because it is applicable to all objects, while painting message, which includes the title, artist, theme and description of the painting will only have one category, because it can only be applied to objects in the household item category.

   The Text Planning component will take all messages that are applicable to a selected object, including messages that are applicable to the category of the object.

   For example, for the object Burnay, the messages would incude: (1).

```
basicMsg(name, what-is, description)                        (1)
purposeMsg(action, object)
make-up(name, description, location, alternative)
akaMsg(aka)
related-itemMsg(name, description)
```

The messages will then be filled with facts about the object from the database. Some facts that are not available in the database will be set as null in the message. Some facts have multiple entries in the database, such as there are more than one purpose for the object Burnay, in this case, only the first entry will be filled in the message. The other entries will only be used if the user asks for more information.

   After the messages for the object Burnay have been filled, it would be (2).

```
basicMsg(burnay, Ilocano earthen jar, null)               (2)
purposeMsg(purify, bagoong)
make-up(red clay, seashores of Vigan, null)
akaMsg(tapayan)
related-itemMsg(null, null)
```

   Some messages, although applicable to the category of the object, may not have facts available in the database. These messages, such as the related-itemMsg in the example, will be removed. The other messages will be ordered according to level of importance, a static value that is based on how the facts included in the messages are presented in the descriptions obtained from curator and captions, and passed on to the Surface Realizer.

   VIGAN will tag each element in the message with its part of speech, for example, in basicMsg, burnay will be tagged as noun, while Ilocano earthen jar will be tagged as noun phrase. After tagging all the elements of a message, it will be passed to the grammar rules. Using the grammar rules, the noun 'burnay' will be tagged as subject, while the noun phrase Ilocano earthen jar will be tagged as predicate with the verb 'is'. The filled up grammar rule will then be passed to SimpleNLG, which will perform surface realization and then generate the description for the selected object. For the example, the basicMsg will produce the sentence: "Burnay is an Ilocano earthen jar."

   The process is similar for the rest of the messages.

   Words and phrases in the sentences can be changed if it has been used often, using the Lexicon, as discussed in Section 4. Also "burnay" can be alternated with its pronoun form.

   The description for the object burnay would be: (3)

```
Burnay is an Ilocano earthen jar. It is used for purifying bagoong.
It is made up of red clay form the seashores of Vigan. It is also
known as tapayan.
```

6. Testing Results

The system was tested using component testing and user acceptance testing.

For the Component testing, the functionality of the system was tested, particularly the internal processing, such as how data was passed from one module to another.

For the User Acceptance Testing, three approaches were used, namely the Reader-focused approach, Text-focused approach and Expert-Judgment approach.

The reader-focused approach was used to properly assess if the user interface is user friendly, the suggested objects are appropriate and descriptions are adequate and formed properly on the perspective of the users. The reader-focused approach was done by asking 20 users, 10 for each age group, to explore and rate the system. From a range of 1 to 5 (5 being the highest score), the average score for the user friendliness of the user interface is 4.7 for the child age group, while 4.3 for the adult age group. The average score for the grammar of the descriptions is 3.4 for the child age group, while 4.4 for the adult age group. This is because the child users explored the museum more and they tend to click on all the objects, even though some of the objects have limited descriptions. The average score for the structure of the descriptions is 4.3 for the child age group, while 3.8 for the adult age group, because some adult users think the sentences should be ordered differently. The average score for the appropriateness of the suggested objects is 5 for both age groups, because the system only suggests objects that are interesting to the users based on the user model. The average score for the descriptions being easy to understand is 4.8 for the child age group, while 4.9 for the adult age group. The average score for the descriptions being adequate is 4.1 for the child age group, while 4.8 for the adult age group. This is because the child users viewed some objects that had limited descriptions.

The text-focused approach was used to check if there is a variation in the descriptions generated for the different types of user age groups and interest. We forced different user types and generated descriptions for objects for each of the user types. We then compared the descriptions generated. Based on the test, we observed that the descriptions vary on number of facts and type of facts based on age group, type of facts based on the interest and words in the sentences based on lexicalization.

The expert-judgment-focused approach was used to assess the quality of the description generated. Linguist evaluation was conducted to assess the grammatical errors and paragraph structures. The feedback is that the sentences were too simple as to become repetitive. As the study does not yet cover difference in sentence structure depending on age group, the researchers made use of simple sentence structures so child users would also be able to understand the generated descriptions. Curator evaluation was also conducted to assess if the content of the description generated is sufficient. On this criterion, the curator commented that descriptions generated should also include some background information (e.g., significance of a particular artifact based on the owner or the era, etc.) to provide context. Since these details were not initially provided, the information were not encoded in the database. However, this can easily be remedied by populating the knowledge base.

7. Conclusion and Future Work

The system is able to generate different descriptions depending on user's age group and on user's preference.

Currently, the system stores the descriptions generated as part of the user model, thus making the database quite large, but it facilitates non-redundant generation of object descriptions if the object was viewed by the same user before. The researchers have considered storing the descriptions in a central database that is accessed depending on the user preference category to make the database smaller. However, this study aims to show that the system is able to generate different sentences for each type of object, at the same time keeping the generated description consistent per user.

The system is able to generate the object descriptions through the use of SimpleNLG. Although SimpleNLG is an existing system, grammar structure rules based on the English language and addtional rules had to be created to automatically feed the facts from the messages to the SimpleNLG.

The system is also able to add variations to the sentences produced by replacing commonly used words with its synonyms. The proponents created a Word Bank that contains the commonly used words along with their sense based on WordNet. The Word Bank was created manually. The system would access WordNet during runtime to replace commonly used words with their synonyms based on the sense of the word stored in Word Bank.

Currently, the system produces based on the sentences based on message types that are based on fact types. Another format can be recommended for the messages, such that it is not based on fact types, but generalized instead based on the structure of the sentence to be produced. For example, in the message, the first content is always the subject of the sentence, the second content is always the object, the third indirect object, and so on. Using this format, the facts can be mapped to the message based on its part of sentence. However, each type of facts should also include the part of sentence, such as subject and object; it will be used to map the facts to the message.

In the present system, it is only capable of producing simple sentences. In future, compound and complex sentences will also be included in the object descriptions so that sentences that are related can be combined and better structured. Also, to improve on the quality of the text in terms of coherence, Rhetorical Structure Theory, which is appropriate for multi-sentential and monologic texts, may be implemented. The sentence structures and lexical choices will also vary depending on age group.

The system built a Word Bank of frequently used words manually and accesses the synonyms of the words from the WordNet during runtime. In the improved system, the researchers may opt not to use a Word Bank, and instead will count the occurrences of the words included in the descriptions during run time to determine whether a word is to be replaced with its synonym or not. In doing so, word sense disambiguation would have to be done so that the words replaced would be appropriate.

In the future, it might be more feasible (in actual deployment) to do the generation of object descriptions offline, with an administrator verifying the generated descriptions, based on grammar, structure, lexicalization and context. This entails a minor adjustment in the current work and an incorporation of an interface for the administrator.

References

Bandelli, A. (1999). Virtual spaces and museums. *Journal of Museum Education*, 24 (1&2), pp. 20-26.

Dale, R., Green, S.J., Milosavljevic, M., and Paris, C. (1999) When virtual documents meet the real world. Proceedings of the Workshop on Virtual Documents, Hypertext Functionality and the Web, held in conjunction with the Eighth International World Wide Web Conference.

Dersch, H. (2001). *PTViewer Documentation*. Technical University Furtwangen. Retrieved March 22. 2008 from http://webuser.hs-furtwangen.de/~dersch/PTVJ/doc.html.

Finin, T. and R. Kass. (1988). Modeling the user in natural language systems. *Computational Linguistics* 4(3), pp. 5-22.

Fulvio, S. (2006). *PTViewer 2.8*. Retrieved March 22, 2008 from http://www.fsoft.it/panorama/ptviewer.htm.

International Council of Museums (ICOM). (2001). Development of the museum definition according to ICOM statues. Retrieved June 20, 2007, from http://icom.museum/hist_def_eng.html.

Miller, G. (2005). WordNet 2.0. Princeton University. Retrieved April 19, 2008 from http://wordnet.princeton.edu.

Mine, M. R. (1995). Virtual environment interaction techniques. UNC Chapel Hill Computer Science Technical Report, TR95-018.

Ocampo, A. (2007, April 13). Looking back museums. *Philippine Daily Inquirer*. Retrieved June 20, 2007, from http://opinion.inquirer.net/inquireropinion/columns/view_article.php?article_id=60116.

Reiter, E. (2007). SimpleNLG v3.5. University of Aberdeen. Retrieved April 19, 2008 from http://www.csd.abdn.ac.uk/~ereiter/simplenlg.

Sources of Individuation in Mandarin Chinese, a Classifier Language [*]

Pierina Cheung[a], Peggy Li[b], and David Barner[c]

[a]Department of Psychology, University of Toronto, 100 St. George Street, Toronto, ON M5S 3G3.
[b]Department of Psychology, Harvard University, 25 Francis Ave, Cambridge, MA 02138, USA.
[c]Department of Psychology, University of California, San Diego, 9500 Gilman Drive, La Jolla, CA 92093-0109

pierina.cheung@utoronto.ca, pegs@wjh.harvard.edu, barner@ucsd.edu

Abstract. When presented with an entity (e.g., a wooden honey-dipper) labeled with a novel noun, how does a listener know that the noun refers to an instance of an object kind (honey-dipper) rather than to a substance kind (wood)? While English speakers draw upon count-mass syntax for clues to the noun's meaning, linguists have proposed that classifier languages, which lack count-mass syntax, provide other syntactic cues. Three experiments tested Mandarin-speakers' sensitivity to the diminutive suffix *-zi* and the general classifier *ge* when interpreting novel nouns. Experiment 1 found that *-zi* occurs more frequently with nouns that denote object kinds. Experiment 2 demonstrated Mandarin-speaking adults' sensitivity to *ge* and *-zi* when inferring novel word meanings. Experiment 3 tested Mandarin three- to six-year-olds' sensitivity to *ge*. We discuss differences in the developmental course of these cues relative to cues in English, and the impact of this difference to children's understanding of individuation.

Keywords: individuation, numeral classifiers, Mandarin –zi morpheme, mass-count syntax.

1. Introduction

Language allows us to express different perspectives towards things in the world. For example, a single object, like a wooden table, can be described both as *a table* (i.e., a kind of object), and as *some wood* (i.e., a kind of material). The ways in which these perspectives are expressed, however, differs from language to language, leading some to claim that speakers of different language may *think* differently about objects in the world (Lucy, 1992; Imai & Gentner, 1997; Quine 1960). This paper contributes to this debate by probing the representation and development of syntactic cues to individuation in Mandarin Chinese.

In English, a distinction can be made between count nouns and mass nouns. Typically, words like *dog*, *table* and *idea* are used as count nouns, and refer to kinds of things that have "atomic structure", with "atoms" or "individuals" that come in natural units for counting. When hearing one of these words (e.g., *dogs*), we know that it refers to a quantity of discrete, naturally bounded individuals, and not some arbitrary portions thereof (e.g., pieces of dog). In contrast, mass syntax does not specify individuation (see Bloom 1994; Gordon 1988; Link 1983). Mass nouns can refer to unindividuated stuff like water, wood, and fun, or to sets of individuals like

---

[*] Thank you to Frankie Chen for his help with preparing the word list in Experiment 1. Thank you also to Becky Huang and Xiaowen Xu for their help with data collection in Taipei, Taiwan. We are grateful to the parents and children who participated, and to the daycares and preschools in Taipei for their support and help with recruitment. This work was supported by a Connaught Grant awarded to D.B.

22nd Pacific Asia Conference on Language, Information and Computation, pages 151–160

footware, furniture, and ammunition. Ususally, words used in mass syntax do not refer to individuals. In English count nouns can occur directly with numerals (e.g., *one dog*), in singular or plural forms (*a dog*, *some dogs*), or with quasi-cardinal determiners (*these dogs*) that signal reference to sets of individuals. Mass nouns, in contrast, usually[1] cannot be used directly with numerals, with singular or plural morphology, or with quasi-cardinal determiners. Also, mass and count constructions selectively specify different quantifiers (many/*much table vs. *many wood/much wood).

Not all languages, however, have such transparent syntactic cues to individuation. In classifier languages like Chinese and Japanese, there is no mass-count distinction at the level of the noun, regardless of what the noun refers to. Instead, nouns in classifier languages syntactically resemble mass nouns in English. For example, in Mandarin Chinese, nouns cannot co-occur directly with numerals, but require a discretizing unit (i.e., a "classifier") for counting, like English mass nouns (e.g. two *pieces* of toast). Classifiers encode information such as the shape, animacy, functionality, or the unit of measure of the referent noun. For example, to label *three pens* in Mandarin requires both the numeral *san* (three) and the classifier *zhi* (stick) as in *san zhi bi* (or "three stick pen"). Also, unlike English count nouns, which obligatorily specify number via singular-plural marking (e.g., *a cat* vs. *some cats*), classifier languages normally lack obligatory plural marking. As a result, bare nouns in classifier languages are unspecified for number. If a classifier language has a plural marker, its use is often optional, infrequent, and restricted (e.g., to animates). Finally, nouns in classifier languages, irrespective of whether they denote countable individuals or unindividuated stuff, typically permit the same quantifiers.[2]

If count syntax specifies individuation in English, are there equivalent syntactic structures to encode individuation in languages that lack a mass-count distinction? According to Cheng and Sybesma (1998, 1999) Mandarin Chinese may make an analogous distinction at the level of the classifier. They argue that Mandarin features two types of classifier, which they call "count classifiers" and "mass classifiers". Count classifiers form a closed-class and mark reference to individuals, whereas mass classifiers form an open-class and function as measure words that are used to denote portions of unindividuated stuff (e.g., a cup of sugar) or portions of objects (e.g., a cup of marbles).

To test the hypothesis that classifiers are semantically analogous to mass-count syntax, Li, Barner and Huang (in press) examined how Mandarin speakers interpret them in a word extension task. Typically, when speakers of English learn new count nouns (e.g., "*Look, this is a wug*"), they assume that these words refer to kinds of objects that share a common form. When they learn mass nouns ("*Look, this is some wug*"), in contrast, they are less likely to assume that the word denotes a solid thing. Based on this, Li et al asked if Mandarin speakers would extend count classifiers, like *gen* (rod) and *pian* (slice) to solid things with matching shape (e.g., rod shapes or slice shapes), and whether they would do so less for mass classifiers like *dui* (pile) and *tuan* (wad). When asked to find "one CL something" (CL = classifier) among several choices, adults selected solid, shape-matched objects when presented count classifiers, but rejected things that were non-solid or that didn't match in shape. However, this distinction was less available to young children, who were willing at age four to accept portions of non-solid stuff when the experimenter requested something with a count classifier, so long as the substance matched the shape specified by the classifier (e.g., toothpaste that was shaped like a rod when the experimenter asked for *gen*). It was not until approximately six years of age that children

---

[1] The mass-count status of some words is fixed by the type of thing that they denote. However, many nouns can also be used flexibly in either mass or count frames (e.g., "some beer"; "three beers", etc.).

[2] The fact that nouns in classifier languages pattern syntactically like mass nouns in English, has led some researchers to propose that nouns in classifier languages do not provide criteria for individuation unless explicitly accompanied by a classifier. There are reasons to believe this proposal is incorrect. Several studies now show that nouns in all languages are broadly alike -- they all have nouns that provide criteria for individuations as well as ones that do not (see Doetjes, 1997; Barner and Snedeker, 2005, 2006; Inagaki and Barner, in press; Li, Dunham and Carey, in press). In fact, most Japanese nouns, like English nouns, name object kinds (Colunga and Smith, 2005; Barner, Inagaki and Li, under review).

began to extend classifiers like adults. Li and colleagues concluded that, before 6 years of age, most Mandarin-speaking children still have not learned that count classifiers are cues to individuation. As a result, syntactic cues to individuation may emerge much later in Mandarin than in English

One problem in comparing classifiers to count syntax is that whereas count syntax specifies only individuation, classifiers also encode item-specific conceptual information, such as the shape, animacy, etc. Classifiers may emerge later in Mandarin acquisition in part because they pose a more difficult learning problem. In the present studies, we explored this question by testing children and adults with the generic or default classifier *ge* rather than on shape-based classifiers tested in Li et al's study. *Ge* is by far the most frequent count classifier in the language. As it provides no shape information, it may function mainly to encode individuation. Therefore, we might expect children to learn the role of this classifier in individuation earlier.

In addition to *ge*, we also tested Mandarin speakers' sensitivity to another potential source to individuation – the diminutive suffix *-zi* (Doetjes, 1997; Sybesma, 2007). Linguists have noted that in several languages diminutive markers function much like unitizers in making mass nouns into count nouns (Wiltschko, 2006). Historically, *-zi*, (meaning "son" or "child") functioned as a diminutive marker in Chinese. However, simplification of the phonological system in the language during the Han Dynasty, and a movement away from monosyllabic nouns led to the adaptation of *-zi* as an ending for many nouns (Li & Thompson, 1981). In contemporary Mandarin it is debateable whether the suffix is still productive (Nishimoto, 2003). When asked about the function of *-zi*, native speakers are often unable to state its contribution to the meaning of the noun. Nonetheless, linguists have observed that many nouns used with *-zi* often refer to "concrete, non-abstract things, that can be counted individually" (Dragunov, 1960, p. 81; Sybesma, 2007). It is possible that speakers of Mandarin are implicitly sensitive to this property of *-zi* and that *-zi* could function as a cue to individuation. However, no experiments have ever examined *-zi* and its relation to object individuation. We, therefore, included *-zi* in our study and compared it to the general classifier *ge*, in the domain of word learning.

The present study investigated whether the general classifier *ge* and the diminutive suffix *-zi* are cues to individuation in Mandarin-speaking children and adults. Experiment 1 tested the hypothesis that *-zi* tends to occur with nouns that denote discrete individuals by asking whether this relation held true for the 256 most frequent nouns in Mandarin child-directed speech. Experiment 2 then examined how adult speakers interpret both *-zi* and *ge* by contrasting them with bare nouns in two word learning tasks. Experiment 3 extended Experiment 2 by testing Mandarin-speaking children's developing comprehension of the classifier *ge*, in order to establish the role of classifiers in children's emerging understanding of individuation.

2. Experiment 1

The first experiment tested whether the diminutive suffix *-zi* is more likely to be used with nouns that refer to object kinds than with nouns that refer to substance kinds. One group of native Mandarin speakers judged whether nouns referred to a kind of object, a kind of substance, both, or neither. A second group rated whether these same nouns could be used with the *-zi* suffix. We asked whether words that were categorized as object nouns were more likely to be acceptable with *-zi* than substance nouns.

2.1.Methods

2.1.1. Participants

Participants were 52 native Mandarin speakers (mean age: 25.9 years old) recruited from student and staff populations in National Taiwan Normal University, in Taipei, Taiwan. Participants were randomly assigned to one of two noun judgment tasks; 27 performed the object-substance categorization task and 25 participated in the zi-rating task.

2.1.2. Stimuli and Procedure

The 256 most frequent nouns were taken from a list provided by Sandhofer, Smith, and Luo (2000), who culled 50 transcripts in CHILDES of Mandarin child-directed speech. The following nouns were excluded: proper nouns, pronouns, and compound nouns. Reduplicated forms of nouns (e.g., *go3-go3* or 'dog-dog') were changed to non-reduplicated (e.g., *go3* or 'dog') forms. Nouns that had *-zi* endings (66 of them) were stripped of the ending.

The list of 256 words was randomly divided into two lists of 128 words each (List A and List B), which were assigned to participants between subjects. To verify that no sytematic difference existed between groups, ten words from each list were randomly selected and added to the other list so that each list had 138 words, with 20 words overlapping between the two lists.

Object-Substance Categorization. Fourteen participants were assigned to List A and 13 participants to List B. For each list, they were randomly assigned to one of two randomized orders. Participants were asked to rate whether each of 138 words referred to an object (*wu4ti3*), substance (*wu4zhi3*), both, or neither. If they selected neither, they were asked to describe in writing what kind of entity the noun could denote.

-Zi Rating. Thirteen participants were assigned to List A and 12 participants to List B. They were asked to rate how likely *-zi* could be affixed to each word, using a scale of 1 to 7 (1 being highly acceptable and 7 being highly unacceptable).

2.2. Results

2.2.1. Object-Substance Categorization.

Words were assigned to a category (object, substance, both, or neither) if at least 66.7% of participants provided the same judgment. Words that received less than 66.7% agreement were categorized as "unclassified".

Comparing the 20 overlapping words of the two lists, participants showed remarkable agreement in their object-substance categorization: 19 of the 20 overlapping words received the same classification. The only exception was *bei4* (which means quilt/blanket in English): participants of List B categorized it as "object", whereas those of List A did not reach a 2/3 agreement and it was thus "unclassified" (50% of the participants rated it as "object").

Of the 256 words, 130 words (50.8%) were categorized object words, 20 were categorized as substance words (7.8%), 0 as both, and 21 nouns as neither (8.2%). A remaining 85 nouns were unclassified (33.2%).

2.2.2. -Zi Rating.

The average *-zi* rating, out of a total score of 7, was calculated for each word. First we verified whether participants were providing sensible ratings. Of the 66 nouns that originally had a *-zi* ending, the average rating was 1.5, suggesting participants highly agreed that the words should be affixed with *-zi* and that their performance was consistent with how *-zi* is used in everyday speech. The average ratings for the 20 overlapping words of the two lists were also highly correlated (Pearson's $r = .90, p < .001$).

To examine the relation between object ratings and *-zi* ratings, we compared the two rating tasks. Words that were rated as object kinds received the lowest average *-zi* rating (2.87), meaning that participants found it highly acceptable to suffix *-zi* to the given noun. Likewise, words that were rated as substance kinds received the highest average *-zi* rating (6.03), meaning that participants found substance nouns highly unacceptable with the *-zi* suffix. The *-zi* ratings of the object noun category differed significantly from the ratings of the substance nouns ($t(148) = -6.43, p < 0.0001$) and the neither object nor substance nouns ($t(149) = -5.32, p < 0.0001$).

An alternative way to compare the two tasks is to first classify the noun as to whether it takes *-zi* as an ending. Given that words that naturally occur with the *-zi* suffix received a score of 1.5, we used an average score of 2 or less as the cut-off criterion. We then ask the following question: Are nouns that have a *-zi* ending more likely to name a kind of object rather than a kind of substance? Indeed, as indicated in Table 1, words that are compatible with *-zi* tend to be nouns that have object kind meanings (N = 75) but not substance kind meanings (N = 0). Interestingly, it should also be noted that having the *-zi* suffix does not provide a necessary condition for a word to refer to object kinds. Out of all nouns that are categorized as words that refer to object (N = 130), participants rated 42.3% of them as less likely to accept *-zi* as a suffix. As compared to singular-plural morphology in English, which is obligatory for all count nouns, *-zi* is a linguistic device that only applies to a subset of count nouns.

Table 1: Number of words in each category based on –zi ratings (> or <= 2)

	Object	substance	both	neither	unclassified
zi highly acceptable (rating <= 2)	75	0	0	2	24
zi less acceptable (rating > 2)	55	20	0	19	61

2.3.Discussion

Experiment 2 revealed two main findings. First, the object-substance categorization task found that many Mandarin nouns denote object kinds, consistent with what is typically found for mass-count languages such as English (Samuelson and Smith, 1999).

Second, the two rating tasks showed that when a word refers to an object, it is more likely to take *-zi* as a suffix, and substance words never take a *-zi* ending. These results support the contention that *-zi* specifies individuation in Mandarin Chinese.

3. Experiment 2

As shown in Experiment 1, words that take the diminutive suffix *-zi* are more likely to refer to object kinds. Experiment 2 examined Mandarin-speaking adults' sensitivity to such linguistic devices as a source of individuation by using two tasks: the word extension task (Imai and Gentner, 1997; Soja, Carey and Spelke, 1991) and the quantity judgment task (Barner and Snedeker, 2005; Gathercole, 1985).

In a standard word extension task, participants are first shown a standard item (e.g., a cork pyramid) labeled with a novel word (*blicket*) and then two alternatives: a shape matched object (e.g., metal pyramid), and a material matched object (e.g., cork square). Participants are then asked to extend the word to one of the two choices, indicating whether they think the noun refers to a kind of object (shape choice) or a kind of material (material choice).

In a quantity judgment task, two characters are shown: one of them with the standard item and the other with a larger number of identical objects that are smaller, and thus have a lesser combined mass or volume than the standard. Participants are asked to decide which of two characters has more (e.g., three tiny cork pyramids vs. one large cork pyramid), indicating whether the noun refers to a kind of individual (choice by number) or a kind of material (choice by mass or volume).

We asked whether novel words that are used with a general classifier *ge* or with *-zi* are more likely to be extended by shape in the word extension task and more likely to be quantified by number in the quantity judgment task, when compared to bare nouns.

3.1.Methods

3.1.1. Participants

Adult participants were 48 Mandarin-English bilingual speakers (mean age: 19.7 years old) recruited from the University of Toronto's Psychology subject pool. The participants were all native Mandarin speakers, and the whole experiment was conducted in Mandarin. Participants were randomly assigned to one of three conditions, with sixteen participants per condition: bare noun, classifier *ge*, and the diminutive *-zi* condition.

3.1.2. Stimuli and Procedure

Six sets of stimuli were hand-crafted, one for each trial. They were simple-shape solid objects that were designed to be unrecognizable as known artifacts or substance. At the beginning of each trial set in each condition, there was a familiarization phase in which the participant was introduced to a standard object that was named four times with a novel term (e.g., *fen2yan2* in the bare noun condition, *yi2 ge4 fen2yan2* in the classifier condition, *fen2yan2 zi* in the diminutive condition). They were then presented with either a block of word extension trials or a block of quantity judgment trials, with block order counterbalanced across participants .

For word extension, participants were shown a shape alternative (that matched in shape but not in substance) and a substance alternative (that matched in substance but not in shape). In the bare noun condition, participants were asked to "Point to blicket" (Mandarin: *qing2 ni3 zhi3 zhe fen2yan2.*). In the classifier condition, the 'numeral + general classifier' combination was used to describe the novel object: "Point to one-CL blicket" (Mandarin: *qing2 ni3 zhi3 zhe yi2 ge4 fen2yan2*), whereas in the diminutive condition, *-zi* was suffixed at the end of each novel word: "Point to blicket-zi" (Mandarin: *qing2 ni3 zhi3 zhe fen2yan2 zi*). The side of the shape alternative was counterbalanced across trials.

For quantity judgment, two characters (Farmer Tom and Captain Peter) were shown. One character had two standard items, and the other had four miniature versions of the item. Participants were asked to judge which character has more of the object named by the novel term. In the bare noun condition, they were given the following instructions: "Farmer Tom has blicket. Captain Peter has blicket. Who has more blicket?" (Mandarin: *nong2 fu1 tang1 mu3 you3 fen2yan2, jiang1 jun1 bi3 de2 ye3 you3 fen2yan2, shei2 you3 bi3 jiao4 duo1 fen2yan2?*). In the classifier condition, the general classifier *ge* was included only in the test question: "Who has more CL-blicket?" (Mandarin: *shei2 you3 bi2 jiao3 duo2 ge fen2yan2*). In the diminutive condition, *-zi* was suffixed at the end of each novel word (Mandarin: *nong2 fu1 tang1mu3 you3 fen2yan2 zi, jiang1jun1 bi3 de2 ye3 you3 fen2yan2 zi, shei2 you3 bi3 jiao4 duo1 fen2yan2 zi?*).

3.2.Results

For word extension, the dependent variable was the percentage of trials in which participants extended a novel word on the basis of shape. Data were submitted to an ANOVA for word extension with three between-subject variables: condition (bare noun vs. classifier vs. diminutive), block order (word extension first vs. quantity judgment first), and item order (order 1 vs. order 2). A parallel ANOVA was conducted for quantity judgment with the percentage of trials in which participants chose the array with the greater number of objects as the dependent variable.

Figure 1 presented data for both word extension and quantity judgment. For word extension, there was a significant main effect of condition ($F(1,36) = 135.69$, $p < 0.038$). No other significant main effects or interaction was found. There was no significant difference in percentage of shape judgments between the classifier condition and the diminutive suffix condition (64.6% vs. 64.6%; $t(30) = 0$, $p = 1.000$). Mandarin-speaking adults extended words on the basis of shape significantly more in both the classifier condition (64.6%; $t(30) = 2.46$, $p < 0.020$) and the diminutive suffix condition (64.6%; $t(30) = 2.35$, $p < 0.026$) than in the bare noun condition (37.5%).

Results from quantity judgment showed a similar pattern: there was a significant main effect of condition ($F(1,36) = 93.85$, $p < 0.021$). There was no significant difference in percentage of number judgments between the classifier condition and the diminutive suffix condition (60.4% vs. 71.9%; $t(30) = 0.84$, $p < 0.408$). Mandarin-speaking adults quantified significantly more by number in both the classifier condition (60.4%; $t(30) = 2.23$, $p < 0.033$) and the diminutive suffix condition (71.9%; $t(30) = 2.99$, $p < 0.005$) than in the bare noun condition (29.2%).

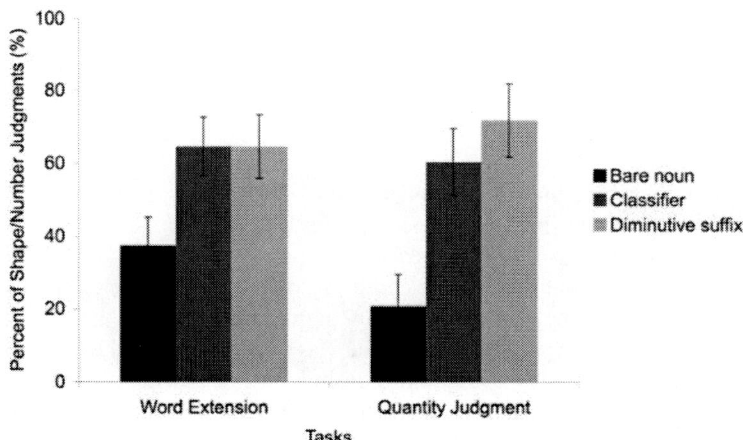

Figure 1: Mandarin speaking adults' performance on word extension and quantity judgment in bare noun, classifier, and diminutive suffix conditions.

3.3. Discussion

Two results emerged from this experiment. First, as predicted, we found that adults were more likely to extend novel words based on shape and quantified them by number when the words were accompanied by the general classifier *ge*. This supports the view proposed by Cheng and Sybesma (1998, 1999) that mass/count distinction in English appears in Mandarin Chinese on the classifier level. Second, we showed that not only does classifier mark individuation, results from word extension and quantity judgment demostrated that adults were also sensitive to the diminutive suffix *-zi* as a cue for novel word learning, suggesting that different languages have their own systems of individuation: Mandarin Chinese provides other syntactic cues (e.g., *ge* and *-zi*) to substitute for mass-count syntax.

4. Experiment 3

The second experiment indicated that adults were aware of the role of the general classifier *ge* as a means to encode shape and to individuate objects. In this last experiment, we explored the developmental trajectory of such sensitivity in Mandarin-speaking children. Studies have generally found that children starting as young as age of 2 1/2 begin to produce classifiers and reach adult understanding at the age of 6 of 7 (e.g., Chien, Lust and Chiang, 2003; Erbaugh, 1986). Thus, using the word extension task, we tested four groups of children between the ages of three and six, and compared their performance to the results obtained from adults in Experiment 2. We only conducted word extension with children, since pilot work with eight five-year-old Mandarin-speaking children indicated a strong bias to base quantification on number (100% of the time) in the bare noun condition in quantity judgment; this suggests the task may not be an appropriate measure of sensitivity to syntactic cues with children.

4.1. Methods

4.1.1. Participants

Child participants were all native speakers of Mandarin, including 31 3-year-olds (mean age: 3;6; range: 3;1-3;11), 32 4-year-olds (mean age: 4;6; range: 4;1-4;12), 32 5-year-olds (mean age: 5;7; range: 5;0-6;0), and 31 6-year-olds (mean age: 6;7; range: 6;1-6;10) recruited from seven daycares and preschools in Taipei, Taiwan.

4.1.2. Stimuli and Procedure

Children were randomly assigned to one of two conditions (bare noun and classifier), and were tested on the word extension task only. The stimuli and procedure were identical to Experiment 2.

4.2.   Results

For children's performance on word extension, an ANOVA was submitted with three between-subject variables: condition (bare noun vs. classifier), item order (order 1 vs. order 2) and age group (3-year-olds vs. 4-year-olds vs. 5-year-olds vs. 6-year-olds).

There was a significant main effect of condition on word extension ($F(1,110) = 638.7$, $p < 0.058$) for children as a group, and a marginally significant effect of age group ($p < 0.062$) and item order ($p < 0.058$). No significant difference was found between the two conditions for each of the four age groups, suggesting that children may not be sensitive to the use of the general classifier to individuate entities. However, the difference in percentage of shape judgments between the bare noun and classifier conditions became gradually bigger from 3-year-olds (3.19%) to 6-year-olds (20.0%; see Figure 2). Compared to a difference of 27.1% found in adults, our current data clearly show a developmental progression and suggest that when children become older, they are more likely to show sensitivity to the classifier *ge* as a cue for individuation.

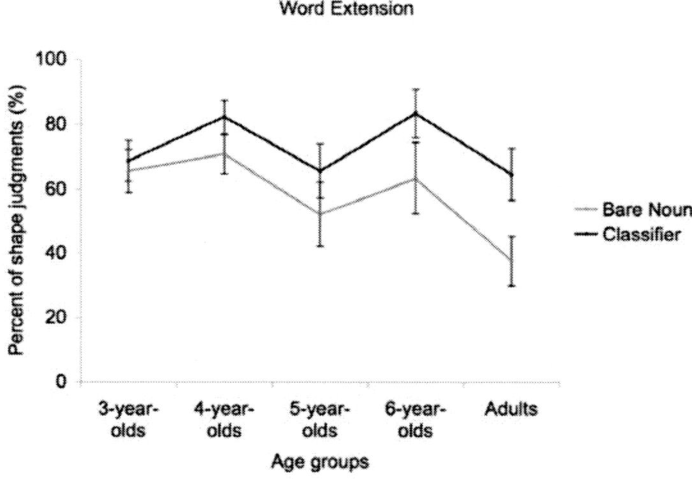

Figure 2: Percentage of judgments based on shape for the bare noun and classifier conditions in Mandarin-speaking 3-, 4-, 5-, 6-year olds and adults.

4.3.Discussion

Experiment 3 examined the developmental progression of Mandarin-speaing children in their sensitivity to using the general classifier *ge* as a cue to individuation. Surprisingly, even 6-year-olds did not possess adult's degree of sensitivity to ge, although previous research has found that *ge* is only used for concrete entities and is the first classifier children acquire (see Chien et al., 2003; Yamamoto, 2005 for reviews), Therefore, even though Mandarin may encode the mass-count distinction at the level of the classifier, the acquisition progression is by far slower than English children acquiring mass-count syntax. As Li et al (in press) proposed, one contributor for the delay may simply be the fact that the frequency of classifier syntax in Mandarin Chinese is far less frequent than that of count syntax in English. Importantly, our data reflect that the sensitivity to syntactic cues to individuation gradually develops.

5.   Conclusion

The current study tests the parallels between Mandarin and English systems of individuation and examines whether morphosyntactic devices such as *ge* and *-zi* in Mandarin Chinese provide cues to individuation as count syntax in English. Experiment 1 aimed at verifying claims raised by previous researchers regarding the function of the diminiutive suffix *-zi*, and how it was related to object individuation. We found that adults were more likely to suffix *-zi* to a noun if it was categorized as an "object". We also found, in Experiment 2, that adults were sensitive to using both syntactic cues, *ge* and *-zi* to encode individuation in learning novel words. Results from word extension and quantity judgment provided strong support for this claim. Our next question is: when does this knowledge that classifiers encode individuation develop in children? Experiment 3 examined this question by testing 3-year-olds to 6-year-olds using word extension and found that even 6-year-olds did not posses adults' sensitivity to ge. However, our results also showed that as children grew older, the gap of their perfomance between bare noun and classifier conditions became bigger, suggesting that the development of sensitivity is relatively gradual.

On one hand, results from all three experiments strongly supported the claim that Mandarin speakers have a distinct linguistic system in acquiring individuation. Classifiers and the diminutive suffix in Mandarin Chinese function in much the same way as count syntax in English, and as suggested in Li et al (in press), count classifiers (e.g., *ge*, *tiao*, *tou*) alone may provide such support. On the other hand, results obtained from Mandarin-speaking children suggested that the distinct syntactic system of individuation may be qualitatively different from mass-count syntax in English. Barner and Snedeker (2005) found that English-speaking 4 year olds based their quantity judgments on number when words were presented in count syntax. Our finding that even Mandarin-speaking children 6 year olds did not possess adults' sensitivity suggested that classifier is a relatively complex linguistic structure. It entails more specific information about the referents than what mass count syntax provides in English. Thus, it seems likely that although classifiers provide cues to individuation, Mandarin-speaking children may take a longer time to understand individuation than their English peers acquiring mass-count syntax.

Future studies could examine why the acquisition of the role of classifiers in encoding individuation is more protracted than that of mass-count syntax. A comparison of *-zi*, which is present in many nouns and required even when not enumerating, to *ge* may yield some insights into the rate of acquisition of the various linguistic structures. Additionally, it is worth examining whether the presence of these syntactic devices could shift meanings of known nouns (e.g., whether the addition of *-zi* to a substance denoting noun could create object-denoting nouns – a recent one in Mandarin is *dian4* = electricity, and *dian4zi* = electron). Finally, these methodologies could be adapted to (1) examine how lexical items interact with syntax to generate meaning across several languages, (2) characterize whether the various languages could express the same conceptual content despite structural differences, and (3) conduct cross-linguistic studies to compare the developmental course of how children acquire these language-specific syntactic structures.

6. References

Barner, D., S. Inagaki and P. Li. Under review. Language, thought, and real nouns.

Barner, D. and J. Snedeker. 2005. Quantity judgments and individuation: Evidence that mass nouns count. *Cognition, 97*, 41–46.

Barner, D. and J. Snedeker . 2006. Children's early understanding of mass–count syntax: Individuation, lexical content, and the number asymmetry hypothesis. *Language Learning and Development, 2*, 163–194.

Bloom, P. 1994. Semantic competence as an explanation for some transitions in language development. In Y. Levy ed., *Other children, other languages: Theoretical issues in language development.* Hillsdale, NJ: Erlbaum.

Cheng, L. L.-S. and R. Sybesma. 1998. Classifiers and massifiers. *Tsing-Hua Journal of Chinese Studies, New Series XXVIII, 3*, 395-412.

Cheng, L. L.-S. and R. Sybesma. 1999. Bare and not-so-bare nouns and the structure of NP. *Linguistic Inquiry, 30*, 509-542.

Chien, Y-C., B. Lust and C-P. Chiang. 2003. Chinese children's comprehension of countclassifiers and mass-classifiers. *Journal of East Asian Linguistics, 12,* 91–120.

Colunga, E and L. B. Smith. 2003. The emergence of abstract ideas: Evidence from networks and babies. In L. Saitta ed., *Philosophical Transactions by the Royal Society B. Theme Issue: 'The abstraction paths: fro experience to concept'*, pp. 1205- 1214.

Doetjes, J. 1997. *Quantifiers and selection: On the distribution of quantifying expressions in French, Dutch and English.* Ph. D. thesis, Leiden University, HAG, The Hague.

Dragunov, A. A. 1960. *Untersuchungen zur Grammatik der modernen Chinesischen Sprarache* [orig. 1952, in Russian; tr. Wolfgang Lippert]. Berlin: Akademie-Verlag.

Erbaugh, M. 1986. Taking stock: The development of Chinese noun classifiers historically and in young children. In C. Craig ed., *Noun Classes and Categorization*, pp. 399-436. Amsterdam/ Philadelphia: John Benjamins.

Gathercole, V. C. 1985. 'He has too much hard questions': The acquisition of the linguistic mass-count distinction in much and many. *Journal of child Language, 12*, 395-415.

Gordon, P. 1988. Count/mass category acquisition: Distributional distinctions in children's speech. *Journal of Child Language, 15*(1), 109-128.

Imai, M. and D. Gentner. 1997. A cross-linguistic study on early word meaning. Universal ontology and linguistic influence. *Cognition, 62*, 169–200.

Inagaki, S. and D. Barner. In press. Countability in absence of count syntax: Evidence from Japanese quantity judgments. In M. Hirakawa, S. Inagaki,Y. Hirakawa,H. Sirai,S. Arita,H. Morikawa,M. Nakayama and J.Tsubakita eds., *Studies in Language Sciences (8): Papers from the Eighth Annual Conference of the Japanese Society for Language Sciences*. Tokyo: Kurosio.

Li, P., D. Barner and B. Huang. In press. Classifiers as count syntax: Individuation and measurement in the acquisition of Mandarin Chinese. *Language Learning and Development.*

Li, C. and S. A. Thompson 1981. Mandarin Chinese: A Functional Reference Grammar. Berkeley, CA: University of California Press.

Li, P., Y. Dunham and S. Carey. In press. Of substance: The nature of language effects on entity construal. *Cognitive Psychology.*

Link, G. 1983. The logical analysis of plurals and mass terms: A lattice-theoretical approach. In R. Bauerle, C. Schwarze, A. Stechow eds., *Meaning, use, and interpretation of language.* Berlin: de Gruyter.

Lucy, J. 1992. *Grammatical Categories and Cognition.* Glasgow, Scotland: Cambridge University Press.

Nishimoto, E. 2003. Measuring and comparing the productivity of Mandarin Chinese suffixes. *Journal of Computational Linguistics and Chinese Language Processing, 8* (1), 49–76.

Quine, W. V. O. 1960. *Word and object.* Cambridge, MA: MIT Press.

Samuelson, L and L. Smith. 1999. Early noun vocabularies: Do ontology, category structure and syntax correspond? *Cognition, 73*, 1-33.

Sandhofer, C., L. Smith and J. Luo. 2000. Counting nouns and verbs in the input: Differential frequencies, different kinds of learning? *Journal of Child Language, 27*, 561-585.

Soja, N. N., S. Carey and E. Spelke. 1991. Ontological categories guide young children's inductions of word meaning: Object terms and substance terms. *Cognition, 38*, 179–211

Sybesma, R.P.E. 2007. 北方方言和粤语中名词的可数标记 Běifāng fāngyán hé Yuèyǔ zhōng míngcí de kěshùbiāojì (Markers of countability on the noun in Mandarin and Cantonese). *Yǔyánxué lùncōng, 35*, 234-245.

Wiltschko, M. 2006. *Why should diminutives count? Organizing Grammar. Linguistic Studies in Honor of Henk van Riemsdijk.* Berlin: Walter de Gryter.

Yamamoto, K. 2005. *The acquisition of numeral classifiers: The case of Japanese children.* Berlin: Mouton de Gruyter.

How to Overcome the Domain Barriers in Pattern-Based Machine Translation System[*]

Sung-Kwon Choi[a], Ki-Young Lee[a], Yoon-Hyung Roh[a],
Oh-Woog Kwon[a], and Young-Gil Kim[a]

[a]Natural Language Processing Team, Electronics and Telecommunications Research Institute,
161 Gajeong-dong, Youseong-gu, Daejon, Korea
{choisk, leeky, yhroh, ohwoog, kimyk}@etri.re.kr

Abstract. One of difficult issues in pattern-based machine translation system is maybe to find how to overcome the domain difference in adapting a system from one domain to other domain. This paper describes how we have resolved such barriers among domains as default target word of any domain, domain-specific patterns, and domain adaptation of engine modules in pattern-based machine translation system, especially English-Korean pattern-based machine translation system. For this, we will discuss two types of customization methods which mean a method adapting an existing system to new domain. One is the pure customization method introduced for patent machine translation system in 2006 and another is the upgraded customization method applied to scientific paper machine translation system in 2007. By introducing an upgraded customization method, we could implement a practical machine translation system for scientific paper translation within 8 months, in comparison with the patent machine translation system that was completed even in 24 months by the pure customization method. The translation accuracy of scientific paper machine translation system also rose 77.25% to 81.10% in spite of short term of 8 months.

Keywords: Customization, Machine Translation, Pattern-based MT, Scientific Paper MT.

1. Introduction

The use of on-line systems is the biggest growth area in the use of machine translation. People are translating web pages or very large documents by using machine translation system as the solution, as human translation of pages which need to be continually updated or are very large scale is not feasible (Mellebeek et.al., 2005).

Electronics and Telecommunications Research Institute (ETRI, henceforth) in Korea has developed the web-based English-Korean machine translation system till 2004, under assumption that as the size of patterns grows, the performance of the system can be incrementally improved (Hong et. al., 2003). During 2 years (2005- 2006) it implemented an English-Korean patent machine translation system on the basis of the web-based English-Korean machine translation system. The English-Korean patent machine translation system was installed in International Patent Assistance Center (IPAC, henceforth) under Ministry of

---

[*] This work was supported by the IT R&D program of MKE/IITA, Domain Customization Machine Translation Technology Development for Korean, Chinese, and English.

Commerce, Industry and Energy in Korea and provides the patent attorneys and the patent examiners with the on-line English-Korean machine translation service for electro-electric patent documents (http://www.ipac.or.kr) because it helped them understand the existing English patent documents easier and more rapidly (Choi et. al., 2007).

It was due to the customization method (Kwon et. al., 2007) that we could change successfully an existing machine translation system from general domain to patent domain. Figure 1 shows us an example of patent machine translation service at IPAC.

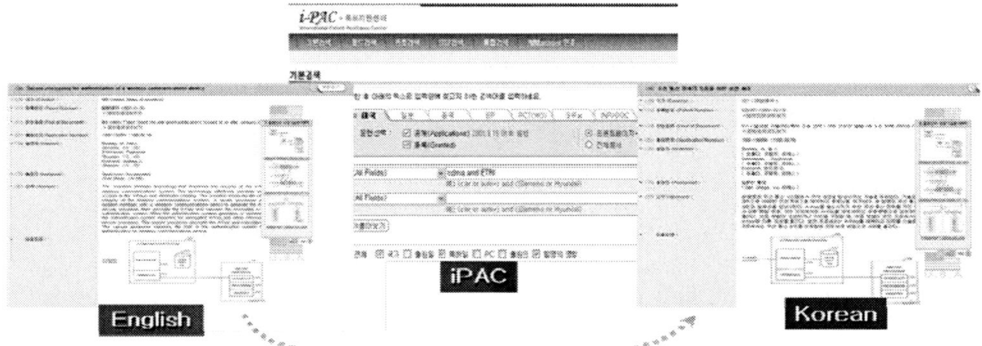

Figure 1: An Example of Patent Machine Translation Service at IPAC

ETRI had upgraded the customization method applied to the English-Korean patent machine translation system since 2007 and completed the practical level of English-Korean scientific paper machine translation system within 8 months. The English-Korean machine translation service for scientific paper translation is expected to be launched for students since September, 2008.

This paper describes how we have resolved such barriers among domains as default target word of any domain, domain-specific patterns, and domain adaptation of engine modules in pattern-based machine translation system, especially English-Korean patterns-based machine translation system. Especially, we will describe a difference between the pure customization method for patent machine translation system and the upgraded customization method applied to scientific paper machine translation system.

The construction of this paper is as follows: in section 2 the pure customization method will be sketched and its experiment will be showed. The limits of the pure customization method will be uncovered in the section 3. To deal with the problems found in the experiment, an upgraded customization method will be proposed in the section 4. In section 5 another experiment will be conducted to evaluate the proposed method. The discussion of the previous sections will be summarized in the concluding section 6.

2. Pure Customization Method

2.1. Customization Steps

As mentioned before, a domain customization method means a method adapting an existing system to new domain. The pure customization method was designed in the course of changing the web-based English-Korean machine transaltion system with general domain into the domain-specific English-Korean machine translation system such as patent domain. It was basically dependent on an idea of Zajac R. (2003) consisting of following steps:

Step 1. Collecting a large scale of domain-specific documents
Step 2. Linguistically studying about characteristics of the collected documents
Step 3. Automatically extracting unknown words and semi-automatically constructing their equivalent words

Step 4. Manually constructing domain-specific translation patterns
Step 5. Customizing the translation engine modules of the existing MT system
Step 6. Human evaluation of translation quality

2.2. Experiment 1

To assess the feasibility of pure customization method, we conducted an experiment. The goal of the experiment was to see how much improvement of translation accuracy can be achieved before and after applying the pure customization method to the web-based machine translation system. Following table shows changes of accuracy before and after applying pure customization steps.

Table 1: Before and after applying pure customization method.

Steps	Item	Before	After	Reference
Step 3	Number of terms	836,000	2,052,604	up 1,216,604 for 13 months
Step 4	Number of patterns	39,127	50,214	up 11,087 for 18 months
Step 5	Accuracy of tagging	95.85%	99.62%	
	Accuracy of parsing	69.00%	85.00%	
	Accuracy of target word selection (noun)	71.70%	92.40%	
Step 6	Translation quality	54.25%	82.20%	

3. Problems of Pure Customization Method

We tried to analyze the automatic translation results of scientific paper translated by patent machine translation system to find the problems of the pure customization method. We evaluated 200 blind test sentences of scientific paper with the patent machine translation system. The average length of the sentences was 21.69 words. The translations were evaluated by 3 translators with the scoring scale from 0 (no translation) to 4 (perfect translation) point. The result was as follows:

Table 2: Error Analysis of Translation Result of Scientific Paper by Patent MT System

Item		Number of Errors	%
Translation Engine	Tagging	10	6.10%
	Parsing	28	17.07%
	Target Word Selection	3	1.83%
	Generation	15	9.15%
Translation Knowledge	Dictionary entries	77	46.95%
	Patterns	23	14.02%
etc		8	4.88%
Total		164	100.00%
Translation Accuracy			78.63%

Table 2 shows that errors of dictionary entries amount to 46.95% and errors of patterns cover 14.02%. That is, 60.97% of total translation errors are caused by translation knowledge.

This means that the extraction of unknown dictionary entries and unknown patterns as well as the adaptation of existing dictionary entries and patterns to new domain are very important to tune the existing machine translation system to new domain. It would be first problem of the pure customization method not to have the step such as the tuning of existing dictionary entries (Ayan et. al., 2003) and the corpus-assisted expansion of existing patterns (Yamada et. al., 2002).

The second problem of pure customization method is that it has no step of automatic tuning for existing translation engine modules. We corrected the existing system modules such as tagger, parser, transfer and generator whenever we found their errors. Its problem was to spend a long tuning time. Therefore, we needed a new step for semi-automatic tuning of translation engine modules to cut tuning time.

Finally, the weakness of pure customization method was related to only human evaluation for translation assessment. To reduce the expenses and much time, we added an automatic evaluation like BLEU (Papineni et.al., 2002) to the human evaluation.

4. Upgraded Customization Method

To resolve the problems mentioned in above section, we introduce new steps and propose the new process as upgraded customization method as follows:

Step 1. Collecting a large scale of domain-specific documents
Step 2. Linguistically studying about characteristics of the collected documents
Step 3. Automatically extracting unknown words and semi-automatically constructing their equivalent words
Step 4. Semi-automatic tuning of existing terminology
Step 5. Semi-automatic constructing domain-specific translation patterns
Step 6. Semi-automatic customization of the translation engine modules based on answer set
Step 7. Human evaluation and automatic evaluation of translation accuracy

4.1. Overall Customization Flow

The Figure 2 illustrates the overall customization flow.

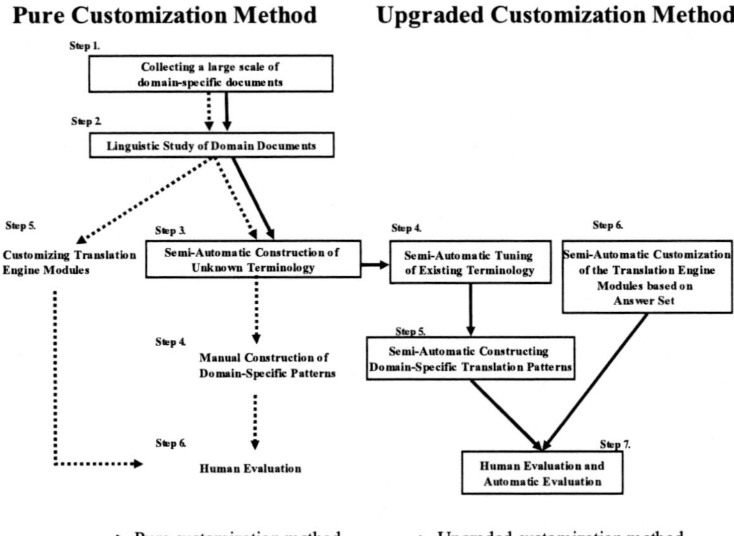

Figure 2: Pure Customization Method vs. Upgraded Customization Method

4.2. Semi-Automatic Tuning of Existing Terminology

We performed the domain tuning for target words of noun, verb and adjective terms adapted to patent domain by using English-Korean comparable corpus. In case of adapting English-Korean bilingual terms to technical document domain, we didn't define the categories. We extracted English ambiguous words with high frequency in the technical document corpus, and then we sorted their Korean equivalents with Korean word frequency extracted from Korean technical document corpus. Next, human translator selected dominant Korean word from the sorted Korean word list.

For the ambiguous English words which couldn't be resolved by dominant Korean word of translation dictionary, we made a target word selection module using context knowledge constructed from corpus. We extracted context information from English-Korean comparable corpus. The context information was converted to sense vectors. The sense means Korean translation word for the ambiguous English word. The sense vectors were used to disambiguate the possible senses of ambiguous English words (Lee et al., 2006). Sense vector is defined by the following formula:

$$SV = \left(w(c_1), w(c_2), w(c_3), ..., w(c_n) \right) \tag{1}$$

where $w(c_k)$ is a weighting function for co-occurring word c_k. And $w(c_k)$ can be calculated by the following formula:

$$w(c_k) = \Pr\left(s = s_i \middle| w = c_k \right) \tag{2}$$

where s_i is an i-th sense (a group of target words sharing same semantic code) of source word. When $w(c_k)$ is 1, it means that if co-occurring word c_k appears with ambiguous word, the probability that the sense of ambiguous word will be s_i is 1.

In the test phase, the test vector for ambiguous word in input sentence is constructed and has same dimension as the sense vector of the corresponding ambiguous word. The elements of test vector are 0 or 1, where 0 indicates that corresponding co-occurring word c_k does not appear in the input sentence and 1 represents that corresponding co-occurring word c_k appears in the input sentence. The similarity between test vector constructed from input sentence and each sense vector of the ambiguous word is calculated using following formula:

$$sim(v, w) = \frac{\sum_{i=1}^{N} v_i w_i}{\sqrt{\sum_{i=1}^{N} v_i^2 \sum_{i=1}^{N} w_i^2}} \tag{3}$$

4.3. Semi-Automatic Construction of Domain-Specific Patterns

Domain-specific patterns are one of factors to make a translation quality higher. The construction of the unknown domain-specific patterns for scientific papers was performed by automatically extracting the domain-specific patterns from tagged corpus of large scientific papers and manually building theirs target patterns.

Figure 3 outlines the method of automatically extracting the domain-specific patterns from scientific papers.

1. make large raw corpus of scientific papers their tagged corpus.
2. extract from the tagged corpus the following pattern candidates:
   - fixed part-of-speech patterns (e.g. COMMA_CONJUNCTION_PRONOUN_VERB_COMMA such as ",as you know,") or
   - meaningful patterns between boundary conditions (e.g. starting with preposition, verb, and conjunction, and ending with preposition, verb, conjunction, noun, verb, auxiliary verb, and number such as "in reference with", "compared with").

> 3. filter pattern candidates such as 'preposition preposition', 'preposition noun', and 'noun of' (e.g. "in on", "for it", "term of").
> 4. count the number of each lexical pattern candidate.
> 5. conduct a base NP chunking for the lexical pattern candidates (ex. "accuse him of" -> "accuse NP of")
> 6. subtract a frequency of long pattern from a frequency of its short pattern to delete unnecessary short patterns (e.g. 1,050 "in spite" − 1,000 "in spite of").
> 7. order patterns according to frequency
>   (e.g. 115334 <I3> in_order_to, 67935 <P4> it_be_shown_that, 61882 <I3> with_respect_to, 60860 <V2> apply[VN]_to, 59730 <V3> paly_NP_in, 53573 <J2> consistent_with)

Figure 3: Method of automatically extracting the domain-specific patterns from scientific papers

4.4. Semi-Automatically Customizing Translation Engine Modules Based on Answer Set

Answer set is a morphologically and syntactically tagged corpus of 5,000 sentences that two human lexicographers constructed. From the answer set we collected the correct answers of morphologically or syntactically ambiguities. On the basis of them, the English part-of-speech tagger and parser were able to be checked automatically.

For customization of the morphological tagger we have first collected the tagging errors with morphological ambiguities of scientific papers that occur frequently. Then the tagging errors were corrected manually if they were matched with the corresponding parts of the answer set. For example, a word with '-ing' can be a noun (NN) or a gerund (VBG). We could find that the par-of-speech of the word with a form '-ing' became noun (NN) or adjective (JJ) before lexical words 'system' and 'method'.

The semi-automatic customization of parser could be achieved by semi-automatically controlling the probabilistic weight of parsing rules including the different attachment ambiguities, such as infinitive phrase attachment and prepositional phrase attachment.

5. Experiment 2

In this section our concern was to see how much the translation accuracy can be enhanced by introducing an upgraded customization method in the place of a pure customization method. To find out this, we evaluated 400 blind test sentences for human evaluation and 1,000 sentences with 5 references for automatic evaluation. The translations for human evaluation were scored at the same manner described in the section 3. In the first experiment described in the section 3, the 616 patterns increased every month, while about 4,000 patterns are growing every month due to a step 'semi-automatic construction of domain-specific patterns' in upgraded customization method. After introducing an upgraded customization method, the translation accuracy by human evaluation improved from 77.25% to 81.10% in spite of short term of 8 months. As well, the morphological BLEU score also rose from 0.4946 to 0.5185.

Table 3: Translation Accuracy of Pure and Upgraded Customization Method

Steps	Item	Pure Customization Method	Upgraded Customization Method	Reference
Step 3	Number of terms	2,052,604	2,510,496	up 457,892 for 5 months

Step 5	Number of patterns	50,214	74,337	up 24,123 for 6 months
Step 6	Accuracy of tagging	99.20%	99.27%	
	Accuracy of parsing	72.00%	82.00%	Up 10.00%
	Accuracy of target word selection (noun)	79.00%	87.75%	
Step 7	Human evaluation	77.25%	81.10%	
	Automatic evaluation (Morphological BLEU)	0.4946	0.5185	

6. Conclusion

In this paper we elaborated on the limits and potentials of pure customization method and introduced an upgraded customization method including some of steps of pure customization method. The pure customization method suffers from manually increasing domain-specific dictionary entries and patterns, while the upgraded customization method is oriented at semi-automatic construction of them. By introducing an upgraded customization method, we could implement a practical machine translation system for scientific paper translation within 8 months. The translation accuracy amounts to 81.10%.

We launched a pilot service named "iMT (interactive Machine Translation)" from September 2007 using English-Korean technical document MT system. The pilot service provides Korean-English technical document translation service and English-Korean technical document translation service to users. The English-Korean technical document MT service automatically translates the English PDF file to Korean text as shown in Figure 4. In Figure 4, the service extracts only text fields (right top window of the Figure 4) from the user's PDF file (left window of Figure 4), next translate into Korean text (right bottom window of Figure 4). In the pilot service, about 50 users among total 2,055 users translate nearly 300 English articles a day. Through the pilot service, we transferred the technology to a machine translation related company at January 2008, and the service will be commercialized at the end of 2008.

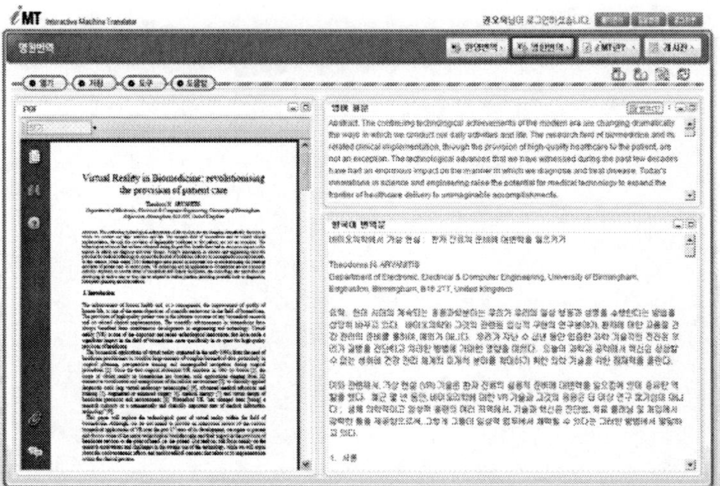

Figure 4: An Example of Machine Translation Service for English-Korean Scientific Paper Translation

In the near future, we are planned to add a new item for customization like a natural generation based on statistical post-editing (Dugast et.al., 2007) to the upgraded customization method.

References

Ayan, N.F., B.J. Dorr and O. Kolak. 2003. Domain Tuning of Bilingual Lexicons for MT. *CS-TR-4449, UMIACS-TR-2003-19, LAMP-TR-096.*

Choi, S.K., O.W. Kwon, K.Y. Lee, Y.H. Roh and Y.G. Kim. 2007. Customizing an English-Korean Machine Translation System for Patent Translation. *The 21st Pacific Asia Conference on Language, Information and Computation (PACLIC 21)*, pp. 105-114.

Dugast L., J. Senellart and P. Koehn. 2007. Statistical Post-Editing on SYSTRAN's Rule-Based Translation System. *In Proceedings of the Second Workshop on Statistical Machine Translation.* pp.220-223.

Hong, M.P., K.Y. Lee., Y.H. Roh, S.K. Choi and S.K. Park. 2003. Sentence Pattern-based MT revisited. *In Proceedings of 20st International Conference Computer Processing of Oriental Languages (ICCPOL '03).* pp. 1-7.

Kwon, O.W., S.K. Choi, K.Y. Lee, Y.H. Roh and Y.G. Kim. 2007. English-Korean Patent Translation System: FromTo-EK/PAT. *MT Summit XI Workshop on Patent Translation,* pp.1-8.

Lee K.Y., S.K. Park and H.W. Kim. 2006. A Method for English-Korean Target Word Selection Using Multiple Knowledge Sources. *IEICE TRANS. FUNDAMENTALS,* Vol.E89-A, No.6.

Mellebeek B., A. Khasin, J.V. Genabith and A. Way. 2005. TransBooster: Boosting the Performance of Wide-Coverage Machine Translation Systems. *EMAT 2005 Conference Proceedings.* pp.189-197.

Papineni, K., S. Roukos, T. Ward and W.J. Zhu. 2002. BLEU: a Method for Automatic Evaluation of Machine Translation. *In Proceedings of the 40th Annual Meeting of the Association for Computational Linguistics (ACL)*, Philadelphia, USA, pp.311-318.

Yamada S., K. Imamura and K. Yamamoto. 2002. Corpus-Assisted Expansion of Manual MT Knowledge. *In Proceedings of the 9th International Conference on Theoretical and Methodological Issues in Machine Translation (TMI 2002).* pp.199-208.

Zajac R. 2003. MT Customziation. *Machine Translation Summit Workshop.*

Multi-Engine Approach for Named Entity Recognition in Bengali[*]

Asif Ekbal [a], and Sivaji Bandyopadhyay [a]

[a]Department of Computer Science and Enginneering, Jadavpur University, Kolkata-700032, India
asif.ekbal@gmail.com and sivaji_cse_ju@yahoo.com

Abstract. This paper reports about a multi-engine approach for the development of a NER system in Bengali by combining the classifiers such as Maximum Entropy (ME), Conditional Random Field (CRF) and Support Vector Machine (SVM) with the help of weighted voting approach. The training set consists of approximately 272K wordforms, out of which 150K wordforms have been manually annotated with the four major named entity (NE) tags such as *Person*, *Location*, *Organization* and *Miscellaneous* tags. An appropriate tag conversion routine has been defined in order to convert the 122K wordforms of the IJCNLP-08 NER shared task[1], into the desired forms. The classifiers make use of the different contextual information of the words along with the variety of features that are helpful in predicting the various NE classes. Lexical context patterns, which are generated from an unlabeled corpus of 3 million wordforms in a semi-automatic way, have been used as the features of the classifiers in order to improve their performance. In addition, we have developed a number of techniques to post-process the output of each of the classifiers in order to reduce the errors and to improve the performance. Finally, we have applied weighted voting approach to combine the systems. Results show the effectiveness of the proposed approach with the overall average recall, precision, and f-score values of 93.98%, 90.63%, and 92.28%, respectively, which shows an improvement of 14.92% in f-score over the best performing *baseline* SVM based system and an improvement of 18.36% in f-score over the least performing *baseline* ME based system. The proposed system also outperforms the other existing Bengali NER system.

Keywords: Named Entity Recognition, Maximum Entropy, Conditional Random Field, Support Vector Machine, Weighted Voting, Bengali

1. Introduction

Named Entity Recognition (NER) is an important tool in almost all Natural Language Processing (NLP) application areas including machine translation, question answering, information retrieval, information extraction, automatic summarization etc. The current trend in NER is to use the machine-learning (ML) approach, which is more attractive in that it is trainable and adoptable and the maintenance of a ML based system is much cheaper than that of a rule-based one. The representative ML approaches used in NER are Hidden Markov Model (HMM) (BBN's IdentiFinder in (Bikel, 1999)), ME (New York University's MENE in (Borthwick, 1999)), CRFs (Lafferty et al., 2001) and SVM (Yamada et al., 2002). The process of stacking and voting method for combining strong classifiers like boosting, SVM and TBL, on NER task can be found in (Wu et al., 2003). Florian et al. (2003) tested different methods for combining the results of four systems and found that robust risk minimization worked best. The work reported in this paper differs from the existing works in the sense that here, we have conducted a number of experiments to improve the performance of the classifiers with the lexical context patterns, which are generated in a semi-automatic way from an unlabeled corpus of 3 million wordforms, and used several post-processing techniques to improve the performance of each classifier before applying weighted voting.

Named Entity (NE) identification in Indian languages in general and in Bengali in particular is difficult and challenging as:

- Unlike English and most of the European languages, Bengali lacks capitalization information, which plays a very important role in identifying NEs.

---

[*] This work is partially supported by the CLIA Project, funded by DIT, MCIT, Govt. of India, Vide Sanction letter no-14 (5)/2006- HCC (TDIL)/29.08.2006.

[1]http://ltrc.iiit.ac.in/ner-ssea-08

- Indian person names are more diverse and a lot of these words can be found in the dictionary with specific meanings.
- Bengali is a highly inflectional language providing one of the richest and most challenging sets of linguistic and statistical features resulting in long and complex wordforms.
- Bengali is a relatively free order language.
- Bengali, like other Indian languages, is a resource poor language - annotated corpora, name dictionaries, good morphological analyzers, Part of Speech (POS) taggers etc. are not yet available in the required measure.
- Although Indian languages have a very old and rich literary history, technological developments are of recent origin.
- Web sources for name lists are available in English, but such lists are not available in Bengali forcing the use of transliteration.

A pattern directed shallow parsing approach for NER in Bengali is reported in Ekbal and Bandyopadhyay (2007a). A HMM based NER system for Bengali has been reported in Ekbal et al. (2007b), where additional contextual information has been considered during emission probabilities and NE suffixes are kept for handling the unknown words. More recently, the related works in this area can be found in Ekbal et al. (2008a), Ekbal and Bandyopadhyay (2008b) with the CRF, and SVM approach, respectively. Other than Bengali, the works on Hindi can be found in Li and McCallum (2004) with CRF and Cucerzan and Yarowsky (1999) with a language independent method. As part of the IJCNLP-08 NER shared task, various works of NER in Indian languages using various approaches can be found in IJCNLP-08 NER Shared Task on South and South East Asian Languages (NERSSEAL)[2].

2. Named Entity Recognition in Bengali

Bengali is the seventh popular language in the world, second in India and the national language of Bangladesh. We have used a Bengali news corpus (Ekbal and Bandyopadhyay, 2008c), developed from the web-archive of a widely read Bengali newspaper for NER. Out of 34 million wordforms of this corpus, 200K wordforms have been manually annotated with the four NE tags namely, *Person, Location, Organization* and *Miscellaneous*. The annotation was carried out by a technical person and edited by a linguist. The data has been collected from the International, National, State and Sports domains. We have also used the annotated corpus of 122K wordforms, collected from the IJCNLP-08 NERSSEAL (http://ltrc.iiit.ac.in/ner-ssea-08). This data was a mixed one and dealt mainly with the literature, agriculture and scientific domains. Moreover, this data was originally annotated with a fine-grained NE tagset of twelve tags. We have defined an appropriate tag conversion routine in order to convert this data into the forms tagged with the four NE tags. The tagset mapping table is shown in Table 1.

Table 1: Tagset mapping table

IJCNLP-08 tagset	Our tagset	Meaning
NEP	*Person*	Single/multiword person name
NEL	*Location*	Single/multiword location name
NEO	*Organization*	Single/multiword organization name
NEA, NEN, NEM, NETI	*Miscellaneous*	Single/multiword miscellaneous name
NED, NEB, NETP, NETE, NETO	NNE	Other than NEs

In order to properly denote the boundaries of NEs, the four NE tags are further divided into the forms:
B-XXX: Beginning of a multiword NE, I-XXX: Internal of a multiword NE consisting of more than two words, E-XXX: End of a multiword NE, XXX→PER/LOC/ORG/MISC. For example,

---

[2] http://ltrc.iiit.ac.in/ner-ssea-08/proc/index.html

the name *sachin ramesh tendulkar* is tagged as *sachin*/B-PER *ramesh*/I-PER *tendulkar*/E-PER. The single word NE is tagged as, PER: Person name, LOC: Location name, ORG: Organization name and MISC: Miscellaneous name. In the output, sixteen NE tags are mapped to the four NE tags with some simple rules.

2.1. Approaches of NER in Bengali

NLP research around the world has taken giant leaps in the last decade with the advent of effective machine learning algorithms and the creation of large annotated corpora for various languages. However, annotated corpora and other lexical resources have started appearing only very recently in India.

In this paper, we have used ME, CRF and SVM frameworks in order to identify NEs from a Bengali text and to classify them into *Person, Location, Organization* and *Miscellaneous*. We have developed two different systems with the SVM model, one using **forward parsing** that parses from left to right and other using **backward parsing** that parses from right to left. Lexical patterns, generated from an unlabeled corpus of 3 million wordforms, have been used to improve the performance of each of the classifiers. In addition, a number of post-processing techniques have been adopted in order to improve the performance of the classifiers. Finally, the classifiers are combined together with the three different weighted voting schemes.

We have used the C++ based ME package (http://homepages.inf.ed.ac.uk/s0450736/software/maxent/maxent-20061005.tar.bz2) and C++ based CRF++ package (http://crfpp.sourceforge.net) for NER. The SVM system has been developed based on (Jochims, 1999; Valdimir, 1995), which perform classification by constructing an N-dimensional hyperplane that optimally separates data into two categories. We have used *YamCha* toolkit (http://chasen-org/~taku/software/yamcha), an SVM based tool for detecting classes in documents and formulating the NER task as a sequential labeling problem. Here, the *pair wise* multi-class decision method and *polynomial kernel function* have been used. We have used TinySVM-0.07 (http://cl.aist-nara.ac.jp/~taku-ku/software/TinySVM) classifier that seems to be the best optimized among publicly available SVM toolkits.

2.2. Named Entity Features

•Context words: Preceding and following words of a particular word. This is based on the observation that the surrounding words are very effective in the identification of NEs.

•Word suffix and prefix: Word suffix and prefix information are helpful to identify NEs. A fixed length (say, *n*) word suffix/prefix of the current and/or the surrounding word(s) can be treated as feature(s). If the length of the corresponding word is less than or equal to *n-1* then the feature values are not defined and denoted by ND. The feature value is also not defined (ND) if the token itself is a punctuation symbol or contains any special symbol or digit. Another way to use the suffix information is to modify the feature as binary valued. Variable length suffixes of a word can be matched with predefined lists of useful suffixes (e.g., *-babu, -da, -di* etc. for persons and *-land, -pur, -lia* etc. for locations). These features are useful to handle the highly inflective Indian languages as like Bengali.

•Named Entity Information (dynamic feature): NE tag(s) of the previous word(s).

•First word (binary valued): Current token is the first word of the sentence or not. First word is most likely a NE.

•Length of the word (binary valued): Length of the token is less than three or not. This is based on the observation that very short words are rarely NEs.

•Infrequent word (binary valued): A cut off frequency has been chosen in order to consider the infrequent words in the training corpus. Frequently occurring words are rarely NEs.

•Digit features: Several digit features have been considered depending upon the presence and/or the number of digit(s) in a token. These binary valued features are helpful in recognizing miscellaneous NEs such as time, monetary and date expressions, percentages, numerical numbers etc.

•Position of the word (binary valued): Position of the word in a sentence is a good indicator of NEs. Generally, verbs occur at the last position of the sentence. This feature is used to check whether the word is the last word in the sentence.

•Part of Speech (POS) Information: We have used a CRF-based POS tagger (Ekbal et al., 2007c) that was originally developed with the 26 POS tags, defined for the Indian languages. For SVM based systems, we have used this POS tagger. However, for CRF and ME models, we have considered a coarse-grained POS tagset that has the following tags: Nominal, PREP (Postpositions) and Other. Postpositions are considered as these often appear after the NEs.

•Gazetteer Lists: Gazetteer lists, developed from the news corpus (Ekbal and Bandyopadhyay, 2008c), have been used as the features in each of the classifiers. These features can improve the performance of the classifiers when used as the features or used to post-process the outputs. Any particular gazetteer does not include the ambiguous entries, i.e., those that can appear in more than one gazetteer list. If the current token is in a particular list, then the corresponding feature is set to 1 for the current and/or the surrounding word(s); otherwise, it is set to 0. Following is the list of gazetteers along with the number of entries:

 (1). Organization clue word (e.g., *kong, limited* etc): 94, Person prefixes (e.g., *sriman, sreemati* etc.): 245, Middle names: 1,491, Surnames: 5,288, Common location (e.g., *sarani, road* etc.): 547, Action verb (e.g., *balen, ballen* etc.): 241, Function words: 743, Designation words (e.g., *neta, sangsad* etc.): 947, First names: 72,206, Location names: 7,870, Organization names: 2,225, Month name (English and Bengali calendars): 24, Weekdays (English and Bengali calendars): 14

 (2). Common word (521 entries): Most of the Indian language NEs appears in the dictionary with some other valid meanings. For example, the word *kamol* may be the name of a person but also appears in the dictionary with another meaning *lotus*, the name of a flower; the word *dhar* may be a verb or also can be the part of a person name. We have manually prepared a list, containing the words that can be NEs as well as valid dictionary words.

 (3). Lexicon (128,000 entries): We have used a lexicon that has been developed from the Bengali news corpus in an unsupervised way. The feature 'LEX' has value 0 for those words that appear in the lexicon; otherwise, the value is 1. This feature has been included as the words that appear in the lexicon are rarely NEs.

3. Unsupervised Lexical Pattern Learning from the Unlabeled Corpus

We have developed a method to generate the lexical context patterns from a portion of the unlabeled Bengali news corpus (Ekbal and Bandyopadhyay, 2008c) containing 3 million wordforms. Given a small seed examples and an unlabeled corpus, the algorithm can generate the lexical context patterns in a bootstrapping manner. The seed name serves as a *positive example* for its own NE class, *negative example* for other NE classes and *error example* for non-NEs.

(1). **Seed list preparation:** We have collected the frequently occurring words from a part of this Bengali news corpus and the annotated training set of 272K wordforms to use as the seeds. There are 123, 87, and 32 entries in the person, location, and organization seed lists, respectively.

 (2). **Lexical pattern generation:** The unlabeled corpus is tagged with the elements from the seed lists. For example, *<Person> sonia gandhi </Person>*, *<Location> kolkata </Location>* and *<Organization> jadavpur viswavidyalya </Organization>*. For each tag T inserted in the training corpus, the algorithm generates a *lexical* pattern p using a context window of maximum width 6 (excluding the tagged NE) around the left and the right tags, e.g.,

   $p = [l_{-3} l_{-2} l_{-1} $ <T> $...$ </T> $ l_{+1} l_{+2} l_{+3}]$,

where, $l_{\pm i}$ are the *context* of p. Any of $l_{\pm i}$ may be a punctuation symbol. In such cases, the width of the lexical patterns will vary. All these patterns, derived from the different tags of the training corpus, are stored in a Pattern Table (or, set P), which has four different fields namely, pattern *id* (identifies any particular pattern), pattern *example* (pattern), pattern *type* (*Person/Location/Organization*) and *relative frequency* (indicates the number of times any pattern of a particular *type* appears in the entire training corpus relative to the total number of patterns generated of that *type*). This table has 28,986 entries, out of which 17,031 patterns are distinct. We have also generated the context patterns by extracting the examples from the labeled training data of 272K wordforms and it yields 15,488 patterns. Finally, the set P has 21,233 distinct patterns.

(3). **Evaluation of patterns**: Every pattern p in the set P is matched against the same unannotated corpus. In a place, where the context of p matches, p predicts the occurrence of the left or right boundary of name. The POS information of the words as well as well as some linguistic rules and/or length of the entity have been used in detecting the other boundary of the entity. The extracted entity may fall in one of the following categories:

- *positive example*: The extracted entity is of the same NE *type* as that of the pattern.
- *negative example:* The extracted entity is of the different NE *type* as that of the pattern.
- *error example*: The extracted entity is not at all a NE.

(4). **Candidate pattern acquisition:** For each pattern p, we have maintained three different lists for the *positive, negative* and *error* examples. The *type* of the extracted entity is determined by checking whether it appears in any of the seed lists (person/location/organization); otherwise, its *type* is determined manually. The *positive* and *negative* examples are then added to the appropriate seed lists. We then compute the pattern's *accuracy* as follows:

$$accuracy(\text{p})= |positive\ (\text{p})|/[|\ positive\ (\text{p})| + |negative\ (\text{p})| + |error(\text{p})|]$$

A threshold value of *accuracy* has been chosen and the patterns below this threshold values are discarded. A pattern is also discarded if its total *positive count* is less than a predetermined threshold value. The remaining patterns are ranked by their *relative frequency* values. The n top high frequent patterns are retained in the pattern set P and this set is denoted as *Accept Pattern*.

(5). **Generation of new patterns:** All the *positive* and *negative* examples extracted by a pattern p in Step 4 can be used to generate further patterns from the same training corpus. Each new *positive* or *negative* instance (not appearing in the seed lists) is used to further tag the training corpus. We repeat steps 2-4 for each new NE until no new patterns can be generated. The threshold values of *accuracy, positive count* and *relative frequency* are chosen in such a way that in each iteration of the algorithm at least 5% new patterns is added to the set P. A newly generated pattern may be identical to a pattern that is already in the set P. In such case, the *type* and *relative frequency* fields in the Set P are updated accordingly. Otherwise, the newly generated pattern is added to the set with the *type* and *relative frequency* fields set properly. The algorithm terminates after the 17 iterations and there are 27,098 distinct entries in the set P.

4.   Evaluation Results and Discussions

We have manually annotated approximately 200K wordforms of the Bengali news corpus (Ekbal and Bandyopadhyay, 2008c) with *Person, Location, Organization* and *Miscellaneous* NE tags with the help of *Sanchay Editor*[3], a text editor for the Indian languages. Out of 200K wordforms, 150K wordforms along with the IJCNLP-08 shared task data has been used for training the models. Out of 200K wordforms, 50K wordforms have been used as the development data. The system has been tested with a gold standard test set of 35K wordforms. Statistics of the training, development and test sets are presented in Table 2. A number of experiments have been carried out taking the different combinations of the available words, context and orthographic word level features to identify the best-suited set of features in the ME, CRF and SVM frameworks for NER in Bengali. The SVM models that use **forward**

---

[3]Sourceforge.net/project/nlp-sanchay

parsing, and **backward parsing** are denoted by SVM-F, and SVM-B, respectively. The systems developed with these features are defined as the *baseline* models.

Table 2: Training, development and test set statistics

Set	#of sentences	#of wordforms (approx.)	# of NEs	Avg. length of NE
Training	21,340	272K	22,488	1.5138
Development	3,367	50K	3,665	1.6341
Test	2,501	35K	3,178	1.6202

Evaluation results of the development set for the *baseline* models are presented in Table 3 in terms of recall (R), precision (P) and F-Score (FS). Evaluation results of the development set have demonstrated that the ME based *baseline* system performs best (f-score=**73.32%**) for the context window of size three (i.e., previous, current and next word), NE information of the previous word, POS information of the current word, prefixes and suffixes of length upto three characters of the current word along with other features. The *baseline* CRF model has shown best performance (f-score=**75.71%**) for the context window of size five, POS information of the current and previous words along with the other set of features like ME. The SVM-F based *baseline* system has performed best among the three models and has demonstrated the f-score value of **76.3%** for the context window of size six, NE information of the previous two words, POS information of the current, previous and the next words along with the other set of features as like ME and CRF. The SVM-B has shown the f-score value of 76.1% with the same set of features used in SVM-F. In SVM models, we have conducted experiments with the different *polynomial kernel* functions and observed the highest f-score value with degree 2.

Evaluation results are reported in Table 3 by including the gazetteers to the *baseline* models. We have observed that all the gazetteers are not equally important to improve the performance of the classifiers. The use of gazetteers increases the performance by 2.49%, 4.11%, 4.45%, and 4.11% in the ME, CRF, SVM-F, and SVM-B classifiers, respectively. Evaluation results suggest that adding all the available features may not be always helpful to improve the performance in a ME framework as careful feature selection has an important role. On the other hand, CRF and SVM can avoid overfitting more efficiently and this fact is established by their performance improvement.

Table 3: Results of the development set for *baseline* models and by adding gazetteers

	Baseline models			Baseline + Gazetteers		
Model	R (in %)	P (in %)	FS (in %)	R (in %)	P (in %)	FS (in %)
ME	73.57	73.07	73.32	76.09	75.53	75.81
CRF	75.97	75.45	75.71	79.03	80.62	79.82
SVM-F	77.14	75.48	76.30	81.37	80.14	80.75
SVM-B	77.09	75.14	76.10	81.29	79.16	80.21

4.1. Use of Context Patterns as Features

Patterns in the *Accept Pattern* set (discussed in section 3) can be used as the features of the individual classifier. Words in the left and/or the right contexts of person, location and organization names carry effective information that could be helpful in their identification. High ranked patterns, which are generated in a bootstrapped manner from the unlabeled corpus, contain these types context words. These words are used as the *trigger words* and very useful to identify the NEs. A particular *trigger* word may appear in more than one pattern *type*. A feature 'ContextInformation' is defined by observing the three preceding and following words of the current word. The feature is set depending upon the type of the *trigger* word. Experimental results of the system for the development set are presented in Table 4 by including the context features. Results show the effectiveness of context features with improvement of f-scores by **2.27%, 3.08%, 2.82%,** and **3.28%** in the ME, CRF, SVM-F, and SVM-B models, respectively.

Table 4: Results of the development set by adding context features

Model	Recall (in %)	Precision (in %)	F-Score (in %)
ME	78.59	77.58	78.08
CRF	82.07	83.75	82.90
SVM-F	84.56	82.60	**83.57**
SVM-B	84.42	82.58	83.49

4.2. Post-processing Techniques

We have performed error analysis for all the classifiers with the help of confusion matrices. In order to improve the performance of the classifiers, several post-processing techniques have been adopted depending upon the nature of errors involved. It has been observed that SVM models suffer most with the tendency of assigning NE tags to the non-NEs. Though SVM models perform better than CRF in terms of f-score, their precisions suffer. SVM performs better than ME with more than 5% f-score value but the rate of improvement of precision is less compared to recall. In ME model, a lot of NEs are not identified at all. CRF model also suffers from this problem. The most confusing pairs of classes in these two models are LOC vs NNE, B-PER vs NNE, PER vs NNE, E-ORG vs NNE and B-MISC vs MISC. On the other hand the most confusing pairs are LOC vs NNE, PER vs NNE, MISC vs NNE and E-ORG vs NNE in the SVM models. Depending upon the errors involved in the models, we have adopted various mechanisms to improve the recall and precision values of the classifiers.

(1). **Class splitting technique for SVM**: Unlike CRF or ME, SVM model does not predict the NE tags to the constituent words depending upon the sentence. SVM predicts the class depending upon the labeled word examples only. If target classes are equally distributed, the *pairwise* method can reduce the training cost. Here, we have a very unlabeled class distribution with a large number of samples belonging to the class 'NNE' (other than NEs) (Table 2). This leads to the same situation like the *one-vs-rest* strategy. One solution to this unbalanced class distribution is to split the 'NNE' class into several subclasses effectively. Here, we have splitted the 'NNE' class according to the POS information of the word. That is, given a POS tagset POS, we produce new $|POS|$ classes, 'NNE-C'$|C \in POS$. So, we have 26 sub-classes which correspond to non-NE regions such as 'NNE-NN' (common noun), 'NNE-VFM' (verb finite main) etc. Experimental results have shown the recall, precision, and f-score values of **87.09, 86.73%**, and **86.91**, respectively, in the SVM-F system and **87.03, 85.98%**, and, **86.5**, respectively, in the SVM-B system.

(2). **Post-processing with the n-best outputs for CRF and ME**: There are inconsistent results in the CRF and ME models. We have performed a post-processing step to correct these errors. The post-processing tries to assign the correct tag according to the n-best results for every sentence of the test set. We have considered the top 15 labeled sequences for each sentence with the confidence scores. Initially, we collect the NEs from the high confident results and then we re-assign the tags for low confident results using the NE list. The procedure is given below:

S is the set of sentences in the test set, i.e., $S = \{s_1, s_2, ..., s_n\}$; R is set of n-best result (n=15) of S, i.e, $R = \{r_1, r_2, ..., r_n\}$, where r_i is a set of n-best results of s_i; c_{ij} is the confidence score of r_{ij}, that is the jth result in r_i.

Creation of NE set from the high confident tags:

for $i = 1$ to n {if (r_{i0} >=0.6) then collect all NEs from r_{i0} and add to the set NESet }.

Replacement:

for i=1 to n {if (r_{i0} >=0.6) then Result(s_i)=r_{i0}; else { TempResult(s_i)=r_{i0};

   for j=1 to m {if (NEs of r_{ij} are included in NESet) then Replace the NE tags of TempResult with these new tags}.

  Result(s_i)=TempResult(s_i)}}.

Evaluation results have demonstrated the recall, precision, and f-score values of 84.32%, 81.31%, and 82.72%, respectively, in ME and 86.75%, 85.91%, and 86.33%, respectively, in the CRF model. Thus, these are the improvement of **4.64%**, and **4.43%** f-score in the ME, and CRF models, respectively.

(3). **Second confident tags**: If a word is tagged as NNE by any model and the confidence of the second best tag is greater than a predetermined threshold value then the second best tag is considered as the correct tag. We have heuristically determined the threshold values of confidence in each model by observing their effects on the evaluation results. This post-processing technique is executed after the techniques 1 and 2. Evaluation results are presented in Table 5. Results show the loss in precision value by less than **1%** and the gain in recall by more than **2.5%** in each case. This results in the overall improvement of the performance in each of the models.

(4). **Use of gazetteers and lexicon for handling unknown words**: We have used person, location and organization name lists along with the lexicon to deal with the unknown words. If the confidence of the tag assigned to an unknown word is less than a predefined threshold value then its tag is determined by checking the gazetteers. This approach is followed only when the confidence of the second best tag is also below some threshold value (i.e., only when less than or equal to the thresholds used in technique 3). In some cases, an unknown word that is assigned the NE tag can also appear in the lexicon. The NE tag of such unseen word is changed to NNE, if its confidence is below a predetermined threshold value and the word is not found in the 'Common word' gazetteer list as discussed in Section 2.2. Appropriate threshold values have been determined by observing the effects on the evaluation results in each of the models. Approximately, there are 21% unknown words in the development set. Experimental results are presented in Table 5.

Table 5: Evaluation results using second confident tags and unknown word handling

	With second confident tags			Unknown word handling		
Model	R (in %)	P (in %)	FS (in %)	R (in %)	P (in %)	FS (in %)
ME	88.53	80.52	84.33	89.46	81.92	85.44
CRF	89.64	85.03	87.27	90.03	86.18	88.06
SVM-F	90.82	86.01	88.35	91.01	87.23	89.08
SVM-B	90.63	85.73	88.11	90.99	86.97	88.95

4.3. Voting Techniques

Voting scheme becomes effective in order to improve the overall performance of any system. Here, we have combined four systems using three different voting mechanisms. In our experiments, we have applied weighted voting to the four systems. But before applying weighted voting, we need to decide the weights to be given to the individual system. We can obtain the best weights if we could obtain the accuracy for the 'true' test data. However, it is impossible to estimate them. Thus, we have used following weighting methods in our experiments:

(1). **Uniform weights (Majority voting)**: We have assigned the same voting weight to all the systems. The combined system selects the classifications, which are proposed by the majority of the models. If four outputs are different, then the output of the SVM-F system is selected.

(2). **Cross validation f-score values**: The training data is divided in to N portions. We employ the training by using N-1 portions, and then evaluate the remaining portion. This is repeated N times. In each iteration, we have evaluated the individual system following the similar methodology, i.e., by including the various gazetteers and the same set of post-processing techniques. At the end, we get N f-score values for each of the system. Final voting weight for a system is given by the average of these N f-score values. Here, we have considered the value of N to be 10. We have defined two different types of weights depending on the cross validation f-score as follows:

(a). Total F-Score: In the first method, we have assigned the overall average f-score of any classifier as the weight for it.

(b). Tag F-Score: In the second method, we have assigned the average f-score value of the individual tag as the weight.

Experimental results of the voted system are presented in Table 6. Results show that the system achieves the highest performance for the voting scheme 'Tag F-Score', which considers the individual tag f-score value as the weight of the corresponding system. Voting shows (tables 5-6) an overall improvement of the f-scores of **6.76%** over the least performing ME based system and **3.12%** over the best performing SVM-F system.

Table 6: Results of the voted system for the development set

Voting Scheme	R (in %)	P (in %)	FS (in %)
Majority	93.15	89.33	91.2
Total F-Score	93.78	89.91	91.8
Tag F-Score	93.82	90.24	92.2

4.4. Experimental Results of the Test Set

Four systems are tested with a gold standard test set of 35K wordforms. Approximately, 25% of the NEs are unknown in the test set. Experimental results of the test set for the *baseline* models have shown the f-score values of 73.92%, 76.35%, 77.36%, and 77.23% in the ME, CRF, SVM-F, and SVM-B based systems, respectively. Evaluation results have demonstrated the fact that the use of gazetteers, context features and post-processing can improve the performance of each individual system by the impressive margins of 11.79%, 12.28%, 12.25%, and 12.19% in f-scores over the *baseline* ME, CRF, SVM-F, and SVM-B base systems, respectively. These post-processed systems are then combined together into a final system by applying three weighted voting approaches. Experimental results are presented in Table 7. Results show that the voting scheme that considers the f-score value of the individual NE tag as the weight of a particular classifier, i.e., 'Tag F-Score' gives the best result among the three voting methods. The multi-engine system has demonstrated the improvement in the f-scores by 6.57%, 3.65%, 2.67%, and 2.86% in the ME, CRF, SVM-F, and SVM-B systems, respectively.

Table 7: Results of the voted system for the test set

Voting Scheme	R (in %)	P (in %)	FS (in %)
Majority	93.21	89.75	91.45
Total F-Score	93.92	90.11	91.98
Tag F-Score	93.98	90.63	92.28

The most recent existing Bengali NER systems have been trained and tested with the same datasets. Evaluation results are presented in Table 8. Results have shown the effectiveness of the proposed multi-engine NER system that outperforms the other existing Bengali NER systems by the impressive margins. Thus, it can be decided that purely statistical approaches cannot yield very good performance always. Evaluation results also suggest that the contextual words along with their information and several post-processing methods can yield a reasonably good performance for each of the classifiers. Results also suggest that combination of several classifiers is more effective than the single classifier.

Table 8: Comparisons with other Bengali NER systems

Model	R (in %)	P (in %)	FS (in %)
HMM, Ekbal et al. (2007c)	74.02	72.55	73.28
CRF, Ekbal et al. (2008a)	80.02	80.21	80.15
SVM, Ekbal and Bandyopadhyay (2008b)	81.57	79.05	80.29
Voted System (proposed)	93.98	90.63	92.28

5. Conclusion

In this paper, we have reported a multi-engine NER system for Bengali by combining the outputs of the classifiers such as ME, CRF and SVM. Performance of the individual classifier has been improved significantly with the use of context patterns learned from an unlabeled corpus of 3 million wordforms and the various post-processing methodologies incorporated by observing the different kinds of errors involved in each classifier. All the four systems are then combined together into a final system by the three different weighted voting methods. The voted system has exhibited the improvement in f-scores by 18.63% over the least performing *baseline* ME system and 14.92% over the best performing *baseline* SVM based system. Future works include investigating the methods that will enable to reduce the errors that still exist because of the abbreviated names and short names. Also, we would like to conduct experiments with the other weighted voting methods.

References

Bikel, Daniel M., R. Schwartz, Ralph M. Weischedel. 1999. An Algorithm that Learns What's in Name. *Machine Learning (Special Issue on NLP), 1-20.*

Bothwick, Andrew. 1999. A Maximum Entropy Approach to Named Entity Recognition. *Ph.D. Thesis*, New York University.

Cucerzan, S., Yarowsky, D. 2002. Language Independent NER using a Unified Model of Internal and Contextual Evidence. In *Proceedings of the Sixth Conference on Natural Language Learning,* San Francisco, Morgan Kaufmann.

Ekbal, Asif, and S. Bandyopadhyay. 2007a. Lexical Pattern Learning from Corpus Data for Named Entity Recognition. In *Proc. of 5th ICON*, India, 123-128.

Ekbal, Asif, Naskar, Sudip and S. Bandyopadhyay.2007b. Named Entity Recognition and Transliteration in Bengali. *Named Entities: Recognition, Classification and Use, Special Issue of Lingvisticae Investigationes Journal, 30:1 (2007), 95-114.*

Ekbal, Asif, R. Haque and S. Bandyopadhyay. 2007c. Bengali Part of Speech Tagging using Conditional Random Field. In *Proc. of 7th SNLP*, Thailand.

Ekbal, Asif, Haque, R and S. Bandyopadhyay. 2008a. Named Entity Recognition in Bengali: A Conditional Random Field Approach. In *Proc. of 3rd IJCNLP-08*, 589-594.

Ekbal, Asif, and S. Bandyopadhyay. 2008b. Bengali Named Entity Recognition using Support Vector Machine. In *Proc. of NERSSEAL, IJCNLP-08*, 51-58.

Ekbal, Asif, and S. Bandyopadhyay. 2008c. A Web-based Bengali News Corpus for Named Entity Recognition. *Language Resources and Evaluation Journal*, Vol. (40).

Florian, Radu, Ittycheriah, A., Jing, H. and Zhang, T. 2003. Named Entity Recognition through Classifier Combination. In *Proc. of CoNLL-2003*.

Joachims , T. 1999. Making Large Scale SVM Learning Practical. In *B. Scholkopf, C. Burges and A. Smola editions, Advances in Kernel Methods-Support Vector Learning*.

Lafferty, J., McCallum, A., and Pereira, F. 2001. Conditional Random Fields: Probabilistic Models for Segmenting and Labeling Sequence Data. In *Proc. of 18th ICML,* 282-289.

Li, Wei and Andrew McCallum. 2003. Rapid Development of Hindi Named Entity Recognition Using Conditional Random Fields and Feature Inductions. *ACM TALIP*, 2(3), (2003), 290-294.

Munro, R., Ler, D., and Patrick, J. 2003. Meta-learning Orthographic and Contextual Models for Language Independent Named Entity Recognition. In *Proc. of CoNLL-2003*.

Vapnik, Valdimir N. 1995. The Nature of Statistical Learning Theory. *Springer.*

Wu, D., Ngai, G., and Carpuat, M. 2003. A Stacked, Voted, Stacked Model for Named Entity Recognition. In *Proc. of CoNLL-2003*.

Yamada, Hiroyasu, Taku Kudo and Yuji Matsumoto. 2002. Japanese Named Entity Extraction using Support Vector Machine. In *Transactions of IPSJ*, Vol. 43 No. 1, 44-53.

Incorporation of WordNet Features to *n*-gram Features
in a Language Modeler [*]

Kathleen L. Go[a] and Solomon L. See[a]

[a] De La Salle University – Manila
2401 Taft Avenue, Malate
1004 Manila, Philippines
go.kathleen@gmail.com, sees@dlsu.edu.ph

Abstract. *n*-gram language modeling is a popular technique used to improve performance of various NLP applications. However, it still faces the "curse of dimensionality" issue wherein word sequences on which the model will be tested are likely to be different from those seen during training (Bengio *et al.*, 2003). An approach that incorporates WordNet to a trigram language modeler has been developed to address this issue. WordNet was used to generate proxy trigrams that may be used to reinforce the fluency of the given trigrams. Evaluation results reported a significant decrease in model perplexity showing that the new method, evaluated using the English language in the business news domain, is capable of addressing the issue. The modeler was also used as a tool to rank parallel translations produced by multiple Machine Translation systems. Results showed a 6-7% improvement over the base approach (Callison-Burch and Flournoy, 2001) in correctly ranking parallel translations.

Keywords: language modeling, statistical methods, translation quality, WordNet

1. Introduction

n-gram language modeling is a popular statistical language modeling (SLM) technique used to improve performance of various natural language processing (NLP) applications such as speech recognition (SR), machine translation (MT), and information retrieval (IR). However, it still faces the "curse of dimensionality" issue wherein word sequences (i.e. *n*-grams) on which the model will be tested are likely to be different from those seen during training (Bengio *et al.*, 2003). This means that these sequences would always be assigned low probabilities.

There have already been attempts to address this problem. A number of works made use of smoothing techniques such as the one presented in (Callison-Burch and Flournoy, 2001) which made use of linear interpolation of trigram, bigram and unigram probabilities. (Bengio *et al.*, 2003) presents an approach that combines neural networks and smoothing techniques to a trigram model while the work in (Brockett *et al.*, 2001) made use of additional linguistic features, such as syntax trees, in order to construct a decision tree that will classify sentences.

Another possible solution is to make use of other linguistic resources such as WordNet (Fellbaum et al., 2006) and devise an approach that combines WordNet features (i.e. synsets and their relations) with the *n*-grams used in language modelers. By incorporating WordNet features, the language modeler can generate related sequences which can possibly give it a higher score even if there are no exact matches seen during training. (Hoberman and Rosenfeld, 2002) presents a study on the integration of WordNet features to address the data sparseness of nouns in bigrams. The study covered the IS-A relationship of nouns and reported

---

22nd Pacific Asia Conference on Language, Information and Computation, pages 179–188

improvement in the language model perplexity, although the improvement was below expectation.

This paper presents an extension of the study in (Hoberman and Rosenfeld, 2002). A trigram language modeler has been developed that considers other parts of speech (i.e adjective, adverb, verb) and relationships (i.e. HAS-A, Synonymy/Antonymy), in addition to nouns and the IS-A relationship, to address the "curse of dimensionality" issue. Since there are many existing MT systems with different ways of producing translations, the language modeler was used as a tool to automatically rank parallel translations (i.e. translations produced by multiple MT systems). The ranking of translations was based on the method found in (Callison-Burch and Flournoy, 2001) where sentences are ranked based on their fluency, which are computed using the probabilities of their trigram components. Trigrams were used for the n-gram language modeler since the study in (Callison-Burch and Flournoy, 2001) showed that trigrams are effective when used in ranking parallel translations.

Section 2 discusses the architecture of the language modeler while Section 3 presents an example on how the new approach works. Section 4 presents the evaluation results both in terms of addressing the "curse of dimensionality" issue and when applied to the ranking of parallel translations. Lastly, Section 5 contains the conclusions and the discussion of possible future works for this research.

2. Architecture

The language modeler has two modules: the Training Module and the Language Evaluation Module. The latter, in turn, consists of the Base Language Evaluation Submodule and the WordNet-Integrated Language Evaluation Submodule.

2.1. Training Module

The Training Module, shown in Figure 1, is based on the language modeler presented in (Callison-Burch and Flournoy, 2001). This module handles the extraction of trigrams, bigrams, and unigrams from an input document. Since WordNet only contains lemma and general representations of parts of speech (e.g. "noun" instead of "NNP" for proper nouns), the general representations are needed for the evaluation of trigrams.

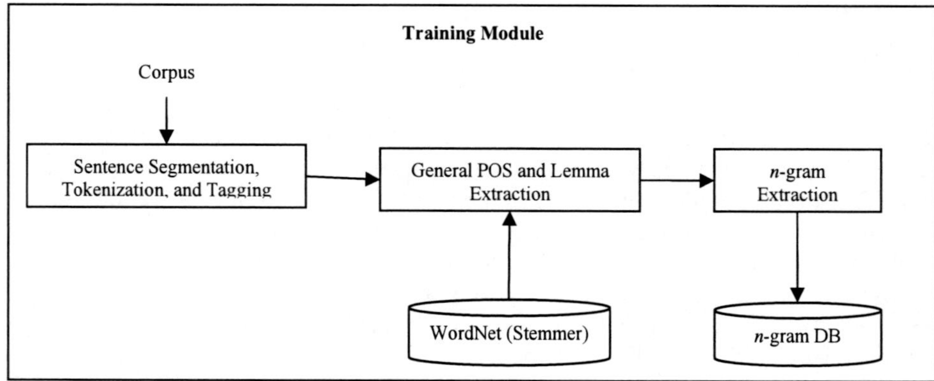

Figure 1: Training Module Architecture.

2.2. Language Evaluation Module

The Language Evaluation Module, shown in Figure 2, consists of the Base Language Evaluation Submodule and the WordNet-Integrated Language Evaluation Submodule.

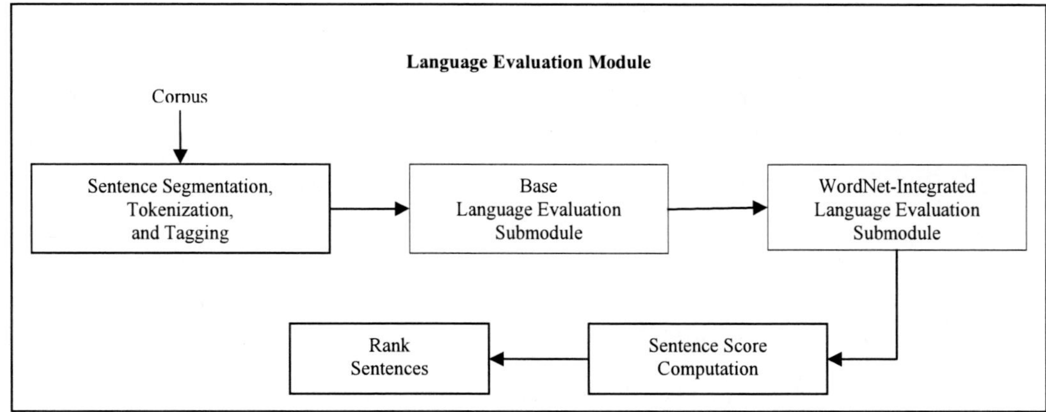

Figure 2: Language Evaluation Module Architecture.

2.2.1. Base Language Evaluation Submodule

The Base Language Evaluation Submodule, shown in Figure 3, is a modified version of the evaluation process in (Callison-Burch and Flournoy, 2001).

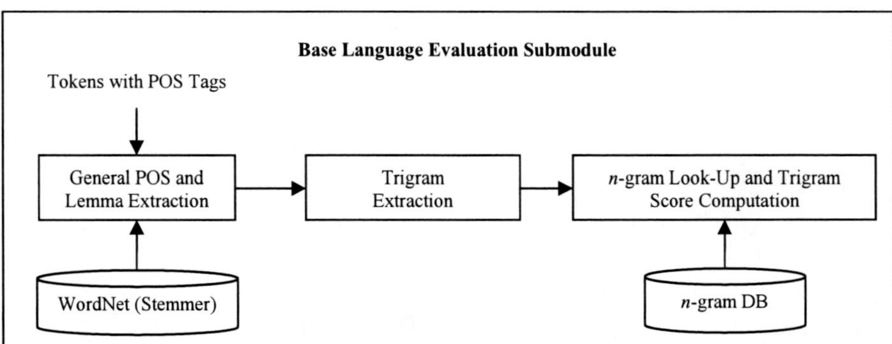

Figure 3: Base Language Evaluation Submodule Architecture.

After the Sentence Segmentation, Tokenization, and Tagging process, the input is passed to the General POS and Lemma Extraction process for the extraction of the generalized representation of its tokens and POS tags. Generalized parts of speech are extracted from the POS tags generated by MontyTagger (Hugo, 2004) while the lemma representations of the tokens are extracted by using WordNet's stemmer. The Trigram Extraction process then extracts the trigrams that will be evaluated, including their POS sequence and general representation. These trigrams are passed to the *n*-gram Look-Up and Trigram Score Computation process that handles the matching of trigrams and their components in the *n*-gram DB to get their frequencies and compute their probabilities. This process performs a *Lemma and General POS Look-Up* whereas the original version performs a *Surface Level without POS Look-Up*. In the former, the *n*-gram Look-Up process matches base on the general representation of the *n*-grams while in the latter, the process matches base only on the surface level (i.e. actual word sequences) of the *n*-grams. The formula used to compute trigram probabilities, which was adapted from (Callison-Burch and Flournoy, 2001), is shown below.

$$P(z|xy) = (0.80 * \text{frequency of } xyz) / (\text{frequency of } xy) + \\ (0.14 * \text{frequency of } yz) / (\text{frequency of } y) + \\ (0.099 * \text{frequency of } z) / (\text{total \# of words seen}) + \\ 0.001 \qquad (1)$$

2.2.2. WordNet-Integrated Language Evaluation Submodule

The WordNet-Integrated Language Evaluation Submodule, shown in Figure 4, contains the additional processes that correspond to the new approach. In summary, the process starts with using the contents of WordNet to generate proxy trigrams for the trigrams that were not seen during training. Depending on the presence of the proxy trigrams or their components in the *n*-gram DB, they may be used to reinforce the fluency of the given trigrams. This is done by using the scores of the proxy trigrams to reinforce the score of the given trigram. Originally, only one proxy trigram was used to reinforce trigram scores. However, initial results showed that using only one proxy trigram, either the highest scoring or the most similar, does not give significant increases in trigram scores. Since proxy trigrams are also faced with the "curse of dimensionality" issue, multiple proxy trigrams were used. If a proxy trigram has matches that contain at least one proxy word, it can be used to reinforce the fluency of the given trigram or its lower order components (i.e. bigram and unigram components). This approach also addresses the data sparseness issue of the given trigram's components wherein even if they have matches in the *n*-gram DB, they are still assigned low scores.

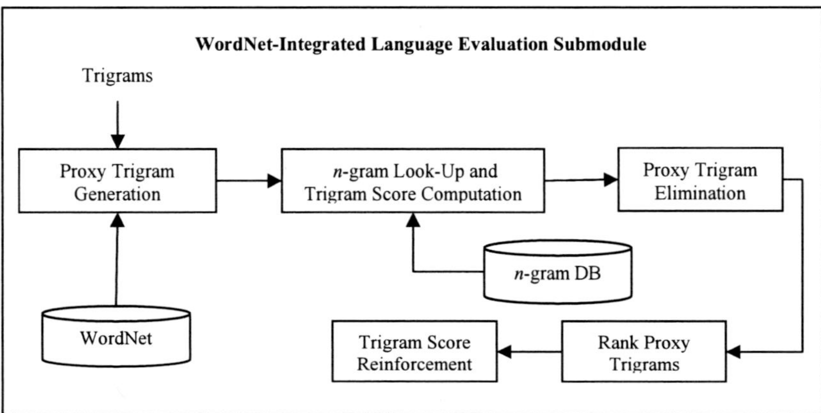

Figure 4: WordNet-Integrated Language Evaluation Submodule Architecture.

In detail, an unseen trigram first goes through the Proxy Trigram Generation process. This process generates proxy trigrams by first looking for partially matching trigrams in the *n*-gram DB (e.g. only the first two words are matched). Words having no position matches (i.e. words that caused the trigrams to not exactly match) are replaced with proxy words (i.e. related words from WordNet). Proxy words are related to the original word through the IS-A and Synonymy/Antonymy relationship. Originally, words related through the HAS-A relationship were also retrieved for nouns. However, initial results showed that the increase in reinforced scores caused by proxy trigrams containing HAS-A related proxy words are insignificant.

The resulting proxy trigrams are then passed to the *n*-gram Look-Up and Trigram Score Computation process, which is the same with the one in the Base Language Evaluation Submodule. In this process, the probabilities of the proxy trigrams are computed.

The Proxy Trigram Elimination process would then remove the proxy trigrams that would not aid in the reinforcement of the given trigram's fluency. These are the proxy trigrams with no matches (i.e. exact, bigram or unigram) in the *n*-gram DB or proxy trigrams with matches but do not contain at least one proxy word. In the initial study, proxy trigrams undergo the Similarity Score Computation process before *n*-gram Look-Up and Trigram Score Computation. In the said process, the similarity between a word and its proxy word is computed using WordNet::Similarity (Banarjee et al., 2006). These scores were used in Proxy Trigram Elimination to further filter the proxy trigrams. This is done by using pre-computed similarity score thresholds for each POS such that if the similarity scores of the proxy words in a proxy trigram do not meet the thresholds, the proxy trigram is assumed to be non-fluent and is removed. The thresholds were derived from the range of the similarity scores of the proxy words belonging to proxy trigrams that produced fluent proxy sentences (i.e. sentences with proxy trigram replacements). The initial results showed that the thresholds were not effective in its purpose such that only an insignificant amount of proxy trigrams were being filtered out. Therefore, the Similarity Score Computation process and the use of similarity score thresholds are removed.

After the Proxy Trigram Elimination process, the remaining proxy trigrams are passed to the Rank Proxy Trigrams process to be ranked based on the probabilities assigned to them from highest to lowest. The Trigram Score Reinforcement process then makes use of the remaining proxy trigrams to reinforce the fluency of the given trigram. This is done by integrating the original score of the given with the scores of the remaining proxy trigrams. The formula used to compute reinforced trigram scores is shown below.

$$P(xyz)_{\text{reinforced}} = (1 - \lambda)P(xyz) + \lambda(\sum_{i=1}^{l} P(xyz_{\text{proxyTriMatch}}) + \sum_{i=1}^{m} P(xyz_{\text{proxyBiMatch}}) + \sum_{i=1}^{n} P(xyz_{\text{proxyUniMatch}})) \quad (2)$$

where:

$$\lambda = 0.9 ,$$

$$\sum_{i=1}^{l} P(xyz_{\text{proxyTriMatch}}) <= 0.9 , \quad \sum_{i=1}^{m} P(xyz_{\text{proxyBiMatch}}) <= 0.01 , \quad \sum_{i=1}^{n} P(xyz_{\text{proxyUniMatch}}) <= 0.006$$

The purpose of λ is to prevent non-fluent trigrams from being reinforced too much in case it has a proxy trigram that is fluent. If a trigram has proxy trigrams that passed the Proxy Trigram Elimination process, the trigram would most likely have a higher reinforced score. This cannot be prevented even for non-fluent trigrams. Therefore, part of the reinforced trigram score must still be influenced by the original score. The value of λ was derived by getting the value with the highest performance in the ranking of parallel translations.

As seen in the formula, the total proxy score for each trigram is derived by getting the sum of: 1) total score of the proxy trigrams with exact matches, 2) total score of the proxy trigrams with bigram matches, and 3) total score of the proxy trigrams with unigram matches. The total scores for each match level are separate since they are assigned different score limits in order to prevent lower level matches from causing a high increase in the reinforced score. If there is only one threshold that covers all the match levels, the reinforced score of a trigram having many proxy trigrams with lower level matches may equal or exceed the score of a trigram that has a proxy trigram with an exact match. This is possible because of the data sparseness issue wherein even if a trigram or proxy trigram has an exact match, the scores assigned to them may still be low. Also, there is a greater chance of a trigram having proxy trigrams with lower level matches than having proxy trigrams with exact matches. Therefore, in order to prevent the scores of the lower level matches to consume the portion of the score that is supposed to be for higher level matches, different score limits are assigned to each match level. These values were derived through multiple tests conducted wherein different values were used to compute reinforced scores of corresponding fluent and non-fluent sets. The results were compared and the set of threshold values that gave a high perplexity reduction while at the same time maintained the perplexity distance was chosen.

2.2.3. Sentence Score Computation

After the scores and reinforced scores of the trigrams are computed, the Sentence Score Computation process computes the fluency scores of the sentences. The fluency score of a sentence is determined by getting the product of the probabilities assigned to all its trigram components. If a trigram has a reinforced score, it is used instead of the original score.

2.2.4. Rank Sentences

Each of the sentence sets (i.e. parallel translation sets) are then passed to the Rank Sentences process to be ranked. The ranking of sentences is based on fluency score from highest to lowest.

3. Example

This section presents an example of the new approach. In this example, the given trigram *"to local capitalists"* – "TO JJ NNS" with a general representation of *"to local capitalist"* – "TO adjective noun", only has a unigram match in the *n*-gram DB with a score of 0.008. This section shows how the reinforced trigram score is computed.

In the Proxy Trigram Generation process, the first step is to look for trigrams with partial matches in the *n*-gram DB. In this case, assume that the *n*-gram DB contains two trigrams having partial matches with the given: 1) *"a foreign capitalist"* – "DT JJ NN" (*"a foreign capitalist"* – "DT adjective noun") and 2) *"to local investors"* – "TO JJ NNS" (*"to local investor"* – "TO adjective noun"). But since the second trigram has more position matches compared to the first (i.e. 2 position matches vs. 1 position match), only the second is used as a pattern (i.e. *"to local {x}"*). There can be more than one pattern used as long as they have the same number of matching words (e.g. *"to {x} investors"*). WordNet is then accessed to retrieve words related to the words with no position matches. Table 1 shows a list of some of the proxy words for the word *"capitalists"* including their relationships.

Table 1: List of Sample Proxy Words

Proxy Word	Relationship		Proxy Word	Relationship
conservative	hypernymy		holder	hyponymy
conservativist	hypernymy		materialist	hyponymy
person	hypernymy		businessperson	hyponymy
individual	hypernymy		investor	hyponymy
someone	hypernymy		financier	hyponymy

The proxy words are used to generate proxy trigrams by using the patterns (i.e. *"to local {x}"*) and replacing their counterparts. Table 2 shows the generated proxy trigrams for the example.

Table 2: Results of the Proxy Trigram Generation Process

ID	Proxy Trigram	Proxy Trigram POS	Proxy Trigram Lemma	Proxy General POS
1	to local conservative	TO JJ NNS	to local conservative	TO adjective noun
2	to local conservativist	TO JJ NNS	to local conservativist	TO adjective noun
3	to local person	TO JJ NNS	to local person	TO adjective noun
4	to local individual	TO JJ NNS	to local individual	TO adjective noun
5	to local someone	TO JJ NNS	to local someone	TO adjective noun
6	to local holder	TO JJ NNS	to local holder	TO adjective noun
7	to local materialist	TO JJ NNS	to local materialist	TO adjective noun
8	to local financier	TO JJ NNS	to local financier	TO adjective noun
9	to local businessperson	TO JJ NNS	to local businessperson	TO adjective noun
10	to local investor	TO JJ NNS	to local investor	TO adjective noun

The proxy trigrams are then passed to the *n*-gram Look-Up and Trigram Score Computation process. Assume that the *n*-gram DB has contents that produced the results in Table 3.

Table 3: Results of the *n*-gram Look-Up and Trigram Score Computation Process

ID	Proxy Trigram Lemma	Proxy General POS	Score	Match Level
1	to local conservative	TO adjective noun	0.008	Unigram
2	to local conservativist	TO adjective noun	0.001	None
3	to local person	TO adjective noun	0.008	Unigram
4	to local individual	TO adjective noun	0.001	None
5	to local someone	TO adjective noun	0.008	Unigram
6	to local holder	TO adjective noun	0.008	Unigram
7	to local materialist	TO adjective noun	0.001	None
8	to local financier	TO adjective noun	0.001	None
9	to local businessperson	TO adjective noun	0.001	None
10	to local investor	TO adjective noun	0.948	Trigram

Given the results shown in Table 3, the Proxy Trigram Elimination process removes the proxy trigrams that would not be useful in reinforcing the given trigram's fluency. These are the proxy trigrams with no matches in the *n*-gram DB. Also, if the match of a proxy trigram does not contain at least one proxy word, the proxy trigram is eliminated. Table 4 shows the remaining proxy trigrams after the Proxy Trigram Elimination and the Rank Proxy Trigrams processes.

Table 4: Results of the Proxy Trigram Elimination Process

ID	Proxy Trigram Lemma	Proxy General POS	Score	Match Level
10	to local investor	TO adjective noun	0.948	Trigram
1	to local conservative	TO adjective noun	0.008	Unigram
3	to local person	TO adjective noun	0.008	Unigram
5	to local someone	TO adjective noun	0.008	Unigram
6	to local holder	TO adjective noun	0.008	Unigram

The Trigram Score Reinforcement process would then use the remaining proxy trigrams to reinforce the score of the given. The equation for the reinforced trigram score is shown below. The value 0.008 represents the original score of the given trigram. For the total score of the proxy trigrams with trigram matches, the threshold value (i.e. 0.9) was used because the sum (i.e. 0.948) exceeded the threshold value. Since there are no proxy trigrams with a bigram match, the total score is 0. For the total score of the proxy trigrams with unigram matches, the threshold value (i.e. 0.006) was used because the sum (i.e. 0.032) exceeded the threshold value. The reinforced score of the given trigram is 0.8162.

$$P(\text{"to local capitalists"})_{reinforced} = (0.1 * 0.008) + (0.9)(0.9 + 0 + 0.006) = 0.8162 \qquad (3)$$

4. Evaluation Results

The trigram language modeler has been trained with online articles in the English language and under the business news domain. The training set consists of 1.86 million words while the evaluation set consists of four sets of English sentences, each set having 100 sentences. The four sets of sentences are parallel translations of 100 Filipino sentences selected from online articles, which are also under the business news domain. The first two sets are manual translations while the remaining are translations of the REAL Translation system (Alcantara *et al.*, 2006) and TExt Translation (Go *et al.*, 2006). The first set of manual translations contains more fluent sentences compared to the other set while almost all of the sentences in the two sets of automatic translations are non-fluent.

The language modeler underwent two evaluation processes: automatic evaluation through the comparison of perplexity values and manual evaluation through comparison of the automatic and manual ranking of the parallel translation sets.

For automatic evaluation, the reduction in the perplexity values caused by the new approach (i.e. WordNet-Integrated Language Evaluation) was measured. Table 5 shows the perplexity reductions resulting from comparisons to the two versions of the Base Language Evaluation: Version 1 uses *Surface Level without POS Look-Up* (Callison-Burch and Flournoy, 2001) while Version 2 uses *Lemma and General POS Look-Up*. The big reductions in perplexity (e.g. 50.25% reduction for Set 1 when compared to the perplexity of Base Language Evaluation Version 1) show that the WordNet-Integrated approach was successful in reinforcing trigram scores. However, a reduction in perplexity does not necessarily mean that there would be a reduction in the error rate for the specific application of the language modeler. Also, since it cannot be avoided that the perplexity of the input be reduced, including those that are not fluent, the distance between the perplexity of the fluent and non-fluent sets must be inspected.

Table 5: Perplexity and % Perplexity Reduction of the WordNet-Integrated Language Evaluation Submodule over the Evaluation Set

	WordNet-Integrated Language Evaluation	
	Perplexity	% Perplexity Reduction
Set 1	44.05073	
Base Language Evaluation Version 1		50.23%
Base Language Evaluation Version 2		45.54%
Set 2	43.97654	
Base Language Evaluation Version 1		52.45%
Base Language Evaluation Version 2		47.91%
Set 3	210.6316	
Base Language Evaluation Version 1		42.27%
Base Language Evaluation Version 2		39.02%
Set 4	262.4471	
Base Language Evaluation Version 1		42.59%
Base Language Evaluation Version 2		37.26%

Table 6 shows that the new approach is consistent in maintaining the distance between the perplexities of Set 3 and Set 4 when compared to Set 1 and Set 2. For example, Set 3 is about 378% more perplexed than Set 1 and Set 2. However, Set 2, which was supposed to contain less fluent sentences, became even less perplexed compared to Set 1. This is because the sentences in Set 2, although less fluent than those in Set 1, contains only a small number of errors that cause them to become less fluent. The decrease in perplexity is caused more by the fluent trigrams.

For manual evaluation, five monolingual English speakers were asked to rank the fluency of the parallel translations in the evaluation set. The same set was also ranked by three language modelers using the different versions of Language Evaluation. The results of the automatic rankings were compared to the results of the manual ranking to get the accuracy of the modelers. Table 7 shows the results of the comparison. Aside from the number of correctly ranked parallel translations, the number of correctly ranked sentences on each set was checked in order to determine which sets the modelers had difficulty in ranking. The WordNet-Integrated Language Evaluation version has 67% accuracy which means that it has a 7% improvement over the Base Language Evaluation using *Surface Level without POS Look-Up*

(Callison-Burch and Flournoy, 2001) and a 6% improvement over the Base Language Evaluation using *Lemma and General POS Look-Up*.

Table 6: Comparison of the Perplexity of the Evaluation Set From the WordNet-Integrated Language Evaluation Submodule

Set #	Set 1	Set 2	Set 3
Set 1			
Set 2	-0.17%		
Set 3	378.16%	378.96%	
Set 4	495.78%	496.79%	24.6%

The results in Table 7 confirmed the results in the automatic evaluation. The WordNet-Integrated approach was able to correctly discriminate fluent sentences from the non-fluent ones (Set 1 and Set 2 vs. Set 3 and Set 4) as seen from the high accuracy rating for Set 3 and Set 4. Another factor for the high accuracy is that according to the manual evaluators, 92% of the parallel sentences belonging to these two sets have the same rank (i.e. same level of fluency). Therefore, for almost all of the parallel translations from the two sets, the language modeler was not required to identify which one is more fluent than the other. However, this is not the case with the translations from Set 1 and Set 2 wherein only 40% have the same fluency level. This means that for 60% of the parallel translations between Set 1 and Set 2, the modelers are required to correctly choose between the translations from the two sets. The accuracy ratings for Set 1 and Set 2 show that the modelers, including the one using the WordNet-Integrated approach, are having difficulty in choosing between sentences with almost the same fluency level (e.g. between the first and second most fluent).

Table 7: Comparison of Manual and Automatic Rankings of the Evaluation Set

Version	# (%) of correctly ranked parallel translations	# (%) of correctly ranked translations per set			
		Set 1	Set 2	Set 3	Set 4
Base Language Evaluation Version 1	60	67	65	93	91
Base Language Evaluation Version 2	61	69	65	93	92
WordNet-Integrated Language Evaluation	67	72	68	95	94

Since the new approach was developed to address the "curse of dimensionality" issue, an additional evaluation was conducted on Set 1 and Set 2 to check if it will be more effective in ranking the translations if there are more unseen trigrams in the input sentences. There are originally 610 trigrams having an exact match from Set 1 and 649 trigrams from Set 2. These trigrams, which make up about 50% of the total number of trigrams in Set 1 and Set 2, were reduced by about 50% more. The language modeler using the WordNet-Integrated Language Evaluation Submodule had 73% accuracy, which is even less than the 74% accuracy of the two versions of Base Language Evaluation.

In order to get the causes for the errors made by the new approach, the 33 incorrectly ranked parallel translations were inspected. We learned that not all causes for the incorrect rankings belong to the scope of the study. For example, less fluent sentences that are shorter were assigned higher ranks than the longer fluent ones. However, there are also instances that must be solved. For example, there are cases wherein higher reinforced trigram scores were assigned to the less fluent trigrams. Another case is when less fluent trigrams are assigned higher reinforced scores than their more fluent and exact matching counterparts.

5. Conclusion and Future Work

A new approach has been developed that integrated WordNet features to an *n*-gram language modeler to address the "curse of dimensionality" issue. It was also able to address the data sparseness issue of lower order components of *n*-grams. Evaluation results show that it is successful in addressing "curse of dimensionality" by reinforcing trigram scores. When used to rank parallel translation sets, it had a 6-7% improvement over the base approaches in terms of accuracy. This new methodology is not effective in choosing between translations with almost the same level of fluency.

One possible extension to this research is to use an ontology specific to the domain the language modeler is intended to be used on. Since WordNet does not contain domain classifications, there are cases wherein less fluent trigrams are assigned high reinforced scores. WordNet contains too many words such that even those that are not related to the sense or domain of the given are still used in the fluency reinforcement process. There is also no way of determining if a proxy trigram is fluent or not since initial results proved that using similarity scores as thresholds is not effective in discriminating between fluent and non-fluent proxy trigrams. Therefore, all of the proxy trigrams with a match may be used in the reinforcement of trigram scores. By using an ontology, the number of applicable proxy trigrams will be reduced and a new set of similarity score thresholds can be derived. These changes may prove to be more effective in approximating the fluency of trigrams.

Another possible extension is to also reinforce the scores of those trigrams already seen in the training. Due to the data sparseness issue in *n*-gram language models, there are cases wherein reinforced trigram scores are higher that their exact matching counterparts.

References

Alcantara, D., B. Hong, A. Perez, and L. Tan. 2006. REAL Translation: Rule Extraction Applied in Language Translation. De La Salle University.

Banarjee, S., J. Michelizzi, S. Patwardhan and T. Pedersen. 2006. WordNet::Similarity 1.04 [online]. Available: http://sourceforge.net/projects/wn-similarity. (May 20, 2007).

Bengio, Y, R. Ducharme, P. Vincent and C Jauvin. 2003. A Neural Probabilistic Language Model. *Journal of Machine Learning Research*.

Brockett, C., S. Corston-Oliver and M. Gamon. 2001. A Machine Learning Approach to the Automatic Evaluation of Machine Translation. *Proceedings of the 39th Annual Meeting on Association for Computational Linguistics*.

Callison-Burch, C. and R. Flournoy. 2001. A Program for Automatically Selecting the Best Output from Multiple Machine Translation Engines. *Proceedings of the Machine Translation Summit VIII*.

Fellbaum, C., B. Haskell, H. Langone, G. Miller, R. Poddar, R. Tengi and P. Wakefield. 2006. WordNet 2.1 [online]. Available: http://wordnet.princeton.edu/obtain. (May 20, 2007).

Go, K., M. Morga, V. Nuñez, and F. Veto. 2006. Text Translation: Template Extraction for a Bidirectional English-Filipino Example-Based Machine Translation. De La Salle University.

Hoberman, R. and R. Rosenfeld. 2002.Using WordNet to Supplement Corpus Statistics [online]. Available: http://www.cs.cmu.edu/~roseh/Papers/wordnet. pdf, 2002. (March 15, 2007).

Hugo, L. 2004. MontyLingua V.2.1 [online]. Available: http://web.media.mit.edu/~hugo/montylingua/. (January 6, 2008).

An Ontology of Chinese Radicals:

Concept Derivation and Knowledge Representation based on the Semantic Symbols of Four Hoofed-Mammals

Chu-Ren Huang, Ya-Jun Yang and Sheng-Yi Chen
Institute of Linguistics, Academia Sinica
Taipei, Taiwan
{churen, Yajun, eagles}@gate.sinica.edu.tw

Abstract. Semantic symbols are essential components of Chinese characters. ShuoWenJieZi (Xyu Shen 121), the oldest dictionary of Chinese, is organized according to the radical forms as semantic symbols. Characters are classified according radicals, and their meanings cluster around the basic concept of the semantic symbol. We believe that ShuoWenJieZi radicals systemreflect conventional conceptualization when Chinese character orthography was invented. In this research, we use the semantic symbols representing four hoofed-mammals in ShuoWenJieZi ,"bovid," "deer," "cattle," and "horse," as our research objects. In principle we assume that semantic symbols represent basic concepts, and further more we distinguish the relations between derived characters and each basic concept to construct a conventionalized ontology headed by basic concepts expressed by the semantic symbols. Our analysis and comparative studies of the semantic symbol ontologies for the four hoofed-mammals show that they share similar conceptual structures strongly motivated by their functions in human society. In particular, we show that the conceptual dependencies between the basic concept of a radical and the meanings of the derived characters can be explained by an enriched version of the Generative Lexicon.

Keywords: Ontology; HanZi ; Semantic Lexicon

1. Introduction

Chinese radical (yi4fu2,ideographs ;semantic symbols) system offers a unique opportunity for systematic and comprehensive comparison between formal and linguistic ontologies. Previous studies adopt either WordNet-based representation (Wong et al, 2002, and Hsieh, 2006) or SUMO-based mapping (Chou, 2005). Among these studies, Chou and Huang (2007) suggest that the family of Chinese characters sharing the same radical can be linked to a basic concept by Qualia relations. This approach has great implications of accounts for radicals as linguistically conventionalized ontology. In this paper, we take this approach further and try to account for each radical group as domain ontology headed by one basic concept. In particular, we examine in details 4 radicals of animals: 羊 (yang2, bovid) , 鹿(lu4, deer), 牛(niu2, cattle) and 馬 (ma3, horse). Among these four animals, "羊," "牛,"and "馬"are domesticated and serve specific functions in human society. They are highly related to daily lives of human. One of the interesting research issues is to see if the derived concepts of these four animal radicals reflect the differences which show the interaction between animals and human.

Our theoretical foundation is Pustejovsky's Quilia Structure (Pustejovsky, 1995), and the original analysis of 'ShuoWenJieZi'(Xu, 121). In ShuoWenJieZi, all Chinese characters are classified as derived from 540 radicals. In this study, we assume that these radicals each represent a basic concept and that all derivative characters are conceptually dependent on that basic concept. Our study aims at accounting for the exact nature of these conceptual dependencies. Combined with previous work, we suggest that conceptual extensions from the basic concept encoded by a radical can be classified into seven main types: formal, constitutive, telic, participant, participating, descriptive (state/manner) and agentive.

2. The Semantic Symbol Ontology

The Semantic Symbol Ontology is a system expressing the relations of Hanzi and its meaning cluster.This ontology system extended the basic structure constructed, (Chou, 2005), which maps the meanings of 540 radicals in *ShuoWenJieZi* with IEEE SUMO. We use the results from analyzing derivative concepts to express the Semantic Ontology for each radical. Our current working interface allows easy query of existing database as well as recording of new entries.

2.1.Radical Search

There are two searching methods for the semantic symbol ontology:
(i) Search on SUMO concepts classification
  Choose certain SUMO concept, then this concept and its lower SUMO concept will show up on the interface.
(ii) Search on the radical word forms
  Key in the radical word form, and users can get the data of that radical directly.

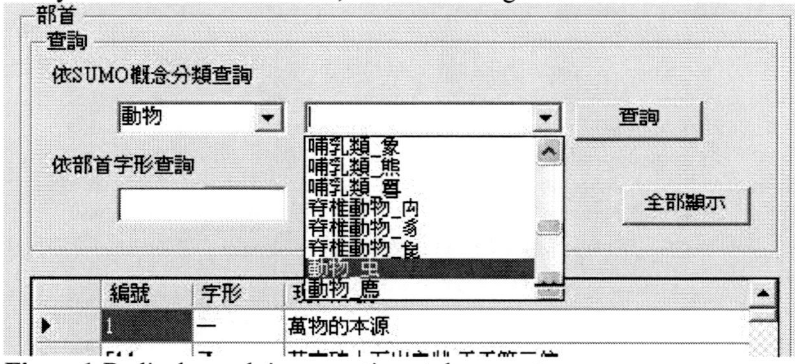

Figure1: Radical search in semantic ontology system

2.2. Basic Concept

According to the definitions in *ShuoWenJieZi* and our analysis of meaning cluster of the characters derived from the same radical, we can posit the basic concept for each radical. For example, the basic concept for "羊" is "mammal with hoof."

2.3. The classification of Hanzi semantic symbols

Based on the definition in *ShuoWenJieZi,* our structure classifies the relationship between deriving meaning cluster and the basic concept of a radical. We use Pustejovsky's *Quilia Structure* as base and observe the analysis on the definitions in *ShuoWenJieZi,* and then classify the deriving concepts of Hanzi radicals into 7 categories, expanded from the orginal four qualia aspects of Formal, Constitutive, Agentive, and Telic:
  (i) Formal: This category can be further divided into 5 small categories: "sense," "characteristic," "proper names," and "atypical." The "sense" categories can be further divided into 5 small categories: "vision," "hearing," "smelling," and "taste."
  (ii) Constitutive: This category can be further divided into 3 small categories: "part," "member," and "group."
  (iii) Telic: Concepts related to function or usage.

(iv) Participant: Words are classified into this category when the definition in *ShuoWenJieZi* mentions the participant involved.

(v) Participating: According to different events, concepts are divided into 6 small categories: "action," "state," "purpose," "function," "tool," and "others."

(vi) Descriptive: This category can be further divided into two categories: "active" and "state."

(vii) Agentive: The relationship between the radical and its meaning cluster coming from production or giving birth are classified in to agentive.

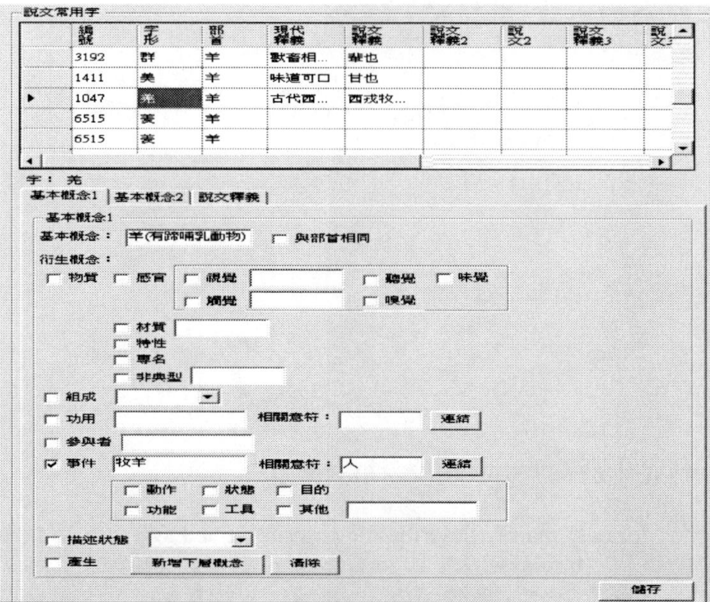

Figure2: The classification of Hanzi semantic symbols

2.4. The link of related semantic symbol

Under "telic" and "participating," we add a column for "related semantic symbol" to show and link the related deriving concepts. For example, **the character "羌" is explained as "西戎羊種人也."(the person whoe herds sheep in Xiyu)** and involves two basic concepts that are represented in the character: bovid and human sincethe Chinese character form of "羌," contains bothe "羊"(bovid) and "人" (human). Our ontology system links "羌"with its related semantic symbol "人" to offer cross-referencing in oreder to build a more realistic ontology of the conceptual convention.

3. Domian Ontologies of Four Hoofed-Animals as Conventionalized by Radical

3.1. Bovid Domain Ontology Conventionalized by Radical "羊"

According to our analysis, the deriving concepts of "羊" on the category system includes "formal," "participating," "constitutive," "agentive," and "telic." Among these five classes, the most prevalent conceptual derivation can be classified as "formal", which is further classified as Sense, Characteristic and Proper Name by us. Two-thirds of the derived characters denote this conceptual groop..

The following is the concept deriving illustration of radical "羊", with the top concept of BOVID.

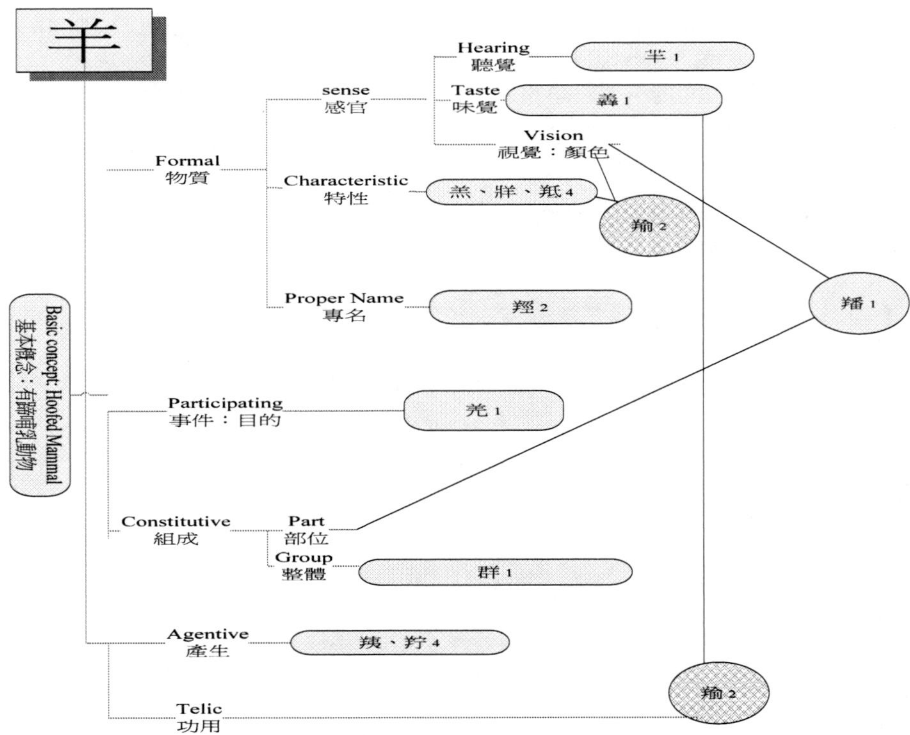

Figure3: The BOVID Domain Ontology Conventionalized by radical "羊"

(i)The cocnept cluster belong to "formal" mainly describe the color, sex, and age of bovid. Foe example, "{羊兆}，羊未足歲也。" **(bovid which is less than one year old)** expresses a concept involving the age of the bovid. "羳，黃腹羊也。" **(bovid which has yellow belly)** involves both the constitutive part of a bovid's belly and its visual attribute. As in many other animal concepts, sex is also an important concept. For example, "羒，牡羊也。"**(male bovid)** "牂，牝羊也。" **(female bovid)**

(ii) A smaller cluster of concepts denotes events which bovid can be involved in and is classified as Participating. For example, "羌，西戎羊種人也。" **(shepherd in Xiyu)** The concept of a particular type of human is defined by referring to their relation with bovid, We categorize this word into participant-goal. Besides, '羌"combines two semantic symbols "羊" and "人." Note that it could be argued that the basic concept should be HUMAN. However, as mentioned earlier, we made the commitment of describing the concept classification of SuoWenJiezi in this first study and will make adjustment after the complete ontologies are completed.

(iii)The concept cluster related to "birth" are classified as Agentive. For example, "羜，五月生 羔也。" **(lamb born in May)** In addition, there are words related to castration, such as "羠，騬羊也。"**(castrated bovid).** We classify it into "Agentive" since it denotes how this kind of bovid comes to being.

3.2. Deer Domain Ontology Conventionalized byRadical "鹿"

There are only 28 concepts in the clusters of radical "鹿." Ict is not very productive compared with the other three animal radicals. It should be observed that deers were not domesticated and hence has a much less linked to direct human experience in archaic Chinese society. This is reflected by the fact that concept cluster conventionalized by the radical "鹿" belong predominantly to the "Formal" calss with only one controversial case of "Participating."

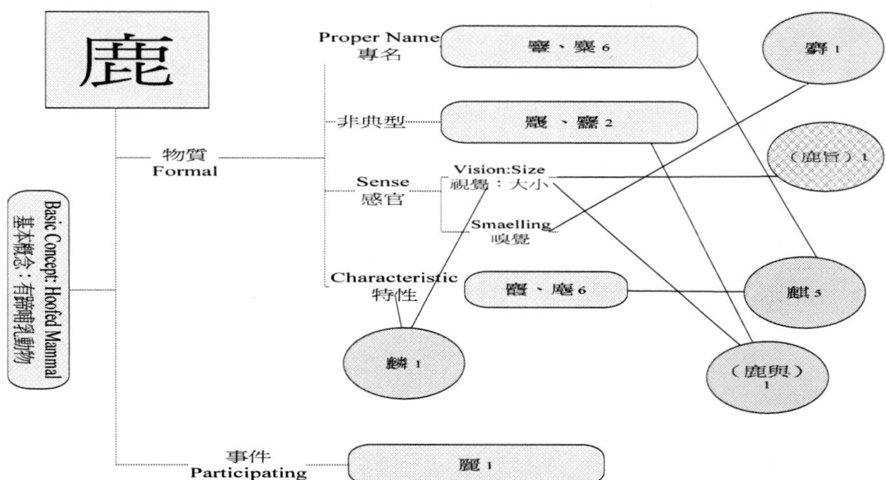

Figure4: Deer Domain Ontology Conventionalized by Radical "鹿"

(i)Most of the cocepts governed by the radical "鹿" are "Formal", mostly in the "Proper name" and "Characteristic" classes. For example, "麋，鹿屬." ""麋 is a "Proper name." "麀：牝鹿也。"**(female deer)**. This describes the sex, in the "Characteristic" class. There are also concepts cross "Proper name" and "Characteristic" two categories. For example, "麖，麋牡者." "麋" (moose) is a "Proper name," and"牡"describes sex. This is a cross categories example.
(ii)There are also atypical category in deriving concept of radical "鹿." For example, "麠，山羊而大者."**(big goat)** Goat is not a kind of deer. So it could be a mis-classification, either by convention or by Xyu Shen.
(iii)There is a single example of concept derived from participating:"麗，旅行也"**(traveling)** The Chinese Dictionary explains traveling here as "travel with companion.". The etymology and conceptual conventionalization cannot be clearly defined.

3.3. Cattle and Horse Domain Ontologies Conventionalized by Radicals "牛" and "馬"

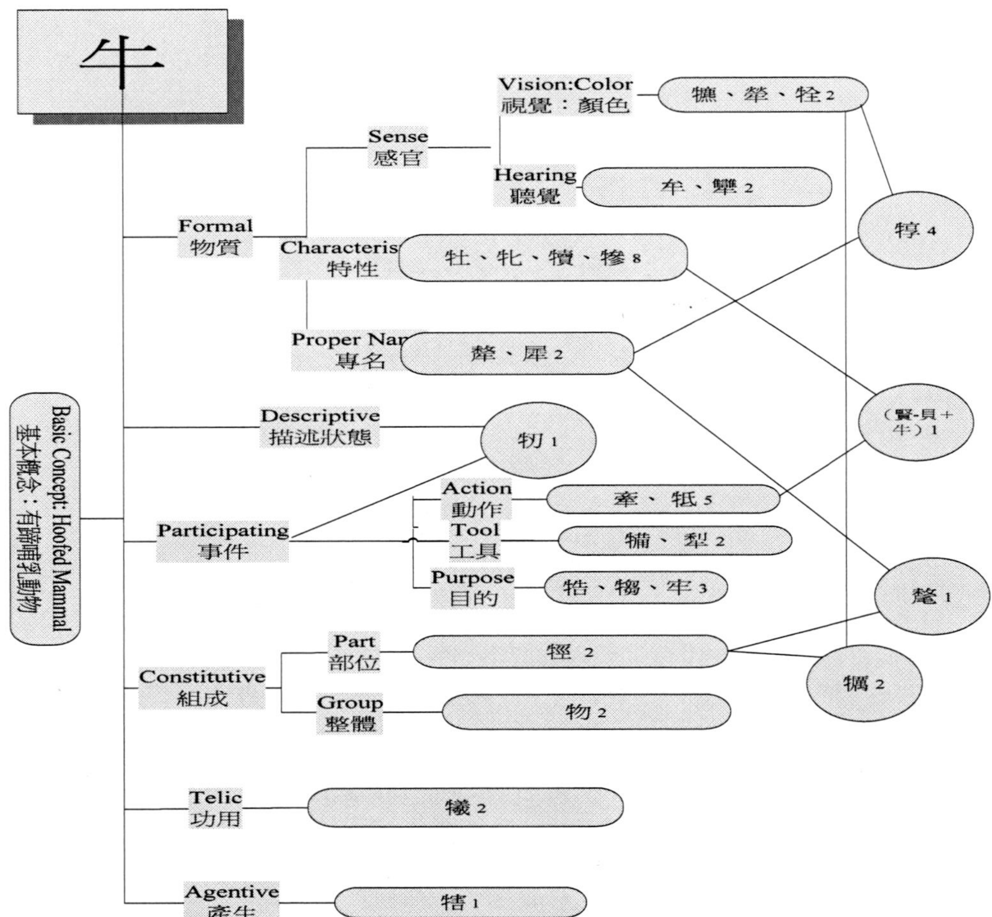

Figure5: Cattle Domain Ontology Conventionalized by of radical "牛"

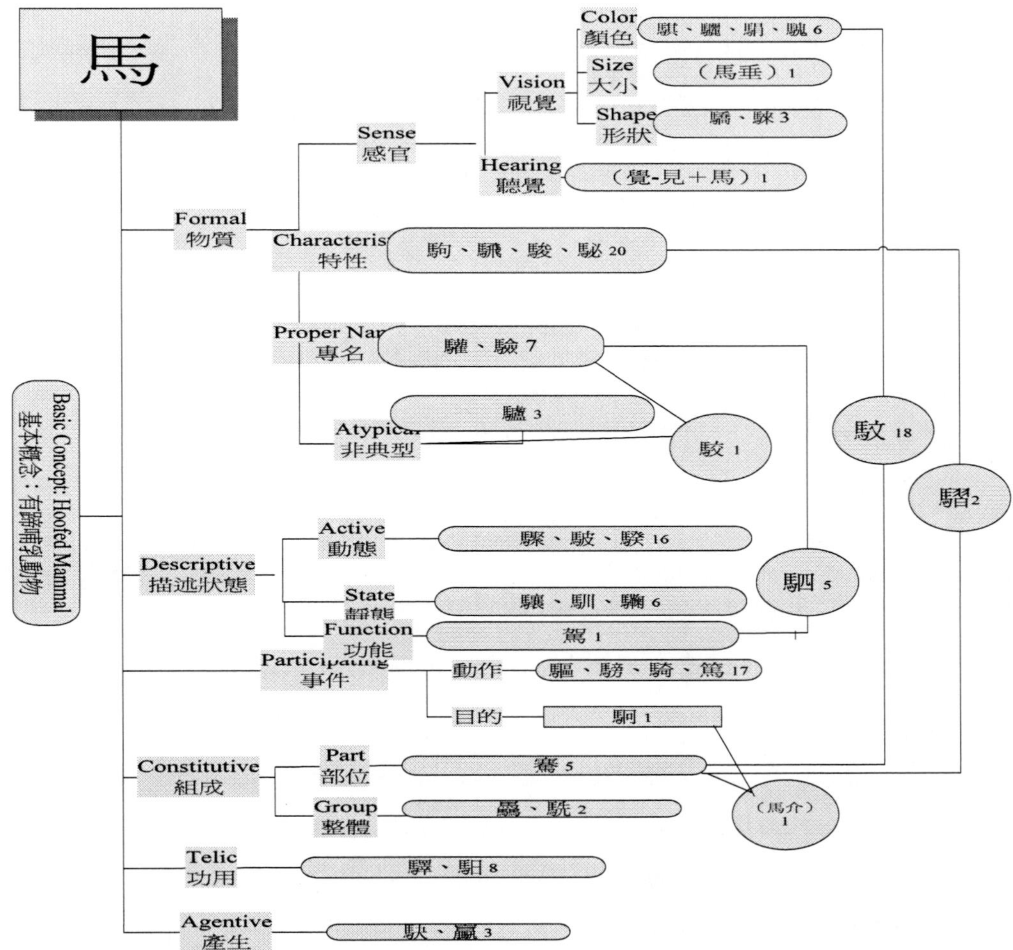

Figure6: Horse Domain Ontology Conventionalized by Radical "馬"

The Cattle and Horse Domain ontologies are much richer than the BOVID and DEER domain onotologies, which shows that these two animals are central to archaic Chinese society. The typical concepts are related to cattle being used to till the land and horses being used in transportation. Because of the close and rich first hand information, there are also descriptive events referring to experiences involves these two animals. For instance, the concept of 'to scare' and 'being scared' is actually represented by 驚 and derived of the drastic and vivid event of a startled horse.

4. Conclusion

In conclusion, we found that the definitions of the semantic primes of these four mammals with hoof are descriptions of the appearance of these animals:**(bovid represents the shape of (an animal with) four legs and a tail) (cattle represents the shape of (an animal with) horns which triangulates with a tail) (horse represents the shape of (an animal with) a maned head, tail, and four legs) (deer represents the shape of (an animal with) horns and four legs).** It is natural that the meaning clusters of concepts they derive belong to the "Formal" aspect, especially the "Vision" and "Characteristic" categories. Note that there are also many examples cross two categories, "Formal" and "Constitutive-Part," reflect the basic concept definitions involved constitute parts.

Among the four semantic primitives, radical "deer" derives the least number of concepts. This reflects the knowledge of the speakers of the language as bovid, cattle, and horse, are known to be already domesticated whiles deers are not.

Among the three domesticated animals, cattle and horse are more similar to each other in how their drived concepts cluster and distribute. The distribution of these two radicals are both include "formal," "Descriptive," "Participating," "Constitutive," "Telic," and "Agentive." Bovid is different, perhaps owning to the fact that bovid was domesticated mostly for food while cattle and horse serve the functions of farming and transportation.

It is also important to note that religion and rituals do play central role in human experience at that time. These can be observed from the definitions of the derived concepts. We observe these functions from "telic" category and find that the occasion people use cattkle is when making a religious offering. For example, **"牲, 牛完全也."(the whole cattle used for offering)**. However, horses do not seem to be offered as sacrifice but can testify to a developed system of transportation, **"驛, 置騎也." (Yi, a place wherehorses are posted).**

In conclusoin, our study of four hoofed anminals support our original thesis that the basic concepts as conventionalized by radicals represents a domain ontology of a cluster of concepts derived and marked by that radical. It is important to note that this conventionalized ontology reflects the human experience and knowledge at the time of conventionalizaiton. Hence we see that the domain ontology of domesticaed and non-domesticated animals differ from each other, while further distinctions can be made between food animial and labor animal. These direct experience and knowledge is reflected in the qualia used to derive these concepts.

5. References

Chou, Ya-Min (2005). Hantology: A Chinese Character-based Knowledge Framework and its

Applications. Ph.D thesis, National Taiwan University.

Chou, Ya-Min and Chu-Ren Huang. (2007). Hantology: An Ontology based on

Conventionalized Conceptualization. Presented at the Fourth OntoLex Workshop. Jeju,

Korea.

Hsieh, Shu-Kai. (2006). Hanzi, Concept and Computation: A preliminary survey of Chinese Characters as a Knowledge Resource in NLP. Ph.D thesis, Universität Tübingen.

Pustejovsky,J. The Generative Lexicon, The MIT Press, 1995.

Xu, Shen. 121. 說文解字 ShuoWenJieZi (in Chinese).

Xu, Zhong-Shu, 漢語大字典 The Chinese Dictionary, Taipei, Jian-Hong Press, 1992

Wong, Shun-Ha and Karel Pala. 2002. Chinese Characters and Top Ontology in EuroWordnet. In Singh, U.N. (ed).Proceedings of the First Global WordNet Conference.

Mysore, India.

Typology of Comparatives

Satomi Ito

Graduate School of Humanities and Sciences, Ochanomizu University,
2-1-1 Ohtsuka, Bunkyo-ku, Tokyo 112-8610, Japan
ito.satomi@ocha.ac.jp

Abstract. It is well-known that an adjective is not a universal part of speech. As pointed out in the previous researches, many oceanic languages do not have a morphologically distinguished adjective class. The only criteria which distinguish adjectives from verbs and nouns could be whether they appear in comparative construction or not. However, even comparative construction is not universal. Whereas most languages have a specific morpheme to construct comparatives like inflection, some languages do not. In this paper I investigate various languages in the Pacific Asia region and discuss the difference in comparative construction in the framework of formal semantics. I suggest two parameters to distinguish the four language groups and propose a new typology of comparative construction.

Keywords: Oceanic languages, Comparatives, Formal semantics, Typology

1. Introduction

It is well-known that many oceanic languages have no adjective class which is distinguishable from noun and verb classes (Wetzer, 1996). The only criteria which distinguish adjectives from nouns and verbs could be comparative constructions (Dixon, 2004). However, comparative construction is not universal. Some languages in Papua New Guinea do not have any comparative morpheme or any comparative-specific structure. In this paper I focus on the comparative forms of various languages in the Pacific Asia region and suggest a new typology of comparatives in the framework of formal semantics.

  The structure of the paper is as follows: in section 2, I summarize the previous studies on semantics of comparatives and define the denotation of adjectives; in section 3, I show the data from various languages in the Pacific Asia region and classify them into four groups depending on the morphological/syntactic markedness; in section 4, I show how to analyze each type of comparative construction in the framework presented in section 2; in section 5, I show that two parameters are relevant to the classification of adjectival systems.

2. Semantics of Comparatives

The denotation of an adjective is property, i.e. an expression of type $<e,t>$. In comparative construction, however, adjectives need to be abstracted over degrees, because what is compared is the degree of property of more than one object. I call this process degree abstraction and define the degree abstraction operator as follows:

1) Degree Abstraction operator Π is a function from expressions of type $<e,t>$ to $<e <d,t>>$
   $$\Pi_{<<e,t>, <e,<d,t>>>} = \lambda A_{<e,t>}\lambda x_{<e>}\lambda d_{<d>} [R_A(d)(x)]$$
   where the domain of type $<d>$ is a set of degrees and R_A is a function which relate objects to degrees on the scale of A.

22nd Pacific Asia Conference on Language, Information and Computation, pages 197–206

Ex. $\lambda x_{<e>} [tall(x)] \rightarrow \lambda x_{<e>}\lambda d_{<d>} [R_{tall}(d)(x)]$

After an adjective undergoes the process of degree abstraction, we obtain a function from individuals to a set of degrees. An adjective *tall* now means a set of degrees which the individual x has on the scale of tallness. However, this procedure is not enough for an adjective to be comparative. When we compare two sets of degrees, we need to pick up the maximal degree in each degree set. This process is conducted by the maximization operator 'MAX' (Rullmann, 1995).

2) $MAX (\lambda d_{<d>} [R_A(d)(x)]) = \iota d [R_A(d)(x)]$

Degree abstraction and maximization work together with comparative morphemes to construct comparatives. For example, English comparative morpheme *–er* is defined as (3) (Kennedy, 1999)[1]. Each argument of *–er* has to be abstracted over degrees and maximized.

3) Definition of comparative morpheme
   $\|MORE(MAX(D2))(MAX(D1))\| = 1$ iff $MAX(D1) > MAX(D2)$

   Ex. $\|Bill\ is\ taller\ than\ John\|$
       $= MORE (MAX(\lambda d_{<d>} [R_{tall}(d)(John)]))(MAX(\lambda d_{<d>} [R_{tall}(d)(Bill)]))$
       $= \iota d_{<d>} [R_{tall}(d)(Bill)] > \iota d_{<d>} [R_{tall}(d)(John)]$

3. Four Types of Comparative Forms

Investigation on a wide variety of languages reveals that there are at least four types of comparative constructions: Enlish-type, Chinese-type, Japanese-type and Dom-type. The former three languages have adpositions to introduce standards of comparison, while Dom-type languages has none. In other words, Dom-type languages cannot describe comparison in one sentence, as there is no way to introduce a standard of comparison into adjectival construction. The sense of comparison is described by coordination of positive and negative adjectives. Other three languages are different in morphological markedness of adjectives. English-type languages mark comparative form and Chinese-type languages absolute form, while Japanese-type languages do not have any morpheme or word to distinguish aboslute and comparative.

Table 1: Typology of Comparative Forms

	The standard of comparison is introduced by...	morphological markedness
English-type	adpositional phrase	comparative
Chinese-type	adpositional phrase	absolute
Japanese-type	adpositional phrase	none
Dom-type	coordination	none

A large number of languages belong to English-type or Japanese-type, while only a few appear as examples of Chinese and Dom-type languages.

4) **English-type**: absolute form as basic
       English, Karo Batak, Madurese, Sundanese, Semelai, Chamorro, ...
5) **Chinese-type**: comparative form as basic

---

[1] The order of D1 and D2 is different from the original suggestion by Kennedy (1999). Following Bresnan (1973), Heim (2000) and Bhat & Pancheva (2004), I assume that comparative/absolute morphemes are first combined with degree clauses.

Chinese, Qiang
6) **Japanese-type**: no morpheme
    Japanese, Worora, Muna, North-East Ambae, ...
7) **Dom-type**: juxtaposing a positive sentence and a negative one
    Dom, Korowai, Sinaugoro, Nabak

3.1. English-type Adjectives
In English-type languages, an adjective designates an abolute quality so that it has to undergo morphological change. For example, English absolute form is bare adjective while comparative form is adjective+*er*.

8) a. Bill is tall.
    b. Bill is taller than John.

This group of languages includes Karo Batak (*-en*), Madurese (*-an*), Semelai (*ra* -) and Chamorro (*-ña*). The comparative form of each language is as follows: [2]

9) Karo Batak
    Ia Gegeh-en asang aku.
    he strong-er than I
    'He is stronger than me.'

10) Madurese
    Hasan sənəng-an katembang Ali.
    Hasan happy-er   than   Ali
    'Hasan is happier than Ali.'

11) Semelai
    □ŋaŋ,   cim ra□-tʰəy   t□m kl□ŋk□ŋ.
    enggang hornbill bird more-be.big from pied-hornbill
    'The enggang hornbill, (it's) bigger than the pied-hornbill.'

12) Chamorro
    Dikike□ña si Rosa kinu si Rita.
    Small-er   the Rosa than the Rita
    'Rosa is smaller than Rita.'

3.2. Chinese-type Adjectives
Chinese-type adjectives stand in sharp contrast to English-type ones. In Chinese, adjectives are inherently comparative and need to be modified by the degree adverb *hen* 'very' to describe absolute qualities.

13) Chinese
    a. Zhangsan hen shuai.
       Zhangsan very cool
       'Zhangsan is cool.'
    b. Zhangsan bi Lisi shuai.

---

[2] The following languages might also have English-type adjectival system: Indonesian (*lebih*), Baumaa Fijian (*ca'e* 'up, more'), Sundanese (*leuwih* 'more'), Tinrin (*siwai--nai* 'comparative--superior'), Māori (*ake* 'up'). These languages utilize adverbs to describe comparison. They might be in pre-gramaticalized stage of comparative morphemes.

Zhangsan than Lisi cool
'Zhangsan is cooler than Lisi.'

Only a few languages have Chinese-type adjectival system. Qiang is another example of this type. The adverb *wa* 'very' clarifies the absolute meaning in (14b), while a bare adjective appears in comparative construction (14c).

14) Qiang
    a. The: tiwi.
      3SG tall
      'He is tall/taller.'
    b. The: tiwi-wa.
      3SG tall-very
      'He is very tall.'
    c. The:-ŋuə□i qa-sə□   ba-□a.
      3SG-TOP   1SG-than big-1SG
      'He is bigger than me.'

3.3. Japanese-type Adjectives

Japanese-type adjectives do not undergo any morphological change to distinguish between absolute and comparative. The only difference between absolute and comparative is whether there is a standard of comparison in the sentence or not. In the following pair of sentences, the adjective *wakai* 'young' appears in both absolute and comparative sentences without undergoing any morphological change.

15) a. Taro-wa wakai.
      Taro-TOPIC young
      'Taro is young.'
    b. Taro-wa Jiro-yori wakai.
      Taro-TOPIC Jiro-than young
      'Taro is younger than Jiro.'

Worora, Muna, North-East and Ambae belong to this group. The standards of comparison are introduced by *man'daga* in Worora, *bhe* in Muna, and *dene* in North-East Ambae respectively. [3]

16) Worora
    Kum'baiu 'inia   man'd□ga Pu'nauera.
    Kumbaiu good than   Punauera
    'Kumbaiu is better than Punauera.'

17) Muna
    No-bhala anoa bhe inodi
    3SG-big he   with I
    'He is bigger than I am.'

18) North-East Ambae
    Vanua-ra, bataha   u   garea u   garea u   garea dene na   vanua-da.

---

[3] The following languages might also belong to this class: Fehan dialect of Tetun (*liu* 'go further'), Seediq (*rmabang* 'surpass'), Abun (*wai* 'pass'), Tawala (*lagona* 'surpass'), Jabêm (*-leleq...su* 'surpass') and Sye (*telwog-* 'go past'). These languages use verbs of motion to introduce standard of comparison. They might be in pre-gramaticalized stage of comparative morphemes which add an extra argument to adjectives.

land-their I.reckon TEL good TEL good TEL good from ACC land-our
'I reckon their land is much, much better than ours.' TEL=telic

3.4. Dom-type Adjectives

In Dom-type languages, a comparison of degrees is described by a coordination of two sentences, one positive and one negative. For example, in (19b), the first adjective is *bl* 'big' and the second one is the opposite, *kepl* 'small'.

19) Dom
 a. John bl mol-gwe.
  John big be-3SG.-INDICATIVE
  'John is big.'
 b. John bl mol-gwe, Bill kepl mol-gwe.
  John big be-3SG.-INDICATIVE Bill small be -3SG.-INDICATIVE
  'John is bigger than Bill.'

Although it might seem to be inappropriate to regard this kind of coordination as comparative, if we assume that there is a notion of comparison in every human language, this structure should be analyzed as comparative construction.

Sinaugoro, Nabak and Korowai belong to this group. The adjective in the second sentence can be the negation of the first adjective as in the example of Korowai.

20) Sinaugoro
  Boregaina tu vanu☐a bara-na, Saroa tu kei-na.
  Boregaina TOPIC village big-3SG Saroa TOPIC small-3SG
  'Boregaina is bigger than Saroa.'

21) Nabak
  Pi imbelaŋaŋ, Ke nugŋaŋ.
  This easy that difficult
  'This is easier than that.'

22) Korowai
  If-e-kha abül-efè khonggél-khayan waf-e-kha abül be-khonggé-tebo-da.
  This-tr-CONN man-TOPIC big-very that-tr-CONN man Neg-big-be.3SG. REAL-NEG
  'This man is bigger than that man.' tr=transitional sound, CONN=connective

4. Typology of Comparatives
4.1. English-type Adjectival System

In English-type adjectival system, adjectives are not abstracted over degrees nor maximized. They must undergo degree abstraction (23b) and maximization (23c) to be arguments of comparative morpheme.

23) a. $\|\text{Adjective}_E\| = \lambda x_{<e>} [A(x)]$
 b. $\|\Pi(\|\text{Adjective}_E\|)\| = \lambda x_{<e>}\lambda d_{<d>} [R_A(d)(x)]$
 c. $\|\text{MAX}(\Pi(\|\text{Adjective}_E\|))\| = \lambda x_{<e>}\iota d_{<d>} [R_A(d)(x)])$
24) $\|\text{-er}\| = \lambda d'_{<d>}\lambda d_{<d>} [d > d']$
 a. $\|\text{-er than John } \text{is tall}\| = \|\text{-er}\|(\|\text{John is tall}\|)$
  $= \lambda d'_{<d>}\lambda d_{<d>} [d > d'](\iota d_{<d>}[R_{tall}(d)(John)])$
  $= \lambda d_{<d>}\lambda x_{<e>} [d > \iota d_{<d>}[R_{tall}(d)(John)]]$
 b. $\|\text{Bill is taller than John } \text{is tall} \| = \|\text{-er than John } \text{is tall}\|(\|\text{Bill is tall}\|)$
  $= \lambda d_{<d>} [d > \iota d_{<d>}[R_{tall}(d)(John)]](\iota d_{<d>}[R_{tall}(d)(Bill)])$

$$= \mathrm{\iota d}_{<d>}[R_{tall}(d)(Bill)] > \mathrm{\iota d}_{<d>}[R_{tall}(d)(John)]$$

As shown by 'is tall', the adjective in *than*-clause is usually interpreted as the same one as the main clause, it can be different from the one in the main clause.

25) The door is wider than the table is long.

(25) is well-formed because we can apply degree abstraction and maximization on main clause and *than*-clause respectively. It means both operators are available in syntax in English-type languages.

4.2. Chinese-type Adjectival System

In 3.2, I mentioned that Chinese adjectives are inherently comparative. However, Chinese adjectives are not homogeneous. In this section I first discuss the different types of adjectives and then define the Chinese adjectival system.

Chinese adjectives can be classified into two major groups: simple adjectives and complex adjectives. Simple adjectives are well-known for their 'nouny' behavior: they can modify nouns directly (26) (a noun can modify another noun directly in Chinese). Complex adverbs are known as 'verby', as they take the form of relative clauses when they modify a noun (27).

26) shuai ge
     cool guy
     'cool guy'
27) shuaishuai de   ge
     cool-cool REL guy
     'very cool guy'   REL=relative clause marker

Observing several different behaviors of the two types of adjectives, Huang concluded that simple adjectives are expressions of type <e>, while complex adjectives are of type <e,t> (Huang, 2006). However, this conclusion is not attested by the most basic criterion which distinguishes the two types of adjectives, i.e. (26)-(27). As nouns are expressions of type <e,t> and modification is possible by generalized conjunction (Partee and Rooth, 1983), simple adjectives may well be expressions of type <e,t>. Huang's conclusion cannot explain why only simple adjectives can appear in comparative construction either.

28) Zhangsan bi   Lisi shuai.
     Zhangsan compare Lisi cool
     'Zhangsan is cooler than Lisi.'
29) *Zhangsan bi   Lisi shuaishuai.
     Zhangsan compare Lisi cool-cool
     'Zhangsan is much cooler than Lisi.'

I assume that simple adjectives in Chinese are abstracted over degrees and maximized in lexicon as (30a). They are already prepared for comparison, hence they sound natural in comparative construction. On the other hand, complex adjectives go too further. They not only designate the property but also mention that the degree to which the object is cool exceeds the usually expected degree. Hence they cannot take another standard of comparison.

30) a.$\|\mathrm{Adjective}_{SIMPLE}\| = \lambda x \iota d[R_A(x)(d)] \rightarrow \lambda d' \lambda x \iota d[R_A(x)(d)] > d'$
     b.$\|\mathrm{Adjective}_{COMPLEX}\| = \lambda x \iota d[R_A(x)(d)] >$ the usually expected degree

Another important point is that degree abstraction is applied in lexicon. When degree abstraction is applied to an adjective in lexicon, the abstracted degrees must be on the scale of the adjective. This is the reason why the counterpart of (25) is not well-formed in Chinese. Chinese native speakers do not consider "long" and "wide" are on the same scale even if they describe degrees on the same dimension.

31) *Zheige men bi [neige zhuozi chang] kuan.
      this door compare that table long wide
    'This door is wider than that table is long'

Let us now see how simple adjectives behave in absolute construction. As mentioned above, a simple adjective cannot construct a predicate in Chinese. It needs the support of a degree adverb like *hen* 'very' to be absolute.

32) ?Zhangsan shuai.
      Zhangsan cool
      'Zhangsan is cooler.'
33) Zhangsan hen shuai.
      Zhangsan very cool
      'Zhangsan is cool.'

As simple adjectives are already abstracted over degrees and maximized, they tend to be interpreted as comparative (34). Degree adverb *hen* 'very' takes the adjective and fills the argument of standard degree, makes the adverb to be absolute.

34) $\|$Zhangsan shuai$\|$ = $\iota d_{<d>}$ $[R_{cool}(d)(Zhangsan)] > ?$
35) a. $\|$hen$\|$ = $\lambda A_{<d,t>}$ $[A(c)]$ c = the standard degree given by the context
     b. $\|$hen shuai$\|$ = $\|$hen$\|$($\|$shuai$\|$)
              = $\lambda A_{<d,t>}$ $[A(c)](\lambda d_{<d>}$ $[\iota d_{<d>}[R_{cool}(d)(x)] > d])$
              = $\iota d_{<d>}$ $[R_{cool}(d)(x)] > c]$

4.3. Japanese-type Adjectival System

Japanese-type adjectives can occur both in absolute and comparative construction without morphological change. Hence we can assume that maximization is not lexical, as lexical maximization usually induce comparative reading as mentioned above. On the other hand, degree abstraction is lexical in Japanese-type languages as argued in Beck et al (2004). The most striking evidence is the ill-formedness of subcomparatives. Since degree abstraction is applied in lexicon, adjectives in different dimensions cannot be compared in Japanese.

36) *Kono doa-wa [ano tsukue-ga nagai]-yori hiroi.
      this door-TOP that table-NOM long than wide
      'This door is wider than that table is long'

Another important aspect of their claim is the way *yori*-clause is interpreted. *Yori*-clause is different from English than-clause in that it provides a clue to obtain the standard of comparison but does not provide the exact degree to compare with. According to their analysis, the standard of comparison is obtained by pragmatic inference.

In sum, the denotation of Japanese adjectives in comparative construction is as follows:

37) a. $\|$Adjective$_J\|$ = $\lambda x_{<e>} \lambda d_{<d>}$ $[R_A(d)(x)]$
     b. $\|$MAX(($\|$Adjective$_J$ $\|$))$\|$ = $\lambda x_{<e>} \iota d_{<d>}$ $[R_A(d)(x)]$
38) $\|$Taroo-wa Jiroo-yori wakai$\|$ = $\iota d_{<d>}$ $[R_{young}(d)(Taroo)]) > c$

where c is provided by *yori*-clause.

4.4. Dom-type Adjectival System

In Dom-type languages, comparative construction consists of positive and negative adjectives on the same dimension. We can formalize the construction as (39). In this construction neither degree abstraction nor maximization seems to be relevant. Instead, they use abstraction over properties (40) and conjunction (41).

39) $||\text{Adjective}_D|| \ \& \ ||{\sim}\text{Adjective}_D||$

40) $A(x) = \lambda P_{<e,t>} \lambda x_{<e>} \ [P(x)] \ni A$

41) $A(x) \ \& \ {\sim}A(y)$
$= \lambda x_{<e>} \ [A(x)] \ \& \ \lambda y_{<e>} \ [{\sim}A(y)]$
$= \lambda P_{<e,t>} \lambda x_{<e>} \ [P(x)] \ni \ ||A|| \ \& \ \lambda Q_{<e,t>} \lambda y_{<e>} \ [Q(y)] \not\ni \ ||A||$

$= \{P: x \text{ has property } P\} \ni A \ \& \ \{Q: y \text{ has property } Q\} \not\ni A$

42) $||\text{John is big, Bill is small}||$

$= \{P: \text{John has a property } P\} \ni \ ||\text{big}|| \ \& \ \{Q: \text{Bill has a property } Q\} \not\ni \ ||\text{big}||$

(42) means that the set of properties that John has includes the property 'big' and the set of properties that Bill has does not include the property 'big'. Dom-type adjectives are defined as (43), in which neither degree abstraction nor maximization is available al through lexicon and syntax.

43) $||\text{Adjective}_D|| = \lambda x_{<e>} \ [A(x)]$

5. Conclusion

In this paper I classified languages into four groups depending on the presence/absence of adpositional phrases and morphological markedness on adjectives in comparative construction. Availability of degree abstraction and maximization distinguishes these four language types.

Table 2: Typology of Adjectives

	Degree Abstraction	Maximization
English-type	syntax	syntax
Chinese-type	lexicon	lexicon
Japanese-type	lexicon	syntax
Dom-type	none	none

English-type adjectival system can utilize degree abstraction and maximization in syntax, while both of them are only applied at lexical level in Chinese-type adjectival system. As early maximization induces comparative reading, comparative forms in Chinese-type languages are unmarked so that adjectives need 'absolute operator'. In Japanese-type adjectival system degree abstraction is limited to lexical level so that they do not allow subcomparatives, whereas maximization is not obligatory in lexicon so that adjectives can feed both absolute and comparative operator. Dom-type languages utilize a unified strategy to noun conjunction and adjective conjunction, which leads these languages to develop a particular way to express comparative.

References

Bhatt, R., and R. Pancheva. 2004. Late Merger of Degree Clauses. *Linguistic Inquiry* 35(1), 1-45.

Beck, S., T. Oda and K. Sugisaki. 2004. Parametric Variation in the Semantics of Comaprison: Japanese vs. English. *Journal of East Asian Linguistics* 13: 289-344.

Berry, K. and C. Berry. 1999. *A description of Abun: A West Papuan Language of Irian Jaya.* Pacific Linguistics B-115.

Bradshaw, J. and F. Czobor. 2005. *Otto Dempwolff's Grammar of the Jabem Language in New Guinea.* Honolulu:University of Hawai'i Press.

Bresnan, J. 1973. The Syntax of Comparative Clause Construction in English. *Linguistic Inquiry* 4: 275-343.

Crowley, T. 2004. *Bislama Reference Grammar.* Honolulu:University of Hawai'i Press.

Dauies, W. 1999. *Madurese.* Munchen:LINCOM EUROPA,

Dixon , R. M. W. 2004. Adjective Classes in Typological Perspective. In R. M. W. Dixon and A. Y. Aikhenvald eds., *Adjective Classes*, pp 1-49. Oxford University Press.

Dixon, R. M. W. 1988. *A Grammar of Boumaa Fijian.* The University of Chicago Press

England, N. C. 2004. Adjectives in Mam. In R. M. W. Dixon and A. Y. Aikhenvald eds., *Adjective Classes*, pp125-146. Oxford University Press.

Ezard, B. 1997. *A Grammar of Tawala.* Pacific Linguistics (C-137)

Fabian, G., E. Fabian and B. Waters. 1998. *Morphology, Syntax and Cohesion in Nabak, Papua New Guinea.* Pacific Linguistics (C-144)

Harlow, R. 1996. *Maori.* Munchen:LINCOM EUROPA.

Heim, I. 2000. Degree Operators and Scope. In B. Jackson and T. Mathews, eds., *SALT X*, pp. 41-64. CLC Publication, N.Y. Ithaca.

Holmer, A. J. 1996. *A parametric Grammar of Seediq.* Lund University Press

Hunag, S.Z. 2006. Property Theory, Adjectives, and Modification in Chinese. *Journal of East Asian Linguistics* 15:343-369.

Hyslop, C. 2004. Adjectives in North-East Ambae. In R. M. W. Dixon and A. Y. Aikhenvald eds., *Adjective Classes.* Oxford University Press

Kennedy, Christopher 1999 Projecting the Adjective. New York Garland.

Klamer, Marian 1998 *A Grammar of Kambera.* Mouton de Gruyter

Kruspe, Nicole 2004 'Adjectives in Semelai.' In R. M. W. Dixon and A. Y. Aikhenvald (eds.) *Adjective Classes*, pp283-305. Oxford University Press.

LaPolla, R. J. and C. Huang. 2004. Adjectives in Qiang. In R. M. W. Dixon and A. Y. Aikhenvald eds., *Adjective Classes*, pp306-322. Oxford University Press.

Love, J. R. B. 2000. *The Grammatical Structure of the Worora Language of North-Wetern Australia.* Munchen :LINCOM EUROPA.

Macdonald, R. R. and D. Soenjono. 1967. *A student's Reference Grammar of Modern Formal Indonesian.* Georgetown University Press

Muller-Gotama, F. 2001. *Sundanese.* Munchen:LINCOM EUROPA.

Osumi, M. 1995. *Tinrin Grammar.* Honolulu:University of Hawai'i Press.

Partee, B. H. and M. Rooth 1983. 'Generalized conjunction and type ambiguity.' In Bauerle, R., C. Schwarze, and A. von Stechow, (eds.) *Meaning, Use and Interpretation of Language.* Berlin:Walter de Gruyter.

Ramos, V. T. 1971. *Tagalog Structures.* Honolulu:University of Hawaii Press.

Rullmann, H. 1995. *Maximality in the Semantics of WH-Constructions.* Ph.D. thesis, University of Massachusetts.

Sneddon, J. N. 1996. *Indonesian.* Routledge.

Tauberschmidt, G. 1999. *A Grammar of Sinaugoro.* Pacific Linguistics C-143

Crowley, T. 1998. *An Erromangan (Sye) Grammar.* Honolulu:University of Hawai'i Press.

Tida, S. 2006. *A Grammar of Dom Language-A Papuan Language of Papua New Guinea.* Ph.D. thesis, Kyoto University.

Topping, D. M. 1973. Chamorro Reference Grammar. Honolulu:The University Press of Hawai'i

Woolams, G. 1996. *A Grammar of Karo Batak, Sumatra*. Pacific Linguistics C-130

Wetzer, H. 1996. *The Typology of Adjective Predication*. Mouton de Gruyter.

van Enk, J. Gerrit and L. de Vries. 1997. *The Korowai of Irian Jaya*. Oxford University Press

van Klinken. and C. Lumien. 1999. *A Grammar of the Fehan dialect of Tetun: An Austronesian Language of West Timor*. Pacific Linguistics C-155

van den Berg, R. 1989. *A Grammar of the Muna Language*. Ph.D. thesis,

Unsupervised Chinese Verb Metaphor Recognition Based on Selectional Preferences[*]

Yuxiang Jia, Shiwen Yu

Institute of Computational Linguistics, Peking University, Beijing, China, 100871
{yxjia, yusw}@pku.edu.cn

Abstract. Metaphors are pervasive in human language and developing methods to recognize and deal with metaphors is an indispensable task in Natural Language Processing (NLP). This paper proposes an unsupervised method to recognize metaphors from real texts. Firstly, source domain candidates are determined based on automatically acquired selectional preferences. And then metaphors are recognized with the source domain knowledge. Experiment results show that this unsupervised method outperforms the baseline by a great improvement. In addition, the source domain knowledge can also be used for metaphor comprehension.

Keywords: Selectional Preference, Source Domain, Metaphor Recognition, Concept Concreteness

1. Introduction

Conceptual Metaphor Theory (Lakoff and Johnson, 1980) considers metaphor as a mapping from the concrete source domain to the abstract target domain. Abstractions and enormously complex situations are routinely understood via metaphors. Metaphorical expressions are pervasive in human languages and must be treated for Natural Language Understanding (NLU) (Carbonell, 1982). As an important figure of speech, metaphor processing has interesting applications in many Natural Language Processing (NLP) tasks like machine translation, paraphrasing, information retrieval and question answering.

Metaphor processing can be divided into three tasks, recognition, comprehension and generation, among which recognition is the basic step. Metaphor recognition is to decide whether a sentence contains metaphorical expressions (a word, phrase or the whole sentence). This paper focuses on verb metaphor, to decide whether a verb is in metaphorical usage or literal usage. In selectional preference violation view, a satisfied preference indicates a literal semantic relation, while a violated preference indicates a metaphorical one. Take the following two sentences as examples.

(1) 农民　在　精心　培植　幼苗。
Nong2min2　zai4　jing1xin1　pei2zhi2　you4miao3
Farmer　at　carefully　cultivate　young plants
"Farmers are cultivating young plants carefully."

---

[*] This research is funded by National Basic Research Program of China (No.2004CB318102). The authors are grateful to the two anonymous reviewers for their helpful comments and suggestions.

22nd Pacific Asia Conference on Language, Information and Computation, pages 207–214

(2) 我们　要　大力　培植　人才。
Wo3men2　yao4　da4li4　pei2zhi2　ren2cai2
We　　　should　devote great effort　train　talents
"We should devote great effort to train talents."

Sentence 1 is a literal usage while sentence 2 is a metaphorical one. The fact that literally 培植 'cultivate' requires the object to denote some plants suggests that selectional preferences offer a cue to the presence of a metaphor. But the selectional preferences automatically induced by conventional computational models may not reflect semantics in the literal usage. On the other hand, concept concreteness or abstractness is an important indicator of literal usage, where concrete concepts usually indicate literal usage while abstract concepts correspond to non-literal usage. This paper makes use of concept concreteness based on automatically acquired selectional preferences for verb metaphor recognition.

Though metaphorical usage could be considered as a different sense of the target word, but when performing inference, it is beneficial to differentiate literal usage from metaphorical usage, because they share inferential structure. For example, the aspectual structure of 培植 'cultivate' is the same in either domain whether it is literal or metaphorical. Further, this sharing of inferential structure between the source and target domains simplifies the representational mechanisms used for inference making it easier to build the world models necessary for knowledge-intensive tasks like question answering.

The rest of this paper is organized as follows. Section 2 is a review of related work. Section 3 describes the details of selectional preferences acquisition. Section 4 shows the method of source domain determination based on selectional preferences. Section 5 uses this source domain knowledge for metaphor recognition. Experiments and conclusions are given in section 6 and 7 respectively.

2. Related Work

Previous work on automatic metaphor recognition using selectional preferences idea includes (Martin, 1990), (Fass, 1991), (Mason, 2004) and (Krishnakumaran and Zhu, 2007). (Martin, 1990) detects metaphors by comparing new sentences with an empirically collected metaphor knowledge base and gives some interpretation of metaphorical sentences. (Fass, 1991) uses collative semantics to identify metaphors and distinguish metaphor from metonymy. But they both require hand-coded knowledge bases and thus have limited coverage.

(Mason, 2004) develops a corpus-based system CorMet for discovering metaphorical mappings between concepts. It finds selectional preferences of given verbs from automatically compiled domain-specific corpora, and then identifies metaphorical mappings between concepts in two domains based on differences in selectional preferences. (Krishnakumaran and Zhu, 2007) uses lexical resources like WordNet and bigram counts generated from a large scale corpus to classify sentences into metaphorical or normal usages. It does not compute selectional preferences explicitly and the bigram counts omit grammatical relations.

Later researches treat metaphor recognition task as a classification problem between normal and metaphorical usage. (Gedigian et al., 2006) uses a maximum entropy classifier to identify metaphors and takes verb arguments as features. (Wang et al., 2006) also uses a maximum entropy approach to recognize Chinese noun phrase metaphors. However, both need manually annotated corpus to train the classifier. In order to reduce manual work on annotation, (Birke and Sarkar, 2006) use a clustering approach with a smaller seed corpus to classify verb usages.

One advantage of selectional preferences based method is that it does not need training. One thing that sets our work apart is that all previous selectional preferences based methods do not make use of concept concreteness information. In contrast, we use it and show that it is effective information for metaphor processing.

3. Selectional Preference Acquisition

The automatic corpus-based induction of selectional preferences was first proposed by (Resnik, 1993). All later approaches have followed the same two-step procedure, first collecting argument head words from a corpus, then generalizing to other similar words. They are different mainly in the generalization step, some using manual semantic taxonomy like WordNet, while others using clustering methods.

Different from previous approaches, the first step in this approach is based on grammatical collocations. It makes use of various statistical measures for computing collocations or combination of some of them, not just word frequency used in previous approaches. For generalization, a semantic lexicon containing synonym and hypernym relations is employed.

3.1. Grammatical Collocation

Grammatical collocation means that the target word and its collocation are in a certain grammatical relation, such as subject-verb, verb-object or modifier-noun. In order to obtain grammatical collocations for the target word, this paper uses Sketch Engine (Kigarriff and Tugwell, 2001), a query system extracting collocations of different grammatical relations from a large scale corpus.

Collocations are sorted in descending order according to the salience value, which is estimated as the product of Mutual Information and log frequency. However, (Kilgarriff and Tugwell, 2001) modify the Mutual Information value by considering of the overall frequency of the grammatical relation as compared to other relations. The purpose of doing so is to avoid cases of low frequency collocations such as those which occur once but have high mutual information values because it is the only time they appear together with the target word. Therefore, the salience value is a reliable calculator instead of the frequency value.

The corpus for grammatical collocation extraction is the Simple Chinese Gigaword corpus, which has 706,427,624 tokens. The input parameters for Sketch Engine are as follows: the minimum frequency is 5; the minimum salience value is 0.0; the maximum number of items in a grammatical relation is 999, which is the upper bound due to licensing limitation.

As an example, table1 shows the top 20 collocations of the target verb 培植 pei2zhi2 'cultivate' in the verb-object relation.

Table 1: Top 20 collocations, object of 培植 'cultivate'

Collocation	Frequency	Salience	Collocation	Frequency	Salience
人才	186	42.33	盆景	8	22.15
税源	29	39.92	幼苗	7	21.71
财源	55	38.18	新秀	12	20.57
干鱼	5	30.16	木耳	6	20.56
草坪	17	28.24	生长点	5	20.19
后进	13	27.58	人材	6	19.7
产业	86	24.29	蘑菇	6	19.4
新人	18	24.26	接班人	8	19.4
球员	36	23.91	细胞	16	18.17
增长点	12	23.69	势力	15	17.29

3.2. Semantic Mapping

Collocation words need to be generalized into semantic level to reflect the semantic preferences of the target word. A Chinese semantic lexicon named TongYiCiCiLin is used for this purpose. In the lexicon, about 80,000 words are arranged into 5-level tree structures (see figure1) according to semantic relations like synonym and hypernym. In the tree structure, the bottom level is called Atomic Word Group Level, where a node represents a synonym set. The parent node is the hypernym of the children. In total, 12 root nodes partition all words into 12 super classes, and the lower nodes further partition words into more detailed classes. The super classes include Human, Substance, Time and Space, Abstraction, Features, Motions, Psychological Activity, Activity, etc.

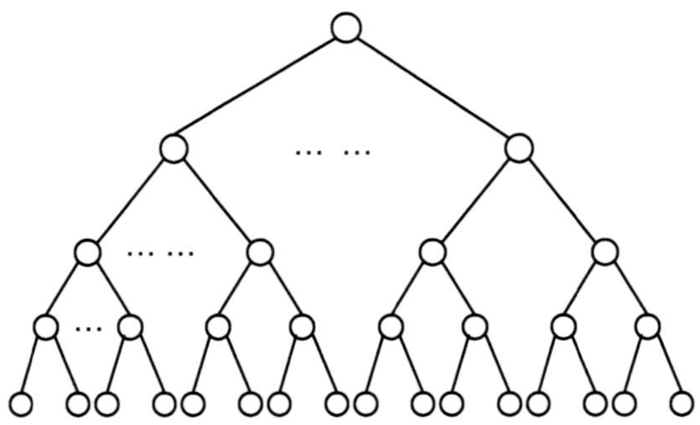

Figure1: The 5-level tree structure of TongYiCiCiLin

With the tree structure, collocations can be mapped to different semantic levels as required. After semantic mapping, collocations are grouped and semantic classes are sorted according to the number of collocations they contain. The sequence of semantic classes reflects the selectional preferences of the target word. The more collocations a semantic class contains, the more it is preferred. Table2 shows the top 10 semantic classes of level 2 of the target word 培植 'cultivate'. The first column is the semantic class ID in TongYiCiCiLin. The second column is the semantic class name. Column 3 and column 4 respectively show the number of collocations and collocations themselves of this semantic class.

Table 2: The top 10 semantic classes of 培植 'cultivate'

SCID*	SCName*	#of collocations	Collocations
Al	才识 'ability and insight'	6	人才 新秀 人材 骨干 艺术家 好手
Bh	植物 'plant'	6	幼苗 木耳 蘑菇 兰花 花卉 蔬菜
Db	事理 'reason and logic'	5	税源 财源 货源 资源 办法
Di	社会 政法 'society, politics and law'	5	工业 党 工作 地方 组织
Dd	性能 'performance'	5	实力 项目 方面 地方 组织
Ae	职业 'profession'	4	球员 选手 干部 厂商
Ba	统称 'general terms of substance'	4	农产品 产品 资源 植物
Cb	空间 'space'	3	生长点 方面 地方
Bk	全身 'body'	3	细胞 皮肤 骨干
Da	事情 境况 'event'	3	势力 过程 信息

*SCID=Semantic Class ID, SCName=Semantic Class Name.

4. Source Domain Determination

Semantic classes acquired in the last section need to be refined for metaphor processing. Some preferred semantic classes may denote metaphorical usage. For example, in table2, semantic class Al, ability and insight, is used metaphorically as the object of the target word 培植 'cultivate'. Only source domain candidates, semantic classes denoting literal usage, are useful knowledge for metaphor recognition and comprehension (Chung and Ahrens, 2006).

Usually, a concrete concept is used as the source domain while an abstract concept as the target domain. So the concept concreteness or abstractness is useful to determine source domains. Information of concept concreteness can be found in TongYiCiCiLin, where class Substance is concrete while class Abstraction is abstract.

We choose all concrete concepts in the top N (N=10 by default) semantic classes as the source domain candidates, and the choosing method is flexible. If no concrete concepts exist, the first semantic class is considered as the source domain candidate. The most preferred source domain candidate is considered as the real source domain when a metaphor occurs. The blocked lines in table3 show the source domain candidates of the target verb 培植 'cultivate' and the semantic class 'Bh' is the most preferred source domain, which agree well with human judgment. The semantic class ID beginning with 'B' denotes concrete class Substance.

Table 3: Source domain candidates of 培植 'cultivate'

SDC*	SCID*	#of collocations	Collocations
No	Al	6	人才 新秀 人材 骨干 艺术家 好手
Yes	**Bh**	**6**	**幼苗 木耳 蘑菇 兰花 花卉 蔬菜**
No	Db	5	税源 财源 货源 资源 办法
No	Di	5	工业 党 工作 地方 组织
No	Dd	5	实力 项目 方面 地方 组织
No	Ae	4	球员 选手 干部 厂商
Yes	**Ba**	**4**	**农产品 产品 资源 植物**
No	Cb	3	生长点 方面 地方
Yes	**Bk**	**3**	**细胞 皮肤 骨干**
No	Da	3	势力 过程 信息

*SDC=Source Domain Candidate, SCID=Semantic Class ID.

5. Recognition Algorithm

After the source domain candidates are determined, whether the target verb is literally or metaphorically used can be decided. If the object or the subject of the verb belongs to the source domain candidates, then it is literal usage; otherwise, it is metaphorical usage.

For example, the source domain candidates of 培植 'cultivate' are {Bh, Ba, Bk} as shown in table3. In 培植幼苗 'cultivate young plants', the object 幼苗 'young plants' belongs to semantic class Bh. So this is a literal expression. However, in 培植人才 'train talents', the object 人才 'talents' does not belong to Bh, Ba or Bk. So this is a metaphorical expression.

The pseudo code for the unsupervised metaphor recognition is as follows:
1. Parse the sentence and obtain object or subject headword of the verb.

2. Search the headword in source domain candidates. If found, then it is literal usage; else it is metaphorical usage.

6. Experiments

Experiments are set up to test performance of source domain determination and metaphor recognition.

6.1. Source Domain Determination

Twenty frequently metaphorically used verbs (see table4) are chosen to test source domain determination results. Measures are coverage and precision, which are defined in formula 1 and 2.

$$\text{Coverage} = \frac{\#\text{Verb whose real source domain occurs in top N semantic classes}}{\#\text{All verbs}} \quad (1)$$

$$\text{Precision} = \frac{\#\text{Verb whose real source domain is correctly determined}}{\#\text{All verbs}} \quad (2)$$

Table 5 shows the performance of source domain determination. As can be seen, only 7 verbs out of 20 have the most preferred semantic class as the real source domain, which indicates the necessity to introduce the conceptual concreteness information. 17 verbs have their real source domains occur in the top 5 preferred semantic classes, and 16 ones are correctly determined. All real source domains are covered in the top 10 semantic classes, and 17 ones are correctly found, with a precision of 85%. Errors occur when some concrete semantic classes are more preferred than the real source domains.

Table 4: 20 metaphorically used verbs

泛滥 fan4lan4	搁浅 ge1qian3	流失 liu2shi1	起飞 qi3fei1	起伏 qi3fu2
overflow	run aground	be washed away	take off	rise and fall
倾斜 qing1xie2	燃烧 ran2shao1	渗透 shen4tou4	瘫痪 tan1huan4	滑坡 hua2po1
slope	burn	permeate	paralyze	landslide
编织 bian1zhi1	点燃 dian3ran2	兜售 dou1shou4	兑现 dui4xian4	腐蚀 fu3shi2
weave	cause to burn	peddle	cash	corrode
解剖 jie1pou1	培植 pei2zhi2	提炼 ti2lian4	消化 xiao1hua4	净化 jing4hua4
dissect	cultivate	refine	digest	purify

Table 5: Source domain determination performance

Top N semantic classes	1	5	10
Coverage	7/20	17/20	20/20
Precision	7/20	16/20	17/20

6.2. Metaphor Recognition

Ten out of the twenty verbs in table4 are chosen to test the recognition performance. For each verb, about 40 sentences are extracted from People's Daily corpus and annotated as literal usage or metaphorical usage. The real usage distribution is shown in table6. As can be seen, 270 out of 413 samples are metaphorical ones, which account for 65.38%.

Table 6: Distribution of metaphorical usages for 10 verbs

Word	#Sample	#Metaphorical	#Literal
bian1zhi1	27	23	4

dian3ran2	33	10	23
jie3pou1	33	27	6
pei2zhi2	44	37	7
ti2lian4	38	26	12
fan4lan4	55	50	5
ge1qian3	45	31	14
qi3fei1	48	7	41
qi3fu2	40	23	17
tan1huan4	50	36	14
Total	413	270	143

Source domain candidates are checked and argument headwords of verbs are extracted manually to remove noises introduced by these steps, so that the capability of this recognition method can be examined given correct knowledge. Totally automatic experiments will be conducted in the near future. Measures of performance are defined as follows in formula 3 to 6.

$$\text{Precision} = \frac{\text{\#Correctly recognized metaphorical samples}}{\text{\#Recognized metaphorical samples}} \quad (3)$$

$$\text{Recall} = \frac{\text{\#Correctly recognized metaphorical samples}}{\text{\#All metaphorical samples}} \quad (4)$$

$$\text{F-measure} = \frac{2*\text{Precision}*\text{Recall}}{\text{Precision}+\text{Recall}} \quad (5)$$

$$\text{Accuracy} = \frac{\text{\#Correctly classified samples}}{\text{\#All samples}} \quad (6)$$

Table 7: Recognition performance

	Precision	Recall	F-measure	Accuracy
Baseline	65.38%	100%	79.07%	65.38%
Source domain	78.95%	100%	88.24%	82.57%
Source domain candidates	86.82%	100%	92.95%	90.07%

Three experiments are carried out (see table7). The baseline assumes that all samples are metaphorical usages and the F-measure is 79.07%. Experiment two only uses the most preferred source domain in the top 10 semantic classes as the source domain knowledge and achieves F-measure of 88.24%. Experiment three uses all source domain candidates in the top 10 semantic classes and the F-measure improves to 92.95%. The recognition method tries to removes recognized literal usages and leaves all others as metaphorical usages, so it always has high recall values.

7. Conclusions

This paper proposes an unsupervised metaphor recognition method based on selectional preferences. Different from other selectional preferences based methods, this approach utilizes concept concreteness information. Firstly, selectional preferences are extracted from a large scale corpus. Then source domain candidates are determined based on the acquired selectional preferences and concept concreteness information in a lexicon. Finally, source domain candidates are used for metaphor recognition and good performance is achieved. In addition, source domain knowledge is also helpful for metaphor comprehension.

More extensive experiments will be carried out to test the effectiveness of this approach. For comparison, supervised and semi-supervised classification methods will be examined.

Contextual information is useful for metaphor recognition, so more contextual information will be exploited to improve the method proposed in this paper.

References

Birke, J. and A. Sarkar. 2006. A Clustering Approach for the Nearly Unsupervised Recognition of Nonliteral Language. *Proceedings of the 11th Conference of the European Chapter of the Association for Computational Linguistics*, pp. 329-336.

Carbonell, J.G. 1982. Metaphor: An Inescapable Phenomenon in Natural Language Comprehension. In W.Lehnert and M.Ringle eds., *Strategies for Natural Language Processing*, pp. 415-434, Hillsdale, N.J.: Lawrence Erlbaum.

Chung, Siaw-Fong and Kathleen Ahrens. 2006. Source Domain Determination: WordNet-SUMO and Collocation. *Proceedings of the 2nd International Conference of the German Cognitive Linguistics Association*, pp. 1-4.

Fass, D. 1991. met*: A Method for Discriminating Metonymy and Metaphor by Computer. *Computational Linguistics*, 17(1), 49-90.

Gedigian, M., J. Bryant, S. Narayannan and B. Ciric. 2006. Catching Metaphors. *Proceedings of the 3rd Workshop on Scalable Natural Language Understanding*, pp. 41-48.

Kilgarriff, A. and D. Tugwell. 2001. Word Sketch: Extraction and Display of Significant Collocations for Lexicography. *Proceedings of the ACL Workshop COLLOCATION: Computational Extraction, Analysis and Exploitation*, pp. 32-38.

Krishnakumaran, S. and X.J. Zhu. 2007. Hunting Elusive Metaphors Using Lexical Resources. *Proceedings of the Workshop on Computational approaches to Figurative Language*, pp. 13-20.

Lakoff, G. and M. Johnson. 1980. *Metaphors We Live By*. Unversity of Chicago Press.

Martin, J. 1990. *Computational Model of Metaphor Interpretation*. San Diego: Academic Press.

Mason, Z.J. 2004. CorMet: A Computational, Corpus-based Conventional Metaphor Extraction System. *Computational Linguistics*, 30(1), 23-44.

Mei, J.J., Y.M. Zhu and Y.Q. Gao. 1983. *Tongyici Cilin*. Shanghai: Shanghai Cishu Press.

Resnik, P. 1993. *Selection and Information: A Class-Based Approach to Lexical Relationships*. Ph.D. thesis, University of Pennsylvania, Philadelphia, PA.

Wang, Z.M., H.F. Wang, H.M. Duan, S. Han and S.W. Yu. 2006. Chinese Noun Phrase Metaphor Recognition with Maximum Entropy Approach. *Proceedings of the 7th International Conference on Intelligent Text Processing and Computational Linguistics*, pp. 235-244.

Korean Parsing Based on the Applicative Combinatory Categorial Grammar[*]

Juyeon Kang, Jean-Pierre Desclés

LaLIC Laboratory, Paris-Sorbonne University
28, Rue Serpente, 75006, Paris, France
kjuyeon79@yahoo.fr, jean-pierre.descles@paris4.sorbonne.fr

Abstract. The **Applicative Combinatory Categorial Grammar (ACCG)** is a new approach to Categorial Grammars by using exclusively the Combinatory Logic. This extended categorial grammar that was originally developed by J.-P. Desclés and I. Biskri, allows us to tackle the problem of the Korean language parsing in which there exist many difficulties from a computational point of view. In this paper, we handle in particular some parsing problems in Korean such as the problem of case, the free word order phenomenon, the coordination structure and the long distance scrambling in the coordination structure. We will show throughout this work some new and robust solutions for the Korean parsing in the ACCG formalism by introducing combinators such as **B**, **C***, **Φ** of Combinatory Logic developed by H.-B. Curry and R. Feys.

Keywords: Korean, Parsing, Categorial Grammar, Combinatory Logic, ACCG.

1. Introduction

In this paper, we propose a new approach to Categorial Grammars by introducing Curry's Combinatory Logic (Curry & Feys 1958) in order to improve the parsing of Korean texts from a computational point of view.

Since the introduction of simple Categorial Grammars, different propositions were made to improve this formalism by adopting applicative languages such as the calculus of syntactic types proposed by J. Lambek (1961), the lambda-calculus proposed by A. Church, the combinatory logic created by the mathematician H.-B. Curry (1958), some attempts by the logician W. V. O. Quine, etc. These works are based on the mechanism of the application of an operator to an operand. Combinatory logic and lambda-calculus were applied to the analysis of grammatical and lexical meaning in natural languages by S. K. Shaumyan (1987) with his model of the Universal Applicational Grammar using Curry's combinatory logic, which extends the simple Categorial Grammars: this model is easily implementable on computational tools using functional programming languages such as CAML, HASKELL and SCHEME. In the 80's, important extensions were given by R. Montague, M. Moortgat (1988), J. Lambek and M. Steedman (1989). Combinatory Categorial Grammar (CCG) developed by Steedman (1989, 2001) was most often quoted and studied for the analysis of Korean sentences.

There exist several studies on Korean parsing based on the Categorial Grammar formalism. For example, the Korean Combinatory Categorial Grammar (KCCG) was developed by (Cha 2001 and Cha & Lee 2002) by extending the CCG of Steedman for the Korean parsing. The KCCG, having a purely computational approach, shows the ability to handle important linguistic phenomena of the Korean such as coordination, long distance scrambling, free word

---

22nd Pacific Asia Conference on Language, Information and Computation, pages 215–224

order, etc. Cho and Park (2000) tried also to improve the complexity in the coordination, and Lee and Park (2003) proposed a morphological analysis of the irregular conjugation of Korean in order to conceive a morphological parser.

The studies presented above and most of the related works are based exclusively on the CCG formalism of Steedman and developed in the purpose of a computational realization. Thus they often ignore the linguistic aspect of language and cannot capture some fine points such as morphological cases in Korean.

Compared to these works based on the CCG formalism, the **ACCG** formalism that we develop in this paper, is not only a computational but also a linguistic approach, namely it better reflects the linguistic aspect in the Korean natural language processing. Consequently, this advantage allows us to parse the Korean language in a more explicit way and to show clearly the morpho-syntactic structure of the Korean through our calculations. Thus, the **ACCG** formalism is a new approach which is both linguistic and computational.

This formalism allows us to scope the difficult characteristics of the Korean that we can often find during automatic processing. In particular, we are interested in the problem of cases in Korean including the phenomenon of double case. Despite of their importance in parsing texts, cases have not been well studied from a computational point of view. Once we analyze the cases in the **ACCG** formalism, we will use some of the results of these analyses to handle the problem of free word order structure and coordination structure. This formalism leads us to easily analyze the free word order structure by a simple application of the combinatory rules we developed. This approach allows us to handle even long distance scrambling in the coordination structure, which is one of the most difficult problems in Korean parsing and has not been completely analyzed in other works (e.g. Cha 2001).

2. Applicative Combinatory Categorial Grammar

The Applicative Combinatory Categorial Grammar formalism is an extension of the Combinatory Categorial Grammar developed by Steedman. This **ACCG** formalism was originally developed by J-P. Desclés and I. Biskri (1995, 1996) for the analysis of coordination and subordination structure in French with the tools of Combinatory Logic by introducing canonical associations between some rules and the combinators.

The purpose of this work is the automatic analysis of Korean sentences in which there exist the problems of case, free word order structure and coordination structure. Firstly, the **ACCG** provides the possibility to go beyond the well-known limits (such as the processing of a coordination, etc.) of simple Categorial Grammars. Secondly, this formalism allows the construction of logico-grammtical representations that provide a way to building semantico-cognitive representations in the general model of Applicative and Cognitive Grammar developed by J-P. Desclés (1990, 2003) with the three following levels: 1) morpho-syntactic configurations, 2) logico-grammatical representations, 3) semantico-cognitive representations. The **ACCG** builds applicative representations on the second level from the concatenated expressions given on the first level.

We present here the rules[3] of the **ACCG,** for the analysis of Korean sentences.

Table 1: ACCG's rules.

Application rules

---

[3] **B** is a composition combinator. Its β-reduction is: **Bfgx→f(gx)**. It is joined to the functional composition rule. This combinator allows us in particular to handle the free word order structure in the Korean sentence. **C*** is a type raising combinator joined to the type raising rules. Its β-reduction is: **C*fg→gf.** This combinator transforms the operand (argument) to operator (function). It is used essentially to analyze nouns of the Korean as the operators.

$[X/Y : u_1]$-$[Y : u_2]$ ----------------------> $[X : (u_1\ u_2)]$	$[Y : u_1]$-$[X\backslash Y : u_2]$ ----------------------< $[X : (u_2\ u_1)]$
Type raising rules	
$[X : u]$ ---------------------->**T** $[Y/(Y\backslash X) : (\mathbf{C}^*\ u)]$	$[X : u]$ ----------------------<**T** $[Y\backslash(Y/X) : (\mathbf{C}^*\ u)]$
Functional composition rules	
$[X/Y : u_1]$-$[Y/Z : u_2]$ ------------------------->**B** $[X/Z : (\mathbf{B}\ u_1\ u_2)]$	$[Y\backslash Z : u_1]$-$[X\backslash Y : u_2]$ ------------------------<**B** $[X\backslash Z : (\mathbf{B}\ u_2\ u_1\ )]$

Consider the following analysis of a Korean sentence in the **ACCG**.

Sumi-ga   *Minju-lil*   *man-ass-da.* (Sumi met Minju.)
Sumi-NOM   Minju-ACC   meet-PS-DC.

1.$[N^{*}$[4]$:$ Sumi-ga$] -$[5] $[(N^*:$ Minju-lil$] - [(S\backslash N^*)\backslash N^*:$ man-ass-da $]$
2.$[S/(S\backslash N^*):(\mathbf{C}^*$Sumi-ga$)]-[(N^*:$Minju-lil$]-[(S\backslash N^*)\backslash N^*:$man-ass-da $]$ (>**T**)
3.$[S/(S\backslash N^*):(\mathbf{C}^*$Sumi-ga$)]-[(S\backslash N^*)/((S\backslash N^*)\backslash N^*):(\mathbf{C}^*$Minju-lil$)]-[(S\backslash N^*)\backslash N^*:$man-ass-da $]$ (>**T**)
4.$[S/((S\backslash N^*)\backslash N^*): (\mathbf{B}(\mathbf{C}^*$Sumi-ga$)(\mathbf{C}^*$Minju-lil$))]-[(S\backslash N^*)\backslash N^*:$man-ass-da$]$ (>**B**)
5. [S: ((B(C*Sumi-ga)(C*Minju-lil))(man-ass-da))]   (>)
6. [S: ((C*Sumi-ga)((C*Minju-lil)(man-ass-da)))]   (B)
7. [S: ((C*Minju-lil)(man-ass-da))Sumi-ga]   (C*)
8. [S: (((man-ass-da)Minju-lil)Sumi-ga)]   (C*)

  We start from the concatenated sentence with assigned syntactic types. Then, we apply consecutively the type raising rules to *"Sumi-ga"* and *"Minju-lil"* which are operands, by introducing the combinator **C***. This operation allows us to transform an operand into an operator. Then, we apply the functional composition rule to form a new operator "(**B(C*Sumi-ga)(C*Minju-lil))**" that will be applied to the operand "man-ass-da" at step 5. We reduce (in the Combinatory Logic formalism) consecutively the combinators **B** and **C*** to build a well-formed applicative expression at step 8. This expression gives a formal interpretation in terms of predicates, arguments and cases.

3.   ACCG and the Korean Parsing

3.1.Case

The Korean is an agglutinative language in which the words are formed by the linking of affixes to a radical such as the cases (or postpositions). In the syntactic and semantic analysis of the Korean sentence, the cases determine the grammatical roles of nominal syntagms (Sung 1999, Hong 1999, Nam 2001). In this paper we study five major cases[6]: *-ga* as nominative marker, *-lil/-ul* as accusative marker, *-eke* as dative marker, *-uy* as genitive marker and *-eso* as locative marker.

  We use predefined notations to facilitate our categorial analysis.

$$X^{\circ}=S$$
$$X^1=(S\backslash N^*)$$
$$X^2=(S\backslash N^*)\backslash N^*$$
$$X^3=((S\backslash N^*)\backslash N^*)\backslash N^*$$

---

[4] The N*s are qualified Nouns such as N*nom, N*acc, etc.
[5] The hyphen (-) means a concatenation at the syntactic level.
[6] A description of Korean cases and their categorial analyses in the **ACCG** are presented in detail and with more examples in the Master's thesis of KANG (2005).

To the two classical basic types N(nominal) and S(sentence), we add a new basic type N* for the complete nominal syntagms.

Let us analyze the following sentence including the five major cases:

Gyosil-eso, Sumi-ga   Minju-eke   na-uy   chaek-ul   ju-aes'-da. (In the class, Sumi gave my book to Minju.)
Class-LOC Sumi-NOM Minju-DAT me-GEN book-ACC give–PS-DC

1.[N:Gyosil]-[(S/S)\N):-eso]-[N:Sumi]-[N*\N:-ga]-[N:Minju]-[N*\N:-eke]-[N:na]-[(N*/N*)\N:-uy]-[N:chaek]-[N*\N:-ul]-[X³: ju-aes'-da]

2. [S/S: -eso Gyosil]- [N:Sumi]-[N*\N:-ga]-[N:Minju]-[N*\N:-eke]-[N:na]-[(N*/N*)\N:-uy]- [N:chaek]-[N*\N:-ul]- [X³: ju-aes'-da]   (<)

3. [S/S:-eso Gyosil]- [N*:-ga Sumi]- [N:Minju]-[N*\N:-eke]-[N:na]-[(N*/N*)\N:-uy]-[N:chaek]-[N*\N:-ul]- [X³: ju-aes'-da]   (>)

4. [S/S:-eso Gyosil]-[N*:-ga Sumi]-[N*:-eke Minju]-[N:na]-[(N*/N*)\N:-uy]-[N:chaek]-[N*\N:-ul]-[X³: ju-aes'-da]   (>)

5. [S/S:-eso Gyosil]- [N*:-ga Sumi]- [N*:-eke Minju]- [N*/N*: -uy na]- [N:chaek]-[N*\N:-ul]- [X³: ju-aes'-da]   (>)

6. [S/S:-eso Gyosil]- [N*:-ga Sumi]- [N*:-eke Minju]- [N*/N*: -uy na]- [N*: -ul chaek]- [X³: ju-aes'-da]   (>)

7. [S/S:-eso Gyosil]- [N*:-ga Sumi]- [N*:-eke Minju]- [N*/N*: -uy na]- [N*: -ul chaek]- [X³: ju-aes'-da]   (>)

8. [S/S:-eso Gyosil]- [N*:-ga Sumi]- [N*: -eke Minju]- [N*: ((-uy na)-ul chaek)]- [X³: ju-aes'- da]   (>)

9. [S/S:-eso Gyosil]- [S/X¹: **C***-ga Sumi]- [N*: -eke Minju]- [N*: ((-uy na)-ul chaek)]- [X³: ju-aes'-da]   (>**T**)

10. [S/S:-eso Gyosil]- [S/X¹: **C***-ga Sumi]- [X¹/X²: **C***-eke Minju]- [N*: ((-uy na)-ul chaek)]- [X³: ju-aes'-da]   (>**T**)

11. [S/S:-eso Gyosil]- [S/X¹: **C***-ga Sumi]- [X¹/X²: **C***-eke Minju]- [X²/X³: **C***((-uy na)-ul chaek)]- [X³: ju-aes'-da]   (>**T**)

12 [S/S:-eso Gyosil]- [S/X²: **B**((**C***-ga Sumi)(**C***-eke Minju))]- [X²/X³: **C***((-uy na)-ul chaek)]- [X³: ju-aes'-da]   (>**B**)

13. [S/S:-eso Gyosil]- [S/X³: (**B**(**B**((**C***-ga Sumi)(**C***-eke Minju)))(**C***((-uy na)-ul chaek))]- [X³: ju-aes'-da]   (>**B**)

14. [S/S:-eso Gyosil]- [S: ((**B**(**B**((**C***-ga Sumi)(**C***-eke Minju)))(**C***((-uy na)-ul chaek))ju-aes'- da)]   (>)

15. [S:(-eso Gyosil ((B(B((C*-ga Sumi)(C*-eke Minju)))(C*((-uy na)-ul chaek))ju-aes'-da))]   (>)

16.[S:(-eso Gyosil ((B(C*-ga Sumi)(C*-eke Minju))((C*((-uy na)-ul chaek)))ju-aes'-da))]   (B*)

17.[S:(-eso Gyosil ((C*-ga Sumi)((C*-eke Minju)((C*((-uy na)-ul chaek))ju-aes'-da)))]   (B*)

18.[S:(-eso Gyosil ((C*-eke Minju)(((C*((-uy na)-ul chaek))ju-aes'-da))-ga Sumi)]   (C*)

19.[S:(-eso Gyosil ((((C*((-uy na)-ul chaek))ju-aes'-da)-eke Minju)-ga Sumi)]   (C*)

20.[S:(-eso Gyosil((((ju-aes'-da)((-uy na)-ul chaek))-eke Minju)-ga Sumi))]   (C*)

We show in the above analysis that the categorical calculus of the given sentence allows us, on one hand, to verify the correct syntactic structure of the sentence by obtaining the result "S" at step 15, and on the other hand, to obtain an applicative expression that underlies this sentence structure. Furthermore, this analysis allows us to deduce the syntactic types of the used cases as follows:

Nominative marker   **(S/X¹)\N**
Dative marker   **(X¹/X²)\N or (X²/X³)\N**
Accusative marker   **(X²/X³)\N or (X¹/X²)\N**
Genitive marker   **((X²/X³)/(X²/X³))\N or ((X¹/X²)\(X¹/X²))\N or ((S/X¹)/(S/X¹))\N**
Locative marker1   **(X¹/X¹)\N**
Locative marker2   **(S/S)\N**

This means that the cases in Korean function as operators that are applied to operands such as nouns including proper nouns, common nouns, collective nouns, materials nouns, etc. The types of cases are given here as a first approximation, namely we intend to go deeper into the assignation of types to cases. Our purpose is to find some invariants of these types in order to reduce the ambiguity and the complexity in the choice of one of the assigned types to each case during their application. This paper presents the first step in this direction.

These types can be reused in other analyses which contain these same categories, namely the cases, to build an applicative expression corresponding to this sentence. Consequently, the construction of an applicative parsing tree is reduced to a simple calculus on the types.
In the next sections, we handle the problem of the double cases, the free word order structure and the coordination considering the proposed types of cases.

3.1.1. Double nominative

The problem of a double subject corresponding to a double nominative and of a double object corresponding to a double accusative is actually very important in the syntactic and semantic study of Korean (Sung 1999, Hong 1999, Lee 2002, Chung 2003). This subject has not been well studied in the aspect of the natural language processing, so it is worth proposing a new analysis in the computational linguistic point of view.

In this paper we give a solution to the problem of the double nominative marker such as *-ga*.
Sumi-ga   maumsi-ga   jo-ta.   (Sumi has a good heart.) (Sumi's heart is good.)
Sumi-NOM   heart-NOM   be good-DC
The above sentence having double nominative (-ga) of *Sumi-ga* and (-ga) of *maumsi-ga* can be interpreted in the other form *"Sumi-uy maumsi-ga jo-ta"*, namely the first *-ga* can be replaced by the genitive marker *-uy* without changing the meaning of the original sentence. This analysis leads us to calculate the syntactic types of the two occurrences of *-ga*.

We consider now the above sentence with a double nominative and the following processing.
Sumi-ga maumsi-ga jo-ta.

1. $[N :Sumi]-[(N^*/N^*)\backslash N :-ga]-[N :maumsi]-[N^*\backslash N :-ga]-[X^1 :jo-ta]$
2. $[N^*/N^* :-ga\ Sumi]-[N :maumsi]-[N^*\backslash N :-ga]-[X^1 :jo-ta]$ (<)
3. $[N^*/N^* :-ga\ Sumi]-[N^*:-ga\ maumsi]-[X^1 :jo-ta]$ (>)
4. $[N^* : (-ga\ Sumi)-ga\ maumsi]-[X^1 :jo-ta]$ (>)
5. $[S/X^1 : \mathbf{C^*}((-ga\ Sumi)-ga\ maumsi)]-[X^1 :jo-ta]$ (>T)
6. $[S : \mathbf{C^*}((-ga\ Sumi)-ga\ maumsi)jo-ta]$ (>)
7. $[S : (jo-ta((-ga\ Sumi)-ga\ maumsi))]$ (C*)

This analysis shows that the second *-ga* is a real nominative marker that forms the subject of the sentence *"maumsi-ga"* and the first *-ga* is used as an element that forms the determinant *"Sumi-ga"* of the subject. Thus, we assign the syntactic type $((S/X^1)/(S/X^1))\backslash N$ to the first *-ga* and the syntactic type $(S/X^1)\backslash N$ to the second *-ga*.

The nominative case becomes more complex when we must process double nominative. The new assignation of type is: $\mathbf{(S/X^1)\backslash N}$ or $\mathbf{((S/X^1)/(S/X^1))\backslash N}$.

The above analysis is new and different of the proposed analyses for the formal double cases in Korean (Cha 2001, Kang 2001) by the Categorial Grammars; it corresponds to the intuitive interpretation.

3.2. Free Word Order

Free word order is a widespread phenomenon in Korean, so the processing of the Korean language becomes difficult. The position of the linguistic elements in the Korean sentence does not play an essential grammatical role because it is generally possible to permute these linguistic elements, namely subjects, direct/indirect objects, etc. except that verbs take always a position at the end of the sentence.

Consider the following examples having the free word order structure.
a. *Sumi-ga   Minju-eke   jilmun-ul   hae-ss-da.* (Sumi asked to Minju a question.)
   Sumi-NOM   Minju-DAT   question-ACC   do-PS-DC
b. *Sumi-ga jilmun-ul Minju-eke hae-ss-da.*
c. *Minju-eke Sumi-ga jilmun-ul hae-ss-da.*
d. *Minju-eke jilmun-ul Sumi-ga hae-ss-da.*
e. *Jilmun-ul Minju-eke Sumi-ga hae-ss-da.*
f. *Jilmun-ul Sumi-ga Minju-eke hae-ss-da.*

In the above examples the sentences have the same predicative interpretation (but the topic/comment interpretation is not invariant). So, the position of the elements is not very important in the Korean analysis. We propose now to analyze these sentences in the **ACCG**.

a) Sumi-ga   Minju-eke   jilmun-ul   hae-ss-da.
  Sumi-NOM   Minju-DAT   question-ACC   do-PS-DC
  « Sumi asked to Minju a question. »

1. $[N: Sumi]-[N^*\backslash N:-ga]-[N:Minju]-[N^*\backslash N:-eke]-[N:jilmun]-[N^*\backslash N:-ul]-[X^3: hae-ss-da]$
2. $[N^*:-ga\ Sumi]-[N^* : -eke\ Minju]-[N^*:-ul\ jilmun]-[X^3: hae-ss-da]$ (<)

3.[S/X^1:(**C***-ga Sumi))]-[N*:-eke Minju]-[N*:-ul jilmun]-[X^3:hae-ss-da] (>T)
4.[S/X^1:(**C***-ga Sumi))]-[X^1/X^2:(**C***-eke Minju))]-[N*:-ul jilmun]-[X^3:hae-ss-da] (>T)
5.[S/X^1:(**C***-ga Sumi))]-[X^1/X^2:(**C***-eke Minju))]-[X^2/X^3: (**C***-ul jilmun)]-[X^3:hae-ss-da] (>T)
6.[S/X^2:**B**(**C***-ga Sumi)(**C***-eke Minju))]-[X^2/X^3: (**C***-ul jilmun)]-[X^3:hae-ss-da] (>B)
7.[S/X^3 :**B**(**B**(**C***-ga Sumi)(**C***-eke Minju)) (**C***-ul jilmun)]-[X^3:hae-ss-da] (>B)
8.**[S: B(B(C*-ga Sumi)(C*-eke Minju)) (C*-ul jilmun) hae-ss-da]** **(>)**
9.**[S: (B(C*-ga Sumi)(C*-eke Minju)) ((C*-ul jilmun) hae-ss-da)]** **(>)**
10.**[S: (C*-ga Sumi)((C*-eke Minju) ((C*-ul jilmun) hae-ss-da))]** **(B)**
11.**[S: ((C*-eke Minju) ((C*-ul jilmun) hae-ss-da)) -ga Sumi]** **(C*)**
12.**[S: (((C*-ul jilmun) hae-ss-da) -eke Minju) -ga Sumi]** **(C*)**
13.**[S: ((((hae-ss-da) -ul jilmun) -eke Minju) -ga Sumi)]** **(C*)**

b) Sumi-ga   jilmun-ul   Minju-eke   hae-ss-da.
Sumi-NOM question-ACC Minju-DAT   do-PS-DC
« Sumi asked a question to Minju. »
1.[N:Sumi]-[N*\N:-ga]-[N:jilmun]-[N*\N:-ul]-[N:Minju]-[N*\N:-eke]-[X^3: hae-ss-da]
2.[N*:-ga Sumi] – [N*:-ul jilmun]-[N*:-eke Minju] - [X^3: hae-ss-da] (<)
3.[S/X^1:(**C***-ga Sumi)]-[N*:-ul jilmun]-[N*:-eke Minju]-[X^3:hae-ss-da] (>T)
4.[S/X^1:(**C***-ga Sumi)]-[X^2/X^3:(**C***-ul jilmun)]-[N*:-eke Minju]-[X^3:hae-ss-da] (>T)
5.[S/X^1:(**C***-ga Sumi)]-[X^2/X^3:(**C***-ul jilmun)]-[X^1/X^2:-eke Minju]-[X^3:hae-ss-da] (>T)
6.[S/X^1 :(**C***-ga Sumi)]-[X^1/X^3:(**B**(**C***-eke Minju)(**C***-ul jilmun))]-[X^3:hae-ss-da] (<B)
7.[S/X^3:**B**((**C***-ga Sumi-ga)(**B**(**C***-eke Minju-eke)(**C***-ul jilmun)))]-[X^3:hae-ss-da] (<B)
8.**[S:B((C*-ga Sumi)(B(C*-eke Minju)(C*-ul jilmun)))hae-ss-da]** **(>)**
9.**[S:(C*-ga Sumi)((B(C*-eke Minju)(C*-ul jilmun))hae-ss-da)]** **(B)**
10.**[S:((B(C*-eke Minju)(C*-ul jilmun)) hae-ss-da) -ga Sumi]** **(C*)**
11.**[S:((C*-eke Minju)((C*-ul jilmun) hae-ss-da)) -ga Sumi]** **(B)**
12.**[S: (((C*-ul jilmun) hae-ss-da) -eke Minju) -ga Sumi]** **(C*)**
13.**[S: ((((hae-ss-da) –ul jilmun) -eke Minju) -ga Sumi)]** **(C*)**

c) <u>Minju-eke</u> <u>Sumi-ga</u>   <u>jilmun-ul</u>   hae-ss-da.
Minju-DAT Sumi-NOM question-ACC do-PS-DC
« It's to Minju that Sumi asked a question. »
1. [N:Minju]-[N*\N:-eke]-[N:Sumi]-[N*\N:-ga]-[N:jilmun]-[N*\N:-ul]-[X^3: hae-ss-da]
2. [N* : -eke Minju] – [N* : -ga Sumi] – [N*:-ul jilmun] - [X^3: hae-ss-da] (<)
3. [X^1/X^2:(**C***-eke Minju)]-[N*:-ga Sumi]-[N*:-ul jilmun]-[X^3:hae-ss-da] (>T)
4. [X^1/X^2:(**C***-eke Minju)]-[S/X^1:(**C***-ga Sumi)]-[N*:-ul jilmun]-[X^3:hae-ss-da] (>T)
5. [X^1/X^2:(**C***-eke Minju)]-[S/X^1:(**C*** -ga Sumi)]-[X^2/X^3:(**C***-ul jilmun)]-[X^3:hae-ss-da] (>T)
6. [S/X^2:(**B**(**C***-ga Sumi)(**C***-eke Minju))]-[X^2/X^3:(**C***-ul jilmun)]–[X^3:hae-ss-da] (>B)
7. [S/X^3:(**B**(**C***-ga Sumi)(**C***-eke Minju))(**C***-ul jilmun)]- [X^3:hae-ss-da] (>)
8. **[S:(B(C*-ga Sumi)(C*-eke Minju))(C*-ul jilmun)hae-ss-da]** **(>)**
9. **[S:(C*-ga Sumi)((C*-eke Minju)(C*-ul jilmun))hae-ss-da)]** **(B)**
10. **[S:((((C*-eke Minju)(C*-ul jilmun))hae-ss-da) -ga Sumi]** **(C*)**
11. **[S: :(((C*-ul jilmun)hae-ss-da) -eke Minju) -ga Sumi]** **(C*)**
12. **[S: ((((hae-ss-da) -ul jilmun) -eke Minju) -ga Sumi)]** **(C*)**

d) <u>Minju-eke</u> <u>jilmun-ul</u>   <u>Sumi-ga</u>   hae-ss-da.
Minju-DAT question-ACC Sumi-Nom do-PS-DC

« It's to Minju that Sumi asked a question. »
1. [N:Minju]-[N*\N:-eke]-[N:jilmun]-[N*\N:-ul]-[N:Sumi]-[N*\N:-ga]-[X^3: hae-ss-da]
2. [N* : -eke Minju] – [N* : -ul jilmun] – [N*:-ga Sumi] - [X^3: hae-ss-da] (<)
3. [X^1/X^2:(**C***-eke Minju)]-[N*:-ul jilmun]-[N*:-ga Sumi]-[X^3: hae-ss-da] (>T)
4. [X^1/X^2:(**C***-eke Minju)]-[X^2/X^3:(**C***-ul jilmun)]-[N*:-ga Sumi]-[X^3: hae-ss-da] (>T)
5. [X^1/X^2:(**C***-eke Minju)]-[X^2/X^3:(**C***-ul jilmun)]-[S/X^1:(**C***-ga Sumi)]-[X^3: hae-ss-da] (>T)
6. [X^1/X^3:**B**(**C***-eke Minju)(**C***-ul jilmun)]-[S/X^1:(**C***-ga Sumi)]–[X^3: hae-ss-da] (>B)
7. [S/X^3: **B**(**B**(**C***-ga Sumi)(**C***-eke Minju))(**C***-ul jilmun)]-[X^3: hae-ss-da] (>B)
8. **[S: B(B(C*-ga Sumi)(C*-eke Minju))(C*-ul jilmun) hae-ss-da]** **(>)**
9. **[S: B(C*-ga Sumi)(C*-eke Minju)((C*-ul jilmun)hae-ss-da)]** **(B)**
10. **[S: (C*-ga Sumi)((C*-eke Minju)(C*-ul jilmun)hae-ss-da)]** **(B)**
11. **[S: ((C*-eke Minju)(C*-ul jilmun)hae-ss-da) -ga Sumi]** **(C*)**
12. **[S: (((C*-ul jilmun)hae-ss-da) -eke Minju)-ga Sumi]** **(C*)**
13. **[S: ((((hae-ss-da) -ul jilmun) -eke Minju) -ga Sumi)]** **(C*)**

e) <u>Jilmun-ul</u>   <u>Sumi-ga</u>   <u>Minju-eke</u>   hae-ss-da
question-ACC Sumi-NOM Minju-DAT do-PS-DC
« It's a question that Sumi asked to Minju. »
1. [N:jilmun]-[N*\N:-ul]-[N:Sumi]-[N*\N:-ga]-[N:Minju]-[N*\N:-eke]-[X^3: hae-ss-da]
2. [N*:-ul jilmun] – [N* : -ga Sumi] – [N*:-eke Minju] - [X^3: hae-ss-da] (<)
3. [X^2/X^3:(**C***-ul jilmun)]-[N*:-ga Sumi]-[N*:-eke Minju]-[X^3: hae-ss-da] (>T)
4. [X^2/X^3:(**C***-ul jilmun)]-[S/X^1:(**C***-ga Sumi)]-[N*:-eke Minju]-[X^3: hae-ss-da] (>T)
5. [X^2/X^3:(**C***-ul jilmun)]-[S/X^1:(**C***-ga Sumi)]-[X^1/X^2: -eke Minju]-[X^3:hae-ss-da] (>T)
6. [X^2/X^3:(**C***-ul jilmun)]-[S/X^2:**B**(**C***-ga Sumi)(**C***-eke Minju)]-[X^3: hae-ss-da] (>B)
7. [S/X^3:**B**(**B**(**C***-ga Sumi)(**C***-eke Minju))(**C***-ul jilmun))]-[X^3: hae-ss-da] (>B)
8. **[S: B(B(C*-ga Sumi)(C*-eke Minju))(C*-ul jilmun)hae-ss-da]** **(>)**
9. **[S: (B(C*-ga Sumi)((C*-eke Minju)((C*-ul jilmun)hae-ss-da)))]** **(B)**
10. **[S: (C*-ga Sumi)((C*-eke Minju)((C*-ul jilmun)hae-ss-da))]** **(B)**
11. **[S:((C*-eke Minju)((C*-ul jilmun)hae-ss-da)) -ga Sumi]** **(C*)**
12. **[S:(((C*-ul jilmun)hae-ss-da)) -eke Minju) -ga Sumi]** **(C*)**
13. **[S: ((((hae-ss-da)-ul jilmun) -eke Minju) -ga Sumi)]** **(C*)**

f) <u>Jilmun-ul</u>   <u>Minju-eke</u>   <u>Sumi-ga</u>   hae-ss-da
question-ACC Minju-DAT Sumi-ga do-PS-DC
« It's a question that Sumi asked to Minju. »
1. [N:jilmun]-[N*\N:-ul]-[N:Minju]-[N*\N:-eke]-[N:Sumi]-[N*\N:-ga]-[X^3: hae-ss-da]
2. [N*:-ul jilmun] – [N* : -eke Minju] – [N*:-ga Sumi] - [X^3: hae-ss-da] (<)
3. [X^2/X^3:(**C***-ul jilmun)]-[N*:-eke Minju]-[N*:-ga Sumi]-[X^3: hae-ss-da] (>T)
4. [X^2/X^3:(**C***-ul jilmun)]-[X^1/X^2:(**C***-eke Minju)]-[N*:-ga Sumi]-[X^3: hae-ss-da] (>T)
5. [X^2/X^3:(**C***-ul jilmun)]-[X^1/X^2:(**C***-eke Minju)]-[S/X^1:(**C***-ga Sumi)]-[X^3: hae-ss-da] (>T)
6. [X^2/X^3:(**C***-ul jilmun)]-[S/X^2: **B**(**C***-ga Sumi)(**C***-eke Minju)]-[X^3: hae-ss-da] (>B)
7. [S/X^3: (**B**(**B**(**C***-ga Sumi)(**C***-eke Minju))(**C***-ul jilmun))]-[X^3: hae-ss-da] (>B)
8. **[S: (B(B(C*-ga Sumi)(C*-eke Minju))(C*-ul jilmun))hae-ss-da]** **(>)**
9. **[S: (B(C*-ga Sumi)((C*-eke Minju)(C*-ul jilmun)))hae-ss-da]** **(B)**
10. **[S: (C*-ga Sumi)(((C*-eke Minju)(C*-ul jilmun))hae-ss-da)]** **(B)**
11. **[S: (C*-ga Sumi)((C*-eke Minju)(hae-ss-da(-ul jilmun)))]** **(C*)**
12. **[S: ((C*-ga Sumi)((hae-ss-da(-ul jilmun)) -eke Minju))]** **(C*)**
13. **[S: ((((hae-ss-da)-ul jilmun) -eke Minju) -ga Sumi)]** **(C*)**

For the six sentences, the six different analyses lead us to one unique and identical applicative expression. So with the simple application of the functional composition rules we presented above, we obtain one applicative parsing tree in the form of applicative expression from six sentences having each one different permutation of elements. Thus, we observe that the **ACCG** formalism gives a new and more efficient approach to the processing of the free word order structure. Moreover, these results can be automatically obtained by computer.

3.3.Coordination

During the automatic processing of the natural language, the coordination structure is one of the most difficult characteristics not only in Korean (Cho & Park 2000), but also in French (Biskri & Desclés 2005) and (Biskri & Rochette 2007), and in English (Steedman 2001).
Coordination structure makes the analysis very complicated with the ellipsis of predicates, coordination between non constituted elements, long distance scrambling and the grammatical and syntactical ambiguity notably from a practical point of view.

In this paper, we are particularly interested in the problem of the ellipsis of predicates, non constituted elements and of a long distance scrambling in the Korean coordination.

For the categorial analysis of the Korean coordination structure, we use a rule which was originally developed for the French coordination analysis. We do not need to modify the rule; we use just a different strategy in the calculus for the Korean. This rule makes possible the coordination analysis notably of elements having the same function and type.

The combinators used for the coordination analysis are **B**, **C*** and **Φ**[7]. This combinator **Φ** can be explained in the following coordination rules proposed for Korean.

Table 2: Coordination rule[8] for Korean.

```
[X :u1]-[CONJD : , / -go ]-[X :u2]
-----------------------------------------<CONJD>
[X: (Φ , u1u2)]
```

Consider the following example of the Korean coordination. In this example, we can see the ellipsis of the predicate in the first proposition, and "Sumi-ga gongbu-lil" and "Minju-ga yori-lil" are non-constituents.

Sumi-ga   gongbu-lil   ,   Minju-ga   yori-lil   han-da. (Sumi studies, Minju cook.)
Sumi-NOM study-ACC CONJ Minju-NOM   cook-ACC do-DC

1. $[N:Sumi]-[N^*\backslash N:-ga]-[N:gonbu]-[N^*\backslash N:-lil]-[CONJ:,]-[N:Minju]-[N^*\backslash N:-ga]-[N:yori]-[N^*\backslash N:-lil]-[X^2:han-da]$
2. $[N^*:-ga\ Sumi]-[N^*:-lil\ gongbu]-[CONJD:,]-[N^*:-ga\ Minju]-[N^*:-lil\ yori]-[X^2:han-da]$ (<)
3. $[S/X^1:(C^*-ga\ Sumi)]-[X^1/X^2:(C^*-lil\ gongbu)]-[CONJ:,]-[S/X^1:(C^*-ga\ Minju)]-[X^1/X^2:(C^*-lil\ yori)]-[X^2:han-da]$ (>T)
4. $[S/X^2:(B(C^*-ga\ Sumi)(C^*-lil\ gongbu))]-[CONJ:,]-[S/X^2:(B(C^*-ga\ Minju)(C^*-lil\ yori))]-[X^2:han-da]$ (>B)
5. $[S/X^2:Φ,(B(C^*-ga\ Sumi)(C^*-lil\ gongbu))(B(C^*-ga\ Minju)(C^*-lil\ yori))]-[X^2:han-da]$ (<CONJD>)
6. $[S:(Φ,(B(C^*-ga\ Sumi)(C^*-lil\ gongbu))(B(C^*-ga\ Minju)(C^*-lil\ yori)))han-da]$ (>)
7. $[S:,((B(C^*-ga\ Sumi)(C^*-lil\ gongbu))han-da)((B(C^*-ga\ Minju)(C^*-lil\ yori))han-da)]$ (Φ)
8. $[S:,((C^*-ga\ Sumi)((han-da)-lil\ gonbu))((B(C^*-ga\ Minju)(C^*-lil\ yori))han-da)]$ (B)
9. $[S:,(((han-da)-lil\ gongbu)-ga\ Sumi)((B(C^*-ga\ Minju)(C^*-lil\ yori))han-da)]$ (C*)
10. $[S:,(((han-da)-lil\ gongbu)-ga\ Sumi)((C^*-ga\ Minju)((han-da)-lil\ yori)]$ (C*)
11. $[S:,(((han-da)-lil\ gongbu)-ga\ Sumi)(((han-da)-lil\ yori)-ga\ Minju)]$ (C*)

The conjunction **,** coordinates two expressions having the same type: **(((han-da)-lil gongbu)-ga Sumi)** and **(((han-da)-lil yori)-ga Minju)**. These expressions are applicative expressions of propositions: ***Sumi studies*** and ***Minju cook*** that were presented here in the form of a logico-grammatical predicative relation. The introduction of the combinator **Φ**, at step 5, builds a new complex operator "**Φ,(B(C*-ga Sumi)(C*-lil gongbu))(B(C*-ga Minju)(C*-lil yori))**". Then, at step 6, the reduction of the combinator allows us to apply the operators "**B(C*-ga Sumi)(C*-lil gongbu)**" and "**B(C*-ga Minju)(C*-lil yori)**" to the operand "**han-da**".

3.3.1. Long Distance Scrambling

The long distance scrambling is one of the types of Free Word Order phenomenon (e.g. short distance scrambling, etc.). In this paper, we are particularly interested in the long distance scrambling in the coordination structure in Korean. This phenomenon that we can often find in Korean makes very complicated the Korean parsing notably when it appears in a complex coordination structure. Through this paper, we try to give a simple and robust solution to this problem with some examples in Korean.

Let us consider the sentence which shows the long distance scrambling phenomenon.

Sunsaengnim-i Sumi-nun Minsu-lil   pyunaehan-da-go saengakha -go, Minsu-nun   Sumi-lil pyunaehan-da-go saengakhan-da.
Professor-TOP Sumi-NOM Minsu-ACC prefer-DC-COMP think -CONJ Minsu-NOM Sumi-ACC prefer-DC-COMP think-DC
(Sumi thinks that the professor prefers Minsu and Minsu thinks that the professor prefers Sumi.)

---

[7] This is a combinator of coordination in the sense of Desclés and Biskri. The β-reduction rule is defined as follows: **Φfgh→f(gx)(hx). f,g,h,** are operators that will form a new complex operator **Φfgh** and **x** is its operand.

[8] This coordination rule was originally presented for the analysis of a French coordination by Biskri and Desclés in the paper "*Analyse de la coordination et de la subordination au moyen de la Grammaire Catégorielle Combinatoire Applicative*" (written in French, 2005).

Fig. 1. shows the original structure of the above sentence by allowing us to understand the origin of the movement of elements in the sentence.

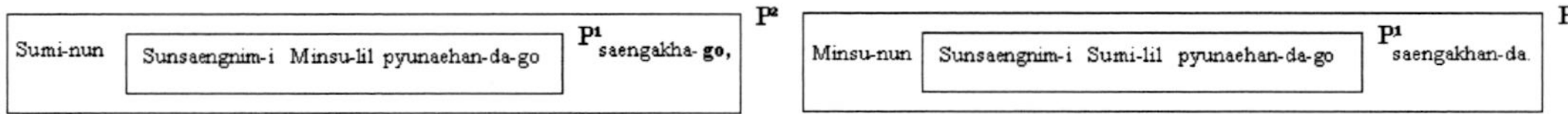

Figure 1: Original structure of the above sentence.

As shown in the above figure, this is a coordination having the movement of subject (NP: *Sunsaengnim-i*) of the embedded sentence (P^1) from both propositions to the head of the sentence. Namely, it concerns the topicalisation of *Sunsaengnim-i.*

We propose now to analyze this sentence in the **ACCG** formalism.
Sunsaengnim-i Sumi-nun Minsu-lil pyunaehan-da-go saengakha-go, Minsu-nun Sumi-lil pyunaehan-da-go saengakhan-da.

1. $[S/X^1$: $C\star$ -i Sunsaengnim]-$[S/X^1$: $C\star$ -nun Sumi]-$[X^1/X^2$: $C\star$ -lil Minsu]-$[X^2$: pyunaehan-da-go]-$[X^1\backslash S$:saengakha]-[CONJ: -go ,]-$[S/X^1$: $C\star$ -nun Minsu]-$[X^1/X^2$: $C\star$ -lil Sumi]-$[X^2$: pyunaehan-da-go]-$[X^1\backslash S$: saengakhan-da]   (>T)
2. $[S/X^1$: $C\star$ -i Sunsaengnim]-$[S/X^1$: $C\star$ -nun Sumi]-$[X^1$: ($C\star$ -lil Minsu pyunaehan-da-go)]-$[X^1\backslash S$: saengakha]-[CONJ:-go,]-$[S/X^1$: $C\star$ -nun Minsu]-$[X^1$: ($C\star$ -lil Sumi pyunaehan-da-go)]-$[X^1\backslash S$: saengakhan-da]   (>)
3. $[S/X^1$: $C\star$ -i Sunsaengnim]-[S: ($C\star$ -nun Sumi ($C\star$ -lil Minsu pyunaehan-da-go))]-$[X^1\backslash S$: saengakha]-[CONJ: -go,]-[S: ($C\star$ -nun Minsu ($C\star$ -lil Sumi pyunaehan-da-go))]-$[X^1\backslash S$: saengakhan-da]   (>)
4. $[S/X^1$: $C\star$ -i Sunsaengnim]-$[X^1$: saengakha-go ($C\star$ -nun Sumi ($C\star$ -lil Minsu pyunaehan-da-go))]-[CONJ:-go,]-$[X^1$: saengakhan-da ($C\star$ -nun Minsu ($C\star$ -lil Sumi pyunaehan-da-go))]   (<)
5. $[S/X^1$: $C\star$ -i Sunsaengnim]-$[X^1$: Φ -go, (saengakha-go ($C\star$ -nun Sumi ($C\star$ -lil Minsu pyunaehan-da-go))) (saengakhan-da ($C\star$ -nun Minsu ($C\star$ -lil Sumi pyunaehan-da-go)))]   (<CONJD>)
6. **[S: $C\star$ -i Sunsaengnim (Φ -go, (saengakha-go ($C\star$ -nun Sumi ($C\star$ -lil Minsu pyunaehan-da-go))) (saengakhan-da ($C\star$ -nun Minsu ($C\star$ -lil Sumi pyunaehan-da-go))))]**   (>)
7. **[S: (Φ -go, (saengakha-go ($C\star$ -nun Sumi ($C\star$ -lil Minsu pyunaehan-da-go))) (saengakhan-da ($C\star$ -nun Minsu ($C\star$ -lil Sumi pyunaehan-da-go))) –i sunsaengnim)]**   (C★)
8. **[S: (-go, (saengakha-go ($C\star$ -nun Sumi ($C\star$ -lil Minsu pyunaehan-da-go))-i sunsaengnim) (saengakhan-da ($C\star$ -nun Minsu ($C\star$ -lil Sumi pyunaehan-da-go))) –i sunsaengnim)]**   (Φ)
9. **[S: (-go, (saengakha-go ((pyunaehan-da-go)-lil Minsu)-nun Sumi)-i sunsaengnim) (saengakhan-da ((pyunaehan-da-go)-lil Sumi)-nun Minsu) –i sunsaengnim)]**   (C★)

In this analysis, we have shown only the most important steps, without detailing the preliminary calculations. At step 5, the application of the coordination rule allows us to coordinate two propositions and at step 8, to distribute *"Sunsaengnim-i"* to the first and second coordinated propositions. At step 9, we obtain a grammatically well-formed applicative expression, which is the parsing tree of the given sentence.

Then, consider the example of the Korean coordination having the ellipsis of the predicate and the long distance scrambling.

Sunsaengnim-i Sumi-nun Minsu-lil   pyunaeha -go,   Minsu-nun   Sumi-lil   pyunaehan-da-go saengakhan-da
Professor-TOP Sumi-NOM Minsu-ACC prefer   CONJ   Minsu-NOM Sumi-ACC prefer-DC-COMP think-DC
(Sumi think that the professor prefers Minsu and Minsu think that the professor prefers Sumi.)

In this sentence, we observe the ellipsis of predicate in the first proposition that make a difference from the above example and also the long distance scrambling phenomenon as the above sentence. This kind of structure has not been well analyzed in other related works from computational point of view because of the complexity of the long distance scrambling phenomenon.

Let us analyze the above sentence.
Sunsaengnim-i Sumi-nun Minsu-lil pyunaeha-go, Minsu-nun Sumi-lil pyunaehan-da-go saengakhan-da.

1. $[S/X^1$: $C\star$ -i Sunsaengnim]-$[S/X^1$: $C\star$ -nun Sumi]-$[X^1/X^2$: $C\star$ -lil Minsu]-$[X^2$: pyunaeha]-[CONJ: -go ,]-$[S/X^1$: $C\star$ -nun Minsu]-$[X^1/X^2$: $C\star$ -lil Sumi]-$[X^2$: pyunaehan-da-go]-$[X^1\backslash S$: saengakhan-da]   (>T)
2. $[S/X^1$: $C\star$ -i Sunsaengnim]-$[S/X^1$: $C\star$ -nun Sumi]-$[X^1$: ($C\star$ -lil Minsu pyunaeha)]-[CONJ:-go,]-$[S/X^1$: $C\star$ -nun Minsu]-$[X^1$: ($C\star$ -lil Sumi pyunaehan-da-go)]-$[X^1\backslash S$: saengakhan-da]   (>)
3. $[S/X^1$: $C\star$ -i Sunsaengnim]-[S: ($C\star$ -nun Sumi ($C\star$ -lil Minsu pyunaeha))]-[CONJ: -go,]-[S: ($C\star$ -nun Minsu ($C\star$ -lil Sumi pyunaehan-da-go))]-$[X^1\backslash S$: saengakhan-da]   (>)
4. $[S/X^1$: $C\star$ -i Sunsaengnim]-[S: Φ -go, ($C\star$ -nun Sumi ($C\star$ -lil Minsu pyunaeha)) ($C\star$ -nun Minsu ($C\star$ -lil Sumi pyunaehan-da-go))]-$[X^1\backslash S$: saengakhan-da]   (<)
5. $[S/X^1$: $C\star$ -i Sunsaengnim]-$[X^1$: saengakhan-da (Φ -go, ($C\star$ -nun Sumi ($C\star$ -lil Minsu pyunaeha)) ($C\star$ -nun Minsu ($C\star$ -lil Sumi pyunaehan-da-go)))]   (<CONJD>)
6. **[S: $C\star$ -i Sunsaengnim (saengakhan-da (Φ -go, ($C\star$ -nun Sumi ($C\star$ -lil Minsu pyunaeha)) ($C\star$ -nun Minsu ($C\star$ -lil Sumi pyunaehan-da-go))))]**   (>)
7. **[S: (saengakhan-da (Φ -go, ($C\star$ -nun Sumi ($C\star$ -lil Minsu pyunaeha)) ($C\star$ -nun Minsu ($C\star$ -lil Sumi pyunaehan-da-go)))) –i sunsaengnim)]**   (C★)
8. **[S: (saengakha-go (-go, ($C\star$ -nun Sumi ($C\star$ -lil Minsu pyunaeha))-i sunsaengnim) ($C\star$ -nun Minsu ($C\star$ -lil Sumi pyunaehan-da- go))) –i**   (Φ)

sunsaengnim)]
9. [S: (saengakha-go(-go, ((pyunaeha-go)-lil Minsu))-i sunsaengnim)-nun Sumi) ((pyunaehan-da-go)-lil Sumi)) –i sunsaengnim]-nun Minsu)]   (C*)

In this work, as shown in our categorial analyses, we could handle the long distance scrambling phenomenon in the complex coordination structure with simple applications of the coordination rule and the type raising rule.

4. Conclusion

As we have shown in this paper, this formalism allows us to scope the difficult characteristics of the Korean language. In particular, we could consider the cases in Korean as operators which play an essential role in the Korean analysis. The cases including double cases have not yet been well studied from a practical point of view. That is why our study is new and different.

We have shown the simple process of the calculation for the free word order structure which can be useful for the automatic processing. The process of calculation reveals clearly the syntactic order of the categories. We could also handle the coordination sentences having non constituent elements, ellipsis of predicates and even scrambling of the elements found in the coordination structure.

Compared to other related works for the Korean language parsing using exclusively Steedman's Combinatory Categorial Grammar, our attempts present a considerable challenge and a new approach resulting in the calculations of the Korean sentence that improve the above mentioned problems.

For the moment, it is possible to assign the several syntactic types to one case in this formalism. To resolve this complexity and ambiguity, we try to find some invariants for each case by calculating more complex sentences. Our results can automatically generate the applicative parsing tree in the form of the applicative expression. This kind of analysis by the categorial grammars can be combined in a more operational model such as the Applicative and Cognitive Grammar developed by J.-P. Desclés for a semantic analysis as a preliminary step to an analysis of a higher level.

References

Biskri, I. 1995. *La Grammaire Catégorielle Combinatoire Applicative dans le cadre de la Grammaire Applicative et Cognitive*, Ph.D.thesis, EHESS, Paris.

Biskri, I. and Desclés, J-P. 2005. Analyse de la coordination et de la subordination au moyen de la Grammaire Catégorielle Combinatoire Applicative, *Colloque Typologie et modélisation de la coordination et de la subordination*, LACITO-ParisIII (UMR 7107, CNRS), Paris.

Biskri, I. and Rochette, M, A. 2007. The operational annotation and the analysis of the correlative coordination in French, *In Proceedings of the 2007 FLorida Artificial Intelligence Society*, AAAI Press.

Cha J.W. 2001. *Statistical Parsing for Korean Categorial Grammar*, Ph.D.thesis, Pohang University of Science & Technology, Pohang, Korea.

Cha J.W. and Lee G.B. 2002. Structural disambiguation of morpho-syntactic categorial parsing for Korean, *International Conference On Computational Linguistics*, Proceedings of the 18th conference on Computational linguistics – Vol. 2, 1002~1006, Saarbrücken, Germany.

Cho, H.J and Park. J.C. 2000. Combinatory Categorial Grammar for the Syntactic, Semantic and Discourse Analyses of Coordination in Korean, *Journal of KISS: Software and Applications*, 27(4), 448-462, Korea.

Chung, G. 2003. *Analyse des constructions à double nominatif/accusatif par l'opération de restructuration en Coréen. Classification syntaxique des constructions à adjectifs sôngsang*, Ph.D.thesis, Marne-La-Vallée University, Paris.

Curry, H. and Feys, R. 1958. *Combinatory Logic*, Vol.I, North-Holland.

Desclés, J.P. 1990. *Langages applicatifs, langues naturelles et cognition*, Hermès, Paris.

Desclés, J-P and Biskri, I. 1996. Logique Combinatoire et linguistique : La Grammaire Catégorielle Combinatoire Applicative, *Mathématiques, Informatiques et Sciences Humaines*, n° 132, 39-68, Paris.

Desclés, J.P. 2003. *La Grammaire Applicative et Cognitive construit-elle des représentations universelles?*, LINX 48, Université Paris X, 139-160, Paris.

Hong, J.S. 1999. Generative Grammar and Korean Cases, in *Korean Cases and Particles* by Institute of Korean Language, Wolin, 83-112, Korea.

Kang, B.M. 2001. *Categorial Grammar* (written in Korean), Institute of Korean Culture, Korea University, Seoul, Korea.

Kang, J.Y. 2005. *Grammaires Catégorielles appliquées au coréen en comparaison avec le français*, Master's thesis, Paris-Sorbonne University, Paris.

Lambek, J. 1961. On the calculus syntactic types, *Proceeding of symposia in Applied Mathematics,* vol. XII, America Mathematical Society, Providence, Rhode Island, 166-178.

Lee H.J. and Park J.C. 2003. Morphological Analysis of Irregular Conjugation in Korean with Micro Combinatory Categorial Grammar, *Proceedings of the Korea Information Science Society (KISS) Spring Conference*, volume 30, number 1(B), 531-533, Korea.

Lee, S.H. 2002. Korean Though Constructions and Double Nominative Constructions, *In Proceedings of the 9th International Conference On HPSG*, Seoul, Korea.

Moortgat, M. 1988. *Categorial Investigation, Logical and Linguistic Aspects of the Lambek calculus*, Foris Publications.

Nam, G.S. 2001. *The Syntax* (written in Korean), Taehaksa, Seoul, Korea.

Shaumyan, S. K. 1987. *A Semiotic Theory of Natural Language*, Bloomington, Indiana Univ. Press.

Steedman, M. 1989. *Work in Progress: Combinators and grammars in natural language understanding*, Summer institute of linguistic, Tucson University.

Steedman, M. 2001. *The Syntactic Process*, MIT Press/Bradford Books.

Sung, K.S. 1999. *Expression of Cases and Meaning of Particles* (written in Korean), Wolin, Seoul, Korea.

Stress Processing Sensitivity in Reading Korean and English Words[*]

Yongsoon Kang[a], Seunghyun Baek[a], and Mira Yim[a]

[a]Department of English Language and Literature, Sungkyunkwan University
53 Myungryun 3-ga, Chongno-gu, Seoul, 110-745, Korea
E-mail: yskang@skku.edu; sh3940@hanmail.net; yimmira@hanmail.net

Abstract. The present study explored the sensitivity to stress patterns of sixty-four ninth-graders learning to speak and read in Korean as a first language (L1) and English as a second language (L2) concurrently. Students' productive stress processing abilities were assessed in reading Korean real words, English unfamiliar real words, and English pseudo-words. Results unveiled that the Korean-speaking English language learners (ELLs) performed differently between Korean and English in terms of number of syllables and stress placement within a syllable structure. More specifically, their stress processing performances between the two languages clearly differed when the number of syllables increases and their stress assignment differences across the two languages were much larger on dissimilar stress patterns than similar ones. These findings suggest that unfamiliar L2-specific prosodic information such as stress may present additional challenges to L2 learners, especially when their L1 is not stress-based.

Keywords: stress processing sensitivity, prosodic information.

1. Introduction

Spoken words can be characterized in terms of suprasegmental or prosodic features, markedly stress, determined by acoustic frequency, intensity, and/or duration. Such a stressed-syllable is relatively louder and longer than other syllables in the same word or phrase (Ladefoged, 2001). In some languages such as Korean, French, and Czech, stress pattern of words is somehow predictable and syllable-based. For example, in Korean, stress mostly falls on the first syllable, otherwise on the second syllable, displaying no significant linguistic difference (Lee, 1990; Park, 2004). In French, stress dominantly falls on the final syllable with a full vowel, with no distinctive minimal pairs of words differed by its stress pattern and in Czech, stress almost always falls on the first syllable of a word (Jannedy, Poletto and Weldon, 1994). These syllable-based languages do not show meaning and grammatical differences influenced by their stress patterns.

In other languages such as English, although the placement of stress is less predictable, stress can involve in lexical contrasts, causing a difference in meaning (i.e., TRUsty-truSTEE). In addition, it can change grammatical functions of words. For example, the word *progress* functions as a noun when the stress is placed on the first syllable, whereas as a verb when the stress is placed on the second syllable. The other stress-based languages in which speech sounds is controlled by stress are Spanish and Dutch (Goetry, Wade-Woolley, Kolnsky and Mousty, 2006). These languages do also illustrate lexical contrasts defined by their stress patterns.

Current understanding of the stress pattern across languages suggests that the linguistic role of stress pattern widely differs with respect to lexical and grammatical functions and the rule of stress assignment is language specific. Recent studies on first-language (L1) stress sensitivity have demonstrated that L1 speakers of stress-based languages (i.e., English, Spanish, and

---

[*] First author: Yongsoon Kang, Correspondence Author: Seunghyun Baek. This research was supported by Sungkyunkwan University Brain Korea 21 Project in 2008.

Dutch) are more sensitive to stress patterns than those of syllable-based languages (i.e, Korean and French). For example, given the discrepant lexical function of stress between Spanish and French, adult L1 speakers of French produced more errors in judging whether a string of pseudo-words differing in stress pattern display the same stress pattern or not than adult L1 speakers of Spanish (Dupoux, Pallier, Sebastian-Galles and Mehler, 1997). In another follow-up study of phoneme-and stress-contrast sensitivity, Dupoux and colleagues (Dupoux, Peperkamp and Sebastian-Galles, 2001) found that adult L1 speakers of Spanish and French performed similarly on the phoneme contrast judgment (i.e., /kypi/-/kyti/). However, the Spanish-native monolinguals significantly outperformed the French-native monolinguals on the stress contrast judgment (i.e, /'kipi/-/ki'pi/).

In the meantime, the sensitivity to stress patterns has not received much attention in L2 reading research until recently because suprasegmental information is not manifested in most written systems. In a recent pioneering study of sensitivity of prosodic features among monolingual and bilingual first graders, Goetry and associates (Goetry, Wade-Woolley, Kolinsky and Mousty, 2006) compared the stress and phonemic awareness of French-native, Dutch-native monolingual, French-native children taught in Dutch, and Dutch-native children taught in French. The results showed that the four groups of first-graders performed similarly on phonemic awareness judgment (i.e., /'tepy/-/'tapy/) but differed on stress sensitivity judgment (i.e., /'tipy/-/ti'py/). The Dutch monolinguals notably outperformed the French monolinguals. The other bilingual first-graders had the intermediary performances. More importantly, Goetry et al. (2006) also suggest that early literacy development in a second stress-based language can be influenced by stress sensitivity by observing the correlation between stress awareness and word reading in the French monolinguals schooled in Dutch, not in the Dutch monolinguals schooled in French.

Based on the findings of existing research on cross-linguistic comparisons of L1 and L2 stress awareness, stress processing ability may play a crucial role in learning to read in a second stress-based language such as English, Dutch, or Spanish, especially when students' L1 is not stress-based. Moreover, spoken word processing is largely related to written word identification (Morais, 2003). At this point, it is significant to explore the stress assignment sensitivity of word reading in Korean, a syllable-based language, compared with that in English, a stress-based language as there has been little exploitation of learning to concurrently speak and read in an L1 with transparent stress rule and an L2 with opaque stress rule. In addition, previous studies have mainly focused on the perceptive sensitivity of stress contrasts. Consequently, more attention needs to be raised in interpreting the productive sensitivity of stress assignment.

As discussed earlier, the stress pattern of Korean is somewhat predictable and regular without distinguishing meanings and grammatical functions of words. On the other hand, because the stress rule in English varies depending on word classes (Roca and Johnson, 1999), to some degree, it is less predictable and irregular with lexical and grammatical contrasts. Indeed, if Korean-speaking English language learners (ELLs) face exclusively distinctive stress patterns of English, which is not relevant to their L1, they may confront drastic restructuring of their interlanguage stress assignments and deal with unstable prosodic representations across the two languages. As a result, they would be at risk for difficulties in learning to speak and read in English as a stress-sensitive L2 and displaying prosodic information of English words.

Given the discrepant stress assignment between Korean and English, the primary goal of this current study is to investigate the stress processing sensitivity of Korean-speaking ELLs in terms of number of syllables in a word and syllable structure in the word. The three research questions addressed in this study are as follows:

(1) Given the distinctive stress assignment between Korean and English, what are the stress processing abilities of Korean-speaking ELLs in the L1 (Korean) and in the L2 (English)?
(2) Depending on the number of syllables, how does students' stress sensitivity differ between the two languages?
(3) Within a syllable structure, how sensitive are they to stress patterns across the two languages?

Investigating language-specific stress awareness engaged in L1 and L2 word reading can shed light on the degree of cross-language transfer and can furthermore suggest that dissimilar L2-specific prosodic features increase particular difficulties in L2 stress processing due to overgeneralized stress rules gained from L1.

2. An Overview of Stress Assignment Rule Differences

In Korean, regardless of word classes (i.e., noun or verb), stress is typically assigned depending on number of syllables. In disyllabic words, for example, stress is almost always placed on the first syllable and in Korean polysyllabic words, depending on the weight of the first syllable, stress patterns of the words are divided into two categories. In other words, if the first syllable is heavy[1], stress is almost always placed on that syllable. If not, either on the first or on the second syllable, displaying no significant linguistic meaning and function changes (Lee, 1990). The stress assignment rules in Korean are represented as follows:

(a) Two syllable morphemes: Stress falls on the first syllable.

(b) Three or more syllable morphemes: If the first syllable is heavy, stress falls on that syllable. Otherwise, either on the first or on the second syllable, with no important linguistic difference implied (Lee, 1990, pp. 50-51).

However, stress rules in English are varying with classes of words, playing a role of meaningful and grammatical contrasts. Stress of nouns and verbs is governed by different rules, respectively (cf. Roca and Johnson, 1999).

(a) Nouns and suffixed adjectives: The penultimate syllable is stressed if it is heavy; otherwise stress falls on the antepenultimate syllable.

(b) Verbs and unsuffixed adjectives: The ultimate syllable is stressed if it is heavy; otherwise stress falls on the penultimate syllable.

Based on the three research questions addressed earlier, this present study would predict that depending on number of syllables in a word and syllable structure in the word, the sensitivity to stress patterns of Korean-speaking ELLs differs between Korean and English. More specifically, the performance on stress processing across the two languages would noticeably differ on dissimilar and non-overlapping stress patterns than similar and overlapping ones because unfamiliar stress-sensitive L2 (i.e., stress assignment rule) may present additional challenges to bilinguals whose L1 is less stress-sensitive.

3. Methods

3.1. Participants

In the context of English as a foreign language (EFL), sixty-four ninth-graders learning to speak and read in Korean and English simultaneously were recruited to voluntarily participate in this study (mean age: 15.97 years; 32 boys, 32 girls). All of the participants were native speakers of Korean with similar socio-cultural backgrounds, attending the same middle school located in Kyunggi-do (province). Based on the results of a demographic questionnaire the participants were individually asked to fill out, the mean stay of English-speaking countries was 0.04 years and all of them have been staying at Seoul metropolitan area and Kyunggi-do in which standard Korean is spoken. All of their family members including the subjects spoke Korean at home. In short, all of the subjects had limited exposure to English as an L2 and spoke standard Korean.

3.2. Testing Items

---

[1] A heavy syllable is one with a branching rhyme (VC) or a branching nucleus (VV), contrasted with V, which` is a light syllable. The number of segments on onset does not matter with regard to the weight of syllables (Spencer, 1996).

In order to examine how Korean-speaking ELLs process a stress in a Korean word, twenty-five Korean real words were selected and split into 5 subcategories with respect to their syllable structures, the number of syllables, the placement of stress in a word (see Appendix A). In particular, nouns are dominantly employed for Korean (L1) testing items to match comparability of English (L2) items in terms of their syllable structures and stress patterns. That is, the Korean verbs and adjectives corresponding to a syllable structure and stress pattern in English do exist but rarely. Additionally, because there exist no Korean words stressed on the second syllable, only the syllable structure of 'CV.CVC under the two syllable category in Korean was used.

In the same way, thirty English real words were selected to observe Korean-speaking ELLs' stress awareness of English (see Appendix B) and fall into 6 subcategories. Twenty items for each subcategory, total of 120 words, were initially field-tested with the participants and then the items with which more than 50% of the subjects were familiar were excluded. Equally important, the selected thirty unfamiliar real words are manipulated by changing the onset of stressed syllable and considering place of articulation and, if it does not work, then manner of articulation (i.e., 'magic -> 'nagic).

3.3. Procedure

The participants were individually assessed in reading Korean real words, English unfamiliar real words, and English pseudo-words. The order of the three language tasks was counterbalanced and the randomized items were visually presented on the screen of a laptop. Within a language task, the students were asked to read target words one by one. Prior to the administrations of each of the two English real and pseudo-word tasks, two trial items per each syllable structure were given to the students. All of the three tasks were conducted by a fluent Korean-English bilingual experimenter, who recorded the students' responses over the three tasks in a quiet room. Each session was audio-taped for later coding of accuracy via a MP3 player.

3.4. Coding

The recorded responses of the participants' production of each Korean and English stimulus were transferred onto a computer. In order to identify a placement of stress in a word, Praat program[2], commonly used for acoustic analysis (Ladefoged, 2003; Yang, 2000) was downloaded from the following link at http://www.fon.hum.uva.nl/praat/. Because a stressed syllable has a longer vowel than the other vowels in a word (Ladefoged. 2001), the waveforms retrieved from the recorded files were edited to measure the durations of vowels in a word. That is, a stress is typically assigned to the longer vowels than the neighboring vowels in the word.

Each item within a syllable structure was scored as 1 when each participant has a correct placement of stress in a word. The score of the Korean syllable structure of 'CV.CVC was used twice because there are no Korean words stressed on the second syllable in two-syllable words. Thus, total score of each language task was 30. Accuracy of stress placement of each item was calculated per subject, then summed up, and averaged in terms of syllable structure, number of syllable, and language task. The mean of stress awareness was   converted into correct percentage of stress sensitivity.

4. Results and Discussion

In investigating stress processing sensitivities of Korean-speaking ELLs, a series of repeated-measures ANOVAs was conducted to measure differences between language tasks, number of syllables, and syllable structures separately. In addition, Bonferroni multiple comparisons were

---

[2] The program was developed by Paul Boersma and David Weenink at the Institute of Phonetic Sciences, University of Amsterdam.

carried out to compare specific language tasks, number of syllables, and syllable structures respectively.

Table 1 shows the means observed for the three language tasks depending on number of syllables and stress placement within a syllable structure. Inspection of Table 1 indicates that overall, Korean-Speaking ELLs performed better on the Korean words than on the English real/pseudo-words and regardless of language task, the mean accuracy of stress awareness generally decreases when number of syllable increases. More important, their productive sensitivity of stress placement was more accurate in responding to similar stress patterns between Korean and English than dissimilar ones.

Table 1: Means observed for the three language tasks depending on number of syllable and stress placement within a syllable structure (N = 64).

Language Task									
	Korean Real Word			English Real Word			English Pseudo Word		
Number of Syllables	To-Be-Stressed-Syllable	M	SD	To-Be-Stressed-Syllable	M	SD	To-Be-Stressed-Syllable	M	SD
2 Syllables	1st	5.00	.00	1st	4.44	.99	1st	4.19	1.41
	1st	5.00	.00	2nd	3.00	1.27	2nd	2.58	1.32
3 Syllables	2nd	4.89	.57	1st	3.45	1.21	1st	3.64	1.25
	1st	5.00	.00	2nd	1.39	0.79	2nd	1.17	.77
4 Syllables	1st	4.94	.24	2nd	.48	.62	2nd	.36	.55
	1st or 2nd	4.98	.13	3rd	1.73	1.22	3rd	1.41	1.19

Note: Maximum score of each stress placement within a syllable structure = 5.

4.1. Results for Research Question 1

In order to answer the Research Question 1 regarding comparison of stress awareness between Korean and English, the accuracy percentages of the three languages tasks are presented in Figure 1. Results in Figure 1 show that the participants' productive awareness of stress assignment was most accurate in Korean real word ($M = 29.82$), followed by English unfamiliar real word ($M = 14.50$) and English pseudo-word ($M = 13.34$). A repeated-measures ANOVA showed the significant within-subjects effects of language task, $F(2, 126) = 952.49$, $p < .001$. Additionally, Bonferroni analyses across the three tasks confirmed that the Korean-speaking ELLs differently performed across the three language tasks (Real Korean vs. Real English: $p < .001$; Real English vs. Pseudo English: $p < .001$; Real Korean vs. Pseudo English: $p < .001$).

Within a language task, a series of repeated-measures ANOVAs were employed to examine stress processing differences between 3 syllables and between 6 syllable structures separately. For Korean real word, there were no significant within-subjects effects of number of syllable and syllable structure. For English real word, however, there were significant within-subjects effects of number of syllables, $F(2, 126) = 264.24$, $p < .001$, and of syllable structure, $F(5, 315) = 160.16$, $p < .001$. Similarly, for English pseudo-word, there were also significant within-subjects effects of number of syllables, $F(2, 126) = 187.85$, $p < .001$, and of syllable structure, $F(5, 315) = 140.18$, $p < .001$. The results of three language tasks suggest that Korean-speaking ELLs perform similarly on Korean real word regardless of the number of syllables and syllable structures, whereas they perform differently on English real and pseudo-word depending on the number of syllables and syllable structures. In other words, their stress processing abilities are stable in Korean and unstable in English.

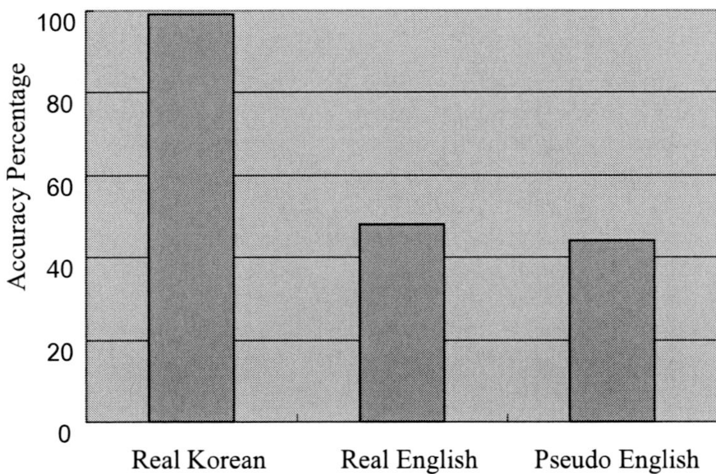

Figure 1: Performance of the stress awareness in Korean real words, English unfamiliar real words, and English pseudo-words.

4.2. Results for Research Question 2

In order to examine the Research Question 2 concerning the stress sensitivity between Korean and English in terms of number of syllables, the correct percentages of the number of syllables across the three language tasks are shown in Figure 2. Findings in Figure 2 provide that for 2-syllable word, the subjects' stress processing accuracy in Korean real word ($M = 10.00$) was higher than that in English real ($M = 7.44$) and pseudo-word ($M = 6.77$). For 3- and 4-syllable word, the similar performances on stress placement were observed (for 3-syllable word: Korean, $M = 9.89$, Real English, $M = 4.84$, Pseudo English, $M = 4.81$; for 4-syllable word: Korean, $M = 9.94$, Real English, $M = 2.21$; Pseudo English, $M = 1.76$).

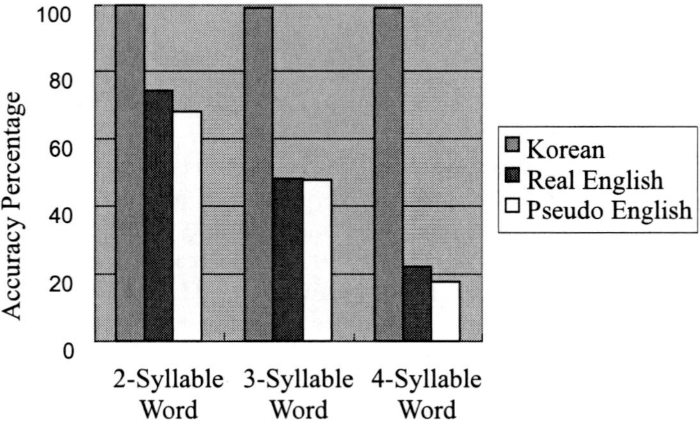

Figure 2: Performance of the stress awareness across Korean real word, English unfamiliar real word, and English pseudo-word in terms of the number of syllables.

In the following step, a string of repeated-measures ANOVAs was conducted to compare their stress processing differences of the three language tasks within a given number of syllables. One ANOVA for 2-syllable word revealed the significant within-subjects effects of language task, F (2, 126) = 92.08, $p< .001$. In addition, Bonferroni analyses also showed the mean differences among the three tasks (Real Korean vs. Real English: $p < .001$; Real English vs. Pseudo English: $p < .05$; Real Korean vs. Pseudo English: $p < .001$). Similarly, for 3-syllable word, the significant differences were obtained between tasks, $F (2, 126) = 408.93$, $p < .001$. In particular, multiple comparisons measured by Bonferroni analyses demonstrated the mean differences between Korean real word and English real word ($p < .001$), and between Korean real word and English pseudo-word ($p < .001$), but not between English real and pseudo-word. In examining differences of 4-syllable word, another ANOVA also showed the significant differences between tasks, $F (2, 126) = 1537.50$, $p < .001$. Moreover, Bonferroni analyses also showed the mean differences among the three tasks (Real Korean vs. Real English: $p < .001$; Real English vs. Pseudo English: $p < .05$; Real Korean vs. Pseudo English: $p < .001$). The findings suggest that overall, in all 2-, 3-, and 4-syllable words, the Korean-speaking ELLs perform better on Korean real word than on English real word and pseudo-word. Furthermore, the effects of language task are more pronounced as the number of syllables increases by observing the effect size of 2-, 3-, and 4-syllable word ($\eta^2 = .59$, $.87$, and $.98$ respectively). In a word, the stress processing performances between Korean and English obviously differ when the number of syllables increases.

4.3. Results for Research Question 3

As far as the Research Question 3 regarding the sensitivity to stress placement within a syllable structure across the two languages is concerned, firstly, Figure 3 presents the accurate percentages of the similar and dissimilar stress patterns in 2-syllable words across the three language tasks. Results in Figure 3 demonstrate that in a similar stress pattern (for both Korean and English: 1st syllable stressed), the participants' production of stress assignment was more accurate in Korean real word ($M = 5.00$) than in English real ($M = 4.44$) and pseudo-word ($M = 4.19$). In a similar stress pattern, a repeated-measures ANOVA showed the significant effects of language task, $F (2, 126) = 14.27$, $p < .001$, $\eta^2 = .19$. Besides, Bonferroni pairwise comparisons confirmed the mean differences between Korean real word and English real word ($p < .001$), and between Korean real word and English pseudo-word ($p < .001$). However, there was no mean difference between English real and pseudo-word. The findings propose that even though there is a similar stress pattern between the two languages, the Korean-speaking ELLs perform differently across the two languages, but similarly between the two English tasks.

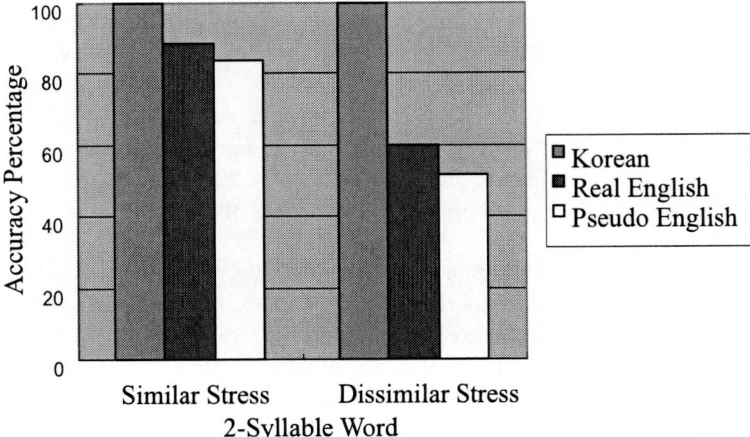

Figure 3: Performance of the stress awareness across Korean real word, English unfamiliar real word, and English pseudo-word in terms of stress placement within 2-syllable words.

Meanwhile, in a dissimilar pattern (for Korean: 1st syllable stressed; for English: 2nd syllable stressed), the subjects' stress assignment accuracy in Korean real word ($M = 5.00$) was higher than in English real (M = 3.00) and pseudo-word (M = 2.58). Another repeated-measures ANOVA unveiled the significant effects of language task, F (2, 126) = 129.29, p< .001, η^2 = .67. Additionally, Theses effects were confirmed by Bonferroni analyses (Real Korean vs. Real English: p< .001; Real English vs. Pseudo English: p< .05; Real Korean vs. Pseudo English: p< .001). The results suggest that in a dissimilar stress pattern, the participants' stress processing accuracy apparently differs between Korean and English. In comparing effect size of similar (η^2 = .19) and dissimilar pattern (η^2 = .67), as expected, the performance differences between the two languages are much larger on dissimilar stress pattern than similar one.

Secondly, Figure 4 illustrates the correct percentages of the two distinctive stress patterns in 3-syllable words across the three language tasks. Results in Figure 4 shows that in a dissimilar stress pattern (for Korean: 2nd syllable stressed; for English: 1st syllable stressed), the performance on Korean real word (M = 4.89) is much better than the two other English tasks (for Real English: M = 3.45; for Pseudo English: M = 3.64). A repeated-measures ANOVA uncovered the significant effects of language task, F (2, 126) = 54.82, p< .001, η^2 = .47. Bonferroni analyses also showed the mean differences between Korean task and the two other English tasks (p< .001) but not between the two English tasks.

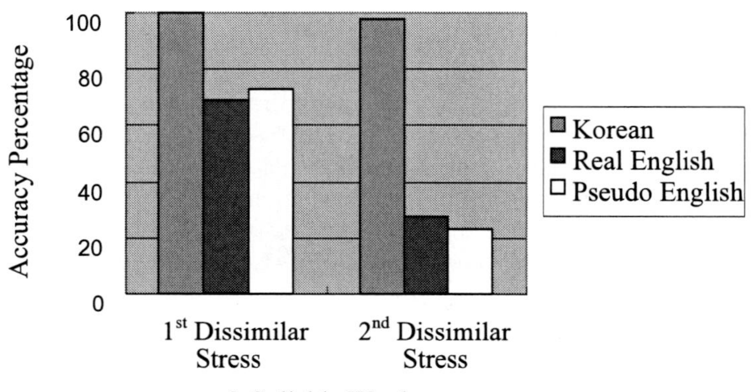

Figure 4: Performance of the stress awareness across Korean real word, English unfamiliar real word, and English pseudo-word in terms of stress placement within 3-syllable words.

In another dissimilar stress pattern (for Korean: 1st syllable stressed; for English: 2nd syllable stressed), the similar performance on stress awareness was also observed by the repeated-measures ANOVA, F (2, 126) = 769.59, p< .001, η^2 = .92 (for Real Korean: M = 5.00; for Real English: M = 1.39; for Pseudo English: M = 1.17) and was verified by Bonferroni analyses (Real Korean vs. Real English: p< .001; Real Korean vs. Pseudo English: p< .001; Real English vs. Pseudo English: p> .1). The findings of the two conflicting stress patterns in 3-syllable words imply that the subjects' stress processing abilities are noticeably uneven across the two languages.

Finally, Figure 5 explains the accurate percentages of the two idiosyncratic stress patterns in 4-syllable words across the three tasks. Findings in Figure 5 provide that in a dissimilar stress pattern (for Korean: 1st syllable stressed; for English: 2nd syllable stressed), the subjects' stress processing in Korean real word (M = 4.94) was most accurate, compared with English real (M = .48) and pseudo-words (M = .36), which was proved by the significant effects of language task in the repeated-measures ANOVA, F (2, 126) = 1947.78, p< .001, η^2 = .97, and by the mean differences in Bonferroni analyses (Real Korean vs. Real English: p< .001; Real Korean vs. Pseudo English: p< .001; Real English vs. Pseudo English: p> .1).

In the other dissimilar pattern (for Korean: either 1st or 2nd syllable stressed; for English: 3rd syllable stressed), similarly, the performance on stress sensitivity in Korean real word (M = 4.98) was much higher than English real (M = 1.73) and pseudo-word (M = 1.41), which was witnessed by the repeated-measures ANOVA, F (2, 126) = 353.52, $p<$ .001, η^2 = .85, and by Bonferroni analyses (Real Korean vs. Real English: $p<$ .001; Real Korean vs. Pseudo English: $p<$ .001; Real English vs. Pseudo English: $p>$ .05). Again, the results of the two incompatible stress patterns in 4-syllable words suggest that the participants' productive awareness of stress assignment clearly differ between the two languages.

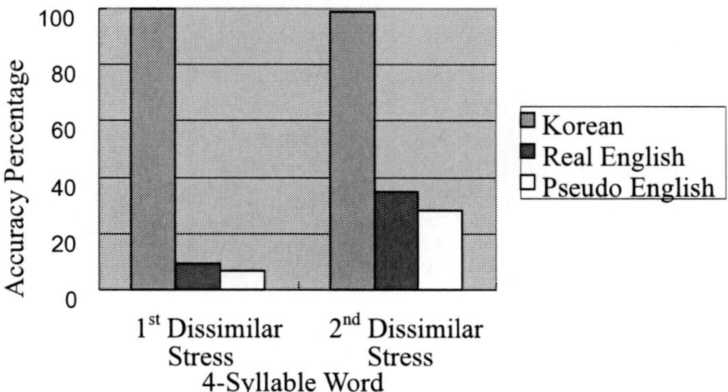

Figure 5: Performance of the stress awareness across Korean real word, English unfamiliar real word, and English pseudo-word in terms of stress placement within 4-syllable words.

4. Conclusion and Implications

The current study investigated the sensitivity to stress placement demonstrated by Korean-speaking ELLs and furthermore, examined the prosodic representations with respect to language, number of syllables, and stress pattern within a syllable structure. The study found that in general, they performed better on Korean than English. More important, when the number of syllables increases, their stress processing abilities between the two languages apparently differed. That is, their stress awareness in Korean was stable regardless of the number of syllables, whereas that in English was unstable, thus decreases when the number of syllables increases. Equally important, their stress assignment differences across the two languages are evidently pronounced when the two languages have distinctive stress patterns.

The present findings suggest that the acquisition of L2 suprasegmental information may depend on the degree to which the L1 and L2 prosodic properties such as stress share structural similarities, identifying the potential prosodic errors which may cause the difficulty in L2 prosodic processing. Especially, if students' L1 is not a stress-sensitive language, they may face difficulties in learning to read in a stress-sensitive L2 like English and dealing with prosodic features of the stress-based L2. Moreover, as the overgeneralized stress assignment rules from the L1 may lead to inappropriate lexical and grammatical functions of the L2 prosodic features, the inclusion of practices focused on developing sensitivity to the placement of stress may be helpful to facilitate L2 speaking and reading abilities.

References

Dupoux, E., Pallier, C., Sebastian-Galles, N., and Mehler, J. 1997. A distressing "deafness" in French? *Journal of Memory and Language, 36,* 406-421.

Dupoux, E., Peperkamp, S., and Sebastian-Galles, N. 2001. A robust method to study stress "deafness". *Journal of the Acoustical Society of America,* 110, 1606-1618.

Goetry, V., Wade-Woolley, L., Kolinsky, R., and Mousty, P. 2006. The role of stress processing abilities in the development of bilingual reading *Journal of Research in Reading,* 29(3) 349-362.

Jannedy, S., Poletto, R. and Weldon, T. L. 1994. *Language files.* Columbus, OH: Ohio State University.

Ladefoged, P. 2001. *A course in phonetics.* 4th ed. Boston, MA: Heinle & Heinle.

Ladefoged, P. 2003. *Phonetic data analysis.* Oxford, UK: Blackwell.

Lee, H. 1990. *The structure of Korean prosody.* Unpublished doctoral dissertation, University of London.

Morais, J. 2003. Levels of phonological representations in skilled reading and learning to read. *Reading and Writing: An Interdisciplinary Journal,* 16, 123-151.

Park, S. 2004. Errors of English stress by Korean speakers. *English Language & Literature Teaching,* 10(3), 177-190.

Roca, I. and Johnson, W. 1999. *A course in phonology.* Oxford, UK: Blackwell.

Spencer, A. 1996. *Phonology.* Oxford, UK: Blackwell

Yang, B. 2000. An acoustic analysis method of numeric sounds by Praat. *Korean Journal of Speech Sciences* 79(2), 127-137.

Appendix A: Korean Items

Number of Syllables	Syllable Structure	Korean
Two	'CV.CVC	사진, 하늘, 시간, 도심, 시골
Three	CV. 'CV.CV	너구리, 지우개, 가자미, 바구니, 개구리
	'CVC. CV.CV	갈매기, 연구소, 잠자리, 문화사, 접미사
Four	'CVC.CV.CV(C).CV(C)	날개개미, 동의보감, 길모퉁이, 장구머리, 한해살이
	(')CV. (')CV.CV.CV	쥐며느리, 귀뚜라미, 가시고기, 가로쓰기, 자유주의

Appendix B: English Items

Number of Syllables	Syllable Structure	Real Words	Pseudo-Words
Two	'CV.CVC	marriage, passive, tunnel, ribbon, heaven	narriage, tassive, kunnel, dibbon, feaven
	CV.'CVC(C)	commit, detach, demand, possess, corrupt	connit, depach, denand, poffess, connupt
Three	'CV. CV.CV(C)	negative, calorie, cinema, summary, capital	megative, talorie, finema, fummary, tapital
	(C)VC.'CV(C).CVC(C)	condition, ambitious, volcanic, advantage, incumbent	conbition, amditious, voltanic, adzantage, intumbent
Four	(C)VC.'CV(C).(C)CV(C).CVC(C)	significant, conditional, consistency, adventurous, complexity	sigmificant, conbitional, confistency, adzenturous, comklexity
	(C)V.CV.'(C)CV(V).CVC	generation, beneficial, democratic, academic, politician	genenation, benesicial, demopratic, acabemic, polipician

A Preliminary Study on the Impact of Lexical Concreteness on Word Senses Disambiguation [*]

Oi Yee Kwong

Department of Chinese, Translation and Linguistics, and
Language Information Sciences Research Centre
City University of Hong Kong
Tat Chee Avenue, Kowloon, Hong Kong
rlolivia@cityu.edu.hk

Abstract. Psychologists have shown that abstract words are harder to understand and often acquired later than concrete words. In this work, we study how the difficulty of automatic word sense disambiguation (WSD) might be affected by this intrinsic property of words, namely the concreteness of a word and its individual senses. We also explore the feasibility of inducing a numerical index for sense and lexical concreteness from dictionary definitions. Analysis of system performance in previous SENSEVAL exercises suggests that concrete words are often easier to disambiguate. The high overall agreement between human ratings and definition-induced ratings is also encouraging. The concreteness factor is worth the attention of computational linguists, particularly in terms of how it bears on the differential information demand of individual words in WSD and how the knowledge of this property could be employed to fine-tune WSD systems to better deal with the lexical sensitivity of the task.

Keywords: Lexical concreteness, Word sense disambiguation

1. Introduction

The SENSEVAL (and recently SemEval) exercises have revealed a lot of issues on automatic word sense disambiguation (WSD), and allowed researchers to learn more about the linguistic and technical aspects of the task. System performance often depends on many factors, including the feature set, availability of training instances, and language models, amongst others. One important linguistic factor is the fine-grainedness of the sense inventory and the semantic closeness among the senses of a word. To this end, Resnik and Yarowsky (1997) suggested that closely related senses are more difficult for WSD, and therefore systems should be penalised less if they fail to distinguish between similar senses than if they fail to tell distinct senses apart.

Despite being a psychologically valid and intrinsic property of words and senses, *concreteness* is seldom addressed in WSD literature. Psychologists have shown, from lexical decision and naming tasks, that abstract words are harder to understand than concrete words, and are often acquired later (e.g. Bleasdale, 1987; Kroll and Merves, 1986; Yore and Ollila,

---

[*] The work described in this paper was fully supported by a grant from the Research Grants Council of the Hong Kong Special Administrative Region, China (Project No. CityU 1508/06H).

22nd Pacific Asia Conference on Language, Information and Computation, pages 235–244

1985). This thus implies differential underlying mechanisms in the representation, development, and processing of word meanings in the mental lexicon. By analogy, the inclusion of the concreteness information in computational lexicons should also benefit natural language processing (NLP) tasks like WSD, in addition to maneuvering only linguistic and technical factors. It should also allow us to study polysemy and sense similarity in a more comprehensive and cognitively plausible way.

Hence, we start on a preliminary study on the relationship between concreteness and WSD. In particular, given the lexical sensitivity of the task, we are interested to see how this psycholinguistic factor bears on the difficulty of WSD, how it could be employed in fine-tuning WSD systems to accommodate the different information demand of individual target words, as well as its potential impact on evaluative measures.

In the first part of this study, we analyse system performance reported in previous SENSEVAL exercises with respect to the concreteness of the target words. In the current study, we focus on noun samples only. In the second part, we explore the feasibility of automatically inducing a more objective and robust concreteness measure from dictionary definitions, which is needed for enhancing lexical resources and benefiting WSD in the long run. In general it was observed that concrete words are often easier to disambiguate. The high overall agreement between human ratings and definition-induced ratings is also encouraging.

In Section 2, we briefly review related work and further set out the background of this study. In Section 3, we report on our analysis of system performance with respect to the concreteness of target words. In Section 4, we outline the relation between definition styles and concreteness, and describe our work on automatically inducing a concreteness measure from surface syntactic forms of dictionary definitions. The results are further discussed with future directions in Section 5, followed by a conclusion in Section 6. In this paper we use "lexical concreteness" and "sense concreteness" as a generic term for the degree of concreteness of words and senses respectively, from highly abstract to highly concrete.

2. Background

Many psycholinguistic studies on lexical processing confirmed that abstract words are harder to understand than concrete ones. For instance, concrete words are often found to lead to shorter reaction times than abstract words in lexical decision tasks (e.g. Bleasdale, 1987; Kroll and Merves, 1986). Such concreteness effect is concurrently under the influence of various lexical, semantic, and even personal factors, including word frequency, imageability, and context availability (DeGroot, 1989; Kroll and Merves, 1986; Schwanenflugel, 1991).

The observed difference between the two kinds of words also implies a somewhat different mechanism by which they are stored, represented, connected, and processed in the mental lexicon. While there were studies investigating the relationship between lexical access and polysemy (e.g. Swinney, 1979), few have addressed the relation between concreteness and polysemy, and WSD. Analysis on word association responses, for instance, has suggested that tangible concepts seem to be more easily activated than abstract concepts; and in the case of polysemy, tangible senses appear to be more accessible than abstract senses (Kwong, 2007). However, concreteness is often discussed only at the lexical level. We must also look into concreteness at the sense level in order to study its impact on the information demand of individual words in WSD, and hence varied information susceptibility (Kwong, 2005).

Concreteness is often measured by means of human ratings on an ordinal scale from highly abstract to highly concrete (e.g. Paivio et al., 1968). Scalability is essential for its application in WSD and other NLP tasks, and to this end, we need to find ways to automatically induce an objective measure of concreteness which is comparable to human judgements. Lexical data reflecting human lexical processing is possibly available from various resources, including dictionary definitions, word association norms, lexical and knowledge bases, as well as corpus data from authentic texts. In the current study, we explore the feasibility of simulating human judgements on concreteness from dictionary definitions.

It has been suggested that WSD systems should be less penalised if they fail to distinguish between closely related word senses than if they fail between distinct senses. This issue of sense similarity is addressed by Resnik and Yarowsky (1999) with quantitative characterisation in terms of sense proximity, and by Chugur *et al.* (2002) in terms of sense stability.

WSD is often considered a lexically sensitive task, in which individual target words might vary in their difficulty and require different treatment. Pedersen (2002) assessed the difficulty of test instances in the SENSEVAL-2 English lexical sample task by analysing the agreement among participating systems.

We base our analysis on the target nouns for the English lexical sample tasks and system performance reported in SENSEVAL-1 and SENSEVAL-4 (officially SemEVAL-2007). Different systems might vary in the disambiguating information and computational approaches they use. Nevertheless, in terms of performance on individual target words, they sometimes complement one another and sometimes achieve similar results. It thus suggests that there is hardly a universal set of parameters which will work in precisely the same way and satisfactorily for all target words. That is to say, words have different *information susceptibility*.

Moreover, with the experience from four SENSEVAL exercises, systems should have matured in one way or another to cope with the lexical sensitivity of WSD. If a difference still persists among target words within individual systems, there must be something else intrinsic to the words and senses themselves that has not been adequately recognised and effectively addressed by automatic WSD systems. We are thus interested in how lexical concreteness, as a psycholinguistic factor and an intrinsic property of words, bears on the difficulty of WSD and information demand of individual target words, in addition to other linguistic and technical factors. More importantly, we should explore how we could capitalise on such a relationship to fine-tune WSD systems and shed light on WSD evaluation.

3. Concreteness and WSD Difficulty

In this section, we outline the procedures in selecting word samples and discuss the results on comparing human concreteness ratings with system performance on individual target words as reported in previous SENSEVAL exercises.

3.1.Materials

Target nouns from the English lexical sample tasks in SENSEVAL-1 and SENSEVAL-4 (Task 17) were selected. There are 15 and 35 target nouns in these two exercises respectively, as listed in Table 1. The column "S" refers to the number of senses in WordNet 3.0, and the column "C" refers to the average of human ratings on lexical concreteness, as discussed below.

Sense definitions were collected for these words from WordNet 3.0. The average number of senses per word for SENSEVAL-1 nouns is 3.67, and the words have 1 to 9 senses. The average for SENSEVAL-4 nouns is 7.94 senses per word, and the words have 1 to 26 senses. Note that the HECTOR sense inventory was used for SENSEVAL-1, and some had very different degrees of polysemy as reported here. For example, "knee" has as many as 22 senses. On the other hand, OntoNotes senses were used for sense distinction in SENSEVAL-4 (Task 17). For the current study, we use WordNet 3.0 senses as a common reference for both sets of words.

For data on WSD difficulty, we made use of the task and system reports, and results summaries from SENSEVAL, assuming WSD difficulty of test words is reflected from system performance on individual words. For SENSEVAL-1 data, we refer to the official scores under "fine-grained, all systems, average" as available from http://www.senseval.org. Precisions and recalls were reported, and we computed the F1 measure for convenience in comparison. System performance for SENSEVAL-4 (Task 17) is based on the average results on individual target words from all systems, as well as results from two individual systems (System 1 and 4, both using Support Vector Machines), reported in Pradhan *et al.* (2007).

Table 1: Target Nouns from SENSEVAL Data

SENSEVAL-1			SENSEVAL-4 (Task 17)					
Word	**S**	**C**	**Word**	**S**	**C**	**Word**	**S**	**C**
accident	2	4.33	area	6	4.00	network	5	3.00
behaviour	4	3.00	authority	7	3.33	order	14	2.67
bet	2	4.50	base	19	3.67	part	12	3.33
disability	1	2.00	bill	10	5.00	people	4	6.67
excess	4	1.50	capital	6	4.00	plant	4	6.67
float	7	4.50	carrier	11	4.67	point	26	4.67
giant	7	4.50	chance	5	1.33	policy	3	2.00
knee	3	7.00	condition	8	1.33	position	16	3.00
onion	3	6.50	defense	11	2.33	power	9	3.00
promise	2	2.00	development	9	2.67	president	4	6.00
rabbit	3	6.50	drug	1	6.33	rate	4	1.33
sack	9	4.50	effect	6	2.00	share	5	2.67
scrap	4	4.00	exchange	10	3.67	source	9	2.33
shirt	1	6.50	future	3	1.33	space	9	3.67
steering	3	4.00	hour	4	2.33	state	7	3.33
			job	9	4.00	system	9	2.67
			management	2	3.33	value	6	1.33
			move	5	4.00			

3.2. Method

Three human judges were asked to rate the words and senses in the sample on a 7-point scale of concreteness, with 1 for highly abstract, and 7 for highly concrete. Ratings were to be given to all words (ignoring individual senses) first, and then independently to each sense. They were asked to do the rating according to their intuition and subjective evaluation, although it was also suggested that imageability could be used as a criterion in their judgement without precluding other relevant factors. One of the judges was an undergraduate student and the other two were graduates. All have studied linguistics before.

Based on the average human ratings, we divided the words into three categories along the concreteness continuum: Abstract (with average rating below 3.0), Medium (with average rating between 3.0 and 5.0 inclusive), and Concrete (with average rating above 5.0).

Analysis and comparison were done with respect to the following: (a) agreement among the human judges at both the word level and sense level; (b) difference in mean performance with respect to word categories based on lexical concreteness; and (c) difference in mean performance with respect to word categories based on sense concreteness.

3.3. Agreement among Human Raters

The Kendall's Coefficient of Concordance W was computed to assess the agreement among the human raters. At the word level, an overall W of 0.767 was found among our three judges on SENSEVAL-1 words, 0.706 on SENSEVAL-4 words, and 0.727 on all words, all statistically significant. This suggests that at the word level, the raters in general agree with one another on positing the word samples on the lexical concreteness continuum, although the absolute ratings they have assigned to individual samples might differ. The agreement, however, is less strong at the sense level, but overall medium to high agreement has been observed.

In the subsequent analysis, we used the average of the rating from the three raters as a measure for concreteness of the words and senses, and divided the words into three categories as explained in Section 3.2.

3.4. Impact of Concreteness on WSD

We compared the mean performance with respect to the three categories of words along the concreteness continuum. Given that we only used secondary data sources for the analysis, we have not controlled for the number of samples in each category, but only depend on the ratings assigned by the human judges on the target nouns. Hence the number of samples in each group is small and the distribution may not be even. Nevertheless, it happens that the datasets in SENSEVAL-1 and SENSEVAL-4 do contain examples for all three groups, and they allow us to start on a preliminary analysis of the relationship between concreteness and WSD difficulty.

The comparison results are shown in Tables 2 and 3. There were only 30 words from SENSEVAL-4 used in the comparison instead of 35, since results for five words were omitted in Pradhan *et al.* (2007).

We also compared the mean performance with respect to the concreteness of the first sense, which is assumed to be the predominant sense according to WordNet ordering, and also the average of the concreteness of all senses. Note that the first sense and the average of all senses may or may not correspond to the concreteness rating at the lexical level, as the lexical concreteness depends on the human raters' intuition, personal experience and their understanding of the word in general without considering individual senses. The results are shown in Tables 4 and 5.

With the datasets and small number of samples, we were not able to establish a statistically significant difference for the mean performance among different word categories on the concreteness continuum. Nevertheless, we had some interesting observations. From SENSEVAL-1 data, it appears that nouns at both ends of the continuum, i.e. either very concrete or very abstract, are better disambiguated than those lying in the mid range of the continuum. With reference to the impact of the first and supposedly predominant sense or the average concreteness of all senses, a similar trend was found. Moreover, words with an abstract predominant sense or more abstract senses in general tend to be even better disambiguated than those with more concrete senses. This is an interesting phenomenon which deserves more in-depth investigation and qualitative analysis.

Table 2: Mean Performance by Word Concreteness for SENSEVAL-1 Data

Group	# Samples	Mean Performance
Abstract	3	0.7235
Medium	8	0.6150
Concrete	4	0.7384

Table 3: Mean Performance by Word Concreteness for SENSEVAL-4 Data

Group	# Samples	Avg	Sys 1	Sys 4
Abstract	12	77.42	85.67	75.00
Medium	15	79.27	87.70	78.00
Concrete	3	92.67	96.00	90.33

Table 4: Mean Performance by Sense Concreteness for SENSEVAL-1 Data

Group	# Samples	Mean Performance
Concreteness Based on First Sense		
Abstract	3	0.7757
Medium	5	0.5815
Concrete	7	0.6871
Concreteness Based on Average of All Senses		
Abstract	4	0.7573
Medium	5	0.6073
Concrete	6	0.6632

Table 5: Mean Performance by Sense Concreteness for SENSEVAL-4 Data

Group	# Samples	Avg	Sys 1	Sys 4
Concreteness Based on First Sense				
Abstract	12	83.83	88.92	80.75
Medium	14	75.29	85.36	74.43
Concrete	4	87.00	89.75	85.50
Concreteness Based on Average of All Senses				
Abstract	5	78.00	86.20	75.00
Medium	20	78.55	86.65	77.00
Concrete	5	87.00	91.40	87.60

On the other hand, analysis on SENSEVAL-4 data seems to yield results closer to our expectation. With reference to word concreteness and average concreteness of all senses, words toward the concrete side tend to be better disambiguated than those in the mid range, which are in turn better disambiguated than those on the abstract end. However, looking at the predominant sense, a similar situation to SENSEVAL-1 data was found, i.e., those with the first sense at either end of the continuum are better disambiguated. One possible reason is that very concrete or very abstract senses are expected to occur in more characteristic linguistic contexts, which could be more successfully captured by the features used in WSD systems. Hence, it remains for us to see in more qualitative terms how this concreteness effect could affect the effectiveness of various kinds of disambiguating information.

4. Concreteness from Definitions

According to McKeown (1991), "a definition can be seen as an attempt to capture the essence of a word's meaning by summarizing all of its applications and possible applications". Although nouns are expected to be relatively easy to define, as compared to other parts-of-speech, various defining styles are observed (Jackson, 2002). A common type is by means of genus (superordinate concept) and differentiae (distinctive features). For words which are not easy to be defined by a genus term, the definition is often composed with one or more synonyms or a synonymous phrase. Another kind of definitions is by means of prototype, which is similar to the genus and differentiae type but in addition specifying what is typical of a referent with words like "typically" or "usually". For others, where a referent is unlikely to be available, lexicographers will capture their meanings in a dictionary by explaining their usage in real text. It is also commonly realised that tangible objects and physical actions are more easily defined in dictionaries, while abstract concepts and other aspects of meaning including connotation, sense relations, and collocations are less readily and often only partially covered by the definitions.

Hence, we assume that the concreteness of a concept will make a difference on the most appropriate defining style. Specifically it will be more difficult to define abstract concepts by means of genus and differentiae, and prototype, and they are more likely to be defined by synonyms and other means. We therefore analysed dictionary definitions and distinguished them into seven categories based on their surface syntactic forms, corresponding to a 7-point scale (7=highly concrete, 1=highly abstract) which is assumed to correlate with various levels on the concreteness continuum from human judgements. The definitions used in this study were obtained from WordNet 3.0. The seven categories are listed and explained in Table 6[1].

Each sense definition for the SENSEVAL-1 nouns was classified into one of the seven types of definitions exemplified in Table 6. The category assigned to each sense definition was thus taken as a numerical indication of the concreteness of the respective meaning on a 7-point scale.

The definition-induced concreteness measures agree relatively strongly with the average human ratings at the sense level, with a statistically significant Kendall's W of 0.680.

With the definition category assigned to each sense definition, lexical concreteness was induced from two conditions. One is to use the category value from the first and presumably dominant sense of a word. We call this condition DefOne. The other is to take the average of the category values from all senses of a word, and we call this condition DefAll. We tested for the correlation with the Spearman rank correlation ρ and agreement with Kendall's W between average human ratings and the definition-induced values. The results are shown in Table 7.

Table 7 shows that the correlation between human ratings and definition-induced ratings is not particularly strong and linear, but the overall agreement is nevertheless quite high. With this particular dataset, apparently the average of sense concreteness models lexical concreteness more reliably. However, this is only a preliminary attempt and more study and refinement remain to be done.

5. Discussion and Future Work

Our results thus show that concreteness bears some relation with WSD difficulty as a psycholinguistic factor superimposing on the linguistic factors like sense distinction and sense similarity, which are often believed to directly affect the difficulty of WSD.

Since psychological evidence suggests that words of different concreteness are represented and accessed by possibly different mechanisms, this factor is worth the attention of computational linguists, particularly in terms of how it bears on the differential information demand of individual words in WSD and how the knowledge of this property could be employed to fine-tune WSD systems to better realise and deal with the lexical sensitivity of the task, as well as its potential impact on evaluative measures. For example, future evaluation might consider balancing the number of concrete and abstract test items.

A potential limitation of our current categorisation of the dictionary definitions is that abstract concepts might be defined by genus and differentiae more often than expected. For instance, one meaning of "accident" is "an unfortunate mishap; especially one causing damage or injury". This may be an artifact of WordNet definitions since WordNet places each sense in a hierarchy of hyponymy relation, which covers both concrete and abstract concepts. Words like "mishap" are nevertheless abstract even when they are used as the genus term for other words. We plan

---

[1] Only a simple version is given here. Refer to Kwong (2008) for more detailed descriptions.

to check against other dictionaries and explore possible ways to deal with various kinds of genus terms, to refine the concreteness index induced from definition categories.

Table 6: Categorisation of Dictionary Definition Styles

Category	Patterns	Explanation and Examples
7	Surface pattern: *Determiner + (Modifier) + Genus + Differentiae + Prototype* e.g. *car* – a motor vehicle with four wheels; usually propelled by an internal combustion engine	Concrete concepts are usually defined in terms of genus and differentiae. High imageability is assumed if a prototype could also be described.
6	Surface pattern: As above with either *Differentiae or Prototype* but not both e.g. *bag* – a flexible container with a single opening; *cup* – a small open container usually used for drinking	Assume slightly less concrete if no distinctive feature or prototype is captured.
5	Surface pattern: 1. a + *(Modifier)* + {kind,type} of + *Genus* + *Differentiae/Prototype* 2. *Determiner + (Modifier) + Genus* 3. someone + *Differentiae/Prototype* e.g. *husband* – a married man; *officer* - someone who is appointed or elected to an office and who holds a position of trust	A less detailed description of the concepts but at least a person or some known membership
4	Surface pattern: 1. a + (Modifier) + {kind, type} of + Genus 2. {somewhere, something, etc.} + Differentiae/Prototype 3. a + (Modifier) + {set, number, collection, etc.} of + Genus + Differentiae/Prototype e.g. body – a collection of particulars considered as a system; mercy – something for which to be thankful	Empty kernels or underspecified objects, but still describable in terms of distinctive features
3	Surface pattern: 1. Det + (Modifier) + {state, instance, etc.} of + Genus(mass noun) 2. (Det) + (Modifier) + Genus(mass noun) + (Differentiae/Prototype) e.g. hour – clock time; glory – brilliant radiant beauty	Unlike tangible objects and physical actions, more abstract concepts are less feasibly and less likely to be defined in terms of countable genus and differentiae.
2	Surface pattern: {your, the} + mass noun + of/to + (Modifier) + mass noun / countable noun in plural form / a gerund e.g. hatred – the emotion of intense dislike; idea – the content of cognition	Mass nouns are often more abstract, and the abstraction often doubles up in patterns in this category involving two mass nouns.
1	All others, including explanation of usage e.g. baby - sometimes used as a term of address for attractive young women	Presumably highly abstract concepts need to be explained more verbosely in other forms.

Given that human ratings on concreteness may be a result of the interaction of many factors including word frequency, context availability, imageability and access to sensory referents, etc., it will be appropriate for us to resort to other sources of external evidence such as word association norm data, authentic linguistic context from corpus data, and domain information, in addition to dictionary definitions, for a more realistic and complete model of lexical concreteness.

As suggested earlier, words at either end of the concreteness continuum might occur in relatively characteristic linguistic contexts. So, more importantly, further studies will be conducted to examine the effect of lexical and sense concreteness on the information demand of automatic word sense disambiguation and the use of concreteness for indicating potentially confusable senses for better evaluation of disambiguation performance.

Future work could thus go in several directions: (1) further investigation in automatically inducing an objective concreteness measure from lexical resources which simulates human ratings, (2) studying the contextual nature of words with different concreteness from natural texts to explore the difference in information demand by individual target words and thus their information susceptibility in WSD, (3) applying the findings on the relation between concreteness and disambiguation performance in WSD in turn, to fine-tune the systems, and (4) enriching lexical resources with the intrinsic property of words in terms of concreteness level.

Table 7: Reliability of Dictionary-Induced Ratings

Condition	ρ	W
DefOne	0.240	0.619
DefAll	0.418	0.709

6. Conclusion

In this paper we have discussed our preliminary study on the impact of lexical concreteness on the difficulty of automatic word sense disambiguation. By comparing system performance on target words of different concreteness from previous SENSEVAL exercises, it was found that concrete words are more easily disambiguated in general, and words at either end of the concreteness continuum are better disambiguated than those in the middle. We also explored the feasibility of simulating human judgements on the concreteness or abstractness of words via dictionary definitions. The overall agreement found between human ratings and definition-induced ratings is encouraging, and more language resources will be employed in future work on the simulation of a numerical index for lexical and sense concreteness. Such an index is believed to inform not only lexicography but also WSD and other NLP tasks. Since psychological evidence suggests that words of different concreteness are processed by possibly different mechanisms, this factor is worth the attention of computational linguists as it bears on the information demand of individual target words in WSD.

References

Bleasdale, F.A. 1987. Concreteness dependent associative priming: Separate lexical organization for concrete and abstract words. *Journal of Experimental Psychology: Learning, Memory, and Cognition, 13*, 582-594.

Chugur, I., J. Gonzalo and F. Verdejo. 2002. Polysemy and Sense Proximity in the Senseval-2 Test Suite. In *Proceedings of the SIGLEX/SENSEVAL Workshop on Word Sense Disambiguation: Recent Successes and Future Directions*, Philadelphia, pp.32-39.

DeGroot, A.M.B. 1989. Representational aspects of word imageability and word frequency as assessed through word association. *Journal of Experimental Psychology: Learning, Memory, and Cognition, 15*, 824-845.

Jackson, H. 2002. *Lexicography: An Introduction.* London and New York: Routledge.

Kroll, J.F. and J.S. Merves. 1986. Lexical access for concrete and abstract words. *Journal of Experimental Psychology: Learning, Memory, and Cognition, 12*, 92-107.

Kwong, O.Y. 2008. A Preliminary Study on Inducing Lexical Concreteness from Dictionary Definitions. In *Proceedings of the 5th International Workshop on Natural Language Processing and Cognitive Science (NLPCS-2008)*, Barcelona, Spain, pp.84-93.

Kwong, O.Y. 2007. Sense Abstractness, Semantic Activation and Word Sense Disambiguation: Implications from Word Association Norms. In *Proceedings of the 4th International Workshop on Natural Language Processing and Cognitive Science (NLPCS-2007)*, Funchal, Madeira, Portugal, pp.169-178.

Kwong, O.Y. 2005. Word Sense Classification Based on Information Susceptibility. In A. Lenci, S. Montemagni and V. Pirrelli (Eds.), *Acquisition and Representation of Word Meaning.* Linguistica Computazionale, pp.89-115.

McKeown, M.G. 1991. Learning Word Meanings from Definitions: Problems and Potential. In P.J. Schwanenflugel (Ed.), *The Psychology of Word Meanings.* Hillsdale, NJ: Lawrence Erlbaum Associates, Inc., pp.137-156.

Paivio, A., J.C. Yuille and S.A. Madigan. 1968. Concreteness, Imagery, and Meaningfulness Values for 925 Nouns. *Journal of Experiment Psychology, Monograph Supplement, 76(1, Pt.2)*, 1-25.

Pedersen, T. 2002. Assessing System Agreement and Instance Difficulty in the Lexical Sample Tasks of SENSEVAL-2. In *Proceedings of the SIGLEX/SENSEVAL Workshop on Word Sense Disambiguation: Recent Successes and Future Directions*, Philadelphia, pp.40-46.

Pradhan, S.S., E. Loper, D. Dligach and M. Palmer. 2007. SemEval-2007 Task 17: English Lexical Sample, SRL and All Words. In *Proceedings of the 4th International Workshop on Semantic Evaluations (SemEval-2007)*, Prague, pp.87-92.

Resnik, P. and D. Yarowsky. 1999. Distinguishing systems and distinguishing senses: new evaluation methods for Word Sense Disambiguation. *Natural Language Engineering, 5(2)*, 113-133.

Resnik, P. and D. Yarowsky. 1997. A perspective on word sense disambiguation methods and their evaluation. In *Proceedings of the SIGLEX Workshop on Tagging Text with Lexical Semantics: Why, What, and How?*, Washington D.C.

Schwanenflugel, P.J. 1991. Why are Abstract Concepts Hard to Understand? In P.J. Schwanenflugel (Ed.), *The Psychology of Word Meanings.* Hillsdale, NJ: Lawrence Erlbaum Associates, Inc., pp.223-250.

Swinney, D.A. 1979. Lexical access during sentence comprehension: (Re)consideration of context effects. *Journal of Verbal Learning and Verbal Behavior, 18*, 645-659.

Yore, L.D. and L.O. Ollila. 1985. Cognitive development, sex, and abstractness in grade one word recognition. *Journal of Educational Research, 78*, 242-247.

Constructing an Ontology of Coherence Relations:
An example of 'causal relation'[*]

Hae-Yun Lee and Sueun Jun

Dept. of Linguistics and Cognitive Science, Hankuk Univ. of Foreign Studies,
Korea

haeyun@hufs.ac.kr, kazoopablo@hotmail.com

Abstract. The goal of this paper is to present the methodology of constructing a language ontology of 'coherent relations'. We construct an ontology of more abstract concepts by combining an upper-level ontology and a middle-level ontology. At the former we use theoretical considerations following Sanders et al. (1992, 1993), and at the latter we use lexical items through the substitutability test of Knott and Dale (1994).

Keywords: ontology, coherence relations, connectives

1. Introduction

1.1. Ontology

'Ontology' has recently become one of the most attractive research areas. Even though the notion originates from philosophy, there have been many researches within AI or Computer Science. Ontology is usually defined as "an explicit specification of a conceptualization," where a "conceptualization is an abstract, simplified view of the world that we wish to represent for some purpose" (Gruber 1993: 199). But many constructed ontologies are not consistent, because the conceptualization is different according to the interests of researchers. Therefore most ontologists make use of languages which are considered to reflect the objects of conceptualization objectively.

If we consider that an element of conceptualization is a concept, it is followed that the notion of ontology is related closely with languages. As we know, the modern linguistics is based on the 'meaning triangle' (Ogden and Richards 1923). At the triangle, the connection of a symbol with an object is mediated by a concept, and each element constructs its own system. So the system of symbols, i.e. a network of words, is similar to the system of concepts, i.e. an ontology. Therefore we can assume, that an ontology can be constructed indirectly by means of words.

The network of words is often called 'Language Ontology'. Nickles et al. (2007) considers Language Ontology as an answer to the following question: "What kinds of things do people talk as if there are?" Further the notion of Language Ontology is defined as "a conceptualization or categorization of what normal everyday human language can talk about" (Zaefferer 2002).

22nd Pacific Asia Conference on Language, Information and Computation, pages 245–252

1.2. Goals

The goal of this paper is to present the methodology of constructing the language ontology about 'coherent relations'. Some previous language ontologies such as WordNet, etc. have been restricted to the lexical categories such as nouns, verbs, adjective, and adverbs. There were no ontologies about abstract notions such as coherent relations which are realized mostly as minor categories such as suffixes or connectives.

For the construction of ontology of coherent relations, we will adopt the following strategy: At the upper-level, we will construct the ontology in a top-down manner, reflecting the theoretical considerations which are relatively language-independent. But at the middle-level, we will proceed with the work in a bottom-up manner. That is we will construct the middle part of the ontology by investigating lexical items. Since the construction of all the coherent relations is an enormous project, we will focus on the 'causal relations' in this paper.

With the ontology to be constructed we can make a typological analysis about coherence relations. For example we can compare the Korean ontology with the English or the Dutch ontology presented in Knott (1996). The trend of typological researches is based on the so-called 'ontolinguistical' approach.[1]

2. Coherence

2.1. Coherence relations

Discourse is more than a random set of utterances, and shows connectedness. The connectedness is captured by the concept of 'cohesion' and 'coherence'. In comparison with cohesion, coherence is an abstract concept which language users establish by relating the different information units in the text.

Coherence is divided into 'referential coherence' and ' relational coherence' (Sanders and Maat 2006). The latter has been investigated under the theme 'coherence relations'.[2] That is, under the assumption, that the interpretation of the related segments needs to provide more information than is provided by the sum of the segments taken in isolation, text grammarians adopt the view that text segments are connected by coherence relations like CAUSE-CONSEQUENCE between them. Such coherence relations can be made explicit by linguistic markers, so-called connectives or cue phrases, but not always, as we see in (1).

(1) (a) The buzzard was looking for prey. The bird was soaring in the air for hours.
    (b) Gareth grew up during the 1970s, *so* he loves disco music.

It has been disputed, what coherence relations are. Some have insisted that coherence relations should be considered as cognitive entities (Hobbs 1979, Mann and Thompson 1988, Sanders et al. 1992, 1993). In addition to that, we can find a similar view in Lyons (1977). He divided entities into 3 subtypes: first-order entities, second-order entities, and third-order entities. He took the third-order entities to be "such abstract entities as proposition, which are outside space and time" (ibid. 443p.). Furthermore, he mentioned the possibility of distinction in those entities, for example between psychological and non-psychological entities. We think that coherence relations in the sense of Sanders et al. (1993) can correspond to those psychological third-order entities.

---

[1] "the most reliable basis for any cross-linguistic research lies in the common core of the different individual human ontologies. This is the basic tenet of all approaches that can properly be called ontology-based linguistics or *ontolinguistics* for short." (Schalley and Zaefferer 2007: 3)

[2] The notion is also called as 'rhetorical relations' (Mann & Thompson 1988), 'clause relations', 'discourse relations', …

There is no agreement among researchers about the kinds/type of relations and the number of relations. For example, Hobbs (1978), Mann and Thompson (1988) etc. hypothesize dozens of relations (cf. Hovy 1990).

With respect to 'causal relation', Mann and Thompson (1988) presented a more detailed classification by considering speaker's volition and ordering between two clauses: *volitional cause, non-volitional cause, volitional result, non-volitional result, purpose.*

2.2. Linguistic realizations

We can sometimes identify the coherence relations at the surface form. In such cases, coherence relations can be realized at the sentence level and at the discourse level.

As for the sentence level, some adverbial/subordinate clauses show the realization of coherence relations. According to Thompson and Longacre (1985), languages of the world use 3 devices to mark subordinate clauses: (i) subordinating morphemes, (ii) special verb forms, (iii) word order. As for the discourse level, discourse markers or cue phrases are typical means to represent coherence relations, by which sentences are connected to each other. For example, phrases such as *as a result, therefore* etc. belong to this category.

In Korean, there are two groups of lexical items which realize coherence relations. The first group is a list of suffixes which are attached to the verbal stems of subordinate clauses. The concrete coherence relation is determinded by the suffix to be attached. The following shows the difference of verbal suffixes at the main clause and at the subordinate clause.

(2) (a) ku-nun   yelsimhi kongpuha-yss-*ta*.
     He-TOP hard   study-PAST-DEC
     'He studied hard.'
  (b) ku-nun   yelsimhi kongpuha-yss-*ciman*   sihem-ey   tteleci-ess-ta
     He-TOP hard   study-PAST-although   test-ACC   fail-PAST-DEC
     'Although he studied hard, he failed the test.'

The second group is a list of connectives which relate two clauses at the discourse level. The example in (3) shows that type.

(3) ku-nun   yelsimhi kongpuha-yss-ta. *kulemeyto* sihem-ey   tteleci-ess-ta.
   He-TOP hard   study-PAST   however   test-ACC   fail-PAST-DEC
   'He studied hard. However, he failed the test.'

3. Language Ontology

3.1. Upper-level Ontology

As we mentioned above, there are a few ontologies about coherence relations. But strictly speaking, the ontologies are merely taxonomies which include fewer levels and the smaller number of nodes in the hierarchy. Therefore we will try to construct an ontology in the original sense.

As for the upper-lever of the ontology, there is an interesting research which has considered some philosophical discussions. Sanders et al. (1992, 1993) presented the classification of coherence relations, based on more elementary notions. Following Sanders et al. (1992, 1993), we will construct an upper-level ontology. At first we look at their classification. They hypothesized four basic notions, each of which can take two alternative values.

- Basic Operation: CAUSAL/ADDITIVE
  CAUSAL relations are those where a 'relevant' causal connection exists between the spans; all other relations are ADDITIVE.

- Source of Coherence: SEMANTIC/PRAGMATIC
  It is SEMANTIC if the spans are related in terms of their propositional content and PRAGMATIC if they are related because of their illocutionary force.
- Polarity: POSITIVE/NEGATIVE
  A relation is POSITIVE if its basic operation links the content of the two spans as they stand, and NEGATIVE if it links the content of one of the spans to the negation of the content of the other span.
- Order of Segments: BASIC/NON-BASIC
  CAUSAL relations are deemed to have BASIC order if the antecedent is on the left, and NON-BASIC order if it is on the right.

Of 4 basic notions, the notion 'Order of Segment' is related with the superficial realization. So if we neglect the notion and revise the taxonomy of Sanders et al. (1993), we can present the upper-level ontology as follows.

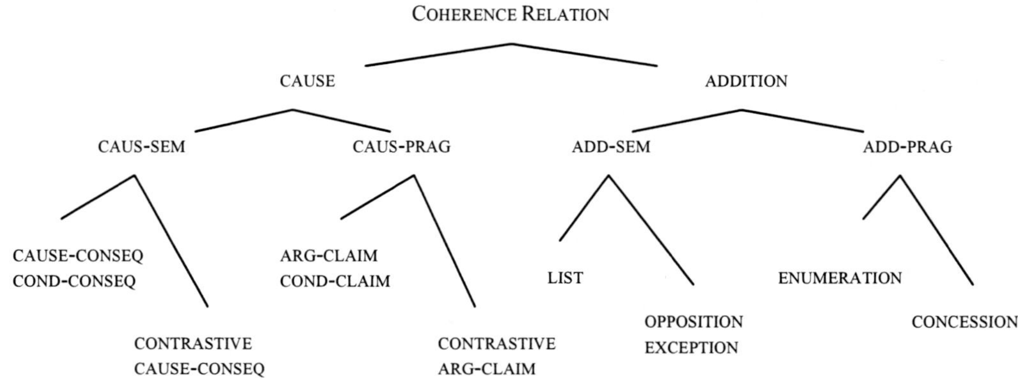

Figure 1: An upper-level ontology

At first, we can divide coherence relations into 'cause' and 'addition' according to the 'source' notion. Next the 'cause' is divided into a semantic concept 'cause-sem' and a pragmatic concept 'caus-prag' according to the 'source' notion. Finally using the 'polarity' notion, we can divide again the former into 'cause-consequence/ condition-consequence' (4ab) and 'contrastive cause-consequence' (4c), and the latter into 'argument-claim/ condition-claim' and 'contrastive argument-claim'. We can see the corresponding examples below (Sanders et al. 1993):

(4) (a) Because there is a low-pressure area over Ireland, the bad weather is coming our way.
    (b) Ready? Then we're now off on safari.
    (c) Although the number of similarities between faces is enormous, we do not have the slightest difficulty in distinguishing a very large number of people.

3.2. Middle-level Ontology

As we have seen above, the upper-level ontology is constructed by philosophical or psychological considerations. So the level of the hierarchy and the number of concepts are sparse. In this section we try to construct a richer middle-level ontology which is connected with the upper-level ontology in Fig. 1. To simplify the explanation, we restrict ourselves to the concept 'cause-sem'.

As is well known, the most explicit markers signaling coherence relations are connectives.[3] Although there is no one-to-one correspondence between coherence relations and connectives, we can construct the middle-level ontology by examining the distribution of connectives. Knott (1996) and Knott and Dale (1994) presented taxonomy of connectives in English and in Dutch. As a starting point, let us review their methodology.

3.2.1. Knott and Dale (1994)

Knott and Dale (1994) classified cue phrases according to their syntactic properties. This classification is made by a simple linguistic test, so-called 'substitutability'. The test calls for the judgment of a writer, if a cue phrase can be replaced by another cue phrase.

(5) The bouncers refused us access to the bar, { *because* / ✓ *on the grounds that* / # *therefore* } we were wearing jeans.

In (5), *on the grounds that* is represented as substitutable for the original cue phrase *because*, whereas *therefore* is not substitutable for the cue phrase. Seeing concretely, there are 4 substitutability relationships (Knott and Sanders 1998):

- X is synonymous with Y if in any context where one can be used, the other can also be used.
- X and Y are exclusive if they can never be substituted for one another in any context.
- X is a hypernym of Y if whenever Y can be used, so can X; but there are some contexts where X can be used and Y cannot.
- X and Y are contingently substitutable if there are some contexts where they can be substituted, other contexts where X can be used and not Y, and still other contexts where Y can be used and not X.

Based on that 'substitutability test', they presented the taxonomy of cue phrases in English and Dutch. But we cannot construct ontology by means of all the 4 relationships. In constructing an ontology, we have no means to represent 'exclusion' and 'a contingent substitutability' differently. Therefore we will merge the two relationships into one, and will use in total 3 relationships in the construction of Korean ontology.

3.2.2. A Korean Ontology

Next, we illustrate the construction of middle level ontology, using the substitutability test of Knott and Dale (1994).

As we have seen above, coherence relations in Korean are realized by suffixes and connectives. For the test we collected such cue phrases from different sources. As for connectives, we selected lexical items signaling causal relations from Im et al. (2001), where the whole list of Korean connectives is presented. The size of selected connectives is 28 tokens which correspond to 20 types. In the case of suffixes, there are no researches which present the whole list. Therefore we collected the items from the tagged corpus 'Sejong corpus'. In details we extracted all the items which are tagged with 'connecting'-suffixes, and selected the suffixes showing the causal relation from the items. By this procedure we have gotten 31 connectives (19 types). The table 1 shows the whole list we got.

Table 1: The list of Korean cue phrases

---

[3] They are also called as 'discourse/ coherence/ lexical markers', 'discourse operators', 'discourse/ pragmatic/ sentence connectives', 'cue phrases', 'clue words', etc.

Connectives	Suffixes
kulayse, kulayya, kulehani/kuleni, kulehancuk/kulencuk/kulihancuk, kulenmankem/kulenimankum/kulenimanchi, kulemulo, kuleca, kulenkolo, kulihaye, ilihaye, iey, kyelkuk, ttalase, hanun-su-epsi, ilehkeytoyca, kulena, kulentey/kulenteto, kulemeyto, kulehciman/kulehcimanun, haciman, kulemeyto pulkuhako	-ase/-ese, -myen/-myenun/-myenya, -ni/-nika, -ulsulok, -tamyen, -mulo, -nula/-nulako, -killay, -cani, -teni/-teniman, -koseya, -nunpa, -may, -layse, -uncuk, -nolani/-nolamyen/-nolanika, -koto, -nunteyto, -ciman/-cimanun

Now we turn to the construction of ontology through the substitutability test. The middle-level ontology to be constructed at this section will be connected to the concept 'CAUSE-CONSEQUENCE/ CONDITION-CONSEQUENCE' at the upper-level ontology (Fig. 1). This methodology can be applied to other concepts of Fig. 1 in a similar way.

As a starting point, we follow Chang (1995) where the suffix '-myen' is considered as the most general suffix among the suffixes representing a causal relation. In addition to '-myen', there are suffixes '-nula'/'-killay' which represent a causal relation, but behave themselves differently. As we see below, the latter group expresses a causal relation on the basis of a temporal connection between events.[4]

(6)(a) syawe-lul   ha-*myen*   kipun-i   sangkway-ha-ta.
      shower-ACC do-SUFF   feeling-NOM refresh-do-DEC
      'If you take a shower, then you feel refreshed.'
  (b) # syawe-lul ha-*nula*   kipun-i   sangkway-ha-ta.
      shower-ACC do-SUFF   feeling-NOM refresh-do-DEC
      'I feel refreshed to take a shower.'
  (c) syawe-lul   ha-*nula*   cenhwa-lul   mos-pat-ass-ta
      shower-ACC   do-SUFF   phone-ACC   not-take-PAST-DEC
      'I couldn't answer the phone, because I took a shower.'

Let us examine the suffix '-myen' in details. If we apply the test of Knott (1996) to Korean, it is revealed that there are subordinate connectives '-kulayse' and '-lyeko' under the connective '-myen'. The tests below show such a sub-classification.

(7)(a) 1-e   2-lul   teha-*myen* 3-i-ta.
      1-ACC 2-OBJ plus-SUFF 3-COP-DEC
      '1 plus 2 is 3.'
  (b) 1-e   2-lul   teha-yss-ta.   *kulayse* 3-i-ta.
      1-ACC 2-OBJ plus-PAST-DEC. so   3-NOM-DEC
      'I plus 1 to 2. so it is 3 now.'
(8)(a) kongpu-lul   yelsimhi ha-*myen* cohun sengcek-ul   et-unu-ta.
      study-OBJ   hard   do-SUFF good grade-OBJ   get-PRES-DEC
      'If you study hard, you will get good grade.'
  (b) cohun sengcek-ul et-*ulyeko*   kongpu-lul   yelsimhi ha-yss-ta.
      good   grade-OBJ   get-SUFF study-OBJ   hard   do-PAST-DEC
      'To get the good grade, I studied hard.'

---

[4] According to Yim (1999), suffixes '-nula' and '-killay' show different syntactic distributions. But such differences are assumed to be recorded under the individual item.

From this observation we can conclude that there are sub-concepts such as 'cause' with '-kulayse' and 'purpose' with '-lyeko' under the concept 'condition' with '-myen'. Furthermore, the following tests show that the two sub-concepts are inter-exclusive each other.

(9)(a) √ pay-ka   kop-ass-ta.   *kulayse* pap-ul   mek-ess-ta.
       stomach-NOM   hungry-PAST-DEC   so   meal-OBJ eat-PAST-DEC
       'I was hungry. So, I had a meal,'
   (b) # pap-ul   mek-*uleko*   pay-ka   kop-ass-ta.
       meal-OBJ eat-SUFF   stomach-NOM hungry-PAST-DEC
       'I was hungry to had a meal..'
(10) (a) √ pap-ul   mek-*uleko*   sang-ul   chali-ess-ta.
         meal-OBJ eat-SUFF   table-OBJ set-PAST-DEC
         'I set the table to eat.'
     (b) #/? sang-ul   chali-ess-ta.   *kulayse* pap-ul   mek-ess-ta.
         table-OBJ set-PAST-DEC.   so   meal-OBJ   eat-PAST-DEC
         'I set the table. That' why I had a meal.'

 Finally the concept 'cause' can be specified into a more concrete concept, as we see in (11). That concept is realized by the connectives such as 'kyelkwuk', 'hanun swu epsi', etc.

(11) (a) pay-ka   kop-ass-ta.   *kulayse* pap-ul   mek-ess-ta.
         stomach-NOM hungry-PAST-DEC   so   meal-OBJ   eat-PAST-DEC
         'I was hungry. So, I had a meal,'
     (b) pay-ka   kop-ass-ta.   *kyelkuk* pap-ul   mek-ess-ta.
         stomach-NOM hungry-PAST-DEC.   finally   meal-OBJ eat-PAST-DEC
         'I was hungry. Finally, I had a meal,'

From the tests above, we can get the following middle-level ontology which is connected with the concept 'cause-consequence'/'condition-consequence' of the upper-level ontology (Fig. 1).

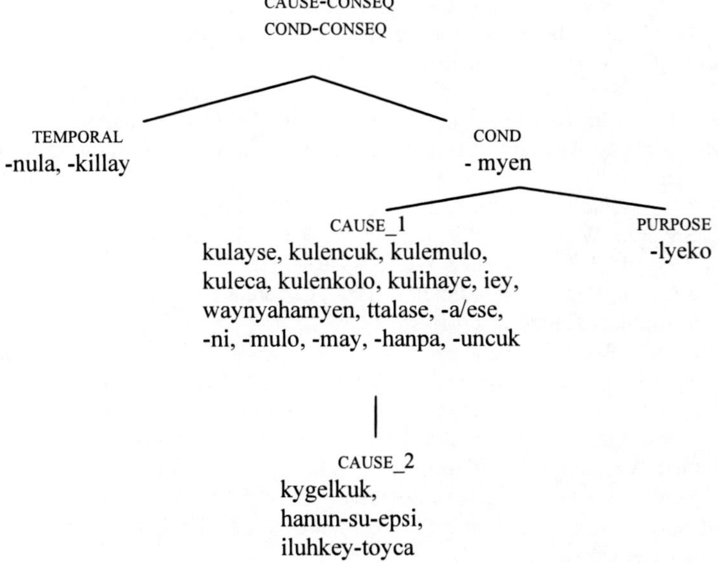

Figure 2: The middle-level ontology

251

4. Conclusion

In this paper, we presented the method of constructing an ontology of coherence relations. We could construct an ontology of more abstract concepts by combining an upper-level ontology and a middle-level ontology. In case of the former we used the theoretical considerations following Sanders et al. (1992, 1993), and in case of the latter we used lexical items through the substitutability test of Knott and Dale (1994).

The resulted Korean Ontology can be used for the typological analysis of coherence relations, because the comparison of languages tends to be based on the ontology. In future we will extend the ontology into the whole coherence relations and try to do a typological analysis between different languages.

References

Chang, Kyeon-hee. 1995. The semantic structure of Korean connective endings. *Hangul 227, 151-174*

Gruber, Thomas R. 1993. A Translation Approach to Portable Ontology Specifications. *Knowledge Acquisition Journal* 5:199-220.

Hobbs, Jerry R. 1978. Why is Discourse Coherent? In *Technical Note.* Menlo Park CA.

Hobbs, Jerry R. 1979. Coherence and coreference. *Cognitive Science* 3:67-90.

Hovy, Eduard H. 1990. Parsimonious and profligate approaches to the question of discourse structure relations. Paper presented at *the 5th International Workshop on Natural Language Generation*, Pittsburgh.

Im, Yoo-jong. Pak, Dong Ho. and Hong, Chai-Song. 2001. A study on connective adverbs in Korean. Linguistics 28, 177-208.

Knott, A. 1996. A Data-Driven Methodology for Motivating a Set of Coherence Relations, Dept. of Artificial Intelligence, Uni. of Edinburgh.

Knott, A., and Sanders, T. 1998. The Classification of Coherence Relations and their Linguistic Markers: An Exploration of Two Languages. *Journal of Pragmatics* 30:135-175.

Knott, Alistair, and Dale, Robert. 1994. Using Linguistic Phenomena to Motivate a Set of Coherence Relations. *Discourse Processes* 18:35-62.

Lyons, John. 1977. *Semantics*.vol. 2. Cambridge: Cambridge University Press.

Mann, William C., and Thompson, Sandra A. 1988. Rhetorical Structure Theory: Toward a functional theory of text organization. *Text* 8:243-281.

Nickles, Matthias, Pease, Adam, Schalley, Andrea C., and Zaefferer, Dietmar. 2007. Ontologies across disciplines. In *Ontolinguistics -How Ontological Status Shapes the Linguistic Coding of Concepts*, eds. Andrea C. Schalley and Dietmar Zaefferer, 23-67. Berlin, New York: Mouton de Gruyter.

Ogden, C.K., and Richards, I.A. 1923. *The Meaning of Meaning.* [n.p.]: [n.p.].

Sanders, T., Spooren, W., and Noordman, L. 1992. Toward a taxonomy of cohrence relations. *Discourse Processes* 15:1-35.

Sanders, T., Spooren, W., and Noordman, L. 1993. Coherence relations in a cognitive theory of discourse representation. *Cognitive Linguistics* 4:93-133.

Sanders, T., and Maat, H. Pander. 2006. Cohesion and Coherence: Linguistic Approaches. In *Encyclopedia of Language & Linguistics*, ed. Keith Brown. Amsterdam et al.: Elsevier.

Schalley, Andrea C., and Zaefferer, Dietmar. 2007. Ontolinguistics - An outline. In *Ontolinguistics - How Ontological Status Shapes the Linguistic Coding of Concepts*, eds. Andrea C. Schalley and Dietmar Zaefferer, 3-21. Berlin, New York: Mouton de Gruyter.

Thompson, Sandra A., and Longacre, Robert E. 1985. Adverbial clauses. In *Language typology and syntactic description: complex constructions*, ed. Timonthy Shopen, 171-234. Cambridge: Cambridge Univ. Press.

Yim, Eun Ha. 1999. A Semantic Analysis of Causal Conjunctive Endings in Korean. *The International Association for Korean Language Education 9th conference, 191-202.*

An Improved Corpus Comparison Approach to
Domain Specific Term Recognition[*]

Xiaoyue Liu, and Chunyu Kit

Department of Chinese, Translation and Linguistics
City University of Hong Kong
Tat Chee Ave., Kowloon, Hong Kong
{xyliu0, ctckit}@cityu.edu.hk

Abstract. Domain specific terms are words carrying special conceptual meanings in a subject field. Automatic term recognition plays an important role in many natural language processing and knowledge engineering applications such as information retrieval and knowledge mining. This paper explores a novel approach to automatic term extraction based on the basic ideas of corpus comparison and emerging pattern with significant elaboration. It measures the termhood of a term candidate in terms of its peculiarity to a given domain via comparison to several background domains. Our experiments confirm its outperformance against other approaches, achieving an average precision of 83% on the top 10% candidates in terms of their termhood.

Keywords: Automatic term recognition, corpus comparison, emerging pattern

1. Introduction

Automatic term recognition (ATR) plays an important role in many natural language processing applications, e.g., information retrieval (IR) (Chowdhury, 1999; Zhou and Nie, 2005), information extraction (Yangarber et al., 2000), domain specific lexicon construction (Hull, 2001), and topic extraction (Lin, 2004). Its technological advancements can facilitate all these applications for performance enhancement.

Despite the large volume of literature on ATR, further significant success in the field still relies heavily on a sound resolution of two basic issues, namely, the unithood and termhood of a term candidate, as identified in Kageura and Umino (1996). The former quantifies the unity of a candidate (especially, a multi-word candidate), indicating how likely a candidate is to be an atomic linguistic unit. It works more like a filter to exclude non-atomic (thus unqualified) term candidates but has little authority to determine which atomic language unit is a true term. The latter measures how likely a qualified candidate is to be a true term in a subject field. It plays a decisive role in licensing a term.

Regardless of the previous progress in term extraction, termhood measurement remains the most critical problem to be solved. Novel technologies and methodologies are needed in order to bring up new insights into our understanding of this problem. This paper is intended to pre-

---

[*] The research described in this paper was supported by the Research Grants Council of HKSAR, China, through the CERG grant 9040861 (CityU 1318/03H) and by the City University of Hong Kong through the Strategic Research Grants 7002037 and 7001879. Correspondence concerning this research should be addressed to Dr. Chunyu Kit.

22nd Pacific Asia Conference on Language, Information and Computation, pages 253–261

sent a novel statistical approach to domain specific term extraction from a collection of thematic documents following the basic ideas of corpus comparison and emerging pattern. It measures the termhood of a term candidate in a subject domain in terms of its peculiarity to this subject domain via comparison to several background domains.

In order to avoid unexpected interference from unithood issues, our study focuses on investigating the termhood measurement for mono-word terms. Nevertheless, this is by no means to imply that mono-word ATR can be any easier than multi-word ATR in any sense. It is pointed out in Daille (1994) that the automatic identification of mono-word terms is possibly more complex than that of multi-word ones. One of the reasons is that all structural information that can be utilized for multi-word ATR is not available for mono-word ATR. In this sense, the latter needs to tackle a fundamental issue, that is, how to differentiate between terms and non-terms without resorting to structure information.

The rest of the paper is organized as follows. Section 2 presents a brief review of previous work on ATR, to give a background for our research. Section 3 formulates our approach and the working procedure involved. A series of experiments are then reported in Section 4 for the purpose of evaluation. Section 5 concludes the paper with a highlight on the advantages of our approach.

2. Previous Work

Various approaches to ATR were developed in the past. From a methodological point of view, the existing approaches can be classified into the following categories.

Linguistic A linguistic approach played a dominant role in the early research on ATR. As early as twenty years ago, Ananiadou (1988) studied the effectiveness of theoretically motivated linguistic knowledge (e.g. morphology) in term recognition. A common procedure involved in this kind of approach is to carry out part-of-speech tagging first and then some pre-defined syntactic patterns, e.g., noun-noun compounds (Dagan and Church, 1994; Wu and Hsu, 2002) and base noun phrases (Justeson and Katz, 1995), can be applied to identify term candidates. All word combinations that match none of the predefined patterns are filtered out. This approach was reported to achieve good results on small scale corpora. However, its disadvantages include inadequate coverage of pre-defined syntactic patterns, low transplantability to other domains or languages, and incapability of excluding non-term candidates consistent with the pre-defined patterns.

Statistical Various kinds of statistical information can be utilized to support term extraction, e.g., frequency (Damerau, 1990), mutual information (Damerau, 1993), C-value (Frantzi and Ananiadou, 1996), NC-value (Frantzi et al., 1998), *imp* function (Nakagawa, 2001), KFIDF measure (Xu et al., 2002), standard deviation (Lin, 2004) and entropy (Chang, 2005), to name but a few. A multi-word term is assumed to carry a key concept and is thus expected to behave like an atomic text unit. Many of these statistical measures are applied to explore such unity or structural stability of a multi-word candidate, namely, its unithood. Besides, a bootstrapping approach is reported in Chen et al. (2003) to learn domain specific terms from unannotated texts on a subject. Wermter and Hahn (2005) identify multi-word terms among n-grams of words in a large biomedical corpus, measuring their termhood in terms of their paradigmatic modifiability. Although statistical approaches share an advantage, i.e., their language independency, they are far from reliable while working on small corpora.

Hybrid Linguistic knowledge is used in conjunction with statistical information in most hybrid approaches to ATR. For example, some syntactic patterns are first applied to identify term candidates, by filtering out those unqualified ones, and then a statistical measure is applied to validate the true terms among them. Daille (1994) presents an integrated approach to ATR that works this way. In addition, a hybrid approach can also be applied to combine several independent term recognizers for a better performance than any of them alone, as reported in Vivaldi et al. (2001).

Corpus Comparison This approach is a popular direction in recent ATR research. Its basic idea is to utilize the distinct distributions of terms and non-terms in different corpora to facilitate term extraction. That is, true terms are more prominent in their own subject field than in others. The original idea of this approach can be traced back to Yang (1986) that attempts to identify scientific terms by their statistical distributional difference between science and general texts. The statistics in use for this purpose include document frequency, average frequency, relative standard-deviation, etc. Ahmad et al. (1994) quantify similar contrasting distributions of terms in different corpora by means of the ratio of relative frequencies of a word in a domain corpus and a background corpus. The words with a score larger than 1.0 are then identified as the most potential terms. Chung (2003) applies a similar scheme called normalized frequency ratio to extract single-word terms in anatomy, reporting a performance of about 86% overlap with the results from a manual rating approach. In Uchimoto et al. (2001), more statistical characteristics (e.g., term frequency, document frequency and field frequency) of a term candidate are explored, achieving an F-score of 58.49%. Kit and Liu (2007) propose to measure mono-word termhood in terms of a candidate's rank difference in a domain and a background corpus.

The approach of corpus comparison can also be accomplished by statistical tests based on the null hypothesis that there is no difference between the observed frequencies for the same word in different corpora. Words with large testing values indicate a statistically significant difference between corpora and hence are more likely to be terms. The statistical tests include log-likelihood ratio (Rayson and Garside 2000), χ^2-test, Mann-Whitney ranks test and t-test (Kilgarriff 2001). Drouin (2003) bases a term extraction process on a statistical test, which uses a normal distribution as an approximation to words' binomial distribution, obtaining an overall precision of 81% on term recognition. Based on Drouin's work, Lemay et al. (2005) examine various corpus comparison approaches in different terminological settings. Among them, one is to use a general corpus as background and another is to break down the specialized corpus into six topical sub-corpora for comparison to the entire specialized corpus.

Methodologically, a corpus comparison approach takes advantage of the intrinsic statistical characteristics of true terms in different corpora and thus has a preferable theoretical grounding over others that utilize only a special domain corpus. Our research reported in this paper falls into the category of corpus comparison approach with necessary elaboration for further enhancement.

3. Term Extraction

Terms are linguistic representations of domain specific concepts to encode our special knowledge about a subject field. Emerging pattern (EP) (Dong and Li, 1999) presents a similar idea to corpus comparison in the field of database for knowledge discovery. EPs are defined as itemsets whose growth rates, i.e., the ratios of their supports[1] in one dataset over those in another, are larger than a predefined threshold. When applied to datasets with classes (e.g., cancerous vs. normal tissues, poisonous vs. edible mushrooms), EPs can capture significant differences or useful contrasts between the classes in terms of their growth rates. In principle, the larger the growth rates, the more significant the patterns. This approach has been successfully deployed in several applications of data mining, e.g., Li and Wong (2002) on identification of good diagnostic gene groups from gene expression profiles.

While the EP approach works on well-structured databases, corpus comparison deals with unstructured texts. Following the essential principle shared by the two, we consider domain specific term recognition from a thematic corpus of documents an issue of identifying words and expressions as EPs in the form of string highly peculiar to their own subject fields than to any others. In this sense, the higher peculiarity of a term candidate to a particular domain but lower to the others, the more likely it is to be a true term in that domain.

Accordingly, we opt to quantify the peculiarity of a term candidate to a subject field in terms of its emerging difference, which is to be scored according to statistical information such as fre-

---

[1] In database studies, the term *support* refers to the frequency of an itemset in a dataset.

quency difference in its own subject field and another field as background. This illustrates the basic idea of corpus comparison. To our knowledge, however, very few existing approaches of corpus comparison to ATR use more than one background corpus. When comparing a thematic corpus with multiple background corpora, we need to find an appropriate way to sum up the comparison results into the final termhood scores for the term candidates in question. This would pay off if such comparison and summing up can make the termhood scoring more reliable. We will follow this idea to derive the termhood for a term candidate in a target subject field.

Given a collection of n documents (or corpora) each representing a subject field, henceforth referred to as thematic documents, we follow the following working procedure to extract mono-word terms from each corpus.

1. Extraction: Extract all mono-words as term candidates, including those appearing only once, via stop word filtering, and then assign to each of them a weight in terms of the statistical measure in use (e.g., frequency, or *tf-idf* score).
2. Normalization: Normalize a weight in each subject field according to the sum of all weights in that field.
3. Computing emerging difference: For a candidate w in a target subject field i, calculate its emerging difference d_{ij} via comparison with another subject field j as

$$d_{ij}(w) = s_i(w) - s_j(w) \qquad (1)$$

   where $s_i(w)$ and $s_j(w)$ are w's normalized weights in fields i and j ($0 < i, j \leq n$), respectively. Consequently each candidate in each field will have n-1 emerging difference scores corresponding to the n-1 background fields involved in the comparison.
4. Ranking: Rank all candidates in each field i in terms of their emerging differences $d_{ij}(\cdot)$, resulting in n-1 ranking lists for each i accordingly to n-1 background corpora in use. In each ranking list, candidate w has a rank $r_{ij}(w)$ corresponding to its score $d_{ij}(w)$.
5. Sorting: Sort all candidates in each field i in terms of their termhood defined as

$$\tau_i(w) = \sum_{j=1}^{n} r_{ij}(w) \qquad (2)$$

   where $j \neq i$.
6. Evaluation: Examine the sorted list for each subject field to check how true terms are pushed to the top of the list by their termhood.

In our approach, a subject corpus is compared with more than one background corpus and all comparison results for each candidate are summed up together to represent its termhood (or peculiarity) in a subject field in question. However, a term candidate may get a negative score from (1) above, which will, unreasonably, weaken the total sum of scores from the comparison to all other background corpora. This certainly would not help to achieve the right ranking outcomes in an ATR output list sorted by the termhood scores so resulted. To alleviate this problem, we opt to rank term candidates first according to their emerging differences before the summing-up is conducted. The ranking in this way keeps the relative position (or relationship) of term candidates in the candidate list while avoiding the unexpected problem. Finally, the termhood of a term candidate is measured by the sum of its ranks that are derived from the comparison to a number of other domain corpora.

4. Evaluation

4.1. Data

A number of experiments following the above working procedure are carried out on the BLIS corpus (Kit et al., 2005) to extract legal terms in HK laws. The corpus consists of all ordinances and subsidiary legislation to prescribe laws and regulations involving almost every aspect of livings in HK. Excluding those repealed, ceased, expired, or not adopted ordinances, there are a total of 503 chapters in the current version of the corpus. Each ordinance can be regarded as a sub-corpus for a "field", e.g., "Public Finance Ordinance", "Forest and Countryside Ordinance", "Hospital Authority Ordinance", and "Marriage Ordinance". We use the English texts from the corpus as data for our experiments.

In order to get reliable statistical information about individual words during the extraction procedure, a series of preprocessing steps are carried out, including word tokenization, lemmatization, and filtering of stop words (including words with only digits or without letters, mono-character words and function words). The evaluation of our approach focuses on the precision of ATR output, for our main concern is how to capture as many true terms as possible at the high end of a candidate list sorted by termhood.

Table 1: Distribution of precision score

Range of precision	$1 \geq p \geq 0.9$	$0.9 > p \geq 0.8$	$0.8 > p \geq 0.7$
Number of chapters	6	16	8

Table 2: Samples of ATR output

Chapter	Terms in the output
Probate and Administration Ordinance	executor, probate, administrator, caveat, testator, *box*, decease, affidavit, estate, renter
Import and Export Ordinance	export, import, manifest, cargo, article, transhipment, trader, smuggle, validate, customs
Theft Ordinance	steal, deception, burglary, theft, deceit, inducement, indictment, menace, robbery, cheat
Adoption Ordinance	adoption, infant, *litem*, accredit, adopt, guardian, parent, adoptive, wedlock, applicant

Table 3: Performance vs. corpus size

Precision	Size	Precision	Size	Precision	Size
1.0000	15	0.8684	38	0.8052	77
0.9655	29	0.8649	148	0.8000	45
0.9474	19	0.8594	64	0.7980	99
0.9320	103	0.8571	42	0.7826	92
0.9048	21	0.8293	82	0.7805	41
0.9000	30	0.8250	40	0.7798	109
0.8889	27	0.8228	79	0.7714	35
0.8727	55	0.8167	60	0.7419	93
0.8718	117	0.8078	26	0.7391	46
0.8710	31	0.8065	31	0.7246	69

4.2. Weighting with *tf-idf*

Applying the ATR procedure given in Section 3 above to the BLIS corpus with *tf-idf* (Salton, 1992) scoring for the initial weighting in the first step, in total we get 503 output lists sorted by termhood. Among them 30 lists are randomly picked for evaluation. For each selected list, the top 10% candidates are manually checked. Chang (2005) presents a modified *tf-idf* model based on inter-domain entropy calculation, giving an average precision of 65.4% on the top 10% of ATR output. It is assumed that around 10% words in each sub-domain are domain specific terms. The exact percentage of true terms among words, however, may vary significantly in different domains. Table 1 presents a distribution of precision scores over the 30 BLIS chapters manually evaluated, each of which corresponds to an ATR output list. The precision score varies from above 70% to 100%, giving an average of 82.98%. As a whole, twenty-two chapters, i.e., 73% of the evaluated lists, have a precision greater than 80%. A few output samples are presented in Table 2, illustrating the top 10 term candidates in the ATR output for four BLIS chapters, with non-terms highlighted in italic font.

An illustration of the performance of the *tf-idf* scoring vs. corpus size is presented in Table 3, resulted from the experiments on the same 30 chapters as above. The number of recognized terms (i.e., 10% of the total number of word types in a corpus) in those chapters varies from 15 to 148. The best performance, a precision of 100%, is achieved on a small chapter of only 15 candidates, whereas a precision of 93% is on a chapter of 103 candidates. This seems to suggest that our approach is able to achieve an excellent performance even on a very small corpus.

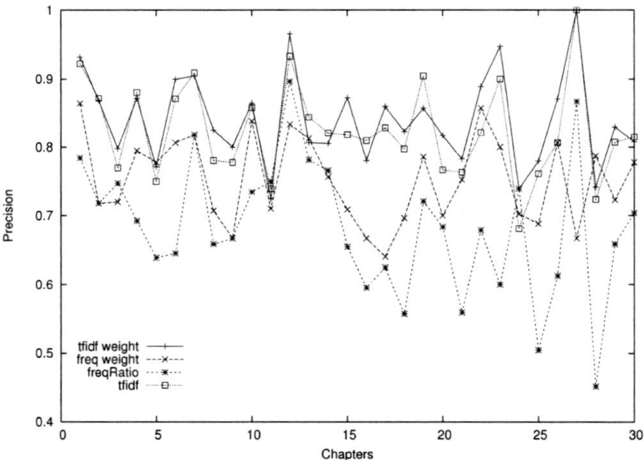

Figure 1: Performance comparison

Table 4: The average precision

Approach	*tf-idf* as weight	freq as weight	freq Ratio	*tf-idf* as termhood
Average precision	82.98%	75.34%	66.93%	81.46%

4.3. Comparison with Other Approaches

On the same data set, several other scoring schemes have also been tested for a comparison with the *tf-idf* scoring above. The comparison is carried out on the same 30 chapters.

1. Frequency for initial scoring: Use frequency as the initial scoring measure, and then follow the above working procedures in Section 3 to derive a term list for each sub-corpus.
2. Corpus comparison using frequency ratio: For each mono-word term candidate, compute the ratio of its frequencies in its own subject sub-corpus and a general background corpus.[2] Candidates with a ratio greater than 1.0 are recognized as true terms.
3. Using *tf-idf* as termhood: Sort the term candidates in a sub-corpus (i.e., an ordinance as a document in our case) in terms of their *tf-idf* scores as given by (3) below, where $freq(w)$ is the frequency of a candidate w in the sub-corpus, N the total number of documents in the entire corpus in use and $d(w)$ the number of documents containing w.

$$tf\text{--}idf(w) = freq(w) \cdot \log \frac{N}{d(w)} \tag{3}$$

---

[2] British National Corpus is used as the background corpus here for comparison. See its official site at http://www.natcorp.ox.ac.uk/ for more information.

Figure 1 presents the performance of the four approaches given above in terms of their precision scores on the 30 chapters, and the average precision achieved by each approach is presented in Table 4. From this figure and table we can see that corpus comparison using frequency ratio directly is outperformed by our working procedure with frequency for initial scoring. Similarly, the working procedure with *tf-idf* for initial scoring outperforms that using *tf-idf* directly as termhood, and performs the best among all the four ATR procedures formulated above. All these verify the significance and effectiveness of the improved corpus comparison approach that we have implemented for enhancing the current ATR technology.

5. Conclusion

We have presented in the above sections an improved approach of corpus comparison to automatic extraction of domain specific terms from thematic corpora, which extends the basic principle of corpus comparison and emerging pattern effectively for performance enhancement. Different from the previous approaches, our approach compares a subject corpus with more than one background corpora and sums up the respective comparison results for each term candidate as its termhood score in the subject field in question.

Accordingly, we have implemented a novel working procedure for term extraction to examine the effectiveness of this approach. The experiments we have carried out on the BLIS corpus of HK laws show that the proposed approach outperforms other approaches of direct corpus comparison and achieves an average precision of 82.98% on the top 10% of candidates according to their termhood in each domain corpus. Also, a nice advantage of this approach is that its performance seems sustainable on a small corpus.

References

Ahmad, K., A. Davies, H. Fulford and M. Rogers. 1994. What is a Term? The Semi-Automatic Extraction of Terms from Text. In M.S. Hornby, F. Pochhacker and K. Kaindl (eds), *Translation Studies: An Interdiscipline*, pp. 267-278. Amsterdam: John Benjamins Publishing Company.

Ananiadou, S. 1988. *A Methodology for Automatic Term Recognition*. Ph.D. thesis, University of Manchester Institute of Science and Technology.

Chang, J. S. 2005. Domain Specific Word Extraction from Hierarchical Web Documents: A First Step toward Building Lexicon Trees from Web Corpora. *Proceedings of the Fourth SIGHAN Workshop on Chinese Language Learning*, pp. 64-71. Korea.

Chen, W. L., J. B. Zhu, T. S. Yao and Y. X. Zhang. 2003. Automatic Learning Field Words by Bootstrapping. *Proceedings of the Joint Seminar on Computational Linguistics 2003*, pp. 67-72. Beijing: Tsinghua University Press.

Chowdhury, G. G. 1999. *Introduction to Modern Information Retrieval*. London: Library Association.

Chung, T. 2003. A Corpus Comparison Approach for Terminology Extraction. *Terminology*, 9(2), 221-246.

Daille, B. 1994. *Approche Mixte pour l'extraction Automatique de Terminologie: Statistique Lexicale et Filtres Linguistiques*. Ph.D. thesis, University Paris 7, France.

Dagan, I. and K. Church. 1994. Termight: Identifying and Translating Technical Terminology. *Proceedings of the 4th Conference on Applied Natural Language Processing*, pp. 34-40. Stuttgart, Germany.

Damerau, F. J. 1993. Generating and Evaluating Domain-Oriented Multi-Word Terms from Texts. *Information Processing & Management*, 29(4), 433-447.

Damerau, F. J. 1990. Evaluating Computer-Generated Domain-Oriented Vocabularies. *Information Processing & Management*, 26(6), 791-801.

Dong, G. and J. Li. 1999. Efficient Mining of Emerging Patterns: Discovering Trends and Differences. *Proceedings of the Fifth ACM SIGKDD International Conference on Knowledge Discovery and Data Mining*, pp. 43-52. San Diego, CA: ACM Press.

Drouin, P. 2003. Term Extraction Using Non-technical Corpora as a Point of Leverage. *Terminology*, 9(1), 99-115.

Frantzi, K. T., S. Ananiadou and J. Tsujii. 1998. The C-value/NC-value Method of Automatic Recognition for Multi-Word Terms. In C. Nikolaou and C. Stephanidis (eds.), *Proceedings of the 2nd European Conference on Research and Advanced Technology for Digital Libraries*, pp. 585-604. Heraklion, Crete, Greece.

Frantzi, K. T. and S. Ananiadou. 1996. Extracting Nested Collocations. *Proceedings of the 16th International Conference on Computational Linguistics*, pp. 41-46. Copenhagen, Denmark.

Hull, D. A. 2001. Software Tools to Support the Construction of Bilingual Terminology Lexicons. In D. Bourigault, C. Jacquemin and M.C. L'Homme (eds), *Recent Advances in Computational Terminology*, pp. 225-244. Amsterdam: John Benjamins Publishing Company.

Justeson, J. S. and S. M. Katz. 1995. Technical Terminology: Some Linguistic Properties and an Algorithm for Identification in Text. *Natural Language Engineering*, 1(1), 9-27.

Kageura, K. and B. Umino. 1996. Methods of Automatic Term Recognition: A Review. *Terminology*, 3(2), 259-289.

Kilgarriff, A. 2001. Comparing Corpora. *International Journal of Corpus Linguistics*, 6(1), 97-133.

Kit, C. and X. Liu. 2007. Mono-Word Termhood as Rank Difference in Domain and Background Corpora. *Proceedings of International Conference: Keyness in Text*, pp. 41-45. Pontignano, Siena, Italy.

Kit, C., X. Liu, K. K. Sin and J. J. Webster. 2005. Harvesting the Bitexts of the Laws of Hong Kong from the Web. *Proceedings of the 5th Workshop on Asian Language Resources*, pp. 71-78. Jeju Island, Korea.

Lemay, C., M.-C. L'Homme and P. Drouin. 2005. Two Methods for Extracting "Specific" Single-Word Terms from Specialized Corpora: Experimentation and Evaluation. *International Journal of Corpus Linguistics*, 10(2), 227-255.

Li, J. and L. Wong. 2002. Identifying Good Diagnostic Gene Groups from Gene Expression Profiles Using the Concept of Emerging Patterns. *Bioinformatics*, 18(5), 725-734.

Lin, S. C. 2004. Topic Extraction Based on Techniques of Term Extraction and Term Clustering. *Computational Linguistics and Chinese Language Processing*, 9(2), 97-112.

Nakagawa, H. 2001. Automatic Term Recognition Based on Statistics of Compound Nouns. *Terminology*, 6(2), 195-210.

Rayson, P. and R. Garside. 2000. Comparing Corpora Using Frequency Profiling. *Proceedings of the Workshop on Comparing Corpora, the 38th Annual Meeting of the Association for Computational Linguistics*, pp. 1-6.

Salton, G. 1992. The State of Retrieval System Evaluation. *Information Processing & Management*, 28(4), 441-449.

Uchimoto, K., S. Sekine, M. Murata, H. Ozaku and H. Isahara. 2001. Term Recognition Using Corpora from Different Fields. *Japanese Term Extraction: Special issue of Terminology*, 6(2), 233-256.

Vivaldi, J., L. Màrquez and H. Rodríguez. 2001. Improving Term Extraction by System Combination Using Boosting. *Proceedings of the 12th European Conference on Machine Learning*, pp. 515-526. Freiburg, Germany.

Wermter, J. and U. Hahn. 2005. Finding New Terminology in Very Large Corpora. *Proceedings of the Third International Conference on Knowledge Capture*, pp. 137-144. Banff, Alberta, Canada.

Wu, S. H. and W. L. Hsu. 2002. SOAT: A Semi-Automatic Domain Ontology Acquisition Tool from Chinese Corpus. *Proceedings of the 19th international conference on Computa-*

tional linguistics, pp. 1-5. Taipei.

Xu, F. Y., D. Kurz, J. Piskorski and S. Schmeier. 2002. A Domain Adaptive Approach to Automatic Acquisition of Domain Relevant Terms and Their Relations with Bootstrapping. *Proceedings of the Third International Conference on Language Resources and Evaluation*, Spain.

Yang, H. Z. 1986. A New Technique for Identifying Scientific/Technical Terms and Describing Science Texts. *Literary and Linguistic Computing*, 1(2), 93-103.

Yangarber, R., R. Grishman, P. Tapanainen and S. Huttunen. 2000. Automatic Acquisition of Domain Knowledge for Information Extraction. *Proceedings of the 18th International Conference on Computational Linguistics*. Germany.

Zhou, G. and Y. Nie. 2005. Improving Retrieval Effectiveness by Using Key Terms in Top Retrieved Documents. *Advances in Information Retrieval*, 3408.

Extending an Indonesian Semantic Analysis-based Question Answering System with Linguistic and World Knowledge Axioms[*]

Rahmad Mahendra[a], Septina Dian Larasati[a], and Ruli Manurung[a]

[a]Faculty of Computer Science, University of Indonesia, Depok 16424, Indonesia
rama42@ui.edu, septina.larasati@gmail.com, maruli@cs.ui.ac.id

Abstract. We adopt a previously developed model of deep syntactic and semantic processing to support question answering for Bahasa Indonesia, and extend it by adding a number of axioms designed to encode useful knowledge for answering questions, thus increasing the inferential power of the QA system. We believe this approach can increase the robustness of semantic analysis-based QA systems, whilst simultaneously lightening the burden of complexity in designing semantic attachment rules that transduce logical forms from syntactic structures. We show how these added axioms enable the system to answer questions which previously could not have been answered.

Keywords: bahasa Indonesia, knowledge representation, QA systems, semantic analysis.

1. Introduction

A question anwering (QA) system seeks to provide answers to questions expressed in natural language, where the answers are to be found in a given collection of documents. QA systems typically require more sophisticated linguistic analysis than conventional information retrieval, as they need to reason about various other factors, among others the types of questions, predicate argument structure, and result aggregation.

In the work presented in this paper, we start from a unification-based grammar augmented with lambda-calculus rules that constructs semantic representations of Indonesian declarative sentences. To these representations we subsequently combine a suite of axioms designed to encode linguistic and world knowledge, and assert them into a knowledge base. A separate QA module answers queries by unifying the question semantic representation with the augmented set knowledge base.

In Sections 2 and 3 we first discuss some relevant past work. Section 4 presents the overall framework of our system, and Section 5 discusses the semantic representation underlying our approach, arguing for some form of axiomatic post-processing. Finally, Sections 6 and 7 present the axioms themselves, along with some examples of how they contribute to the QA process.

2. Lightweight semantic approaches to Question Answering

In general, there are two approaches to QA: the bottom-up approach employs "shallow" statistical methods such as keyword-based retrieval, which benefit from the sheer size of large electronic collections of documents nowadays available (e.g. the web), and are very robust. Unfortunately, these probabilistic methods are sometimes unable to perform the required inference for answering complex questions. On the other hand, the top-down approach uses "deeper" linguistic methods to obtain semantic representations of both the question and (a subset of) documents. The resulting logical forms enable precise identification of answers, sometimes in cases where they are not explicitly stated in the source documents. However, these

---

22nd Pacific Asia Conference on Language, Information and Computation, pages 262–271

deep methods typically require carefully-engineered, language-specific resources that are very costly to produce and not very robust.

More recently, work has been done in developing QA systems that try to combine the two approaches, e.g. (Moldovan et al., 2003), (Narayanan and Harabagiu, 2004), and (Shen and Lapata, 2007). Crucially, these systems capture predicate argument structure that is shown to be essential for complex question answering. Additionally, semantic representations enable logical inference, allowing the QA systems to answer more complex queries by exploiting knowledge encoded in ontologies such as WordNet, SUMO, and various other Semantic Web-based resources.

COGEX, the system reported in (Moldovan et al., 2003), is a QA system that employs a robust syntactic parser that essentially outputs a quasi-logical form containing part of speech information and general predicate argument structure. This output is passed to a theorem prover, and question answering is modelled as a theorem proving task. To aid this process, several axioms are added: NLP axioms establish the semantic content ignored by the robust parser from syntactic constructions such as complex nominals, coordinated conjunctions, appositions, and possesives. World knowledge axioms augment the knowledge extracted from the document collection with knowledge from existing ontologies, e.g. WordNet (Fellbaum, 1998).

3. Question answering in bahasa Indonesia

Bahasa Indonesia (hereinafter simply 'Indonesian') is the official language of Indonesia, spoken by over 100 million people. Given this fact, we believe it is underrepresented in terms of research into Indonesian QA, and Indonesian NLP in general.

There has been some work on developing QA systems for Indonesian. (Wijono et al., 2006) sought to achieve multilingual QA by answering queries in Indonesian based on English documents. Questions are classified based on a manually constructed taxonomy of Indonesian questions. The query is then automatically translated into English using a commercial translator available online[1], and from then on is handled as a purely English QA task. (Purwarianti et al., 2007) uses a machine learning method to develop the question and answer classifier modules based on a corpus of raw text.

(Larasati and Manurung, 2007) presented a purely symbolic approach that adopts a deeper linguistic approach, leveraging a previously built syntactic parser for the Indonesian language (Joice, 2002). We adopt this approach and extend it with some post-processing of the semantic representations with a suite of axioms.

4. Our QA system framework

The overall framework of our Indonesian QA system consists of the following modules: a syntactic parser, a semantic analyser, and a question answering module augmented with axioms. Following (Larasati and Manurung, 2007), we use a unification-based grammar implemented as a set of DCG rules in Prolog. Since wide coverage is currently not the main aim of our research, we developed a relatively small yet usable handcrafted grammar and lexicon based on the official Indonesian grammar (Alwi et al., 1998).

The semantic analyser module transduces semantic representations from parse trees. These semantic representations are designed to abstract away syntactic variations, allowing sophisticated automated processing of Indonesian texts. We adopt a 'flat' semantic representation (Hobbs, 1985). Details of the specific representation we use is presented in Section 5.1. Adopting the well-known rule-to-rule hypothesis, we augmented the lexicon with semantic information (Section 5.2), and developed semantic attachment rules for each grammar rule (Section 5.3).

Although the above Indonesian semantic analyser is intended to be general-purpose, we have a specific concrete aim of developing a question answering system for Indonesian. Currently, we have implemented a prototype query processor in Prolog. The semantic representations of

---

[1] http://www.toggletext.com

Indonesian declarative sentences, i.e. as found within a collection of documents, are stored in a clausal knowledge base. Subsequently, the semantic representation of queries are transformed into Prolog rules which, when unified with the clause database, yields the appropriate answer.

5. Semantic representation

In this section we present all the details concerning the semantic representations of Indonesian sentences, i.e. the syntax of logical expressions, the content of lexical semantics, and how the semantic attachment rules are defined and applied.

5.1. Logical expressions

As mentioned above, we adopt a simple 'flat' semantic representation (Hobbs, 1985), where a logical expression is a conjunction of first order logic literals. The arguments of these literals represent domain concepts such as objects and events, while the functors state relations between these concepts. All variables are existentially quantified with the widest possible scope.

Additionally, following the approach in (van Durme et al., 2003), literals are divided into two categories, extrinsic and intrinsic literals. An extrinsic literal defines a relationship between two variables, whereas an intrinsic literal defines a relationship between a variable and its referent as being some semantic concept in some underlying ontology. Examples of intrinsic literals are $\lambda X\ event(X,Y)$, where X is event object Y, $\lambda X\ object(X,Y)$, where X is inanimate object Y, and $\lambda X\ location(X,Y)$, where X is location object Y. Examples of extrinsic literals are $\lambda X \lambda Y\ agent(X,Y)$, where X is the agent of Y, and $\lambda X \lambda Y\ patient(X,Y)$, where X is the patient of Y. Both types of literals are stored within the lexical semantics entries of the words that convey their meaning, which specify the Y variable (see Section 5.2).

Our semantic representation falls into the category of so called neo-Davidsonian approaches, where intrinsic literals are predicates over objects and events, and arguments and modifiers are specified via the thematic relations specified by the extrinsic literals.

5.2. Lexical semantics

Lexical entries of open class words are associated with exactly one intrinsic literal which asserts a reference to the domain concept the word is 'about'. We arbitrarily choose the root form of a synonym to act as the conceptual symbol. Additionally, words may also be associated with extrinsic literals representing thematic relations that must be specified by complements within its syntactic projection.

For instance, the transitive verb *"memakan"* (to eat) has the following lexical semantic representation:

$$\lambda E \lambda A \lambda P\ event(E,memakan) \wedge agent(E,A) \wedge patient\ (E,P).$$

where *event(E,memakan)* is the intrinsic literal specifying the domain concept, i.e. eating event, and *agent(E,A)* and *patient(E,P)* are extrinsic literals whose variables will be subsequently bound with the subject and object variables through the lambda calculus operation of β-reduction (see Section 5.3 below).

In (Alwi et al. 1998), there are several subcategories of nominals, e.g. temporal, location, object, person, etc. The lexical semantics of nominals is simply the appropriate intrinsic literal, e.g. the semantics of *"dapur"* (kitchen) is $\lambda X\ location(X,dapur)$ and the semantics of *"ayah"* (father) is $\lambda X\ person(X,ayah)$.

Adjunct modifiers such as adjectives and adverbials are associated with a logical expression containing the appropriate intrinsic literal coupled with an extrinsic literal that specifies the thematic relation between the modifier and its head. For example, the semantics of *"indah"* (beautiful) is $\lambda A\ \lambda T\ property(A,indah) \wedge attrib(T,A)$.

The lexical semantics of prepositions and words which coordinate and/or subordinate other clauses is simply the appropriate extrinsic literal which specifies the relation between the prepositional phrase and its head or the clauses being coordinated. For example, the semantics of *"karena"* (because) is $\lambda X \lambda Y cause(X,Y)$.

Question words, i.e. *wh* words in Indonesian, e.g. *"apa"* (what), *"siapa"* (who), *"mana"* (mana), are associated with a logical expression that contains two literals. The first is the appropriate literal which would typically be associated with the answer, but instead of specifying the domain concept as the second argument, it is given a variable *Ans*. The second literal is a special *ans(Ans)* literal that indicates a question that is to be processed by the question answering module. For example the lexical semantics of *"siapa"* is $\lambda X person(X,Ans)$ $\wedge$ *ans(Ans)*.

Finally, there are several special cases of lexical semantics where morphological processes introduce literals. For example, the suffix *"nya"* amounts to a possessive pronoun, requiring the addition of the literals *person(O,owner)* and *possess(O,X)* to the lexical semantics. For example, we assume that the lexical semantics for the word *"bukunya"* (his/her book) is λX *object(X,buku)* $\wedge$ *person(O,owner)* $\wedge$ *possess(O,X)*.

5.3. Semantic attachment rules

Frege's principle of compositionality of semantics states that the meaning of a complex expression is determined by the meanings of its parts, and the way in which those parts are combined. In linguistic terms, rules that determine semantic interpretation are defined on the syntactic rules and structures. As a result, we develop *semantic attachment rules* for each syntactic rule in our grammar.

These semantic attachment rules define how the lexical semantics of the constituent words are combined, and in particular how the correct predicate-argument structure is specified. The most common approach is to use *lambda calculus* notation, where predicate-argument structure is controlled through the operation of β-reduction. See (Jurafsky and Martin, 2000) for a clear discussion of this approach (note that they call the process lambda-reduction).

To see an example of the semantic attachment rules and how they are combined, observe the following example, which constructs the semantic representation of the simple declarative sentence *"Ayah memakan nasi"* (father eats rice).

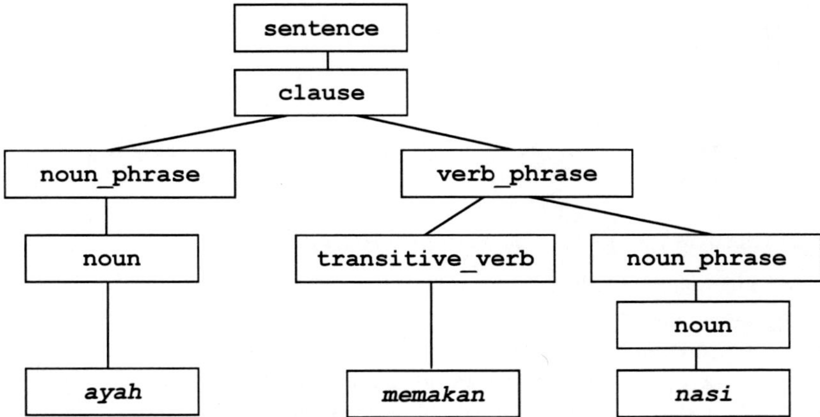

Figure 1: Parse tree for sample sentence *"Ayah memakan nasi"*.

Figure 1 shows how the sentence is parsed by our grammar: a **sentence** can consist of a single **clause**, which in turn expands to **noun_phrase** and **verb_phrase**. The **noun_phrase** category simply consists of a single **noun** lexeme, whereas a **verb_phrase** consists of a **transitive_verb** lexeme and another **noun_phrase** category.

Rules (1)-(3) below show the required syntax rules and corresponding semantic attachment rules, whereas rules (4)-(6) show the lexical semantics entries (see Section 5.2 for discussion of these values):

1. `clause -> noun_phrase, verb_phrase`
   λM `(noun_phrase.sem(K) ^ verb_phrase.sem(M)(K))`

2. `noun_phrase -> noun`
   `noun.sem`

3. `verb_phrase -> transitive_verb, noun_phrase`
   $\lambda H \lambda G$ `(transitive_verb.sem (H)(N)(G) ^ noun_phrase.sem (N))`

4. `noun -> [ayah]`
   λD `person(D, ayah)`

5. `transitive_verb -> [memakan]`
   $\lambda E \lambda P \lambda A$ `(event(E, memakan) ^ agent(E, A) ^ patient(E, P))`

6. `noun -> [nasi]`
   λS `object(S, nasi)`

The `.sem` operator indicates the logical expression of the indicated syntactic category. The β-reduction proceeds as follows:

1. Lexical semantics are copied over to the **noun_phrase** categories:
   (2) & (4): `noun_phrase.sem =` λD `person(D, ayah)`
   (2) & (6): `noun_phrase.sem =` λS `object(S, nasi)`

2. At the **verb_phrase** rule, the semantics **transitive_verb** and **noun_phrase** are substituted and reduced:
   (3), (5) & (2): `verb_phrase.sem =` $\lambda H \lambda G$ `(`$\lambda E \lambda P \lambda A$ `(event(E, memakan)` $\wedge$ `agent(E, A)` $\wedge$ `patient(E, P))(H)(N)(G)` $\wedge$ λS `object(S, nasi)(N))`
   reduces to
   $\lambda H \lambda G$ `(event(G, memakan)` $\wedge$ `agent(G, H)` $\wedge$ `patient(G, N)` $\wedge$ `object(N, nasi))`

3. At the **clause** rule, the semantics **noun_phrase** and **verb_phrase** are substituted and reduced:
   (1), (2) & (3): `clause.sem =` λM `(`λD `person(D, ayah)(K)` $\wedge$ $\lambda H \lambda G$ `(event(G, memakan)` $\wedge$ `agent(G, H)` $\wedge$ `patient(G, N)` $\wedge$ `object(N, nasi))(M)(K))`
   reduces to
   λM `(person(K, ayah)` $\wedge$ `event(M, memakan)` $\wedge$ `agent(M, K)` $\wedge$ `patient(M, N)` $\wedge$ `object(N, nasi))`

The semantic representation of **sentence**, the sentence, is simply the semantics of the **clause** as shown above.

5.4. The problem with syntax-driven semantic analysis

The complex machinery described in the last three subsections essentially plays one role: to abstract away the syntactic variations from paraphrases that essentially convey the same thing. The semantic representations produced from these paraphrases should be a single canonical representation. Due to the complex nature of natural language, however, this is an extremely complicated task, and often fails to scale up to large collections of text.

For example, in the case of possessives, we identified five different representations produced by the syntax-driven semantic analysis. The noun phrase

raket   Rahma
racket   Rahma
"Rahma's racket"

yields the semantic representation λX *object(X,raket)* $\wedge$ *person(A,rahma)* $\wedge$ *possess(A,X)*, whereas the sentence

Rahma   memiliki   raket
Rahma   owns   racket

"Rahma owns a racket"

yields the semantic representation *event(E,memiliki)* $\wedge$ *agent(E,A)* $\wedge$ *patient* $\wedge$ *(E,X)* $\wedge$ *object* $\wedge$ *(X,raket)* $\wedge$ *person(A,rahma)*.

One would hope the two semantic representations form an entailment relationship despite the fact the former focuses on the object whereas the latter focuses on the ownership event. Although theoretically we could reformulate the semantic attachment rules to produce a canonical form, we believe these rules are still too closely mapped to the syntactic structure, and thus not yet at a high enough level of abstraction to establish semantic equivalence. Following the approach in (Moldovan et al., 2003), this task is handled by introducing logical axioms as a form of "post-processing". We argue there are two benefits to this approach. Firstly, it reduces the burden on the design of the semantic attachment rules having to produce canonical forms, i.e. syntactic variations may still be present. This in turn enables the use of wider-coverage grammars. Secondly, it allows us to encode external knowledge not available in the original document collection. The following subsection discusses the axioms we have designed and implemented.

6. Axioms

To refine the semantic representation produced by the previous semantic analysis module, we build a post-processing semantic analysis by defining axioms and adding it to the system. These axioms broadly fall into two categories, NLP axioms and world knowledge axioms.

6.1. NLP axioms

Of the various NLP axioms we have developed, we show two instances. Table 1 lists axioms dealing with possessives, whereas Table 2 handles sentences that use the coordinative conjunction *'dan'*.

Using the axioms listed in Table 1, the two phrases presented in Section 5.4 above yield the same canonical logical form. In fact, all paraphrases signifying possession will entail the canonical logical form. The axioms are similar to production rules: if the combination of facts on the left-hand side are found to appear in the KB, the axiom will assert the right-hand side literals as new facts. For example, the first possessive axiom states that if the literal *possess(A,X)* is found, then *event(E,memiliki)*, *agent(E,A)*, and *patient(E,X)* will also be asserted, with the corresponding variables bound to the concepts specified in the KB.

Table 1: Axioms handling possessives

{possess(a,x)}	$\rightarrow$	*{event(e,memiliki)* $\wedge$ *agent(e,a)* $\wedge$ *patient(e,x)}*
{object(x,CONCEPT1) $\wedge$ *nobject(m,milik)* $\wedge$ *person(a,CONCEPT2)* $\wedge$ *nn(m,a)* $\wedge$ *nn(x,m)}*	$\rightarrow$	*{event(e,memiliki)* $\wedge$ *agent(e,a)* $\wedge$ *patient(e,x)}*
{person(a,pemilik) $\wedge$ *nn(a,x)}*	$\rightarrow$	*{event(e,memiliki)* $\wedge$ *agent(e,a)* $\wedge$ *patient(e,x)}*

Table 2 shows the axiom that handles sentences using the coordinative conjunction *'dan'*. Previously, for any coordination that holds between concepts d_1 and d_2, the syntax-driven analysis simply introduces a new concept d representing the conjunction of the two concepts. The conjunction axiom searches for all literals in which d participates as an argument, and asserts new copies of those literals in which d_1 and d_2 appear in place of d.

Table 2: Axiom handling coordinative conjunction

{dan(d,d$_1$,d$_2$) $\wedge$ *PRED$_1$(...,d,...)* $\wedge$ *...* $\wedge$ *PRED$_n$(...,d,...)}*	$\rightarrow$	*{PRED$_1$(...,d$_1$,...)* $\wedge$ *PRED$_1$(...,d$_2$,...)* $\wedge$ *...* $\wedge$ *PRED$_n$(...,d$_1$,...)* $\wedge$ *PRED$_n$(...,d$_2$,...)}*

6.2. World knowledge axioms

In our work, we also provide additional information to the system that is derived from a prototype Indonesian WordNet in the form of world knowledge axioms[2]. These axioms analyse the semantic representations constructed through syntax-driven analysis and will add literals that improve the inferential capabilities of the system. There are four types of world knowledge axioms: synonym axioms, antonym axioms, hypernym axioms, and derivational morphology axioms.

WordNet (Fellbaum, 1998) is a lexical resource where specific senses of words are clustered together into synonym sets, and semantic relationships between these sets are specified. (Putra et al., 2008) presents work on the development of an initial Indonesian WordNet[3]. For our purposes, this Indonesian WordNet can be viewed as a collection of Prolog facts stating semantic relationships holding between intrinsic symbols denoting domain concepts, e.g.

> *synonym(ibu,bunda).*
> *antonym(panas,dingin).*
> *hypernym(kue,makanan).*

The **synonym** axiom (Table 3) is designed for nouns, verbs, adjectives, and adverbs. For each domain concept appearing in the semantic representation of declarative sentences, it will assert new literals based on the Indonesian WordNet.

Table 3: Axiom handling synonyms

{synonym(k,k₁) ∧ ... ∧ synonym(k,kₙ) ∧ PRED(...,k,...)	→	*{PRED(...,k₁,...) ∧ ... ∧ PRED(...,kₙ,...)*

The **antonym** axioms (Table 4) assert new literals explicitly stating the negation of the opposing concept of adjectives appearing in the semantic representation.

Table 4: Axioms handling antonyms

{antonym(VAR1,VAR2) ∧ not(a,b) ∧ property(a,VAR1) ∧ isAdjNGrade(VAR1)}	→	*{property(b,VAR2)}*
{antonym(VAR1,VAR2) ∧ not(a,b) ∧ property(a,VAR2) ∧ isAdjNGrade(VAR2)}	→	*{property(b,VAR1)}*
{antonym(VAR1,VAR2) ∧ property(a,VAR1)}	→	*{not(a,b) ∧ property(b,VAR2)}*
{antonym(VAR1,VAR2) ∧ property(a,VAR2)}	→	*{not(a,b) ∧ property(b,VAR1)}*

The **hypernym** axiom (Table 5) is designed for nouns and verbs. It adds all new hypernym literals of all the concepts in the semantic representation.

Table 5: Axiom handling hypernyms

{hypernym(k,k₁) ∧ ... ∧ hypernym(k,kₙ) ∧ PRED_def(VAR,k) ∧ PRED₁(...,VAR,...) ∧ ... ∧ PREDₘ(...,VAR,...)}	→	*{PRED_def(VAR₁,k₁) ∧ ... ∧ PRED_def(VARₙ,kₙ) ∧ isA(VAR₁,VAR) ∧ ... ∧ isA(VARₙ,VAR) ∧ PRED₁(...,VAR₁,...) ∧ ... ∧ PRED₁(...,VARₙ,...) ∧ ... ∧ PREDₘ(...,VAR₁,...) ∧ ... ∧ PREDₘ(...,VARₙ,...)}*

The **derivational morphology** axioms (Table 6) can be seen as introducing frame-theoretic knowledge to the QA system. Specifically, it establishes a logical link between the semantic representations of intransitive and transitive verbs. Using this axiom, sentences containing

---

[2] Note that some would take issue with our use of the term '*world knowledge*', as WordNet is, strictly speaking, a lexical semantics resource, unlike, say, OpenCyc.
[3] http://bahasa.cs.ui.ac.id/iwn

verbal phrases that consist of an intransitive verb and obligatory complement noun phrase (*pelengkap*) will have the same semantic representation as a sentence with an active transitive verb. These axioms also handle derivational morphosemantic relations. They are designed to equate the semantic representations of noun phrases signifying *profession* and sentences containing verbs signifying *profession*. Specifically, the presence of *profession(X,Y)* intrinsic noun literal results in the assertion of appropriate *agent* and *event* literals.

Table 6: Axioms handling derivational morphology

{der(VAR1,VAR2) ∧ vintr(VAR1) ∧ vtran(VAR2) ∧ event(e1,VAR1) ∧ theme(e1,t) ∧ object(t,VAR3)}	→	*{event(e2,VAR2) ∧ patient(e2,t)}*
{der(VAR1,VAR2) ∧ person(VAR1) ∧ vtran(VAR2) ∧ profession(a,VAR2) ∧ nn(a,x)}	→	*{event(e,VAR2) ∧ agent(e,a) ∧ patient(e,x)}*
{der(VAR1,VAR2) ∧ person(VAR1) ∧ vintr(VAR2) ∧ profession(a,VAR2) ∧ nn(a,x)}	→	*{event(e,VAR2) ∧ agent(e,a) ∧ theme(e,x)}*
{der(VAR1,VAR2) ∧ person(VAR1) ∧ vintr(VAR2) ∧ profession(a,VAR2)}	→	*{event(e,VAR2) ∧ agent(e,a)}*

7. Axioms in Action

Our QA system is implemented in Prolog. It consists of a DCG grammar, where each syntactic rule has been augmented with semantic attachment rules (see Section 5.3), and we also constructed a small handcrafted lexicon where words were associated with lexical semantics as discussed in Section 5.2. A Prolog parser with semantic representation building, using the associated attachment rules, was developed to handle our resources, and testing revealed that indeed the correct semantic representations were being transduced from input sentences in Indonesian.

The next step was to develop a question answering module that employs the axioms described in Section 6. In general, semantic representations of declarative sentences are asserted as new facts to the KB, but not before passing them through the axiom post-processing. This can be repeated for as many sentences as necessary. Finally, we issue a query to the knowledge base by asking it an Indonesian interrogative sentence.

We first show how the system can still answer simple questions without the need for axioms as defined in Section 6 above. Consider the following sentence:

Lusi mencicipi kue buatan   ibu   dan apel hijau yang dibeli kakak di toko Harun
Lusi taste   cake made by mother and apple green that bought sister at store Harun
"Lusi tastes a cake made by mother and a green apple that sister bought from Harun's store."

Without the aid of axioms, the semantic analyzer constructs the following semantic representation:

```
event(e,mencicipi),  agent(e,a),  patient(e,p),  person(a,lusi),  dan(p,x,y),
object(x,kue),     nobject(n,buatan),     ibu(i,ibu),     nn(x,n),     nn(n,i),
object(y,apel),      property(w,hijau),      attrib(y,w),      event(f,membeli),
agent(f,k),     patient(f,y),     person(k,kakak),     di(f,t),     object(t,toko),
person(h,harun), possess(h,harun)
```

This representation can answer simple questions such as:

Siapa membeli apel   ?
Who   buy   apple ?
"Who bought an apple?"

which yields the correct answer '**kakak**' (sister), since it unifies with the following query:

```
ans(Ans)  :- person(X1,Ans),event(X2,membeli),agent(X2,X1),patient(X2,X3),
             object(X3,apel)
```

However, when asked a different question such as the following one:

Lusi mencicipi apa   ?
Lusi taste   what   ?
"What did Lusi taste?"

which produces the following query:

```
ans(Ans) :- person(X1,lusi),event(X2,mencicipi),agent(X2,X1),
            patient(X2,X3), object(X3,Ans)
```

the system is unable to identify the correct answer, since the patient of the "**mencicipi**" event is **p**, a domain concept introduced to represent the conjunction (see the **dan(p,w,x)** literal). By employing the coordinative conjunction axiom, the semantic representation will be augmented with the literals **patient(e,x)** and **patient(e,y)**, thus making the representation canonical. As a result, the system unifies the query with '**kue**' (cake) and '**apel**' (apple) for the answer.

The final example shows the value of the world knowledge axioms. Firstly, due to the existence of a WordNet fact **synonym(mencicipi,memakan)**, the synonym axiom asserts new literals for the synonym of 'mencicipi' (taste) term that is 'memakan' (eat). Specifically, it asserts **event(e2,memakan)**, **agent(e2,a)**, and **patient(e2,p)**. On the other hand, due to the existence of an Indonesian WordNet fact **hypernym(apel,buah)**, the hypernym asserts new literals for the hypernym of 'apel' (apple) term that is buah (fruit). Specifically, it asserts **object(q,buah)**, **isA(y,q)**, **dan(p,x,q)**, and **patient(e,q)**. As a result, given the following question:

> Buah apa   yang dimakan Lusi ?
> fruit what that eaten by Lusi ?
> *"What fruit did Lusi eat?"*

which produces the following query:

```
ans(Ans) :- event(X1,memakan),agent(X1,X2),patient(X1,X3),person(X2,lusi),
            object(X3,Ans), object(X4, buah), isA(X3,X4).
```

the system will produce the correct answer '**apel**' (apple), whereas without the world knowledge axioms it fails to do so.

8. Discussion and Summary

The implemented axioms have been shown to increase the capability of our Indonesian QA system in answering questions with syntactic variations and use of implicit world knowledge. We believe that handling these aspects as logical axioms is the right strategy, as it is at the appropriate level of abstraction, and lightens the burden on designing the semantic attachment rules that are still fairly tightly coupled to syntactic structure. Moreover, these axioms are not necessarily specific to the Indonesian language. For instance, the world knowledge axioms are fairly language independent, although the NLP axioms may have to be revised for another language, depending on how certain concepts are conveyed, e.g. possessives. Our prototype Prolog system still employs a fairly simple inference mechanism. In the future, we hope to feed the semantic representations into more sophisticated theorem provers, similar to the approach in (Blackburn and Bos, 2005).

References

Alwi, H., S. Dardjowidjojo, H. Lapoliwa and A. Moeliono. 1998. *Tata Bahasa Baku Bahasa Indonesia*. Balai Pustaka.

Blackburn, P. and J. Bos. 2005. *Representation and Inference for Natural Language: A First Course in Computational Semantics*. CSLI Publications.

van Durme, B., Y. Huang, A. Kupść and E. Nyberg. 2003. Towards Light Semantic Processing for Question Answering. *Proceedings of the 2003 Human Language Technologies Conference of the North American Chapter of the Association for Computational Linguistics Workshop on Text Meaning*, pp. 54-61.

Fellbaum, C. 1998. *WordNet: An Electronic Lexical Database*. MIT Press.

Hobbs, J. 1985. Ontological Promiscuity. *Proceedings of the 23rd Annual Meeting of the Association for Computational Linguistics*, pp. 61-69.

Joice. 2002. *Pengembangan lanjut Pengurai Struktur Kalimat Bahasa Indonesia yang menggunakan Constraint-Based Formalism*. Undergraduate thesis, Faculty of Computer

Science, University of Indonesia.

Jurafsky, D.S. and J.H. Martin. 2000. *Speech and Language Processing: An Introduction to Natural Language Processing, Computational Linguistics, and Speech Recognition.* Prentice-Hall.

Larasati, S.D. and R. Manurung. 2007. Towards a Semantic Analysis of Bahasa Indonesia for Question Answering. *Proceedings of the 10th Conference of the Pacific Association for Computational Linguistics (PACLING 2007).*

Moldovan, D., C. Clarke, S. Harabagiu and S. Maiorano. 2003. COGEX: A Logic Prover for Question Answering. *Proceedings of the 2003 Human Language Technologies Conference of the North American Chapter of the Association for Computational Linguistics*, pp. 87-93.

Narayanan, S. and S. Harabagiu. 2004. Question Answering based on Semantic Structures. *Proceedings of the 20th International Conference on Computational Linguistics.*

Purwarianti, A., M. Tsuchiya and S. Nakagawa. 2007. A Machine Learning Approach for Indonesian Question Answering System. *Proceedings of the International Conference on Artificial Intelligence and Applications (AIA 2007).*

Putra, D.D., A. Arfan and R. Manurung. 2008. Building an Indonesian WordNet. *Proceedings of the 2nd International MALINDO Workshop.*

Shen, D. and Lapata, M. 2007. Using Semantic Roles to Improve Question Answering. *Proceedings of the 2007 Joint Conference on Empirical Methods in Natural Language Processing and Computational Natural Language Learning*, pp. 12-21.

Wijono, S.H., I. Budi, L. Fitria and M. Adriani. 2006. Finding Answers to Indonesian Questions from English Documents. *Working Notes of the Workshop in Cross-Language Evaluation Forum (CLEF 2006).*

An Implementation of a Flexible Author-Reviewer Model of Generation using Genetic Algorithms[*]

Ruli Manurung[a], Graeme Ritchie[b], and Henry Thompson[c]

[a]Faculty of Computer Science, University of Indonesia, Depok 16424, Indonesia
maruli@cs.ui.ac.id

[b]Dept. of Computing Science, University of Aberdeen, King's College, Aberdeen AB24 3UE, UK
g.ritchie@abdn.ac.uk

[c]HCRC, University of Edinburgh, Informatics Forum, 10 Crichton St., Edinburgh EH8 9AB, UK
ht@inf.ed.ac.uk

Abstract. This paper proposes performing natural language generation using genetic algorithms to address two issues: the difficulty in controlling global textual features which arise from a large number of interdependent local decisions, and the difficulty in applying conventional NLG wisdom in domains where the communicative goal lacks sufficient detail. It presents details of an implemented system that embodies the aforementioned proposal, and discusses the results of an empirical study conducted using the system.

Keywords: natural language generation, genetic algorithms, poetry, creative language.

1. Background

This paper proposes an approach to natural language generation (NLG) using the genetic algorithm (GA), a widely used stochastic search method.

In this section we discuss two well known issues in NLG, and in Section 2 we discuss why and how genetic algorithms can address these issues. In Sections 3 to 5 we present an implementation of an NLG system that embodies the proposed approach. Our own interest is in developing a generator that conveys a given semantics as a text that simultaneously exhibits a certain metre, i.e. regular patterns in the rhythm of the text. Consequently, some of the design decisions, particularly concerning the evaluation functions, are domain-specific. However, we believe the architecture as a whole is of general-purpose interest. The paper concludes with some examples and discussion in Section 6.

1.1. Achieving fidelity and fluency

Oberlander and Brew (2000) argue that NLG systems must achieve fidelity and fluency goals, where fidelity is the faithful representation of the relevant knowledge contained within the communicative goal, and fluency is the ability to do it in a natural-sounding way such that it engenders a positive evaluation of the system by the user. In practice, applied NLG systems can often sidestep the fluency goal given a very restricted domain of output, with a limited style that may be just enough to serve the purpose of the application.

Unfortunately, fluency may be controlled by global textual features which arise from a large number of local decisions, few of which are based on stylistic considerations. This does not suit

---

[*] The work reported in this paper was carried out while all authors were at the University of Edinburgh.

22nd Pacific Asia Conference on Language, Information and Computation, pages 272–281

"

the prevalent paradigm of NLG as a top-down, goal-driven process, decomposed into the stages of content determination, text planning, and surface realisation, typically implemented within a *pipeline architecture* (Reiter, 1994) (cf. the "generation gap" problem in Meteer (1991)).

Oberlander and Brew propose an architecture which consists of two collaborating modules: an author and a reviewer. The author faces the task of generating a text that conveys the correct propositional content, i.e. achieving fidelity, whereas the reviewer must ensure that the author's output satisfies whatever macroscopic properties have been imposed on it, i.e. achieving fluency. Recent corpus-based NLG systems (Langkilde and Knight, 1998) essentially embody this architecture: a symbolic generator acts as the author, and a language model acts as the reviewer.

1.2. Vague communicative goals

Most NLG systems make two basic assumptions: that text generation is communicative goal-driven, and that these goals are sufficient to dictate a top-down approach for the planning of the text's structure and decomposition of goals. However, Mellish et al. (1998b) claim there is a class of NLG problems for which these basic assumptions do not apply. In the case of the ILEX system, this is due to two factors. Firstly, as ILEX produces explanation labels of jewelry items on display, there is often no clear plan or goal to be conveyed beyond *"say something coherent and interesting about this artifact within the space available"*. Secondly, ILEX can not plan far in advance, as it has to generate text in real-time based on the user's choices.

The alternative approach they adopt is *opportunistic planning*, whose key elements are interleaving of planning and execution, flexible choice of tasks from an agenda, expanding "sketchy plans" as needed, taking into account the current state of the world, and recognition of opportunities through detection of reference features.

2. Using genetic algorithms to do NLG

In addressing the above issues, we advocate treating the NLG process as a constraint satisfaction problem, where a solution is a text that satisfies multiple interdependent constraints relating to various levels of linguistic representation, e.g. semantic, syntactic, pragmatic, stylistic. Finding such a solution requires searching a space that is undoubtedly immense. Our proposed solution is to employ the *genetic algorithm* (GA), a widely-used heuristic search strategy that relies on random traversal of a search space with a bias towards more promising solutions. Specifically, it evolves a population of individuals over time, through an iterative process of evaluation, selection, and evolution. Upon termination, the fittest individual is hoped to be an optimal, or near-optimal, solution (Bäck et al., 1997).

Using GAs to do NLG has been done before, e.g. Mellish et al. (1998a). However, these previous attempts employed GAs as optimisation functions for specific subtasks of NLG. We believe that handling the entire NLG process through GAs opens up the potential for various flexible approaches, which we discuss in Section 2.1. In particular, employing GAs allows a measure of opportunistic planning (Section 1.2), where the evolutionary cycle enables fitness functions to recognize opportunities and provide feedback to the executor, i.e. genetic operators.

Finally, we note that using genetic algorithms for NLG also reflects a *discriminative* model of generation, where domain knowledge is stated declaratively, i.e. what a good text should look like instead of how to write one (cf. the corpus-based systems in Section 1.1).

2.1. Representing linguistic constraints and the encoding of domain knowledge

When using GAs for NLG, a solution is a text that must achieve fluency and fidelity goals. These goals can be expanded as a set of constraints to be satisfied by a text, e.g. it must be grammatical, it must convey some given meaning, it must be readable, etc.

There are two ways constraints can be implemented: ensuring that all possibly evolvable solutions never violate the constraint, or imposing penalties on individuals that violate a constraint. There is a trade-off: the former approach is obviously ideal, but its intractability is often the very reason GAs are employed in the first place. On the other hand, imposing excessively heavy penalties often leads to premature convergence on the first found well-formed solution, whereas if the penalties are too light, the GA may continue to evolve ill-formed solutions that score better than well-formed ones.

Within this framework, there is large scope for flexibility in terms of where domain-specific knowledge is encoded to help satisfy these constraints. For NLG, it seems reasonable to assume that candidate solutions must at least be grammatically well-formed.

Oberlander & Brew's author-reviewer model specifies that the author focuses on achieving fidelity, whereas the reviewer focuses on maximizing fluency goals. In GAs, this suggests devising genetic operators that explicitly work towards realising some input semantics, and fitness functions that measure fluency factors such as readability, length, coherence, etc.

However, other setups are possible. For instance, one could envisage an author (genetic operator) concentrating on fluency whilst a separate reviewer (fitness function) assessed the output for fidelity, or a pair of reviewers assessing a document of grammatical nonsense[1], each concentrating on fluency and fidelity respectively. Such approaches may seem unnecessarily awkward for conventional NLG tasks, but may provide a more suitable platform for NLG systems without well-defined communicative goals (see Section1.2).

Note that the various components, i.e. the ensemble of authors and reviewers, can more or less be defined independently of each other, modulo the need for a common representation of a candidate text. This addresses the "engineering argument", one of the main arguments supporting the pipeline architecture as opposed to an integrated architecture (Reiter, 1994), i.e. it enables a modular decomposition of an NLG system, thus resulting in a more manageable implementation.

3. Linguistic representation

Our system represents candidate texts as lexicalized tree adjoining grammar (LTAG) derivation trees, augmented with the use of feature structures (Vijay-Shanker and Joshi, 1988). A derivation tree can be seen as the basic formal object that is constructed during the course of sentence generation from a semantic representation (Joshi, 1987). However, derivation trees are also the ideal data structure within our system for another reason, i.e. the non-monotonic structure building nature of GAs. Since the genetic operators may involve randomly altering subtrees through subtree deletion and swapping, we must somehow undo the unification of certain feature structures. Using the derivation tree as our primary data structure, we are able to store all local feature structures in their respective elementary trees (cf. Kilger (1992)). When required, e.g. to evaluate certain properties of the resulting text, the derived tree is rebuilt. Redundant computation is minimized by reusing a cached derived tree if it has not been modified between iterations.

Within evolutionary theory, the LTAG derivation tree can be viewed as the *genotypic* representation of candidate solutions, from which we can compute the *phenotypic* information of semantic (Section 5.2) and prosodic (Section 5.1) features via the derived tree.

We adopt a simple 'flat' semantic representation that is often used in NLG (Koller and Striegnitz, 2002). A *semantic expression* is a set of first order logic literals, which is logically interpreted as a conjunction of all its members. The arguments of these literals represent domain concepts such as objects and events, while the functors state relations between these concepts. See Section 5.2 for some examples.

The semantic form of a tree is the union of the semantic expressions of its constituent elementary trees, with binding of variables during substitution and adjunction to control predicate-argument structure; cf. Stone et al. (2001).

Finally, since our system requires information on prosody, each word is associated with its phonetic spelling, taken from the CMU pronouncing dictionary[2].

---

[1] As produced by a statistical language model, or by some combination of monkeys and typewriters.
[2] http://www.speech.cs.cmu.edu/cgi-bin/cmudict

4. Genetic operators for NLG

Genetic operators are functions that are stochastically applied to candidate solutions to explore alternative solutions. In essence, they define the search space. When designing operators for our system, the following desiderata were considered:

1. **Grammaticality:** The operators should ensure that syntactic well-formedness of the candidate texts be preserved. This suggests that genetic operators be based on the derivational rules of the underlying grammatical formalism (LTAG).
2. **Non-monotonicity:** As operators are stochastically applied, it is highly improbable that optimal texts can be constructed using monotonic structure-building operators alone. Rather, they are typically built through the trial and error design mechanism that evolution affords. Therefore, one or more non-monotonic operators must facilitate this, such as deletion, replacement, and swapping of substructures.
3. **Incrementality:** Constructing texts in an incremental fashion enables the generation process to benefit from the guiding hand of evolution. The appropriate granularity of operator incrementality is an open question. Furthermore, incomplete derivations may conflict with requirements of grammaticality.

Within our framework, several sets of operators were implemented.

4.1. Baseline operators

Existing work in *genetic programming* defines genetic operators on tree data structures, such as *grow*, which randomly selects a leaf from a tree and replaces it with a randomly generated new subtree, *shrink*, which does the opposite, and *switch*, which randomly selects two nodes and swaps their position.

Within the context of NLG, although it seems obvious to perform such structural manipulations on phrase structure trees, we argue that they are most appropriately applied to the LTAG derivation tree instead. This maintains the syntactic principle of well-formed LTAG structures being constructed through valid compositions of elementary trees using the operations of substitution and adjunction. The BLINDADD operator adds a node in the derivation tree; variants exist for both substitution and adjunction. The BLINDDELETE operator removes a node in the derivation tree, along with the subtree that it dominates. Finally, the BLINDSWAP operator swaps the positions of two subtrees, either belonging to the same derivation tree, resulting in *mutation*, or to another derivation tree, resulting in *crossover*.

These baseline operators, while grammatically sound (in particular, all involved feature structures must license the operation), are oblivious to fidelity and fluency goals. Consequently, they indiscriminately add, delete, and swap both good and bad content, delegating judgments of quality to the fitness evaluation functions.

4.2. Semantically motivated operators

Given the task of generating the sentence "*John loves Mary*", it seems absurd that an NLG system would attempt to add content concerning, say, Greek archaeological artefacts or medical conditions, yet this is an entirely possible scenario given the baseline operators above.

Accordingly, we implemented a set of operators that deliberately attempts to bring the semantics of a candidate text closer to that of some pre-defined input semantics. This is precisely the task of surface realisation in NLG, and our approach is reminiscent of Nicolov (1998) and Stone et al. (2001).

Our "semantically smart" operator, SMARTADD, explicitly tries to realise some portion of the input semantics S, specifically that which has not yet been realised, while simultaneously maintaining syntactic well-formedness. Nicolov calls this gradual process the *consumption* of semantics. Conversely, SMARTDELETE will only consider removing elementary trees whose lexical semantics are extraneous with respect to S, and SMARTSWAP will only consider swapping subtrees that preserve the predicate argument structure represented by S.

Such operators require a way of reasoning about the relationship between the input semantics and the semantics conveyed by the candidate text, i.e. which portion of the input semantics has been realised, and which portion of the candidate text semantics indeed realises the input, or is extraneous. This is achieved using the semantic mapping algorithm discussed in Section 5.2.

5. Fitness functions for NLG

In GAs, the fitness function is where the bulk of domain-specific knowledge and heuristics is typically encoded. Specifically for NLG, the fitness function serves as a metric, or more precisely a set of metrics, that measure whether a candidate text achieves the goals of fidelity and fluency.

For our implemented system, we measured fidelity in terms of how well a candidate text realised a given propositional input, and fluency in terms of how closely the rhythmic stress patterns of a text matched a given poetic metre.

5.1. Metre similarity

Our system is tasked with conveying a given semantics as a text that exhibits a given metre. For example, Fig. 1 shows the metre of Hillaire Belloc's "*The Lion*", with stressed syllables in bold type, unstressed syllables in normal type, syllables extraneous to the underlying metre in italics, and • indicating a 'missing' syllable.

The	**Lion**, the	**Lion**, he	**dwells** in the	**waste**,
He	**has** a big	**head** and a	very small	**waist**;
But his	**shoul**ders are	**stark**, and his	**jaws** they are	**grim**,
And a	**good** little	**child** • will	**not** play with	**him**.

Figure 1: Metre pattern of Belloc's "*The Lion*"

Our system represents metre patterns as a list of *stress syllables* notated as follows: **w** ('*weak*') is an unstressed syllable, **s** ('*strong*') is a stressed syllable, **x** ('*wildcard*') is any syllable, and **b** indicates a linebreak. Fig. 2 shows example notations for (a) a limerick, and (b) "*The Lion*" (formatted into lines for readability purposes).

```
[w,s,w,w,s,w,w,s,b,          [w,s,w,w,s,w,w,s,w,w,s,b,
 w,s,w,w,s,w,w,s,b,           w,s,w,w,s,w,w,s,w,w,s,b,
   w,s,w,w,s,b,                w,s,w,w,s,w,w,s,w,w,s,b,
   w,s,w,w,s,b,                w,s,w,w,s,w,w,s,w,w,s,b]
 w,s,w,w,s,w,w,s,b]
         (a)                              (b)
```

Figure 2: Encoding for (a) a limerick and (b) "*The Lion*"

Our metre evaluation function measures the degree of similarity between a given metre pattern and the metre exhibited by a candidate text. To compute this, we use the well-known *minimum edit distance*, in which the distance between two strings is the minimal sum of costs of operations (symbol insertion, deletion, and substitution) that transform one string into another. We have devised a suitable cost function that reflects our intuitions of metre. Since the edit distance only accounts for context-free operations, we implemented a metre compensation function to account for the fact that context can affect lexical stress, particularly in poetry.

Our metre evaluation function, $\mathcal{F}_{metre}$, takes the value computed by the minimum edit distance algorithm, adjusts it using our context-sensitive compensation scheme, and normalizes it to the interval [0,1]. Table 1 shows $\mathcal{F}_{metre}$ values for various candidate texts, against the target form in Fig. 2(b). The first is Belloc's actual poem, which itself contains some metrical imperfections; the second is a limerick by Edward Lear; the third is an extract from an academic text, containing roughly the correct number of syllables; the last is chosen for its inappropriateness. The $\mathcal{F}_{metre}$ scores do not conflict with our intuitions of poetic metre.

Table 1: Metre fitness for various texts

Candidate text	$\mathcal{F}_{metre}$
The Lion, the Lion, he dwells in the waste. He has a big head and a very small waist. But his shoulders are stark, and his jaws they are grim, and a good little child will not play with him.	0.787
There was an old man with a beard, who said, "it is just as i feared! two owls and a hen, four larks and a wren, have all built their nests in my beard!"	0.686
Poetry is a unique artifact of the human language faculty, with its defining feature being a strong unity between content and form.	0.539
John loves Mary.	0.264

5.2. Semantic similarity

Following Love (2000), we propose two factors that must be considered: *structural similarity* and *conceptual similarity*. Structural similarity measures the degree of isomorphism between two semantic expressions. Conceptual similarity is a measure of relatedness between two concepts (logical literals). We simply use the following: two concepts are the same if and only if they share the same literal functor. However, one could envisage a refined approach using an underlying ontology such as WordNet, or using statistical models of lexical semantics, e.g. LSA.

Computing a structural similarity mapping between two expressions is an instance of the NP-complete maximal common subgraph problem. However, we have implemented a greedy algorithm that serves our purposes and runs in $O(V^3)$, based on Gentner's structure mapping theory (Falkenhainer et al., 1989). It takes two sets of logical literals, S_{target} and $S_{candidate}$, and attempts to 'align' the literals. We then apply a function $\mathcal{F}_{sem}$, normalised to [0,1], to compute a score based on various aspects of the alignment; this is based on Love's computational model of similarity Love (2000).

Table 2 shows an example of computing semantic similarity for a selection of candidate texts against a target semantics that represents the second line of Belloc's "*The Lion*", i.e. "[The lion] has a big head and a very small waist". The target semantic expression is as follows:

$$S_{target} = \{lion(\_,L), own(\_,L,H), head(\_,H), big(\_,H),$$
$$own(\_,L,W), waist(\_,W), small(S,W), very(\_,S)\}$$

The first two texts convey a subset of the target; the third text conveys an altogether different fact about the lion; the fourth text is purposely inappropriate; and the last text, conveys the semantics of the first text in its object to the verb '*love*'. As with our metre similarity function, we believe that the $\mathcal{F}_{sem}$ scores roughly approximate human intuitions.

Table 2: Semantic fitness for various texts

Candidate text	Candidate semantics	$\mathcal{F}_{sem}$
The lion has a big head	{lion(_,L), own(_,L,H), head(_,H), big(_,H)}	0.525
The lion has a head and a waist	{lion(_,L), own(_,L,H), head(_,H), own(_,L,W), waist(_,W)}	0.598
The lion dwells in the waste	{lion(_,L), dwell(D,L), inside(_,D,W), waste(_,W)}	0.078
John loves Mary	{john(_,J), love(_,J,M), mary(_,M)}	0.0451
John and Mary love the lion's big head	{john(_,J), love(_,J,H), mary(_,M), love(_,M,H), lion(_,L), own(_,L,H), head(_,H), big(_,H)}	0.389

6. Testing and discussion

Throughout our testing, we employed *proportionate selection*, which assigns a distribution that accords parents a probability to reproduce that is proportional to its fitness. Individuals are sampled from this distribution using *stochastic universal sampling*, which minimises chance fluctuations in sampling. To reduce the chances of premature convergence or stagnation, we used an *elitist* population of 20% of the entire population (the latter being 40). See Bäck et al. (1997) for a review of these issues. Each test was run five times, and each run lasted for 500 iterations. The three mutation operators used, along with their probabilities, were substitution (0.5), adjunction (0.3), and deletion (0.2). For crossover, the subtree swapping operator was used. The probabilities of applying genetic operators were $p_{mutation} = 0.6$, $p_{crossover} = 0.4$, for both the "blind" and "smart" variants. A small handcrafted grammar and lexicon was used, with 33 elementary trees and 134 lexical items, 28 of which were closed class words. Most of the content words were taken from Belloc's "*The Bad Child's Book of Beasts*".

6.1. Fluency and fidelity generation

In this test, we measured the ability of our system to generate texts that simultaneously achieve fidelity and fluency goals. We took a very simple approach to combining the metre similarity and semantic similarity functions – the arithmetic mean of their scores, i.e.

$$F_{fitness} = \frac{F_{metre} + F_{sem}}{2}$$

The target metre was that of a limerick, as in Fig. 2(a). The target semantics was a representation of the first two lines of "*The Lion*" (Fig. 1), with a slight alteration where the original opening noun phrase "*The lion, the lion*" was replaced with "*The african lion*". The target semantic expression is as follows:

$$S_{target} = \{lion(\_, l),\ african(\_, l),\ dwell(d, l),\ inside(\_, d, was),\ waste(\_, was),\ own(\_, l, h),$$
$$head(\_, h),\ big(\_, h),\ own(\_, l, wai),\ waist(\_, wai),\ small(s, wai),\ very(\_, s)\}$$

Two variants of the test were conducted: one with the baseline 'blind' operators and one with the semantically-aware 'smart' operators.

Table 3 shows the highest-scoring candidate from the blind operator test. The text is metrically perfect. However, the unmapped S_{target} literals show that the text fails to convey three concepts, i.e. that the lion is *african*, that its head is *big*, and that the waist is *very* small.

Table 3: Solution for blind operators tests

Fitness score:
0.81
Text:
A **lion**, it **dwells** in a **waste**.
A **lion**, it **dwells** in a **waste**.
A **waste** will be **rare**.
Its **head** will be **rare**.
Its **waist**, that is **small**, will be **rare**.
Unmapped S_{target}:
{african(_1, l), big(_6, h), very(_9, s)}
Unmapped $S_{candidate}$:
{rare(_33,_34),   will(_35,_36),   waste(_37,_34),   dwell(_38,_39), lion(_40,_39), inside(_41,_38,_42), waste(_43,_42), rare(_44,_45), will(_49,_50), rare(_51,_52), will(_55,_56)}

Table 4 shows the highest-scoring candidate from the smart operators test. Although the fitness score is very similar to the one in Table 3, the characteristics of the text are markedly different. The smart operators, which increase bias towards semantics, have a detrimental effect on the metre. Unlike the metrically perfect limerick in Table 3, this text requires several edit operations: 2 insertions and 2 deletions (even Belloc's original poem contains similar rhythmic imperfections – see Section 5.1). However, it does a better job of conveying S_{target}, only failing to convey the fact that the waist is *very* small, whilst also conveying fewer extraneous semantics (most of which are repetitions of correct semantics).

Table 4: Solution for smart operators test

Fitness score:
0.83
Text: A **very** • **af**ric**an li**o*n*, *who* is african, **dwells** in a **waste**. Its **head**, that is **big**, is **very** • **big**. A **waist**, *that* is its **waist**, it is **small**.
Unmapped S_{target}: *{very(_9, s)}*
Unmapped $S_{candidate}$: *{very(_137,_135), big(_141,_136), waist(_145,_143), very(_153,_152), african(_154,_140)}*

6.2. Line by line generation

In this test, we had our system generate each line of a limerick individually. The purpose is to see whether the system can perform better given a simpler task. We also based this test on a different limerick to show the flexibility of the system. The new input is shown in Table 5. Note that the target metres represent an *ideal* limerick. The "gold standard" limerick itself is metrically imperfect.

Table 5: Buller's original limerick as individual lines.

Line 1: *There was a young lady called Bright.* *S = {lady(_, l), young (_, l), name(_, l,b), bright(_, b)}* `[w,s,w,w,s,w,w,s,b]`
Line 2: *She could travel much faster than light.* *S = {travel(t,l), faster (f, t, li), light(_, li), much (_, f), can(_, t)}* `[w,s,w,w,s,w,w,s,b]`
Line 3: *She set out one day in a relative way.* *S = {leave (le, l), relative(_, le), oneday(_, le)}* `[w,s,w,w,s,w,s,w,w,s,b]`
Line 4: *She returned on the previous night.* *S = {return (r, l), on(_, r, n), night (_, n), previous(_, n)}* `[w,s,w,w,s,w,w,s,b]`

Table 6 shows the best solution obtained by trying to generate the whole limerick at once, as in previous tests, whereas Table 7 collects the results of generating each individual line. In the latter case, the resulting limerick is metrically much better than the former, as there are only two edits compared to five. Both of these generated texts are metrically superior to the original.

Table 6: Solution for entire limerick.

Fitness score:
0.69
Text: A **la**dy could **be** on an **eve***ning*, that **could** be prece**d**ing, one **day**. A *young* **la**dy called **Bright**, who **set** out one **day**, **tra**velled much **faster** than **light**.
Unmapped S_{target}: *{can(_6, t), relative(_7, le), return(r, l)}*
Unmapped $S_{candidate}$: *{oneday(_199,_210), lady(_201,_197),can(_221,_207),can(_228,_213)}*

Table 7: Collected solution for individual lines.

Fitness score:
Line 1: 0.82, Line 2: 0.66, Line 3: 0.78, Line 4: 0.86
Text: A **lady** <u>called</u> **Bright** could be **young**. She **tra**velled. The **light** could be **light**. She **set** out one **day**. She **set** out one **day**. She **is** on a **previous night**.
Unmapped S_{target}: *{travel(t, l), faster(f, t, li), much(_1, f), relative(_0, le), {return(r, l)}*
Unmapped $S_{candidate}$: *{can(_57, _81), {light(_527, _524), travel(_603, _536), {leave(_359, _323), oneday(_333, _359)}*

However, the system fails to satisfy the semantics, and in fact does worse in the latter case, as there are five unmapped S_{target} literals as opposed to three. This suggests that, particularly given the smaller task of individual line generation, our evaluation function is not guiding the GA to optimize semantics as well as it is for metre. We attempt to address this in the final test.

6.3. Evaluation weighting

The results in the preceding test suggest that the evaluation function is biased towards metre optimisation. In our final test, we simply modified the linear combination by doubling the weight of semantic fitness as follows:

$$F_{fitness} = \frac{F_{metre} + 2 * F_{sem}}{3}$$

Table 8 collects the results of generating each individual line using the modified evaluation function. We believe this text is definitely an improvement over the ones in Tables 6 and 7, and most closely resembles the original limerick in Table 5. Note that semantically it only lacks 2 target literals and only has 1 extraneously conveyed literal. Metrically, it requires 9 edits. Subjectively, however, we believe it still scans reasonably well as a limerick.

This suggests that semantic fitness should carry more weight than metre fitness, perhaps reflecting the intuition that fidelity is more of a 'harder' constraint than fluency is.

Table 8: Collected solution, modified fitness

Fitness score:
Line 1: 0.78, Line 2: 0.79, Line 3: 0.95, Line 4: 0.76
Text: There **is** a <u>young</u> **lady** <u>called</u> **Bright**. She *will* **tra**vel much **faster** than **light**. She **set** out one **day** * **relative**<u>ly</u>. She **is** on *a* preceding * **night**.
Unmapped S_{target}: *{can(_2, t), return(r, l)}*
Unmapped $S_{candidate}$: *{will(_409, _415)}*

7. A (Speculative) Summary

We have proposed a flexible author-reviewer model for performing NLG that is based on GAs to address the two issues presented in Section 1.

We then presented details of an implemented instance of this model, which specifically aims to convey a given semantics as a text that satisfies a given metre pattern. Through a series of small tests, we showed that it has the potential to satisfy the interdependent goals of fidelity and fluency (compare in particular, the output in Table 8 with the gold standard in Table 5).

As implemented, our system does not really address the difficulty of generation when the communicative goal is vague: the semantic similarity function (Section 5.2) still requires an existing propositional input. However, one can envisage other measures of fidelity that account for notions of coherence, interestingness, consistency. As for fluency, one could replace our very specific metre similarity function with a declarative model of, for instance, readability, document length, personality, and language complexity.

References

Back, T., D. Fogel, and Z. Michalewicz, editors. Handbook of Evolutionary Computation. Oxford University Press and Institute of Physics Publishing, 1997.

Falkenhainer, B., K. D. Forbus, and D. Gentner. The structure-mapping engine: Algorithm and examples. Artificial Intelligence, 41:1–63, 1989.

Joshi, A. K. The relevance of tree adjoining grammars to generation. In G. Kempen, editor, Natural Language Generation: New Results in Artificial Intellligence, pages 233–252. Martinus Nijhoff Press, Dordrecht, The Netherlands, 1987.

Kilger, A. Realization of tree adjoining grammars with unification. Technical Report TM-92-08, DFKI, Saarbr¨ucken, Germany, 1992.

Koller, A. and K. Striegnitz. Generation as dependency parsing. In Proceedings of the 40th Anniversary Meeting of the Association for Computational Linguistics, Philadelphia, USA, July 2002.

Langkilde, I. and K. Knight. Generation that exploits corpus-based statistical knowledge. In Proceedings of the 36th Annual Meeting of the Association for Computational Linguistics and 17th International Conference on Computational Linguistics, pages 704–710, Montreal, Canada, August 1998.

Love, B. C. A computational level theory of similarity. In Proceedings of the 22nd Annual Meeting of the Cognitive Science Society, pages 316–321, Philadelphia, USA, August 2000.

Mellish, C., A. Knott, J. Oberlander, and M. O'Donnell. Experiments using stochastic search for text planning. In Proceedings of the Ninth International Workshop on Natural Language Generation, Niagara-on-the-Lake, Canada, 1998a.

Mellish, C., M. O'Donnell, J. Oberlander, and A. Knott. An architecture for opportunistic text generation. In Proceedings of the Ninth International Workshop on Natural Language Generation, Niagara-on-the-Lake, Canada, 1998b.

Meteer, M. Bridging the generation gap between text planning and linguistic realisation. Computational Intelligence, 7(4):296–304, 1991.

Nicolov, N. Approximate Text Generation from Non-Hierarchical Representations in a Declarative Framework. PhD thesis, Department of Artificial Intelligence, University of Edinburgh, Edinburgh, UK, 1998.

Oberlander, J. and C. Brew. Stochastic text generation. Philosophical Transactions of the Royal Society of London, Series A, 358:1373–1385, 2000.

Reiter, E. Has a consensus on NL generation appeared? and is it psycholinguistically plausible? In Proceedings of the Seventh International Natural Language Generation Workshop, pages 163– 170, Kennebunkport, USA, April 1994. Springer-Verlag.

Stone, M., C. Doran, B. Webber, T. Bleam, and M. Palmer. Microplanning with communicative intentions: The SPUD system. Technical Report TR-65, Rutgers University Center for Cognitive Science, New Jersey, USA, 2001.

Vijay-Shanker, K. and A. K. Joshi. Feature structure based tree adjoining grammars. In Proceedings of 12th International Conference of Computational Linguistics, pages 714–720, Budapest, Hungary, August 1988.Blackburn, P. and J. Bos. 2005. *Representation and Inference for Natural Language: A First Course in Computational Semantics.* CSLI Publications.

Semantic Change of the Selected Cebuano Words*

Rowanne Marie R. Maxilom, Ph.D

University of San Carlos
P. del Rosario Street, 6000 Cebu City

{wannex_007@yahoo.com}

Abstract

This study attempted to determine the types of semantic change of the selected Cebuano words from the written texts, specifically the Bisaya magazine and spoken language of Cebuano speakers aged 15 – 40 years old living in Cebu province. Twenty (20) Cebuano words were analyzed using Campbell's (1998) and Crowley's (1997) classifications of the semantic change. The results revealed that metaphor was the dominant type of semantic change in the written text and broadening was frequently-used in the spoken language.

Keywords: broadening, metaphor, semantic change, widening

1. Introduction

"Earlier grammars and dictionaries reveal that Cebuano-Bisaya has undergone rapid changes in the course of the last four centuries." (Wollf, 2001, p. 121). There are words listed in the earlier dictionaries that seem to be unknown in the current time. In fact, some of the young Cebuano speakers who are more exposed to other languages such as English do not understand the speech of their elders who used old Cebuano terms.

Trask (1994) also pointed out that the young generation had a hard time in reading what the ancestors wrote 400 years ago. In the same manner, the descendants would surely find reading what the current generation of speakers is writing presently or the future generation could even hardly understand the tape recordings and films shown these days.

Because of the cultural influences, the language was also affected. There are many Cebuano terms that are currently used by the native speakers that were originated in English and Spanish. In fact, "when the Spaniards left the Philippines in 1898 after almost 350 years of colonization..." as reported by Gonzalez (2004, p. 73), ten percent of the Filipinos spoke in Spanish.

---

* Acknowledgment

This paper was made possible because of the following persons: Dr. Shirley Dita, who invited me to submit an article to PACLIC, Dr. Hsiu-chuan who encouraged me to write a paper in Historical Linguistics, Ms. Ma. Lourdes Apodaca, Mrs. Letty Espina, Mr. Joselito Flores, Miss Haidee Palapar, Dr. Hope S. Yu, and Mrs. Norly Plasencia, who were my informants and consultant, respectively.

However, thirty percent of the Filipinos could speak in English after the Philippines had been colonized by the Americans for forty eight years. In this manner, the colonization by the Spaniards and Americans could possibly account for the semantic change that was undergone by some Cebuano words.

Bloomfield (1933) and Campbell (1998) defined semantic change as a change in the concepts that were associated with a term and the innovations that change the meaning of words.

With regard to the types of semantic change, Campbell (1998) and Crowley (1997) have the following classifications: First, widening or broadening refers to the increase of the meaning of words (Campbell, 1998) and a change in meaning which could result in a word processing additional meanings while retaining the original meaning (Crowley, 1997). For example, the English word 'dog' had a specific meaning of 'a powerful breed of dog' which has a broader meaning that includes 'all breeds of dog'.

Second, narrowing involves the change of meaning that decreases its range of reference into a fewer context (Campbell, 1998) and occurs when a word refers to only part of the original meaning (Crowley, 1997). For instance, the word 'starve' (i.e. to suffer or perish from hunger) came from the Old English word 'steorfan' (i.e. to die).

Third, metaphor is a type of semantic change that involves one kind of thing in relation to another kind of thing that is somehow similar to the previous thing (Campbell, 1997). For example, the Cebuano word 'higante' which is similar to the concept 'big' is used in describing a great writer.

Fourth, litotes is another type of semantic change that refers to exaggeration through understatement (Campbell, 1998). For instance, the phrase 'of no small importance' is mentioned that would mean 'something that is too important'.

Other types of semantic change that were identified by Campbell (1998) are metonymy, synechdoche, degeneratin or pejoration, and elevation or amelioration. Metonymy occurs when there is a change of meaning of a word which includes other senses that are not originally present but are closely associated with the word's previous meaning. An example of metonymy is the Spanish word 'plata' (i.e. silver) that has been elaborated to mean 'money'.

Another type of semantic change is synechdoche (i.e. a part-to-whole relationship). For instance, the word 'tongue' means 'language'. In addition, degeneration or pejoration takes place when the sense of the word has a negative assessment in the minds of the users. For instance, the word 'spinster' has a negative connotation of an unmarried older woman. Elevation or amelioration (i.e. a shift of meaning which has an increasingly positive value judgment) is also another type of semantic change. An example of this type of semantic change is the Spanish word 'casa' (i.e. house) which had a previous meaning in Latin that is 'hut' or 'cottage'.

The other types of semantic change are taboo replacement and avoidance of obscenity which can also be called euphemism, hyperbole or exaggeration (i.e. shifts in meaning because of exaggeration through overstatement), and bifurcation or semantic split classified by Crowley (1997) (i.e. when a term acquires another meaning that relates to the original meaning). To provide a concrete example of taboo replacement is the use of the term 'rooster' instead of 'cock' to avoid obscene association of 'cock' with 'penis'. In addition, an example of hyperbole is the use of word 'terribly' that means little more compared to 'very'. Lastly, an illustration of bifurcation is the English word 'silly' which had a cognate in German word 'selig' (i.e. blessed) and is derived from Seele 'soul'. Semantic shift takes place when the meaning 'blessed' changes its meaning into 'stupid' or 'reckless' in Modern English.

Moreover, Campbell (1998) and Crowley (1997) argued that there were various causes of language change. First, climate and geography could account for language change. The languages of mountainous areas as pointed out by Crowley (1997) tended to change swiftly than the languages spoken closer to the sea level due to higher altitude.

Second, foreign influence or substratum is also one of the causes of language change. According to Campbell (1998), the substratum theory of linguistic change involves the idea that if people migrate into an area and their language is acquired by the original inhabitants of the area, then any changes in the language can be put down to the influence of the original language. For example, the colonization Spaniards to the Philippines has influenced the Cebuano language, especially the counting system.

Third, simplification is another cause of language change. In this cause, the production of sounds in one language (e.g. Spanish /v/) in the word *verde* would be simplified into Cebuano *berde* which means 'green'.

2. Related Literature

This section focuses on the studies concerning the semantic correlates in Cebuano (Adeva, 2005), semantic meanings of Cebuano and Hiligaynon enclitic adverbs (Lising, 2004), and the semantic reconstruction in Austronesian Linguistics (Zorc, 2004).

In Adeva's (2005) study, the semantic correlate in Cebuano and the way the semantic correlate were reflected in the morpho-syntax and semantics of Cebuano were investigated. This study also determined the transitive and intransitive constructions of the Cebuano stories. Using Hoppes and Thompson's (1980) transitivity hypothesis and Dixon's (1994) syntactic-semantic primitive cited in Adeva's (2005) study, the results revealed that in actor focus, two affixes (mi-/ni-~m-replesive) were evident and three affixes (i-, -un, -an) were evident in goal the focus.

However, this study had only few number of Bisaya magazines where the stories were taken from. The parameter could have been clearly described so that the scales are clear and the semantic correlates of the grammar could be systematically presented.

Lising (2004) analyzed the semantic meanings and syntactic distribution of the Cebuano and Hiligaynon counterparts of Tagalog enclitic adverbs in Cebuano short stories and Hiligaynon plays. The data of this study were taken from the published short stories (i.e. Mga Piling Kuwentong Sebuwano, 1986) cited in Lising (2004) and plays (i.e. Dulaang Hiligaynon, 1996) cited in Lising (2004). The results of this study revealed that all 15 Tagalog enclitic adverbs have counterparts in Cebuano and Hiligaynon except for the politeness markers such as 'ho' and 'po'.

However, this study used two different genres (i.e. short stories and plays). The results of this study could be more reliable and valid when only a single genre was used.

Zorc (2004) conducted a study on the semantic reconstruction in Austronesian linguistics. In this study, Zorc (2004) focused on the important points such as 1) the part was relatively silent, yet important steps have recently been made which should guide the researchers in the art and science of assigning meanings to etymon, 2) a full citation of semantic information for each entry should be done, 3) a careful investigation of the breadth and meaning of cognates within any given set should be conducted, 4) all information with synchronic values should be compared and contrasted within the semantic system of the languages shown, 5) having done steps 2, 3, and 4, the extrapolation of a common core could only be successfully undertaken, and 6) the results could be assessed through consulting current and past semantic theory.

In this study, Zorc (2004) also argued that the semantic relationships (e.g. metaphor) could be considered as checks and balances for the semantic reconstruction method. On the contrary, the process of showing a full citation from every dictionary entry was time-consuming for the researchers.

Although these studies dealt with the semantic aspects of language, none of these studies focused on the semantic change. Hence, a study on semantic change of Cebuano words should be conducted.

The semantic aspects of language have not been given much attention by the researchers. Zorc (2004) argued that semantics was considered outside the domain of most formal linguistic analysis. Ward (1971) who conducted a bibliographic survey of the Philippine linguistic studies also found that no studies have been conducted concerning the semantic change in Cebuano. Campbell (1998) and Crowley (1997) added that the semantic aspects of language were overlooked by many of the researchers in historical linguistics. Thus, a study on the semantic change of Cebuano words should be conducted to fill this gap.

This paper attempted to determine and analyze the semantic change of the selected Cebuano words. Also, this paper aimed at determining the types of semantic change undertaken by the Cebuano words from the written texts and spoken data.

3. Methodology

The data were taken from *Bisaya*, a Cebuano-Bisaya magazine issued in 2004 and 2005. Twenty (20) words were chosen (i.e. 10 words from the short stories and feature articles of the authors residing in Cebu province to avoid lexical variation from the other Cebuano-speaking communities and 10 words from the spoken discourse). The list of words from the spoken language was assumed to be used by the Cebuano speakers who are assumed to be aged 15-40 years old living within Cebu province. Textual analysis was used in this study because the data were based on the magazine named *Bisaya*. Word is the unit of analysis since only the Cebuano words that underwent semantic change were chosen.

In analyzing the types of semantic change, the classifications of Campbell (1998), and Crowley (1997) were used. To validate the reason in using a metaphor in writing Cebuano literature such as short stories and feature articles, five (5) informants were asked about their personal reasons in using a metaphor in writing short stories and feature articles. Three informants were Cebuano writers of short stories and feature articles and two informants were writers of Filipino short stories. A consultant who was a student taking up Doctor of Arts in Languages and Literature at De La Salle University – Manila was also chosen to make the analysis of the data more reliable and valid.

4. Results and Discussion

This section focuses on the semantic change of the selected Cebuano words from the written texts and spoken data. Examples of the data would be shown before the presentation of the data.

Examples of Metaphor

Written Text

      Originally, *higante* only refers to the large creature. Its meaning is compared to the well-known writers as in (1).

(1) **higante** sa   natad sa   panulat (Vaño, 2004, p. 5)
    giant   LCV field LCV writing
    'giant in the field of writing'

Spoken Language

      The word *uk-uk* previously refers to the cockroach only. The characteristic of the person who is shy is associated with the cockroach.

(2) Nauwaw ang **uk-uk**
    ashamed ang cockroach
    'The cockroach is ashamed'

Examples of Widening

Written Text

      The word *atakehon* deriving from the word 'attack' in English means 'to siege' has increased its meaning when it is used to describe a person who has a heart ailment.

(3) **atakehon** sa   sakit   sa   kasingkasing (Lape, 2004, p. 11)
    attack   LCV the ailment LCV heart
    'will have heart attack'

Spoken Language

      Kodak is originally a brand name of the camera. Currently, it is used to refer to a camera in general by some Cebuano speakers.

(4) **kodak** (spoken language)
    'a brand name of a camera *Kodak'* → 'camera in general'

      Table 1 presents the types of semantic change of the selected Cebuano words.

Table 1. Types of Semantic Change

Data	Types of Semantic Change												Σ
	B	M	N	BI	S	L	ME	SY	D	E	EU	H	
Written	4	6	0	0	0	0	0	0	0	0	0	0	10
%	40%	60%	0%	0%	0%	0%	0%	0%	0%	0%	0%	0%	100%
Spoken	7	3	0	0	0	0	0	0	0	0	0	0	10
%	70%	30%	0%	0%	0%	0%	0%	0%	0%	0%	0%	0%	100%

Legend: B – broadening   M – metaphor   N – narrowing   BI – birfurcation
         S – shift   L – litotes   ME – metonymy   SY – synechdoche
         D – degeneration E – elevation   EU – euphemism   H – hyperbole

The data on Table 1 revealed that the Cebuano words underwent semantic change in written and spoken data differently. With regard to the data taken from Bisaya magazine, metaphor (70%) was commonly-used while in the words based on the spoken data, widening (60%) was frequently-used.

Based on the data from *Bisaya*, metaphor was frequently-used because Cebuano writers most likely used figurative speech such as metaphor in capturing the attention and building the readers' interest. The Cebuano writers who were interviewed also used metaphors to let the readers understand the text easily, to show the relationship that exists between the people, to raise a higher level of thinking, and to clearly express the ideas.

This study supports Campbell's (1998) theories of linguistic change that refers to the external factors such as the expressive uses of language, and the positive and negative social evaluations.

Concerning the spoken language, widening was the dominant semantic change. This result could be attributed to the Cebuano speakers' expressive use of the language by broadening the original meaning of the word into a more expressive way of conveying the message to the listeners. Language contact (e.g. Spanish colonization which caused the borrowing of the word *chica*), social conventions (e.g. *papa*), technology (e.g. *Kodak*), religion (e.g. *Judas*), expressive use of language (i.e. *berde ug dugo*) could account for the linguistic change among the Cebuano words.

Furthermore, based on the analyzed words from Bisaya magazine, all selected words underwent semantic change through widening due to Cebuano itself since Cebuano language is playful and rich in providing meanings of the words used in written language in order to be appreciated by the readers of any literary works.

On the one hand, the two (2) analyzed Cebuano words which were evident in the spoken language such as 'berde' (i.e. is derived from the Spanish word 'verde') which means 'green', that is, an example of metaphor in spoken language; and the word 'magtsika'
(i.e. is derived from the Spanish word 'chica' which means 'girl') that demonstrates broadening
(i.e magtsika ta which means 'let's talk') underwent semantic change because of Spanish-
speaking colonizers who first introduced Spanish to the Cebuano speakers in Cebu province.
To illustrate, instead of focusing on the literal meaning of the color green in the word 'berde' in the phrase 'berde ug dugo', the meaning was changed into 'gay' or 'homosexual'.
Hence, broadening and metaphor were the frequently-used types of semantic change of the selected Cebuano words found in the written text and spoken speech.

4. Conclusions

In determining the types of semantic change of the selected words in Cebuano, the results revealed that in the written text, metaphor was frequently used while broadening was the predominant type of semantic change in the spoken language.

Metaphor was predominantly used by the Cebuano writers to clearly express the ideas, let the readers clearly understand their points, and raise the readers' thinking into a higher level.

Broadening was usually used in the spoken data due to various reasons such as language contact, social conventions, technology, religion, and expressive use of language. However, this study only used the twenty (20) selected Cebuano words as the data for the analysis. A replication of this study is recommended using discourse analysis of the spontaneous speech of the Cebuano speakers who interact with their fellow native speakers of Cebuano to validate the results of this study.

Hence, this study is consistent with Campbell (1998) and Crowley (1997) studies that metaphor and broadening are the common types of semantic change. However, this study did not provide evidence of the other types of semantic change due to the limited number of Cebuano words.

List of References

Adeva, F. M. 2005. Mga semantic koreleyt ng pagkatransitibo sa mga kwentong Sebwano. *Philippine Journal of Linguistics, 36,* 101- 156.

Bloomfield, L. 1933. *Language.* New York: Holt, Rinehart, and Winston.

Campbell, L. 1998. *Historical linguistics*: *An introduction.* London: Edinburgh University Press.

Crowley, T. 1997. *An introduction to historical linguistics.* Oxford: Oxford University Press.

Flores, O. 2005. Ulahing panag-uban. *Bisaya,* February 2: 17 & 23.

Gallardo, A. 2004. Pres. GMA, gipalabi ang usa ka kinabuhi kaysa mga pagsaway ug kaakohan sa America ug ubang nasod. *Bisaya* September 1:10.

Gonzalez, A. 2004. Applied linguistics and language teaching in the Philippines: Theory and implications. *Philippine Journal of Linguistics, 35,* 69-74.

Lape, E. 2004a. Ang biyahi sa kasingkasing nga nangita sa matuod nga kalipay. *Bisaya* December 22:3-15.

__________. 2004). Unsay purohan karong eleksiyon sa mga artistang kandidato. *Bisaya* February 4:10.

Lising, L. 2004. A comparative analysis of enclitic adverbs in Cebuano and Hiligaynon. *Tanglaw, 10,* 77- 98.

Monternel, F. 2004a. Nganong dunay mga tinagoan sa kinabuhi nga dili mapasabot sa tawhanong kaalam? Unsa ba gayoy misteryo sa kamatayon sa usa ka tawo? *Bisaya* November 3:11-17.

__________. 2004b. Pagduaw. *Bisaya,* November 3: 11.

Trask, R. 1994. *Language change.* London: Routledge.

Reyes, G. 2004a. Ang iring u gang kagabhion. *Bisaya* December 1:3.

__________. 2004d. May baybayon ang pikas bahin sa lawod. *Bisaya* February 11:3.

Vaño, R. 2004. Hinulamang kadaogan. *Bisaya* December 15:4-5.

Ward, J. 1971. Philippine linguistic studies: A bibliographic survey of the coverage in the literature. *Philippine Journal of Linguistics, 2,* 91-115.

Wolff, J. 2001. *Cebuano*. In Jane Gary and Carl Rubino. (Eds.). *Facts about he world's languages*. New York City: New England Publishing Associates, Inc.

Ybañez, J. 2004. Pinaskohan. *Bisaya*, December 29: 11.

Zorc, R. D. (2004). Semantic reconstruction in Austronesian linguistics. *Philippine Journal of Linguistics, 35*, 1-21.

On Japanese Desiderative Constructions [*]

Akira Ohtani [ab] and Mark Steedman [a]

[a]School of Informatics, University of Edinburgh,
Informatics Forum, 10 Crichton Street, Edinburgh EH8 9AB, Scotland, UK
[b]Faculty of Informatics, Osaka Gakuin University,
2-36-1 Kishibe-minami, Suita, Osaka 564-8511, Japan
{aotani, steedman}@inf.ed.ac.uk

Abstract. This paper describes desiderative constructions in Japanese with the main focus on *ta(i)* 'want' desideratives. In spite of the morphological one-word status, desiderative constructions have been claimed to have a complex structure at some abstract level of representation. We claim that there are two types of desideratives, and that their predicates have different lexical representations within the framework of Combinatory Categorial Grammar. Building on the proposed analysis, we also discuss the difference between the two types of desideratives in terms of adverbial modification and passivizability.

Keywords: Japanese Desideratives, *Ta(i)* 'want' Morpheme and Particle, Adverbial Modification, Passivizability, Combinatory Categorial Grammar (CCG)

1. Introduction

Ranging across a number of differing expressions in differing languages, there are various constructions described as complex predicates. Japanese also abounds in such predicates, which consist of a stem verb or gerundive expression followed by another morpheme. Passives and causatives, for example, have been a focus of attention in many linguistic studies. However, only few attempts have so far been made at desideratives by comparison. In this paper we conduct a detailed examination of desiderative constructions in Japanese with the main focus on the suffix, *ta(i)* 'want'.

Ta(i) 'want' is suffixed to a stem verb and forms an adjective as exemplified in (1):

(1) Boku-wa eego-{ga/wo}   hanasi-tai.
    I-TOP   English-NOM/ACC speak-want
    'I want to speak English.'

The active counter part for (1) is the following (2):

(2) Boku-wa eego-{*ga/wo}   hanasi-ta.
    I-TOP   English-NOM/ACC speak-PAST
    'I spoke English.'

As shown in (1), the object argument of the stem verb can be marked with either nominative *ga* or accusative *wo*, though the stem verb originally marks its object by only accusative as in (2).

---

[*] We are indebted to two anonymous PACLIC reviewers and Paul Crook for their invaluable comments on an earlier version of this paper. Our thanks also go to Mr. Yoshiyasu Shirai, the president of Osaka Gakuin University. All remaining inadequacies are our own.

22nd Pacific Asia Conference on Language, Information and Computation, pages 290–301

We call the type with nominative object *ga*-desiderative, and the type with accusative object *wo*-desiderative.

One question here is why the object of desiderative construction can be marked with either nominative or accusative. Under the previous approaches based on series of transformations or movements, the desideratives have been claimed to have different complex structures at some abstract level of derivation or representation. However, there are some data that cannot be accounted for in terms of the only structural distinction.

In this paper we discuss the syntactic and semantic properties of desideratives with the main focus on *ta(i)* 'want', show the lexical representation of the suffix, and answer to the question.

2. Previous Analyses and Adverbial Modification

Kuno treats *ta(i)* as a sentential predicate (Kuno 1973) and then as a 'transitive' Deep Structure predicate (Kuno 1983). The latter predicate, for example, creates a biclausal control-type Deep Structure, which is reduced to a monoclausal Surface Structure by Predicate Raising and Tree Pruning. Inoue (1989a, 1989b) and Nishigauchi (1993) propose that complex predicates such as desideratives are formed by the process of Verb Incorporation, following Baker (1988). Inoue, for example, proposes that the two desideratives share the same D-structure but two patterns of incorporation available for the structure derive two types of S-structure, whose object NP is marked with nominative and accusative, respectively.

There are, however, some problems in those analyses both empirically and theoretically. Putting aside the theoretical problems, we point out that all the above analyses fail to capture adverbial modification. See (3):[1]

(3) Boku-wa { asita-kara　　　 / tonari-no heya-de　　 } eego-{(?)?ga/wo} hanasi-tai.
　　　 I-TOP　　　 tomorrow-from　next-GEN room-LOC　English-NOM/ACC speak-want

　　　 'I want to speak English {from tomorrow / in the next room}.'

One prediction resulting from their view is that both *ga*-desideratives and *wo*-desideratives should allow the same range of time and place adverbials, *asita-kara* 'tomorrow-from' and *tonari-no heya-de* 'in the next room', to be modifiers of the stem verb. Such adverbials, however, are restricted in the case of *ga*-desideratives as shown in (3). Thus, the contrast on adverbial modification in (3) cannot be explained by their analyses.

Sugioka (1984) claims that *ta(i)* is suffixed to a V' as an instance of syntactic suffixation, thereby producing a *wo*-desiderative predicate. She also notes certain monoclausal properties of *ga*-desiderative predicates regarding adverbial modification. Adverbials that modify the stem verb alone cannot be placed between a nominative NP and a desiderative predicate as shown in (4) below:

(4) Boku-wa eego-{(?)*ga/wo} {asita-kara　　　 / tonari-no heya-de　　 } hanasi-tai.
　　　 I-TOP　　English-NOM/ACC tomorrow-from　next-GEN room-LOC　speak-want

　　　 'I want to speak English from tomorrow.'

This observation, together with other considerations, has led her to propose that the nominative case marking results from the restructuring of a complex complement structure to a simplex structure at Surface structures as in (5):[2]

---

[1] One reviewer pointed out that some native speakers judge (3) (and some other examples) as not so bad and the degree of naturalness of (3) is the same as that of (i) for such people.

(i) Boku-wa { asita-kara　　　 / tonari-no heya-de　　 } igirisu eego-{ga/wo}　　 hanasi-tai.
　　　 I-TOP　　 tomorrow-from　next-GEN room-LOC　BritishEnglish-NOM/ACC speak-want

　　　 'I want to speak British English {from tomorrow / in the next room}.'

The reviewer also offered the comment that the relevant difference between (3) and (i) is that the former tends not to carry focus, whereas the latter does. Although a kind of focus theory (of *ga*) may be responsible for the (un)naturalness of the examples, such a theory should be inquired with respect to pragmatics and is beyond our study that investigates the syntactic and semantic properties of desideratives.

[2] The case alternation of the desideratives can be accounted for in terms of 'reanalysis' (Kageyama 1982).

(5) a. [_A' [_V' [_NP eego-wo] [_V hanasi]] [_A ta(i)]]
    b. [_A' [_NP eego-ga] [_A' [_V hanasi] [_A ta(i)]]]

This restructuring converts a structure like (5a) into one like (5b), and therefore an adverbial cannot intervene between an NP and a stem verb.

There are also some empirical problems in her analysis. We only point out here that the analysis fails to capture adverbial modification. Compare (3) with (4), and note the position of adverbials as indicated in (6):[3]

(6) a. NP-wa (Adv) NP-wo (Adv) V-tai
    b. NP-wa (??Adv) NP-ga (*Adv) V-tai

The ungrammaticality of (3) also suggests that adverbials modifying the stem verb alone are restricted in the case of *ga*-desideratives. Note that such adverbials do not interrupt the surface restructuring shown in (5) because they do not intervene between a nominative object NP and a stem verb. Thus, the restructuring analysis cannot straightforwardly account for the restriction observed in (3).

Sugioka's analysis also misses the semantic restriction on the kind of verbs that can be used in *ga*-desideratives (Matsumoto 1996). See (7) below:

(7) a. Boku-wa hurui kitte-{ga/wo}   {atsume/koonyuu-si}-tai.
        I-TOP   old   stamp-NOM/ACC collect/buy-do-want

        'I want to collect/buy old stamps.'

    b. Boku-wa Naomi{(?)?ga/wo} {nagusame/tasuke}-tai.
        I-TOP   Naomi-NOM/ACC console/help-want

        'I want to console/help Naomi.'

    c. Boku-wa Naomi{*ga/wo}   machi-tai.
        I-TOP   Naomi-NOM/ACC wait-want

        'I want to wait for Naomi.'

In (7), while all of the desiderative predicates can take an accusative object, only some can take a nominative object. Matsumoto (1996) points out that those verbs whose meaning allow the object of the stem verb to be the target of the desire to obtain something (e.g., wanting to collect the old stamp means wanting the stamp itself) sound better with a nominative object than do other verbs. Within the restructuring account, it is not clear how such a restriction on *ga*-desiderative predicates could be stated.

For explaining the variable patterning of adjunct modification in (4), Sells (1990) proposes another account in which the two kinds of desiderative predicates may differ in the phrase structure position of their object NP, as shown in (8) below:

(8) a.

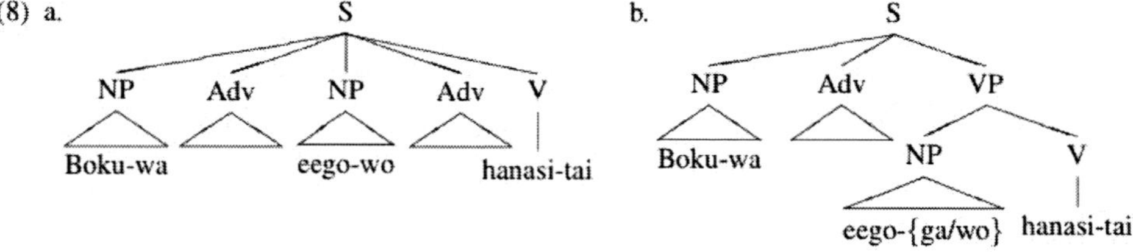

According to Sells's analysis, an accusative object NP in Japanese can appear in two different positions as shown in (8a) and (8b). A nominative object NP, on the other hand, can only appear within a VP governed by a stative predicate *hanasi-tai* 'want to speak' as in (8b). He also assumes that adjuncts such as *asita-kara* and *tonari-no heya-de* are S-level adjuncts and

---

[3] There is a slight difference in the acceptability of the adjuncts in (4) and (i):

(i) Asita-kara   (boku-wa) eego-{??ga/wo}   hanasi-tai.
    tomorrow-from I-TOP   English-NOM/ACC speak-want

    'From tomorrow, I want to speak English.'

Some adjuncts are more clearly ruled out. This can be attributed to a surface constraint disfavoring a long distance interruption between a nominative object and a predicate (Shibatani 1978).

suggests the reason why they cannot intervene between a nominative object and a stative predicate is because the nominative object occurs only under a VP.

Sells's analysis has the same problem as Sugioka's. The contrast found in (3) and (4) also cannot be attributed to constituency difference in (8), since the adjuncts that are excluded in the case of *ga*-desiderative in (4) cannot appear even in sentences where they do not intervene between a nominative object and a stative predicate as shown in (3).

Moreover, the following sentence shows that it is possible to place the adjuncts between a nominative object NP and a desiderative predicate: See (9):

(9) Boku-wa (hontooni) eego-ga   (hontooni) hanasi-tai.
    I-TOP   truly   English-NOM truly   speak-want

    'I want to speak English truly.'

Hontooni 'truly' in (9) modifies the whole desiderative predicate, while *asita-kara* 'from tomorrow' in (4) modifies the stem verb only. Thus, Sells's analysis cannot account for the restriction on adjunct modification.

In this section we have discussed that the nominative and accusative case distinctions of the object of desideratives plays a crucial role for licensing adjunct modification. We have also argued against several previous analyses since they cannot explain the behavior of adverbials.

3. *Gar(u)* Verbalization and Passivizability

3.1. Passivizability of Complex Predicates

Gar(u) is a verbal suffixal element that turns an adjective denoting 'an internal feeling' into a verbal expression which behaves as an ordinary predicate with the meaning 'showing the feeling x' (Sugioka 1984). Consider the following:

(10) a. Ken-wa Naomi-ga   urayamasii.
      Ken-TOP Naomi-NOM envious

      'Ken is envious of Naomi.'

    b. Ken-wa Naomi-wo urayamasi-gatte iru.
      Ken-TOP Naomi-ACC envious-VBZ   is

      'Ken shows the signs of being envious of Naomi.'

(11) a. Ken-wa Naomi-wo { sasot-ta.   / sasoi-tai   rasii. }
      Ken-TOP Naomi-ACC ask.out-PAST   ask.out-want seem

      'Ken asked out Naomi (e.g. for a date). / Ken seems to want to ask Naomi out.'

    b. Ken-wa Naomi-wo sasoi-ta-gatte   iru.
      Ken-TOP Naomi-ACC ask.out-want-VBZ is

      'Ken shows the signs of wanting to ask Naomi out.'

Since *ta(i)* is an adjectival suffix forming an adjective as *sasoi-ta(i)* 'want to ask out' in (11a), the newly created predicate with *gar(u)* also turns the adjective into the verb as *sasoi-ta-gar(u)* 'is envious of' in (11b) through verbalization.

With regard to *gar(u)*-verbalization, there is an interesting contrast which is first brought to attention by Sugioka (1984). Note that the verbalized predicates in (10b) and (11b) show the difference in passivizability. See (12) below:[4]

(12) a. Naomi-wa (Ken-ni) urayamasi-gar-arete iru.
      Naomi-TOP Ken-by envious-VBZ-PASS is

      'Naomi is being envied (by Ken).'

    b.*Naomi-wa (Ken-ni) sasoi-ta-gar-arete   iru.
      Naomi-TOP Ken-DAT ask.out-want-VBZ-PASS is

      'Naomi is being wanted (by Ken) to ask out.'

---

[4] Note that (12b) is acceptable as the so called adversative passive. In this paper, we make a distinction between the adversative passive and the direct passive, and the relevant passive is the latter. See also fn. 6.

One question here is why the sentence with "an adjective + *gar(u)*" in (10b) is passivizable as in (12a) while the one with "a desiderative + *gar(u)*" in (11b) is not as shown by the ungrammaticality of (12b).

The question here is, however, not so simple. There are verbalized desiderative predicates that can undergo passivization (Nishigauchi (1993), Matsumoto (1996)). Consider (13):

(13) a. Hurui kitte-wa   minna-ni   atsume-ta-gar-arete   iru.
         old   stamp-TOP everyone-by collect-want-VBZ-PASS is

         'Old stamps are in such a state that everyone wants to collect them.'

       b. Minna-wa   hurui kitte-wo   atsume-ta-gat-te iru.
          everyone-TOP old   stamp-ACC collect-want-VBZ is

          'Everyone wants to collect old stamps.'

(13a) is a passive counterpart of a desiderative in (13b). Thus, another question here is why (11b) cannot be passivized as shown in (12b) while (13b) can as shown in (13a).

3.2. Conditions on Passivization

As Nishigauchi (1993) argues, one crucial difference between (10a) and (11a) is that the complex predicate *urayamasii* 'envious' in (10a) is derived lexically by combining the verb *urayam* 'envy' with the 'adjectival morpheme' *-asi*, while the predicate *sasoi-tai* in (11a) is a syntactically complex predicate. The resulting expression of the former as a whole is syntactically a simple adjectival predicate *urayamasii*, and the verb *sasow* 'ask out (for a date)' and the desiderative adjectival element *ta(i)* originate as distinct syntactic elements.

For explaining the passivizability in (12), Nishigauchi claims that NP-movement is subject to a locality condition, which is claimed to be Subjacency defined on maximal projections. Consider below:

(14) a.   [$_{VP}$ NP$_i$ [$_{V'}$ [$_{VP}$ [$_{V'}$ [$_{AP}$ PRO [$_{A'}$ t_i urayam-asi]]] gar]] are]
       b. * [$_{VP}$ NP$_i$ [$_{V'}$ [$_{VP}$ [$_{V'}$ [$_{AP}$ PRO [$_{A'}$ [$_{VP}$ PRO [$_{V'}$ t_i sasoi]]] ta]]] gar]] are]

Except the VP headed by *gar(u)*,[5] the object NP-movement in (14a) skips only one projection, AP, while that in (14b) skips two projections, AP and VP headed by *sasoi*. Since NP-movement across one projection is permissible but that across two projections causes violation of Subjacency, only (14b) is ungrammatical.

One prediction resulting from Nishigauchi's account is that syntactically complex *ga-* and *wo*-desideratives should not allow their verbalized form to be passivized, since those have the uniform structure shown in (14b). However, this is the wrong prediction. Remember the semantic restriction on *ga*-desideratives in (7), repeated with slight modification as (15), and then compare them with their passive counterparts with *gar(u)* shown in (16):[6]

(15) a. Boku-ga hurui kitte-{ga/wo}   atsume-tai (koto)
         I-NOM   old   stamp-NOM/ACC collect-want the thing that

         '(that) I want to collect old stamps.'

       b. Boku-ga Naomi{(?)?ga/wo} nagusame-tai (koto)
          I-NOM   Naomi-NOM/ACC   console-want the thing that

          '(that) I want to console Naomi.'

       c. Boku-ga Naomi{*ga/wo}   machi-tai (koto)
          I-NOM   Naomi-NOM/ACC wait-want the thing that

          '(that) I want to wait for Naomi.'

---

[5] This VP does not count as a projection crossed by the object NP-movement. See Nishigauchi (1993).

[6] Another reviewer pointed out that the adversative passive may be more widespread than the direct passive in Japanese and passive sentences as in (12), (16), etc. get marginal readings on that basis. Our claim here is as follows: if the distribution of nominative object exemplified by judgment as in (15) is clear, (16a) is acceptable as the direct passive but unacceptable as the adversative passive because of the animacy requirement for its subject, and (16b) and (16c) do not make a sense as any passives, then a desiderative sentence that has a nominative object can have a direct passive counterpart. Thus, we get the condition in (17).

(16) a. Hurui kitte-ga   (minna-ni) atsume-ta-gar-arete   iru (koto)
        old   stamp-NOM everyone-by collect-want-VBZ-PASS is   the thing that
        '(that) old stamps are in such a state that everyone wants to collect them.'

    b.??Naomi-ga   (minna-ni) nagusame-ta-gar-arete   iru (koto)
        Naomi-NOM everyone-by console-want-VBZ-PASS is   the thing that
        '(that) Naomi is in such a state that everyone wants to console her.'

    c.*Naomi-ga   (minna-ni) machi-ta-gar-arete   iru (koto)
        Naomi-NOM everyone-by wait-want-VBZ-PASS is   the thing that
        '(that) Naomi is in such a state that everyone wants to wait for her.'

As (16) suggests, passivization of the whole verbalized desiderative predicate is possible only when the non-passivized plain desiderative can take a nominative object. In other words, *ga*-desiderative predicates but not *wo*-desiderative predicates are passivizable. Thus, the condition on passivization of desideratives is as follows:[7]

(17) Only the *ga*-desiderative is passivizable.

Now compare the grammaticality of (12b) with that of active counterpart whose object NP is marked with nominative *ga* and accusative *wo* shown in (18):

(18) Ken-ga   Naomi-{*ga/wo} sasoi-tai   (koto)
     Ken-NOM Naomi-NOM/ACC ask.out-want the thing that
     '(that) Ken wants to ask Naomi out.'

(18) cannot take a nominative object and therefore it is not passivizable.

It is worth noting that the object of (10a) occurs in the nominative case like other simple stative predicates. Thus, the contrast between (12a) and (12b) is accounted for by our claim that the passivization of the verbalized stative predicate is possible when the non-verbalized plain stative predicate can take a nominative object.

In this section we have discussed that the nominative and accusative distinction of the base object NP plays a crucial role for licensing the passivization of the verbalized desiderative predicates. That also accounts for the contrast between (12a) and (12b), because such a distinction also depends on the semantic restriction which is placed on the kind of predicate that can have a nominative-marked object.

4. Lexical and Syntactic Desideratives

In this section we seek the answer to the following questions posed in the previous sections examining how the desiderative constructions can be dealt with within the framework of Combinatory Categorial Grammar (CCG) (Steedman 1996, 2000).

(19) a. Why is the object of desideratives able to be marked with either nominative or accusative?
        (in Section 1)

     b. Why is the range of some adverbials restricted in *ga*-desideratives, but not in *wo*-desideratives?
        (in Section 2)

     c. Why are the sentences with "an adjective + *ta(i)*" passivizable while the certain sentences
        with "a desiderative + *ta(i)*" not? (in Section 3)

To answer the first question in (19a), we propose two types of predicates with desiderative constructions, i.e., *ga*-desiderative and *wo*-desiderative constructions in Japanese. These desideratives are correlated with the difference not only in the case marking of the object but also in a number of differences that we have shown in the previous sections. Based on those data, we discuss the lexical entries and the derivations for *ta(i)* 'want' in the following sections.

4.1.Lexical Entries of Desiderative Suffix *Ta(i)*

We claim that *ga*-desideratives are derived via lexical operations with the morpheme *ta(i)* where the crucial operations are the change of the value of case feature of the object NP, the value of

---

[7] It is worth noting that the syntactic condition in (17) is also related with the semantic constraint on *ga*-desideratives discussed in Section 2. See (7) and the following discussion.

sentential feature and semantics of the original predicate. The following is the lexical entry that we propose for such a derivational morpheme:

(20) The Morpheme *-ta(i)* for *Ga*-Desideratives:

$$-ta(i) := ((S_{[+stative]} \backslash NP_{nom}) \backslash NP_{nom}) \backslash ((S_{[-stative]} \backslash NP_{nom}) \backslash NP_{acc})$$
$$: \lambda P_{tv} \lambda x \lambda y \; want'(P'_{tv} xy)x$$

See the following derivation, where the input verb is *hanas(u)* 'speak':

(21) a. $hanas(u) := (S_{[-stative]} \backslash NP_{nom}) \backslash NP_{acc} : \lambda x \lambda y \; speak' xy$
     $hanasi - ta(i) := (S_{[+stative]} \backslash NP_{nom}) \backslash NP_{nom} : \lambda x \lambda y \; want'(speak' xy)x$

   b. Boku ga eego ga   hanasi − tai

$$\frac{\displaystyle \frac{\displaystyle NP_{nom} \quad NP_{nom} \quad (S\backslash NP_{nom})\backslash NP_{nom}}{S\backslash NP_{nom}}{}^{<}}{S}{}^{<}$$

The valence is not affected by the derivation but the object NP is marked with nominative for the lexically derived predicate. The change of the value of sentential feature tentatively referred to as [+/-stative] is important. The feature indicates the stativity referring to the semantics of the predicate.

In Japanese, an object NP of stative predicates is generally marked with nominative:

(22) a. Boku-wa eego-{ga/*wo}   wakaru.   (pure predicate)
      I-TOP   English-NOM/ACC understand

     'I understand English.'

   b. Ken-wa Naomi-{ga/*wo} urayamasii.   (lexically derived predicate)
     Ken-TOP Naomi-NOM/ACC envious

     'Ken is envious of Naomi.'

In the previous sections, we also argued that the nominative case marking of an object in desiderative constructions is restricted to be the object of the stem verb that can be the target of *the desire to obtain something*. The pattern appears here is determined by the stativity of the predicate, and thus we claim that the generalization for the nominative marking of an object in Japanese is as follows:

(23) An object is marked with nominative if and only if it is subcategorized for by a stative predicate.

(23) is certainly consistent with the obligatory nominative case marking of the object of stative predicates as in (22).

In contrast with *ga*-desideratives, *wo*-desideratives involve syntactic embedding. Namely, the desiderative suffix *ta(i)* of the *wo*-desiderative functions as a word with its own lexical contents. The following is the relevant part of the lexical entry and the derivation of the *wo*-desiderative with the syntactic particle *ta(i)*:

(24) The Particle *ta(i)* for *Wo*-Desideratives:

$$ta(i) := (S_{[+stative]} \backslash NP_{nom}) \backslash (S_{[-stative]} \backslash NP_{nom}) : \lambda P_{iv} \lambda x \; want'(P'_{iv} x)x$$

(25) Boku ga eego wo   hanasi   tai

$$\frac{\displaystyle \frac{\displaystyle \frac{\displaystyle NP_{nom} \quad NP_{acc} \quad (S\backslash NP_{nom})\backslash NP_{acc}}{S\backslash NP_{nom}}{}^{<} \quad (S\backslash NP_{nom})\backslash(S\backslash NP_{nom})}{S\backslash NP_{nom}}{}^{<}}{S}{}^{<}$$

We propose that the *wo*-desiderative suffix is a predicate subcategorizing for one NP and a VP, i.e., $S\backslash NP_{nom}$. The embedded VP intuitively corresponds to a sentence headed by the stem verb. The reason for positing a VP-embedding structure instead of a S-embedding is the facts that the former is not available for passivization. Here we do not go into the detail of the passive morpheme and particle but the point is that there is no accessible object NP which is promoted by passivization once $S\backslash NP_{nom}$ is derived with *ta(i)*. Thus, the *wo*-desiderative has no passive counterparts.

One of the crucial points of our approach concerns the advantage of CCG as a lexical grammar formalism. Because of the way pieces of lexical information are put together in constructing successively larger linguistic objects, when the *wo*-desiderative particle *ta(i)* is combined with its VP-complement, the information about the stem verb is supplied. Notice that the semantics in (25) is identical to that of the output of the *ga*-desiderative in (21b) at the end of derivation.

4.2. Adverbial Modification and Complex Constituency

As shown in Section 2, some adverbials are restricted in the case of *ga*-desideratives. *Wo*-desideratives, on the other hand, do not have such a restriction. We have discussed the differing patterns of adverbial modification in the two types of desiderative constructions. This provides support for our analysis in which the two types of desiderative derivation exist. The crucial data is repeated below:

(26) Boku-wa { asita-kara   / tonari-no heya-de   / Naomi-ga   ki-tara   }
         I-TOP   tomorrow-from next-GENroom-LOC   Naomi-NOM come-when

         eego-{(?)?ga/wo} hanasi-tai.
         English-NOM/ACC speak-want

         'I want to speak English {from tomorrow / in the next room / when Naomi comes}.'

(3), repeated as (26) with additional data *Naomi-ga ki-tara* 'when Naomi comes' suggests that both adverbials and an adverbial clause are acceptable in the case of *wo*-desideratives but not *ga*-desideratives.

Note that the acceptability of adverbial modification is also observed in the case of non-stative predicate *hanasi-masu* 'speak'. See (27) below:

(27) Boku-wa { asita-kara   / tonari-no heya-de   / Naomi-ga   ki-tara   }
         I-TOP   tomorrow-from next-GENroom-LOC   Naomi-NOM come-when

         eego-wo   hanasi-masu.
         English-ACC speak-POLITE

         'I will speak English {from tomorrow / in the next room / when Naomi comes}.'

We claim the acceptability found in these data can be attributed to the compatibility of time and place adverbials with non-stative predicates and the complex constituency of *wo*-desideratives. Since the predicate of *ga*-desiderative is lexically derived with the stative specification, it is not compatible with such adverbials. The predicate of *wo*-desiderative, on the other hand, maintains non-stative stem verb in the embedded VP and the adverbials can modify it although desiderative *ta(i)* itself is stative.

Then, consider the difference between (26) and (28):

(28)   a. Boku-wa hontooni eego-{ga/wo}   hanasi-tai.
          I-TOP   truly   English-NOM/ACC speak-want
          'I want to speak English truly.'

       b. Boku-wa hontooni eego-wo   hanasi-masu.
          I-TOP   truly   English-ACC speak-POLITE
          'I will speak English truly.'

The adverb *hontooni* 'truly' in (9), repeated as (28a) can modify both the stem *hanasi* 'speak' and *ta(i)* 'want' and hence the *ga*-desiderative of (28a) is acceptable, while the adverbials in (26) is intended to modify only the stem.

This is the reason for the difference between *ga*-desideratives and *wo*-desideratives in terms of adverbial modification, and this is the answer to the second question in (19b).

4.3. Gar(u)-Verbalization and Passivization

This section is devoted to answer to the third question in (19c) examining *gar(u)*-verbalization and passivization. The objects of the verbalized adjective in (29b) and desiderative in (30b) obligatorily occur in the accusative below:

(29) a. Ken-ga   Naomi-{ga/*wo} urayamasikat-ta (koto)
Ken-NOM Naomi-NOM/ACC envious-PAST   the thing that
'(that) Ken was envious of Naomi.'

b. Ken-ga   Naomi-{*ga/wo} urayamasi-gat-ta.   (koto)
Ken-NOM Naomi-NOM/ACC envious-VBZ-PAST the thing that
'(that) Ken showed the signs of being envious of Naomi.'

(30) a. Boku-ga Naomi-{*ga/wo} machi-takat-ta   (koto)
I-NOM   Naomi-NOM/ACC wait-want-PAST the thing that
'(that) I wanted to wait for Naomi.'

b. Boku-ga Naomi-{*ga/wo} machi-ta-gat-ta   (koto)
I-NOM   Naomi-NOM/ACC wait-want-VBZ-PAST the thing that
'(that) I showed the signs of waiting for Naomi.'

It is also worth noting that *gar(u)* is also attached to intransitive verbs. See below:

(31) a. Boku-wa samukat-ta.
I-TOP   cold-PAST
'I was cold.'

b. Boku-wa samu-gat-ta.
I-TOP   cold-VBZ-PAST
'I showed the signs of being cold.'

Based on these observation, we claim that *gar(u)*-verbalized forms are derived by lexical operations with the following derivational morphemes:

(32) a. The Morpheme -*Gar(u)* for Verbalization   (for Transitive):
$$-gar(u) := ((S_{[-stative]} \backslash NP_{nom}) \backslash NP_{acc}) \backslash ((S_{[+stative]} \backslash NP_{nom}) \backslash NP_{nom})$$
$$: \lambda P_{tv} \lambda x \lambda y \ show\_signs\_of'(P'_{tv} xy)x$$

b. The Morpheme -*Gar(u)* for Verbalization   (for Intransitive):
$$-gar(u) := (S_{[-stative]} \backslash NP_{nom}) \backslash (S_{[+stative]} \backslash NP_{nom})$$
$$: \lambda P_{iv} \lambda x \ show\_signs\_of'(P'_{iv}x)x$$

In (32), the valence of stem verb is not affected by the morphemes but the object NP is marked with accusative for a lexically derived predicate. The change of the value of sentential feature is specified as non-stative.

Next let us see how the derivational morphemes in (32) change the lexical entries of the predicates in (29b) and (30b):

(33) a. $urayamasii := (S_{[+stative]} \backslash NP_{nom}) \backslash NP_{nom} : \lambda x \lambda y \ be\_envious\_of'xy$
$urayamasi - garu := (S_{[-stative]} \backslash NP_{nom}) \backslash NP_{acc}$
$\quad : \lambda x \lambda y \ show\_signs\_of'(be\_envious\_of'xy)x$

b. Ken ga Naomi wo urayamasi $-$ gat $-$ ta

$\overline{NP_{nom}}$	$\overline{NP_{acc}}$	$\overline{(S \backslash NP_{nom}) \backslash NP_{acc}}$

$$\frac{\qquad\qquad\qquad\qquad}{S \backslash NP_{nom}}<$$
$$\frac{\qquad\qquad\qquad\qquad}{S}<$$

(34) a. $ta(i) := (S_{[+stative]} \backslash NP_{nom}) \backslash (S_{[-stative]} \backslash NP_{nom}) : \lambda P_{iv} \lambda x \ want'(P'_{iv}x)x$
$ta - garu := (S_{[-stative]} \backslash NP_{nom}) \backslash (S_{[-stative]} \backslash NP_{nom})$
$\quad : \lambda P_{iv} \lambda x \ show\_signs\_of'(want'(P'_{iv}x)x)x$

b. Ken ga Naomi wo   machi $ta - gat - ta$

$\overline{NP_{nom}}$	$\overline{NP_{acc}}$	$\overline{(S \backslash NP_{nom}) \backslash NP_{acc}}$	$\overline{(S \backslash NP_{nom}) \backslash (S \backslash NP_{nom})}$

$$\frac{\qquad\qquad\qquad\qquad}{S \backslash NP_{nom}}<$$
$$\frac{\qquad\qquad\qquad\qquad}{S \backslash NP_{nom}}<$$
$$\frac{\qquad\qquad\qquad\qquad}{S}<$$

The remarkable difference on the derivations between (33) and (34) is the valence of the matrix predicate. The former *urayamasi-gar(u)* involves an accusative NP, but the latter *ta-gar(u)* does not. It is also involved in the embedded predicate *machi*.

Based on this difference, we can account for the difference between *ga*-desideratives and *wo*-desideratives in terms of passivizability. Since *gar(u)*-verbalization in the case of both stative predicate and *ga*-desideratives take a lexically derived predicate, the whole complex predicate can be passivized through the promotion of the object NP of the predicates. *Wo*-desideratives, on the other hand, involve VP-embedding structure. The object NP cannot be the target of the passivization, since it is located within the valence of embedded stem verb where the passive morpheme or particle cannot access. This is why the passivizability difference exists.

5. Some Implications of the Present Approach

5.1. The Range of Adverbials and Monoclausality

One prediction resulting from our approach is that simple stative predicates should allow the same range of adverbials as *ga*-desideratives. In Section 2, we discussed that adverbials modifying the stem verb alone are restricted in the case of *ga*-desideratives. The crucial data is repeated below:[8]

(35) a.(?)* Boku-wa eego-ga   { asita-kara   / tonari-no heya-de} hanasi-tai.
         I-TOP   English-NOM   tomorrow-from   next-GEN room-LOC speak-want

   'I want to speak English {from tomorrow / in the next room}.'

   b.??{ Asita-kara   / tonari-no heya-de} boku-wa eego-ga   hanasi-tai.
         tomorrow-from   next-GEN room-LOC I-TOP   English-NOM speak-want

   'I want to speak English {from tomorrow / in the next room}.'

This restriction is also observed in the case of simple stative predicate. See (36) below:

(36) a.*Ken-wa Naomi-ga   { asita-kara   / tonari-no heya-de} urayamasii.
        Ken-TOP Naomi-NOM   tomorrow-from   next-GEN room-LOC envious

   'Ken is envious of Naomi {from tomorrow / in the next room}.'

   b.*{ Asita-kara   / tonari-no heya-de} Ken-wa Naomi-ga   urayamasii.
        tomorrow-from   next-GEN room-LOC Ken-TOP Naomi-NOM envious

   'Ken is envious of Naomi {from tomorrow / in the next room}.'

The unacceptability shown in (36) also cannot be attributed to constituency as Sugioka (1984) and Sells (1990) assume because the predicate has the status of a single word syntactically. In addition to this, time and place adverbials cannot co-occur with stative predicate in general. Thus, not only the nominative case-marking of an object NP but also the incompatibility of such adverbials support the analysis that the *ga*-desiderative sentence involves a lexically derived stative predicate, which consists of the derivational morpheme *ta(i)*.

The restriction on adverbial modification of the stem verb is also reflected in the lack of the ambiguity of adverbial scope interpretation in *ga*-desideratives (Matsumoto 1996). Consider (37) below:

(37) a. Boku-wa zutto   sono ko-wo   dakisime-takat-ta.
        I-TOP   for.a.long.time the   child-ACC embrace-want-PAST

   '(i) For a long time, I wanted to embrace the child.'
   '(ii) I wanted to embrace the child for a long time.'

   b. Boku-wa zutto   sono ko-ga   dakisime-takat-ta.
        I-TOP   for.a.long.time the   child-NOM embrace-want-PAST

   '(i) For a long time, I wanted to embrace the child.'

The *wo*-desiderative sentence in (37a) is ambiguously interpreted, with *zutto* 'for a long time' modifying either the desire to embrace the child, interpreted as (i) or the action of embracing a child, interpreted as (ii). The *ga*-desiderative sentence in (37b), on the other hand, does not allow such ambiguity. The time adverb can only be interpreted as indicating the duration of the desire to embrace the child, interpreted as (i).

---

[8] Compared with (35b), (35a) sounds worse because of a surface constraint disfavoring a long distance interruption between a nominative object and a stative predicate. See fn. 3.

5.2. Constituency Tests

Japanese has a structure corresponding to English *do*-support. It is triggered by emphatic particle *mo* 'also'. *Mo* can be attached to the stem of desiderative predicate, but when this happens, an interesting difference turns up between *ga*- and *wo*-desideratives. See (38) below:

(38) a. Boku-wa kitte-{ga/wo}   atsume-tai-kedo,   okane-ga   nai.
       I-TOP   old   stamp-NOM/ACC collect-want-although money-NOM have.no

       'Although I want to collect old stamps, I have no money.'

    b. Boku-wa hurui kitte-{(?)?ga/wo} atsume-mo si-tai-kedo,   okane-ga   nai.
       I-TOP   old   stamp-NOM/ACC collect-also do-want-although money-NOM have.no

       'Although I also want to collect old stamps, I have no money.'

As shown in (38b), the emphatic particle *mo* and the supportive *s(u)* 'do' can intervene between the stem verb and the desiderative suffix only in the *wo*-desiderative.

The differing pattern of the verbal anaphora in the two types of desideratives also provides support for the analysis in which the two types of desiderative predicates exist. Consider (39):

(39) Boku-wa hurui kitte-{?ga/wo}   atsume-takat-ta.   Naomi-mo soo si-takat-ta   rasii.
    I-TOP   old   stamp-NOM/ACC collect-want-PAST Naomi-too so do-want-PAST seem

    'I wanted to collect old stamps, and Mary seems to have wanted to do so, too.'

The desiderative predicate with an accusative object, i.e., *wo*-desiderative in (39) allows the replacement of the complement predicate and its argument by *soo suru* 'do so', but this is not fully possible with those when there is a nominative object, i.e., the *ga*-desiderative.

Asymmetries in the two types of desideratives with these putative 'coordinated VPs' as in (40) provide further support for the present approach (Sugioka 1984):

(40) a.*Boku-wa [koohii-ga   non-de   ][keeki-ga   tabe]-tai.
      I-TOP   coffee-NOM drink-GER   cake-NOM eat-want

    b.*Boku-wa [koohii-ga   non-de   ][keeki-wo tabe]-tai.
      I-TOP   coffee-NOM drink-GER   cake-ACC eat-want

    c.?Boku-wa [koohii-wo non-de   ][keeki-ga   tabe]-tai.
      I-TOP   coffee-ACC drink-GER   cake-NOM eat-want

    d. Boku-wa [koohii-wo non-de   ][keeki-wo tabe]-tai.
      I-TOP   coffee-ACC drink-GER   cake-ACC eat-want

      'I want to drink coffee and eat cake.'

In (40) above, only *wo*-desideratives allow coordination.

The data (38)-(40) suggest that the *ga*-desiderative predicate as a whole is morphologically a single word where it is not possible to separate the two morphemes by inserting a particle, replacing and coordinating only its stem verb. The *wo*-desiderative, on the other hand, has no such restrictions. These observations support for the present analysis, whereby the *wo*-desiderative predicate subcategorizes for a syntactic complement structure, while the *ga*-desiderative predicate is a lexically derived word.

6. Concluding Remarks

The Japanese desiderative construction has been claimed to have a complex structure at some abstract level of the representation in spite of its morphological one-word status of the predicate. In this paper we have conducted a detailed examination of the constructions with the main focus on the suffix *ta(i)*, and then have made the argument that there are two types of *ta(i)*, a morpheme suffixed to the stem verb and a particle which adjoins to VP. The object argument of such complex predicates is marked with nominative *ga* or accusative *wo*, respectively. Building on the CCG analysis proposed, we also discussed the difference of *ga*- and *wo*-desideratives in terms of adverbial modification and passivizability. We believe that our study will be helpful to explore other complex predicates at which only few attempts have so far been made.

References

Baker, M. C. 1988. *Incorporation: A Theory of Grammatical Function Changing.* University of Chicago Press.

Inoue, K. 1989a. Shugo to Bun-koosei ('The Subject and Sentence Structure'). In K. Inoue, ed., *Nihon Bunpoo Shoo-jiten ('A Small Dictionary for Japanese Grammar')*, pp. 79-101. Taishukan, Tokyo..

Inoue, K. 1989b. Shugo no Imi-yakuwari to Kaku-hairetsu ('Semantic Roles of Subject and Case Arrangement'). In Kuno, S. and M. Shibatani, eds., *Nihongogaku no Shintenkai ('New Developments in Japanese Linguistics')*, pp. 130-147. Kuroshio Publishers, Tokyo.

Kageyama, T. 1982. Word Formation in Japanese. Lingua, 57, 215-258.

Kuno, S. 1973. *The Structure of the Japanese Language.* The MIT Press.

Kuno, S. 1983. *Sin-Nihon Bunpoo Kenkyuu ('New Study of Japanese Grammar')*. Taishukan, Tokyo. In Japanese.

Matsumoto, Y. 1996. *Complex Predicates in Japanese: A Syntactic and Semantic Study of the Notion 'Word'.* CSLI Publications.

Nishigauchi, T. 1993. Long Distance Passive. In N. Hasegawa, ed., *Japanese Syntax in Comparative Grammar*, pp. 79-114. Kuroshio Publishers, Tokyo.

Sells, P. 1990. VP in Japanese: Evidence from *-Te* Complements. In Hoji, H. ed., *Japanese/Korean Linguistics,* Vol.1, pp. 79-114. CSLI Publications.

Shibatani, M. 1978. *Nihongo no Bunseki: Seiseibunpoo no Hoohoo ('An Analysis of Japanese: The Method of Generative Grammar')*. Taishukan, Tokyo. In Japanese.

Steedman, M. 1996. *Surface Structure and Interpretation.* The MIT Press.

Steedman, M. 2000. *The Syntactic Process.* The MIT Press.

Sugioka, Y. 1984. *Interaction of Derivarional Morphology and Syntax in Japanese and English.* Ph.D. thesis, University of Chicago.

Generating Story Reviews Using Phrases Expressing Emotion

Hiroshi Ota and Kazuhide Yamamoto

Nagaoka University of Technology,
1603-1, Kamitomioka, Nagaoka, Niigata 940-2188 Japan
{ota, ykaz}@nlp.nagaokaut.ac.jp

Abstract. This paper presents a method for generating reviews of stories. In this work, we focus on generating sentences that include subjective expressions. First, we constructed lexicons using emotion-emerged expressions that are thought to be the origin of the emotional content. The lexicon consists of syntactic pieces that are proposed as units of syntactic structure to represent suitable units of expression for estimating emotions. We confirmed the effectiveness of the lexicons by estimating the emotional content of blog text. Second, we confirmed the relationship between the naturalness of the sentences and the coherence of the emotion it expresses. Finally, we proposed a method of review generation using the lexicons.

Keywords: emotion, syntactic piece, emotion-emerged expression(E3), review, language generation

1. Introduction

In many situations, we use subjective expressions that convey emotions, feelings and evaluations about someone or something. It is essential to be able to understand such expressions, and in particular, to be able to use them in language generation tasks. One kind of text that involves subjective expressions is a review of consumer goods and services. In this work, we focus on the task of generating review sentences.

This study considers emotional expressions as a subset of subjective expressions. Reviews of stories may include many emotional expressions that emerge in response to the story being reviewed. In this sense, we call the expressions of these emerging emotions 'emotion-emerged expressions' (hereafter, E3) in this paper. We first built lexicons for E3, and then made a prototype system to generate story reviews.

2. Related Studies

Sentence generation technology has been approached from the viewpoint of the semantic network (Ozaki et al., 1997) or lexical relations (Seki et al., 1999). However, subjective expressions have not been considered. Sentences should be coherent, as emotional coherence affects the naturalness of a sentence. Consider these three sentences:

- She receives a present that feels joyous.
- She receives a present that is sad.
- She receives a present that is afraid.

We can select the first sentence 'She receives a present that feels joyous.' as the most natural. In this study, we confirm the relationship between the naturalness of a sentence and the coherence of the emotion it expresses.

22nd Pacific Asia Conference on Language, Information and Computation, pages 302–310

Related studies on emotion analysis include those of Kozareva et al. (2007), Yang et al. (2007) and Mihalcea and Liu (2006). Kozareva et al. propose an emotional classification approach based on frequency and co-occurrence. They calculate an emotional score for each word using mutual information. A word can express several types of emotions, and we aim to compile these expressions for text generation.

Some methods are available for extracting sentences and paragraphs that have emotional content from the blog corpus. Yang et al. used an emoticon as a marker for emotional expression and extracted emotion expressing sentences. Mihalcea and Liu used blog tags such as 'happy' or 'sad' and extracted emotion expressing blogs. However, the tagged blog content that can be collected is limited. One characteristic of our method is considering words used not only in blog text but also in their titles.

Yang el al. built a lexicon of emotions, and Mihalcea and Liu compiled phrases identified as happiness factor. They formed lexicons from 1gram, 2gram or 3gram. We form lexicons from syntactic pieces (Aoki and Yamamoto, 2007). Our purpose is to generate a natural sentence that includes subjective phrases. Therefore, we use syntactic pieces that have structural information and generate sentences effectively.

3. Emotion-Emerged Expression Lexicons (E3 Lexicons)

This section presents now, we construct E3 lexicons that are collections of phrases associated with a certain emotion. We design the lexicons using blogs as a large corpus. Figure 1 illustrates the construction method. First, we identify blogs that express a certain emotion. Second, we form a model of classifier using these blogs. Third, the model estimates the emotional content of new blogs. Finally, we construct the E3 lexicons from these new blogs.

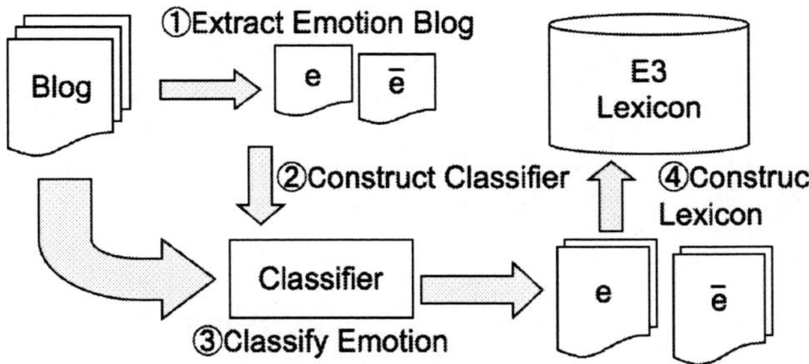

Figure 1: Construction process for an E3 lexicon

3.1. Emotional Word Lexicons

Before constructing the E3 lexicons, we prepared emotional word lexicons. Emotional words clearly represent an emotion; for example, a word 'glad' clearly represents a happy emotion. Therefore, the lexicons provide useful information for extraction of particular emotion expressing blogs(in section 3.2). Emotional words are collected by a human as follows. First, we give adjectives and adverbial words extracted from the IPA thesaurus to 5 examinees. The examinees select the emotion associated with the words from eight possible emotions. Those are defined by Plutchik (1960). We used the words for which there is more than 75% agreement. Table 1 shows the eight possible emotions and the number of words associated with each emotion.

Table 1: The number of words in each emotional word lexicon

Joy	sadness	acceptance	disgust	surprise	anticipation	fear	anger
67	100	6	302	28	14	31	6

For brevity, we treat three emotions, joy, sadness and fear, hereafter. We estimate that these three emotions don't very often co-occur. However, we must note that our method does not depend on the number of emotions.

3.2. Extraction of Emotion expressing Blogs

This section proposes a method for extracting blogs that have a particular emotion e. This method considers the words in the blog, from the title and the text. The title is a summary of the article. Our hypothesis is that a blog expresses emotion e when the title has words somehow associated with emotion e. In addition, the method considers words in the blog text. The blog has emotion e when the text contains words associated with emotion e in greater numbers than words in the lexicon of other emotions $\bar{e}$. $\bar{e}$ mean emotions other than e; when emotion e is sadness, emotions $\bar{e}$ are joy and fear. Thus, there are two requirements, below, for a blog to be considered as having emotion e.

Requirement 1: The title includes emotion-e word(s)
Requirement 2: The body includes emotion-e word(s) in greater numbers than words associated with other emotions $\bar{e}$

We performed a preliminary experiment to test the hypothesis. This experiment aimed at extracting blogs expressing sadness. The words in the lexicon sadness were used as emotion-e words, and those in the lexicons joy and fear as emotion-$\bar{e}$ words. We tried the method in 3 patterns: satisfying (1) only requirement 1, (2) only requirement 2 and (3) both requirements.

Table 2: Extraction of blogs expressing sadness

	Requirement 1	Requirement 2	Requirements 1 & 2
Accuracy (%)	50	60	85

This extraction experiment achieved 85% accuracy when both the requirements were satisfied. As a result, we regarded a blog as being an emotion-e blog when it satisfied both requirements 1 and 2.

3.3. Emotion Classifier Model

This section constructs the emotion classifier model. The classifier classifies the blog according to whether the blog text expresses the emotion-e or -$\bar{e}$. We propose the method for extracting emotion-e blogs in section 3.2. This method obtains good accuracy. However, most blogs fail to fulfil the two requirements. These blogs must be used if we wish to construct a large-scale lexicon(Construct method is written in section 3.4). We want to estimate for all blogs whether the blog emerge the emotion emotion-e or -$\bar{e}$. Therefore, we construct a classifier model by utilizing emotional blogs. This model is binary classifier. We should construct the model for each emotions; joy, sadness and fear. When constructing the model for sadness, emotion-e is sadness, and -$\bar{e}$ is joy and fear. Emotion-e and -$\bar{e}$ blogs, which are collected as described in section 3.2, were used as training data. For our experiments, we used TinySVM, a support-vector machine package. We adopt all the content words of the blogs as the features. Table 3 shows the result of 10-fold cross-validation.

Table 3: Evaluation of the emotion classifier model

	joy	**sadness**	**fear**
Number of Blog text	17270	10810	6460
Accuracy (%)	70.9	71.1	71.1

3.4. Constructing E3 Lexicons

This section proposes an automatic construction method for E3 lexicons. The lexicons are formed using syntactic pieces (Aoki and Yamamoto, 2007), which are defined as pairs consisting of a modifier and a modificand (modified entity) based on dependency analysis. A syntactic piece is the minimum unit of syntactic structure of an expression. This pair is expressed as follows.

syntactic piece : modifier => modificand

A syntactic piece has useful characteristics. In particular, it can deal with a chunk of meaning. Emotion may emerge from a phrase as follows:

・背筋が => こおる
　(a chill goes down one's spine)
・腰を => やる
　(cause low back pain)

These phrases are associated with fear, which cannot be associated with the individual words. Furthermore, this unit has structure, a characteristic that is effective in generating sentences. We adopt syntactic pieces for the lexicons in this task.

We collected syntactic pieces from emotion-e and -$\bar{e}$ blogs (all blogs were classified as either e or $\bar{e}$ by the classifier model) and assigned an emotion-e score to each one. The scoring method used the formula of Fujimura et al. (2004). According to Fujimura, a word that has positive semantic orientation should appear in text expressing a positive opinion. The same can be said even if we replace the positive opinion with emotion e. Furthermore, the same can be said even if we replace a word with a syntactic piece. Based on this hypothesis, we calculate the frequency differences for syntactic pieces between emotion-e and emotion-$\bar{e}$ blogs. In cases of the emotion-sadness score, syntactic pieces expressing sadness have a higher score because they are expected to occur more often in emotion-sadness blogs compared with emotion-joy and emotion-fear blogs. We calculate the emotion-e score as follows:

1) Extract all syntactic pieces from all blog text.
2) Count the occurrence rate of each of the syntactic pieces in emotion-$e/\bar{e}$ blogs.
3) Calculate the $score_e(piece)$ for each of the syntactic pieces with the following expression.

$$score_e(piece) = \frac{P_e(piece) - P_{\bar{e}}(piece)}{P_e(piece) + P_{\bar{e}}(piece)} \tag{1}$$

$$(-1 \leq score_e(piece) \leq 1)$$

where *piece* is a syntactic piece, $score_e(piece)$ is the emotion score of piece for emotion-e, $P_e(piece)$ is the probability of piece appearing in emotion-e blogs and $P_{\bar{e}}(piece)$ is the probability of piece appearing in emotion-$\bar{e}$ blogs.

4) Syntactic pieces that have a positive $score_e(piece)$ are added to the E3 lexicon of emotion-e.

By conducting this process, we can automatically construct the E3 lexicons. This method can be used any emotional classification system.

Table 4: The number of words in each E3 lexicon

joy	sadness	fear
327,702	37,439	13,238

3.5. Evaluation of E3 Lexicons

To evaluate the constructed E3 lexicons, we extracted 50 syntactic pieces from each of the E3 lexicons of joy, sadness and fear. Three examinees described the emotion of the syntactic pieces as RIGHT, WRONG or OTHER. The result is accepted, if 2 or all examinees agree. RIGHT means the lexicon's identification of the emotion and the judgement of the examinees agree. In the case of WRONG, the examinees judged the emotion to be different from the one in the lexicon. OTHER means 'neutral (no emotion)' or 'cannot evaluate'. 'cannot evaluate' means the syntactic piece does not provide sufficient information. One modified entity can't always keep the phrase. Table 5 shows the results of the evaluation. According to these results, the constructed lexicons include a few WRONG emotions. There are fewer WRONG emotions than RIGHT ones, indicating the accuracy of the lexicons. However, in many cases, a single E3 expression is not clearly associated with an emotion.

Table 5: Results of evaluation of the E3 lexicons

	joy	sadness	fear
RIGHT	19	8	7
WRONG	0	2	3
OTHER	27	35	30

We show a part of the evaluated result as follows:
・RIGHT
　joy: 喉を => 潤す
　　　(wet one's whistle)
　sadness: ツキが => ない
　　　　(get no luck)
・WRONG: The syntactic piece belongs in the sadness lexicon, but it was classed as joy.
　joy: 容疑者が => 逮捕される
　　　(crime suspect is arrested)

・OTHER

    sadness: 原因を => 調べる
        (examine its cause)

4. Generating Reviews

Figure 2 shows the process of review generation. The system collects material from the corpus. The collected reviews are used as templates to generate phrases. The system's input is syntactic piece, which it uses as a review target. The system decides the relevant emotion and selects a review that has same emotion as the target. Syntactic piece and template are fitted together as review sentence.

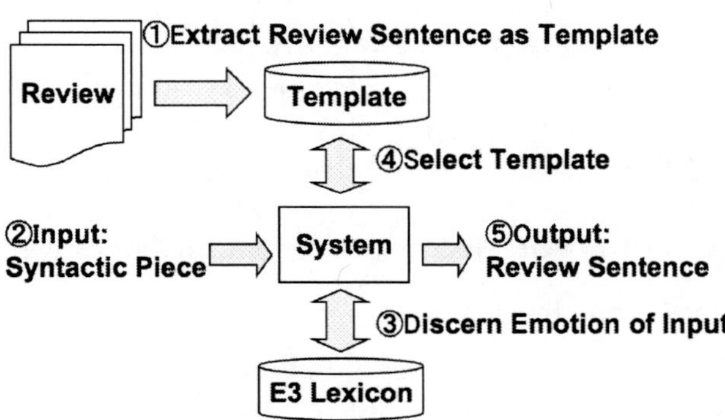

Figure 2: The review generation process

4.1. Review Sentences

In this paper, we define opinion sentences as reviews of stories, such as book or movie reviews. A review consists of four elements: attitude, nominative, object and reason (Nakayama et al., 2005). In their analysis, reviews almost always include the attitude, nominative and object. However, the nominative is not always apparent. Therefore, we regard attitude and object as the basic elements of a review. Nakayama et al. define a sub-element of object as scene, and a sub-element of attitude as emotion. In this study, we consider review sentences, which include object and attitude, especially scene and emotion. The following sentence is an example of a review sentence.

・別れの場面が悲しかった。
    (The parting scene is sad.)

Review sentences exist in review articles. We decide on a rule for extracting them heuristically; the rule is based on specific nouns, which exhibit the point of the scene in the review. '場面 (the scene)' is one of the specific nouns. In Japanese, the scene is written before the noun and the impression is written after the noun using a word expressing emotion. We extract the review sentences by the rule from Amazon customer reviews. Amazon customer reviews provide an easy-to-use review corpus. Of the categories used by Amazon, we selected the categories of books and DVDs. A review sentence is used as a template for generating text. Each review sentence includes an emotion word. We describe the requirements for a review sentence as follows:

・The review sentence has a specific noun that exhibits the scene: '場面(scene/locale)', 'シーン(scene)', 'ところ(where)' and 'くだり(line)'.

・The particle ('が', 'は' or 'で') are joined to specific nouns. The particles suggest the object.
・The specific noun modifies the emotion word.

Table 6 shows the number of review sentence templates for each of the emotions we consider. We also show examples of the collected review sentences that are used as templates.

Table 6: The number of review sentence templates for each emotion

joy	sadness	fear
987	105	49

・joy: バスでの掛け合いの場面が楽しい。
　　　(The scene of the dialogue on the bus is pleasant.)
・sadness: 誰も信じたくないというくだりは悲しいです。
　　　　(The scene where he said 'I do not believe anyone!' is sad.)
・fear: 刀でザックリのシーンはちょっと怖いですね。
　　　(The scene where they were 'slashed with a sword' is a bit scary.)

4.2. The Naturalness of the Review Sentences

We confirm the relationship between emotional coherence and the naturalness of a sentence. In this paper, we regard E3 as one scene. (We treat the accepted E3 elements in section 3.5.) That is, each E3 is associated with one emotion. Three review sentences are generated based on one scene, each containing a different emotion word (joy, sadness or fear). Each emotion is expressed by '喜ばしい(joyous)', '悲しい(sad)' or '恐い(scared)'. For example, the sentences in section 2 were generated by using the scene 'to receive a present'. We evaluate 90 sentences generated from 30 scenes: 30 sentences are emotionally coherent, and 60 sentences are incoherent. All the coherent sentences, but only 11 of the incoherent sentences, were evaluated as natural. This shows that coherence of emotion affects the naturalness of the sentence. Therefore, review sentences described in section 4.3 are generated from scenes and templates that agree emotionally.

4.3. Review Sentence Generation

To generate emotionally coherent review sentences, a 'scene' is input to the system to obtain a review sentence about the scene. A phrase from E3 is used to express the scene as a part of story. A review sentence is made from the phrase and the template, which have the same emotional content, as described in section 4.2. The review sentence is generated by the following processes:

1) Input the syntactic piece into the system.
2) Discern the emotion of input by E3 lexicons.
3) Select a review sentence template that has the same emotion as the E3 phrase.
4) In the selected template, replace the word before the specific noun phrase with the E3 phrase.
5) Output the resulting sentence as the review sentence.
We show examples of generated sentences below.

・Input syntactic piece (E3 phrase): メダルを逃す
　　　(miss the medal)
・Selected template: 涙をこらえるシーンは切なすぎる
　　　　(The scene where he holds back his tears is agonizing.)

・Output review sentence: <u>メダルを逃す</u>シーンは切なすぎる

(The scene where he <u>misses the medal</u> is agonizing.)

5. Discussions

5.1. Estimating Emotion in Blogs

This section confirms the effectiveness of the E3 lexicons by estimating the emotions expressed in blogs. We treat the emotion of sadness below. We selected 120 blogs, including 45 sad blogs, for which the emotional content is evaluated.

This experiment applies requirement 2 in section 3.2 using the E3 lexicons. That is, the text includes words from the E3 lexicon for emotion e in greater numbers than E3 lexicon words for other emotions. As a result, 20 of the 120 blogs were identified as sad, using the E3 lexicons. Of the 20 blogs, 14 are identified correctly, for an accuracy of 0.70. Moreover, the examined blogs included 3 that were not identified using the emotion lexicons. Therefore, the E3 lexicons have different characteristic compared with the emotion lexicons. The accuracy of 0.70 is not bad, however the E3 lexicons estimated 14 of 45; we obtained the recall of 0.31.

As a result, we can not say whether the E3 lexicons are good for estimating emotion, because the recall is low. However, the obtained result suggests the possibility of effective estimation when we use the E3 lexicons together with emotion lexicons.

5.2. Generated Review Sentences

Generated review sentences are evaluated as natural, because the template used was made from reviews that were collected by strict rules. The review template has emotion words, which are constructed in section 3.1. Emotion word lexicons express clear emotions that do not differ between examinees. Therefore, the collected reviews can be used as templates. Collected templates are nice; there is no incorrect. However, we have a problem. We cannot select the best template. We doesn't consider the selecting the template in this paper. Therefore, when input one syntactic piece, multiple reviews are generated, one for each template. Take the example of the following generated review.

・初戦を落とすシーンは<u>つらい</u>です。
   (The scene where he drops the 1st round is <u>heartbreaking</u>.)
・初戦を落とすシーンが<u>悲しい</u>です。
   (The scene where he drops the 1st round is <u>sad</u>.)

Both sentences are natural reviews. We cannot select the better one because we lack input information. In this experiment, input information is one syntactic piece containing only two segments. Therefore, the expressed scene is not clear. In future work, we will input multiple syntactic pieces and generate a review. Increasing the information should make the review target clear.

6. Conclusion

This paper presents a method for generating story reviews using emotion-emerged expressions (E3) that are thought to be the origin of the emotional content. In this work, we have confirmed that the coherence of emotions is an important factor in generating natural sentences. Future work will include increasing the information about the review target to generate more natural sentences.

We have also constructed E3 lexicons using blogs. The lexicons are made up of syntactic pieces that are proposed as units of syntactic structure to represent suitable units of expression for estimating emotions. We finally illustrate the possibility of effective estimation when we use the E3 lexicons together with emotion lexicons.

Tools and language resources

1) IPA Thesaurus, Ver.2.7.0, Matsumoto Lab., Nara Institute of Science and Technology. http://chasen.naist.jp/stable/ipadic
2) Amazon.co.jp. http://www.amazon.co.jp/
3) CaboCha, Ver.0.53, Matsumoto Lab., Nara Institute of Science and Technology. http://chasen.org/~taku/software/cabocha/
4) TinySVM, Ver.0.09, Matsumoto Lab., Nara Institute of Science and Technology. http://chasen.org/~taku/software/TinySVM/
5) livedoorBlog. http://blog.livedoor.com

References

Suguru Aoki and Kazuhide Yamamoto. 2007. Opinion extraction based on syntactic pieces. Proc. of PACLIC21, pages 76–86.

Shigeru Fujimura, Masashi Toyota, and Masaru Kitsuregawa. 2004. A consideration of extracting reputations and evaluative expressions from the web. Technical Report of The Institute of Electronics, Information and Communication Engineers, 104:141–146.

Zornitsa Kozareva, Borja Navarro, Sonia Vazquez, and Andres Montoyo. 2007. A headline emotion classification through web information. 4th International Workshop on Semantic Evaluations, pages 334–337.

Rada Mihalcea and Hugo Liu. 2006. A corpus-based approach to finding happiness. Proceedings of AAAI 2006 Spring Symposium on Computational Approaches to Analyzing Weblogs, pages 139–144.

Norio Nakayama, Kouji Eguchi, and Noriko Kando. 2005. Emotion expression model. 11th Annual Meeting of the Association for Natural Language Processing, pages 149–152. (in Japanese)

Syoutarou Ozaki, Sadao Kurohashi, and Makoto Nagao. 1997. Text generation using semantic network. IPSJ SIG Notes, 97(69):133–140.

Robert Plutchik. 1960. The multifactor-analytic theory of emotion. The Journal of Psychology, 50:153–171.

Yohei Seki, Tadashi Iijima, and Ken'ichi Harada. 1999. Semantic focus-driven sentence generation. IPSJ SIG Notes, 99(49):79–85. (in Japanese)

Changhua Yang, Kevin Hsin-Yih Lin, and Hsin-Hsi Chen. 2007. Building emotion lexicon from weblog corpora. Proc. of 45th Meeting of the Association for Computational Linguistics, pages 133–136

Integrating Prosodics into a Language Model for
Spoken Language Understanding of Thai[*]

Siripong Potisuk

Department of Electrical and Computer Engineering
The Citadel, the Military College of South Carolina
171 Moultrie Street
Charleston, South Carolina 29409 USA
siripong.potisuk@citadel.edu

Abstract. This paper describes a preliminary work on prosody modeling aspect of a spoken language understanding system for Thai. Specifically, the model is designed to integrate prosodics into a language model based on constraint dependency grammar. There are two steps involved, namely the prosodic annotation process and the prosodic disambiguation process. The annotation process uses prosodic information (stress, pause and syllable duration) obtained from the speech signal during low-level acoustic processing to encode each word in the parse graph with a prosodic feature called strength dynamic. The goal of the annotation process is to capture the correspondence between the phonological and phonetic attributes of the prosodic structure of utterances and their intended meanings. The prosodic disambiguation process involves the propagation of prosodic constraints designed to eliminate syntactic ambiguities of the input utterance. It is considered a pruning mechanism for the parser by using prosodic information. The aforementioned process has been tested on a set of ambiguous sentences, which represents various structural ambiguities involving five types of compounds in Thai.

Keywords: Spoken language understanding, Prosody, Thai.

1. Introduction

In the realm of artificial intelligence, there is no denying that the ultimate goal for man-machine communication is to use natural human languages. Humans aspire to build a machine capable of understanding and responding to commands issued in the form of spoken language. Research towards this goal encompasses various research disciplines, and the fruits of such labor include machine translation, speech synthesis and recognition, and spoken language understanding.

Spoken language understanding has been a challenge for scientists and engineers for many decades. Early efforts were primarily aimed at simply recognizing speech, and extensive research has been conducted to improve performance of speech recognition systems. Much of the improvements can be attributed to combining various research disciplines including linguistics, psychology, computer science, and signal processing, as well as improvements in modeling techniques, such as statistical and symbolic pattern recognition. Speech models now incorporate linguistic modeling to account for coarticulation and grammatical constraints to reduce the search

---

[*] The author would like to thank the Citadel Foundation for its financial support in the form of a presentation grant.

22nd Pacific Asia Conference on Language, Information and Computation, pages 311–320

space for the correct utterance. Also, steady advances in the computational efficiency of computers and hardware have enabled researchers to implement computationally intensive models that were deemed nearly impossible in the past.

With the remarkable advances in speech recognition, the focus has now shifted toward the development of spoken language understanding systems. The goal is to build a machine capable of understanding naturally spoken language by combining together speech recognition and natural language processing technologies. Such systems must be capable of recognizing a large number of words (on the order of tens of thousand), and they also need to make better use of additional information present in the speech signal, such as prosody. It is well known that prosodic information, such as pause, stress, intonation, etc., facilitates human speech communication by helping disambiguate utterances.

Prosody is an important aspect of speech that needs to be fully explored and utilized as a disambiguating knowledge source in spoken language understanding systems. Statistical modeling of prosodic information has the potential to be used as an additional knowledge source for both low-level processing (recognizing) and high-level processing (parsing) of spoken sentences. A knowledge source may be thought of as a module in spoken language understanding system, which contributes to the understanding of a spoken sentence.

Low-level use of prosodic information potentially allows for more accurate recognition at the phonetic and phonological levels. It may also prove to be useful at the stage of lexical access during word hypothesization. The most relevant prosodic information at this level is intra-word and syllable-level stress. A lexicon containing word stress patterns may help the recognizer discard word hypotheses with poorly matched stress patterns. A syllable is considered stressed if it is pronounced more prominently than adjacent syllables. Stressed syllables are usually louder, longer, and higher in pitch.

High-level use of prosodic information can help resolve ambiguities inherent in natural language independent of contextual information since computers do not currently utilize all the knowledge sources that humans do. Relevant prosodic information at this level includes pauses, sentential stress, and intonation contours. Sentential or inter-word stress information can be used in speech recognizers to resolve lexical and syntactic ambiguities. For example, the degree of stress among words in a spoken sentence provides an acoustic cue for distinguishing between content (noun, verb) and function (auxiliary, preposition, etc.) words. Furthermore, the marking of prosodic phrases may improve parsing performance by reducing syntactic ambiguities since prosodic groupings may rule out some of the syntactic groupings for a syntactically ambiguous sentence. Also, the identification of sentence mood (i.e., declarative, interrogative, command, etc.) from intonation contours may reduce syntactic and pragmatic ambiguity.

The overall objective of this research is to study the role of prosody in the implementation of a spoken language understanding system for Thai since prosodic information has the potential to be used as a pruning mechanism at both the low and high levels of spoken language processing. In particular, we specifically examine how salient prosodic features of Thai (e.g., stress) can be integrated with the overall language modeling scheme. Thai is the official language of Thailand, a country in the Southeast Asia region. The language is spoken by approximately 65 million people throughout different parts of the country. The written form is used in school and all official forms of communication.

Language modeling is one of the many important aspects in natural (both written and spoken) language processing by computer. For example, in a spoken language understanding system, a good language model not only improves the accuracy of low-level acoustic models of speech, but also reduces task perplexity (the average number of choices at any decision point) by making better use of high-level knowledge sources including prosodic, syntactic, semantic, and pragmatic knowledge sources. A language model often consists of a grammar written using some formalism which is applied to a sentence by utilizing some sort of parsing algorithm.

To overcome the difficulties in parsing Thai, we believe that a constraint dependency grammar (CDG) parser proposed by Potisuk (1996) appears to be an attractive choice for analyzing Thai sentences, considering vantage points from both written and spoken language processing aspects of an automatic system. CDG parsers rule out ungrammatical sentences by propagating constraints. Constraints are developed based on a dependency-based representation of syntax. The motivation for our choice of dependency grammar, instead of phrase-structure grammar, stems from the fact that it appears that Thai syntax might be better described by the former representation.

Our work in this paper extends the adopted CDG parsing approach by incorporating prosodic constraints into a grammar for Thai. Prosodic information is specifically used as part of a disambiguation process. Disambiguation is accomplished through the use of prosodic constraints which identify the strength of association between prosodic and syntactic structures of the sentence hypotheses. We next describe the proposed basic framework for a Thai spoken language understanding system and detail the necessary steps for achieving the goal of integrating prosodic information with other aspects of the language model.

2.   A Conceptual Model of a Thai Spoken Language Understanding System

The elusive goal of building a machine capable of understanding naturally spoken language that covers a very large vocabulary has not yet been realized. Presently, state-of-the-art spoken language interfaces merely recognize, rather than understand speech, and such systems only achieve high recognition on tasks that have low perplexity. To achieve understanding, we need to improve performance of speech recognition systems as well as combine speech recognition with natural language processing technology.

A spoken language understanding system may generally be thought of as comprising low-level (recognizing) and high-level (parsing) processing components although the detailed configuration may vary from system to system. The low-level processing usually involves acoustic modeling of the speech signal for recognition purposes. At the high level of processing, high-level knowledge sources (such as prosody, syntax, semantics, and pragmatics) are utilized not only for improving recognition performance, but also for analyzing the structure of the sentence hypotheses to obtain the best parse to map to a semantic representation in order to achieve understanding. This is commonly known as the language modeling aspect of the system.

Spoken language understanding should be viewed as a computer-human interaction problem. Understanding how various cues contribute to system performance in the context of spoken language interfaces to task-oriented mixed-initiative systems is crucial in the design of a language model. Such systems are best evaluated and judged in terms of their success in supporting users in accomplishing tasks.

A language model usually consists of a grammar which is applied to a sentence by utilizing a parsing algorithm to account for syntactic representation of the recognized string of words. In addition to syntactic parsing, the language model must be designed to be capable of using other high-level knowledge sources. The goal should be to not only improve the accuracy of low-level acoustic models of speech, but also reduce task perplexity. The choice of the approach to language modeling depends on how easily the model can be integrated with the acoustic model. Of primary concern are the issues of separability, scalability, computational tractability, and inter-module communication. These issues specify the level of interaction between the speech component and the language model, which can be classified into three categories: tightly-coupled, semi-coupled, or loosely-coupled systems.

In this research, we choose a constraint-based system of integration, which can be classified as a loosely-coupled system of integration. It utilizes the language model, which is based on a CDG parsing algorithm, as a post-processing step to the acoustic model. The high-level knowledge sources are isolated into relatively independent modules which communicate with one another through the use of a uniform framework of constraint propagation. Figure 1 illustrates a conceptual model of a Thai spoken language understanding system based on a constraint-based system of integration.

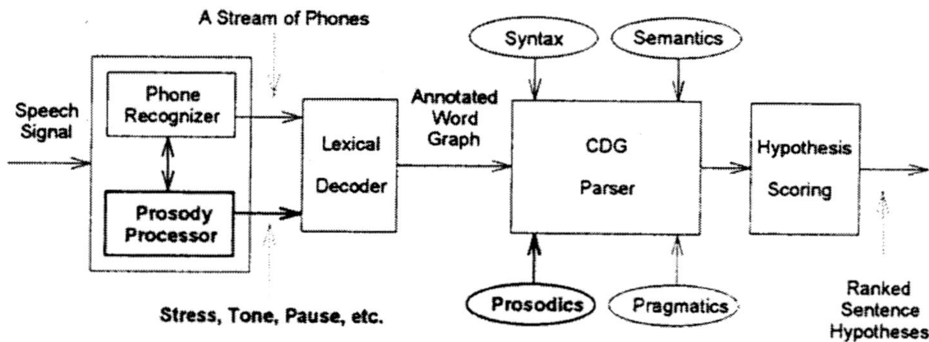

Figure 1: A Conceptual Model of a Thai Spoken Language Understanding System.

It is noted that the prosody processor has been designed to extract the tone feature from the input speech signal. Tone recognition is difficult to incorporate into a phone recognizer (usually HMM-based model), because tone is a property of a syllable, not of an individual phone. As a result, a lexical decoder or word hypothesizer is added to the system as a separate module in order to combine the output of the phone recognizer and that of the prosody processor together.

Because the overall system is loosely-coupled and the language model is based on a constraint dependency parsing algorithm, this approach is a very attractive choice for Thai. The first advantage is that the parser uses a word graph (a directed acyclic graph) augmented with parse-related information. For spoken Thai sentences, a word graph provides a very compact and less-redundant data structure for simultaneously parsing multiple sentence hypotheses generated by a lexical decoder. Secondly, since the knowledge sources are independent, their individual impact is more easily measured. The individual modules can be tested in a stand-alone fashion. Furthermore, the modularity potentially makes the system easier to understand, design, debug, and scale up to larger problems. In addition, the system becomes more versatile since they can easily accommodate more than one task or language by simply replacing individual modules. Thirdly, the system appears to be more computationally tractable because it selectively uses level-appropriate information at every stage of processing. For example, no acoustic decisions are made in the syntactic module.

In the above model, prosodic modeling involves the development of two components (highlighted in bold): the prosody processor and the prosodic knowledge source for CDG parsing. The first module is a part of the acoustic model that deals with automatic detection and classification of the prosodic cues of interest. The second module is a part of the language model that deals with representing and utilizing automatically-detected prosodic cues from the prosody processor to improve the accuracy of the parser by means of prosodic disambiguation. The information is transferred to the parser by annotating the word graph, the central processing structure of the parser. The process of prosodic disambiguation (i.e., choosing a parse or parses with the most likely prosodic patterns from among several candidate parses) is accomplished by propagating prosodic constraints. Prosodic constraints check the agreement between the annotated prosodic structure from the prosody processor and the prosodic structure of each of the competing sentence hypotheses of the ambiguous utterance, which is generated indirectly from its syntactic structure. A sentence hypothesis is rejected if its prosodic structure is poorly matched by the annotated prosodic structure. This paper deals with the second module only, and in the following sections the use of prosodic information for resolving structural ambiguities in a Thai spoken language understanding system will be described. Two specific issues will be addressed: the prosodic annotation process and the prosodic disambiguation process.

3. CDG Parsing with Prosodic Constraints

Due to the scope of the paper, a description of the basics of CDG parsing of Thai will be briefly described with a parsing example. Interested readers are referred to the paper by Potisuk (1996) for a complete discussion of the basic CDG framework.

3.1. A description of CDG parsing

CDG is defined as a 4-tuple, $G = < \Sigma, R, L, C >$, where Σ represents a finite set of terminal symbols or lexical categories, $L = $ a finite set of labels, $\{l_1, \ldots \ldots, l_q\}$, $R = $ a finite set of uniquely named roles (or role-ids), $\{r_1, \ldots \ldots, r_p\}$, and $C = $ a constraint set of unary and binary constraints. Within this grammar, a sentence $s = w_1 w_2 w_3 w_4 \ldots .. w_n$ is defined as a word string of finite length n.

The elements of Σ are the parts of speech of the words in a sentence. Associated with every word i in a sentence s are all of the p roles in R. Hence, every sentence contains $n*p$ roles. A role can be thought of as a variable which is assigned a role value. A role value is a tuple $<l, m>$, where l is a label from L and m is an element of the set of modifiees, $\{1, 2, \ldots \ldots, n,$ nil$\}$. A modifiee is a pointer to another word in the sentence (or to no word if nil). Role values will be denoted in the examples as label-modifiee.

Two types of roles (role-ids) per word are used: *governor* and *need* roles. The governor role indicates the function a word fills in a sentence when it is governed by its head word (e.g., a subject is governed by the main verb). Several need roles (i.e., need1 and need2) may be used to make certain that a head word has all of the constituents it needs to be complete. Each of the need roles keeps track of an item that its word needs in order to be complete (e.g., a verb generally needs a subject for the sentence to be complete).

The function that a word plays within the sentence is indicated by assigning a role value to a role. The label in the role value indicates the function the word fills when it is pointing at the word indexed by its modifiee (e.g., a *subj* label). When a role value is assigned to the governor role of a word, it indicates the function of that word when it modifies its head word. Likewise, when a role value is assigned to a need role of a word, it indicates how that need is being filled.

To parse a sentence using CDG, the constraints (members of C) must be specified. A constraint set C is a logical formula of the form: (and $C_1 C_2 \ldots C_t$). Each C_i is a constraint represented in the form: (if *Antecedent Consequent*), where *Antecedent* and *Consequent* are either single predicates or a group of predicates joined by the logical connectives (a conjunction or disjunction of predicates). The possible components of each C_i are variables, constants, access functions, predicate symbols and logical connectives. Variables (i.e., x, y, etc) used in the constraints stand for the role values. A constraint involving only one variable is called a unary constraint; two variables, a binary constraint. A maximum of two variables in a constraint allows for sufficient expressivity. That is, using predicate symbols and access functions, unary and binary constraints for a CDG grammar can be constructed. Constants are elements and subsets of $\Sigma \cup R \cup L \cup \{nil, 1, 2, \ldots \ldots, n\}$, where n is the number of words in a sentence. Allowable access functions are *pos* – word position, *rid* – role-id, *lab* – label, *mod* – modifiee position, and *cat* – lexical category. The predicate symbols allowable in constraints are: *eq* ($x = y$), *gt* ($x > y$), *lt* ($x < y$), and *elt* ($x \in y$). Lastly, the logical connectives are $\wedge$, $\vee$, and $\sim$.

Using the predicate symbols and access functions mentioned, unary and binary constraints for a CDG grammar can be constructed. Unary constraints are often used to restrict the role values allowed by a role given its part of speech whereas binary constraints are constructed to describe how the role values assigned to two different roles are interrelated. Examples of unary and binary constraints are given below.

In CDG, a sentence s is said to be generated by the grammar if there exists an assignment **A** given a set of constraints C. An assignment **A** for the sentence s is a function that maps role values to each of the $n*p$ roles such that the constraint set C is satisfied. There may be more than one assignment which satisfies C, in which case there is more than one parse for the sentence.

To illustrate the use of CDG grammars, consider the following simple example grammar G used for parsing a Thai sentence, เสื้อนีสาย.

```
Σ = {det, noun, verb}
R = {governor}
L = {det, root, subj}
C =   ∀x, y  (∧
        ;; [U-1] A noun receives the label 'subj' and modifies a word to
           its right.
        (if  (eq (cat  (pos x))  noun)
             (∧ (eq  (lab x)  subj)
                (lt  (pos x)  (mod x))))
        ;; [U-2] A determiner receives the label 'det' and modifies a word
           to its left.
        (if  (eq (cat  (pos x))  det)
             (∧ (eq  (lab x)  det)
                (lt  (mod x)  (pos x))))
        ;; [U-3] A verb receives the label 'root' and modifies no word.
        (if  (eq (cat  (pos x))  verb)
             (∧ (eq  (lab x)  root)
                (eq  (mod x)  nil)))
        ;; [B-1] A subj is governed by a verb.
        (if  (∧ (eq  (lab x)  subj)
                (eq (mod x) (pos y)))
             (eq (cat  (pos y))  verb)))
```

The constraints in this grammar were chosen for simplicity, not to exemplify constraints for a wide coverage grammar. Note that U-1, U-2, U-3 are unary constraints while B-1 is a binary constraint. Also, each word is assumed in this example to have a single lexical category, which is determined by dictionary look-up. For G above to generate the sentence, there must be an assignment of a role value to the governor role of each word, and that assignment must simultaneously satisfy each of the constraints in C. Figure 2 depicts the initialization of roles for the given sentence and its assignment which satisfies C in the form a final parse graph for the constraint network. Details of the constraint network after the propagation of each constraint are omitted for the sake of brevity.

After all the constraints are propagated across the constraint network and filtering is completed, the network provides a compact representation of all possible parses. Syntactic ambiguity is easy to

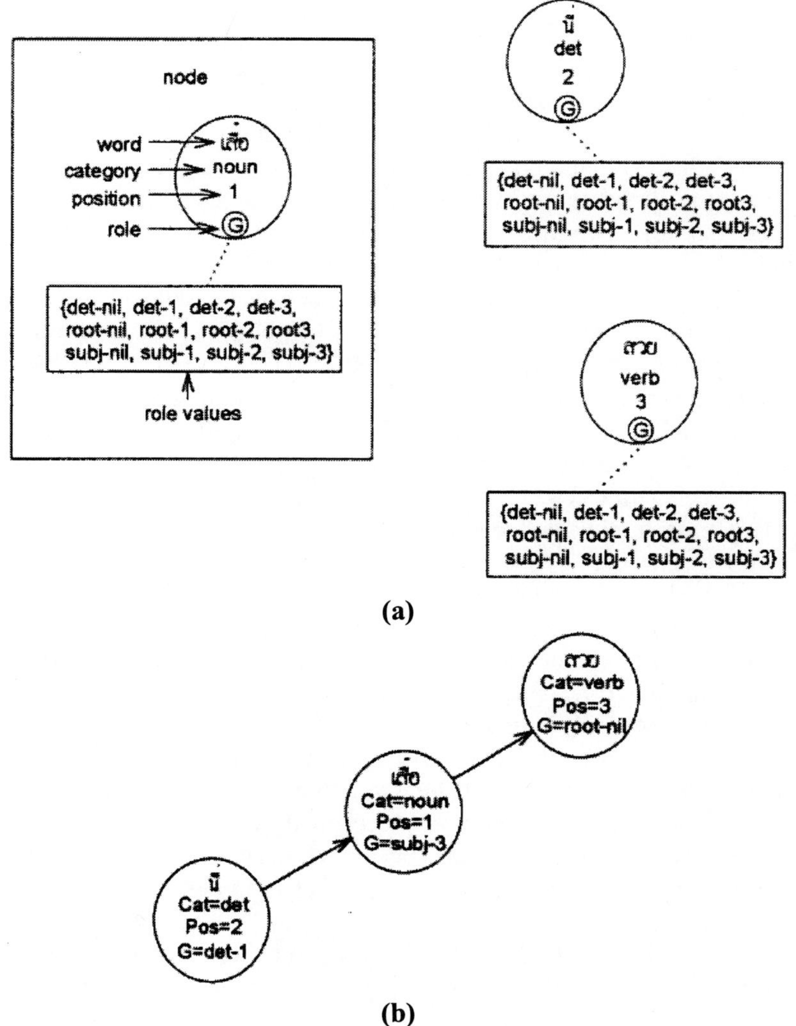

(a)

(b)

Figure 2: (a) Initialization of roles and (b) the final parse graph for the sentence เตือนีสาย.

spot in the network. If multiple parses exist, then additional constraints, such as semantic constraints, can be propagated to further refine the analysis to the intended meaning of the input sentence. The resulting parse trees are then ready to be prosodically annotated. The annotation process is described next.

3.2. Prosodic Annotation

Prosodic annotation or encoding is a mechanism for passing up prosodic information from low-level acoustic module for high-level processing. It provides to the parser relevant information that adequately captures the essence of the prosodic structure of the input utterance. Prosodic encoding usually involves the process of labeling prosodic patterns in the speech signal. The labeling criteria provide a mechanism for mapping a sequence of acoustic correlates of prosody into abstract prosodic labels. As a result, prosodically-labeled sentences contain information concerning the correspondence between the phonological and phonetic attributes of the prosodic structure of utterances and their intended meanings. Prosodic labels should be chosen to represent abstract linguistic categories of prosody, such as rhythmic groupings (or phrasing) and prominence. Also, they should be chosen such that they are used consistently within and across human labelers, and they make the automatic labeling process tractable and consistent.

Following the annotation process proposed by Potisuk (2007) for a text-to-speech system for Thai, a brief description of the annotation process will be described. The encoding of the prosodic structure is accomplished by annotating each word candidate in the word graph with a prosodic feature called *strength*. The strength feature is chosen based on the dependency representation of syntax. There are four levels of strength dynamics: strong dependence (SD), dependence (DE), independence (ID), and strong independence (SI). SD describes a strength dynamic at the word boundary within a clitic group, within a compound, between a content and a function word, or between two function words that are interdependent (i.e., both depend on the same governor). DE describes strength dynamic at minor phrase boundaries, i.e., between a subject noun phrase and a verb phrase, between a verb and an object noun phrase, or between two content words. ID describes strength dynamic at major phrase boundaries (intonational phrases). And, SI describes strength dynamic at the sentence boundary. In addition to the strength feature, a word at the end of a phrase or an utterance will receive the feature '*final*' to indicate that it is affected by the final lengthening effect. Final lengthening is always accompanied by a pause. A word with a '*final*' feature also automatically receives a strength dynamic of ID or SI.

The criteria for labeling a parse with the above strength features using the acoustic information are now described. The criteria establish the correspondence between the phonological (strength dynamics) and the phonetic (acoustic correlates) attributes of prosody by minimizing speech disrhythmy while maintaining the congruency with syntax. Since Thai is a stress-timed language, a phonological unit called foot can be used to describe rhythmic groupings within an utterance. A foot is neither a grammatical nor a lexical unit. The domain of a foot extends from a salient (stressed) syllable up to but not including the next salient syllable. A pause is considered a salient syllable, and the beginning of an utterance is always preceded by a pause. The acoustic realization of a rhythmic foot assuming that each rhythmic foot is arbitrarily three units long, regardless of the number of syllables comprising the foot (one through five) can be summarized as follows:

| S |	→	| 3 |	→ | 2 | if the foot is in an utterance-initial position.
| S |	→	| 3 |	→ | 4 | if the foot is in an utterance-final position and it does not have a CVS structure.
| S W |	→	| 2 : 1 |	→ | 2 : 2| if the salient syllable has a CVS structure; or the weak syllable is the first element of a compound that does not have a CVS structure; or both the salient syllable and the weak syllable are function words.
| S W W |	→	| 1½ : ¾ : ¾ |	→ | 1⅔ : 1⅔ : 1⅔ | if the salient syllable has a CVS structure; or it is in an utterance-initial position; or it is a function word and the two weak syllables are two function words or a function word and a linker syllable.

where S and W indicate salient (stressed) and weak (unstressed) syllables, respectively. It is noted that the four-syllable and five-syllable feet are very rare and are omitted from discussion. Note also that foot boundaries are usually inserted in front of the salient syllables. The above rule can be used to obtain a derived syllable duration information (phonological level) from the corresponding syllable duration (phonetic level) obtained during the low-level acoustic processing.

By using stress, pause, and derived syllable duration information, the input utterance can be divided into feet. Then, the strength dynamics can be assigned as follows. Since we only distinguish between two classes of stress, the salient syllable immediately after a weak syllable receives a strength dynamic of SD. A word before a pause receives a strength dynamic of DE as well as the *'final'* feature. A word after a pause receives a strength dynamic of SI if it is in the utterance-initial position; otherwise, it receives a strength dynamic of ID.

3.3. Prosodic Disambiguation Process

In this section, we describe our prosodic disambiguation process in CDG parsing. We assumed that the word graph for our CDG parser was perfectly annotated with prosodic information (i.e., strength dynamics). Our method of incorporating prosodics into the CDG formalism is quite similar to the work proposed by Zoltowski et.al (1992) for handling English. To construct prosodic constraints, two additional access functions were introduced:

`(abut x y)` returns true if x and y abut each other (i.e., x and y are adjacent),

`(strength x y)` returns the strength dynamic between x and y given that x and y are adjacent.

Given the above access functions, prosodic constraints are constructed in the form of binary constraints (i.e., constraints relating two variables).

The parsing process begins by propagating syntactic constraints to eliminate syntactically ill-formed sentence hypotheses. Then, prosodic constraints are propagated to check the agreement based on the strength dynamics between every pair of word candidates in each of the remaining competing sentence hypotheses of the ambiguous utterance. A sentence hypothesis is rejected if its syntactic structure is incompatible with the prosodic structure encoded via the annotated strength dynamics.

4. Experiments and Results

The above approach of incorporating prosodics into a CDG grammar has been tested on a set of ambiguous sentences, which represents various structural ambiguities involving five types of compounds in Thai: noun-noun, noun-propernoun, noun-verb, non-verb-noun, and verb-noun. There are two test sentences for each type of ambiguity resulting in a total of 10 sentence types for the whole set. These sentences consist of only monosyllabic words in which structural ambiguity in Thai often involves. For a complete list of test sentences, see Potisuk (2007).

To illustrate how the strength dynamic information extracted from the input speech signal is used in a CDG grammar to eliminate prosodically implausible parses, we provide two prosodic constraints to help disambiguate two example sentence hypotheses.

1)　　$_{SI}$ keeŋ $_{DE}$ pʰèt $_{SD}$ mâak $_{DE}$ paj　　'The curry is too spicy.'

| subj. | verb | adv. | aux. |

2)　　$_{SI}$ keeŋ $_{SD}$ pʰèt $_{DE}$ mâak $_{DE}$ paj　　'There is too much curry.'

| subj. (compound) | verb | aux. |

In this example, structural ambiguity results from the relationship between the first two words, subject-verb vs. a noun-verb compound. To handle this type of ambiguity, the following two prosodic constraints were constructed. The first indicates the requirements for a compound, and the second indicates the requirements for a subject-verb combination of words.

```
;; To have a label root, a verb abutting a modifier of a compound to its
left must have strength of DE.
      (if (∧ (abut (pos x) (pos(y))
             (eq (lab x) root)
             (eq (rid y) governor)
             (gt (pos x) (pos y))
             (~ (eq (mod y) (pos x))))
          (eq (strength x) DE)).

;; To have a label root, a verb abutting a subject modifier to its left
must have strength of DE.
      (if (∧ (abut (pos x) (pos(y))
             (eq (lab x) root)
             (eq (rid y) governor)
             (eq (lab y) subj)
             (gt (pos x) (pos y)))
          (eq (strength x) DE)).
```

Given the strength dynamics as in the first sentence, the word /pet/ must have a label root because it has strength of DE, while the word /maak/ cannot have a label root based on the second constraint. Thus, the compound interpretation is eliminated. On the other hand, given the strength dynamics as in the second sentence, the first constraint only permits the word /pet/ to be labeled as a verb modifier of a compound because it has strength of SD. As a result, the word /maak/ can only become the main verb of the sentence, thus eliminating the subject-verb sequence interpretation.

5. Summary and Discussion

A system combining constraint dependency parsing of Thai spoken sentences with prosodic constraints has been described. Prosodic constraints have been developed to rule out prosodically implausible sentence hypotheses in the face of syntactic ambiguity. These prosodic constraints check for the agreement between every pair of words in each of the competing sentence hypotheses of an ambiguous utterance based on the annotated strength dynamics. A sentence hypothesis is rejected if its syntactic structure is not congruent with the prosodic structure given by the annotated strength dynamics.

Since the algorithm is in a very early stage of development, we are unable to assess its true performance. We are planning to generalize the approach to cover a wider variety of sentences. Specifically, we are modifying our constraint network to tolerate multiple word candidates, which are prevalent in the spoken language domain, both for words in a particular word position (aligned) as well as for word candidates that overlap each other in time (unaligned). The problem of multiple word candidates is likely to occur when we extend our system to account for ambiguity involving polysyllabic words.

6. References

Potisuk, S. and M. P. Harper. 1996. CDG: An Alternative Formalism for Parsing Written and Spoken Thai. *Proceedings of the Fourth International Symposium on Languages and Linguistics*, pp. 1177-1196.

Potisuk, S. 2007. Prosodic Annotation in a Thai Text-to-speech System. *Proceeding of the 21ˢᵗ Pacific Asia Conference on Language, Information and Computation.* pp. 405-414.

Zoltowski, C.B., Harper, M.P., Jamieson, L.H., and Helzerman, R.A. (1992) PARSEC: A Constraint-based Framework for Spoken Language Understanding. *Proceedings of the International Conference on Spoken Language Processing.* pp. 249-252.

Using a Word-Space Model to Determine the Relevance of Messages in Anchored Asynchronous Online Discussions [*]

Rodolfo Raga[a], Jennifer Raga[a], Erick Bonus[a], and Raymund Sison[b]

[a]Computer Science Department, Jose Rizal University,
80 Shaw Boulevard, Mandaluyong City, Philippines
[b]College of Computer Studies, De La Salle University-Manila,
2401 Taft Avenue, Manila, Philippines
{jundy.raga, jennie.raga,erick.bonus}@gmail.com; sisonr@dlsu.edu.ph

Abstract. This paper presents results of the first phase of our study aimed at investigating the applicability of word-space models, particularly those generated using Random Indexing (RI) technique, for the task of determining the relevance of messages posted in anchored asynchronous online discussion forums. In this phase, we addressed several questions intended to establish baseline figures: How efficient will the word-space model perform in this task? How much of its classification decisions align with the decisions of the human annotators? More importantly, does the paradigmatic and syntagmatic contexts of words have a direct effect on its output and which produces the best results? Using Cohen's Kappa and Holsti's Coefficient Reliability measure, our experiments generated an initial reliability performance (K=0.41, CR=0.72). It further indicated that the syntagmatic context is more applicable for this task. We concluded with a discussion of the weaknesses identified and possible means of improving the level of performance.

Keywords: Asynchronous Online Discussion, Word-Space Model, Random Indexing, Paradigmatic Context, Syntagmatic Context.

1. Introduction

Asynchronous Online Discussions (AOD), also known as forums or threaded discussion boards, are a popular form of web-based computer-mediated communication (CMC). More recently, this form of communication has come into focus in education as an alternative form of assessment that can be used to supplement traditional classroom discussions. The advantage of this communication medium lies in its anytime and anywhere accessibility which provides logistic flexibility for students to communicate with each other and for teachers to assess their interaction.

A disadvantage of this medium however is that the focus of discussion is prone to topic drifting; this drifting is primarily due to the time-lags inherent in the asynchronous mode of discussion. Another problem is that the manual monitoring and assessment of message contributions are time-consuming and often tedious, especially for teachers. For these reasons, automated analysis for discussion understanding and better methods of topic-focus monitoring to enable more efficient information assessment are much sought for (Ravi & Kim, 2007).

In our study, we aim to investigate the feasibility of utilizing the functionality of word-space models for the task of analyzing online discussion transcripts. More particularly, we want to determine how word-space models can be used to detect the relevance of individual message posts

22nd Pacific Asia Conference on Language, Information and Computation, pages 321–330

relative to the overall topic of discussion. Several methods for generating word-space models are available and have been successfully tested on detecting similarity between terms in groups of texts, but to our knowledge very few have been applied and tested on analyzing online discussion transcripts, a rare example is that of (McArthur and Bruza, 2003) which applied Latent Semantic Analysis on a small dataset of email correspondence to detect conversational implicatures. In our experiments, we chose to use the Random Indexing (RI) technique. RI is a word-space modeling technique primarily designed to measure similarity between terms and not between documents. In our work, we extended the capability of RI to work both at the document and message size levels.

The rest of the paper has the following organization: The second section endeavored to put our study into context by providing a brief background on the problem of topic drifting in online discussions and cites a recent approach used to address it. The third section discussed the concept of word-space models and provides a brief introduction on how it can be implemented using RI. The fourth section presented a description of the experiments we conducted. In the fifth section we presented the results of the experiments and provided some discussion. We ended the paper with our conclusion and expected future directions.

2. Review of Literature

The topic focus of online discussions constantly changes from one topic to another (Beaudin, 1999). This phenomenon is what (Potter, 2007) referred to as *topic drifts* or the tendency of online discussions to stray from their announced topic.

In academic settings, researchers try to limit the occurrence of this problem by implementing anchored discussions (Guzdial and Turns, 2000). These educational online discussions are structured to align the contributions of participants to a single topic represented by the contents of a reference document called the *anchor document*. Literature shows that this method yields a more coherent discussion than traditional forums by promoting conscious topic monitoring (van der Pol et al, 2006). However, participants are unconsciously still prone to introduce irrelevant posts which often induce off-topic discussion. As such, tools that can help mediators automatically detect, at the earliest, such irrelevant contributions are still needed.

An initial requirement for the development of such tools is a method for determining the alignment of each message to the overall topic focus of the discussion. This necessitates a content analysis approach similar to the strategy proposed by (Teufel and Moens, 1998) whereby the alignment of one text with another was measured by a mechanism that analyzes several characteristics of the aligned sentences such as the presence of particular phrases and occurrence of thematic words and proper names. For our purpose, we are looking towards utilizing the functionalities of word-space models for the same task. The context of the work we're pursuing is the anchored discussion mentioned above. As such, the basis of the relevance value we are trying to measure is the closeness of the semantic information between the contents of each message to the contents of an anchor document.

Word-space models have previously been observed to provide two modes of semantic similarity between terms. Sahlgren (2006) noted that these modes depend on whether the paradigmatic or syntagmatic relationship of the terms within a context are captured. Syntagmatic context refers to the linear relationship of words and applies to linguistic entities that occur in sequential combinations while paradigmatic context refers to the substitutional relationship of words and applies to words that can be used in the same context but not at the same time. We aim to initially investigate, among other things, whether or not these two modes will provide different levels of performance for this task, and if so, which provides the best result.

3. Word-Space Models and Random Indexing (RI)

In this section, we present a simple introduction to the concept of word-space modeling, how it is used to assign meaning to a term, and how it can be implemented using Random Indexing.

3.1. Word Space Model

A word-space model is a spatial representation that derives the meaning of words by plotting these words in an *n*-dimensional geometric space (Sahlgren, 2005). This process is similar to the way points are plotted in a two dimensional graphing paper. The main difference is that, in the case of a word-space, the dimension *n* can be arbitrarily large. The size of this dimension is determined by the number of unique word type in the set of words to be plotted.

Usually, the coordinates used to plot each word depends upon the frequency of the contextual feature that each word co-occur with within a text. For example, words that do not co-occur with the word to be plotted within a given context are assigned a coordinate value of zero. The set of zero and non-zero values corresponding to the coordinates of a word in a word-space are recorded in a *context vector*. Because most of the words in any text dataset will never co-occur with a particular word, the context vectors are often sparse or full of zero values.

By itself, the position of a word in a word space does not indicate anything about its meaning. To deduce a certain level of meaning, this position needs to be measured relative to the position of other words. In this sense, a linguistic concept known as the *distributional hypothesis* which states that *"words that occur in the same contexts tend to have similar meanings"* is applied. Having similar contexts means that words are surrounded or that they co-occur with same set of words. Thus, if we plot these words in a word-space they would be positioned close to each other. The level of closeness of words in the word-space is often referred to as the spatial proximity of words. This spatial proximity is what is used to represent the semantic similarity of words. A common approach used to determine spatial proximity is to measure the cosine of the angle generated between the plotted context vectors. The formula for computing cosine is as follows:

$$CoSim(Q,D) = \frac{Q * D}{|Q| * |D|} \quad (1)$$

Where: Q is a vector representing one term or document, D is a vector representing another term or document related to Q, and |Q| and |D| are the magnitudes of Q and D.

Currently, there are three major approaches to implement a word space. These include: Latent Semantic Analysis (LSA), Hyperspace Analogue to Language (HAL), and Random Indexing (Sahlgren, 2005). For our purpose, we opted to use the Random Indexing approach.

3.2. Random Indexing

Random Indexing (RI) is a word space modeling technique that can be used with any type of linguistic context. It is inherently incremental and incorporates a built-in dimension reduction phase (Sahlgren, 2005).

There are two basic steps involved in using Random Indexing to implement a word-space:

1. The first step involves the assignment of a unique and randomly generated label called an *index vector* to each word in the data. These vectors are sparse, high-dimensional, and ternary. High-dimensional means that it uses a large number of dimensions while ternary means that the label consists of a small number of randomly distributed +1s and -1s, with the rest of the elements of the vectors set to 0.

2. Then, context vectors with the same number of dimensionality as the index vectors are automatically produced by scanning through the text, and each time a word occurs in a context (e.g. in a document, or within a sliding context window), that word's index vector is added to the context vector for the word in question.[1]

RI has attracted much attention with successful applications in term similarity measurement. For our purpose, we have selected RI because of its incremental approach; this means that the

---

[1] Please refer to (Sahlgren,2005) for more details

context vectors can be used for similarity computations even after just a few examples have been encountered. This characteristic is useful in experiments and applications such as ours where the size of the dataset is small. Secondly, as already mentioned, Random Indexing can be used with any type of context. This characteristic is useful in our experiment because we want to separately capture the paradigmatic and the syntagmatic contexts of words.

4. Experiments

4.1. Research Questions

The experiments described below are meant to address the following questions:

1. Using only the contents of an external anchor document as basis, how efficient is the word-space model's baseline performance in identifying relevant and irrelevant messages in an online discussion transcript?
2. To what extent will the classification decisions generated by the word-space models for this task align with the classification decisions made by the human annotators?
3. Does the paradigmatic and syntagmatic relationship of words have a direct effect on the performance of the word space model for this task? If so, which of the two provides the best performance?

4.2. Model Implementations

To provide an answer to the above enumerated questions, we need to separately capture the syntagmatic and paradigmatic relationships of words and use it to build a word-space. This entailed implementing two variants of context windows that dissected the sentences in each document into its syntagmatic and paradigmatic context as described below:

4.2.1. Syntagmatic Context Window

Following the definition specified in (Sahlgren, 2006), we defined the syntagmatic context vector v as constituting of n context regions c as follows:

$$\vec{v} = (c_1, c_2, ..., c_n) \quad (2)$$

We then defined each context region c as a window that we deem would capture the syntagmatic context of words in a sentence as follows:

$$c = (t_1, t_2, ..., t_m) \quad (3)$$

where c is a single context, $t_1..t_m$ are m terms occurring in sequential order within the text being modelled and m is a number defining the size of the window. This window slides through each sentence in the text, one word at a time. As such, some windows will necessarily have null values in them (those that are near the end of the sentence).

In RI terminology, the value we assign to each context c is the sum of the index vector of m terms occurring sequentially in it. For weighing function, we multiplied the index vector of each term to its position index within the context (i.e. the 1st term by 1, the 2nd by 2, and so on).

4.2.2. Paradigmatic Context Window

Similarly, following the definition specified in (Sahlgren, 2006), we defined the paradigmatic context vector v as constituting of n word types fw as follows:

$$\vec{v} = (fw_1, fw_2, ..., fw_n) \quad (4)$$

The value we assigned to each word fw is determined by its surrounding words as contained in a window that we deem would capture the paradigmatic context of the word as follows:

$$w = (wp_m, wp_{m-1}, ... wp_1, \boldsymbol{fw}, ws_1, ws_2, ..., ws_m) \quad (5)$$

here, fw is the focus word and $wp_m, wp_{m-1}, ... wp_1$ and $ws_1, ws_2, ..., ws_m$ are groups of m sequential words that precede and succeed the focus word respectively within the text to be modeled. This window is also a sliding window and rolls through each sentence in the text, one word at a time.

In RI terminology, the value we assign to each focus word fw is the sum of the index vectors of m sequential terms surrounding fw in some $m + m$ context window. For weighing function, we multiplied the value of each surrounding word to their distance from the focus word.

4.3. The Discussion Transcript

The discussion transcript we used as dataset in our experiments was culled from a public forum. We deemed this transcript as suitable for our purpose since the discussion that generated it revolved around an online article which was cited in the first message. The online article consists of 34 sentences with a total of 602 words and served as the *anchor document*. Table 4 provides some statistical details on the discussion transcript.

Table 1. Some statistical details of the discussion transcript.

Total number of messages posted	87
Total number of participants	16
Discussion duration	5 days
Average message length	86.3 words

4.4. Methods

The methods we used in this study involved four steps requiring as input a text-based transcript of an online discussion and an external anchor document. The output included a relevance measure for each message in the transcript as well as calculations of reliability statistics.

4.4.1. Initial Setup

First, the text of the selected discussion transcript was downloaded along with the online article that served as the *anchor document*. These were then encoded into separate tables in a database. This task was accomplished using the Microsoft Access software.

We then asked three people to annotate the messages in the discussion transcript. The annotators were instructed to read first the anchor document, after which they were asked to give a binary judgment as to whether they think each message is relevant or irrelevant to the topic expressed in the document {1 = relevant, 0 = irrelevant}. The annotators performed this task independently, without convening with each other. The technical background of the annotators also vary; one is a computer programmer that had extensive hands-on experience with the software tool discussed in the anchor document, one is a computer science instructor having theoretical understanding but little industry-based experience, and the last is a call-center agent who has no background knowledge nor experience in programming.

4.4.2. Dataset Preprocessing

Second, a tool was constructed to browse through each message body in the database as well as through the anchor document to perform dataset pre-processing. Pre-processing included replacing special symbols and numeric characters with null values, rolling upper-case alphabetic characters into lower case, and segmenting each text into its sentential units. The delimiters used to identify sentential units include the symbols [., ?, !, :].

No stopping or stemming of words was applied to the text. However, within the RI computations, the random index of stopwords was set to zero. This has the same effect as removing those words from the text. The stoplist we used was culled from (Sanderson, n.d.).

4.4.3. Experimental Setup

In our experiments we first divided the discussion transcript into two distinct dataset. The first dataset included messages that were unanimously classified by the annotators as being either relevant or irrelevant; this dataset served as our Gold Standard and we refer to it as the *unanimous dataset* (n=66). The annotators unanimously coded 49 messages as relevant and 17 messages as irrelevant. The other dataset included all the messages; we refer to this dataset as the *standard dataset* (n=87).

We then conducted two sets of experiments: one using the paradigmatic context and the other the syntagmatic context. In both cases, the RI system was first trained on the anchor document before being applied to the datasets. Also, the generated word space was first tested on the *unanimous dataset* before applying it to the *standard dataset*. The purpose of the first test is to establish a baseline on the performance of the word space model in identifying the exact category of a message. The second test was meant to probe the reliability of the decisions of the model as compared to humans with all the noise present.

We also experimented on various window sizes. For the syntagmatic context the window sizes we used are $w = \{2, 4, 6, 8\}$ while the paradigmatic counterpart are $w = \{1, 2, 3, 4\}$. The Random Indexing system we used in our experiments was constructed using the JavaSDM package (Hassel, 2004) and the parameters we applied are shown in Table 2:

Table 2: Parameters used in the RI implementation

RI Parameters	Values Used
Number of Dimensions used	900
Degree of Randomness Used	8
Seed-value used to generate random number	123

4.4.4. Reliability Measures

In this final step, we first measured the precision and recall of the classification decisions of the model in classifying messages in the *unanimous dataset*. Then, reliability measures were taken comparing the classification decisions of the human annotators with those produced by the word space model in the *standard dataset*. Two reliability measures were employed for this purpose: Holsti's coefficient of reliability (CR) which measures the agreement between two annotators divided by the total number of messages analyzed and Cohen's kappa (K) which computes the proportion of agreement actually observed between annotators after adjusting for the proportion of agreement expected by chance [2].

To compare the RI system's classification decisions with those of our human annotators, we treated any message with a computed cosine between 0.1 and 1.0 to be relevant (category = 1). Otherwise, it was treated as not-relevant (category = 0). Processing and computations in this final stage was done using the Microsoft Excel software.

5. Results and Discussions

---

[2] Acceptable values for (K) are between 6.0 – 7.0 while (CR) values can range from 0.00 (indicating no agreement) to 1.00 (indicating complete agreement).

5.1. Classification Precision and Recall

Tables 3 and 4 below shows the precision and recall gathered using the *unanimous dataset*.

Table 3: Precision and Recall of the classification results using the syntagmatic context

	$w = 2$	$w = 4$	$w = 6$	$w = 8$
P-R	0.57	0.57	0.55	0.52
R-R	0.71	0.71	0.71	0.65
P-IR	0.89	0.89	0.89	0.87
R-IR	0.82	0.82	0.80	0.80

w = window size, P-R = precision on relevant messages, R-R = recall on relevant messages, P-IR = precision on irrelevant messages, R-IR = recall on irrelevant messages.

Table 4: Precision and Recall of the classification results using the paradigmatic context

	$w = 2$	$w = 4$	$w = 6$	$w = 8$
P-R	0.30	0.31	0.31	0.31
R-R	0.47	0.47	0.47	0.47
P-IR	0.77	0.78	0.78	0.78
R-IR	0.61	0.63	0.63	0.63

w = window size, P-R = precision on relevant messages, R-R = recall on relevant messages, P-IR = precision on irrelevant messages, R-IR = recall on irrelevant messages.

5.2. Reliability

Tables 5 and 6 below present the reliability measures gathered using the *standard dataset*.

Table 5: Average Kappa and Coefficient Reliability measures with the human annotators using the syntagmatic context.

	$w=2$	$w=4$	$w=6$	$w=8$
Ave. Kappa	0.41	0.37	0.33	0.30
Ave. CR	0.72	0.71	0.69	0.69

Table 6: Average Kappa and Coefficient Reliability measures with the human annotators using the paradigmatic context.

	$w=2$	$w=4$	$w=6$	$w=8$
Ave. Kappa	0.12	0.14	0.14	0.14
Ave. CR	0.57	0.58	0.58	0.58

5.3. Discussion

Initial interpretations we derived from our experiments are three-fold, relative to the three questions presented in section 4.1. In our analysis, we divided the messages into four groups: (1) those that were correctly classified as relevant (true positive), (2) those that were correctly classified as irrelevant (true negative), (3) those that were incorrectly classified as relevant (false positive), and (4) those that were incorrectly classified as irrelevant (false negative).

Question #1: Using only the contents of an external anchor document as basis, how efficient is the word-space model's baseline performance in identifying relevant and irrelevant messages in an online discussion transcript?

As shown in tables 3 and 4, the highest precision-recall tandem for classifying relevant messages (P=0.57, R=0.71) as well as classifying irrelevant messages (P=0.89, R=0.82) from the *unanimous dataset* was returned by the RI system implementing the syntagmatic context and using a window size of 2 and 4. The paradigmatic counterpart of these settings returned lower values both for relevant (P=0.31, R=0.47) and irrelevant messages (P=0.78, R=0.63).

These results seem to indicate that the word-space model is more efficient at identifying irrelevant messages for this situation. To establish some basis for this performance, we manually analyzed the results on the syntagmatic context. We found that messages that were categorically assigned to the *true positive* group all contain several technical keywords that also occurred in the anchor document; we initially assumed that the presence of these keywords is the primary reason why these messages were classified as relevant. However, we also found that the *true negative* group is not exclusive to the messages that contained no shared technical keywords; some messages in this group also contained technical keywords that occurred in the anchor document, one of them even contained as much as three keywords. This finding seemed counter-intuitive with the first assumption we made; it implies that while the model relies on the presence of technical keywords to identify relevant messages, it doesn't necessarily rely on the absence of the same to identify irrelevant messages.

Further analysis led us to consider the way technical keywords are used in each message as a probable cause of this phenomenon. We noticed that the anchor document, being a technical document utilized and prescribed technical keywords in proximity with each other. This characteristic can also be observed in most messages that contained technical discussions. As such, when compared with the anchor document, technical messages got a higher chance of being classified as relevant. All messages assigned to the *true positive* group are of this type.

On the other hand, most non-technical messages are loosely constructed. Some of these messages also cited technical keywords but often presented them either in wide intervals or in isolation. Thus, when compared with the compact structure of the anchor document, the system has a higher tendency to tag them as irrelevant even though they contained technical keywords.

What we deduced from this observation is that the word-space model may be more efficient at identifying irrelevant messages in this situation because it can utilize two sources of information: the first is the absence of technical keywords, and, if technical keywords are presented, it can analyze the proximity of these keywords to determine whether they project the same topic as those of the anchor document. The analysis on relevant messages, on the other hand, solely relied on the presence of technical keywords. It has no alternative for recognizing the relevance of messages that have no keywords present. This problem is further compounded by the presence of dominant words (i.e., in our dataset, the word "sqldatasource") in the messages. Messages assigned to the false positive group seemed to indicate that the model have a tendency to classify as relevant those messages that contained the most frequently occurring word in the anchor document even if this word occurred in isolation.

Question #2: To what extent will the classification decisions generated by the word-space models for this task align with the classification decisions made by the human annotators?

As indicated in the values presented in Tables 5 and 6, both the paradigmatic and syntagmatic implementations of RI produced unacceptable values of reliability at this phase. With the RI system implementing the syntagmatic context and using a window size of (w=2) producing the higher reliability score (K=0.41, CR=0.72) with the human annotators. Manual inspection of the messages assigned to the false positive and false negative groups revealed that most of the discrepancies incurred on these tests were made on messages that either expounded on a particular concept or led the discussion to an off-topic direction. In the case of the latter, participants introduced other technical keywords in their messages that are related to but are not found in the anchor document. We assumed that this caused discrepancy because the RI system has no way of recognizing these keywords, especially if they are embedded within analogies. In the former, messages contained questions or brief comments that presented isolated technical keywords. If the technical keyword used is dominant (i.e., the highest occurring), the RI system classified the message as relevant otherwise it is classified as irrelevant. Human annotators, however, are still able to methodically discriminate the true value of these messages. We surmised that unconsciously they do this by utilizing the coherence or semantic relatedness of successive messages within the transcript.

At any rate, we found that the best performance of the model aligned more closely to the decisions made by the computer science instructor-annotator. Table 7 provides the details of this observation. Although this finding is still open to interpretations, we deem that this gives a good background and motivation for the application that we are envisioning.

Table 7: Best performance of the word-space model using syntagmatic context (w=2)

	Programmer	Instructor	Call Center Agent
Kappa	0.41	0.44	0.37
CR	0.72	0.74	0.70

Question #3: Does the paradigmatic and syntagmatic relationship of words have a direct effect on the performance of the word space model for this task? If so, which between the two provides the best performance?

Clearly, the results presented in Tables 3, 4, 5, and 6 indicated that context has a direct influence on the performance of the model. Another interesting observation that can be deduced from these results is that the RI implementing the syntagmatic context outperformed the RI implementing the paradigmatic context. Two related and supporting hypotheses may be derived from this discrepancy. One, is that the syntagmatic context, for this task, are better geared to model the human annotators' classification decisions than the paradigmatic context, the other is that human annotators may be relying more on the syntagmatic context of words in determining the relevance of messages under the circumstances given. Further studies are needed to prove these hypotheses.

By intuition, we believe that since information coming from both forms of contexts is available to them, the human annotators are utilizing both of these in finalizing their classification decisions (i.e., the arrangement of the words + the acquired meaning of each word). We argue that this, to a greater extent, caused the misalignment between the decisions exhibited by the word-space model and those made by the human annotators in our experiments.

6. Conclusions and Future Directions

Analyzing the applicability of the word-space model for the task of determining the relevance of forum messages, undoubtedly, requires a multi-phase process. In this paper, we have started exploring the capabilities of the model and gathered figures that will serve as our baseline data. Initially, we have shown the insufficiency of the word-space model's functionality to produce reliable results given the conditions specified. In succeeding phases of our study, we aim to explore other means that may improve the performance level of the word-space model. Some of our prospects include the following:

1. <u>Other datasets</u>. It would be interesting to experiment with other datasets, preferably, on larger discussion transcripts but of similar anchor document sizes. This will enable us to determine whether the observations cited in answering question #1 represented recurring patterns or merely an artifact of the dataset we used.
2. <u>Word sense information</u>. In the current model, we tested the performance of the syntagmatic and paradigmatic contexts separately. In future experiments we aim to find ways of combining the functionalities of the two contexts. For example, the paradigmatic

context seems more applicable to determining word similarity or antonymity. It would be interesting to determine whether this context can serve as an effective source of word-sense information for the syntagmatic context. This may help improve the precision and recall of the word-space model's performance.

3. <u>Message hierarchy information</u>. In the current model, we treated each message as an independent document. However, in reality, messages in a discussion transcript are inter-related, with previous messages possibly providing a context to succeeding messages. Humans implicitly recognize this relationship but our RI system cannot. We aim to also take this into consideration in future experiments and to enable the system to adjust the relevance scores based on the contextual relationship of each message to its preceding messages. This may help improve the reliability measure.

The rising popularity of Asynchronous Online Discussion as a tool for supporting student learning necessitates the development of tools that can be used to efficiently monitor and assess online discussions. Word-space models provide an alternative approach for developing these tools. Current applications of word-space models focus on extracting meaning using large-scale corpora, more so, traditional tests of how well each particular model represents meaning largely revolves around word level comparison. The contribution of this paper is that it provides an initial bench-mark on the performance of this approach on small-sized datasets but on larger linguistic structures. We believe that such benchmarks are vital for fine-tuning word-space models for this particular task and application.

References

Beaudin, N.B. 1999. Keeping Online Asynchronous Discussions on Topic. *Journal of Asynchronous Learning Networks*, Volume 3, Issue 2 - November 1999

Guzdial, M., and J. Turns. 2000. Effective discussion through a computer-mediated anchored forum. *Journal of the Learning Sciences*, 9, 4, 437-470.

Hassel, M. 2004. JavaSDM - A Java package for working with Random Indexing and Granska. http://www.nada.kth.se/~xmartin/java/JavaSDM/

McArthur, R., and P.D. Bruza. 2003. Discovery of tacit knowledge and topical ebbs and flows within the utterances of online community, in: *Chance Discovery*, Y. Ohsawa and P. McBurney eds., Springer Verlag, pp. 115–132.

Potter, A. 2007. *An Investigation of Interactional Coherence in Asynchronous Learning Environments*. Ph.D. thesis, Nova Southeastern University

Ravi, S. and J. Kim. 2007. Profiling Student Interactions in Threaded Discussions with Speech Act Classifiers. In Proceedings of *Artificial Intelligence in Education Conference*, 2007.

Sahlgren, M. 2006. The Word-Space Model. Using distributional analysis to represent syntagmatic and paradigmatic relations between words in high dimensional vector spaces. Ph.D. thesis, Stockholm University.

Sahlgren, M. 2005. An Introduction to Random Indexing. In Methods and Applications of Semantic Indexing Workshop at the *7th International Conference on Terminology and Knowledge Engineering*, Copenhagen, Denmark, 2005.

Sanderson, M. (n.d.) IR linguistic utilities – Stop word list. Retrieved on June 1, 2008 from http://www.dcs.gla.ac.uk/idom/ir_resources/linguistic_utils/stop_words

Teufel, S., and M. Moens. 1988. Sentence extraction and rhetorical classification for flexible abstracts. In AAAI *Spring Symposium on Intelligent Text Summarization*, Stanford.

van der Pol, J., W. Admiraal and P.R.J. Simons. 2006. The affordance of anchored discussion for the collaborative processing of academic texts. *Computer-Supported Collaborative Learning, 2006.* 1: 339–357

Trend-based Document Clustering for Sensitive and Stable Topic Detection [*]

Yoshihide Sato[a], Harumi Kawashima[b], Hidenori Okuda[b], and Masahiro Oku[b]

[a] NTT West Corporation [b] NTT Cyber Solutions Laboratories, NTT Corporation
1-1, Hikarino-oka, Yokosuka, Kanagawa, 239-0847 Japan
y.sato@west.east.ntt.co.jp, {kawashima.harumi, okuda.hidenori, oku.masahiro}@labs.ntt.co.jp

Abstract. The ability to detect new topics and track them is important given the huge amounts of documents. This paper introduces a trend-based document clustering algorithm for analyzing them. Its key characteristic is that it gives scores to words on the basis of the fluctuation in word frequency. The algorithm generates clusters in a practical time, with $O(n)$ processing cost due to preliminary calculation of document distances. The attribute allows the user to settle on the best level of granularity for identifying topics. Experiments prove that our algorithm can gather relevant documents with F measure of 63.0% on average from the beginning to the end of topic lifetime and it largely surpasses other algorithms.

Keywords: trend, clustering, gradient model, word frequency

1. Introduction

Due to the information explosion on the WWW, the cost of catching up with the latest trends has risen. Consumer Generated Media (CGM), such as weblogs and social networking service (SNS), are only accelerating this explosion. The best approach to recognizing trends from among the huge number of documents being created is to analyze the topics in them.

The goal of Topic Detection and Tracking (TDT) is to find state-of-the-art events in a stream of broadcast news stories (Allan et al., 1998). The study defines segmentation, new event detection, and event tracking as the major tasks. Segmentation proceeds by automatically dividing a text stream into topically homogeneous blocks. New event detection identifies stories in several continuous news streams that pertain to new or previously unidentified events. Event tracking identifies any and all subsequent stories describing the same event as sample instances of stories describing the event. Document clustering is an efficient approach to find topics in many documents.

In the tasks, new event detection is intimately related to clustering, and involves the functions of retrospective detection and on-line detection. The input to retrospective detection task is the entire corpus, and it is desired to divide them into event-specific groups. The input to on-line detection is a chronologically ordered document stream, and the change point of topics should be found.

On the WWW, where documents are numerous and increasing hourly, our goal is to provide an environment that supports users on finding and tracking the topics. In particular, sensitive detection of new topics is needed there. Then, our research is categorized as both on-line event detection and event tracking in TDT. As a matter of fact, both aspects are essential for adequately grasping the topics. This paper introduces a trend-based document clustering algorithm that enables the detection of topic occurrence at the earliest possible stage and the observation of topic transition.

The remainder of this paper is organized as follows: Section 2 describes related work; Section 3 describes our clustering algorithm; Section 4 describes our experiments and their results; and we conclude in Section 5.

2. Related Work

New event detection is the target of incremental clustering algorithms for on-line documents. In new event detection, conventionally, the similarity between new document and existing clsuters are

---

22nd Pacific Asia Conference on Language, Information and Computation, pages 331–340

calculated, and it is judged that which cluster is appropriate to include the document or any one is inappropriate. Developments of similarity measure (Dharanipragada et al., 1999) and term weighting (Brants et al., 2003) have proposed for better detection performance.

Many clustering algorithms have been applied for the task, such as single-pass based algorithm (Papka and Allan, 1998) and incremental k-means algorithm (Walls et al., 1999). They do not consider trends in on-line documents. However, it is required to focus attention on "time" for the sensitive topic detection.

The time-focused approach attempts to enhance detection performance by attenuating document similarities on the basis of time interval between documents (Yang et al., 1998). The strategy yielded measurable improvements in their on-line detection experiments. Word distribution in a corpus is used to choose core lexicon in the corpus (Zhang et al., 2004). The algorithm is applied to choose topical words in document if the documents are divided into some parts by their timestamps, though time temporal continuity is not considered.

Another incremental clustering algorithm F^2ICM (Ishikawa et al., 2001; Khy et al., 2006) is characterized by its ease in updating the statistics value used for calculating document similarities when new documents arrive. It defines the forgetting model as being exponential. It attenuates worth of documents exponentially as time passes, as if they are forgotten. In their model, recent documents are likely to be situated closer to each other, and older ones are likely to be more widely separated. The algorithm tends to generate clusters containing especially newer documents. On the other hand, persistent clusters are seldom generated. Thus, the algorithm is not the best way to observe topics continuously in terms of event tracking.

3. Trend-based Clustering Algorithm

What the prior studies lack in is the responsiveness to the current trends. Our approach to accomplish the goal is based on the trends in documents.

More and more documents describing the same event are created when people's interest in the event arises. In on-line documents, a rapid increase in the frequency of a word indicates a trend toward one or more topics relevant to the word. Taking such trends into account, when clustering documents, yields the sensitive detection of new topics.

The most remarkable feature in our algorithm is that it senses current trends by word frequency fluctuation and gathers relevant documents based on the latest trends. Since its clustering process finishes in a short time after the classification granularity is indicated, it helps users to find adequate clustering results interactively that meet their intentions.

Word weights in our algorithm involve word appearance growth and its accumulative appearance. We declare the gradient model in the following part before describing word weights. The concept of gradient, essential idea in our algorithm, represents the growth of the two aspects. Word weighting algorithm is described in the second subsection, and the clustering algorithm is detailed in the third subsection.

3.1. Gradient Model

The impression of word appearance in a document declines over time. Suppose that the initial intensity of the impression is one, the intensity after time Δt can be defined as $e^{-\Delta t/T_l}$ following the forgetting model in F^2ICM (Ishikawa et al., 2001). T_l denotes the parameter deciding the rate of intensity attenuation.

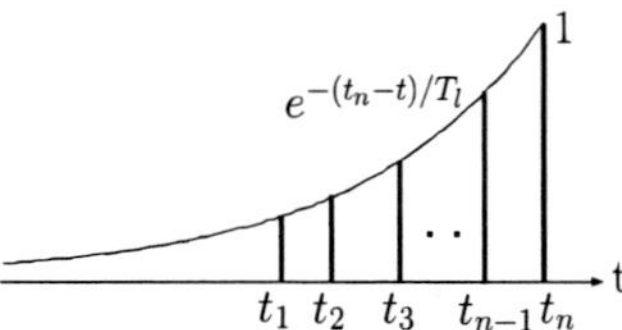

Figure 1: Impression Intensity.

Figure 1 shows the residual impression of each appearance of word w. Here, t_n is the time of the nth appearance. Given that the current time is t_n, the current appearance is assigned the maximum

332

impression (the intensity is one), and the impression of w appearance at t remains $e^{-(t_n-t)/T_l}$. Then the total impressions score up to now, we define this as memory M, is described as follows.

$$M(w,t_n) = \sum_{t=1}^{n} e^{-(t_n-t)/T_l}. \qquad (1)$$

In consecutive appearance of words, the memory M is efficiently updated if the previous result is stored. Updating follows Equation 2. If the word appears at t_{n+1}, time Δt after t_n, the new $M(w,t_{n+1})$ is represented as the sum of the previous result multiplied by the attenuation coefficient for the elapsed time Δt and the latest intensity.

$$
\begin{aligned}
M(w,t_{n+1}) &= \sum_{i=1}^{n+1} e^{-(t_{n+1}-t_i)/T_l} \\
&= \sum_{i=1}^{n} e^{-(t_n+\Delta t-t_i)/T_l} + 1 \\
&= e^{-\Delta t/T_l} \cdot \sum_{i=1}^{n} e^{-(t_n-t_i)/T_l} + 1 \\
&= e^{-\Delta t/T_l} \cdot M(w,t_n) + 1. \qquad (2)
\end{aligned}
$$

On the other hand, the memory can be also regarded as the amount of word w appearances with time attenuation. With strong attenuation parameter T_s ($<T_l$), the memory is approximate recent frequency of the word; the recent frequency F is represented in Equation 3, as well as M.

$$F(w,t_n) = \sum_{i=1}^{n} e^{-(t_n-t_i)/T_s}. \qquad (3)$$

Suppose that the recent frequency of a word is higher compared to the amount of permanent memory which the word has given up to now. Then the word is in the growth phase.

Here, we declare the concept of gradient as the difference of the memory from the recent frequency.

$$G(w,t_n) = \frac{\alpha F(w,t_n) - \beta M(w,t_n)}{M(w,t_n)}. \qquad (4)$$

The denominator is a normalizing element for eliminating the effects of general words with high frequency. α and β are coefficients.

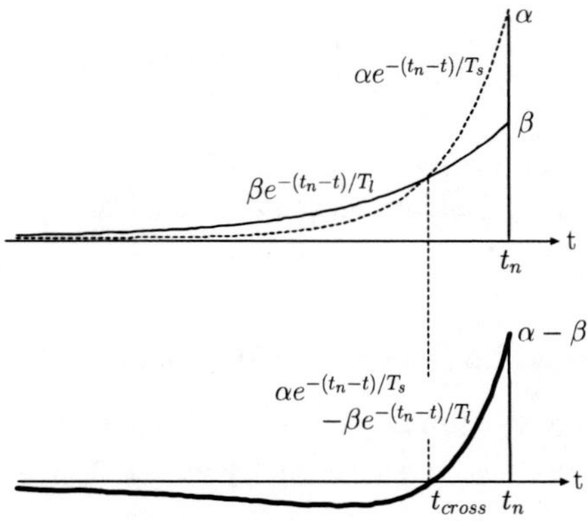

Figure 2: Differential Curve.

In the definition of gradient, the numerator, $\alpha F(w,t_n) - \beta M(w,t_n)$, is also explained by Figure 2. Two curves are drawn in the upper part. The solid line curve corresponds to the memory of w, with attenuation parameter T_l. The other dashed line corresponds to the recent frequency of the word, with strong attenuation parameter T_s. In fact, the curves do not directly plot memory or recent frequency rather the intensity attenuation used in calculating them. α and β in the definition of $G(w,t_n)$ correspond to intercepts respectively in the upper part of Figure 2. The bold line curve in the bottom part, we define this as differential curve, corresponds to the difference between the dashed and solid lines.

By the way, M and F, represented in summations, can be represented in integrations if a word appears continuously. Moreover, $G(w,t_n)$ score of a word with invariable frequency should be zero. Then the following equality is true.

$$\alpha \int_{-\infty}^{t_n} e^{-(t_n-t)/T_s}\,dt - \beta \int_{-\infty}^{t_n} e^{-(t_n-t)/T_l}\,dt = 0. \qquad (5)$$

The first term is deformed as follows.

$$\alpha \int_{-\infty}^{t_n} e^{-(t_n-t)/T_s}\,dt = \alpha \int_{-\infty}^{0} e^{\tau} T_s\,d\tau$$
$$= \alpha T_s. \qquad (6)$$

Deforming the second term in Equation 5 in the same way, the ratio of α to β is derived.

$$\frac{\alpha}{\beta} = \frac{T_l}{T_s}. \qquad (7)$$

For simplification, we regard the current ($t=t_n$) difference between two curves in Figure 2 as one.

$$\alpha - \beta = 1. \qquad (8)$$

Incidentally, α and β are derived as follows, respectively, from Equation 7 and 8.

$$\alpha = \frac{T_l}{T_l - T_s}, \quad \beta = \frac{T_s}{T_l - T_s}. \qquad (9)$$

$G(w,t_n)$ is interpreted as differential operator for frequency transition. $G(w,t_n)$ is zero if w appears with invariable frequency. The value is above zero if the frequency is increasing as time passes, and below zero if decreasing.

The time t_{cross} when differential curve crosses horizontal axis is also derived as follows.

$$t_{cross} = \frac{T_l T_s}{T_l - T_s}\left(\ln T_s - \ln T_l\right). \qquad (10)$$

The current growth rate is evaluated as an accumulation of past appearances by the differential curve. The appearance until t_{cross} affects negatively, and the appearance after t_{cross} is enhanced positively.

3.2. Trend Scores for Words and Document Expression

$G(w,t_n)$ quantifies the degree of growth. That is, the value does not accurately reflect the current trend. Word scores for trend-based clustering should reflect both growth and accumulative appearance.

Therefore, we define the trend score of word w, $TREND(w,t_n)$ in Equation 11, as the accumulation of its gradient scores with time attenuation. as well as recent frequency F.

$$TREND(w,t_n) = \sum_{i=1}^{n} G(w,t_i) \cdot e^{-(t_n-t_i)/T_s}. \qquad (11)$$

Trend score can be easily updated as well as memory or recent frequency by multiplying attenuation coefficient for elapsed time to the previous result, and then adding the latest gradient.

$$TREND(w, t_{n+1}) = e^{-\Delta t / T_s} \cdot TREND(w, t_n) + G(w, t_{n+1}). \qquad (12)$$

All the system has to do is to preserve the latest M, F, and $TREND$ for each word, and the timestamp when they were last updated. When a new document arrives, M and F for the words in the document are updated as shown in Equation 2, and then the latest $TREND$ is calculated as shown in Equation 12.

For trend-based document clustering, documents are expressed as vectors based on $TREND$. The vector of document d_n (arrived at t_n) is defined in the following equation.

$$\vec{v_n} = (W(w_1, t_n), W(w_2, t_n), W(w_3, t_n), \cdots, W(w_m, t_n)). \qquad (13)$$

Here, m denotes the number of unique words in d_n, and weight $W(w_x, t_n)$ is defined as follows.

$$W(w_x, t_n) = \begin{cases} TREND(w_x, t_n) & \text{if } TREND(w_x, t_n) > 0 \\ 0 & \text{else} \end{cases}. \qquad (14)$$

Equation 14 means that words with negative trend scores are eliminated from the document. This is because words with negative score can be considered to be completely irrelevant to current trends. However, the same word in another document is used for vector element if its trend score rises above zero due to the arrival of the second document.

3.3. Clustering based on Trend Scores

Many clustering algorithms have been invented, which are roughly classified into hierarchical or partitioning-optimization. The former generate a document tree called a dendrogram, whereas the latter give flat document clusters without any hierarchy.

For observing topic transition, the clustering algorithm should offer cluster reproducibility. There are two perspectives to reproducibility. First, the documents, already classified into clusters, should not be moved to another cluster when a new document arrives. If documents in a cluster move continuously, we cannot observe topic expansion and declination. Next, the documents should also remain stable when classification granularity is changed. If cluster coherency is preserved during the merging and partitioning processes, we can find the most effective level of granularity easily.

For the twin goals of reproducibilities, our approach is based on the single linkage clustering algorithm as a hierarchical scheme. Most hierarchical algorithms have processing cost of $O(n^2)$ where n is the number of documents. However, the single linkage algorithm has processing cost of $O(n)$ after a threshold is given and the nearest document for each document has been already identified.

Our clustering algorithm is composed of two steps. In the first step, distances between a new document and prior ones are calculated upon its arrival, and the nearest one is recorded in a nearest-neighbor table. In the second step, document clusters are generated based on the threshold given by the user. This admits of interactive analysis through the flexible threshold changes in a practical time by using the nearest-neighbor table as a cache.

The distance between two clusters, in the single linkage algorithm, is defined as the distance between the closest documents in the clusters. One of the problems in this algorithm is the chaining phenomenon, which is due to the definition of distances between clusters. Even if each two documents in a cluster are substantially relevant, the farthest documents in the cluster may cover decidedly irrelevant topics. The focus of the single linkage algorithm is the result of giving preference to both high speed clustering performance and reproducibility rather than trying to suppress the influence of chaining.

The two key steps in our clustering algorithm are detailed below.

Step1: Updating Nearest-Neighbor Table

The left of Figure 3 visually shows the structure of a nearest-neighbor table. The nodes denote documents, and d_n inside the circles denote document identifiers. The larger n is, the later the document arrived. Newer documents are placed right of others in the figure. The arrows denote the nearest links from newer document to older one, and the values beside the arrows denote the distance between two documents.

When the latest document d_6 arrives, the nearest-neighbor table is updated as follows.

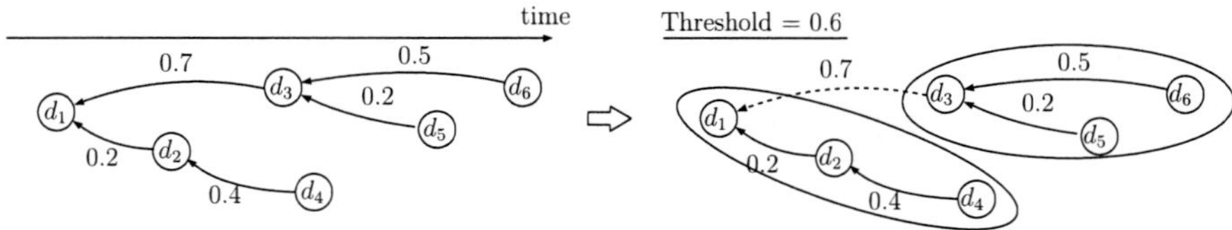

Figure 3: Nearest-Neighbor Table and Clusters

First, for the words in d_6, M, F, and *TREND* are updated based on their previous results and the elapsed time since they were last updated. In the definition of trend scores in Equation 11, the score for a word with the first appearance is one. The timestamp of d_6 is stored for the next update. Then, the current trend scores are assigned to d_6; the weighted words form the vector of the document. Though trend scores of words are updated whenever new documents arrive, $\vec{v_6}$ (the vector of d_6) is never updated even if the new documents contain same words in d_6. In other words, weighted words in a document reflect the trends at the time of its arrival. Therefore, scores in different documents may be different if the documents arrive at different times.

Second, $\vec{v_6}$ is compared to the vectors of older documents respectively, and the distances are calculated. The distance between two documents is defined by subtracting cosine similarity of respective vectors from one. The cosine similarity is normalized between zero and one.

$$\mathrm{dis}(d_m, d_n) = 1 - \mathrm{sim}(\vec{v_m}, \vec{v_n}) \qquad (15)$$

When the nearest document as d_6 is identified from among the older documents, the identifier of the nearest document and the corresponding distance are added to the nearest-neighbor table. In the Figure 3, the nearest neighbor as d_6 is d_3, and the distance is 0.5.

Step2: Clustering based on Nearest-Neighbor Table

The clustering process begins after the threshold is given. Since the nearest-neighbor table specifies the most similar older documents, document clusters can be generated in a short time.

The right of Figure 3 shows the composition of clusters after threshold 0.6 is given. Links shorter than 0.6 are valid, and only the link from d_3 to d_1 is regarded as invalid. As a result, two clusters, "d_1, d_2, d_4" and "d_3, d_5, d_6", are generated. Since it is not necessary to update distances between clusters during clustering processes, the algorithm can generate clusters with $O(n)$ processing cost. Even if the threshold is changed, the algorithm can process again with the same cost.

4. Evaluation

For the evaluation, we reviewed the clusters generated by our algorithm, and examined the sensitivity performance as regards new topics.

We used the Mainichi newspaper tagged corpus (in Japanese) in our experiments. All articles are tagged with issued date and category of the page on which they were placed, such as world topics, politics, economics, and sports. Several keywords are attached to each article.

We extracted 1,037 articles which are classified as world topics in January and February in 1994. The number of keywords in articles varies from 8 to 243, and the average article includes 54.2 keywords. We used the keywords as the elements of the document vectors. Though we stated that trend scores are updated each time a new document arrives, the scores are updated once a day in this experiment because the documents in the corpus had only day-based timestamps.

4.1. Reviewing Clusters

To comprehend the characteristics of our clustering algorithm, we reviewed the clusters formed with different thresholds.

In this experiment, we set T_l as 10(days) and T_s as 5(days) so as to set t_{cross} to 7(days) approximately. The appearance in the last seven days is thus emphasized in calculating trend scores. Our word weighting algorithm performs reasonably well only when the positive and negative regions of the differential curve are populated by existing documents; word scores calculated in the earlier period are not proper. Therefore, the articles prior to the last thirty days (about half of whole period) were not used for constructing the nearest-neighbor table, though all articles were processed to obtain trend scores during the last thirty days. Consequently, 567 articles (from the total of 1,037) were included in the nearest-neighbor table, and used for clustering.

Table 1 and Table 2 summarize the largest top 10 clusters yielded by our algorithm. They are the results at the end of the two months. In the results in Table 1, instead of giving distance threshold directly, we indicate the threshold that made the number of clusters half the number of articles in the nearest-neighbor table. In the results in Table 2, we set the threshold to make the number of clusters one quarter the number of articles. Clusters are sorted by size, the number of articles in it, in descending order. Span is the days from the timestamp of the latest article to that of the earliest one in each cluster. Clusters are manually summarized at the rightmost column.

Table 1: The Summary of Top 10 Clusters (clusters: 1/2).

No.	articles	span(days)	summary
1-1	84	22	Sarajevo, Bosnia-Herzegovina, Russia, etc
1-2	57	21	Bosnia, China, Vietnam, etc
1-3	13	3	Hebron random shooting
1-4	10	28	USA(North Korea, China), UN
1-5	6	5	Russian election
1-6	6	9	relationship between China and Taiwan
1-7	6	21	Austria, Ukraine, Russia
1-8	6	3	Myanmar(Aung San Suu Kyi)
1-9	6	5	USA(lifting of the economic sanctions for Vietnam)
1-10	6	23	North Korea(IAEA), China, Iran & Iraq

Table 2: The Summary of Top 10 Clusters (clusters: 1/4).

No.	articles	span(days)	summary
2-1	160	30	North Korea(IAEA), China, South Korea
2-2	87	22	Sarajevo, Bosnia-Herzegovina, PKO, etc
2-3	21	24	relationship between China and Taiwan, North Korea
2-4	14	8	Russian politics
2-5	13	3	Hebron random shooting
2-6	10	9	Italy, China, NATO
2-7	9	19	North Korea, Russia
2-8	9	14	Taiwan, Israel
2-9	7	21	NATO, Russia
2-10	6	3	Myanmar(Aung San Suu Kyi)

As for the clusters in Table 1, a review finds that No.1-3, 1-5, 1-6, 1-8, and 1-9 cover single topics; the other clusters are composed of several topics. The results are relative to cluster span. Clusters with short span gather relative articles quite precisely. Longer cluster spans indicate more topics. Larger clusters, such as No.1-1 and 1-2, cover especially wide various topics due to the chaining effect.

The clusters in Table 2 are larger. Though some larger clusters are created by general words such as country name, and other larger ones are affected by chaining, two of top ten clusters, No. 2-5 and 2-10, completely correspond to No.1-3 and 1-8 in Table 1. Both events described in these two clusters occurred at the end of February, the last one week in our dataset. Our algorithm sensitively gathered the events at the earliest possible stage just after their occurrences and separated them from the other events definitely.

4.2. Sensitivity to New Topics

The purpose of the next experiment was to evaluate the algorithm's sensitivity to new topics. Sensitivity is achieved when the word scores reflect current trends. We started by comparing the relationship between daily document frequency of a word and its scores. Next, we examined the performance of gathering documents related to new topics.

In the experiment, as benchmark word weighting algorithms, we prepared simple "IDF", "weighted-DF(W-DF)" using the summation of document frequency with time attenuation, and "*Gradient*" as the growth of word appearance, in addition to our word weighting algorithm "*Trend*". W-DF corresponds to $F(w,t_n)$, and *Gradient* corresponds to $G(w,t_n)$; they are obtained in the process of trend score calculation. In scoring words by IDF, the total number of documents and document frequency of words were updated each day by using articles up to the day because it is not feasible to obtain future given our assumption. Therefore, scores by IDF changed daily. We also regarded minus scores as zero in *Gradient*, as well as *Trend*.

Word Scores
Word scores yielded by the four algorithms are drawn in Figure 4.

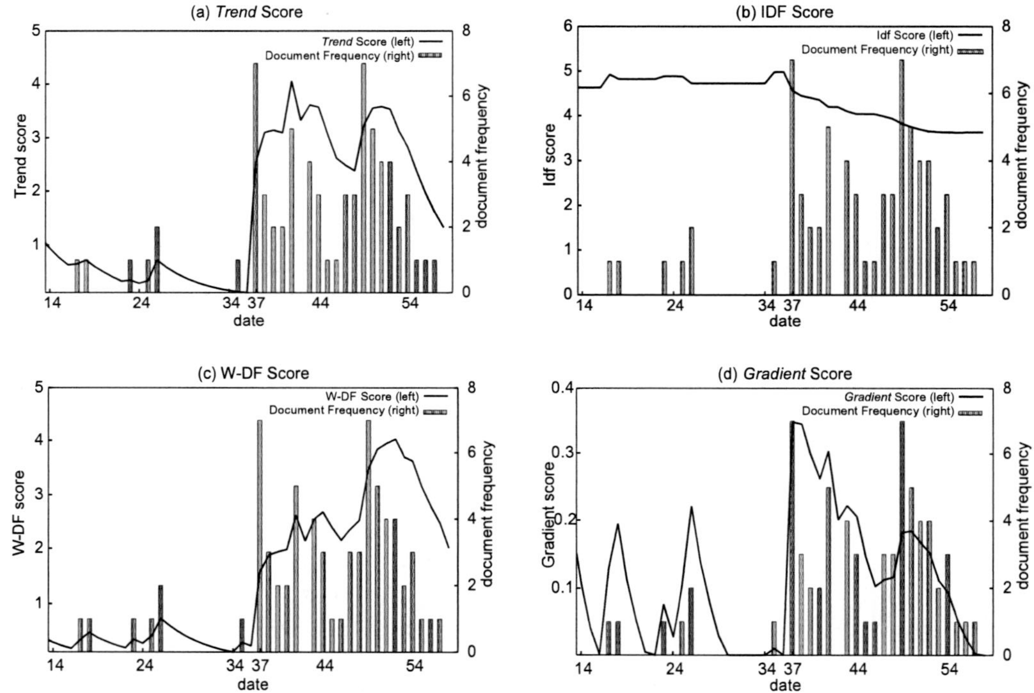

Figure 4: Document Frequency and Word Scores: "Sarajevo" (a)*Trend* (b)IDF (c)W-DF (d)*Gradient*.

They are the results for the word "Sarajevo", which was frequently used in news articles in the period. The bars denote daily document frequency where the word appears. The lines denote the scores output by each algorithm. *Trend*(a) surges at the first peak in document frequency at 37th day, and hovers at a relatively high level on following days. IDF(b) changes fluidly while it declines as document frequency increases. The specific difference between *Trend* and W-DF(c) is the sensitivity to dramatic increase of document frequency. W-DF rises gradually as time passes after the first high peak on the 37th day because it reflects the accumulation of frequency. *Gradient*(d) reflects the peak on the 37th day as well as *Trend*. However, it also overreacts to smaller peaks in the earlier period. It reflects the behavior seen when the scores are obtained from just the rate of frequency change. *Gradient* scores rise strongly at small peaks only if it was missing articles on prior days. On the other hand, due to the negative coefficient in the differential curve, it seldom reaches high scores after big peaks pass.

Eventually, *Trend* scores faithfully follow document frequency change, and they reflect the beginning and the end of trend lifetime. Moreover, they are unaffected by smaller peaks.

Clustering Performance

We evaluated clustering performance precisely.

For this experiment, we prepared a target article group with fifteen articles among the corpus. They are manually gathered so as to cover a single topic. For the four algorithms, nearest-neighbor tables were constructed for the last thirty days, as in the previous experiment. After constructing them, we generated clusters by adding articles day by day. The first results contain the articles in the first day of the thirty day period. The second ones contain the articles the first two days.

The previous experiments proved that using the large threshold, which yielded the cluster number of 25% of all documents, could gather articles related to new topics. Since reducing cluster number makes it easier to comprehend, we also used the large threshold in this experiment.

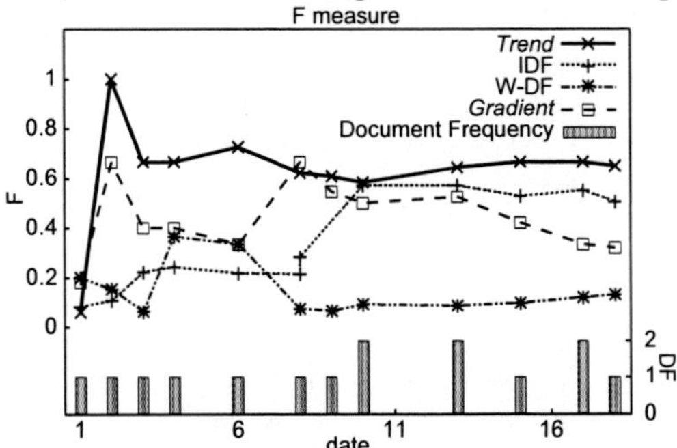

Figure 5: Target Group Detection Performance.

Table 3: Target Group Detection Performance.

date	Trend	IDF	W-DF	Gradient
1	0.059	0.083	0.20	0.18
2	**1.0**	0.11	0.15	**0.67**
3	0.67	0.22	0.062	0.40
4	0.67	0.24	**0.36**	0.40
6	0.73	0.22	0.33	0.33
8	0.63	0.21	0.073	**0.67**
9	0.61	0.28	0.065	0.55
10	0.58	**0.57**	0.091	0.50
13	0.64	**0.57**	0.086	0.53
15	0.67	0.53	0.097	0.42
17	0.67	0.55	0.12	0.33
18	0.65	0.51	0.13	0.32
Ave.	0.63	0.44	0.34	0.18

Figure 5 plots F measure day by day. The horizontal axis plots the days since the first article in the target group appeared. The bars are the number of articles in the target group. Data details are shown in Table 3; several dates are missing because the performance was estimated for the dates when the articles in the target group were issued. The bold values indicate the best performance achieved by each algorithm.

Trend performed well, especially for a few days after the first target article was issued, and recorded the highest performance throughout almost the entire period. The averaged performance was 63%. Though IDF demonstrated excellent performance after several articles were issued, it did not work well initially. The performance of W-DF was significantly below that of *Trend* while there was not so much of a difference between their word scores in Figure 4(a) and Figure 4(c). This is because the scores of general words tend to be overweighted by IDF. Though *Gradient* proved high performance compared to IDF or W-DF initially, it does not last so long, as also seen in word scores in Figure 4(d).

The experiment proved the performance of our algorithm to detect topics sensitively and follow them over time.

5. Conclusion

This paper introduced a trend-based clustering algorithm for detecting and tracking new topics in online documents. Our algorithm is marked by its word weighting algorithm based on the gradient model, that represents word appearance growth. The clustering process adopts the single linkage algorithm, that offers high speed clustering in a practical time.

The experiments proved that word weights in our algorithm reflect their frequency transitions and that the clustering algorithm can gather related news articles persistently as well as sensitively identify new topics. The performance meets the purpose of detecting new topics effectively and tracking them sustainably for documents increasing hourly.

Our next goal is to optimize the adequate parameters related to attenuation power for different types of documents.

References

Allan, James., Jaime Carbonell, George Doddington, Jonathan Yamron, and Yiming Yang. 1998. Topic Detection and Tracking Pilot Study Final Report, *Proceedings of the DARPA Broadcast News Transcription and Understanding Workshop.*

Brants, Thorsten., Francine Chen, and Ayman Farahat. 2003. A System for New Event Detection, *Proceedings of SIGIR 2003, the 26th Annual International ACM SIGIR Conference on Research and Development in Information Retrieval.*

Dharanipragada, S., M. Franz, J.S. McCarley, S. Roukos, and T. Ward. 1999. Story Segmentation and Topic Detection in the Broadcast News Domain, *Proceedings of the DARPA Broadcast News Workshop.*

Ishikawa, Yoshiharu., Yibing Chen, and Hiroyuki Kitagawa. 2001. An On-Line Document Clustering Method Based on Forgetting Factors, *5th European Conference on Research and Advanced Technology for Digital Libraries.*

Khy, Sophoin., Yoshiharu Ishikawa, and Hiroyuki Kitagawa. 2006. Novelty-based Incremental Document Clustering for On-line Documents, *Proceedings of the 22nd International Conference on Data Engineering Workshops.*

Papka, Ron., and James Allan. 1998. On-Line New Event Detection using Single Pass Clustering, *UMASS Computer Science Technical Report 98-21.*

Walls, Frederick., Hubert Jin, Sreenivasa Sista, and Richard Schwartz. 1999. Topic Detection in Broadcast News, *Proceedings of the DARPA Broadcast News Workshop, 193-198.*

Yang, Yiming., Tom Pierce, and Jaime Carbonell. 1998. A Study on Retrospective and On-Line Event Detection, *Proceedings of the 21st Annual International ACM SIGIR conference on Research and development in information retrieval.*

Zhang, Huarui., Churen Huang, and Shiwen Yu. 2004. Distributional Consistency: As A General Method for Defining A Core Lexicon, *Proceedings of the 4th International Conference on Language Resources and Evaluation.*

Sentiment Sentence Extraction Using a Hierarchical Directed Acyclic Graph Structure and a Bootstrap Approach [*]

Kazutaka Shimada[a], Daigo Hashimoto[a], and Tsutomu Endo[a]

[a] Department of Artificial Intelligence, Kyushu Institute of Technology
680-4 Iizuka Fukuoka 820-8502, Japan
{shimada, d_hashimoto, endo}@pluto.ai.kyutech.ac.jp

Abstract. As the World Wide Web rapidly grows, a huge number of online documents are easily accessible on the Web. We obtain a huge number of review documents that include user's opinions for products. To classify the opinions is one of the hottest topics in natural language processing. In general, we need a large amount of training data for the classification process. However, construction of training data by hand is costly. The goal of our study is to construct a sentiment tagging tool for particular domains. In this paper, we propose a method of sentiment sentence extraction for the 1st step of the system. For the task, we use a Hierarchical Directed Acyclic Graph (HDAG) structure. We obtained high accuracy with the graph based approach. Furthermore, we apply a bootstrap approach to the sentiment sentence extraction process. The experimental result shows the effectiveness of the method.

Keywords: Sentiment analysis, sentence extraction, similarity, HDAG.

1. Introduction

As the World Wide Web rapidly grows, a huge number of online documents are easily accessible on the Web. Finding information relevant to user needs has become increasingly important. The most important information on the Web is usually contained in the text. We obtain a huge number of review documents that include user's opinions for products. Buying products, users usually survey the product reviews. More precise and effective methods for evaluating the products are useful for users. To classify the opinions is one of the hottest topics in natural language processing. Many researchers have recently studied extraction and classification of opinions (Hatzivassiloglou and McKeown 1997, Kobayashi et al. 2005, Pang et al. 2002, Wiebe and Riloff 2005).

There are many research areas for sentiment analysis; extraction of sentiment expressions, identification of sentiment polarity of sentences, classification of review documents and so on. The goal of our study is to easily construct a corpus for sentiment information for particular domains that users want. For the purpose we need to extract sentiment sentences from documents as the 1st step of the corpus construction. Extraction of sentiment expressions or sentiment sentences is one of the most important tasks in the sentiment analysis because classification tasks usually need a large amount of training data to generate a high accuracy classifier. There are several reports for classification of sentences (Kudo and Matsumoto 2004, Osajima et al .2005). However, the purpose of these studies is to classify sentences into positive and negative opinions. Our purpose in this paper is to classify sentences into opinions and non-

[*] Copyright 2008 by Kazutaka Shimada, Daigo Hashimoto, and Tsutomu Endo. This research was partially supported by the Ministry of Education, Science, Sports and Culture, Grant-in-Aid for Scientific Research (C), 18500115, 2008.

opinions. Touge et al. (2004) and Kawaguchi et al. (2006) have proposed methods for opinion extraction. However, these approaches essentially need a large amount of training data for the process. Construction of training data by hand is costly. Kaji and Kitsuregara (2006) have reported a method of acquisition of sentiment sentences in HTML documents. The method required only several rules by hand and obtained high accuracy. Also they have proposed a method for building lexicon for sentiment analysis (Kaji and Kitsuregawa 2007). The knowledge extracted from the Web by using the proposed methods contains the huge quantities of words and sentences. Takamura et al. (2005) also have reported a method for extracting polarity of words. These dictionaries are versatile and valuable for users because they do not depend on a specific domain. Here, assume that we need to construct a system for a domain. In that case, we often desire domain-specific knowledge for the system. Therefore, we need to efficiently extract sentiment sentences, which depend on a particular domain or topic.

In this paper, we propose a method of sentiment sentence extraction. It uses several sample sentences for the extraction process. In the process, we compute a similarity between the sample sentences and target sentences. Yu and Hatzivassiloglou (2003) have reported a similarity based method using words, phrases and WordNet synsets for sentiment sentence extraction. However, word-level features are not always suitable for the extraction process because of lack of relations between words. For the similarity calculation we, therefore, employ the graph-based approach, called Hierarchical Directed Acyclic Graph (HDAG), which has been proposed by Suzuki et al. (2006). Furthermore, we apply a bootstrap approach into the sentiment sentence extraction process. The number of extracted sentiment sentences increases with the bootstrap approach.

2. A Graph-based Data Structure

In this section, we explain a graph-based data structure to compute a similarity.

2.1. Hierarchical Directed Acyclic Graph

In natural language processing, bag-of-words representation is the most general way to express features of a sentence for the similarity calculation. However, it is insufficient to represent the features of a sentence because of lack of relations between words.

To solve the problems, Suzuki et al. (2006) have reported a new graph-based approach, called Hierarchical Directed Acyclic Graph kernels (HDAG). The method can handle many linguistic features in a sentence and includes characteristics of tree and sequence kernels. The HDAG is a hierarchized graph-in-graph structure. It represents semantic or grammatical information in a sentence. In this paper, we use the HDAG structure for the sentiment sentence extraction. We compute a similarity between HDAGs generated from sentences. See (Suzuki et al. 2006) for more information about the HDAG.

2.2. Layer

Layers in the HDAG denote grammatical information in a sentence. To compute similarity between sentences correctly, we add some layers to a naive HDAG structure. The HDAG in this paper consists of three layers as follows:

- **Combined POS tag layer**

  This layer consists of part of speech tags of words. We unify the POS tags of words in a bunsetsu[1] into one node. This layer expresses a pack of POS tags in each bunsetsu.

- **POS tag layer**

  This layer consists of the POS tags of each word or each compound noun.

- **Word/Compound noun layer**

  This layer contains the surface expression of each word. We can use the surface information for calculation of similarity by adding this layer. The layer is used for handling compound

---

[1] A bunsetsu is a linguistic unit in Japanese. It usually consists of one content word and its function words.

nouns in bunsetsus. This layer often resolves a problem of difference between surface expressions. We unify nouns belonging to a compound noun and then dispose it under the POS node of its compound nouns. For example, we flexibly treat the difference of the following expressions in similarity calculation by adding this layer: "file downloading software", "downloading software" and "software".

Figure 1 shows an example of an HDAG expression in this paper. In the HDAG, the elements, such as "Bunsetsu" and "Common noun", in each rectangle are the attributes of each node. The directed links are a kind of the dependency relation between elements. The double-headed arrows denote the link between a node and a sub-graph enclosed with a dashed line.

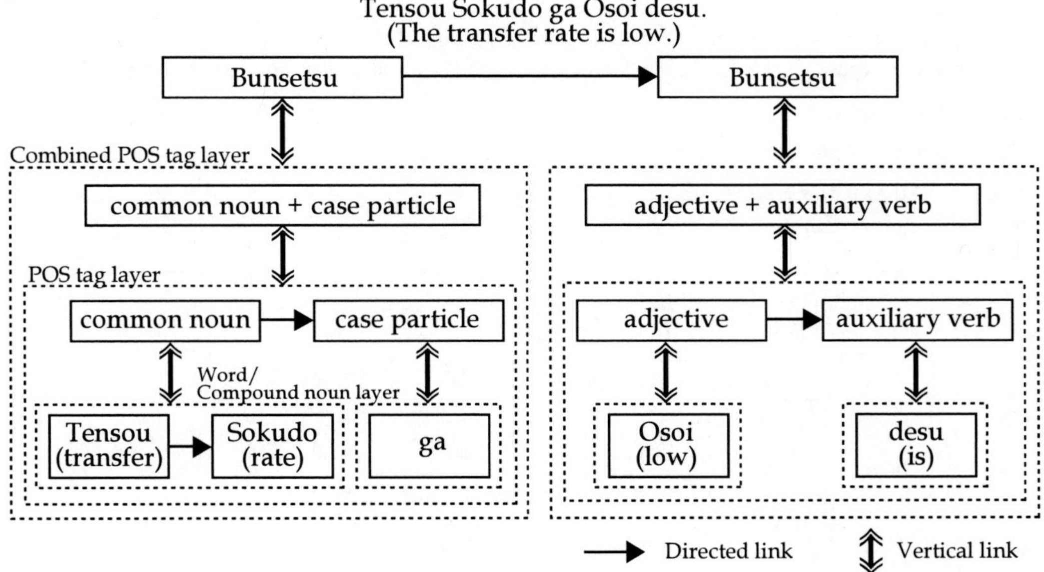

Figure 1: An example of an HDAG expression.

3. Similarity Calculation

In this section, we explain a method of similarity calculation based on the HDAG structure. First, we describe a conversion method of sentences into the HDAGs. Next, we explain an extraction method of hierarchical attribute subsequences from HDAG structures for the similarity calculation. Finally, we introduce a method of similarity calculation and the extraction process using it.

3.1. Preprocessing

There are two processes as the preprocessing for similarity calculation; conversion and extraction of hierarchical attribute subsequences. First we explain the conversion process. To convert sentences into the HDAG structure, we need to analyze them, that is morphological analysis and dependency analysis. In this paper we use JUMAN[2] as the morphological analyzer and KNP[3] as the dependency analyzer.

   Next we need to extract hierarchical attribute subsequences for the similarity calculation. A hierarchical attribute subsequence is an attribute list with hierarchical structures. The similarity is computed from correspondence of hierarchical attribute subsequences extracted from sentences that we want to compare.

---

[2] http://nlp.kuee.kyoto-u.ac.jp/nl-resource/juman.html
[3] http://nlp.kuee.kyoto-u.ac.jp/nl-resource/knp.html

Here Suzuki et al. (2006) introduced two factors; β and γ. The β ($0 < \beta \leq 1$) is the factor for the correspondence. The value of each hierarchical attribute sequence is multiplied by $\sqrt{\beta^m}$ where m represents the number of attributes in the hierarchical attribute sequence. The λ is the decay factor ($0 \leq \lambda \leq 1$). The system allows not only exactly matching structures but also similar structures by using this factor. The actual decay value of a skipping node v_i is $\Lambda(v_i) = \lambda^{n+1}$ where n is the number of nodes in a graph   if vertical link exists, or $\Lambda(v) = \lambda$ otherwise.

Figure 2 shows an example of hierarchical attribute subsequences and the factors[4]. In the figure, a dependency relation and a hierarchical relation are expressed by using a comma and a nested structure, respectively. For the two HDAGs, the hierarchical attribute subsequence <Bunsetsu <Noun, Particle>, Bunsetsu <Adj, Aux>> appears in both sentences. Since the number of attributes in the hierarchical attribute subsequence is 6, the value of β is $\sqrt{\beta^6} = \beta^3$. The hierarchical attribute subsequence of the 2nd sentence in the figure is generated by skipping a node, Adverb. Therefore, the weight contains $\lambda^{1+1} = \lambda^2$. These weights are used in the similarity calculation process.

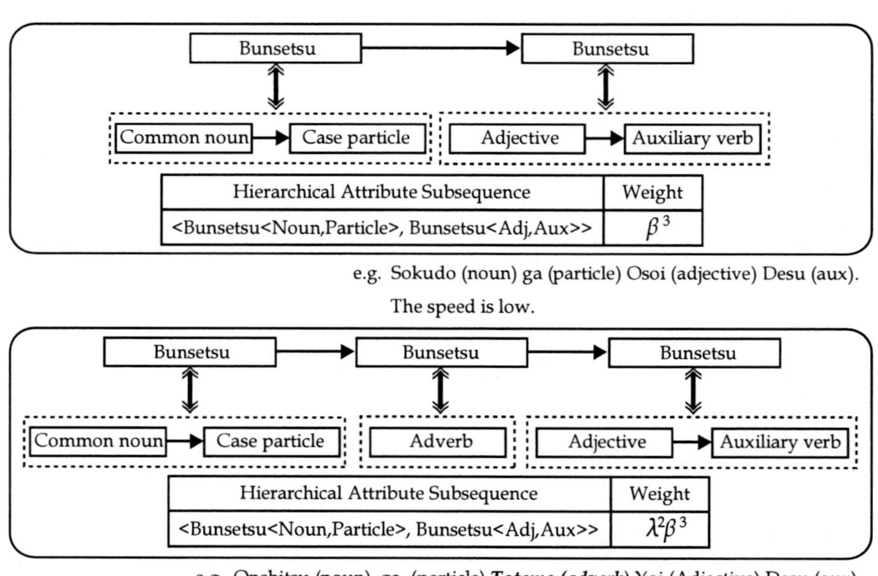

e.g. Sokudo (noun) ga (particle) Osoi (adjective) Desu (aux).
The speed is low.

e.g. Onshitsu (noun) ga (particle) *Totemo (adverb)* Yoi (Adjective) Desu (aux).
The sound quality is *very* good.

Figure 2: An example of corresponding hierarchical attribute subsequences and the weight.

3.2. Similarity between Two Sentences

Next, we compute a similarity between two HDAG structures. First, we search the common hierarchical attribute subsequences between HDAGs (See Figure 2). Then we multiply the weight values of them. For example, the correspondence of them in Figure 2 is $\lambda^2 \beta^6$. Finally, we divide the sum total of correspondence values by the product of the numbers of bunsetsus of the two sentences. We handle this value as the similarity between them.

---

[4] In this simplified explanation, the graph structure for an example is expressed without the layers described in the previous section.

Here we consider the factor β. Suzuki et al. (2006) defined the range as $0 < \beta \leq 1$ to avoid overfitting in machine learning methods. However, we define the range as $\beta > 0$ in this paper. Also we categorize the range into two types; $0 < \beta \leq 1$ and $\beta > 1$. Our method computes the similarity focusing on structural information (SI) if $\beta \leq 1$. If the β is more than 1, it computes the similarity focusing on surface expressions (SE). This is due to layers that we constructed. In our layers, the word layer and compound noun layer are lower layer than the structural layer, i.e., the POS tag layer. Therefore surface expressions are treated as important element in the case that $\beta > 1$ because the elements in deeper layers possess high weight values. We apply these two types of the parameter β to our method.

3.3. Sentence Extraction

In this subsection, we explain the sentence extraction process based on the HDAG and the similarity calculation. The process is as follows:
1. prepare sample sentences as seeds for similarity calculation,
2. compute the similarity between each seed and target sentences,
3. extract n-best lists of each seed as sentiment sentence lists,
4. combine n-best lists obtained by two different parameters of β.

For the combination in the last step, we compare two strategies.
- **CombAND** We extract the intersection of each n-best list as the output.
- **CombOR** We extract the union of each n-best list as the output.

Figure 3 shows the outline of the extraction process.

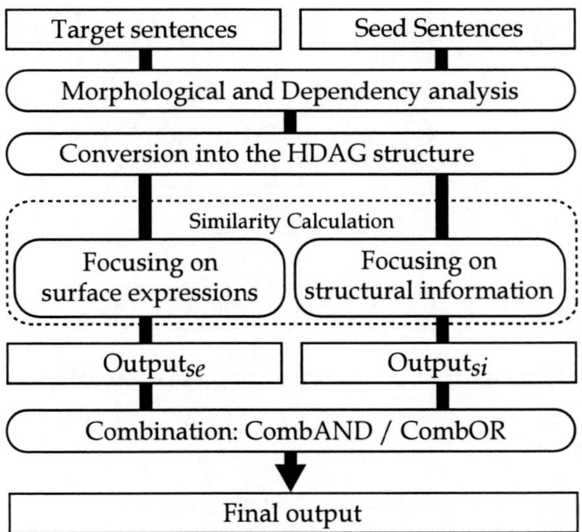

Figure 3: The outline of the sentence extraction process.

4. Bootstrap Approach

The method proposed in the previous section contains a problem; the number of sentences extracted from target sentences. It depends on the number of seed sentences and the number of n of n-best. Preparing many seed sentences is usually high cost for users. If the number of n becomes large, the number of extracted sentences increases. However, it leads to decrease of the accuracy.

To solve this problem, we apply a bootstrap approach to our method. In the bootstrap approach, we use both CombAND and CombOR as the situation demands. We use the CombAND to acquire new seed sentences because it usually generates the high accuracy. On the other hand, we use the CombOR in the final step of the bootstrap process because it usually extracts more sentences than the CombAND. In addition, we change the value of n in each step of the bootstrap approach. In other words, we decrease the value in the bootstrap process. In the bootstrap approach, the method often extracts incorrect sentences as sentiment sentences, and add them into the seed sentence list. The method tends to extract incorrect sentences in the later steps of the bootstrap process. Therefore we set a larger value to the n in the early steps and a smaller value to it in the later steps.

The process is as follows:
1. extract sentences with CombAND by using current seed sentences,
2. add the extracted sentences into the seed sentence list as new seeds,
3. decrease the value of n,
4. iterate the process 1-3, m-times,
5. extract sentences with CombOR as the final output.

Figure 4 shows the outline of the bootstrap process.

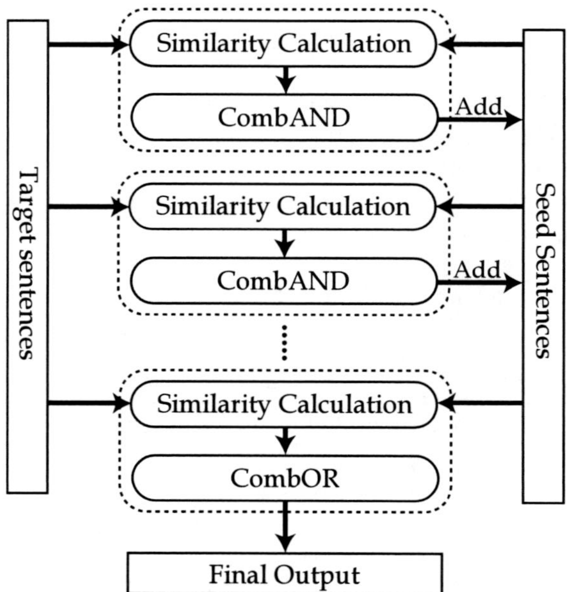

Figure 4: The outline of the bootstrap approach process.

5. Experiment

In this section we evaluated the proposed method with a review document set.

5.1. Dataset and Criteria

We used review documents of a portable audio player[5] posted in the bulletin board system of kakaku.com[6]. We extracted 1052 Japanese sentences from the review documents. The dataset consists of 610 sentiment sentences and 442 non-sentiment sentences. For the experiment, we prepared 10 sample sentences as seeds for the sentence extraction process. All the seed sentences in this experiment were sentiment sentences. We generated the seed sentences on the basis of some evaluation criteria which were mentioned in the review documents; e.g., "design of the product", "Sound quality" and so on.

---

[5] SONY Walkman NW-A808
[6] http://www.kakaku.com/

In this experiment, we set $\lambda = 0.5$. Also we set $\beta = 0.5$ as the parameter for focusing on structural information and $\beta = 1.5$ as the parameter for focusing on surface expressions. The number of sentences we extracted in this experiment is 5 for each seed sentence, that is 5-best list. In other words, we extracted the top 5 sentences that possessed high similarity as the sentiment sentences that were estimated from each sample sentences. We did not employ any thresholds for the similarity in the extraction process. For the bootstrap approach, we set the number of iterations as 3. The values of n in each step were n=7 in the 1st step, n=5 in the 2nd step and n=3 in the final step, respectively.

We used the following three criteria for this evaluation.

•$Sent_{real}$: This criterion is the number of sentiment sentences extracted correctly from target sentences.

•$Sent_{non}$: This criterion is the number of non-sentiment sentences extracted from target sentences.

•Acc: This criterion is the accuracy computed from $Sent_{real}$ and $Sent_{non}$.

$$Acc = \frac{Sent_{real}}{Sent_{real} + Sent_{non}}$$

•$Recall$: This criterion is the recall rate computed from $Sent_{real}$ and the number of sentiment sentences in the dataset.

5.2. Experimental Results

Table 1 shows the experimental result. In the table, the BOW denotes a similarity calculation method based on the cosine measure and bag-of-words features. This is a baseline in this experiment. The accuracy rates of each non-bootstrap approach in our method outperformed the baseline method based on BOW features. Our methods obtained high accuracies even without combinations, namely CombAND and CombOR. In addition, the method focusing on surface expressions (SE) outperformed the method focusing on structural information (SI) in terms of all criteria.

For the combinations, the accuracy of the CombOR was the lowest of the methods although the number of sentiment sentences extracted correctly was the best of them. On the other hand, the accuracy of the CombAND produced the best performance. Although the number of extracted sentences with the CombAND drastically decreased, the output possessed high reliability.

By using the bootstrap approach, the number of correct sentences nearly tripled although the accuracy decreased somewhat. This result shows the effectiveness of applying the bootstrap approach to our method. As an additional experiment, we evaluated our method with a fixed n; n=5, that is an experiment without decrease of n in each step. In the additional experiment, the accuracy rate became 0.78. This result shows the importance of changing n in each step of the bootstrap approach. Therefore we need to consider the determination of the appropriate n in each step.

One reason of the decrease of the accuracy with the bootstrap approach is that our method occasionally added non-sentiment sentences as seed sentences in each step. One of the solutions to this problem is to apply feedback from users to the bootstrap process, such as relevance feedback. This is one future work for our method.

The number of extracted sentences increased by using the bootstrap approach. However, the recall rate was insufficient. It was 0.256 even if we applied the bootstrap approach to the extraction process. One approach to improve the recall rate is use of the extracted sentences for the training data of the sentiment classification task. Wiebe and Riloff (2005) have proposed a method for creating subjective and objective classifiers from unannotated texts. They used some rules for constructing initial training data. Then they used the data for generating a classifier. We think that the outputs from our method also can be used for the training data of a classifier for this sentiment sentence classification task.

Table 1: The experimental result.

	$Sent_{real}$	$Sent_{non}$	Acc	$Recall$
Structural information	32	4	0.889	0.052
Surface expression	43	4	0.915	0.070
CombAND	22	*1*	*0.957*	0.002
CombOR	53	7	0.883	0.087
Bootstrap	*156*	30	0.839	*0.256*
BOW (Baseline)	42	7	0.857	0.069

6. Conclusions

In this paper, we proposed a method of sentiment sentence extraction based on a graph-based approach, called Hierarchical Directed Acyclic Graph (HDAG). Our method can extract sentiment sentences by using several sample sentences. We obtained high accuracy in the experiment. However, the number of extracted sentences was not enough, that is the recall rate was extremely low. To solve this problem, we applied a bootstrap approach to out method. As a result, we acquired more sentiment sentences by adding the extracted sentences as new seeds. By using the bootstrap approach based on the combination of CombAND and CombOR, we obtained large quantities of sentences as compared with the non-bootstrap approach. However, even the recall rate with the bootstrap approach was insufficient. Therefore we need to discuss solutions to the problem. One approach is to apply feedback from users to the method. We need to consider a semi-automatic approach based on human-aid to accomplish high recall and accuracy rates. Some researchers have reported approaches with structured features (Zhang et al. 2006 and Zhou et al. 2007). We need to compare our method with them.

In this experiment, we evaluated our method with fixed parameters. However, they are not always the best parameter values. In previous work, we compared several values of these parameters (Shimada et al. 2008). By tuning the parameters, we obtained higher accuracy for the SI and SE. However, these values depended on the dataset in the experiment. Therefore we need to consider an automatic determination method of these parameters to achieve higher accuracy for the bootstrap approach.

Our future work includes (1) evaluation of our method in a large-scale dataset and other datasets, (2) improvement of the accuracy by adding other layers to the HDAG structure, such as semantic features of words (Ikehara et al. 1997), and (3) construction of a sentiment sentence maintenance tool based on this approach.

References

Hatzivassiloglou, V. and K. R. McKeown. 1997. Predicting the Semantic Orientation of Adjectives. *In Proceedings of the 35th Annual Meeting of the Association for Computational Linguistics* (ACL) and *the 8th Conference of the European Chapter of the Association for Computational Linguistics* (EACL), pp.174-181.

Ikehara, S., M. Miyazaki, S. Shirai, A. Yokoo, H. Nakaiwa, K. Ogura, Y. Ooyama and Y. Hayashi, editors. 1997. Goi-Taikei . A Japanese Lexicon (in Japanese). *Iwanami Shoten.*

Kaji, N. and M. Kitsuregawa. 2006. Automatic Construction of Polarity-tagged Corpus from HTML Documents. *In Proceedings of the 21st International Conference on Computational Linguistics* (COLING/ACL2006), pages 452.459.

Kaji, N. and M. Kitsuregawa. 2007. Building Lexicon for Sentiment Analysis from Massive HTML Documents. *In Proceedings of the Conference on Empirical Methods in Natural Language Processing* (EMNLP-CoNLL2007).

Kawaguchi, T., T. Matsui and H. Ohwada. 2006. Opinion Extraction from Weblog Using SVM and Newspaper Article (in Japanese). *In The 20th Annual Conference of the Japanese Society for Artificial Intelligence.*

Kobayashi, N., R. Iida, K. Inui and Y. Matsumoto. 2005. Opinion Extraction Using a Learning-based Anaphora Resolution Technique. *In Proceedings of the Second International Joint Conference on Natural Language Processing* (IJCNLP-05), pp. 175-180.

Kudo, T. and Y. Matsumoto. 2004. A Boosting Algorithm for Classification of Semi-structured Text. *In Proceedings of the Conference on Empirical Methods in Natural Language Processing* (EMNLP).

Osajima, I., K. Shimada and T. Endo. 2005. Classification of Evaluative Sentences Using Sequential Patterns. *In Proceedings of the 11nd Annual Meeting of The Association for Natural Language Processing* (in Japanese).

Pang, B., L. Lee, and S. Vaithyanathan. 2002. Thumbs up? Sentiment Classification Using Machine Learning Techniques. *In Proceedings of the Conference on Empirical Methods in Natural Language Processing* (EMNLP), pp. 79-86.

Shimada, K., D. Hashimoto and T. Endo. 2008. A Graph-based Approach for Sentiment Sentence Extraction. *First International Workshop on Algorithms for Large-Scale Information Processing in Knowledge Discovery* (ALSIP 2008), Working Note, pp. 42-51.

Suzuki, J., Yutaka Sasaki and Eisaku Maeda. 2006. Hierarchical Directed Acyclic Graph Kernel. *Systems and Computers in Japan*, 37(10), pp. 58-68.

Takamura, H., T. Inui and M. Okumura.2005. Extracting Semantic Orientations of Words Using Spin Model. *In Proceedings of the 43rd Annual Meeting of the Association for Computational Linguistics* (ACL2005), pp. 133-140.

Touge, Y., K. Ohashi and K. Yamamoto.2004. Extracting Opinion Sentence Adapted to Topic Using Iteration Learning (in Japanese). *In IPSJ SIG Notes*, pp. 43-50.

Turney, P. D. 2002. Thumbs up? or Thumbs down? Semantic Orientation Applied to Unsupervised Classification of Reviews. *In Proceedings of the 40th Annual Meeting of the Association for Computational Linguistics*, pp. 417-424.

Wiebe, J. and E. Riloff. 2005. Creating Subjective and Objective Sentence Classifiers from Unannotated Texts. *In Sixth International Conference on Intelligent Text Processing and Computational Linguistics* (CICLing-2005).

Yu, H. and V. Hatzivassiloglou. 2003. Towards Answering Opinion Questions: Separating Facts from Opinions and Identifying the Polarity of Opinion Sentences. *In Proceedings of the Conference on Empirical Methods in Natural Language Processing* (EMNLP), pp.129-136.

Zhang, M., J. Zhang, J. Su, G. Zhou. 2006. A Composite Kernel to Extract Relations between Entities with Both Flat and Structured Features. *In Proceedings of the 21st International Conference on Computational Linguistics and the 44th annual meeting of the Association for Computational Linguistics*, pp. 825-832.

Zhou, G., M. Zhang, D. Ji and Q. Zhu. 2007. Tree Kernel-Based Relation Extraction with Context-Sensitive Structured Parse Tree Information. *In Proceedings of the 2007 Joint Conference on Empirical Methods in Natural Language Processing and Computational Natural Language Learning* (EMNLP-CoNLL 2007), pp. 728-736.

An Effective Speech Understanding Method with a Multiple Speech Recognizer based on Output Selection using Edit Distance[*]

Kazutaka Shimada[a], Satomi Horiguchi[a], and Tsutomu Endo[a]

[a] Department of Artificial Intelligence, Kyushu Institute of Technology
680-4 Iizuka Fukuoka 820-8502, Japan
{shimada, s_horiguchi, endo}@pluto.ai.kyutech.ac.jp

Abstract. In this paper, we propose a simple and effective method for speech understanding. The method incorporates some speech recognizers. We use two recognizers, a large vocabulary continuous speech recognizer and a domain-specific speech recognizer. The integrated recognizer is a robust and flexible method for speech understanding. For the integration process, we use a simple edit distance measure of each output sentence from each recognizer. Our method has high scalability and accuracy. The experimental results show the effectiveness of the proposed method.

Keywords: Multiple speech recognizer, Integration, Output selection, Edit distance.

1. Introduction

Speech understanding and dialogue systems have been developed for practical use recently. These systems often recognize user utterances incorrectly. It is important to deal with speech recognition errors for speech understanding systems. Extracting keywords and understanding an utterance using them reduce speech recognition errors (Bouwman et al. 1999, Komatani and Kawahara 2000). Another approach is to use domain-specific grammars and linguistic models. However these methods can not handle out of domain and spontaneous utterances.

One approach for the improvement is to repair recognition errors by users. There are many studies on detection of recognition errors in a speech output. Goto et al. (2005) have proposed some systems with nonverbal speech information, such as "SPEECH STARTER" and "SPEECH SPOTTER". Ogata and Goto (2005) have proposed a speech input interface with a speech-repair function. Although repairing recognition errors by humans is effective in terms of development of a speech understanding system with high recognition accuracy, it is costly for users.

Combining some recognizers is one of the best approaches to improve the accuracy of speech understanding systems (Isobe et al. 2007, Utsuro et al. 2004). Utsuro et al. (2004) have obtained high accuracy by using some speech recognizers' outputs. However they dealt with word error reduction only. Although Isobe et al. (2007) have proposed a multi-domain speech recognition system by using some domain-specific recognizers, their system cannot treat out-of-domain utterances such as a chat between users. However the chat utterances often include a significant role as the context of the dialogue.

In this paper we propose a simple and effective speech understanding method based on a large vocabulary continuous speech recognizer (LVCSR) and some domain-specific speech

[*] Copyright 2008 by Kazutaka Shimada, Satomi Horiguchi, and Tsutomu Endo. This research was supported by the New Energy and Industrial Technology Development Organization (NEDO), Intelligent RT Software Project, 2008.

22nd Pacific Asia Conference on Language, Information and Computation, pages 350–357

recognizers (DSSR). The task of this system is speech understanding for a livelihood support robot. The DSSRs recognize particular utterances about orders; e.g., order utterances from elders who need care and order utterances from nurses. Figure 1 shows the outline of the proposed method. We construct the grammar-based DDSR for order utterances with small vocabulary and high accuracy for each order type. We use the LVCSR for recognition of utterances that the DDSR can not recognize, such as a chat between users. The information recognized by the LVCSR is of assistance for context construction of a dialogue. If we handle these different speech recognizers selectively and integratively, we realize a flexible and robust speech understanding method. Figure 2 shows the effectiveness of the proposed multiple recognizer. The DDSR achieves the order recognition with high accuracy and the LVCSR supplies lack of information in the order utterances.

In this paper we use two recognizers, a large vocabulary continuous speech recognizer and a domain-specific speech recognizer for user's order utterance understanding. In the experiment we focus on the selective usage of the multiple speech recognizer. In other words, it is to select outputs from each recognizer. For example, with respect to the utterance "Please pick up the remote" in Figure 2, it is important which result to select. For the selection we propose the *One Commoner and Some Specialists* (OCSS) model. In our system, the LVCSR is the commoner, namely domain-independent, and the DSSRs are specialists, namely domain-dependent. We focus on the difference between outputs generated from the commoner and specialists. For the method, we compare several features to judge whether an input utterance is an order to the robot or not.

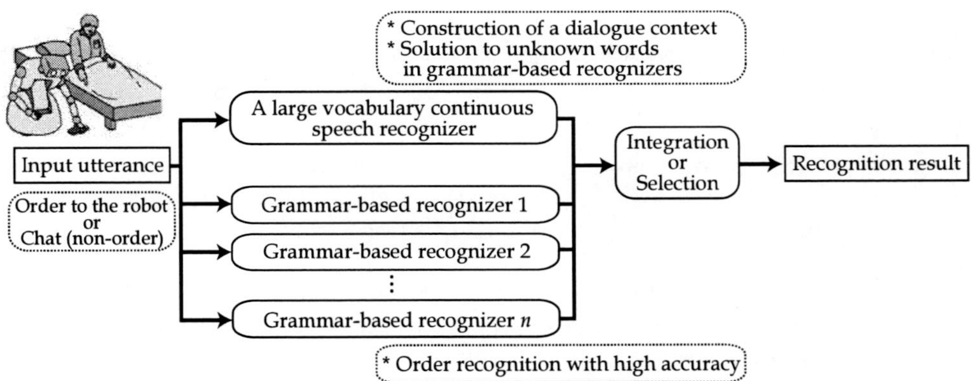

Figure 1: The outline of the proposed system.

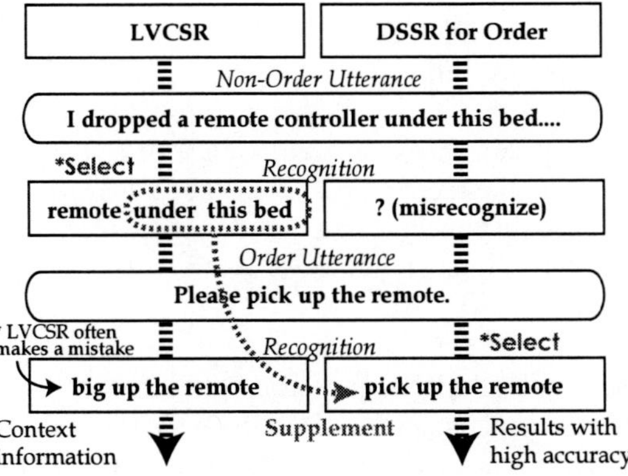

Figure 2: The effectiveness of a multiple recognizer.

2. Grammar-based recognizer

We use Julius as the LVCSR and Julian as the DSSR (Lee et al. 2001). The Julian consists of a vocabulary and a grammar file. For the grammar file we describe sentence structures in a BNF style, using word category names as terminate symbols. The vocabulary file defines words with its pronunciations (i.e., phoneme sequences) for each category.

Here we design grammar and vocabulary files of the Julian which accepts only order utterances from users. The acceptable utterances by our DSSR recognizer for order sentences are as follows:

- [Noun] wo [Verb] shi te kudasai or kureru ? [e.g., Please pick up the cellular telephone.]

- [Noun] wo [Verb] shitai [e.g., I want to eat the snack.]

- [Noun] wo [verb] kudasai or kureru? [e.g., Give me it.]

- [Location] ni aru [Noun] wo [Verb] shite kudasai or kureru? [e.g., Please bring the remote controller on the table.]

- [Noun] [e.g., The cellular telephone.]

We evaluated this grammar-based recognizer with 50 test utterances and 2 test subjects (male and female). The accuracy rate was 97% on the utterance-level. Here the utterance-level denotes that we judged that the output was correct if all words in an utterance were correct. This result shows that the DSSR used in our multiple recognizer is a robust and high accurate speech recognizer for the order utterances.

3. Output Selection

In our system, we need to judge whether an input utterance is an order to the robot or not. In this section we explain features and rules for the output selection.

3.1. Features

For the output selection, we compared each output in a preliminary exrperiment. As a result, we obtained 4 effective features for the selection; (1) confidence, (2) the number of candidates, (3) existance of a short pause mark and (4) a similarity between outputs.

- **Confidence**:

This is a confidence measure that is computed from the speech recgnizer Julius/Julian. This score is based on a posterior probability of each word (Lee et al. 2004). The range is from 0 to 1.

- **The number of candidates**:

The 2nd feature is the number of candidates of each DSSR. The number of candidates in a DSSR's output usually becomes small in the case that an input utterance is an order sentence. The reason is that the DSSR has high accuracy for target utterances because of small vocabulary. On the other hand, the number of candidates of a DSSR becomes large if the input is not an order utterance. In this situation, the DSSR generates many misunderstood results because the DSSR can not accept the input essentially.

- **Short paused mark**:

Julius/Julian can deal with a short pause in an utterance. If a short pause exists in an utterance, it output a short pause mark in the recognition result. The DSSR often contained the short pause mark in the result in the case that an input was not an order utterance[1]. Therefore the existance of the short pause mark in the output of the DSSR is effective to judge whether a input utterance is an order to the robot or not.

- **Similarity**:

The 4th feature is based on a similarity measure between outputs of the LVCSR and DSSR. Even human beings tend to misunderstand words which consist of similar pronunciations (Komatani et al. 2005). Here we focus on the output of the LVCSR. If an input is an order utterenace, the DSSR and the LVCSR generate similar outputs on phoneme-level because the

---

[1] I think that the reason is that the system replaced the part which it cannot analyze, with the mark.

LVCSR is domain independence. On the other hand, if the input is not an order utterenace, they often generate different outputs even on the phoneme-level because the DSSR never generates the correct result for non-order uttereances.

Komatani et al. (2007) have reported an utterance verification method based on difference of acoustic likelihood values computed from two recognizers. Kumar et al. (2005) have utilized Bhattacharyya distance to measure an acoustic similarity of different languages for multilingual speech recognition. In this paper, we use the edit distance as the similarity measure. The correspondence such as the edit distance is one of the most effective measures to identify high confidence words in outputs (Utsuro et al. 2004) and to extract similar word pairs (Komatani et al. 2005). In our method, if an input is an order utterance, the edit distance between the outputs from the DSSR and the LVCSR becomes small. However if the input is not an order utterance, that between the outputs from the DSSR and the LVCSR becomes large.

In our method, we compute the edit distance of utterance-level and word-level by using a DP matching algorithm. In the process, we compute the edit distance between phonemes of words for both levels.

3.2. Rules for the Selection

We apply the features to our selection process in the OCSS model. In the selection process, the rules to judge an utterance are applied in the following order:

1. If a short pause mark exists in the output of the DSSR or the output contains a word of which the confidence is 0, we select the output of the LVCSR as the final output.
2. If the number of candidates in the DSSR's output is less than 9, we select the output of the DSSR as the final output.
3. Compute the edit distance of the utterance-level (ED_{utter}) between the LVCSR and each DSSR. For the outputs of which the edit distance is less than $thresh_{utter}$, we select the output of the DSSR which contains the minimum $thresh_{utter}$, as the final output.
4. Compute the edit distance of the word-level (ED_{word}) between the LVCSR and each DSSR. For the output of which the edit distance is less than $thresh_{word}$, we select the output of the DSSR which contains the minimum $thresh_{word}$ as the final output. Otherwise, the LVCSR as the final output.

The ED_{utter} is the edit distance value on the utterance-level. The ED_{word} is the average of the edit distance value computed on word-level. These values are normalized by the number of phonemes in the outputs. The $thresh_{utter}$ and $thresh_{word}$ are threshold values for the judgment. These values are decided experimentally.

In the computation of the word-level, we eliminate word pairs that are matched completely first. Next, we compute all the combinations of the other. Finally, we employ the minimum combinations as the word-level edit distance. Figure 3 shows an example of the calculation of the ED_{utter} and ED_{word}. In the figure, the dotted line denotes completely matched words. The numerals with arrows denote the original edit distance of the word pair. In the alignment process of word pairs, we select pairs which have the minimum value of the edit distance. In other words, we admit overlap of word pairs. For example, "noue vs. no" and "no vs. no" in Figure 3.

*Utterance-level
Input: saifu wo mottekite
(Bring my wallet)

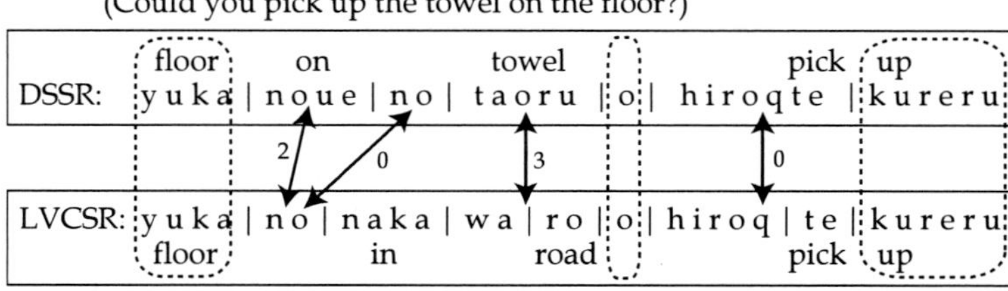

ED_{utter} = Distance / # of phonemes in two results
= 6 / 26 = 0.23

*Word-level
Input: yuka no ue no taoru wo hirotte kureru?
(Could you pick up the towel on the floor?)

Best Combinations: noue vs. no, no vs. no, taoru vs. wa|ro, hiroqte vs. hiroq|te
Distance/Phoneme: 2/6=0.33, 0/4=0, 3/9=0.33, 0/14=0
ED_{word}= Sum / # of words in the DSSR result = (0.33+0.33)/7 = 0.09

Figure 3: An example of the calculation of the word-level and utterance-level edit distance.

4. Experiment

We used 50 order utterances and 50 non-order utterances in this experiment. The DSSR accepts all the order utterances that used in this experiment. The non-order utterances consist of common greetings and daily conversation[2]. The number of test subjects was 4 persons (2 men and 2 women). We evaluated our method with cross-validation.

Table 1: The result of classification of the outputs.

Type	Precision	Recall	F-Value
Order	0.888	0.965	0.924
Non-Order	0.962	0.877	0.917

Table 1 shows the experimental result of the judgment process. Although our method was simple, we obtained high accuracy. In the experiment, the ranges of $thresh_{utter}$ and $thresh_{word}$ which were determined from training data were 0.24-0.26 and 0.08-0.13, respectively. In other words, the changes of these thresholds were little in the cross-validation. These results show the effectiveness and robustness of our method.

Next, we analyzed the correctness of each feature. Table 2 shows the distribution of each feature. As a result, we obtained the knowledge that the accuracy rates without the edit distance features were not always high.

On the basis of this result, we evaluated our method with the edit distance measures only. In other words, we used the rule 3 and 4 in Section 3.2. The thresholds, namely $thresh_{utter}$ and $thresh_{word}$, were the same as the previous experiment. Table 3 shows the experimental result. As a result, we obtained extremely high accuracy although the method was very simple.

---

[2] For example, "Today is busy." and "I think that it rains in the afternoon of today."

The standard deviation of the F-values in the cross-validation was approximately 0.007. Furthermore, the change of the F-value was at the most 0.01 even if the thresholds were fixed. These results show the effectiveness of our method.

Table 2: The correctness of each feature.

Feature	# of correct	# of incorrect
Confidence	48	15
Short pause	93	6
# of candidates	384	57
ED_{utter}	192	14
ED_{word}	388	3

Table 3: The result of classification of the outputs by using the edit distance only.

Type	Precision	Recall	F-Value
Order	0.963	0.985	0.974
Non-Order	0.985	0.963	0.974

5. Discussion

Our method is very simple and robust. In addition, our method has high scalability. This results from comparing the edit distance between the LVCSR and each DSSR. In general, a multiple recognizer consists of only DSSRs. Isobe et al. (2007) have proposed a multi-domain speech recognition system based on the model likelihoods of the different domain specific language models. Our method differs from it in use of the LVCSR. By using the LVCSR for a multiple recognizer, the system becomes simple and has high scalability. Figure 4 shows the advantage of our method as compared with previous studies. In general, systems in previous studies need to recalculate a model to select an output. In our method, when users add other grammar-based recognizers, what they need to change is 2 thresholds only ($thresh_{utter}$ and $thresh_{word}$)[3]. In fact, after the experiment, we added a new DSSR (the 3rd recognizer) to recognize some system commands for a robot such as "Stop", "Move to the right by 50cm" and "Please go back a little". As a result we also obtained high accuracy of output selection from 3 outputs without any changes of the thresholds; there was little decrease of the F-Value. Also we evaluated our method with 5 recognizers. The 4th recognizer was for question utterances such as "Where is my cellphone?". The 5th recognizer was for order utterances from nurses such as "Carry these meals to patient's rooms". In the additional experiment, we obtained approximately 0.95 on F-value with no change of the thresholds. Table 4 shows the details of the result. The test data consisted of 50 utterances (10 utterances for each category; daily conversation, orders from patients, system commands, orders from nurses and questions). The number of test subjects was 6 persons. These results show the effectiveness of the OCCS model with the edit distance.

Sako et al. (2006) have reported a method to discriminate a request to a system from a chat using AdaBoost. Tong et al. (2008) have reported a SVM-based method to separate a target language from other languages for spoken language recognition. Machine learning techniques generally need a large amount of training data to generate a classifier with high accuracy. However constructing training data by handwork is costly. As compared with them, our method can be realized with low cost. Besides, our method does not depend on particular speech recognizers although we used Julius/Julian in the experiment because it needs only phonemes of each output from the recognizer to select the final output.

Although we evaluated our method for output selection in this paper, we do not discuss integration of several outputs. To supplement information (e.g., "under the bed" in Figure 2)

---

[3] Note that if users want to select an output from DSSRs only, our method does not need any changes because the thresholds are used to distinguish between an order utterance and a chat. If the system does not need to recognize a chat in a dialogue, all it needs to do is just select the output that contains the highest similarity with the LVCSR as the final output.

and to construct a context of a dialogue by using the LVCSR are our future work. In the experiment, the word accuracy rates of the LVCSR were 65%[4] for order utterances and 32% for non-order utterances, respectively. This result shows the importance of improvement of the accuracy of the LVCSR. To apply the method in related work (Utsuro et al. 2004) to the LVCSR is also significant future work.

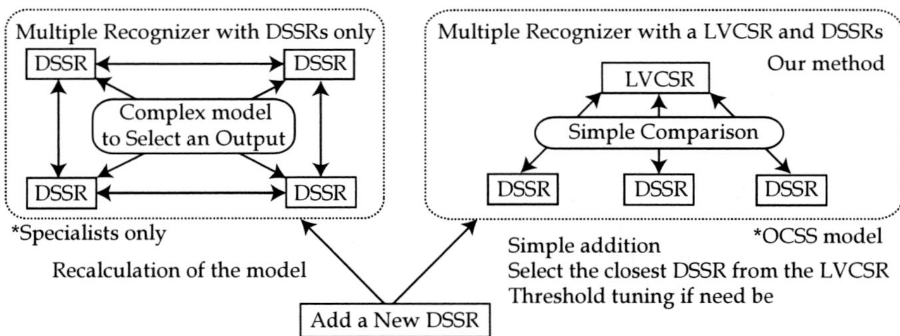

Figure 4: Comparison of a previous method and our method.

Table 4: The result of classification with 5 recognizers (edit distance only).

Type	Precision	Recall	F-Value
1st (LVCSR)	0.838	0.950	0.891
2nd (Patient's Order)	0.983	0.966	0.975
3rd (Command)	1.000	0.933	0.966
4th (Question)	0.948	0.917	0.932
5th (Nurse's Order)	1.000	0.983	0.992
Average	0.954	0.950	0.951

6. Conclusions

In this paper, we proposed a simple and effective method for speech understanding with some speech recognizers. Our method, OCSS model, does not need any complex computation and models. It uses an edit distance measure only. Furthermore, it can deal with out-of-domain utterances by using the LVCSR's output. We obtained the high precision and recall rates in the experiment. Future work includes (1) construction of the context using LVCSR and (2) development of multi modal interface with other sensors in the robot.

References

Bouwman, C., J. Sturm and L. Boves. 1999. Incorporating Confidence Measures in the Dutch Train Timetable Information System Developed in the ARICE project. *Proceedings of ICASSP*.

Goto, M., K. Itou and T. Kobayashi. 2005. Speech Interface Exploiting Intentionally-Controlled Nonverbal Speech Information. *Proceedings of the 18th Annual ACM Symposium on User Interface Software and Technology* (UIST 2005), pp.35-36.

Isobe, T., K. Itou and K. Takeda. 2007. A Likelihood Normalization Method for the Domain Selection in the Multi-Decoder Speech Recognition System. *IEICE TRANSACTIONS on Information and Systems* (Japanese Edition) Vol.J90-D No.7 pp.1773-1780.

Komatani, K. and T. Kawahara. 2000. Flexible Mixed-initiative Dialogue Management Using Concept-level Confidence Measures of Speech Recognizer Output. *Proceedings of*

---

[4] Note that this accuracy rate is on word-level, i.e., word accuracy. On the other hand, the accuracy of the DSSR mentioned in Section 2 is utterance-level. In other words, even if the output utterance contains one mistake, it is incorrect. There is a significant difference between the LVCSR and the DSSR for the accuracy in this experiment.

COLING 2000, Vol. 1, pp. 467-473.

Komatani, K., R. Hamabe, T. Ogata, and H. G. Okuno. 2005. Generating Confirmation to Distinguish Phonologically Confusing Word Pairs in Spoken Dialogue Systems. *Proceedings of 4th IJCAI Workshop on Knowledge and Reasoning in Practical Dialogue Systems*, pp. 40-45

Komatani, K., Y. Fukubayashi, T. Ogata, and H. G. Okuno. 2007. Introducing Utterance Verification in Spoken Dialogue System to Improve Dynamic Help Generation for Novice Users. *Proceedings of the 8th SIGdial Workshop on Discourse and Dialogue*, pp. 202--205.

Kumar, S. C., V. P. Mohandas and H. Li, 2005. Multilingual Speech Recognition: A Unified Approach. *Proceedings of InterSpeech 2005 - Eurospeech - 9th European Conference on Speech Communication and Technology*, pp. 3357-3360.

Lee, A., T. Kawahara and K. Shikano. 2001. Julius - an open source real-time large vocabulary recognition engine. *Proceedings of European Conference on Speech Communication and Technology* (EUROSPEECH), pp. 1691--1694, 2001.

Lee, A., and K. Shikano and Kawahara, T. 2004. Real-time word confidence scoring using local posterior probabilities on tree trellis search. *Proceedings of IEEE International Conference on Acoustics, Speech, and Signal Processing* (ICASSP2004), I, pp. 793-796.

Ogata, J. and M. Goto. 2005. Speech Repair: Quick Error Correction Just by Using Selection Operation for Speech Input Interfaces. *Proceedings of Interspeech 2005*, 2005, 133-136.

Sako, A., T. Takiguchi and Y. Ariki. 2006. System Request Discrimination Based on AdaBoost. *IEICE technical report. Natural language understanding and models of communication* (in Japanese), Vol. 106, No. 411, pp. 19-24.

Tong, R., B. Ma, H. Li, and E. S. Chng. 2008. Target-oriented phone tokenizers for spoken language recognition. *Proceedings of IEEE International Conference on Acoustics, Speech, and Signal Processing* (ICASSP 2008), pp. 4221-4224.

Utsuro, T., H. Nishizaki, Y. Kodama and S. Nakagawa. 2004. Estimating Highly Confident Portions Based on Agreement among Outputs of Multiple LVCSR Models. *Systems and Computers in Japan*, Vol.35, No.7, pp. 33-40.

The Relationship between Semantic Similarity and Subcategorization Frames in English: A Stochastic Test Using ICE-GB and WordNet[*]

Sanghoun Song, Jae-Woong Choe

Dept. of Linguistics, Korea University,
Anam-dong, Sungbuk-gu, Seoul, KOREA
{yooseon21, jchoe}@korea.ac.kr

Abstract. In this paper, we test a working hypothesis that there is a significant relationship between semantic similarity and subcategorization frames in English. This paper is under the assumption that if a group of verbs form a cluster sharing a similar meaning, they tend to share subcategorization frames. In the process, we propose a statistical method to test this assumption, making use of two language resources, namely, ICE-GB and WordNet. We come to the conclusion that the proposed hypothesis holds true to the degrees of 42~73%, based on our stochastic analysis.

Keywords: semantic similarity, subcategorization frames, ICE-GB, WordNet, statistical method, clustering, dendrogram, selectional preference strength

1. Introduction

The following examples taken from Lasnik and Uriagereka (2005) bring out an issue concerning the relationship between semantic similarity of verbs and the corresponding subcategorization frames.

(1) a. She asked what time it was.
    b. She asked the time.
    c. She wondered what time it was.
    b. *She wondered the time.

Sentences in (1) show that verbs like *ask* and *wonder*, which are similar in meaning, show different ways of argument realization. Although it is true that arbitrariness is at the core of the form-meaning mapping in any language, there are other aspects of language where formal or grammatical realization seems to be largely determined by meaning. Levin (1993) provides many

[*] Acknowledgments: We owe special thanks to Jieun Jeon   for her assistance and partial participation in the preparation of this paper, especially for extracting relevant data from ICE-GB.   We also would like to express our thanks to Prof. Seok-Hoon You for his support for our project.   Finally, comments from three anonymous reviewers for PACLIC 22 are much appreciated.

22nd Pacific Asia Conference on Language, Information and Computation, pages 358–367

examples of semantic classes of English verbs that lead to the same or similar pattern of argument realizations. For example, the *cut* verbs (e.g. *chip, cut, scrape, snip*, etc.), a semantically identifiable group of words in the sense that they all involve notions of motion, contact, and effect, do not allow causative alternations. That is, their subcategorization frames are affected by their meaning.

(2) a. Carol cut the bread.
    b. *The bread cut.

The question we raise in this paper is if the meaning restriction applies in a significant way to the realization of argument structure, if it does, to what extent it holds. In other words, how much is a syntactic pattern tied up with the semantic properties of the English verbs? In order to test this research question in a rather comprehensive way, we make use of large sets of language resources, in particular, ICE-GB and WordNet. In the process, we propose a more articulated methodology to take advantage of the language resources statistically and computationally. Also introduced in this paper are a software package to measure similarity of lexicons, an algorithm to cluster words in natural languages, and a kind of stochastic model to calculate selectional preference strength.

2. Methodology

There are two main methods used in this study; one is clustering, and the other is the use of frequency value.

In order to measure semantic relatedness between verbs, clustering method was used to divide verbs into various subsets in accordance with semantic similarity. As a way to ensure consistency in defining semantic similarity, WordNet (ver. 2.1) has been adopted as the basis for similarity measurement. The measurement itself was carried out by a module called WordNet::Similarity[1] that calculates similarity between words in WordNet (Pedersen et al. 2004). The results from the module, then, went through a clustering process on the basis of the hierarchical bottom-up clustering algorithm, adopted from Manning and Schütze (1999).

This study also required a method that can calculate the selectional preference strength of subcategorization frames. Selectional preference, in this paper, refers to the degree of relationship between a lexicon and its relevant items. In other words, this study seeks to figure out not merely whether a subcategorization frame can be realized or not, but how much relevance a verb has with the subcategorization frame.

3. Data

The initial set of English verbs for this study was extracted from the Collins Cobuild English Dictionary (henceforth CCED), which divides English words into five level groups according to each word's frequency. CCED includes approximately 1,600 words that belong to the highest or the second highest level groups. We then compared the list with the verb list in WordNet, and only those that appear in both lists were selected, resulting in 799 verbs. Starting with these 799 verbs, we tried to build up the hierarchical cluster and as a result obtained 61 meaningful clusters that cover 157 verbs out of 799. The next section provides an explanation of the whole procedure in detail.

4. The Analysis

4.1.Semantic Similarity

---

[1] The WordNet::Similarity module coded in the Perl language is freely available on the Internet (http://www.d.umn.edu/~tpederse/similarity.html).

There are three steps in the clustering process. The first step measures semantic similarity between the initial 799 verbs, using the WordNet::Similarity module and the Parse-Tree algorithm. The second step is to draw a dendrogram that indicates the hierarchy of semantic similarity, on the basis of the matrix algorithm. The final step distinguishes significant clusters from insignificant ones, after finding a critical value on the basis of the Z-score.

4.1.1. WordNet::Similarity

The WordNet::Similarity module offers several algorithms to measure similarity between words. Among them, the Lesk algorithm was adopted in this study, which measures incorporate information from WordNet glosses. That is, this algorithm 'finds overlaps between the glosses of concepts A and B, as well as concepts that are directly linked to A and B (Pedersen et al. 2004)', as shown in the following formula (Banerjee and Pedersen 2003).

$$realatedness(A, B) = score(gloss(A), gloss(B))$$
$$+ score(hype(A), hype(B)) + score(hypo(A), hypo(B)) \quad (3)$$
$$+ score(hype(A), gloss(B)) + score(gloss(A), hype(B))$$

The reason we chose the Lesk algorithm in this study is that the resulting value of the Lesk algorithm is relatively bigger than those of the others, which is of great advantage to clustering. The process of measuring is given below, where sim(A,B) is equal to sim(B,A).

```
V = {v₁,v₂,…,vₙ}
S = {sim(v₁,v₂),sim(v₂,v₃),…,sim(vₙ₋₁,vₙ)}
for i = 1 to n-1:
   for j = i+1 to n:
      sim(vᵢ,vⱼ)=lesk(vᵢ,vⱼ)
```

4.1.2. A Dendrogram

The above algorithm gives a similarity matrix as below.

	v_2	v_3	v_4	...	v_n
v_1	sim(v₁,v₂)	sim(v₁,v₃)	sim(v₁,v₄)	...	sim(v₁,vₙ)
v_2		sim(v₂,v₃)	sim(v₂,v₄)	...	sim(v₂,vₙ)
v_3			sim(v₃,v₄)	...	sim(v₃,vₙ)
...				...	sim(v…,vₙ)
v_{n-1}					sim(vₙ₋₁,vₙ)

Figure 1: A similarity matrix.

Using this matrix, this section shows the process to draw a dendrogram that represents the hierarchy of semantic similarity. Since a dendrogram is a kind of tree diagram to illustrate the arrangement of clusters, it can be built up by the so-called Parse-Tree algorithm. Data structure of the Parse-Tree algorithm is composed of three elements; the mother node, the left daughter node, and the right daughter node. Each node in the tree diagram is connected with another, forming an operator-operand relation. For example, a node can be both an operator of its daughter nodes and an operand of its mother node.

This is how the Parse-Tree algorithm is applied to draw a dendrogram: A set S is given as below, its elements being defined on the basis of a relation °.

```
S = {a°b=7, a°c=8, a°d=15, b°c=12, b°d=100, c°d=3}
```

The dendrogram will be produced by a similarity matrix as follows.

STATE 1

	a	b	c	d
a		7	18	15
b			12	100
c				3
d				

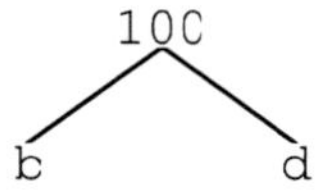

STATE 2

	b,d	a	c
b,d		7	3
a			18
c			

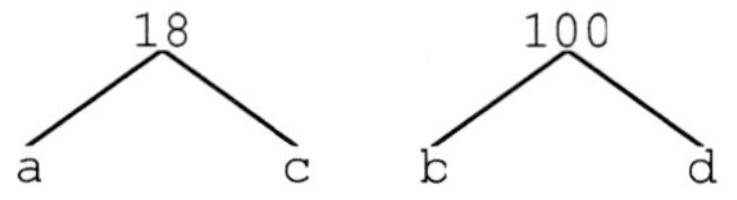

STATE 3

	a,c	b,d
a,c		3
b,d		

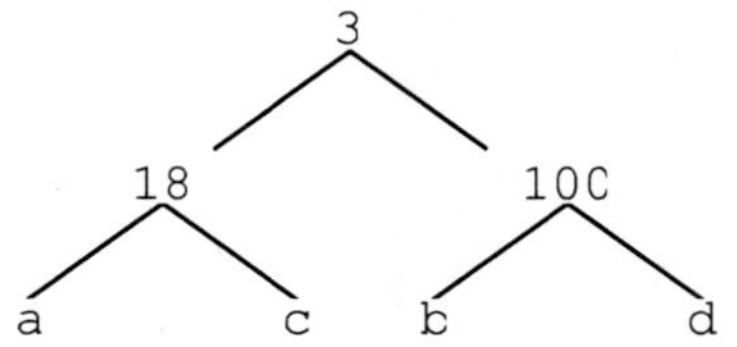

Figure 2: The procedure of drawing a dendrogram.

STATE 1 in Figure 2 is the initial matrix. The maximum value on the matrix, which is 100 at this state, will be selected, and since the value is given by the relation between **b** and **d**, they would form an initial dendrogram. Now that the relational value between **b** and **d** has been defined, those two elements are treated as a single element in the following process. Thus, in STATE 2, the pair, **b** and **d**, moves to the first place on the matrix, and each cell will be filled with the minimum value in each relation. For instance, in relation with 'a∘b=7' and 'a∘d=15', 7 will be allotted into the first cell in STATE 2. After all the relevant cell values have been filled up, the maximum value 18 from the matrix will be selected, introducing a new pair node **a** and **c**. In the same way, STATE 3 builds up the final dendrogram.

The algorithm to draw a dendrogram in the above is as follows.

```
V_i = {v_i}
M  = {v_1, v_2, ..., v_n-1, v_n}
while n > 1:


    V_1 = V_pos_i ⊕ V_pos_j


    for i = 1 to n-1:
        for j = i+1 to n:
            sim(V_i,V_j) = min(V_i,V_j)
            if max < sim(V_i,V_j):
                max = sim(V_i,V_j)
                pos_i = i
                pos_j = j
    parse_tree(pos_i, pos_j)
    n = n - 1
```

Repeating the process described above, we could draw a dendrogram for the initial 799 verbs.

4.1.3. Clusters

On the basis of the dendrogram found in the previous section, we could distinguish significant clusters from others. To begin with, we set up a critical value for discrimination. That is, if a value of a node is over the critical value, we assume the node and its descendant nodes are of significance.

The critical value in this study is the so-called Z-score. (4) stands for Z-score, in which x is for a value of a node, m is for the mean value of whole nodes, and s is for the standard deviation. Using this formula, we could obtain 61 clusters consisting of 157 verbs in total.

$$\frac{x - m}{s} > 1 \quad (4)$$

4.2. Subcategorization Frames

In order to get basic data which include subcategorization frames of English verbs, we employed the ICECUP III program, a search program for ICE-GB. To begin with, we listed up the inflectional paradigm of the 157 verbs found as a result of the process described in the previous section, such as *take*, *takes*, *took*, *taken*, and *taking*. With this paradigm, we could take advantage of the Text searching function. ICECUP III provides a function to extract concordances from the corpora in the form of set. (e.g. {*ask, asks, asked, asking*}, {*take, takes, took, taken, taking*}, or {*cut, cuts, cutting*}), which makes it easier to extract all the sentences that include at least one of the 157 verbs. We saved the search result as a separate file one by one in the form of treebanks (e.g. 'take.tre'). Plate 1 illustrates the searching and saving processes.

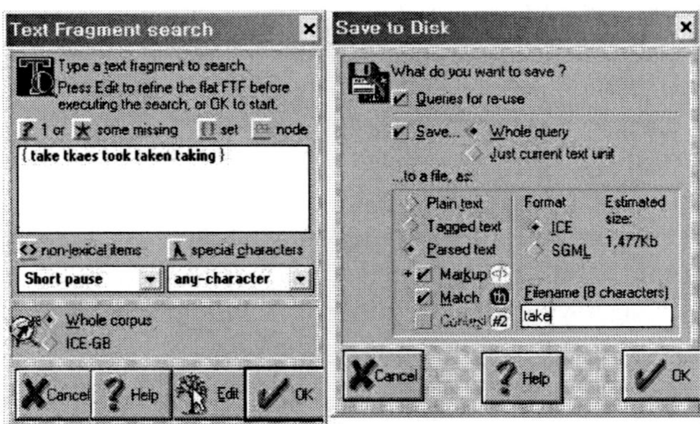

Plate 1: ICECUP III – Text searching / saving

Now that we have 157 files that contain concordances of verbs in the form of treebanks, we can calculate frequency of each verb's subcategorization frames. However, there are some issues and potential problems that need to be settled regarding the subcategorization information from ICE-GB. The next section discusses these issues and shows how they were handled in this study.

4.2.1. Some Issues

4.2.1.1 Subjects

English verbs subcategorize for a subject almost invariably; hence, subjects can be omitted from subcategorization frames. Besides, no subject appears on the surface in some VPs, such as infinitival constructions or gerundives. For these reasons, this study excludes subjects from the subcategorization frames.

4.2.1.2 Relative Clauses

Relative clauses can raise a troublesome issue in terms of extracting subcategorization frames from corpora, because one of the arguments appears outside of the relative clauses. However, the way relative pronouns are tagged in ICE-GB allows us to be able to retrieve the missing arguments in a systematic way. ICE-GB annotates pertinent information to relative pronouns as shown in Plate 2. The relative pronoun 'which' is tagged as 'OD,NP', meaning it is the direct object of the verb 'had',.

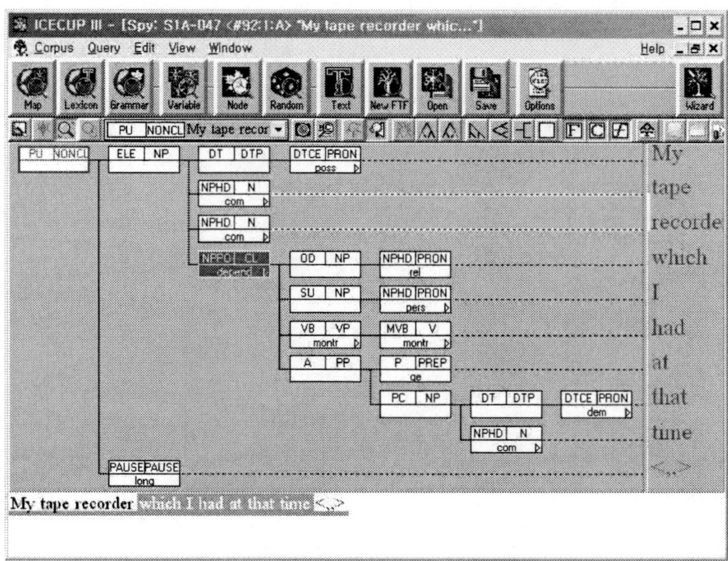

Plate 2: My tape recorder which I had at that time. (S1A-047 #92)

4.2.1.3 Oblique Complements

Let us consider the *Put* class verbs in English (Levin 1993). (5b-c) are ungrammatical because the obligatory arguments are missing. That is, an adverbial phrase 'on the desk' in (5a) functions as an oblique complement.

    (5) a. John put the book on the desk.
         b. *John put on the desk.
         c. *John put the book.

The way ICE-GB deals with this kind of complements helps us to avoid any potential problem concerning this kind of constructions. They are straightforwardly marked as such. For example, in Plate 3, 'on me' is tagged as 'CO,PP'.

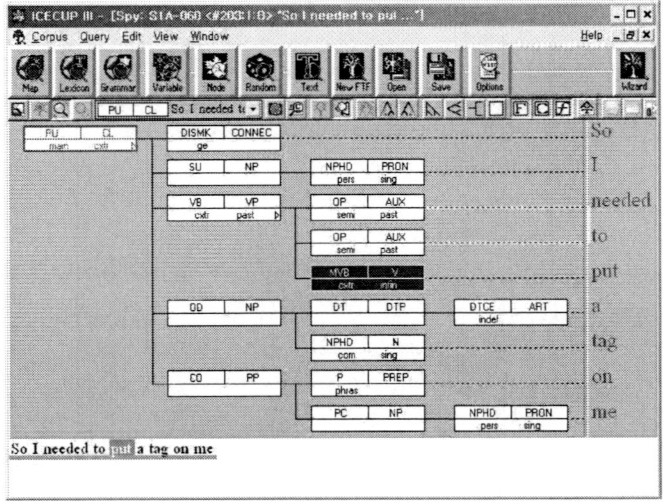

Plate 3: So I needed to put a tag on me. (S1A-060 #203)

4.2.1.4 Passives

The passive construction shows argument alternations in most languages. These alternations should be taken into consideration, because there may be a moved argument or a deleted argument in passive constructions. ICE-GB lays focus on the surface form, and we found it is rather difficult to reconstruct the 'deep, active' counterpart for all the passive constructions found in ICE-GB. Hence, we chose to exclude passive constructions from our consideration. There is also an empirical reason for our decision; some typical transitive verbs tend to be used as passive forms. If we would not get rid of these cases, the result would be biased. For instance, if we include 'be regarded' in our analysis, the most frequent subcategorization pattern of 'regard' will be something other than the most typical 'regard NP as NP'.

4.2.2. Extracting Subcategorization Frames

This section provides an explanation of how to extract subcategorization frames from the result in the form of treebanks. To take an instance, one of the sentences in which 'regard' is used is shown in the following Plate 4, and its parsed text version is as in the below.

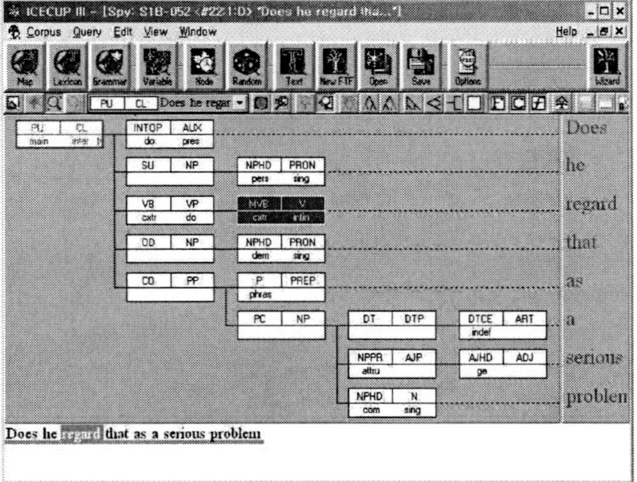

Plate 4: Does he regard that as a serious problem? (S1B-052 #22)

```
<ICE-GB:S1B-052 #022:1:D>
[<#22:1:D> <sent>]
 PU,CL(main,inter,cxtr,pres)
  INTOP,AUX(do,pres) {Does}
  SU,NP
   NPHD,PRON(pers,sing) {he}
  VB,VP(cxtr,do)
*   MVB,V(cxtr,infin) {regard} **
  OD,NP
   NPHD,PRON(dem,sing) {that}
  CO,PP
   P,PREP(phras) {as}
   PC,NP
    DT,DTP
     DTCE,ART(indef) {a}
    NPPR,AJP(attru)
     AJHD,ADJ(ge) {serious}
    NPHD,N(com,sing) {problem}
```

From the above parsed text, we have to extract 'OD,NP' corresponding to 'that' and 'CO, PP' corresponding to 'a serious problem'. Note in particular the depth of each node in the above. 'OD,NP' and 'CO, PP' underlined in the above lie at the second depth, which is tantamount to the previous depth of 'regard' marked with asterisks. That means it is necessary to design the algorithm to collect relevant items while traversing inside the maximal projection of a verb. The algorithm is given below.

```
ARGS = ['OD', 'OI', 'CO', 'CS', 'CI', 'CT', 'PROI', 'NOOD']
N_i = {PARSED_TEXT_i, DEPTH_i}
T = {N_1, N_2, ...}
num = 1
for nd in T:
  if nd has *:
      tmp = num - 1
      do until N_tmp is the maximal projection of nd
        if PARSED_TEXT_tmp is relevant to ARGS and DEPTH_tmp == DEPTH_num - 1
          SF += PARSED_TEXT_tmp
        tmp = cnt + 1
      do until Ntmp is the maximal projection of nd
        if PARSED_TEXT_tmp is relevant to ARGS and DEPTH_tmp == DEPTH_num - 1:
          SF += PARSED_TEXT_tmp
        tmp = num - 1
  num = num + 1
```

Each subcategorization item includes functional information as well as categorical information (e.g. 'OD,NP', 'CS,AJP', or 'CO,AJP / OD,NP'). On the other hand, if there is no subcategorization item (i.e. intransitive verbs that need only the subject), the representation of the frame is as '–'. Now that we get the whole subcategorization frames of 157 verbs with their frequency values, we are ready to measure selectional preference strength.

4.2.3. Selectional Preference Strength

This study makes use of the Kullback-Leibler Divergence model in order to discriminate which subcategorization frame is significantly relevant to a verb. In this study, the formula (6) from Resnik (1996) was applied to measuring each strength, in which S stands for 'strength', v a 'verb', and sf a 'subcategorization frame'.

$$S(v, sf_i) = \frac{P(sf_i \mid v) \log \dfrac{p(sf_i \mid v) + 1}{q(sf_i)}}{\sum P(sf \mid v) \log \dfrac{p(sf \mid v) + 1}{q(sf)}} \quad (6)$$

Using the above formula, we could sort out the subcategorization frames of a verb ordered by strength. For instance, 'regard' takes the following as its major frames.

Table 1: The major subcategorization frames of 'regard'.

	frame	strength	Σ
1st	CO,PP / OD,NP	0.448312089	0.448312089
2nd	CO,PP	0.33378163	0.782093719
3rd	CO,PP / NOOD,CL	0.07252358	0.854617299

4.3. The Relationship

The section investigates the relevance between semantic similarity discussed in Section 4.1 and subcategorization frames dealt with in Section 4.2. In order to test the relevance, we figured out how much each cluster shares subcategorization frames. According to how much each verb is compatible with the other verb(s) in the same cluster, 157 verbs were classified into four subgroups; 'Y', 'N', 'M', and '?'. First, 'Y' means the coincidence accounts for more than 0.8. Even if a verb does not belong to 'Y', if the sum of the largest value and the second largest value is over 0.5, the verb comes under 'M' groups. Third, '?' represents the situation where the word does not appear in ICE-GB as a verb (e.g. 'queen'). Finally, the others that do not belong to any of them will be labeled as 'N'. Table 2 shows the distributional property.

Table 2: The relevance between clusters and selectional preference.

	num	%	Σ
Y	66	42.04%	42.04%
M	49	31.21%	73.25%
N	39	24.84%	98.09%
?	3	1.91%	100%

Table 2 indicates that the significant relevance between semantic similarity and subcategorization frames accounts for approximately 42%, and the likelihood that verbs in a cluster share subcategorization frames is more than 73%. These measures imply that there is a considerable relationship between them, and the selection of subcategorization frames depends on semantic characteristics to some degree.

Another interesting observation we were able to make is that the bigger the Z-score is, the more significant the cluster is. The proportion of 'Y' in the high-ranking 10 clusters ordered by Z-score is about 63%, whereas that in the low-ranking 10 clusters is about 22%.

Table 3: The comparison between high-ranking and low-ranking clusters.

	high-ranking 10		low-ranking 10	
	num	%	num	%
Y	17	62.69%	6	22.22%

| M | 7 | 25.93% | 8 | 29.63% |
| N | 3 | 11.11% | 13 | 48.15% |

Table 3 shows that two or more verbs whose meanings are much similar to each other have a tendency to use the same subcategorization frame. In a nutshell, semantic properties of the verbal lexical items constrain their choice of syntactic patterns to a significant degree.

5. Conclusion

In this study, we tested a working hypothesis that there is a positive relationship between semantic similarity and subcategorization frames in English. This paper is under the assumption that if a group of verbs form a cluster sharing a similar meaning, they tend to share subcategorization frames. In the process, we proposed a statistical method to prove this assumption. We made use of two language resources, namely, ICE-GB and WordNet. We came to the conclusion that the proposed hypothesis holds true to the degrees of 42~73%. This generalization is based on our statistical analysis of two results; one is a list of 61 verbal clusters built up on the basis of the WordNet::Similarity module and the hierarchical bottom-up clustering algorithm, the other is a set of subcategorization frames gathered from the one million word corpus of ICE-GB and ordered by the Kullback-Leibler Divergence model.

The implication of this study for some similar future studies can be summarized as follows: First, this paper provides a well-structured method to test the validity of a linguistic hypothesis based on large-scale language resources, such as ICE-GB, WordNet, or CCED. The stochastic approach introduced in this paper can also be applied to other linguistic research. Second, we believe this kind of descriptive and inductive approach complements the more theoretically oriented approaches, based mostly on intuition.

References

Banerjee, S. and T. Pedersen. 2003. Extended gloss overlaps as a measure of semantic relatedness. *Proceedings of the 18th International Joint Conference on Artificial Intelligence*, pp. 805-810.

Fellbaum, C. 1998. *WordNet: An Electronic Lexical Database*. Cambridge: The MIT Press.

Lasnik, H. and J. Uriagereka. 2005. *A Course in Minimalist Syntax*. Malden: Blackwell Pub.

Lesk, M. 1986. Automatic sense disambiguation using machine readable dictionaries: how to tell a pine cone from an ice cream cone. *Proceedings of the 1986 Special Interest Group on Design of Communication Conference*, 24-26.

Levin, B. 1993. *English Verb Classes and Alternations: a Preliminary Investigation*. Chicago: University of Chicago Press.

Manning, C. D. and H. Schütze. 1999. *Foundations of Statistical Natural Language Processing*. Cambridge: The MIT Press.

Nelson, G., S. Wallis and B. Aarts. 2002. *Exploring Natural Language: Working with the British Component of the International Corpus of English*. Philadelphia: John Benjamins Pub. Co.

Pedersen, T., S. Patwardhan and J. Michelizzi. 2004. WordNet::Similarity - measuring the relatedness of concepts. *Proceedings of the 19th National Conference on Artificial Intelligence*, pp. 1024-1025.

Resnik, P. 1996. Selectional constraints: an information-theoretic model and its computational realization. *Cognition*, 61, 127-159.

Automatic Bilingual Lexicon Extraction
for a Minority Target Language[*]

Eileen Pamela Tiu[a], and Rachel Edita O. Roxas[a]

[a]College of Computer Studies, De La Salle University-Manila
2401 Taft Avenue, Malate, Manila, Philippines
roxasr@dlsu.edu.ph

Abstract. An automated approach of extracting bilingual lexicon from comparable, non-parallel corpora was developed for a target language with limited linguistic resources. We combined approaches from previous researches which only concentrated on context extraction, clustering techniques, or usage of part of speech tags for defining the different senses of a word. The domain-specific corpora for the source language contain 381,553 English words, while the target language with minimal language resources contain 92,610 Tagalog word, with 4,817 and 3,421 distinct root words, respectively. Despite the use of limited amount of corpora (400k vs Sadat's (2003) 39M word corpora) and seed lexicon (9,026 entries vs Rapp's (1999) 16,380 entries), the evaluation yielded promising results. The 50 high and 50 low frequency words yielded 50.29% and 31.37% recall values, and 56.12% and 21.98% precision values, respectively, which are within the range of values from previous studies, 39 - 84.45% (Koehn et al., 2002 and Zhou et al., 2001). Ranking showed an improvement to overall F-measure from 7.32% to 10.65%.

Keywords: Automatic lexicon extraction.

1. Introduction

Automatic bilingual lexicon extraction is the automated process of acquiring bilingual word pairs from corpora in order to construct a lexicon. The product of this process, a bilingual lexicon (or a dictionary), is commonly used for Machine Translation, Natural Language Processing, and other linguistic usages. Since acquiring lexicon from parallel corpora already yields 99% accuracy (Rapp, 1999), this study focused into processing non-parallel corpora, specifically on comparable corpora.

In addition, a lexicon is more helpful if it has the feature of grouping similar senses together. This feature is called word sense discrimination. In this study, the syntax and senses of the word are the contributing factors to discriminate words that have several meanings.

Throughout the years, linguists and translators compile different types of lexicons manually from experts and automatically from corpora, which are collections of texts and other forms of writings. *Parallel corpora* refer to a source text and its translation into one or more target languages (Ahrenberg, et al., 1999). Parallel corpora are used for lexicon extraction due to the following characteristics (Fung, 1998): (1) Words have one sense per corpus; (2) Words have single translation per corpus; (3) No missing translations in the target document; (4) Frequencies of bilingual word occurrences are comparable; and (5) Positions of bilingual word occurrences are comparable.

However, acquiring parallel corpora is labor intensive and time consuming. It is also unlikely that one can find parallel corpora in any given domain in electronic form especially for minority languages. This problem can be solved by using non-parallel corpora. Non-parallel corpora

22nd Pacific Asia Conference on Language, Information and Computation, pages 368–376

come in two forms: comparable and non-comparable corpora. *Comparable* corpora are collections of documents that have common domains or topics but different authors and published dates, while *non-comparable* corpora have totally different domains, authors, and published dates. This factor is crucial for languages with minimal language resources, and the utilization of existing language resource (such as non-comparable corpora) should be maximized to automatically generate other language resources (such as a bilingual lexicon).

Several methods have been developed to utilize these types of corpora to automatically construct a lexicon such as the co-occurrence model (Rapp, 1999), the Convec algorithm (Fung, 1998), the exploration of other clues (Koehn and Knight, 2002), the dependency grammar approach (Zhou, 2001), and the word filtering approach (Sadat et al., 2003). Others utilize these types of resources for word sense disambiguation (WSD) (Kikui, 1999 and Kaji, H et al., 2005). Rapp (1999) yielded 65% accuracy when the first word in the ranked list was considered and 72% when other senses were considered. Convec (Fung, 1998) yielded a 30-76% precision when the top 20 ranks of the translations were considered. Zhou et al. (2001) achieved a 70.8% accuracy for high frequency verbs and 81.48% for low frequency words. Koehn et al. (2002) achieved 39% noun translation accuracy. The average precision of Sadat et al. (2003) was 41.7%.

The main idea behind these techniques is to collect words that co-occur with the source word in the corpora and to establish the correlation between the patterns of word co-occurrences in the corpora of another language. Words that occur in a certain context window in one language have translations that are likely to occur in a similar context window in another language (Koehn et al., 2002).

Nevertheless, relying on context alone is not sufficient to handle ambiguity. For example, the word "find" in the sentence "How did you find the Philippines?" may be interpreted automatically as either "discovery" or "observe". The process of assigning correct senses to an ambiguous word, called *disambiguation,* is addressed by the following word sense disambiguation approaches (Kikui, 1999 and Kaji, H et al., 2005).

On the other hand, discrimination is a subtask of disambiguation that clusters (or groups) similar senses of a word into a number of classes (Schutze, 1998). Part-of-speech (POS) provides syntactic information and serves as a useful clue to sense disambiguation (Stevenson et al., 2001), and imply its usefulness to sense discrimination. However, current studies on discrimination are applied to monolingual corpora and syntactic information is not included in classifying word senses.

This study used the basic concepts introduced by Rapp (1999) to build a lexicon from two comparable, non-parallel corpora of the same domain. Thus, it assumes the existence of a bilingual lexicon as its initial seed lexicon. The application domain of this study is on tagged English and Tagalog corpora. Also, a small scale set of tagged English and Tagalog corpora is used to simulate the presented approach.

The research did not support phrasal translations, and bi-directional translations such as Tagalog to English.

The evaluation based on Rapp (1999) and Zhou et al. (2001) used 50 high and 50 low word frequency occurrences from the corpora and manually validated by human experts. The criteria of their judgment were based on the acceptability of the outputs.

Section 2 discusses the approach taken in this study, and the various modules of the developed system. Section 3 presents the evaluation results. And finally, Section 4 presents some recommendations and conclusions.

2. The Modules of the Lexicon Extraction System

The modules of the lexicon extraction algorithm are presented in Figure 1. Before processing, the initial linguistics resources were first collected and the corpora were pre-processed where POS tagging and stemming were performed. Both source and target corpora underwent context extraction where co-occurrence analysis of each of the words is performed. Alignment is performed on the contexts of the words to be translated with the target corpora through the aid of an initial bilingual lexicon. Initial clustering is performed wherein similar senses of the target translations are grouped together. Feature vector computation and word ranking computes for the ranks of candidate translations.

The initial resources involved in this process include the corpora and the lexicon. The types of corpora used in this research involve comparable types. The corpora contain 381,553 English and 92,610 Tagalog terms, with corresponding 4,817 and 3,421 distinct root words, respectively.

An initial bilingual lexicon, taken from a previous project IsaWika! (Roxas, 1997) served as a seed lexicon and contains 9,026 English elements, and unique meanings and parts of speech. In addition, both English and Tagalog entries were stemmed with the stemming algorithms.

The corpora underwent preprocessing to remove punctuation marks, convert the words to lowercase, stemming, removal of function words, and part of speech assignment. Function words were removed from the source corpus by removing words that were found in the function word lists obtained (Mitton, 1987). Function words in the target language were removed manually by computing for the highest word frequencies and removing the undesired terms. The Porter's Algorithm (Anu, 2003) was used to stem the English documents, while TagSA, a Tagalog stemmer (Bonus, 2003), was used to stem the Tagalog documents. An online English Memory Based Tagger (Zavrel et al., 1999) was used to tag the source documents.

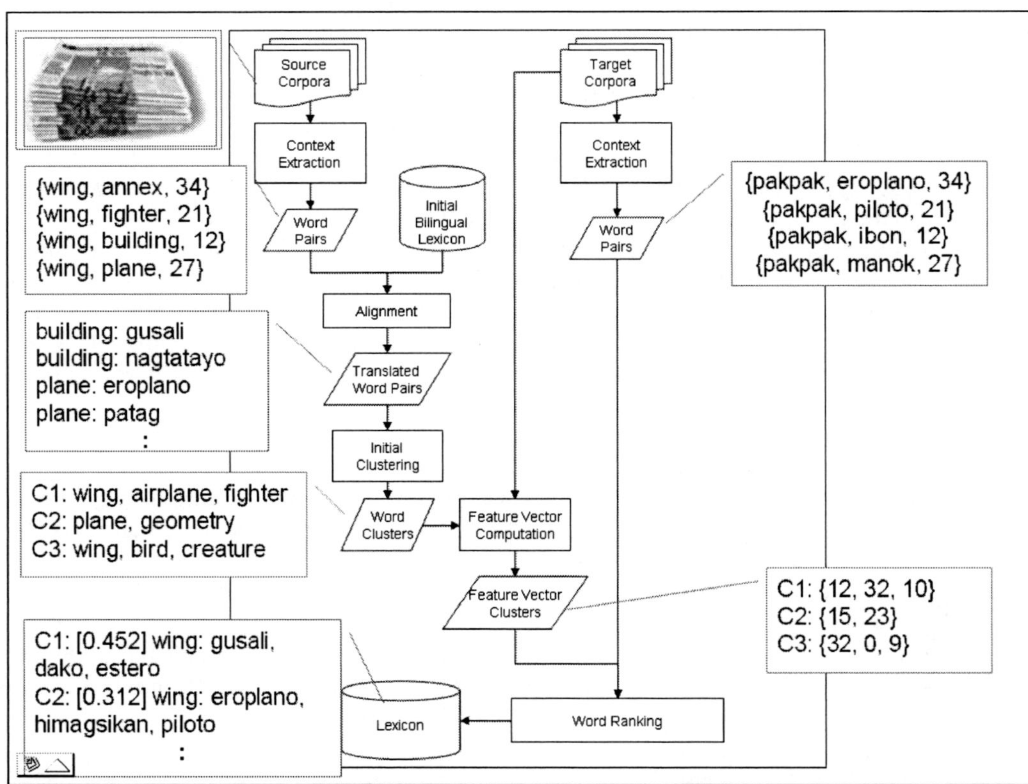

Figure 1: Automatic Bilingual Lexicon Extraction for a Minority Target Language.

2.1. Context Extraction

In the source corpora, context extraction was performed on every word found in the corpora to generate *source word pairs* that represent a set of words that are gathered in a window size of 25 in conjunction with the work of (Kaji et al., 2005). Word pairs are represented in the form:

{SourceWord, Source POS Tags, ContextWord, Context POS Tags, Co-occurrence Frequency} which indicates the number of times a word co-occurs with its neighboring words. For example, as shown in Table 1, we can say that "aaron" co-occurs with "abihu" 20 times in the entire corpora.

Source words are then collected and selected from the set of source word pairs. Similarly, in the target corpora, context extraction was performed on every word found in the corpora to generate *target word pairs*.

Table 1: Representation of Word Pairs.

(English) Source Word Pairs				
Source Word	Source POS Tags	Context Word	Context POS Tags	Frequency
aaron	nnp	abiasaph	nnp	1
aaron	nnp	abihu	nnp	20
aaron	nnp	abiram	nnp	3
aaron	nnp	abishua	nnp	5
aaron	nnp	abl	jj	7
aaron	nnp	about	in	10
aaron	nnp	account	nn	2
aaron	nnp	across	in	2
aaron	nnp	act	vbg	3
aaron	nnp	addit	nn	1

2.2. Alignment Process

The alignment process functions as a bridge between the source and target languages based on the word pairs from the context extraction module and the initial bilingual lexicon. This process finds all translations to the contexts of the *source words*. This was done at an early stage to reduce the dimensionality of the data and thus increase the speed of the processes to be performed later. An issue in this stage is the existence of multiple translations per context. It was decided, however, to consider all translations since the lexicon was built in such a way that the translations were all referring to a similar sense. Thus, it should enhance the algorithm since it provided other possible translations for a single term projecting one sense. Context words derived from the *source word pairs* are translated to the target language with the help of the *initial bilingual lexicon*. Words not found in the initial bilingual lexicon are discarded from the word pair list. Table 2 shows a sample output of the alignment algorithm.

2.3. Sense Grouping

The usual way of clustering starts by collecting random points from the collection that will serve as its initial points in clustering. This proved detrimental to the results thus, later algorithms, like CBC (Pantel, 2003), were modeled in such a way to solve the deficiency by first using agglomerative algorithms to compute for initial points that will serve as their starting points in clustering. The sense grouping algorithm is based on this idea, and is composed of three stages. The first stage locates clusters from the source corpora and assigns different ClusterIDs to different clusters. The second stage computes for the *feature vectors* (or the average) of each cluster collected in the target corpora. The third stage involves ranking the elements computed within these *feature vectors* by comparing the *feature vector* to the set of word pairs extracted from the target corpora. Note that the word pairs were extracted from the target corpora through the *context extraction* module.

Table 2: Bridging the Two Languages.

Word to be Translated		Contexts of the Word to be Translated		Tagalog Translations of the Contexts Words from the Lexicon
Source Words	Source POS Tags	Context Words	Contexts POS Tags	
said	nnp	agreement	nn	sundu
		altar	nn	dambana
		angel	nn	anghel
		ark	nn	arka
		captain	nn	pit
		come	vbp	daan
		delight	nn	lugod
		ey	nns	butas
		face	nns	mukha
		faith	nn	anampalataya
		fear	nn	takot

The *translated word pairs* contain the source word pairs that were translated using the *initial bilingual lexicon* so as to reduce the dimensionality of the data. The elements within the *translated word pairs* are clustered into their most similar senses with the clustering algorithm. And the output of the process is the *word clusters* wherein words with similar senses are grouped into a cluster.

The clustering technique used to group similar terms together is called *single link clustering*. The aligned words are first grouped into their most similar senses. This aims to merge terms whose similarity is beyond a certain threshold into the cluster table. Cluster tables are used to store word clusters. The table will begin to fill up as elements are being assigned and merged inside the table. The threshold was set experimentally to 0.8, 0.85 and 0.9. The clusters generated by the 0.90 threshold were found to be favorable since it generated clusters with fewer number of elements than the other thresholds. It will only stop merging the clusters once all the elements are not similar with any of the other clusters.

The contexts of the source word having translations in the lexicon were clustered with their most similar senses with neighboring words using the clustering algorithm. After which, words having a common sense were assigned a single ClusterID. A partial output consisting of one cluster, ClusterID 759, is shown in Table 3. As observed, the word "sai", with Part of Speech *vbz*, consisting of cosine similarity 0.93129767, occurs more than once with the same Part of Speech but different Cosine Similarity of 0.87990112. This happens as the cosine similarities of the words are computed based on their common neighboring contextual words. Each source word has many contextual neighbors, thus generating different cosine similarities. Words with higher cosine similarity indicate the "nearness" of the context to the source word. Thus, words with higher similarity score, 0.9, will be clustered together. The contexts were clustered from the source and the *feature vectors* were computed based on the target corpora in order to determine the existence and the frequency of the translated words in the target corpora.

From the *ClusterTable* containing the generated *Word Clusters*, the *TargetCorpora*, and the translations of the elements within those clusters generated, a *feature vector* for each cluster of the source word are computed by getting the average co-occurrence frequency of the results generated. The *centroid* or the average of the generated translation is computed such that the summation of the frequency counts of each translation is divided by its number of occurrences. For example, the word "*sabi*" co-occurs 291 times with other words as shown in Table 4, as each word is recounted each time it appears together with the target words, thus possibly generating a higher co-occurrence value than the word_count. This value is then divided by the actual word count of "*sabi*", which is counted individually within the cluster window of the Target Corpora, which is 12 times, yielding 24.25 for the first word. The same procedure is repeated for all the other elements. Note that overstemming has occurred for the first and last words in the context of the words "*sai*" and "*salvat*" which are supposed to be words "*said*" and "*salvation*", respectively.

Table 3: Example of an Output Cluster Table

Source Word			Contexts of the Source Word		
Word	Part of Speech	ClusterID	Word	Part of Speech	Cosine Similarity
said	vbd	759	sai	vbz	0.93129767
			right	jj	0.92557105
			turn	vbg	0.92209296
			work	nns	0.91110829
			turn	vbg	0.89938562
			love	nn	0.89279824
			turn	vbg	0.89015483
			heaven	nn	0.88574855
			heaven	nns	0.88109349
			salvat	nn	0.88105634
			sai	vbz	0.87990112

Table 4: Feature Vector of the Translated Terms.

Word to be Translated			Context of the Words to be Translated			
Word	POS Tags	ClusterID	Words	POS Tags	Tagalog Translations	Centroid
said	vbd	759	sai	vbz	sabi	24.25
			right	jj	may	11.12
			turn	vbg	gawa	10.51
			work	nns	gawa	10.51
			turn	vbg	tayo	10.30
			love	nn	Ibig	9.39
			turn	vbg	bigay	7.64
			heaven	nn	langit	6.56
			heaven	nns	langit	6.56
			salvat	nn	ligtas	5.81

After computing for all the feature vectors of the clusters, these were then compared to the set of word pairs extracted. The word pairs that correspond to a similarity higher than a given threshold would serve as the possible senses of the *source word*. The inputs required were the cluster feature vectors computed and the word pairs gathered. The feature vectors were compared against the vectors of the word pairs in the target language and their cosine similarity computed. The computed values were arranged in descending order to indicate that those with higher values have higher similarity. The word alignments of the *Source Words* with probable translations are generated. It loops through the elements belonging to a feature vector and compares it against the words in the target corpora and computes its cosine similarity. As illustrated in Table 5, the *Target Translations* are the words that matched with the *feature vector* computed and its cosine similarity was computed based on the *feature vector* and the vector of the target words. Note that among the candidate translations, "*sabi*" and "*tinig*" which ranked 0.47 and 0.46, respectively, are closest semantically to the source word "*said*" where *"sabi"* is the literal translation, while *"tinig"* (with literal meaning *"voice"*) is semantically related.

Table 5. Similarity of the Translations to the Source Words

Words to be Translated			Translations	
Word	POS Tags	ClusterID	Word	Cosine Similarity
said	vbd	759	takot	0.47
			anghel	0.47
			sabi	**0.47**
			tinig	**0.46**
			ulan	0.46
			yari	0.45
			may	0.44
			taka	0.44
			labas	0.44
			propeta	0.43

3. Evaluation Results

Various evaluation approaches have been used to assess the performance of the automatic lexicon extraction algorithm, and no existing standard has been developed. Thus, a test plan was designed that is similar to the approaches presented by Rapp (1999) and Zhou (2001). The approach of Rapp performed an evaluation using 100 randomly selected words whereas the approach of Zhou performed an evaluation using a combination of frequently and rarely occurring words. A hybrid approach was used because this study aims to determine the effectiveness of the algorithm on words having different number of occurrences in the corpora. The number of candidate words was limited to 100 because of performance considerations, that is, the processing time needed for each word. Furthermore, it permits opportunities for fine-tuning the algorithm and performing re-executions.

From the source corpora, 50 words with the highest occurrence frequencies and 50 words with the lowest occurrence frequencies were identified. The effectiveness of the lexicon extraction algorithm was tested on these 100 words, by comparing the expected translations which were taken from an initial bilingual lexicon with the actual results of the algorithm. These words then underwent the *context extraction* process that outputs *feature vectors* for the contexts of the 100 terms. The context words, together with their part of speech tags, within these feature vectors are translated to the target language with the help of an initial bilingual lexicon to yield their target language counterparts and thus transforming the feature vector from the source language to a corresponding feature vector in the target language. The target feature vector is then compared to all the vectors found in the target corpora by computing their similarities. The generated sets of translations are then clustered first according to their syntax, then with their most similar senses. The translation corresponding to the top similar senses per cluster were gathered.

The F-measure was used in the research to determine the effectiveness of the approach to both high and low frequencies. In addition, a portion of the test cases were presented to point out some features offered by the extraction algorithm.

As a summary, the yielded translations captured most of the expected translations and placed them in high ranking positions. Furthermore, the Part of Speech tags and the discriminating algorithm complemented each other in grouping similar senses together. It was also able to select the correct translations for some low frequency words that have correct senses associated with the cluster scattered in the target corpus.

The F-measure was used to evaluate the overall performance of the system. The initial F-measure calculated was 7.32%. The generated value was influenced by several factors. The first reason was that it was strictly based on the output of the initial lexicon provided in the beginning of the study, thus, other correct translations for a particular source word were not considered. Secondly, alternate translations were also not considered in evaluation, in order to reduce the inconsistencies in testing. Thirdly, the sizes of some of the generated clusters were large. Thus, another form of testing was done on the results. The F-measure was modified to include the ranks generated by the algorithm. And the ranked F'-measure was calculated to be 10.65%, improving the results generated by the former evaluation. For the recall test, the system was able to yield 50.29% for high frequency words and 31.37% for low frequency words of the expected translations in all clusters. For the ranked precision test, the system was able to yield 56.12% for high frequency words and 21.98% for low frequency words of the expected translations within clusters. The precision and recall values were found to be within the range of values reported from previous researches, which range from 39 - 84.45% (Koehn et al., 2002 and Zhou et al., 2001). In contrast to the size of the corpora and lexicon used, the system used significantly smaller sized corpora (100K for source and 300K for target), versus the resources used in the related literature, wherein the smallest corpora resource used was 39M (Sadat et al., 2003) and the lexicon resource was 16,380 (Rapp, 1999).

It should also be noted that several factors were involved in generating the output. First, the algorithm performs well on high frequency words. Second, the sparseness of the data contributes to the drawback of the performance.

4. Conclusion

This research has presented an algorithm that automatically selects translations from comparable corpora involving a minority target language. Previous researches have only concentrated on acquiring translation from one language to another incorporating the use of parts of speech for defining the different usages of a word in a sentence.

An improvement introduced in this study involves the use of clustering algorithm to group together similar senses of a word. One of the contributions of this research is the combination of the word context extraction (Rapp, 1999) with the clustering technique (Pantel, 2003) and other clues like the part of speech tags in the source corpora. Other researches only concentrated on either context extraction or on clustering techniques only. This research first extracts the contexts of the source word, clusters them into their most similar sense, and then ranks the output through the assistance of the target corpora.

The system was tested on a set of 50 high frequency words and 50 low frequency words. The F-measure was used as the evaluation measure on the output translations of the initial lexicon. The initial F-measure calculated was 7.32%. And the ranked F'-Measure was calculated to be 10.65%, improving the results generated by the former evaluation. It was shown that the algorithm performs on a satisfactory level. This could be attributed to several factors such as the quality of corpora, preprocessing errors, and the inclusion of some function words in the target corpora.

The algorithm is dependent on the quality of translation generated by the initial lexicon and it would generate better results if a high quality lexicon is provided for evaluation. An alternative approach is to develop an algorithm that does not completely rely on the use of an initial lexicon, as introduced by (Koehn et al., 2002). In this study, function words in the target corpora were manually removed and it would be better if a basis could be found for these set of function words. Schachter (1972) has listed a set of function words that can be used as the basis for the removal of function words. Data sparseness affected the quality of translations, thus, some smoothing techniques could also be implemented in order to complement the lexicon extraction algorithm.

Disambiguation techniques, the introduction of a Tagalog part of speech tagger and the removal of function words on the target corpora based on the available list would be good sources of improvement to the present system. In addition, an algorithm could also be developed to handle bi-directional translations, i.e. from Tagalog to English.

References

Ahrenberg, L., M. Merkel, D. Ridings, A. Sågvall Hein and J. Tiedemann. 1999. Automatic Processing of Parallel Corpora: A Swedish Perspective. Linkoping Electronic Articles in Computer and Information Science, ISSN 1401-9841, 4(2).

Anu, J. 2003. Porter's Stemming Algorithm (Visual Basic Version). [online]. Available: http://www.tartarus.org/~martin/PorterStemmer. (February 27, 2004).

Bonus, E. 2004. A Stemming Algorithm for Tagalog Words. *Proceedings of Philippine Computing Society Congress 2004.*

Fung, P. 1998. A Statistical View on Bilingual Lexicon Extraction: From Parallel Corpora to Non-Parallel Corpora. In Farwell, D., L. Gerber and E. Hovy, editors, *Third Conference of the Association for Machine Translation in the Americas*, 1-16.

Kaji, H and Y. Morimoto. 2005. Unsupervised Word Sense Disambiguation Using Bilingual Comparable Corpora. *IEICE Transactions on Information and Systems 2005*, E88-D(2): 289-301.

Koehn, P and K. Knight. 2002. Learning a Translation Lexicon from Monolingual Corpora. *In the Proceedings of ACL Workshop on Unsupervised Lexical Acquisition.*

Kikui, G. 1999. Resolving Translation Ambiguity Using Non-parallel Bilingual Corpora. *In Proceedings of ACL99 Workshop on Unsupervised Learning in Natural Language Processing.*

Mitton. 1987. Function word list from: Spelling Checkers, Spelling Correctors and the Misspellings of Poor Spellers. Function Word List. [online]. Available: http://www.cse.unsw.edu.au/~min/ILLDATA/Function_word.htm. (February 28, 2004).

Rapp, R. 1999. Automatic Identification of Word Translations from Unrelated English and German Corpora. *In Proc. of ACL-99*, 519-526.

Roxas, R. 1997. Machine Translation from English to Filipino: A Prototype. *International Symposium of Multi-lingual Information Technology (MLIT '97)*, Singapore.

Sadat, F., M. Yoshikawa and S. Uemura. 2003. Learning Bilingual Translations from Comparable Corpora to Cross-Language Information Retrieval: Hybrid Statistics-based and Linguistics-based Approach. *In the Proceedings of the Sixth International Workshop on Information Retrieval with Asian Languages*, 57-64.

Schutze, H. 1998. Automatic Word Sense Discrimination. *Computational Linguistics*, 24(1), 97-123.

Stevenson, M. and Y. Wilks. 2001. The Interaction of Knowledge Sources in Word Sense Disambiguation. *Computational Linguistics*, 27 (1).

Zavrel, J & Daelemans, W. 1999. Recent Advances in Memory-Based Part-of-Speech Tagging. *In VI Simposio Internacional de Comunicacion Social*, 590-597.

Zhou, M., Y. Ding, and C. Huang. 2001. Improving translation selection with a new translation model trained by independent monolingual corpora. *Journal of Computational linguistics and Chinese language processing*, pp 1-26, 6(1).

Using 'Low-cost' Learning Features for Pronoun Resolution

Ramon Ré Moya Cuevas and Ivandré Paraboni

University of São Paulo, Escola de Artes, Ciências e Humanidades (USP / EACH)
Av. Arlindo Bettio, 1000, São Paulo, Brazil.
{fusion, ivandre} @usp.br

Abstract. We investigate a machine learning approach to Portuguese pronoun resolution. We presently focus on so-called 'low-cost' learning features readily obtainable from the output of a part-of-speech tagger, and we largely bypass deep syntactic and semantic analysis. Preliminary results show significant improvement in resolution precision and recall, and are comparable to existing rule-based approaches for the Portuguese language spoken in Brazil.

Keywords: Anaphora resolution, Machine Learning.

1. Introduction

The computational resolution of anaphoric expressions lies at the heart of a variety of NLP applications, including text understanding, Machine Translation, text summarization and many others. Although it has received a great deal of attention for many years now, anaphora resolution remains a computational problem yet to be overcome (Mitkov, 2002), and a challenge that is considerably increased if we speak of languages for which basic NLP resources (such as parsers, taggers or large corpora) are still under development, or may have only recently become available. This is the case, for instance, of Portuguese, one of the most widely-spoken languages in the world, and which still lacks somewhat behind as a relatively resource-poor language in NLP.

In this work we extend our previous investigation on learning approaches to Portuguese personal pronoun resolution in (Cuevas et. al., 2008.) In doing so, we focus on so-called 'low-cost' learning features, that is, we will limit the proposed solution to the knowledge readily obtainable from basic NLP tools such as part-of-speech taggers, and we will largely bypass deep syntactic or semantic analysis. In this sense, our work resembles the knowledge-poor approach in Kennedy & Boguraev (1996), which consists of a re-interpretation of the 'classic' algorithm proposed in Lappin & Leass (1994) using shallow rather than in-depth analysis. In addition to that, as we do not intend to explicitly write any anaphora resolution algorithms or rules (but rather induce them automatically) our work is mainly related to machine learning approaches such as Soon et. al. (2001), McCarthy and Lehnert (1995) and Ng & Cardie (2002). However, in discussing a possible 'low-cost' learning approach to Portuguese third person plural pronouns ("Eles/Elas"), we will focus more on the *choice* of learning features, and less on the *results* of a particular machine learning approach, which are to be discussed elsewhere.

The rest of this paper is structured as follows. Section 2 reviews previous work taken as the basis for our present investigation. Section 3 proposed an extended set of features for the problem at hand. Results of a standard decision-tree induction algorithm using the new features are presented in Section 4. Finally, Section 5 draws a number of comparisons with related work in Portuguese pronoun resolution and Section 6 describes our future work.

2. Previous Work

As in Cuevas et. al. (2008), we will follow Soon et. al. (2001) and regard anaphora resolution as a machine learning *classification* task. Accordingly, a pronoun *j* and a potential antecedent term *i* may be classified as co-referent or not, that is, for each pair (i, j) in the text, we intend to label a binary class *coref* as being *co-referential* or *non co-referential*.

Positive instances of co-reference will consist of pairs (i, j) explicitly defined as co-referential in the training data by human annotators, and negative instances will consist of all pairs (i, j) in which *i* is an intermediate NP between *j* and its actual antecedent in the text.

For instance, the pronoun *j1* in the following text gives rise to one positive *(i1, j1)* and two negative (*(i2, j1)* and *(i3, j1)* instances of anaphora. Analogously, pronoun *j3* also co-refers with *i1'*, and pronouns *j2 and j4* both co-refer with *i2*:

> *Scientists$_{i1}$ know that the phenomenon$_{i2}$ occurs once every three to seven years$_{i3}$: they$_{j1}$ can detect when it$_{j2}$ is coming, they$_{j3}$ perceive when it$_{j4}$ is going away.*

The starting point of the work in Cuevas et. al. (2008) was the Portuguese portion of an English-Portuguese-Spanish parallel corpus tagged using the PALAVRAS tool (Bick, 2000), comprising 646 articles (440,690 words in total) from the Environment, Science, Humanities, Politics and Technology supplements of the on-line edition of the "Revista Pesquisa FAPESP", a Brazilian journal on scientific news. Focusing on instances of third person plural pronouns (male) "Eles" and (female) "Elas", two independent annotators created a data set of 2595 instances of co-reference, being 483 positive and 2112 negative, with an average of 4.4 intermediate antecedents between each pronoun and the actual antecedent. About 10% of the positive instances were set aside with their negative counterparts for testing purposes. Thus, the test data comprised 234 instances and the reminder 2361 instances (being 435 positive or co-referential, and 1926 negative or non co-referential) became our training data. As we are still in the process of defining which precise features are applicable to the task at hand, our investigation is currently based on the training data set only, leaving the test data reserved for future use.

It was also shown in Cuevas et. al. (2008) that a simple set of syntactically-motivated features (based on distance, gender and number agreement) may achieve overall positive results in pronoun resolution (85.81% success rate) using C.4.5. ten-fold cross-validation decision-tree induction (Quinlan, 1993). However, this simple approach still suffers from low precision for the co-referential cases, making the resulting algorithm only partially useful for practical purposes. A more conservative (and possibly more reliable) analysis of these results focusing on the positive (i.e., co-referential) instances only shows a 70.5% score in F-measure. The following Table 1 summarizes those findings.

Table 1: Results from Cuevas et. al. (2008.).

Class	Precision	Recall	F-measure
Co-referential	0.572	0.910	0.703
Non Co-ref.	0.977	0.846	0.907

---

[1] In fact, pronoun *j3* co-refers with pronoun *j1* as well, although we presently do not deal with the resolution of full co-reference chains.

3. An Extended Set of 'Low-Cost' Learning Features

What kinds of learning feature may boost pronominal anaphora resolution? From the results in the previous section it is clear that additional features are needed to improve the system's ability to tell actual antecedents apart from all potential candidates. Thus, the first step in our present investigation was to extend the original set of features to gather as much information as possible about the anaphoric relations regardless of their usefulness to solve the problem at hand (which will be left to be 'learned' automatically.) However, as our ultimate goal is the induction of a Portuguese pronoun resolution algorithm based on existing - and easily accessible - Portuguese NLP resources, we shall limit our set of features to those based on the knowledge obtainable from the Portuguese tagger PALAVRAS (Bick, 2000.) More specifically, we have not defined any feature based on semantic knowledge other than what PALAVRAS may provide, or which may require full syntactic analysis.

Our extended set of features consists of 20 classes (plus the *coref* class to be learned), which are summarized in Table 2 below.

Table 2: An extended set of learning features for pronominal anaphora resolution given a candidate *i* and a pronoun *j*.

Feature name	Description
distance	sentences between i and j.
words_between	number of words between i and j.
same_sentence	true if i and j occur in the same sentence.
number_agreement	true if i and j agree in number.
gender_agreement	true if i and j agree in gender.
pronoun_type	1=personal ('eles/elas', or 'They'); 2=possessive ('deles/delas', or 'theirs'); 3=location ('neles/nelas', or 'in them' or 'on them'.)
i_name	true if i is a proper name.
i_defined	true if i is a definite description.
i_demonstrative	true if i follows a demonstrative.
i_subject	true if i is the sentence subject.
i_direct	true if i is a direct object.
i_indirect	true if i is an indirect object.
j_subject	true if j is the sentence subject.
j_direct	true if j is a direct object.
j_indirect	true if j is an indirect object.
function_agreement	true if j and i are both subject or object.
is_hh	true if i is a group of humans.
is_org	true if i is an organisation.
is_inst	true if i is an institution.
is_civ	true if i is a city, country, province etc.

The feature *distance* counts the number of sentences between the pronoun and the candidate, under the assumption that an anaphoric relation becomes less likely as we move further away from the reference. Similarly, the *words_between* feature counts the number of words between pronoun and candidate, which may be particularly helpful for resolving *intrasentencial* anaphora, and so does (perhaps rather redundantly) the boolean feature *same_sentence*.

Given that Portuguese personal pronouns must always agree in number and gender with their antecedents, the features *number_agreement* and *gender_agreement* are expected to play a crucial role in the resolution of "Eles/Elas" references.

The feature *pronoun_type* accounts for the different pronoun usages most commonly found in our corpus: personal, possessive or locative. The features *i_name*, *i_defined* and *i_demonstrative* give additional information about the referring expression that represents the candidate term: a proper name, a definite description or a description following a demonstrative pronoun (e.g., "that company".)

In Cuevas et. al. (2008) the feature *function_agreement* was found to be unhelpful for anaphora resolution. However, this is not to say that subject/object information is irrelevant to our problem. On the contrary, such information is most likely essential to capture a number of syntactic constraints on pronoun resolution, especially considering that in-depth parsing information is not available. A possible reason why *function_agreement* was not useful in our previous work may be related to the excess of information that we attempted to convey as a single feature. Thus, in the presently extended set of features this information is split into six separate features (namely, *i_subject*, *i_direct*, *i_indirect*, *j_subject*, *j_direct* and *j_indirect*), from which we expect to derive the required syntactic constraints as originally intended, whilst allowing each individual feature to influence the solution independently.

The last four features (*is_hh*, *is_org*, *is_inst* and *is_civ*) are based on the semantic tags <hh>, <org>, <inst> and <civ> provided by PALAVRAS, and are intended to aid in the resolution of cases of anaphora in which there is no number agreement between antecedent and pronoun, as in, e.g., "The family" referred to as "They".

Finally, note that the above feature set is readily obtainable from a part-of-speech tagger such as PALAVRAS (Bick, 2000), in this sense corresponding to the 'low cost' aspect of our approach.

4. Testing

In order to select the most useful features for solving the problem at hand we started by taking the entire set of 20 learning features into account. Using C.4.5. ten-fold cross-validation decision-tree induction (cf. Quinlan, 1993) over the training data set alone, we confirmed the findings in Cuevas et. al. (2008) suggesting that the information conveyed by the *function_agreement* feature is not directly useful to our learning approach.

As for the additional features now under consideration, we manually tested several possible combinations to refine the resolution model. Speaking of the information about the anaphor (*j*), we found that *j_direct* and *j_indirect* did not improve resolution. This is largely explained by the fact that we focused on third person pronouns that do not occur in object position, that is, the syntactic function of the anaphor does not play a significant role in the resolution process[2].

Regarding the information about the candidate (*i*), four other superfluous features were identified: *i_indirect*, *is_org*, *i_name* and *i_demonstrative*. Once again, this was to be fully expected as, in a machine learning approach, we were not concerned with any linguistic investigation on how precisely pronoun resolution should be carried out, that is, one of the main goals of our investigation was precisely to determine which features are relevant or not.

The seven superfluous features (*function_agreement*, *j_direct*, *j_indirect*, *i_indirect*, *is_org*, *i_name* and *i_demonstrative*) were hence removed from the data and our test was re-run using the remaining 13 features. The following Table 3 summarizes our findings, using once again C.4.5. ten-fold cross-validation decision-tree induction (cf. Quinlan, 1993) over the training data set alone. The corresponding confusion matrix is shown in Table 4.

Table 3: Results from the extended set of features.

Class	Precision	Recall	F-measure
Co-referential	0.710	0.713	0.712
Non Co-ref.	0.936	0.935	0.936

---

[2] In principle these features are still relevant if, for example, we are to extend the existing approach to cover other kinds of reference phenomena.

Table 4: Confusion matrix.

	True	False
True	311	125
False	127	1830

The above confusion matrix is to be interpreted as follows: 2141 instances (being 311 co-referent and 1830 non co-referent) were correctly classified (89.47% success rate); 125 co-referent instances were misclassified as non co-referent (5.22%), and 127 non co-referent instances were misclassified as co-referent (5.31%.)

5. Discussion

At first glance, the present results are only marginally better than those achieved in Cuevas et. al. (2008). However, they do show improvement over our previous tests in the sense that they represent a better balance between precision and recall for positive instances of anaphora.

Regarding, existing work on Portuguese pronoun resolution, three of the best-known studies in the field are summarized as follows:

- Coelho & Carvalho (2005) describe an implementation of the Lappin & Leass algorithm (Lappin & Leass, 1994) for Portuguese third person pronoun resolution. The proposed algorithm was tested against 297 pronouns, achieving 35.15% success rate.

- Santos & Carvalho (2007) focus on an implementation of the Hobbs' algorithm (Hobbs, 1978) for Portuguese pronoun resolution. The test involved a set of 916 instances of non-reflexive pronouns in three linguistic genres, with accuracy rates ranging from 40.4% (texts on legislation) to 50.96% (magazine articles.)

- Chaves (2007) describes an implementation of the algorithm of R. Mitkov (Mitkov, 2002) for Portuguese third person pronouns. Results in this case range from 38% (novels domain) to 67.01% (newspapers articles) success rates.

A comparison between the best results achieved by these approaches and ours suggests that our present work is at least comparable to those. Moreover, being trainable from corpora, our work is in principle domain-independent, and much less prone to the wide fluctuations in results experienced by the above-mentioned studies.

On the other hand, it should be pointed out that when building the present training data, the annotators were selective in the choice of training instances of anaphora to be addressed. In particularly, our work does not include instances of reference to compound antecedents (e.g., "The boy and the girl" referred as "They"), which may partially explain the higher success rates[3].

Another important difference between learning and non-learning approaches to anaphora resolution is that in the former what counts as 'success' is simply the correct true/false labeling of the class 'coref', which is not the same as finding the right antecedent (as in the above mentioned non-learning approaches.) For example, our approach may successfully find the intended antecedent but, at the same time, mark a second candidate as co-referent as well, which may be correct (i.e., if they form a single co-reference chain) or not.

Bearing in mind these differences, the following summary in Table 8 is presented for illustration purposes only. Regarding our own work, we take a conservative view and show the F-measure score for co-referential cases only (cf. Table 6) and not the overall success rate of 89.47% since the data are heavily imbalanced (with on average 4.4 false antecedents for each pronoun.)

---

[3] To minor this difficulty, a separate annotation task is underway, in which a wider variety of reference phenomena will be taken into account to create a complementary test data set.

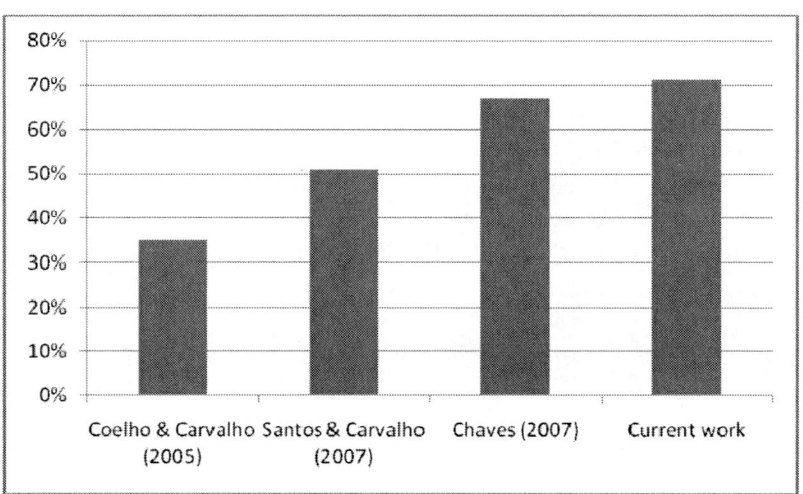

Figure 1: Maximum accuracy reported in previous anaphora resolution algorithms for the Portuguese language.

6. Conclusion

We have described an extension of previous work in Cuevas et. al. (2008) regarding a machine learning approach to Portuguese personal pronoun resolution. Using an enlarged set of features, our present results show improvement in resolution accuracy whilst avoiding the need for deep syntactic or semantic parsing information, which may not be easily obtainable for large-scale NLP projects involving the (Brazilian) Portuguese language.

We are now in the process of analyzing the remaining classification errors to define additional features to improve results even further. Among these, our approach may require information about adjunct and embedded expressions, as well as quantifiers and indefinite noun phrases usage. Since all the required information is (in principle) readily available from our tagged corpus, we expect to benefit from these additional features whilst keeping our knowledge acquisition costs low.

Once our set of features is stabilized and suitably tested, we intend to run our resulting pronoun resolution algorithm using the Portuguese portion of our parallel corpus as input, and use its output information to resolve their Spanish and English counterparts without any explicit knowledge about these languages. In doing so, we expect to improve the performance of an ongoing Machine Translation project for these three languages.

Finally, although in this work we have built our training data from a collection of third person plural pronouns only, we notice that our resulting algorithm should be capable of dealing with singular cases as well (i.e., "ele/ela" or he/she), and that should remain the case despite the fact that some of our current features (i.e., those conveying semantic 'group' information) are unlikely to play a role in the resolution of these cases. To make this point clear, a separate evaluation work on a different domain (namely, using a corpus of Brazilian newspapers articles) is underway, and will be described elsewhere once finalized.

Acknowledgements

The authors acknowledge support by FAPESP (2006/03941-7, 2007/07356-4) and CNPq (484015/2007-9.)

References

Bick, E. 2000. The parsing system PALAVRAS: automatic grammatical analysis of Portuguese in a constraint grammar framework. PhD Thesis, Arhus University.

Chaves, Amanda. 2007. A resolução de anáforas pronominais da lingual portuguesa com base no algoritmo de Mitkov. Msc. dissertation, University of São Carlos, São Carlos, Brazil.

Coelho, T.T. and Ariadne M.B.R. Carvalho. 2005. Uma adaptação de Lappin e Leass para resolução de anáforas em português. Anais do XXV Congresso da Sociedade Brasileira de Computação (III Workshop em Tecnologia a Informação e da Linguagem Humana – TIL 2005), São Leopoldo, Brazil, pp. 2069-2078.

Cuevas, Ramon Ré Moya, Willian Yukio Honda, Diego Jesus de Lucena, Ivandré Paraboni and Patrícia Rufino Oliveira. 2008. *Portuguese Pronoun   Resolution: Resources and Evaluation*. 9th International Conference on Intelligent Text Processing and Computational Linguistics (CICLing-2008) Haifa, Israel. Springer LNCS vol. 4919, pp. 344-350. Springer-Verlag Berlin Heidelberg.

Hobbs, J. 1978. Resolving pronoun references. Lingua, vol. 44, pp. 311-338.

Kennedy, Christopher and Branimir Boguraev. 1996. Anaphora for Everyone: Pronominal Anaphora Resolution without a Parser. 16th International Conference on Computational Linguistics (COLING-1996) Copenhagen, pp. 113-118

Lappin, S. and H. J. Leass. 1994. An algorithm for pronominal anaphora resolution. Computational Linguistics, 20(4), pp. 535-561.

McCarthy, J. F. and W. G. Lehnert. 1995. Using Decision Trees for Coreference Resolution. 14th International Conference on Artificial Intelligence IJCAI'1995.

Mitkov, Ruslan. 1999. Multilingual Anaphora Resolution. Machine Translation volume 14, numbers 3-4. Springer, pp. 281-299.

Mitkov, Ruslan. 2002. Anaphora Resolution. Longman.

Ng, Vincent and Claire Cardie. 2002. Improving Machine Learning Approaches to Coreference Resolution. 40th Annual Meeting of the Association for Computational Linguistics (ACL), Philadelphia, pp.104-111.

Quinlan, J.R.. 1993. C4.5: programs for machine learning. Morgan Kaufmann Publishers Inc., San Francisco, CA, USA.

Santos, D.N.A. and Ariadne M.B.R. Carvalho. 2007. Hobbs' algorithm for pronoun resolution in Portuguese. 6th Mexican International Conference on Artificial Intelligence, MICAI-2007, Aguascalientes, pp. 966-974.

Soon, Wee Meng et. al. 2001. A Machine Learning Approach to Correference Resolution of Noun Phrases. Computational Linguistics 27(4).

Natural Language Database Interface for the
Community Based Monitoring System [*]

Krissanne Kaye Garcia, Ma. Angelica Lumain,

Jose Antonio Wong, Jhovee Gerard Yap, Charibeth Cheng

De La Salle University – Manila. 1410 Taft Avenue Malate, Manila

{10533834, 10517197, 10514848, 10506349, koc}@dlsu.edu.ph

Abstract. In most information systems, databases are accessed and manipulated typically through systems developed to tailor-fit the company's needs. The usual problem in these cases is the limitation on data accessibility because the users are constrained to the forms created for the system. Another way of accessing the database is through Structured Query Language (SQL), a language that is not familiar to end users, thus still limiting the access to the data. Natural Language Database Interfaces were developed to address limited database accessibility for end users. This paper presents AlLaDIn, a web-based natural language interface to the Community-Based Monitoring System of a city in the Philippines.

Keywords: natural language database interface, SQL, CBMS, natural language query

1. Introduction

CBMS is a poverty monitoring system that is now used in Pasay City. It tracks poverty by surveying the people living in a certain area. Once this is done, they input them using the programs Census Professional (CSPro) and CMS-Natural Resource Database (NRDB), which are customized free software used to encode the data and to digitize spot maps. The output of CSPro is a text file, which is then used as an input to the program STATA, which they use to actually statistically monitor poverty. Since STATA needs technical skills to be used effectively, the data is very hard to access. Thus, people who actually must have direct access to these pieces of information must first ask the people/person who are/is capable of using the software to get the data for them, which might take some time. To address this problem, a Natural Language Database Interface (NLDBI) was developed for CBMS that will allow users to access the CBMS data without having to learn STATA.

A NLDBI allows users to access a database using natural language query. It accepts a user query, extracts pertinent data from the query, converts the extracted data to SQL, then retrieves the data from the database. AlLaDIn is domain-dependent, database-dependent natural language interface for CBMS-Pasay.

2. System Architecture

AlLaDIn is concerned with translating the English query by the user into its corresponding SQL query to retrieve the data from the database. The result will then be displayed to the user. This system has four major modules, as shown in the architectural design of the system in Figure 1. This design is partially based on the Masque/SQL system (Androutsopoulos *et al.*, 1995) and the FST mapping technique (Gala, 2005).

2.1 Parser and Semantic Analyzer

This phase involves the (1) the tokenization of input, (2) parsing and analyzing the semantics of

---

22nd Pacific Asia Conference on Language, Information and Computation, pages 384–390

words, (3) retrieval of syntactic and semantic properties of words in the lexicon, and (4) checking the grammatical and semantic rules of the input. A context-free grammar for the English language is used to check if the sentence is grammatically correct.

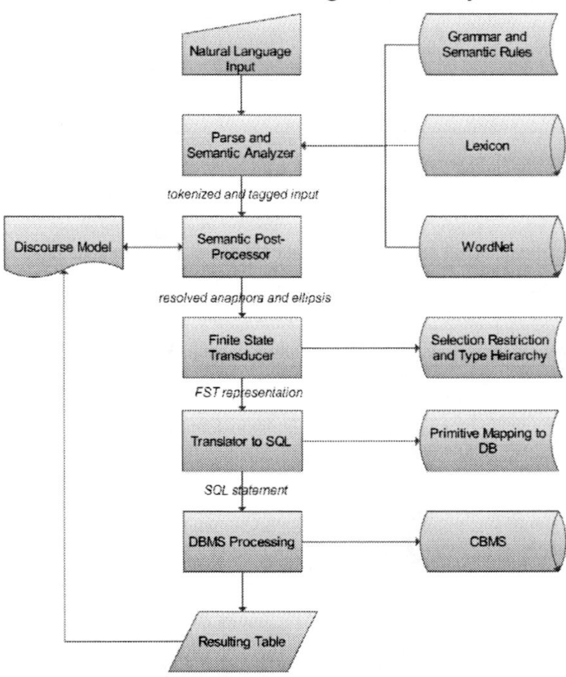

Figure 1: Architectural Design of NLDBI-CBMS

Once the sentence has been inputted, the Parser and Semantic Analyzer would tokenize the sentence. Each token would then be passed to WordNet for it to be properly tagged with its part-of-speech (POS), other information tag (eg. singular, person), and the token's synonyms. After being tagged by WordNet, it would then be passed to the lexicon. The lexicon contains domain-specific words or terminologies that are not found in WordNet. It would then tag each token that was not tagged by WordNet. After tagging all tokens, the sentence would then be parsed and checked if it is grammatically correct.

2.2 Semantic Post-Processor

Once the natural language query is accepted and confirmed by the system as grammatically and semantically correct, the query is then passed to the semantic postprocessor. The semantic post-processor is necessary for queries present the referencing problems of anaphora and ellipses (Androutsopoulos *et al.*, 1995). Consider the compound user query `"How many people live in Barangay 1? What about Barangay 2?"` The second query is ambiguous, however, the handling of such ambiguities presents a simpler way of querying for the users by allowing follow-up questions to be used and short.

If the user's input query does not have any anaphoric expression or ellipsis, the query is scanned. The query would be looked up in the discourse model to fill up the succeeding queries that have to be further resolved.

Template of the discourse model is shown in Table 1 and a sample discourse template is shown in Figure 2.

Table 1: Discourse Model Template.

Tag	Possible values	Description
`<Discourse>`		Marks the start of a discourse entry
`<Sentence>`		Marks the start of an input sentence
`<Token>`		Marks the start of a token in a sentence
`<Term>`	`person`	Indicates the term in the token

<POSTag>	noun	Indicates the term's part-of-speech tag
<OtherInfo>	singular, common, number, plural, proper}	Indicates other information related to the token
<Synonym>	Members	Lists all possible synonyms of the token. These synonyms are taken from WordNet if the token is in WordNet, otherwise, these synonyms came from the lexicon.

```
<Discourse>
    <Result>
        <Row>
            <Col>
                <Term>489</Term>
                <POSTag></POSTag>
                <OtherInfo>singular, noun, proper</OtherIr
                <Synonym>members</Synonym>
            </Col>
        </Row>
    </Result>
    <Resolved>
        <Token>
            <Term>how many</Term>
            <POSTag>wh</POSTag>
            <OtherInfo></OtherInfo>
            <Synonym>null</Synonym>
        </Token>
        <Token>
            <Term>person</Term>
            <POSTag>noun</POSTag>
            <OtherInfo>singular, common</OtherInfo>
            <Synonym>members</Synonym>
        </Token>
        <Token>
            <Term>live</Term>
            <POSTag>verb</POSTag>
            <OtherInfo>singular</OtherInfo>
            <Synonym>live, know, experience, live, be, li\
```

Figure 2. Sample Discourse template.

2.3 Finite State Transducer

A finite state transducer (FST) consists of states that maps one string to another string. It transduces or replaces a certain string to another.

AlLaDIn uses FST to replace keywords extracted with their corresponding SQL terms and database table attributes and conditions. The FST is represented by the rules defined in the Selection Restriction and Type Hierarchy, and the Translation Rules.

The Selection Restriction and Type Hierarchy is in charge of looking for words that are searchable in the CBMS Database. These words were manually created based on the CBMS database schema. The words that we placed here are those that have a particular mapping to the database, whether it be a table, attribute, or a condition. A sample of this is found in Table 2.

The Translation Rules is a table containing SQL keywords with a list of its corresponding English terms. These English terms are just synonyms of the SQL keyword's English literal. For example, the SQL keyword max has an English literal maximum, the list of English terms were derived from the synonyms of maximum. A sample of this is found in Table 3.

Table 2: Sample entries of the Selection Restriction with the mapping.

word	map1
boarder	BOARDERS
tenant	BOARDERS
calamity	CALAMITIES
cleanliness program	CLEANPROGRAMS
computer income	COMPUTERINCOME
construction income	CONSTRUCTIONINCOME
credit program	CREDITPROGRAMS

Table 3: Sample entry of the Translation Rules.

rule	output	synonyms
avg_stmt	avg	,average,
between_stmt	between	,between,between,betwixt,tween,
count_stmt	select count(*)	,count,count,number,enumerate,numerate,matter,weigh,consi
equal_stmt	=	,equal,equal,be,touch,rival,match,equalize,equalise,equate,
except_stmt	except	,except,demur,except,exclude,leave out,leave off,omit,take o
exists_stmt	exists	,exists,
greater_stmt	>	,greater,greater,bigger,older,more,more(a),more than,
having_stmt	having	,having,have,have,have got,hold,feature,experience,receive,
less_stmt	<	,less,less(a),smaller,younger,
like_stmt	like	,contains,begins,
max_stmt	max	,maximum,maximal,maximum,biggest,most,most(a),largest,
min_stmt	min	,minimum,minimal,minimum,smallest,least,least(a),
select_stmt	select	,select,choose,take,select,pick out,show,show,demo,exhibit,p

2.4 Translator to SQL

The tokens here are first replaced by their table attributes. This is done by passing each token term as a parameter to the Primitive Mapping to DB, which will return their mapping(s). The Primitive Mapping to DB is basically a table, which contains the word and their corresponding mappings. This is shown in Table 2. The first column represents the token while the other column represents the mappings. There are 40 more columns here that represent the mappings of the token, but due to space constraint it cannot be displayed all here. 41 was used as the maximum number of mappings because there are 41 tables in the CBMS database and we assumed that a token can only be mapped to one attribute per table.

After replacing all keywords with their table attributes, the Translator to SQL module will group the keywords into two groups, namely, the *Object* group and the *Components* group. The Object group contains the `select` and `from` clauses, while the Components group contains the `where` clause.

3. Simulation

To further understand how each module works, the inputs and outputs of each module will be shown based on the query "`How many people live in Barangay 1? What about Barangay 2?`".

3.1 Paser and Semantic Analyzer

As the sentences enter the Parser and Semantic Analyzer module, the sentences are separated so processing may be performed one sentence at a time. Figure 3 shows the sentences after separation.

```
[1]      How many people live in Barangay 1?
[2]      What about Barangay 2?
```

Figure 3: Sentences after being separated.

After separating the sentences, the sentences would then tokenized and passed to WordNet for part-of-speech tagging and retrieve of semantic information and synonyms. The underlined entries in Table 4 are the data taken from WordNet.

Table 4: The extracted tokens with WordNet information.

Term	Part-of-Speech tag	Other Information tag	Synonyms
How many	WH	Null	Null
People	Noun	Plural	Members
Live	Verb	Null	Null
In	Preposition	Null	Null
Barangay 1	Unknown	Null	Null
What about	WH	Null	Null
Barangay 2	Unknown	Null	Null

As seen in Table 4, "Barangay 1" is tagged as unknown. This is because WordNet does not contain the domain-specific terminologies used by the CBMS, which can be found in the lexicon. Table 5 shows the tokens with the lexicon information (underlined entries).

After tagging all tokens, the sentences will be parsed to check if the sentences are grammatically correct. If one of the sentences is grammatically incorrect, the sentences proceed to the Post-Semantic Analyzer for anaphora or ellipsis resolution.

Table 5: The extracted tokens with WordNet and lexicon information

Term	Part-of-Speech tag	Other Information tag	Synonyms
How many	WH	Null	Null
People	Noun	Plural	Members
Live	Verb	Null	Null
In	Preposition	Null	Null
Barangay 1	Noun	Singular	Null
What about	WH	Null	Null
Barangay 2	Noun	Singular	Null

3.2 Semantic Post-Processor

Upon entering the second module, the system checks if the sentences contain an anaphora or an ellipsis for them to be resolved. Consider the second sentence "*What about Barangay 2?*". This sentence contains an ellipsis and need to be processed. The Semantic Post-Processor determines the missing components of the sentence with ellipsis from the previous query. In our example, the previous query is "*How many people live in Barangay 1?*". The processed sentence is shown in Table 6.

Table 6: Query 2 after ellipsis resolution.

Term	Part-of-Speech tag	Other Information tag	Synonyms
How many	WH	Null	Null
People	Noun	Plural	Members
Live	Verb	Null	Null
In	Preposition	Null	Null
Barangay 2	Noun	Singular	Null

The Semantic Post-Processor compares each token of the previous query with the current query, and then merging distinct tokens from both queries into one to formulate the new and resolved query. However, the result of this process might not always be correct or complete.

3.3 Finite State Transducer

In the finite state transducer module, tokens are replaced, when possible, with their corresponding SQL equivalents based on the Translation Rules table. In our example, **how many** was replaced **select count(*)**. Its part-of-speech tag is then changed to SQL to indicate that the token is already an acceptable SQL token. Other tokens are replaced with database-specific tokens, based on the Selection and Type Hierarchy entries and the synonyms of the tokens. For our sample queries, the token **people** was replaced to the CBMS table **member**, since it has a synonym of **members**. Its part-of-speech tag is then changed to **selection restriction**. Tokens that are tagged as adverb, adjective, or prepositions are filtered out of the token list. Table 7 shows the resulting set of tokens for both sentences.

Table 7: Tokens after passing through FST.

Term	Part-of-Speech tag	Other Information tag	Synonyms
select count(*)	SQL	Null	Null
member	Selection Restriction	Plural	Members
live	Verb	Null	Null
Barangay 1	Noun	Singular	Null
select count(*)	WH	Null	Null
member	Selection Restriction	Plural	Members
live	Verb	Null	Null
Barangay 2	Noun	Singular	Null

3.4. SQL Translation

The fourth module, *Translator to SQL*, converts those tokens tagged **Selection Restriction** to its corresponding SQL syntax. Each token is checked in the *Primitive Mapping to DB* if it has a corresponding SQL syntax. After which, all tags that are not tagged as **SQL** are removed from the token list. Table 8 shows the partial output of the module.

Table 8: Partial output of SQLTranslator module.

Term	Part-of-Speech tag	Other Information tag	Synonyms
select count(*)	SQL	Null	Null
MEMBERS	SQL	Null	Null
MEMBERS.brgy = 1	SQL	Null	Null
select count(*)	SQL	Null	Null
MEMBERS	SQL	Null	Null
MEMBERS.brgy = 2	SQL	Null	Null

The tokens will then be separated to the Objects and Component groups. Table 9 shows the separation of tokens into groups.

Table 9: Object and Component groups.

Object	Component
select count(*)	MEMBERS.bgry = 1
MEMBERS	

After grouping the tokens, it will then converted to its SQL statement which is *select count(*) from MEMBERS where MEMBERS.brgy = 1.*

4. Results and Conclusion

AlLaDIn is domain-specific natural language database interface. The information that it knows is heavily dependent on the data stored in and the structure of the CBMS database. If the database schema is revised and/or when the data is updated, it is not guaranteed that the system would still work perfectly. Entries in the lexicon came from the CBMS data, which means that it needs to be update manually through the Administrator module when the CBMS database is updated. The *Primitive Mapping to DB* table relies heavily on the database schema and if the schema is changed, it also has to be revised.

The Parser and Semantic Analyzer module accepts simple interrogative and imperative sentences. This module is dependent on WordNet and the lexicon in recognizing and tagging words in the given sentence. If a word in the sentence is not matched or is matched but tagged incorrectly, the system may generate an incorrect SQL statement thus generating incorrect results or no results at all.

The Semantic Post-Processor module, in regards with sentence ambiguity detection and resolution process, the module does not have any sentence ellipsis detection mechanism and the resolution process is still imperfect. In the sentence ellipsis detection, the module just assumes that every input natural language is an ellipsis sentence ambiguity problem. Therefore, all input undergoes the resolution process even though the input natural language originally is not an ellipsis. And with the resolution process, both resolution processes uses simple algorithms that might not be enough to handle all possible cases. So there is a possibility that the input natural language might not be resolved well, especially those inputs that are too complex. To further improve the module, future works can be done to find a proper way of detecting the ellipsis sentence ambiguity problem and to develop resolution algorithms that can handle and resolved complex inputs.

The Finite State Transducer is able to handle the words that are found in the CBMS database and the translation rules. If a given word is synonymous (according to WordNet) to a word found in the database, the system would be able to successfully process it.

The Translator to SQL works as expected if at least one of the tokens is the query refer to a table found in the CBMS database. If the tokens do not contain any database-specific attribute, a default set of attributes is used by the system per table. The translator is also capable of distinguishing if an attribute is used as an attribute or as a condition. For example, the query `"List the age of the people."` and `"List the people with age greater than 30."` In the first query **age** is used as an attribute, while in the second query **age** is used as a condition. Although the system can handle this, it cannot distinguish if there are 2 or more attributes used as conditions. If a query is ambiguous (i.e. tokens may be mapped to 2 or more tables), the translator will be able to create 2 or more queries and determine which attributes and/or condition belongs to a specific query.

To further improve AlLaDIn, it is recommended that the parser handle compound sentences. Reliance of the system to CBMS data may also be lessened by automating the lexicon update whenever the CBMS data has been updated. Ellipsis resolution and detection may also be improved. Finally, the tokenization process may be enhanced. Since the conversion of the tokens to SQL is highly dependent on the tokenization phase, it could be further improved if the system can distinguish two or more attributes used as conditions.

5. Reference

Androutsopoulos, G.D., Ritchie, & P. Thanisch, "Natural Language Interfaces to Databases – An Introduction". *Natural Language Engineering,* 1(1), Cambridge University Press (1995).

CBMS Brochure (2003). Philippine Institute for Development Studies. Makati, Philippines.

CBMS Network Conference Overview.(2006) The CBMS Network Conference 2006: Philippine Institute for Development Studies. Makati, Philippines.

CBMS Network Coordinating Team (2005). Gaining Insights on the CBMS Application: The Case of the Philippines Proceedings of the 2004 National Conference on CBMS. *2004 National Conference on CBMS* (pp. 2-51). Makati City: CBMS Network Coordinating Team.

CBMS Network Project Progress Report. (2004). Angelo King Institute for Economic and Business Studies, De La Salle University, Manila.

Gala, S. (2005). *Translation From English to Sql Using Statistical Machine Translation and Finite State Transducers.*[online] Available: http://tangra.si.umich.edu/clair/shyamg/project.pdf

Controlled Korean for Korean-English MT

Munpyo Hong [a] **, Chang-Hyun Kim** [b]

[a] Department of German Lang. & Lit.
Sungkyunkwan University
53 Myeongnyun-dong
Seoul, Korea
skkhmp@skku.edu

[b] Natural Language Processing Team
ETRI
Gajeong-dong 16
Taejeon, Korea
chkim@etri.re.kr

Abstract. This paper addresses the issues in designing the so-called 'Controlled Korean' for a Korean-English MT system. Controlled Language is a sublanguage of a natural language which is supposed to improve the readability and the translatability of a text. Much effort has been made to design a controlled language for major international languages such as English, German, Spanish and etc. However, little effort has been made yet to design a Controlled Korean in the context of machine translation. In this paper we introduce the concept of the Controlled Korean we have developed for a Korean-English MT system and compare the Controlled Korean with the Controlled English and Controlled German from the perspective of the translatability. The result of our experiments shows that in designing a Controlled Language, not only the linguistic characteristics of the language but also the characteristics of an MT-System must be taken into account.

Keywords: Controlled Language, Controlled Korean, Machine Translation, Translatability, Negative Translatability Indicators

1. Introduction

Controlled Language is a sublanguage of a natural language designed to improve the readability and the translatability of a text. Originally, the concept of a controlled language was introduced in the field of technical documentations to prevent the misunderstanding of texts. [1] In the last couple of years the necessity of a controlled language has increased significantly, especially in the technical documentation domain, as the number of pages to be translated has increased enormously.

The increase of the volume of the documents to be translated made it necessary to employ a full automatic translation system like an MT or a machine-aided translation system like translation memory. In Korea, however, MT systems have not been widely welcomed by the experts in the localization business, because the quality of the translations failed to match their expectations.

The recent researches on the controlled languages show that the use of a controlled language can generally lead to the improvement of machine translation quality, thus reducing the cost of

---

[1] cf. Esselink(2000), Göpferich(1995)

22nd Pacific Asia Conference on Language, Information and Computation, pages 391–396

post-editing. The general assumption behind the idea of the controlled language is that the cost of the use of a controlled language that can be paraphrased as 'pre-editing' is lower than that of 'post-editing' in using an MT system for localization.

Previous works on the controlled language in the context of MT have mainly focused on the impact of the controlled language on MT. Aikawa et al. (2007), for example, addressed the impact of the controlled English for MSR-MT. Lehrndorfer (1996), Lehrndorfer&Schachtl (1998) dealt with the controlled German for German-English MT.

In this paper, we will introduce the concept of the 'Controlled Korean' for Korean-English MT. We will not only show the impact of the Controlled Korean on Korean-English MT, but also share our experience in designing the Controlled Korean.

2. Controlled Korean

2.1.Background

Since early 2000, MT has been paid much attention in Korea because of the fast growth of the Internet. However, most of the efforts to bring out the off-the-shelf products into the market have failed mainly due to the difficulty in Korean syntactic parsing and the failure in the domain adaptation.[2] One of the few Korean-English MT systems actively used not only in Korea but also in foreign countries is the Korean-English Patent MT system developed at ETRI.[3] The performance of the patent MT system is good enough for foreign patent examiners to retrieve the patent documents of their interest in English.

The quality of the Korean-English patent MT is good enough for cross-language information retrieval, however not good enough, if it is to be used for other purposes like academic paper authoring. If an MT system is to be used for academic paper writing in English, the quality of the translation must be far superior to that of the patent MT system, the purpose of which is not to produce a perfect translation, but to produce a translation just enough for the understanding. However, we are very well aware of the difficulties and obstacles in improving the performance of an MT system in a short period of time. One way to improve the translation quality is to employ a controlled language for MT. Kim et al. (2007) showed that even some simple writing rules can improve the translation quality for around 10 %.

2.2.Designing Controlled Korean

To design a controlled language for MT, the purpose of the application must be properly understood. Most of the controlled languages introduced so far have without exceptions limited lexicons and writing rules. This is possible and useful, when the controlled language and the MT system are used by a homogeneous group of users like employees in a company. However, in the academic paper authoring setting, the scenario should be somewhat different, i.e., the users have all the different interests of their own. Thus, it is almost impossible to enforce them to use only the allowed lexicon and not to use any words they like. We therefore gave up introducing the restricted Korean lexicon and rather focussed on the writing rules which impact on the translation quality most.

The philosophy in designing the Controlled Korean was to give the authors as much freedom as possible. The authors write an English academic paper that will be automatically checked against Controlled Korean writing rules by a Controlled Korean Checker.[4] Thus we investigated on the translation errors that might be occurred by stylistic errors that are hard for an MT system to treat properly.

To do this, we manually checked 40,000 Korean-English machine translation pairs. We scored all the translations from 0(poor) to 4(very good). The translations above 3 points(good) were

---

[2] Korean-Japanese MT, however, is widely used in both countries
[3] Hong et al. (2005)
[4] cf. Kim et al. (2007) about the Controlled Korean Checker module of IMT system

excluded. We assumed that the syntactic analysis and the transfer of those sentences succeeded without fatal errors. Then we focused on the translations that were scored below 3. Many of them failed in the morphological or syntactic analysis for some reasons. We were interested in those cases where, though the morphological and the syntactic analysis succeeded, but the translation was poor. In such cases generally the so-called 'Konglish (English in Korean style)' was produced. We assumed that the reason why such 'Konglish' was produced was that the source Korean sentence was poor.

We found out 8 most frequent writing errors that Korean authors commit and that have the most significant effects on the performance of an MT system.[5]

Table 1: Most frequent writing errors that effect on MT

Error Types	Description
Subject-Predicate mismatch	Semantic mismatches between the subject and the predicates in a sentence
Topic Markers in the Sentence Initial Position	Sentence initial NPs with topic markers are underspecified w.r.t. their case
Ambiguous expressions	Use of specific ambiguous words such as 'ulo', 'hata', 'tayhata' and etc. [6]
Spoken language expressions	Use of spoken language type expressions
Double subject/object construction	Though these constructions are legitimate, they are difficult to analyze correctly
Punctuation	If a sentence is long, the correct punctuation helps the anlaysis
Minor grammatical errors	Though the grammatical errors are not supposed to be treated by a controlled language checker, some grammatical errors are so frequent and not conceived by the authors that they have to be checked before the syntactic analysis
Light-verb expressions	Frequent use of unknown light-verb contructions that can be substituted by a single verb

Another important issue in designing a controlled language is the learnability of the controlled language. Lehrndorfer(1996), for example, criticized the AECMA Simplified English for its poor learnability. Especially, in the academic paper authoring setting, it will be very difficult to train the users with the Controlled Korean. Therefore, the application of the above rules must be automated with a Controlled Korean Checker. However, the formalization of above rules is not always simple. For example, the semantic mismatch of the subject and the predicates in a sentence is very difficult to detect automatically. It would not be possible without deep semantic processing. However, the deep semantic processing technique is currently not available. Therefore we collected lexical clues with which we can detect the semantic mismatches on the surface level. Currently about 6,000 manually constructed lexical rules and metarules are employed in the Controlled Korean Checker.

---

[5] Strictly speaking, some of these 'errors' are not a grammatical error, but we stick to the term 'error' for the simplicity of the expression

[6] 'ulo' corresponds roughly to English 'as' and 'with'

3. Experiment

3.1. The impact of Controlled Korean on MT

O'Brien(2005) introduced the concept of the 'negative translatability indicators'. The negative translatability indicators are the specific linguistic constructions or phenomena that negatively effect on the quality of MT. We performed an experiment to find out the negative translatability indicators in Korean-English MT. We collected 50 sentences for each error type in the table 1. Each sentence was rewritten only as the Controlled Korean Checker suggests, i.e., even if the sentence contained the error of the given type, if it is not detected by our Controlled Korean Checker, the sentence was not corrected. Table 2 shows the result of our experiment.

Table 2: Negative Translatability Indicators in Korean-English MT

Error Types	Improvements
Ambiguous expressions	+25%
Subject-Predicate mismatch	+21%
Double subject/object construction	+20%
Topic Markers in the Sentence Initial Position	+12.5%
Punctuation	+12.5%
Spoken language expressions	+7.5%
Minor grammatical errors	+4.2%
Light-verb expressions	+4.2%

It turned out that the 'ambiguous expressions', 'subject-predicate mismatch', and 'double subject/object construction' error types are the most important negative translatability indicators. Most of these error types were related to resolving ambiguities in the analysis. As mentioned, in order to detect the subject-predicate semantic mismatch, many rules on the lexical level must be written. In other words, the more lexical rules we have, the better is the the performance of the Controlled Korean Checker, hence Korean-English MT system expected to be.

The overall performance of the Korean-English MT system supported by the Controlled Korean Checker was improved for 4.25%. As Kim et al.(2007) showed, if we can provide the checker with more rules, we can improve the performance of the MT system for more than 10%.

3.2. Controlled English/German

We were interested not only in finding out what are the negative translatability indicators in Korean, but also in learning if the MT paradigm plays a role in designing a controlled language. For this purpose, we conducted another experiment. In this experiment, we analyzed Controlled English by Aikawa et al.(2007) and Controlled German proposed by Lehrndorfer(1996).

Aikawa et al.(2007) introduced the MS Controlled English designed for the MSR-MT System which is a statistics-based MT system. They showed that Controlled English not only improves the performance of a rule-based MT system but also a statistics-based MT system. The following table shows the negative translatability indicators for 4 language pairs.

Table 3: Negative Translatability Indicators in Aikawa et a.(2007)

	Eng.=>Ara.	Eng.=>Chin.	Eng.=>Fr.	Eng.=>Du.
1	Formal Style	Formal Style	Short Ambiguous Sentences	Formal Style
2	Hyphens	Attachment	Formal Style	Capitalization

3	Short Ambiguous Sentences	-ing clauses	Spelling	Spelling
4	Capitalization	Spelling	Adjective/Verb Ambiguity	Short Ambiguous Sentences
5	Spelling	Long Sentences	Capitalization	Long Sentences

Contrary to our expectation, in 3 out of 4 language pairs, the 'Formal Style'[7] was the most influential negative translatability indicator. In case of Controlled Korean, most of the indicators were related to resolving the ambiguities in the source language.

In the experiment with the Controlled German, we employed a rule-based German-English MT system. We were interested in learning what can be the negative translatability indicators in German-English rule-based MT. In the preparation stage, we collected 250 sentences from German technical documents in the IT domain. On the next step, we re-wrote the sentence according to the guidelines proposed by Lehrndorfer(1996). Among 250 sentences 64 sentences were re-written. By applying the Controlled German, we could improve the translation accuracy of the whole sentences for 2.41%. If we consider only those sentences that were re-written with Controlled German, the translation accuracy rose for 9.28%. The following table shows the negative translatability indicators in rule-based German-English MT.

Table 4: Negative Translatability Indicators German-English rule-based MT

	Controlled German Writing Rules
1	Don't use relative sentences
2	Don't use long sentences
3	Follow the coordination construction rules
4	Put the subject in the sentence initial position
5	Don't omit connectives

In the experiment with Controlled German, the rules resolving the ambiguities are the most important negative translatability indicators. Though more comprehensive experiments should follow to back up our conclusion, we assume that in designing a controlled language for MT, the paradigm of the MT should be well taken into account.

4. Conclusion

In this paper we proposed 'Controlled Korean' for Korean-English MT. We also shared our experience in designing a controlled language. We didn't introduce the controlled lexicon as done in many other researches, but we focused on the writing rules. As the learnability is a very important factor for the acceptability by the users, we tried to formalize the Controlled Korean rules as much as possible. As a result, we could improve the translation accuracy of the Korean-English MT system backed up by a Controlled Korean Checker for 4.25%.

Another important issue in designing a controlled language for MT is whether the MT paradigm should be considered. Our experiment and the comparison of our result with Aikawa et al.(2007) showed that the MT paradigm could play a very important role in designing a controlled language for MT. Our experiment with Controlled German for rule-based MT showed different results from that of Aikawa et al.(2007). For a rule-based MT, ambiguities-resolving rules seem to play important roles, whereas for a statistics-based MT, rather the rules

---

[7] 'Formal Style' relates to the use of spoken language expressions or slangs.

that normalize the source expressions so that the decoding can be performed more easily seem
to play more important roles.

References

AECMA (1995): AECMA Simplified English, A Guideline for the Preparation of Aircraft
Maintenance Documentation in the International Aerospace Maintenance Language, Issue
I

Aikawa et al. (2007): " Impact of Controlled Language on Translation Quality and Post-editing
in a Statistical Machine Translation System" , Proceedings of MT-Summit XI, 1-8

Esselink, B. (2000): A Practical Guide to Localization, John Benjamins Publishing Company,
Amsterdam/Philadelphia

Göpferich, S. (1995): Textsorten in Naturwissenschaft und Technik. Pragmatische Typologie -
Kontrastierung -Translation. Tüubingen: Narr.

Hong, M., Kim, Y., Kim, C., Yang, S., Seo, Y., Ryu, C. & S. Park (2005): Customizing a
Korean-English MT System for Patent Translation, Proceedings of MT-Summit X, 181-
187

Kim, Y., Hong, M. & S. Park (2007): CL-Guided Korean-English MT System for Scientific
Papers, Lecture Notes in Computer Science, vol.4394, 409-419, Springer Verlag

Lehrndorfer, A. (1996): Kontrolliertes Deutsch: linguistische und sprachpsychologische
Leitlinien für eine (maschinell) kontrollierte Sprache in der technischen Dokumentation.
Tüubingen: Narr.

Lehrndorfer, A. / R. Mangold (1997): "How to Save Money in Translation Cost", TC-Forum
97-2, URL: http://www.techwriter.de/tc-forum/pdf/editions/ tcf972s.pdf

Lehrndorfer, A. / S. Schachtl (1998): Controlled Siemens Documentary German and TopTrans,
TC-Forum 98-3, URL: http://www.tc-forum.org/topictr/tr9contr.htm

Ley, M. (2005): Kontrollierte Textstrukturen. Ein (linguistisches) Informationsmodell für die
Technische Kommunikation. Dissertation, Justus-Liebig-Universitäat Gießsen.

Mitamura, T. / Nyberg, E. H. (1995): " Controlled English for Knowledge-Based MT:
Experience with the KANT System" , Proceedings of TMI-95.

Mitamura, T. (1999): " Controlled Language for Multilingual Machine Translation" .
Proceedings of MT-Summit 1999

Möller, M. (2003): Grammatical Metaphor, Controlled Language and Machine Translation,
Proceedings of EAMT/CLAW 2003

Nübel, R. (2004): "Evaluation and Adaptation of a Specialised Language Checking Tool for
Nonspecialised Machine Translation and Non-expert MT Users for Multi-lingual
Telecooperation", Proceedings of LREC 2004

O'Brien, S (2005): Methodologies for Measuring the Correlations between Post-Editing Effort
and Machine Translatability, Machine Translation, vol.19, no.1, 37-58

O'Brien, S (2006): Pauses as Indicators of Cognitive Effort in Post-editing Machine Translation
Output, Across Languages and Cultures vol.7, no.1, 1-21

O'Brien, S. & J. Roturier (2007): How Portable are Controlled Language Rules? A Comparison
of Two Empirical MT Studies, Proceedings of MT Summit XI, 345-352

Reuther, U. (2003), "Two in one - can it work? Readability and translatability by means of
controlled language". Proceedings of the 4th International Workshop on Controlled
Language Applications, Dublin, Ireland.

Statistical Analysis on Large Scale Chinese Short Message Corpus and Automatic Short Message Error Correction

Rile Hu[1], Yuezhong Tang[1], Chen Li[1,2] and Xia Wang[1]

[1]NOKIA Research Center, Beijing
[2]Beijing University of Posts and Telecommunications

{rile.hu, yuezhong.tang, ext-chen.9.li, xia.s.wang}@nokia.com

Abstract. Analysis of short message corpus is an important foundation for research of automatic short message processing technology. Based on large scale short message corpus, this paper firstly presents statistical data and performs analysis in detail on basic information of short message corpus and special language phenomena in it. The distributions of the corpus parameters and special language phenomena are also given out. The statistical results presented in the paper are meaningful for research of robust short message understanding and implementation of short message based man-machine dialog system and short message based machine translation system. And we also build an automatic error correction system on mobile phone to correct the misapplication of Chinese character in short messages. The preliminary results show that our method is effective.

Keywords: computer application; Chinese information processing; corpus technology; statistical analysis; short message; error correction.

1. Introduction

With the development and popularization of mobile phones, the short message is widely used for communication and plays more and more important role in people's daily life. As a main part of mobile communication, the short message has become a hot spot of mobile communication service in China at present because of its huge quantity and rapid progress. According to the statistics, there are 0.4 billion mobiles and 300 billion short messages in 2005 in China. The short message is so widely used and rapidly communicated that it makes our lives much convenient. However, on the other hand, there are a series of problems on the use and application of the short message.

The limitation of mobile input leads to wrong words, self-made symbols, non-punctuation and many other non-standard Chinese problems in short message text at present. These non-standard words and application customs spread to all ages and many places with the fast and wide radiation of short messages, which makes a huge negative effect to correctly use and inherit Chinese. (For example, the students form all over the country use many short message words to write compositions of the entrance examination to college.)

With the development of Corpus Linguistics (Kennedy, 2000), more and more corpora are built for research works. The results of the research works are widely used in natural language processing tasks. For example, Brown University in US built BROWN corpus, Lancaster University in UK and Oslo University and Bergen University in Norway built LOB corpus (Johansson, 1991). In China, large scale corpora were built by Tsinghua University, Peking University, Chinese Academy of Sciences and Chinese Academy of Social Sciences. Statistic and analysis had been done on these corpora (Feng,1999) (Feng ,2002) (Yu, 1998) (Yu,2002) (Guo, 2005) (Hu, 2002). The works listed above are focused on written languages. There are also some research works on Chinese spoken language. Qualitative analysis had been taken on

Chinese spoken language in early research (Chen, 1984). A spoken language corpus on specific domain was also built; statistic analysis had been taken on this corpus (Zong, 1999). But for the specific domain of short message, there is not any corpus built and analyzed.

The short message is characterized by informal, highly interactive and other features of oral Chinese. However, it has many differences with the normal oral Chinese. Therefore, how to establish an effective corpus analysis measures on exact statistics analysis is so important to understand and handle the short messages.

2. Basic Information of the Corpus

The corpus contains 410K short messages. And these messages contain more than 7M Chinese character. The average length of these short messages is 16.98 Chinese characters.

Automatic word segmentation and POS tagging tools (Zhang, 2007) are used here to process the short message corpus. According to the characteristic of the Chinese short message, we classify all the word in the corpus into 18 part-of-speeches: adjective (A), conjunction (C), adverb (D), position word (F), idiom (I), abbreviated word (J), common-used phrase (L), measurement word (M), noun (N), onomatopoeia (O), preposition (P), quantifier (Q), pronoun (R), location word (S), time word (T), auxiliary (U), verb (V) and particle (Y).

Statistical results are got from the corpus after segmentation and POS tagging. Some of these results are shown in the coming sub-sections.

2.1. Distributions of Word Length

The distributions of word length of the corpus are shown in Table1:

Table 1: the distributions of word length

Word length (characters)	1	2	3	More than 4
Percentage（%）	67. 01	30. 64	1. 88	0. 47

There are 1.31 Chinese characters per word in the short message corpus. The word length of short message is short than that of the spoken language (about 1.87 characters per word), and much shorter than that of the written language (about 2.45 characters per word) (Chen, 1984) (Zong et.al, 1999).

2.2. Distributions of Message Length

The distributions of message length of the corpus are shown in Table2:

Table 2: the distributions of message length

Length（characters）	1～10	11～20	21～30	31～40	41～50	51～60	61～70
Percentage（%）	31. 27	46. 68	12. 81	4. 54	2. 25	1. 28	1. 17

The messages no more than 30 characters cover the more than ninety percent of the corpus. This shows that people lean to use short and simple message in mobile communication.

2.3. Distributions of Part-of-Speech

The distributions of part-of-speech of the corpus are shown in Figure 1:

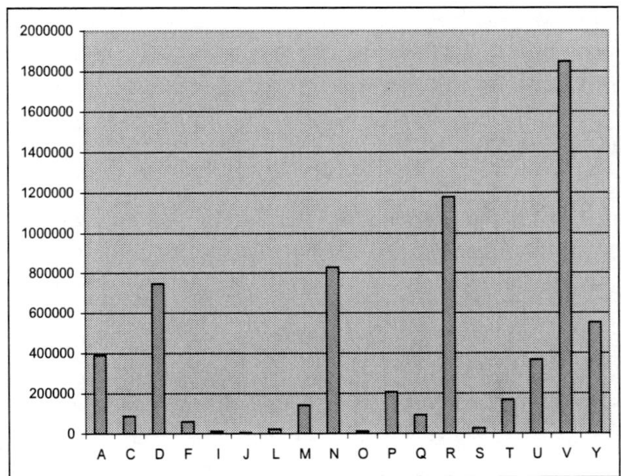

Figure 1: the distributions of part-of-speech

The highest frequent part-of-speeches are verb, pronoun, noun, adverb, particle and adjective. This is similar to spoken language (Zong et.al, 1999).

3. Special Language Phenomena Analysis

There are many special language phenomena contained in short messages, this makes the processing of short messages more difficult. The analysis of these phenomena is important for the development of short message processing technology.

Some manual labeling and modification of these special phenomena are made on the corpus. And also some statistical analysis are made on the manually processed results.

3.1.Classification of the Special Language Phenomena

The special language phenomena of the short message can be classified into the categories below:

（1）Usage of dialect words

Short message and spoken language have many similar characteristics, including the usage of dialect words. Some short messages contain some words and expressions in dialects; this brings difficulty for the automatic processing of short messages.

Example:

阿拉是上海人

Here, the word "阿拉" is a dialect word which is not used in Mandarin Chinese.

（2）Misuse of words with same pronunciation

Example:

你自几对我说　　（你自己对我说）

The character "几" and "己" have the same pronunciation, but their meanings are different. When users input short messages using pinyin input method, if they directly select the characters ranked high but not the actual character, they will misuse the words with same pronunciation. This phenomena also brings some difficulties for automatic short message processing.

（3）Misuse of words with similar pronunciation

Example:

我从启下机子。（ 我重启下机子 。）

Here, the character "从" (cong) and character "重" (chong) have similar pronunciation and the first one are misused instead of the second. This is because that some users in China could not distinguish the Pinyin（z、c、s）and（zh、ch、sh），the Pinyin（in）and（ing），and etc. , so they uses the characters with similar pronunciation instead of the original ones. This also makes the processing of short message harder.

（4）Misuse of words with similar shape

Examples:

a) 这儿件事 (这几件事)

b) 自已 (自己)

This mistake occurs when the users choose the wrongly recognized character when using pen input method to input short messages. This will make the error correction and message understanding very difficult.

（5）Redundancy

Redundancy means that the short message contains redundant words.

Example:

你那儿里是不是有事？　　(你那里是不是有事？)

（6）Incomplete word

This means that there are some incomplete words in short messages.

Example:

我去街买点东西　　　　(我去街上买点东西)

（7）Repeat:

This means that short messages contain some similar meaning parts.

Example:

越来越愈来愈幽默了　　(越来越幽默了)

（8）Usage of net languages

This means that short messages often contain some strings (maybe not real words) widely used in internet.

Example:

偶不知道　　　(我不知道)

This is because that these strings are widely used in some net forums and bbs, and the users take these strings into their daily life. So these strings are used and spread in short messages.

（9）Disorder

This means that there are some disorders in short messages.

Example:

为什么说五周见？　（为什么说周五见？）

Some of these special language phenomena are similar to spoken language (Redundancy, Repeat, Disorder and etc.), some of them are special in short message corpus (Misuse of words with same pronunciation, Misuse of words with similar pronunciation and etc.). These phenomena affect the automatic processing and understanding of the short messages very much. How to solve the problem is an important task.

3.2.Distributions of the Special Phenomena

The distributions of the special phenomena are shown in Table 3:

Table 3: the distributions of the special phenomena.

Phenomena No.	1	2	3	4	5	6	7	8	9
Percentage (%)	3. 66	24. 78	9. 29	0. 71	33. 30	24. 00	1. 99	1. 32	0. 95

The results shows that the highest frequent special phenomena are: redundancy, misuse of words with same pronunciation and incomplete word.

Some of these phenomena (Misuse of words with same pronunciation, Misuse of words with similar pronunciation and Misuse of words with similar shape) are correlative to the input methods of mobile phones. If some improvements are made to solve these problems in input methods, these errors could be perished.

4. Automatic Short Message Error Correction

We focus on the problem of the misuse of words with same pronunciation and the misuse of words with similar pronunciation; build an automatic error correction system on mobile phone. The system uses language model to correct the misapplication of Chinese character. And the preliminary results show that our method is effective.

There are three assumptions in advance:

1) The error in the Chinese character string comes not from the wrong input (For example, if "liu" should be input in the pinyin input approach, it is not "li", "lin" or some others but "liu" input) but from the wrong choice.

2) Most of the wrong Chinese characters cannot compose a word with the neighbour characters.

3) Most of the characters in the string are correct.

These 3 assumptions are usually assured in practice.

In the following, we will take Pin Ying input method as an instance. There should be a mapping table between Pin Yin string (PYMT), never wrong characters set (NWCS) and Chinese words and a language model (LM) based on Chinese words in advance. NWCS includes some characters which never be wrongly used in practical corpus. The algorithm is the same for all the input approaches. The processing procedure is listed as follows:

(1) Word segmentation

Firstly the sentence is segmented to some words group according to a pre-defined lexicon, which can be updated dynamically. According to the assumption 2, the word, which consists of 2 or more Chinese characters, should be correct in most situations, and the word that is a single Chinese character may be the wrong character. They will be treated in different way. The word, which consists of 2 or more Chinese characters, should be checked by language model. Those that have low score in language model will be labelled as doubtful. The word that is single Chinese character will be labelled doubtful except those that belong to NWCS.

(2) Recover to Pin Yin string

The doubtful Chinese words will be transformed to Pin Yin code. If the Chinese Character has more pronunciations, all of the possible Pin Yin codes should be kept. Moreover, the tone of Pin Yin will be removed because the user usually ignores tone while input characters. (The process of tone is particularly for Pin Yin input. For the other input method, it is ignored)

(3) Search Chinese Character based on the Pin Yin

The sentence with Pin Yin will be matched from the beginning to the end according to the PYMT. Any matched Chinese word from the table will be selected. By the way, PYMT can be extended so that some similar codes will be included. For example, "jin" and "jing" can be treated equally. With the existed Chinese words, they will compose several possible sentences. Now the possibilities of all the possible sentences will be calculated based on the language model. The top N best results will be kept. By the way, in calculating with language model, there should be threshold. The candidates which possibility is lower than threshold value should be given up. If all the possibility is lower than threshold, the original characters will be kept.

The language model and mapping table can be different in terminal and server.

(4) Select the best candidate

In the terminal of mobile phone, the users can help to select one from the Top N candidates.

The selection can be done automatically, especially in server. The selection criterion should consider both the possibility based on language model and the match degree with the original sentence, which is related with the assumption 3.

Here is a sample:

Original: 这次华费乐十元

Segment and Pin Yin transform: 这次 hua fei le 十元

Table match: 这次 花 费 了 十元，这次 话 费 了 十元，这次 花 费 乐 十元，这次 华 费 乐 十元 …

Language model check: 这次 花 费 了 十元 has the highest score. It will be chosen

Final result:这次花费了十元, this is what we want.

Now, there are 7 candidates of Chinese characters after inputting any code in mobile phone. If the correct Chinese character is not in the 7 candidates, you have to page down to search. Moreover, with the help of this technology, the input method can be adjusted. For any code, there are only 6 candidates of Chinese characters. The 7th is special character. If it is chosen, it means that the user prefers this character shown in the form of code (PY, WB, or stroke). The correct Chinese character will be found until the text modification is activated. In this way, the user reduces the burden of selection. Moreover the location of character that needs to be modified is clear. This is helpful to improve the modification accuracy.

The preliminary experiment has been done on the mobile phone platform. The accuracy of the system is 54.68%, the recall is 71.17%, and F measure is 70.86%. This is good since that the system runs on mobile phone, the resources are limited.

5. Conclusion

On the basis of the above-mentioned statistics and example analysis, we make the conclusions as follows:

1) The corpus of short message is similar with that of Chinese spoken language. Both of the words used are shorter than that of the formal language, among which the corpus of short message word is much shorter. The distributions of the part-of-speeches are similar.

2) Short message is highly interactive, which the pronoun and particle are frequently used.

3) Short message has many special language phenomena that make great effects on its automatic processing and understanding. The study and process of the corpus according to the special phenomena will benefit the short message use and spread.

We made a statistics analysis on large scale short message corpus in this paper, reflecting the rule of choosing words and making sentences in daily life, and all kinds of special language phenomena. These results are valuable to establish robust short message understanding system, short message based human-computer dialog system and machine translation system as reference.

And we also built an error correction system on mobile phone for Chinese short messages. The preliminary results show that our method is effective.

References

Chengqing ZONG, Hua WU, Taiyi HUANG and et al, 1999. Analysis of Spoken Dialog Corpus in Restricted Domain, *In Proceedings of the 5th Joint Symposium of Computational Linguistics.* Beijing: Tsinghua University Press, pp. 115-122.

George GUO, Hua LIU, Xuemin XIE and et al, 2005. The Initial Statistic Analysis on Tagged Corpus of People's Daily. *Natural Language Understanding and Large-scale Content Computing.* Beijing: Tsinghua University Press, pp. 187-192.

Graeme Kennedy, 2000. An Introduction to Corpus Linguistics. *Beijing: Foreign Language Teaching and Research Press.*

Guohua ZHANG. 2007. Research and Application of Automatic Chinese Word Segmentation and POS Tagging Algorithm. *Beijing: Graduate School of Chinese Academy of Sciences.*

Jianmin CHEN, 1984.Chinese Spoken Language. *Beijing: Beijing Press.*

Johansson S., Stenstorm, 1991. English Computer Corpora. *Berlin: Mouton de Gruyter.*

Rile HU, Chengqing ZONG, Juha Iso-Sipilä, et al, 2002.Investigation and Analysis on Designing Chinese Balance Corpus . *In Proceedings of the International Symposium on Chinese Spoken Language Processing (ISCSLP2002),* Taiwan：, pp. 335-338.

Shiwen YU, Xuefeng ZHU, Hui WANG and et al, 1998. Dictionary of Modern Chinese Grammatical Information. *Beijing: Tsinghua University Press.*

Shiwen YU, Huiming DUAN, Xuefeng ZHU and et al, 2002. The Basic Processing of Contemporary Chinese Corpus at Peking University Specification. *Journal of Chinese Information Processing*, Vol. 16, No. 5, pp. 49-64.

Yuan LIU, Qiang TAN, Xukun SHEN, 1994. The Standard of Chinese Word Segmentation for Information Processing and Automatic Word Segementation Methods. *Beijing: Tsinghua University Press.*

Zhiwei FENG, 2002. Evolution and Present Situation of Corpus Research in China. *Journal of Chinese Language and Computing*, Vol. 12, No. 1, pp. 43-62.

Zhiwei FENG, 1999. Corpus Linguistics and Machine Translation. *In Age of Information Network and Japan Research*, Shandong：Shandong University Press.

Contrastive Approach towards Text Source Classification based on Top-Bag-of-Word Similarity

Chu-Ren Huang[1,2], and Lung-Hao Lee[2]
[1]Hong Kong Polytechnic University
[2]Institute of Linguistics, Academia Sinica
churen.huang@polyu.edu.hk
{churen, lunghao}@gate.sinica.edu.tw

Abstract. This paper proposes a method to automatically classify texts from different varieties of the same language. We show that similarity measure is a robust tool for studying comparable corpora of language variations. We take LDC's Chinese Gigaword Corpus composed of three varieties of Chinese from Mainland China, Singapore, and Taiwan, as the comparable corpora. Top-bag-of-word similarity measures reflect distances among the three varieties of the same language. A Top-bag-of-word similarity based contrastive approach was taken to solve the text source classification problem. Our results show that a contrastive approach using similarity to rule out identity of source and to arrive actual source by inference is more robust that directly confirmation of source by similarity. We show that this approach is robust when applied to other texts.

Keywords: Top-bag-of-word similarity, Text Source Classification, Contrastive Approach, Comparable Corpus, Chinese Gigaword.

1. Introduction

Comparable corpora are corpora which select similar texts in more than one language or language variety[1]. These texts are typically gathered during the same time period. Comparable corpora are different from parallel corpora are widely used as resources for statistical machine translation, bilingual lexicons. Comparable corpora overcome the scarcity and limitations of parallel corpora, since sources for original, monolingual texts are much more abundant (Barzilay and Elhadad, 2003; Munteanu et al., 2004; Shao and Ng, 2004; Talvensaari et al., 2007).

The degree and nature of lexical similarity and contrast among Mandarin Chinese used in different Chinese speaking societies were widely observed but not thoroughly studied due to the lack of comparable corpora. Recently, LDC's Chinese Gigaword (2003)contains three sets of monolingual corpora selected according to the same set of criteria but in different language varieties from China, Singapore and Taiwan. We will explore it as a comparable corpus for variations of Chinese in this paper. In particular, we propose a measure of top-bag-of-word similarity for comparing the language variants contained in Chinese GigaWord corpus. Texts from the same period of time from Central News Agency (Taiwan), Xinhua News Agency (PRC) and Lianhe Zaobao (Singapore) are extracted and compared in our study. By comparing these three varieties of Mandarin Chinese, we hope to find the language significant lexical contrasts and meaning variations. We also propose a constrative approach towards automatic text source classification based on co-occurence similarity measures with documents from the same time period of Chinese Gigaword. Experimental resultes indicated that our proposed constrastive approach is reliable and robust.

The rest of this paper is organized as follows. Section 2 investigates related literature in word similarity measures in comparable corpus and a brief introduction to Chinese Gigaword. Section 3 describe the text source classification based on co-occurence similarity. Section 4 presnts experimental results and further discussion. Finally, Section 5 concludes this study.

---

[1]   Definition of comparable corpus according to EAGLES report, accessed at http://www.ilc.cnr.it/EAGLES/corpustyp/node21.html

22nd Pacific Asia Conference on Language, Information and Computation, pages 404–410

2. Literature Review

2.1 Word Similarity Measures in Comparable Corpus

A comparable corpus is one which gathered the similar texts in more than one language or language variety from the same time periods. Comparable corpora were widely used in researches issues consist of machine translation, natural language processing and cross language information retrieval. Fung and Yee (1998) used a comparable-corpus-based approach to estimate the similarity between a word and its translation candidates. Fung and Cheung (2004) used multi-level bootstrapping to iteratively improve alignment for extracting parallel sentences from a quasi-comparable corpus. Cheng et al. (2004) mined bilingual search results obtained from search engines to translate unknown query terms. Their approach was with Web corpora that can alleviate the problem of the lack of large bilingual corpora and benefit cross-language Web search.

Barzilay and Elhadad (2003) focused on monolingual comparable corpus, i.e. texts in the same language to address the task of sentence alignment. They found that context plays an important role to combine with a sentence similarity measure. Shao and Ng (2004) proposed a method by combining both context and transliteration information for the task of mining new word translations. They translated Chinese Words into English and tested it on Chinese and English Gigaword. Munteanu et al. (2004) improved machine translation performance via parallel sentence extraction from comparable corpora that consist of two large monolingual news texts in English and Arabic. Talvensaari et al. (2007) used Relative Average Term Frequency (RATF) valve to create a comparable corpus from articles by a Swedish news agency and a U.S. newspaper.

Chen and You (2002) proposed using only syntactic related co-occurrences as context vectors and adopted information theoretic methods for measuring word similarity to solve the problem of data sparseness and characteristic precision. Gao et al. (2002) extended the basic co-occurrence model by adding a decaying factor that decreases the mutual information when the distance between the terms increases. The experimental results also indicated that their proposed triple translation model brings further improvements than word-by-word translation. Weeds and Weir (2005) proposed a flexible framework called as co-occurrence retrieval for lexical distributional similarity. Zheng et al. (2007) presented a novel word co-occurrence model based on an ontology representation of word sense and its related applications.

2.2 Introduction to Chinese Gigaword

Automatic annotation is remains a challenging task in Chinese language processing. For instance, ACL SigHan has hosted four bakeoff competition for segmentation, but none for POS tagging. There is only a handful of POS tagging systems and automatic taggers which are widely accepted and accessible. In Taiwan, Academia Sinica's CKIP tagset has been considered the standard and has been used in annotating the Sinica Corpus (CKIP, 1995/1998), which were first annotated in 2006 and contains roughly 10 million words in the latest version (2007). In PRC, the Institute of Computational Linguistics (ICL)'s tagset has been considered the de facto standard and is widely available through the POS tagged People's Daily Corpus (Yu et al., 2002; 2003). However, an even greater challenge occurs with the new demand of very large corpora and the availability of the untagged LDC Gigaword Corpus.

The Chinese Gigaword Corpus (CGW) released in 2003 by Linguistic Data Consortium (LDC). It contains about 1.12 billion Chinese characters, including 735 million characters from Taiwan's Central News Agency (CNA) from 1991 to 2002, and 380 million characters from Mainland China's Xinhua News Agency (XIN) from 1990 to 2002. CNA uses the complex character form and XIN uses the simplified character form. CGW has three major advantages for the corpus-based Chinese linguistic research: (1) It is large enough to reflect the real written language usage in either Taiwan or Mainland China. (2) All text data are presented in a SGML form, using a markup structure to provide each document with rich metadata for further inspecting. (3) CGW is appropriate for the comparison of the Chinese usage between Taiwan and Mainland China, because it provides the same newswire text type, and these news texts were almost published during the overlapping time period.

LDC's Chinese Gigaword Corpus currently has a segmented and tagged version available (Huang, 2007). This version adopts the CKIP tagset and enhanced Sinica Word Segmenter (Ma and Chen, 2005) to segment the corpus into the words. And they utilized HMM method for POS tagging and morpheme-analysis-based method (Tseng and Chen, 2002) to predict POSs for new words. The annotated Chinese Gigaword Corpus was also performed automatically with automatic and partially manual post-checking (Ma and Huang, 2006). The precision accuracy is estimated to be over 95% for Central New Agency part of data from Taiwan. Quality assurance of automatic annotation of Chinese Gigaword Corpus based on heterogeneous tagging system is also proposed to improve the precision accuracy (Huang et al., 2008).

3. Text Source Classification based on Top-bag-of-word similarity

3.1 Top-bag-of-word similarity Measures

Although there is as yet no agreement on the nature of the similarity of comparable corpora, there were several attempts to use comparable corpora for making similarity measures. In these attempts, top-bag-of-word similarity metric was widely used because it is simple and efficient (Gao et al., 2002; Chen and You, 2002; Cheng et al. 2004; Fung and Cheung, 2004; Weeds and Weir, 2005; Zheng et al, 2007).

In our approach, the corpus is firstly represented as "bags of words" (Baeza-Yates and Ribeiro-Neto, 1999, Manning and Schutze, 1999). The top frequency word types (Weeds and Weir, 2005) are continuously selected as the main features for comparing the language variants. Once the corpus is reformatted as top bags of words, their similarity metric is defined in equation 1:

$$\text{Sim} (C_i, C_j) = \text{Co-Num} (C_i, C_j) \ / \ \text{Num} (C_j) \qquad (1)$$

Where $\text{Sim}(C_i, C_j)$ denotes the similarity between corpus i and corpus j; $\text{Num}(C_j)$ denotes the number of representative words of corpus j; and $\text{Co-Num}(C_i, C_j)$ denotes the number of word types which occurr in both corpus i and j. Obviously, the similarity between a corpus and itself, as well as another corpus which contains exactly the same word types, is 1and the similarity is 0 if there are two corpus i and j have not common word types.

3.2 Text Source Classification

We further formulate the similarity matrix and determined intervals for text categorization. Table 1 shows a similarity matrix based on the definition of our top-bag-of-word similarity measures in comparable corpus of three kinds of language variations: C_1, C_2 and C_3. The similarity of corpus itself i.e. Sim (C_1, C_1), Sim (C_2, C_2) and Sim (C_3, C_3) is 1. Sim (C_i, C_j) is equal to Sim (C_j, C_i), that is because of the corpus is reformatted as the same size of top bags of words based on this common word type measure. Assuming the similarity of Corpus C_1 and C_2 is a, similarity of Corpus C_2 and C_3 is b and similarity of Corpus C_2 and C_3 is c.

Table 1: A top-bag-of-word similarity matrix of C_1, C_2 and C_3.

	C_1	C_2	C_3
C_1	1	a	c
C_2	a	1	b
C_3	c	b	1

As this similarity formulation, 1 means that two corpora have the same representing word types. Oppositely, 0 means the no representing word type co-occurs in these two corpora. If the similarity, a, is larger than c, it means C_2 is more close to C_1 than C_3. Our hypothesis is that if

C_1 is applied as a baseline for classifying corpus sources, the text of document belongs to C_1 when its similarity falls into the interval [a, 1]; the text of document belongs to C_2 when its similarity falls into the interval [c, a]; if similarity fall into the interval [0, c], the source of document is classified as C_3. The classification process will adopt similar heuristics to generate determined intervals when C_1, C_2 and C_3 are applied as a classification baseline individually. Different from individual corpus based classification, we further use a contrastive elimination algorithm that simple majority voting mechanism is employed for determining the final classification results. For example, if C_2 receives two votes and C_3 receives only one vote, so C_2 wins as the final classified results.

4. Evaluation

4.1 Data Source

In order to compare the use of Chinese, the same time period of tagged Chinese Gigaword (Huang, 2007) is selected as comparable corpus. Three parts of resource is consisting of Taiwan's Central News Agency (CNA), Mainland China's Xinhua News Agency (XIN) and Singapore's Lianhe Zaobao (ZBN). The same time period is October to November in 2000, January 2001 and April to September in 2003. Table 2 shows the document size of these comparable corpora.

Table 2: Number of Document in data source

	# of Doc. in CNA	# of Doc. in XIN	# of Doc. in ZBN
200010	13,010	6,198	2,091
200011	13,123	5,694	2,060
200012	12,736	5,990	1,991
200101	11,518	5,565	1,972
200304	1,028	7,156	5,189
200305	934	6,202	5,897
200306	735	5,786	5,531
200307	787	6,613	5,637
200308	669	5,060	5,478
200309	361	6,461	5,572

In Table 2, it' not difficult to find the document size is significant difference. The size of CNA in 2003 is obviously smaller than that in 2001 and meanwhile smaller than the other two sources, XIN and ZBN. Since the document size is so different, we further analyzed the number of distinct word types in these comparable corpora.

We adopted the CKIP tagset and enhanced Sinica Word Segmenter (Ma & Chen, 2005) to segment the corpus into the words. By these analyzed results shown in Table 3, we finally decided to use the top 5 thousands distinct word types for representing every comparable corpus individually. And we randomly selected a half of the same time period i.e. 200010, 200012, 200304, 200306 and 200308 from three different sources as training data sets and the remaining parts of these corpora as testing data sets for applying similarity measure to text categorization, that is to say that the documents of testing data sets would be blind predicated into only one of CNA, XIN and ZBN.

4.2 Experimental Results

Table 4 shows the co-occurrences similarity of CNA, XIN and ZBN. It is clear that all similarities of these three trained corpora is larger than 0.6 regardless of different sources. The main reason for high similarity is because all documents from Chinese Gigaword with the same time period and similar topics of documents. When we finished calculating this similarity matrix, determined intervals were generated according to our assumptive heuristics.

Table 4: A top-bag-of-word similarity matrix of CNA, XIN and ZBN

	CNA	XIN	ZBN
CNA	1	0.6068	0.6276
XIN	0.6068	1	0.6814
ZBN	0.6276	0.6814	1

Table 5 shows the experimental results of classifying text sources in testing data sets. In individual source based classification, there is an agreement on classified results excluding CNA based classification. In CNA based classification column, "*" notation denoted incorrect classification results. All incorrect files were classified as XIN by CNA based classification, which is because of the lower top- bag-of-word similarity resulting from variant words for describing topics. Note that although document sizes of comparable corpora vary greatly, they do not distort the expected result from similarity measurement comparison. Hence we are assured of the robustness of the top-bag-of-word similarity measure regardless of corpus size variations.

Table 5: Experimental results of text source classification in Chinese Gigaword

	CNA Based Classification	XIN Based Classification	ZBN Based Classification	Majority Voting
cna_200010	0.9294 (C)	0.5974 (C)	0.6174 (C)	C
cna_200012	0.9246 (C)	0.594 (C)	0.6142 (C)	C
cna_200304	0.4322 (X)*	0.3544 (C)	0.3538 (C)	C (C:2 , X:1)
cna_200306	0.407 (X)*	0.3296 (C)	0.3344 (C)	C (C:2 , X:1)
cna_200308	0.4124 (X)*	0.326 (C)	0.3302 (C)	C (C:2 , X:1)
xin_200010	0.576 (X)	0.8658 (X)	0.6458 (X)	X
xin_200012	0.5828 (X)	0.8632 (X)	0.648 (X)	X
xin_200304	0.5946 (X)	0.8506 (X)	0.6744 (X)	X
xin_200306	0.5898 (X)	0.8626 (X)	0.659 (X)	X
xin_200308	0.5842 (X)	0.8452 (X)	0.6576 (X)	X
zbn_200010	0.6216 (Z)	0.6742 (Z)	0.8138 (Z)	Z
zbn_200012	0.6214 (Z)	0.6626 (Z)	0.802 (Z)	Z
zbn_200304	0.5876 (X)*	0.646 (Z)	0.8704 (Z)	Z (Z:2, X:1)
zbn_200306	0.5982 (X)*	0.648 (Z)	0.8908 (Z)	Z (Z:2, X:1)
zbn_200308	0.5956 (X)*	0.6428 (Z)	0.885 (Z)	Z (Z:2, X:1)

The characters of our proposed contrastive elimination algorithm that simple majority voting mechanism is employed for determining the final classification results are combined with similarity and dissimilarity measures from the suspected text sources. For example, the testing file "cna_200304", if only applied similarity measure from the same text source, that's to say, just CNA based classification was applied, experimental results indicated that this file will be classified as wrong text source XIN. Further analysis found that although the same time period of news text from PRC, Taiwan and Singapore were selected as parts of Chinese Gigaword. There are still existing greatly differentiated topics. The contents of selected documents in CNA corpus consisted of many weather reports. But if we involved dissimilarity measures from the other sources and majority voting mechanism was adjusted final decision, we can get the accurate prediction. It was proven that our proposed method will be reliable for variant words to describe different topics. We are also assured of the robustness of our contrastive elimination algorithm regardless of corpus topic variations.

5. Conclusion and Future Work

We propose a top-bag-of-word similarity measures for classifying texts from different variants of the same language. We take LDC's Chinese Gigaword Corpus composed of three varieties of Chinese from Mainland China, Singapore, and Taiwan, as the comparable corpora. Top-bag-of-word similarity measures are shown reflect distances among the three varieties of the same language. Our results show that proposed contrastive approach using similarity to rule out identity of source and to arrive actual source by inference is more robust that directly confirmation of source by similarity. And the document size does not influence the prediction. This robust result is notable given the similarity and almost very high degree of mutual intelligibility among these variants.

Ongoing work is focusing on verifying the robustness of the top-bag-of-word similarity measure on outside data and with data from more than three different sources since study is an empirical research in Chinese Gigaword corpus. Other similarity measures for comparable corpus study are also being investigated.

References

Baeza-Yates, Ricardo and Berthier Ribeiro-Neto. 1999. Modern Information Retrieval. *The ACM Press.*

Barzilay, Regina and Noemie Elhadad. 2003. Sentence Alignment for Monolingual Comparable Corpora. *In Proceedings of the Conference on Empirical Methods in Natural Language Processing.*

Chen, Keh-Jiann and Jia-Ming You. 2002. A Study on Word Similarity using Context Vector Models. *Computational Linguistics and Chinese Language Processing.* 7(2), 37-58.

Cheng, Pu-Jen, Jei-Wen Teng, Ruei-Cheng Chen, Jenq-Huar Wang, Wen-Hsiang Lu, and Lee-Feng Chien. 2004. Traslating Unknown Queries with Web Corpora for Cross-Language Information Retrieval. *In Proceedings of the 27th annual International ACM SIGIR Conference on Research and Development in Informational Retrieval.*

CKIP (Chinese Knowledge Information Processing Group). 1995/1998. The Content and Illustration of Academica Sinica Corpus. *(Technical Report no 95-02/98-04). Taipei: Academia Sinica.*

Fung, Pascale and Lo Yuen Yee. 1998. An IR Approach for Translating News Words from Nonparallel, Comparable Texts. *In Proceedings of International Conference on of Computational Linguistics*

Fung, Pascale and Percy Cheung. 2004. Multi-level Bootstrapping for Extracting Parallel Sentences from a Quasi-Comparable Corpus. *In Proceedings of International Conference on of Computational Linguistics.*

Gao, Jianfeng, Jian-Yun Nie, Hongzhao He, Weijun Chen and Ming Zhou. 2002. Resolving Query Translation Ambiguity using a Decaying Co-occurrence Model and Syntactic Dependence Relations. *In Proceedings of the 25th annual International ACM SIGIR Conference on Research and Development in Informational Retrieval.*

Huang, Chu-Ren, Lung-Hao Lee, Wei-guang Qu and Shiwen Yu. 2008. Quality Assurance of Automatic Annotation of Very Large Corpora: a Study based on Heterogeneous Tagging Systems. *In Proceedings of the 6th International Conference on Language Resources and Evaluation.*

Huang, Chu-Ren. 2007. Tagged Chinese Gigaword. Linguistic Data Consortium, Philadelphia.

Ma, Wei-Yun and Chu-Ren Huang. 2006. Uniform and Effective Tagging of a Heterogeneous Giga-word Corpus. *In Proceedings of the 5th International Conference on Language Resources and Evaluation.*

Ma, Wei-Yun and Keh-Jiann Chen. 2005. Design of CKIP Chinese Word Segmentation System. *Chinese and Oriental Languages Information Processing Society*, 14(3), 235-249.

Manning, Christopher D. and Hinrich Schutze. 1999. Foundations of Statistical Natural Language Processing. *The MIT Press.*

Munteanu, Dragos Stefan, Alexander Fraser and Daniel Marcu. 2004. Improved Machine Translation Performance via Parallel Sentence Extraction from Comparable Corpora. *In Proceedings of the Human Language Technology Conference of the North American Chapter of the Association for Computational Linguistics.*

Shao, Li and Hwee Tou Ng. 2004. Mining New Word Translations from Comparable Corpora. *In Proceedings of International Conference on of Computational Linguistics.*

Talvensaari, Tuomas, Jorma Laurikkala, Kalervo Jarvelin, Martti Juhola and Heikki Keskustalo. 2007. Creating and Exploiting a Comparable Corpus in Cross-Language Information Retrieval. *ACM Transactions on Information Systems.* 25(1), 1-21.

Tseng, Huihsin and Keh-Jiann Chen. 2002. Design of Chinese Morphological Analyzer. *In Proceedings of 1st SIGHAN Workshop on Chinese Language Processing.*

Yu, Shiwen, Huiming Duan, Xuefeng Zhu, Bin Swen and Baobao Chang. 2003. Specification for Corpus Processing at Peking University: Word Segmentation, POS Tagging and Phonetic Notation. *Journal of Chinese Language and Computing*, 13(2),121-158.

Yu, Shiwen, Huiming Duan, Xuefeng Zhu and BinSun. 2002. The Basic Processing of Contemporary Chinese Corpus at Peking University- Specification. *Journal of Chinese Information Processing.* 16(5&6), 49-64.

Weeds, Julie and David Weir. 2005. Co-occurrence Retrieval: A Flexible Framework for Lexical Distributional Similarity. *Computational Linguistics.* 31(4), 439-475

Zheng, Dequan, Tiejun Zhao, Sheng Li and Hao Yu. 2007. Research on a Novel Word Co-occurrence Model and Its Application. Lecture Notes in Computer Science. 4798, 437-446.

Extracting Troubles from Daily Reports
based on Syntactic Pieces

Kakimoto Yoshifumi and Kazuhide Yamamoto

Nagaoka University of Technology,
1603-1, Kamitomioka, Nagaoka, Niigata 940-2188 Japan
{kakimoto, ykaz}@nlp.nagaokaut.ac.jp

Abstract. It is expensive for companies to browse daily reports. Our aim is to create a system that extracts information about problems from reports. This system operates in two steps. First, it records expressions involving troubles in a dictionary from training data. Second, it expands the dictionary to include information not included in the training data. We experimentally tested this extraction system; in the tests, a two-values classifier attained an F-value of 0.772, and experimental extraction of troubles attained a precision of 0.400 and a recall of 0.827.

Keywords: syntactic piece, extracting troubles, knowledge dictionary

1 Introduction

In resent years, many companies request daily reports of text data from company members. The text data is Email and web form. However, daily reports are browsed by human, it is expensive for companies. Our aim is to cut back the workload of daily reports browsing.

This paper discusses a type of information extraction. Ichimura et al. (2001) developed a system that reduces the cost of access to reports and assists decision-making for users. This system extracts 'good' or 'bad' practices using a human-created knowledge dictionary. However, the knowledge dictionary depends on the specific enterprise because it is constructed using reports from that enterprise. Saito and Watabe (2001) developed a system that extracts and visualizes information indicating troubles using extraction rules defined by humans. They chose the extraction categories 'trouble', 'causality' and 'countermeasure', which their system evaluated with a precision of 0.878, 0.701 and 0.703, respectively. This system depends on the specific domain, because they considered only printer problems. Both systems produce rules or a dictionary only from training data. This approach has two problems. First, because the dictionary and rules are made by humans, the cost is considerable. Second, this system cannot extract troubles that is not included in the training data. Our approach corrects these problems. Our system automatically creates a dictionary, and can extract troubles by expanding the dictionary to add data not included in the training data.

2 Definition of the Trouble

In this paper, we define the trouble as 'content regarding some problem in daily reports'. Troubles must take into account the context of the problem. A single word does not provide adequate troubles because it is too short. For example, when the word '壊れる(break)' occurs in daily reports, we can identify a trouble word. But '椅子が壊れる(The chair breaks)' and 'サーバーが壊れる(The server breaks)' have different meanings, calling for different responses and involving different degrees of risk. Aoki and Yamamoto (2007) investigate syntactic pieces that mine units of syntactic structure. Syntactic pieces are pairs consisting of a modifier and a modificand, as shown in Figure 1.

入力文(input sentence):

古いパソコンのバッテリーがいきなり爆発した。
(The battery of the old computer exploded suddenly.)

出力構文片(output syntactic pieces):

古い(old) ⇒ パソコン(computer)

バッテリーが(battery) ⇒ 爆発する(explode)

いきなり(suddenly) ⇒ 爆発する(explode)

Figure 1: Example of syntactic pieses

Syntactic pieces have the following characteristics:

- They are easy to extract
- They yield statistical information readily
- They are amenable to matching analysis
- They can deal with a chunk of meaning

We can apply these characteristics to troubles. Therefore, we found it more comfortable to deal with syntactic pieces than with words. Furthermore, we dealt with continuous modification of the syntactic pieces because troubles must take into account the context.

3 Method

3.1 System Overview

Figure 2 shows an overview of the system.

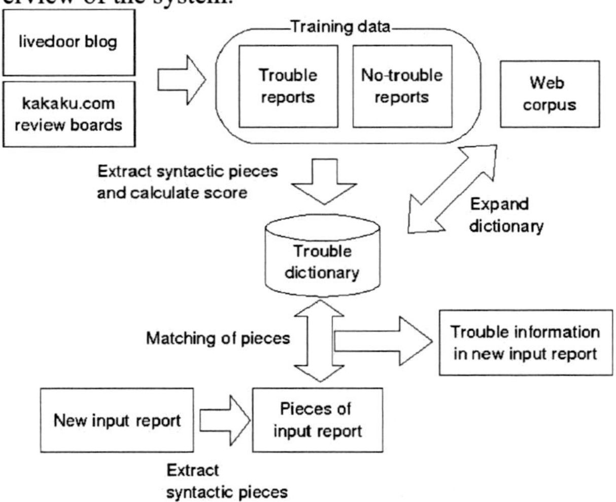

Figure 2: System overview

This paper defines weblogs and bulletin boards as daily reports. Our system uses weblogs and bulletin boards as sources of training data. First, we extract syntactic pieces from the training data, compute scores and construct a dictionary of troubles (the trouble dictionary). Second, we expand this dictionary because we must process troubles that do not appear in the training data. Third, we extract troubles from new reports using the trouble dictionary.

3.2 Training Data

The weblogs we used are part of the 'livedoor blog'[2], and have original tags and titles supplied by each author. We accumulated reports that mentioned problems (trouble reports) in the tag and title text. We defined trouble reports as those with the term 'トラブル(trouble)' in tags or

titles. We defined no-trouble reports as those that did not include 'トラブル(trouble)' in tags, titles or sentences.

Bulletin boards are 'kakaku.com review boards'[3]. These boards have context tags supplied by users. We defined trouble reports as those with the term '悪い(bad)' in the tags. No-trouble reports did not include '悪い(bad)' or '質問(question)' in the tags.

3.3 Trouble Dictionary

We constructed a trouble dictionary using these reports. We collected syntactic pieces from trouble and no-trouble reports and assigned a score to each one as troubles. The score observes deviation between trouble and no-trouble reports. Common pieces appear with similar frequency in trouble and no-trouble reports. Troubles has a higher score because it occurs more often in trouble reports. Therefore, we employed the method of Fujimura et al. (2004). We calculate the trouble score as follows:

1. Prepare the corpus, classified as trouble reports or no-trouble reports
2. Extract the syntactic piece
3. Count the frequency of each piece in each reports
4. Compute the trouble score with the following equation

$$S(w_i) = \frac{P'(w_i) - N(w_i)}{P'(w_i) + N(w_i)} \tag{1}$$

$$P'(w_i) = P(w_i) \times \frac{N_{doc}}{P_{doc}} \tag{2}$$

where w_i is a syntactic piece, $P(w_i)$ is the frequency of trouble reports containing w_i, $N(w_i)$ is the frequency of no-trouble reports containing w_i, P_{doc} is the total number of trouble reports and N_{doc} is the total number of no-trouble reports. Expression (2) defines a population parameter because there really is difference of frequency between P_{doc} and N_{doc}. If the score computed by expression (1) is a positive number, the syntactic piece occurs frequently in trouble reports. However, expression (1) does not consider the frequency of syntactic pieces in the training data. For example, in the two cases

Case1. frequency: 100, score: 0.9 and

Case2. frequency: 10000, score: 0.9,

One may regard the second case is more reliable than the first. We applied the confidence interval estimation method to fix this problem. Expression (3) shows this method (Agresti and Coull, 1998).

$$score(w_i) = S'(w_i) - 2 * 1.96\sqrt{\frac{S'(w_i)(1 - S'(w_i))}{P'(w_i) + N(w_i) + 4}} \tag{3}$$

$$S'(w_i) = \frac{P'(w_i) + 2}{P'(w_i) + N(w_i) + 4} - \frac{N(w_i) + 2}{P'(w_i) + N(w_i) + 4} \tag{4}$$

The second term of expression (3) is the confidence interval. This paper considers only negative values for the confidence interval because we treat syntactic pieces with positive values for $score(w_i)$. The second term of expression (3) is the doubled confidence interval, because $score(w_i)$ is the computed difference of two probabilities. This paper considers only negative values for the confidence interval, because we treat syntactic pieces with positive values for $score(w_i)$. As mentioned previously, we computed the trouble score of syntactic pieces, and added syntactic pieces having positive scores to the trouble dictionary.

3.4 Expansion of Trouble Dictionary with Syntactic Pieces

Extraction of troubles from new input reports was conducted by comparison with the trouble dictionary created as described in section 3.3. However, we cannot extract all troubles in the new reports using the trouble dictionary because it contains troubles from the training data only. Therefore, we expanded the trouble dictionary, tackling troubles not included in the training data, as described in the following sections.

3.4.1 Expansion of Target

We considered syntactic pieces that only included verbal nouns, and we expanded only verbal nouns in syntactic pieces. Verbal nouns means nouns that used in the same manner as verbs. We consider that if a verbal noun changes, the meaning of the syntactic piece changes too. For example, 'メッセージが出ない(don't output message)' is a trouble, but 'クレームが出ない (don't output complaint)' is not a trouble. Therefore, this paper uses only verbal nouns for expanded objects. We do not expand verbs because verbs have many conjugations, and handling them would be too complex. Below, 'expansion' refers only to verbal nouns.

3.4.2 Expansion Method

As we expand the trouble dictionary, the plausibility of troubles in syntactic pieces in the dictionary must not change. We must find verbal nouns that easily apply in the context of the expanded object. Figure 3 outlines the expansion method.

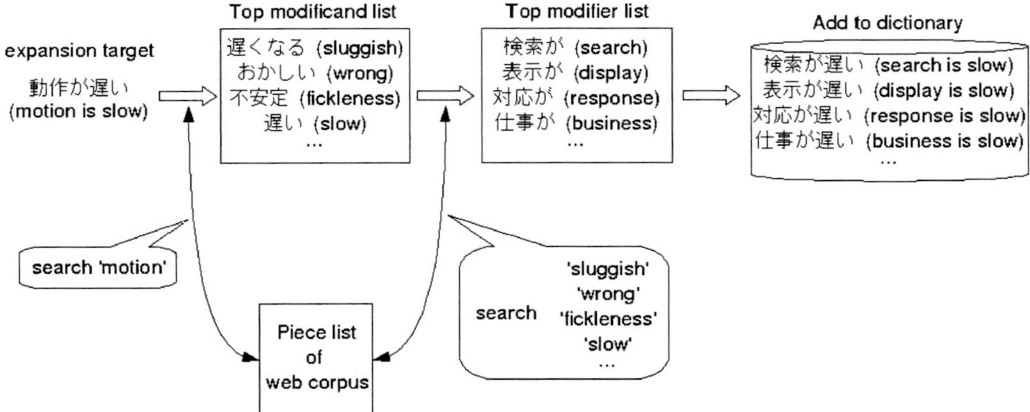

Figure 3: Expansion overview

First, we arrange a large web corpus that does not include the training data. Second, we extract syntactic pieces from this corpus, making a piece list of syntactic pieces. In the piece list, we note the frequency of syntactic pieces in the web corpus. Third, we use one of two methods to expand the dictionary. One method is to expand the modifiers (modifier expansion); the other is to expand the modificands (modificand expansion). Following are details of modifier expansion. For modificand expansion, susbstitute the word 'modifier' for 'modificand' and vice versa.

1. Search the piece list for a modifier (motion), and compute the frequency of each modificand (sluggish, wrong, fickleness, and slow). The 10 most frequent modificands are added to the 'top modificand list'.
2. Search the piece list for each modificand (sluggish, wrong, fickleness, and slow) in the top modificand list, and compute the frequency of each modifier (search, display, response, and business). The 10 most frequent modifiers are added to the 'top modifier list'.
3. Modifiers on the top modifier list are considered highly likely to occur along with a modifier of the expansion target. We connect the modifiers on that list with a modificand of the expansion target, and add these to the dictionary as new syntactic pieces (search is slow, display is slow, response is slow, and business is slow) having the same trouble score as the expansion target piece.

In this section, we construct the trouble dictionary. We extract troubles from new reports using this dictionary. Following are details of extracting troubles.

1. Extract syntactic pieces form the input report.

2. Set thresholds in the dictionary, and used syntactic pieces that scored higher than the thresholds as troubles.
3. If syntactic pieces in the input report occur in pieces of dictionary, we correct input pieces as troubles.

4 Evaluation

We extracted troubles from new input reports with the trouble dictionary described above. We used two evaluation methods.

1. Evaluation of a two-values classifier

We designed a two-values classifier that differentiated trouble reports from no-trouble reports. We decided that input reports that extracted troubles were trouble reports, and other cases were no-trouble reports. We classified input reports as having troubles or no-troubles, and evaluated this result.

2. Evaluation of troubles extracted from input reports

We evaluated troubles for plausibility.

4.1 Evaluation Data

We prepared reports that did not include training data, and chose three human evaluators. Evaluators sorted reports into trouble reports and no-trouble reports. The classification basis is whether a report includes expressions indicating troubles. Classification reports include 400 reports having 'トラブル(trouble)' in the title, and 400 not having the word 'トラブル (trouble)' in the title or main text. These 800 reports are judged in trouble reports or no-trouble reports by evaluators. The evaluators classified 133 as trouble reports and 253 as no-trouble reports. Therefore we used 133 trouble reports and 253 no-trouble reports as evaluation data.

4.2 Evaluation of Two-Values Classifier

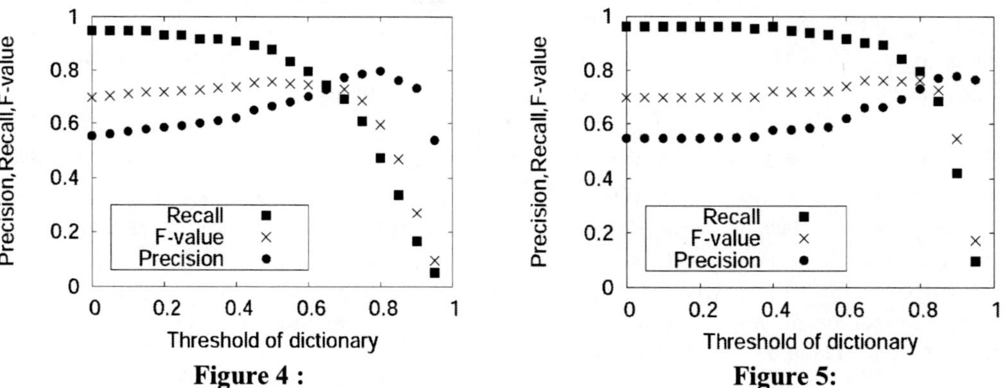

Figure 4 :   Figure 5:

Figure 4: Two-values classifier results (unexpanded dictionary)
Figure 5: Two-values classifier results (expanded dictionary)

Figure 4 shows the result of analysis using the dictionary created in section 3.3. Evaluation of the two-values classifier used precision, recall and F-value. The highest F-value is 0.757, which occurs when the threshold is 0.5. In this case, the precision and recall are 0.665 and 0.880, respectively.

Figure 5 shows the result using the expanded dictionary created in section 3.4. The highest F-value is 0.772 when the threshold is 0.780. In this case, the precision and recall are 0.724 and 0.827, respectively.

4.3 Evaluation of Troubles

This section evaluates troubles extracted from the evaluation reports. We evaluate the result obtained using the expanded dictionary. The threshold of the expanded dictionary is 0.780. This score is the highest point in Figure 5. Four hundred seven pieces of troubles were extracted from the evaluation reports. We evaluated the results by hand, based on the following:

1. The piece is about a problem.
2. The piece is not about a problem, but we can associate it with a problem.
3. The piece is not about a problem, and we cannot associate it with a problem.

The number of pieces corresponding to (1), (2) and (3) is 116, 47 and 244, respectively, indicating that the system can identify troubles but with a precision of only about 0.300. If we consider both (1) and (2) as being the right answer, the precision is about 0.400. The precision is shown expression (5). We cannot evaluate the recall of the extracted troubles, but section 4.2 indicates a recall of 0.827. We believe it represents the recall of extracted troubles. This value of recall is difficult to attain with heuristic rules and a dictionary.

$$Precision = \frac{number\ of\ troubles}{whole\ number\ of\ output\ pieces} \tag{5}$$

5 Discussion

5.1 Extracted Troubles

We show part of the extracted troubles from the evaluation data in Table 1.

Table 1: Example of extracted troubles

basis	trouble information
(1)	画面-が ⇒ 表示-さ-れ-ない (don't appear on the screen) 遅延-が ⇒ 発生-する (is delayed) 音-が ⇒ 途切れる (sound is interrupted)
(2)	サポート-に ⇒ 電話-する (call for support) 販売-店-に ⇒ 返品-する (return goods to selling office) 原因-を ⇒ 特定-する (identify reasons)
(3)	コンセント-を ⇒ 抜く (pull out a plug) 電源-を ⇒ 入れる (turn on power) 一度-も ⇒ 繋がる (connect only once)

Basis (1) included lots of troubles that had a word meaning 'ない(not)'. Syntactic pieces including 'ない(not)' are easily identified as troubles. The syntactic piece '音が⇒途切れる (interrupt the sound)' clearly indicates the nature of the troubles. In Basis (2), we regarded terms as indicating troubles when they occur with Basis (1) terms. In fact, 'サポートに⇒電話する (call for support)' and '画面が⇒表示されない(do not appear on the screen)' occur in the same reports. Therefore, if we connect Basis (2) and Basis (1), we can look on Basis (2) as belonging to Basis (1), with Basis (2) terms clarifying the meaning. Basis (3) includes terms that cannot be considered troubles. As a result, the rate of Basis (3) terms is higher than that of Basis (1) and (2). But there are valid pieces for which the task of two-values classification would work if the pieces cannot be judged as troubles manually. However, we must consider a score that can separate Basis (1) and (2) from Basis (3).

5.2 Expanded Dictionary

We show part of the extracted troubles obtained using the expanded dictionary. In Basis (1) and (2), we obtain the pairs 'サービス(service)→イメージ(imagery)', '検索する(search)→表示する(display)', '連絡する(inform)→相談する(consult)' and 'エラーが(error)→マークが (mark)'. These word usages resemble each other.

Also, troubles in Basis (1) and (2) retains the attribution of troubles in both the unexpanded and expanded dictionaries. In Basis (3), our system can expand the pieces '報告する(inform)→取引する(have a deal)' and '連絡を(contact)→返事を(reply)'; these words resemble each other. However, the expanded pieces are not troubles because the pieces of the expansion target are not troubles. Most pieces in Basis (3) belong to this case. This result indicates that the expansion is good. In other words, our expansion method by syntactic pieces is found to be useful for this task. In this paper, the expanded pieces are few because we expanded only verbal nouns. We must consider other parts of speech: verbs, nouns and adjectives. If other parts of speech are expanded, we can create bigger dictionary.

Table 2: Example of troubles extracted using expanded dictionary

basis	trouble information
(1)	悪い ⇒ サービス (bad service) → 悪い ⇒ イメージ (bad image) 検索-が ⇒ でき-ない (can't search) → 表示-が ⇒ でき-ない (can't display)
(2)	サポートに ⇒ 連絡-する (inform for support) → サポート-に ⇒ 相談-する (consult for support) エラー-が ⇒ 出る (get the error) → マーク-が ⇒ 出る (get the mark)
(3)	私-は ⇒ 報告-する (I inform) → 私-は ⇒ 取引-する (I have a deal) 連絡-を ⇒ くれる (receive the contact) → 返事-を ⇒ くれる (receive the reply)

6 Conclusion

In summary, we developed a system that extracts troubles from reports. Our dictionary is constructed using training data involving syntactic pieces, and is expanded to accommodate unknown troubles. We extract troubles from input reports with the dictionary. We evaluated our system using two methods. The two-values classifier had an F-value of 0.772, and the extracted troubles had a precision of 0.400 and recall of 0.827.

7 Future Work

We are currently working on two future projects. The first problem involves the treatment of Basis (2) in section 5.1. These syntactic pieces can be considered troubles but do not directly indicate a problem. We think that if we can connect Basis (2) and Basis (1) pieces, Basis (2) pieces can be called troubles. The second problem is about the expanded dictionary. The expansion method cannot add many pieces because we consider only verbal nouns. We must consider expanding other parts of speech.

Tools and language resources

(1) CaboCha, Ver.0.53, Matsumoto Lab., Nara Institute of Science and Technology.
   http://chasen.org/~taku/software/cabocha/
(2) livedoor Blog, http://blog.livedoor.com/
(3) kakaku.com review boards, http://bbs.kakaku.com/bbs/

References

Alan Agresti and Brent A. Coull. 1998. Approximate is better than "exact" for interval estimation of binomial proportion. The American Statistician, 52:119-126.

Suguru Aoki and Kazuhide Yamamoto. 2007. Opinion Extraction based on Syntactic Pieces. The 21st Pacific Asia Conference on Language, Information and Computation, pages 76-86.

Shigeru Fujimura, Masashi Toyota, and Masaru Kitsuregawa. 2004. A Consideration of Extracting Reputations and Evaluative Expressions from the Web. Technical Report of The Institute of Electronics, Information and Communication Engineers, 104:141-146.

Yumi Ichimura, Yasuko Nakamura, Toshio Akahane, Miyoko Miyosi, Toshikazu Sekiguchi, and Yousuke Fujiwara. 2001. Text Mining System for Analysis of a Salesperson's Daily Reports. Pacific Association for Computational Linguistics, pages 127-135.

Takahiro Saito and Isamu Watabe. 2001. The mining from trouble control data(in Japanese). Information Processing Society of Japan SIGNL Note, 93:145-152.

What is Needed the Most in MT-Supported Paper Writing

Chang Hyun Kim, Oh-Woog Kwon, Young Kil Kim

ETRI, NLP Team
161 Gajeong-dong, Yuseong-gu, 305-350 Daejeon, Korea
{chkim,ohwoog,kimyk}@etri.re.kr

Abstract. This paper addresses our system which provides an effective method to write an English paper suitable for international conferences and analyze the system's pros and cons through the user's data collected from operating the system for 6 months. The system consists of Korean-English paper MT module supported by user interaction environment. Our original Korean-English paper MT system was quite useful for understanding, but not satisfactory for writing. So, we analyzed our system to trace what caused such dissatisfaction. We classified the analysis results into three main categories, that is, the errors in the source sentence itself, the errors of our MT system, and the absence of the appropriate domain-specific expression information. For each category we provide an alternative method and show the effectiveness through analyzing the user's data. We can confirm that our system can be used quite usefully for paper writing.

Keywords: Machine Translation, User Interaction, Korean-English Translation, Paper writing

1. Introduction

Many Koreans who are not fluent in English have difficulty in writing a scientific paper or technical documents in English. Although the state-of-the-art Korean-English MT system is quite useful for understanding, many people hesitate to use the MT system for paper writing. Understanding does not necessarily require perfect sentences, but writing papers does require impeccable grammars and correct, native expressions.

The main purpose of the original Korean-English paper MT system (Kim, 2007) was to help researchers or students to submit their papers to a conference or an academic journal. This system had been developed through customization of the patent MT system (Hong, 2005), which is currently serviced by KIPO (Korean Intellectual Property Office) and is being used by more than 20 countries with positive feedbacks from foreign users. The customization process includes construction of translation resources specialized in scientific papers, modification of the engine to reflect the linguistic characteristics of academic papers. Moreover, a Controlled-Language (CL) guided Korean rewriting checker is provided to correct the errors in Korean spelling and sentence structure. Language model component reports the unlikely or unnatural English expression.

Several beta testers of the original MT system reported that it was very helpful in writing a paper, but that was not enough. They said that the user interface was inconvenient, and they wanted to understand what caused the mistranslations, and how to correct them. Besides, the MT output still contained erroneous expressions even the users rewrite sentences according to the guidelines of the CL-checker.

We analyzed those reports and found 3 main reasons: the errors in the source sentence itself, the errors of our MT system, and the absence of the appropriate domain-specific expression information.

In this paper, we provide alternative methods to cope with those problems within our user interaction environment. As a result, authors can interact with the system through modification of source sentences, correction of engine errors, and correction of target sentence expression.

22nd Pacific Asia Conference on Language, Information and Computation, pages 418–427

In section 2 we will survey some major works on controlled language and interactive MT. Section 3 deals with the three steps of user interaction process in detail. At each subsection, the simulation of the user interaction will be described with proper examples. We implemented our system and opened the beta site to users for 6 months. In Section 4, we show the statistics we got from operating our system and analysis result. Finally, conclusions and future work are presented in section 5.

2. Related Works

Re-designing the traditional MT system for the improvement of the translation quality can be driven from two perspectives: Firstly, a controlled language can be adopted to enhance the readability and translatability. Secondly, an interactive MT system can be implemented to collect meta-information through user interactions to resolve the ambiguities and errors from the translation process. There is no clear definition as to what a controlled language or the interactive MT system should be like.

A controlled language has usually a restricted vocabulary and syntax rules. Most of the works on a controlled language focus on how to design a grammar rules and lexicon for a given language (Mitamura, 1999; Adriaens & Schreuers, 1992; Fuchs et al, 1999). The emphasis of major controlling could be put on the lexicon (AECMA, 1995) or on the syntax restrictions (Lehrndorfer, 1996). In our current setting, the major controlling takes place on the syntactic level because small set of syntactic restrictions affects the performance seriously. To split a long sentence into a fragment of simple sentences which are controlled by our scheme, we used a set of syntactic rules which has lexical/grammatical features. (Shirai et al., 1998) reports the improvement of translation quality by 20% through applying rewriting rules to Japanese to English translation.

The interactive MT system provides UI functions connected with the engine which includes a translation model and a language model that are used to produce the translation candidates. The target sentence under construction serves as the medium of communication between an MT system and its user (Foster et al., 1997, Langlais et al., 2000). In such an environment, human translators interact with a translation system that acts as an assistance tool and dynamically provides a list of translation candidates. To extend a type of translation models, a hybrid approach was suggested (Yamabana, 1997).

The language model that is adopted at the end of our MT system has been widely used as a post-processing step to enhance the generation performance in MT systems (Liu et al., 2003).

3. Interactive Machine Translation System

The design principles for our system are as follows; maximization of user's engine control, user's optional control, provision of full information about error correction, and user-friendly interface.

Maximization of user's engine control means that users get full control on the intermediate process of the translation, for example, the modification of morphological/syntactic analysis and target word selection. So, if a user wants to check and modify the intermediate results of the engine in the course of translation, engine errors can be corrected and more improved translation is possible.

To provide the function of engine control is one thing and to use it is another. User's optional control means that users can control the process of the translation engine as much as they want and can turn off functions which they don't want. If a user is poor in English, he/she probably wants to focus only on the rewriting of the Korean sentence. If a user knows the translation process well and wants better translation, he/she is going to revise errors from translation engine more deeply. A user can select the level of engine control and the system provides only such items that a user has selected.

Provision of full information means that our MT system provides full information that is related to the improvement of translation to the user. Those are morphological/syntactic analysis results, the translation result, link information between Korean and English words, error candidates in Korean and English sentences. The system also offers information on what the information means exactly and how to handle error candidates effectively by providing examples.

To implement user-friendly interface, the system detects both user's action and the environment and determines what the user wants in such environment. The information is represented as easy and instinctive as possible. The user can see the effect of correction by pressing the translation button right away.

Figure 1 shows the main window of our system. It consists of four sub-windows, that is, Korean window, English window, working window, and sentence structure window. The Korean window on top left shows the Korean sentences to be translated. The English window on bottom left shows the translated English sentences. The modified English sentence by the user is also saved in English window. The working window on top right shows one Korean sentence and the corresponding English sentence which is the user's current concern. The sentence structure window shows the syntactic structure of the Korean sentence on working window. Basically, one node of the tree is a simple sentence which is linked with the corresponding English translation. Link information on simple sentence level is more easy to grasp the structure and find errors than on word level. Word-level syntactic structure can be seen also if a user clicks the '+' on the tree.

Figure 1: Main Window of Korean-English MT System

3.1 Korean Sentence Modification

Korean sentences are scanned and analyzed by using morphological, morpho-syntactic, syntactic information and candidates for modification are reported to the user. Modification candidates include both error correction candidates and quality improvement candidates. Most of the errors in Korean sentences are spelling errors and spacing errors which must be corrected before translation. Such error candidates are reported to the user through triangle marks as in Figure 2. If a user presses the triangle button, the error-related part of the sentence are highlighted and at the same time an information box is popped up which describes the error type and how to handle it.

Figure 2: Reporting the Error Candidates of Korean sentences

Rewriting the Korean sentence needs to be done both for translatability and readability. But, sometimes they conflict with each other where we prefer translatability. For example, the appropriate use of auxiliary postpositions in Korean can enhance the readability for human in many cases, but it sometimes causes errors in translation. But, most of the time, improvement in readability leads to improvement in translatability. Ambiguous words or long sentences often make mistakes for human, much more for machine translation. Examples of ambiguous words are as follows.

(a) 기본적인 HMM 모델**도** 사용하는 경우
(b) 기본적인 HMM 모델**에서** 벗어나지 않고
(c) 얼굴 검출을 **할** 경우에는
(d) 지문의 방향영상을 **구할** 경우

Auxiliary-postpositions cause case ambiguities. In (a), '도' has case ambiguities between subject/object/adverb case, and a user is asked about whether '도' can be replaced by case-postpositions such as '이(subject)','를(object)' or others. If it is better not to modify, then no action is needed. Case-postpositions can cause ambiguities also. In general, '에서' has several meanings and can be replaced by other less ambiguous words for each meaning. In (b), the better alternative of '에서' is '로부터' and the original translation 'deviate in the basic HMM model' is changed to 'deviate from the basic HMM model'. '하다'(which means do) is one of the most frequently used verb in Korean and the abuse of '하다' often leads to deterioration in translatability and even in readability. So, if '하다' is considered to be better to modify, '하다' is reported for modification as in (c). The modified sentence "얼굴을 검출할 경우에는" has the translation 'if the face is detected' instead of the original translation 'if the face detection is done'. Verbs acting like pro-verb also causes ambiguities as '구하다' in (d). The user is asked about whether to change '구하다' into '계산하다(compute)', '얻다(get)', or '구하다(save)'. Modifications on the structure are as follows.

(e) ... **형상을** ... 여러 **형상을** 다단계 모델의 구조로 생성하는 기술을 말한다.

Unlike English, there exist double subject/object phenomena in Korean, the translation of which is various depending on their semantic characteristics. But, many double subject/object sentences are erroneous in reality. (e) is such an example. So, double subject/object sentences with the possibility of error are reported to the user.
In Korean, ellipses are frequently occurred in various ways as the following.

(f) 첫번째 프레임에서 **얼굴** 검출하는 경우
(g) 성능 개선을 수행하는 경우
(h) 오류를 **검출**, 수정하는 과정에서

The ellipsis of postposition and obligatory case as in (f) is easy to detect and the user needs to change '얼굴' into '얼굴을' . Unlike English, subject ellipsis is common in Korean and if a Korean transitive verb has no subject in a sentence, the user is asked about whether to convert it into intransitive or not. The English translation of a Korean transitive verb requires a subject all the time. The intransitive version of (g) is '성능 개선이 수행되는 경우' and the translation doesn't need subject. On the contrary, as in (h), the ellipsis of suffix part in a light verb is not easy to detect and the failure of the detection leads to the wrong syntactic analysis and wrong translation. The unabridged form of '검출(detection, noun)' is '검출하다' (detect, verb) in (h), where the verb '검출하다' is mis-interpreted as noun '검출'(detection). For this kind of ellipsis we use lexical co-occurrence information and also syntactic patterns. Lexical co-occurrence dictionary has entries like '오류-를-검출하다'.
In addition to the fore-mentioned, there are still other kinds of problems in translation as in the following :

(i) 증가를 가져오다
(j) 이렇게 하여 나오는 정보는
(k) 최대수는 3n 이며, 최소수는 n 이 된다

Although the Korean expression is natural to the native Korean, the translation can be awkward in many cases. For example, the translation of (i) is 'bring increment'. The correct translation is 'increase' which is the translation of '증가시키다'. Non-informative expressions can lead the mis-translation also. For example, the translation of (j) is 'information which does in this way and come out' where '하다' is obsolete. The modified sentence '이렇게 나오는 정보들은' get the , translation 'information coming out in this way'. The application of agreement/concord can improve the translation quality also. The translation of sentence (k) is 'The maximum number is $3n$ and the minimum number becomes n' which is very faithful to the source sentence. With respect to the standpoint of agreement/concord, '이 된다' can be modified into '이다' in (k) and the translation is 'The maximum number is $3n$ and the minimum number is n'. Generally, human doesn't want to repeat the same vocabulary in writing. But, the application of agreement/concord and therefore the use of the same vocabulary is a very good way for machine translation.

The modifications described in this section are obtained automatically or semi-automatically through corpus analysis and they are still needed to be complemented.

3.2 Engine Error Correction

Engine errors are not easy for a user to understand and correct. So, items reported to users are needed to be understandable and manageable. We only report such errors like morphological, syntactic analysis errors and word translation errors to the user.

The morphological errors are part-of-speech tagging errors and segmentation errors which can be found indirectly through scanning the translation result. These errors can be modified by correcting the morphological analysis directly. If a user presses the morphological analysis button, the morphological analysis result is popped up. Figure 3 is the morphological analysis result of "본 논문에서는 멸치 다시 국물을 효과적으로 만드는 방법에 대해 기술한다.".

Here, '다시' is wrongly tagged as adverb, the user can fix it.

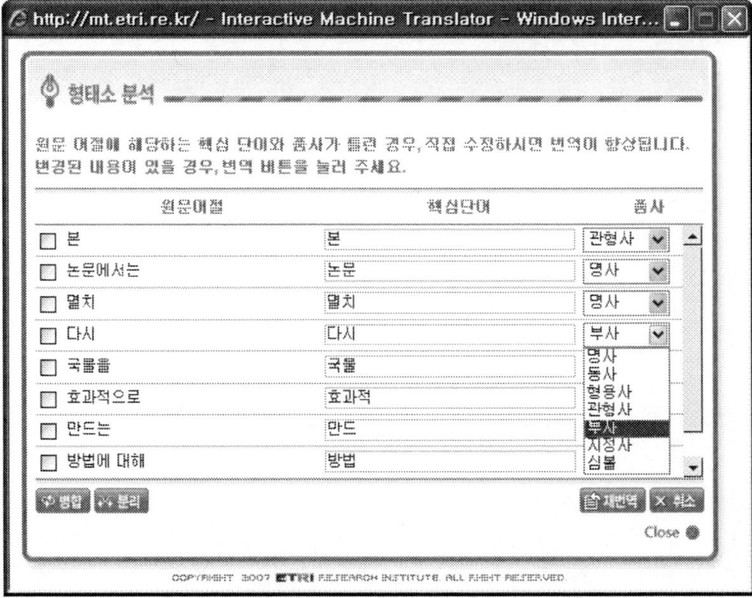

Figure 3: Error Correction for Morphological Analysis

Syntactic analysis result is displayed on the sentence structure window. Each line in a tree corresponds to a simple sentence and its translation is linked with its translation. Figure 4 is the original and modified tree. Dtra&drop is used for structure modification.

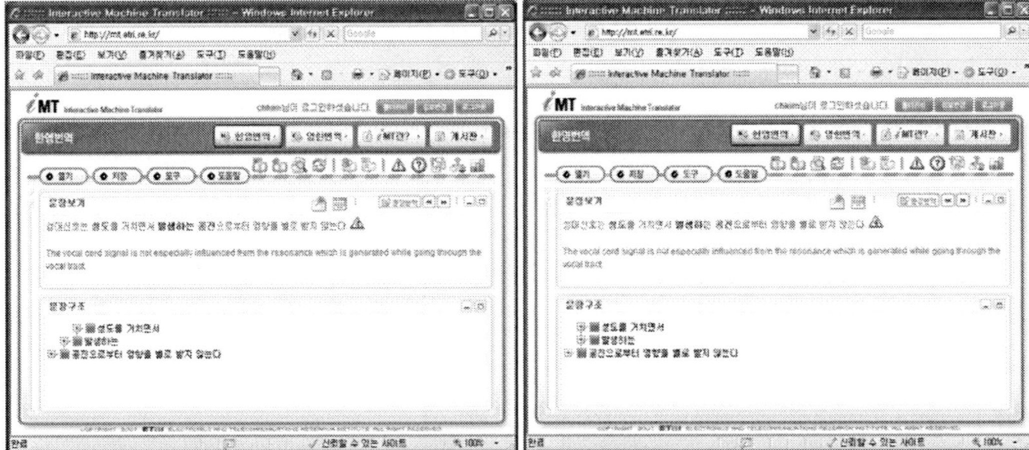

Figure 4: Sentence Structure before and after the Correction

Word translation errors can be modified by pressing the suspicious word and selecting the right one among several candidates or by typing in the right one directly.

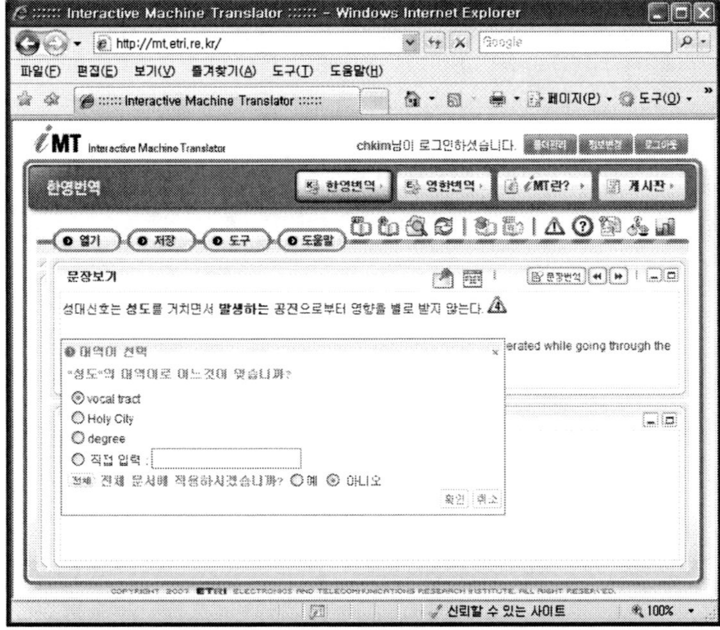

Figure 5: Word Translation Error Correction

3.3 Target Sentence Correction

Source sentence modification and engine error correction can improve the translation, however it still may not be satisfying. This is because our paper MT system is pattern-based system. Our MT system generates target sentences mainly based on pattern resources such as sentence patterns, verbal patterns, noun patterns and etc. When the wrong patterns are matched and used in generation, the translated English sentences may contain erroneous expressions. Even when the patterns are correctly matched, the English counterpart may contain somewhat unnatural translation. For this reason, we employed the language model for post-processing. For example, the translation of "필요성이 대두되고 있다" is "a necessity is occurring". The system reports to the user that "a necessity is occurring" is scarcely used and shows all possible English translation for "필요성이 대두되고 있다" by consulting the dictionary for each Korean word and combining the candidates. In this case, those Korean words '필요성'(necessity) and '대두되다'(occur, come to the front, raise, show itself, be raised) are consulted and combined. Each combination expression is retrieved from the English paper database for its examples. From this information, the user gets a hint on how to correct the expression. Sometimes some expressions look unnatural to the user even though the system regards them as natural. For the user's confidence, the system provides the function to retrieve the same expression as the one in the translation as in Figure 6.

Figure 6: Expression Search

4. Evaluation

We have implemented our system and opened it to users for 6 months. The main users are researchers and university students in the field of science and technology.

Total # of Users	Total Length of Stay(day)	Average(stay/user)
694	1,827	2.633

The total number of users and their length of stay are as the above. It is hard to say that our system is useful for paper writing according to the above statistics. Some few can write an English paper just in 2.6 days but most of people can't.

Total # of Users	Total # of Sentences	Average (Sent./user)
694	39,506	56.925

The average sentence translated per user is as the above. It is still not so promising but a little bit more positive than the previous one. We can think that if a user thinks our system is useful, then the user is sure to use more complex function of the system in addition to the simple translation such as the source sentence modification, the engine error correction or the target sentence modification. These kind of functions entail the re-translation(RT).

# of RT Users	Total # of RT Sentences	Average (RT/user)

344	7,142	20.762

The retranslation statistics are as the above. This is somewhat different from the previous ones. We can think that around 50% of the users consider our system is interesting. Let's narrow our interest to the 344 users(focus user(FU)) and renew the above statistics.

# of FU	Length of Stay	Average Stay	# of FU Sent.	Average Sent.
344	1,442	4.192	38,096	110.744

The average length of stay per FU is 4.192 and the average number of sentence for translation is 110.744 for paper translation. These statistics surely tells that our system can be contributed to some of FU's needs although we do not know their needs exactly. Then let's analyze our system more deeply for those needs. The below is the details for RT sentences.

# of FU Sentences	Total # of RT Sentences(ratio)	# of Non-RT Sentences(ratio)
38,096	7,142(18.75%)	30,954(81.25%)

The above says that FU users use 81.25% of the total FU sentences as it is without modifying anything at all. If we analyse this statistics on the assumption that our system is useful, 81.25% means that the most preferred function of the system is the translation function itself. It can also be said that the users are either satisfied with the translation result or although they are not satisfied with the translation quality, they know the limits of the system and use the translation result usefully according their needs by any means. In fact, phrase-level or simple-sentence level translation is quite correct.

Total # of RT	MorphErr	TreeErr	CaseErr	SenseErr
7,142	37	47	236	97

The above is the statistics for complex functions. MorphErr is the number of RT triggered by morphological errors, TreeErr by structural analysis, CaseErr by case analysis error, SenseErr by sense disambiguation errors. The other sentences except the above 4 cases are the case for the Korean sentence correction. Korean is an agglutinative language and has some somewhat complicated spelling and spacing rules. So Koreans have often difficulties in writing Korean sentences accurately. So, errors in Korean sentences cause poor translation results. By just correcting the Korean sentences, the performance of the system can be improved by a large margin. The most frequently used functions among the above are CaseErr and SenseErr. The reason seems to be that these two functions are quite intuitive and simple for use and also are easy to see the effect of correction directly. On the other hand, the functions MorphErr and TreeErr are somewhat difficult for the layman to understand and use and also the effect of the correction may not be easy to identify directly sometimes.
The post-editing function is not dealt with in this section. In reality we don't have the statistics for the function.

5. Conclusion

In this paper, we presented the Korean-English paper machine translation system allowing the user interaction and evaluated the implemented system by opening it to users for 6 months. To obtain high quality translation we redesigned our MT system and applied the new design principles: maximization of user's engine control, user's optional control, provision of sufficient information about error correction, and user-friendly interface.

The evaluation statistics show that almost half of the users consider our system can be of any help to their needs for English paper writing. 81% of the translation results are used as it is without any modification, which means that the performance of our system can be said satisfactory to some extent. A Korean sentence is somewhat complicated to write and includes errors often. This fact is identified by the RT statistics and just correcting the Korean sentence errors can enhance the degree of satisfaction to the translation quality. Case disambiguation and sense disambiguation functions are frequently used that are easy to understand and see the effects directly. Morphological analysis and structural analysis functions are rarely used partly because of the difficulties in understanding and identifying the effects directly.

From the evaluation we can conclude that the basic translation quality is the most important in paper writing MT systems but, the function of just correcting the source sentence errors can be enormous help. In addition to that, simple functions such as case disambiguation and sense disambiguation can be very helpful, but user are not so interested in complex functions such as morphological analysis and syntactic analysis.

In the future, we will continually improve the translation performance of our MT translation engine and improve the user interaction based on the analysis performed in this paper.

References

AECMA : A Guide for the Preparation of Aircraft Maintenance Documentation in the International Aerosace Maintenance Language, AECMA Simplified English , 1995.

Adriaens, G. and D. Schreuers. 1992. From COGRAM to ALCOGRAM: Toward a controlled Eng-lish grammar checker, *COLING* , 595-601.

Foster, G, Pierre Isabelle and Pierre Plamondon. 1997. Target-Text Mediated Interactive Machine Translation, *Machine Translation*.

Fuchs, N. E., U. Schwertel and R. Schwitter. 1999. Attempto Controlled English (ACE) Language Man-ual, Version 3.0, Technical Report, Department of Computer Science, University of Zurich.

Hong, M., Y. Kim, C. Kim, S. Yang, Y. Seo, C. Ryu and S. Park. 2005. Customizing a Korean-English MT System for Patent Translation, *MT-Summit*.

Kim, Y., M. Hong and S. Park. 2007. CL Guided Korean-English MT system for scientific papers, *CICLing*

Langlais, P., G. Foster, and G. Lapalme. 2000. TransType : a computer-aided translation typing system. *In Workshop on Embedded Machine Translation Systems*.

Lehrndorfer, Anne. 1996. Kontrolliertes Deutsch, Gunter Narr Verlag, Tuebingen.

Liu, Fu-Hua, Liang Gu, Yuqing Gao and Michael Picheny. 2003. Use of Statistical N-gram Models in Natural Language Generation for Machine Translation. *MT-Summit*.

Mitamura, Teruko. 1999. Controlled language for multilingual MT, *MT-Summit*.

Roh, Y., Y. Seo, K. Lee and S. Choi. 2001. Long Sentence Partitioning using Structure Analysis for Machine Translation, *NLPRS*.

Shirai, S., S. Ikekaha, A. Yokoo and Y. Ooyama. 1998. Automatic Rewriting Method for Internal Expressions in Japanese to English MT and Its Effects, *In proceedings of the Second International Workshop on Controlled Language Applications(CLAW98)*.

Seo Y, K. Lee and S. Park. 2001. CaptionEye/EK: English-to-Korean Caption Translation System using the Sentence Pattern, *MT-Summit*.

Yamabana, K., S. Kamei, K. Muraki, S. Doi, S. Tamura and K. Satoh. 1997. A Hybrid Approach to Interactive Machine Translation – Integrating Rule-based, Corpus-based, and Example-based Method, *Proceedings of the Fifteenth International Joint Conference on Artificial Intelligence*.

Semantic Structures of Polysemous Psych-adjectives in Korean: A Conceptual Semantics Approach

Ilkyu Kim

Department of Linguistics and Cognitive Science, Hankuk University of Foreign Studies
Imun-dong, Seoul, South Korea
onefinedayjazz@hufs.ac.kr

Abstract. Although researches have been conducted on the polysemous nature of some Korean psych-adjectives, no consensus has been made on the criteria used for evaluating the polysemy. Furthermore, few formalizations (semantic structures) have been proposed for the polysemous phenomena. The purpose of this paper is twofold: 1) to propose new criteria for distinguishing polysemous psych-adjectives from monosemous ones, and 2) to provide exact semantic structures for the polysemous psych-adjectives. For the second goal in particular, I will work under the framework of Jackendoff's Conceptual Semantics.

Keywords: Korean psych-adjectives, Conceptual Semantics, polysemy.

1. Introduction

The idiosyncratic syntactic behaviors of psych-predicates in many languages have attracted linguists around the world since 1960s. Korean psych-adjectives, however, are also interesting from the semantic perspective; that is, some of them seem to be polysemous between the meanings of one's purely psychological state and the objective property of an entity. Contrary to the arguments for the polysemy (e.g. S Kim 1994, H-K Yoo, J-N Kim 2005), it has not been recognized by many syntacticians and all the psych-adjectives have been treated as monosemous with the meaning of psychological state (e.g. Y-J Kim 1990, J-H Han 1999, Gerdts & Yoon 2001).

Although researches have been conducted on the polysemous nature of some Korean psych-adjectives, no consensus has been made on the criteria used for evaluating the polysemy. Furthermore, few formalizations (semantic structures) have been proposed for the polysemous phenomena. The purpose of this paper is twofold: 1) to propose new criteria for distinguishing polysemous psych-adjectives from monosemous ones, and 2) to provide exact semantic structures for the polysemous psych-adjectives. For the second goal in particular, I will work under the framework of Jackendoff's Conceptual Semantics.

2. Polysemous Korean Psych-adjectives

Although most studies that deal with the syntactic phenomena of psych-adjectives consider them as monosemous, some researchers who focus on the semantics of Korean adjectives have shown that the meanings of psych-adjectives are not just all monosemous (e.g. C Lee 1976, S Kim, H-K Yoo 1998, J-N Kim 2005). In this section, I will examine some of their arguments and show that they are problematic in one way or another.

2.1. S Kim (1994)

Among the researches that deal with the polysemy of Korean psych-adjectives, S Kim (1994) was the first to try to formalize the polysemy. Working under the framework of Conceptual Semantics, S Kim divides Korean adjectives into three groups: property adjectives, psych-adjectives, and quasi-psych-adjectives. According to him, property adjectives and psych-adjectives can be distinguished by whether the predicate requires experiencer as its argument. Quasi-psych-adjectives are adjectives that show characteristics of both property adjectives and psych-adjectives.

S Kim (1994) defines quasi-psych-adjectives as adjectives that basically describe the objective property of an entity but still needs experiencer as its argument. (1) shows predicates that belong to each group suggested by S Kim (1994: 44-49), and Table 1 shows the main criteria used for distinguishing one another.

> (1) a. Property Adjectives: *alumtapta* 'beautiful', *chakhata* 'good-natured', etc.
>   b. Psych-adjectives: *yasokhata* 'unkind, unfeeling', *silhta* 'dislike', etc.
>   c. Quasi-psych-adjectives: *kwiyepta* 'cute', *salangsulepta* 'lovely', etc.

Table 1: Criteria of identifying three kinds of Korean adjectives

	combine with '*-e ha-*'	modification	stage-level vs. individual-level
property	impossible	possible	individual-level only
qusi-psych	possible	possible	both
psych	possible	impossible	both

According to S Kim, the first criterion, possibility of being able to combine with '*-e ha-*' construction, is to find out whether the predicate requires experiencer as its argument, and the second and the third criteria, the possibility of being able to be used in modifying NPs and the possibility of being able to represent stage-level state, are to figure out whether the predicate represents the objective property of an entity.

In addition to this distinction, he further divides psych-adjectives into two groups based on whether the predicate takes stimulus as its obligatory argument or not. Thus, he proposes three lexical conceptual structures (LCSs) for the adjective *mwusepta* as in (2).

> (2) LCS for mwusepta 'scary/scared' (S Kim 1994: 55)
>   a. mwusepta[1] (EXP, THEME)
>   [STATE BE/FEEL (x, [PLACE AT mwusewum] [y])]
>   b. mwusepta[2] (EXP)
>   [STATE BE/FEEL (x, [PLACE AT mwusewum])]
>   c. mwusepta[3] (THEME)
>   [STATE BE/FEEL (x, [AT mwusewum][1] [y])]

By the LCSs S Kim (1994) provides, we can see that he considers mwusepta 'scary/scared' as a quasi-psych-adjective ((2a,b) vs. (2c)) and its stimulus argument as optional rather than obligatory ((2a) vs. (2b)). S Kim's analysis, although well captures the polysemous nature and optionality of stimulus of the predicate, is problematic in two respects.

First, he does not have to posit two independent LCSs for (2a) and (2b) in order to show that the stimulus argument is optional. By positing separate LCSs, he argues that (2a) and (2b) should be thought of as two different lexemes. However, I do not find any reason for that. We can put the stimulus, i.e., [y] in (2a), in a parenthesis and capture the semantic similarity between the two, instead of arguing they are totally different lexemes, which is absolutely against our intuition.

---

[11] His missing the function PLACE seems to be a simple mistake.

Second, there is no difference between the LCS for mwusepta[1] and the LCS for mwusepta[3] at all. With leaving the two LCSs being the same, he just distinguishes the two by positing different argument structures, (EXP, THEME) and (THEME). In fact, the function BE/FEEL is what he made in order to distinguish the objective property of an entity from one's psychological state. That is, BE refers to the objective property while BE/FEEL requires experiencer as its argument and refers to one's psychological state. However, he does not use these two functions in distinguishing mwusepta[1] from mwusepta[3]. Furthermore, the meaning of the predicate in (2c) is an objective property of an entity, which means the LCS, as that of any other property adjectives, is natural with only one argument in the conceptual structure.

2.2. H-K Yoo (1998)

Following S Kim (1994), H-K Yoo (1998) also points out the polysemous nature of some psych-adjectives. She classifies Korean adjectives into two broad categories, subjective and objective adjectives, in terms of the thematic role of the subject the predicate takes. If the predicate requires experiencer as its subject then it belongs to subjective adjectives, and if theme or location is required, the predicate is an objective adjective.

Subjective adjectives are further divided into psych-adjectives, perceptive adjectives and evaluative adjectives according to the types of complements the adjectives take. Objective adjectives fall into various kinds of adjectives depending on their syntactic and semantic characteristics, but the majority of them fall into property/sate adjectives which represent property (individual-level) or state (stage-level) of an entity.

Among property/state adjectives, H-K Yoo (1998) argues, some adjectives are also used as subjective psych-adjectives. The adjectives that she suggests to be able to refer to both objective and subjective state include *yeypputa* 'pretty/adore', *kwiyepta* 'cute/feel cute', *cohta* 'good/like', *mwusepta* 'scared/scary', *mipta* 'ugly/hate'.

The criteria she suggests for determining whether the predicate is ambiguous or not is the case frame; that is, if the predicate can take both 'NP1-NOM NP2-NOM Adjective' and 'NP1-NOM Adjective' frames, it is thought to be polysemous. However, in her actual analysis, she determines whether the predicate is ambiguous by just considering whether the predicate can occur with experiencer argument regardless of the case marked on it. This is problematic because not only psych-adjectives but other objective adjectives can take (DAT)-TOP-marked experiencer as shown in (3).

    (3) a. na-(eykey)-nun i   paci-ka   nemwu kilta
          I-DAT-TOP   this pants-NOM too   long
          'As for me, these pants are too long.'
       b. ku-(eykey)-nun ku kicha-ka nemwu ppaluta
          he-(DAT)-TOP the train-NOM too   fast
          'As for him, the train is too fast.'

According to H-K Yoo's (1998) criteria, the adjectives *kilta* 'long' and *ppaluta* 'fast', which are apparently not psych-adjectives, also must be treated as subjective psych-adjectives, because they can occur with experiencers *na* 'I' (3a) and *ku* 'he' (3b).

2.3. J-N Kim (2005)

J-N Kim (2005) criticizes the approaches taken by S Kim (1994) and H-K Yoo (1998) that regard psych-adjectives as having two different meanings, that is, psychological state/property (S Kim 1994) or objective/subjective (H-K Yoo 1998).

Instead, he contends that the key to the understanding of the polysemous nature of the adjectives is to look into the context, or construction, in which the adjective is used. If the adjective is used as either the subjective (psych) or objective (property) predicate, it is the construction not the adjective itself that gives rise to the different readings.

By this way, he tries to avoid positing quasi-psych-predicates or predicates that have both subjective and objective meanings. This solution, at first glance, seems plausible and even desirable, as J-N Kim argues, in that there is no need to posit an additional category like quasi-psych-adjective or to posit two different meanings for one word. However, his solution eventually ends up positing two different categories for adjectives in order to explain the polysemy-like phenomena and it is fundamentally not different from the former approaches.

The two categories he postulates are "correlative" and "non-correlative" adjectives. Correlative adjectives are adjectives that describe the state or characteristic of an entity with regard to other entities, whereas non-correlative adjectives are adjectives that describe the state or characteristic of an entity without regarding any other entity.

There are two reasons that this solution is no better than the former approaches. First, the distinction between the two categories, correlative and non-correlative, must be made on the basis of the number of "semantic" argument that the predicate requires, and the number of arguments the predicate requires are determined ultimately by the meaning of the predicate itself. That is, instead of using the context or the construction as the criterion of distinguishing the two types of categories as he originally suggests, J-N Kim uses the meaning of the adjectives as the criterion for the distinction between correlative and non-correlative adjectives.

Furthermore, some predicates categorized as correlative adjectives by J-N Kim are also used as non-correlatives (e.g. *maypta* 'hot, feel hot' and *cohta* 'good, like') and among what he classifies as non-correlatives are predicates that can also be used as correlatives (e.g. *tepta* 'hot, feel hot' and *sulphuta* 'sad, feel sad'). Thus, his suggestion is just another kind of typology of Korean adjectives based on the lexical meaning of predicates and not fundamentally different from what the previous researchers have suggested.

2.4. New Criteria for Polysemous Korean Psych-adjectives

Instead of J-N Kim's typology, I prefer the former typologies that divide adjectives into two broad groups whether they belong to psychological (subjective) state or to (objective) property, because I believe this distinction fits better to our intuition.

Following S Kim and H-K Yoo, I argue that many of the predicates that have been treated as monosemous psych-adjectives in most previous researches are in fact polysemous between two meanings: objective property and one's psychological state. Basically agreeing with S Kim and H-K Yoo (1998), I propose further convincing evidence, some of which have also been briefly mentioned by S Nam (2007), that show the polysemy of some psych-adjectives.

The first evidence comes from the fact that some psych-adjectives can take either animate or inanimate NOM-marked arguments as their subject. This is strange if the adjective has only one meaning of referring to one's psychological state, because inanimate entities cannot have any psychological state. For example, we can see by (4) that what is known as a psych-adjective kipputa 'pleased' is acceptable only when it takes an animate NOM-marked argument.

    (4) a. nay-ka/nun (kipputa/mwusepta).
           I-NOM/nun pleased/scared
          'I am pleased.'
      b. ku inhyeng-i/un (#kipputa/mwusepta).
         the doll-NOM/TOP pleased/scary
       'The doll is pleased.'

On the other hand, another psych-adjective *mwusepta* 'scared, scary' can be used with both an animate and an inanimate NOM/TOP-marked NP. This indicates that *mwusepta* 'scared, scary' is somewhat different from kipputa 'pleased' and the difference is that *mwusepta* 'scared, scary', unlike *kipputa* 'pleased', can refer not only to one's psychological state but also to an objective property of an entity. We can see this by the fact that the natural interpretation of (34b) with the predicate *mwusepta* is only 'The doll is scary' but not 'The doll is scared'.

The second evidence comes from the possibility of modification. Modification was already suggested by S Kim as one of the tests that distinguish property from psychological state, but the possibility of being able to modify a NP itself cannot be a valid one. What is important is the fact that some psych-adjectives can be used to modify an inanimate NP and represent the property not the psychological state of the modified NP.

(5a) is clearly different from (5b) in that the adjective *cilwuhata* 'boring/bored' can both represent the properties of the inanimate NPs and the psychological states of the animate NPs that they modify, while *kipputa* 'pleased/happy' can only modify the psychological states of the animate NPs.

(5) a. cilwuhan   pulloku/kkwum/yenghwa/Jane/Tom/tongsayng …
        boring   blog/dream/movie/Jane/Tom/brother …
        'boring   blog/dream/movie'
   b. kippun   #pulloku/#kkwum/#yenghwa/Jane/Tom/ tongsayng…
        happy   blog/dream/movie/Jane/Tom/brother …
        'happy   #blog/#dream/#movie/Jane/Tom/brother '

Some might argue that *kipputa* 'pleased' can be thought of also as a property adjective in the sense that it can modify the inanimate NPs like *nal* 'day' and *sosik* 'news' as in *kippun nal* 'happy day' and *kippun sosik* 'happy news'. However, it is different from other property adjectives since it does not pass the first criterion. Although *kipputa* can modify the NPs *nal* 'day' and *sosik* 'news' it cannot be used as a predicate with the same NPs as in (6).

(6) ku nal/sosik-i kipputa.
   the day/news-NOM happy
   #'The day/news is happy.'
   '(I am) happy with the day/news.'

As shown in (6), the sentence is unacceptable with the adjective's referring to the property of *ku nal* 'the day' or *ku sosik* 'the news'. But it is much more natural if the experiencer argument *na* 'I' is thought to be ellipsed and the predicate refers to the psychological state of the experiencer. This shows that *kipputa* 'pleased' refers to the psychological state of the abbreviated experiencer rather than the objective property of the modified NPs like *nal* 'day' and *sosik* 'news'.

One thing to note is that *kippun* in *kippun sosik* 'happy news' or *kippun nal* 'happy day' nevertheless can be thought of as referring to the property of *sosik* 'news' or *nal* 'day' intuitively. I attribute this characteristic, as H-K Yoo (1998) also noticed, to the semantic change the adjective is going through. That is, *kipputa* 'pleased' originally meant only one's psychological state but its meaning is becoming ambiguous between 'pleased' and 'pleasing' at least when it modifies the NP *sosik* 'news' or *nal* 'day' as time goes by.

In fact, this kind of semantic change, whether from psychological state to property or from property to psychological state, is often found cross-linguistically. For example, the English word sad, which originally meant one's psychological state, is now not only used as referring to one's psychological state but also as referring to the property of an entity in sentences like *This book is sad*.

The third evidence is that DAT experiencer cannot go along with the adjective that is used with the meaning of one's psychological state as in (7). In response to the question (7a), one can use TOP/NOM experiencer but not DAT experiencer as (7b) shows. If the psych-adjective can take DAT experiencer as most previous studies have acknowledged, this must be a crucial problem.

(7) a. ne cikum kipwun-i etteni?
       you now feeling-NOM how
       'How do you feel now?'
    b. na-(*eykey/nun/??ka^2) sulphe/mwusewe/kippe
       I-DAT/TOP/NOM sad/scared/pleased
       'I am sad/scared/pleased.'

This, at least indirectly, shows that the psych-adjective itself in DAT experiencer constructions is not the psych-adjective but the property adjective in S Kim's term or the objective adjective in H-K Yoo's term. The adjective can refer to one's psychological state only when the experiencer argument is assigned NOM or TOP.

Then, there arises a problem of DEC's being understood as a psych-construction and synonymous with its counterpart NEC. How can the construction with no psych-adjective be used as a psych-construction? I argue that this is due to the semantic similarity of one's psychological state and one's subjective evaluation.

What has been called property adjectives in the paper so far are also called evaluative adjectives (e.g. Jackendoff 2007). Evaluative adjectives can represent either subjective or objective evaluation depending on the existence of a specific evaluator in the sentence.

(8) Objectification and Subjectification   (Jackendoff 2007: 240)
    Y BE [Property λz [X BE [F (z)]]] □default
    (e.g. Y is interesting to X)

                            Y BE [Property λz [YA BE [F (z)]]]
                            (e.g. Y is interesting)
    (where Y is the entity being evaluated, X is the experiencer, and YA is the generic
    perceiver)

As shown in (8), Jackendoff (2007) proposes the mechanism that accounts for how evaluative predicates are sometimes used as subjective evaluation and sometimes objective evaluation. If a specific evaluator is introduced by to X form then the construction becomes subjective evaluation whereas the construction is used as objective evaluation with no specific evaluator, which, according to Jackendoff, is a default construction.

I agree with Jackendoff's basic idea on the subjectification and objectification above, but I differ from him on the LCS of the evaluative predicates. Jackendoff originally distinguishes property/evaluative adjectives from psych-adjectives on the level of the thematic tier as in (9), but later he argues that the distinction on the level of the macrorole tier is enough as in (10).

(9) a. Frank is amazing to Sam.
       FRANK BE [λz [SAM BE [AMAZED (z)]]]
       SAM EXP FRANK
    b. Sam is amazed at Frank.
       SAM BE [AMAZED (FRANK)]
       SAM EXP FRANK
(10) a. Frank is amazing to Sam.
       SAM BE [AMAZED (FRANK)]
       SAM EXP FRANK
    b. Sam is amazed at Frank.
       SAM BE [AMAZED (FRANK)]
       SAM EXP FRANK

                                        (Jackendoff 2007: 237)

---

^{2} The reason why NOM on the experiencer argument makes the sentence sound strange seems the matter of pragmatics not of syntax or semantics. That is, the pragmatic information that NOM carries causes conflicts with the question (7a). Explaining the exact mechanism regarding this phenomenon is beyond the scope of this paper.

First, in (9a), Jackendoff paraphrases the sentence as 'Frank is such that Sam is amazed at' and proposes FRANK BE [λz [SAM BE [AMAZED (z)]]] as the thematic tier, in which the notation λz can be read informally as 'such that' and the bound variable z that serves as argument of AMAZED can be read as the resumptive pronoun 'him'.

Although this lambda abstraction very well captures the meaning of evaluation/property and the semantic difference between psychological state and evaluation/property, he does not give any detailed semantic analysis of one's psychological states such as *interested, bored, scared,* etc. Instead, he just uses the state function BE and the words themselves for representing the conceptual structures of the words, which causes the circulation problem and thus cannot be the satisfying semantic (or conceptual) representation of the words.

Moreover, as shown in (10), he argues that (9a) and (10a) are "logically equivalent" and the prominence of stimulus in (9a) can be captured on the level of the macrorole tier by underlining a more prominent argument. This means that "EXP, unlike AFF, does not inherently determine which macrorole is linked to subject position. Rather, each EXP verb must individually mark its subject" (Jackendoff 2007: 235).

3. Formalization of the Polysemy: A New Conceptual Semantics Approach

Among several semantic theories that deal with LCS, we use Jackendoff's (1983, 1990, 2002, 2007) Conceptual Semantics as our framework. The motivation for using Conceptual Semantics comes from our view on the overall architecture of the language faculty. That is, we take the tripartite parallel model as more realistic than Chomskyan syntactocentric models in accounting for human language faculty, and Conceptual Semantics, unlike many other LCS theories that go along with the syntactocentric models (e.g. Hale & Keyser 1992, 1993, Zubizaretta & Oh 2007, Ramchand 2008), is the semantic theory that best fits the model.

Despite its success in analyzing various kinds of domains of concepts like spatial concepts, Conceptual Semantics had made little progress in dealing with psych-predicates before Jackenodff (2007) introduced a new function called EXP which belongs to a new level of conceptual structure called macrorole tier.

Following Culicover & Wilkins (1986) and Talmy (1985), Jackendoff (1990:128) argues that "conceptual roles fall into two tiers: a thematic tier dealing with motion and location, and an action tier dealing with Actor-Patient relations." In addition to Actor and Patient, Jackendoff (2007) adds two more conceptual roles, Experiencer and Stimulus, to the action tier and call it macrorole tier. He proposes an independent motivation for doing so. By postulating the two functions in the macrorole tier, the semantic difference, for instance, between see and look at can be captured as in (11) (Jackendoff 2007: 205).

(11) a. X looks at Y
          X SENSEvisual Y
          X AFF
       b. X sees Y
          X SENSEvisual Y
          X EXP Y
(12) a. What I did was look at/*see the tree.
       b. I am looking at /*seeing the tree.

That is, (11) captures important differences between see and look at. First, the look at denotes an action while see a psychological state (cf. (12)), and this is captured by positing two different functions at the macrorole tier, thus making the subject of look at as Actor and the subject of see as Experiencer. Secondly, one can look around without particularly looking at anything, while one cannot see without seeing anything. Each of these characteristics is also naturally captured on the level of the macrorole tier, in which the second argument of look at does not exist while that of see is Stimulus. Furthermore, positing AFF and EXP on the level of the macrorole tier also helps to account for the semantic difference between psych-adjective constructions and

[psych-adjective + *-e ha-*] constructions that has caused a lot of conflicts among researchers (cf.
I Kim 2007).

Regarding the semantic difference between psychological states (e.g. bored/interested/scared)
and evaluation/property (e.g. boring/interesting/scaring) discussed above, the only previous
formalizations of the difference are Jackendoff's (2007) lambda abstraction (cf. (9)) and S
Kim's (1994) distinction between BE and BE/FEEL.

However, the two formalizations are problematic as discussed above; that is, Jackendoff
(2007) argues the difference is just a matter of prominence (cf. (9) vs. (10)), and S Kim just
posits a new function BE/FEEL for psychological predicates without changing anything else.
Instead, we propose two different conceptual structures for evaluation/property and
psychological state as in (13).

(13) a. Conceptual Structure of Objective Property/Evaluative Adjectives
         (e.g. boring, interesting, scary, …)
         thematic tier: [$_{State}$ BE ([X], [$_{Property}$ FEELING$_d$])]
         macrorole tier: EXP X
      b. Conceptual Structure of Subjective Evaluative Adjectives
         (e.g. boring to y, interesting to y, scary to y, …)
         thematic tier: [$_{State}$ BE ([X], [$_{Property}$ λz [$_{State}$ FEEL ([Y], [FEELING$_d$ (z)]]])])]
         macrorole tier: Y EXP X
      c. Conceptual Structure of Psychological State Adjectives
         (e.g. bored, interested, scared, …)
         thematic tier: [$_{State}$ FEEL ([X], [$_{Property}$ FEELING$_{i/d}$ <(Y)>)]
         macrorole tier: X EXP (Y)

Conceptual structures in (13) have several characteristics that make them better than LCSs that
have been introduced by others so far. First, regarding the conceptual structure of
property/evaluation adjectives, I argue that the default structure is like (13a). This is the same as
the conceptual structures of any other property adjectives such as *long*, *blue*, and *big*. By
positing (13a), I reject Jackendoff's idea that experiencer is a generic perceiver or YA for
objective evaluation. Instead, I argue that when people utter the sentence *This book is boring*,
they do not think that everybody is bored with the book but that the book has boredom as its
inherent property as other properties such as its size, color, etc. My argument is justified by the
following possible conversation between two people.

(14) A: SPE is really boring!
      B: No! It is the most interesting book in the world no matter how you or anybody
         evaluates it!

In B's response to A's utterance, (s)he does not care about anybody's evaluation of the movie
and insists that SPE is the most interesting book in the world. It is important to note that B's
utterance cannot mean that B intends to say the book is interesting to everybody but must be
interpreted that he intends to say that the book is interesting by its inherent nature no matter how
people evaluate it. In this sense, (13a) better represents the conceptual structure of objective
evaluation than (8) does. And in this sense, it is important to note that property/objective
evaluation does not refer to one's mental state and does not have experiencer at its macrorole
tier, whereas subjective evaluation does represent one's mental state and has the function EXP
at the macrorole tier. In addition, the same function EXP on the macrorole tier for both
subjective evaluation and psychological state captures the fact that the two constructions are
construed as synonymous psych-constructions.

Second, the fact that the default structure of evaluative/property adjectives, which is (13a), has
only one argument but (13b) has two arguments implies that the argument Y in (13b) is optional.
That is, it is not the main argument that the adjective necessarily takes; rather, its syntactic
status is closer to adjunct.

Third, as for the subjective evaluation, the highest argument on the thematic tier is the second argument of EXP on the macrorole tier (cf. (13b)). This captures the fact that the first argument on the thematic tier X is not the experiencer but the stimulus which evokes the feeling in Y's mind. On the other hand, the conceptual structure of psychological state has the highest argument on the thematic tier linked to the first argument of the EXP on the macrorole tier (cf. (13c)). This captures the fact that the first argument X is the one who feels the feeling evoked by the stimulus Y.

The Fourth characteristic of the conceptual structures in (13) is that (13a) and (13c) differ from each other with respect to the functions that take ([X], [Property FEELING]) as their arguments. While the function is BE for property/objective evaluation, it is FEEL for psychological state. Here, the function FEEL is a newly proposed function for the meaning of psychological state, and the motivation for the new function comes from the ambiguity that sentences have as in (15).

> (15) na-nun(/ka) caymissta/mwusepta …
>   I-TOP(/NOM) (amusing/amused)/(scaring/scared)
>   'I am (amusing/amused)/(scaring/scared).'

As in (15), polysemous adjectives like *caymissta* 'amusing/amused' or *mwusepta* 'scary/scared' make the sentence ambiguous. Without introducing a new function for the meaning of psychological state, it is impossible to show the ambiguity of the sentences in (15). For the same reason, S Kim (1994) proposed a new function BE/FEEL, but we see no reason to include BE in the new function.

Last, the subscripts on the function FEELING helps to capture the further difference between property/evaluation adjectives and psychological state adjectives. Jackendoff (2007) divides psych-adjectives into two groups according to the nature of the psychological state they refer to. That is, some psych-adjectives can refer to "pure feelings" or feelings connected to a particular stimulus, and others can refer to only feelings that are directed toward a stimulus.

> (16) Distinction between Inherent/Directed Feelings (Jackendoff 2007: 227)
>   a. Inherent or directed feelings (e.g. bored, calm, depressed, happy)
>   [Property F_i, $<(Z)>$]
>   (where $<(Z)>$ denotes an optional argument)
>   b. Directed feelings (e.g. amazed, amused, interested, pleased)
>   [Property F_d, (Z)]

The division of the psychological state into two groups is motivated language-independently as pointed out by Jackendoff (2007).

> This difference between "pure feelings" and "directed feelings" does not appear to have anything to do with language. Rather, it appears to arise from the character of human experience. Research on cultural universals of emotion (Ekman and Davidson 1994) seems to show that certain aspects of experience can be characterized as "moods" or "pure emotions," independent of surroundings; these include being happy, sad, calm, nervous, scared, and upset. Others are intrinsically "directed motions," such as being attracted, disgusted, interested, humiliated, or ashamed; these require connection to a stimulus in the environment (or in one's mind). However, the "pure emotions" can also be directed at or connected to some particular stimulus. (Jackendoff 2007: 225).

The distinction between "inherent feelings" and "directed feelings" in (16) captures the difference between property/evaluation and psychological state in the sense that property/evaluation necessarily requires the FEELING to be directed since the stimulus argument is obligatory in the conceptual structure of objective and subjective evaluation. This is captured by attaching $_d$ to FEELING for property/evaluation as in [Property $FEELING_d$], whereas $_{i/d}$ to FEELING for psychological state as in [Property $FEELING_{i/d}$].

4. Conclusion

In this paper, I have examined previous studies on the Korean polysemous psych-adjectives and their problems. In order to solve the problems, I proposed new criteria that can distinguish polysemous psych-adjectives from monosemous ones. Also, I have tried to provide exact semantic structures of the polysemous psych-adjectives using Conceptual Semantics. In doing so, I proposed a new function FEEL so that it can represent the meaning of one's pure psychological state.

This study deals with only semantic aspects of the psych-adjectives but it can and should be used for explaining idiosyncratic syntactic behaviors of the predicates, their case marking systems in particular. For achieving this goal, further studies have to be conducted on the syntax-semantics interface of these predicates.

References

Culicover, Peter. & Wilkins Wendy. (1986). Control, PRO, and the Projection Principle. *Language* 62, 112-153.

Gerdts, Donna B. & Chenong Youn. (2001). Korean Dative Experiencers: The Evidence for their Status as Surface Subjects. *HSKL VI*, 317-327. Department of Linguistics, Harvard University, Cambridge, Mass.

Han, J-H. (1999). *Morphosyntactic Coding of Information Structure in Korean (Multiple Case Marking, Light Verb Construction, Quantifier Float): A Role & Reference Grammar Account*. Ph.D. dissertation. State University of New York at Buffalo.

Jackendoff, Ray. (2007). *Language, Consciousness, Culture: Essays on Mental Structure*. Cambridge, London: The MIT Press.

Kim, Ilkyu (2007). What Makes Negative Imperative So Natural for Korean [psych-adjective +- e ha-] Constructions? *Paper presentend at PACLIC 2007*. Seoul National University.

Kim, J-N. (2005). *A Research on Korean Adjectives*. Seoul: Yeoklak.

Kim, Sejung. (1994). *The Lexico-semantic Structure of the Psychological Predicate in Korean* (written in Korean). Ph.D. dissertation. Seoul National University.

Kim, Youngjoo. (1990). *The Syntax and Semantics of Korean Case: The Interaction Between Lexical and Syntactic Levels of Representation*. Ph.D. dissertation. Harvard.

Lee, Chungmin. (1976). Cases for psychological verbs in Korean. *Linguistic Journal of Korea* 1(1), 256-296.

Nam, Seunho. (2007). *Event Structure and Argument Structure of Korean Predicates*. Seoul: Seoul National University Press.

Ramchand, Gillian C. 2008. *Verb Meaning and the Lexicon: A First Phase Syntax*. Cambridge: Cambridge University Press.

Talmy, L. 1985. Force dynamic in language and thought. In *Papers from the Twenty-First Regional Meeting of the Chicago Linguistic Society*. Chicago: Chicago Linguistics Society.

Yoo, H-K. (1998). *Research on Korean Adjectives* (written in Korean). Seoul: Hankwuk mwunhwasa.

Zubizarreta, Maria Luisa & Eunjeong Oh. 2007. *The Lexicon-Syntax Interface: The Case of Motion Verbs*. Cambridge, MA: MIT Press.

Sign Language and Computing in a Developing Country: A Research Roadmap for the Next Two Decades in the Philippines

Liza B. Martinez[a] and Ed Peter G. Cabalfin[b]

[a] Philippine Deaf Resource Center, Inc.
27 K-7 Street, West Kamias, Quezon City 1102 Philippines
lizamartinez@phildeafres.org

[b] Computer Vision & Machine Intelligence Laboratory
Department of Computer Science, College of Engineering
University of the Philippines, Diliman, Quezon City 1101 Philippines
ed.cabalfin@gmail.com

Abstract. This paper presents the current situation of Filipino Sign Language in the Deaf community and milestones in sign linguistics research. It highlights key computing research, particularly in Asia as well as enumerates research attempts to date of Philippine academic institutions which have applications in sign language recognition. This paper also touches on technical considerations, economic feasibility, partnerships and other sociocultural considerations appropriate for a developing country such as the Philippines.

Keywords: Filipino Sign Language, Philippines, sign language recognition, research agenda

1. Introduction

1.1. The Filipino deaf community

The last Census on disability reports over 121,000 Filipinos with hearing loss (NSO 2000). The deaf community (as with the other disabled sectors) remains widely marginalized from the mainstream of society, lagging behind recognized disadvantaged groups such as peasants, urban poor, fisher folk and indigenous peoples. Despite this, the Filipino Deaf remain a vibrant and dynamic assemblage of communities throughout the archipelago bound by their visual language. This complex spatial-gestural rule-governed mode of communication endows a strong sense of collective identity. Sign language is at the core of the progressive view of deafness as a culture, and of deaf people as a linguistic minority.

1.2. Research on Filipino Sign Language

There are only several recent milestone studies on the visual-spatial language of the Filipino Deaf community (i.e., Filipino Sign Language or FSL) initiated by Filipinos themselves. In the seventies and eighties, publications by North American writers, drew largely from American Sign Language (ASL) and artificial sign systems to publish highly prescriptive material. The earliest descriptive works are comprised by the pioneering research of Liza Martinez on the sociolinguistics and structure of FSL beginning in the early nineties. To date, the most comprehensive linguistics reference was initiated by Martinez herself (PDRC and PFD, 2004).

Recent papers presented at the 9th Philippine Linguistics Conference covered several topics on the structure and sociolinguistics of FSL. Noteworthy also are the publications of the Philippine Federation of the Deaf on the use of sign language in the Philippines (2008), on regional variation (PFD, 2005, 2007), as well as by the Philippine Deaf Resource Center on applied issues (Tiongson and Martinez, 2007).

1.3.Current Issues on the Status and Use of Filipino Sign Language

Filipino Sign Language has only recently begun to be documented because of the young state of sign linguistics research in the country. It is largely unrecognized by government in the language domains of schools, courtrooms, the workplace, hospitals and mass media. In the community, both deaf and hearing Filipinos may still disregard FSL as an authentic linguistic entity. Despite the considerable research efforts for nearly two decades, the language and its users remain at the periphery of Filipino society. Language policy is virtually non-existent for sign language use (PDRC, 2005).

2. Overview of Current Trends in Automatic Analysis of Sign Language and Related Research

Pavlovic and Sharma (1997) provide a useful review of human-computer interactions for hand gestures although there have been considerable additional discoveries in the past decade. Ong and Ranganath (2005) discuss future scenarios for automatic sign language analysis. Other key studies include Wu et al. 2005, Nolker et al. 2002, Yang et al. 2002 and Chen et al., (in progress).

For specific sign languages, a well established literature on the linguistics of ASL coupled with strong community advocacy for its use have resulted in several computer science collaborations on automatic analysis in the U.S. This include overall gesture recognition (Wei 2008) as well as specific handshape recognition (Athitsos et al., 2008; Potamias and Athistsos 2008; Thangali and Yuan 2008; Vogler, and Goldenstein, In press; Huenerfauth 2005, Vogler & Metataxas, 2001).

In Asia, active collaboration in China by researchers in Beijing and Harbin have been pioneering vision-based recognition systems for Chinese Sign Language (Zhang 2005, 2004) and proposing innovative methods e.g., homography and invariant sign language recognition to minimize problems in viewpoint variance during recognition and testing (Wang 2007, Wang et al, 2006). The research group of Sagawa in Tokyo, Japan has likewise been studying vision-based methods in recognition for Japanese Sign Language for the past several years (e.g., Nakano et al. 2007; Xu et al., 2000).

In the Philippines, current research on FSL number recognition (Sandjaja, 2008) at De La Salle University Manila is studying feature extraction and recognition from a video stream using the Hidden Markov Model and Artificial Neuron Fuzzy Network. Underway are research in the same university for NMS feature extraction (Pamparo, In progress) and recognition of continuous signing (Sarmiento, In progress). Past studies in the same institution with potential contributions to sign language recognition and its applications are strongly motivated by the presence of a large tertiary level program for Deaf students in its academic system: investigations on a sign language modeler (Mejia, et al., 2002), translators (Aguilos, 2007;

Canono, 2004), hand pose graphical interface (Abola, 2004), animation (Cadiz et al., 2003), teaching applications (De Guia et al., 2001; Garin, et al., 1993, Aldea et al., 1993), and communications application (Brosas et al., 2003).

Research by Basa (2000) at the national University of the Philippines has been done on handshape recognition of still images.

3. Considerations

3.1.Technical Considerations

There are two general approaches to capturing hand shape and gesture data: direct measure devices and vision based devices. Direct measure devices provide exact information about hand shape, orientation, location and movement; however, they are often impractical to use outside the lab since people rarely go about their business wearing motion-capture gloves. Computer vision provides a more natural approach.

Sign languages (SL) are fully visual languages. A sentence in SL often contains much more information than a similar spoken or written sentence. Sign languages make extensive use of classifiers, inflections, various spatial grammatical devices through the simultaneous channels of the hands, face and body, thus making vision-based analysis of SL several times more complex than recognition of spoken or written languages. Orientation of the signer relative to the viewer may partially or completely occlude the hands of the former introducing additional challenges. Stereo or multi-camera setups may be required to get around this problem.

Sign language recognition systems need to examine five elements: gross arm movement, hand location, hand shape, hand orientation, and non-manual signals (NMS) which include facial expressions and body posture. However, most previous research have concentrated on the hand and arm gestures. Very little research has been done on NMS, and their integration with the hand gesture data.

Signer independence is another critical area in need of further research. Most prior research use a single signer for training and testing. Error rates increased dramatically when a different signer was introduced.

Increasingly larger vocabulary sets and discourse data also need to be eventually targeted by future research. Research to date have limited their scope to a small number of isolated signs.

3.2.Socioeconomic feasibility and relevance

Where is the place of scientific inquiries on machine intelligence, and human-machine interactions in a small Asian country with a runaway population, a volatile political structure and a large proportion of its citizens faced with the most abject poverty? In an environment where a typical family might earn no more than $8 a day, and barely have enough food on the table or access to the basics of clean water, electricity and education, *on top of* having a member with a hearing disability, what *is* the role of this research?

Ironically, it is precisely this plight of seeming hopelessness that such scientific endeavors need to be pursued. To the Deaf, sign language *is* the core of their existence and connection to the world. And in order to penetrate the barrier of discrimination, the Deaf community needs innovative and visionary science to draw it back into the realm of mainstream society.   This kind of scientific research that has *real* applications in the lives of Filipinos, shall lessen (rather than widen) the often mentioned chasm between the technological *haves* and *have-nots*.

Since machine intelligence and human machine interactions do not aim to replace human interpretation or be mechanical rivals, but rather supplement or compliment such resources, then it could bypass typically unproductive aspects of human interactions in Philippine society such as: corruption, endless politicking, and others.

The technology and skills needed to develop, build, and deploy sign language recognition systems fall under the domain of science and engineering. The Philippines must increase the number of science and engineering professionals in order to meet the demand. Policy changes must be made to support research and development; more than just business process outsourcing. The educational system, starting at the lowest levels, must be improved with additional emphasis on science and math.

Attitudes towards science and technology must also change. More than anything else, interest in science and technology beyond simple consumerism is critical to success in the fields of computer vision and intelligent systems. Filipinos must escape the mindset that we are *only* consumers of technology. We *must* nurture the mindset that we are creators, developers, and builders of technology.

Filipino talent in the IT domain has been gaining recognition (Cristobal, 2006; Damarillo, n.d.). Harnessing this creativity is a logical and relevant strategy in a country beset with numerous economic and political challenges. It is an important thrust based on the fact that "creative-sector occupations in science and technology... have grown since 1980 from 12 percent of the work force to between 30 and 40 percent in most advanced countries today..." and at the same time, "...disturbing that the poorest countries and regions around the world continue to export more than half of their scientific and engineering talent to advanced economies" (Florida, 2006).

Directions in the Philippine IT industry have also been gearing towards tapping this resource. For instance, the 1st Cebu Open Source Summit last month (Cebu Sunstar 2008) recommended the creation of innovation systems and the promotion of technology entrepreneurship as the pillars of development. Metropolitan Cebu's software development sector is generating around $60 million annually, and the population of software developers jumped from 1,000 in 2003, to 3,276 in 2007.

3.3.Sociocultural impact on the Filipino Deaf community

Understanding of natural language processing and modeling of human intelligence will be a strong validation of the Deaf mind and its cognitive processes. This shall help dispel the stigma that Deaf people are mentally *deficient* simply because they use a visual language, and are not native users of written language. By bringing the Deaf into active partnership with academe, scientists, engineers, there shall be further validation of this language community.

Proving structural differences of FSL and ASL from the phonological through the syntactic levels require highly systematic methodologies which can handle dissecting subtle differences in the lexicon and linguistic hierarchy. Applied aspects of computational linguistics will have much to offer in this arena.

Specific targeted language domains for application are: education – development of classroom tools for literacy; legal – stenographic notation during court trials; medical – hospital interviews; workplace – office communications; media / telecommunications: mini-translators, videophones and public facilities / services – instructions / directories.

3.4. Partnerships

The potential impact on, and benefit to the Deaf community of intelligent systems shall hinge on critical partnerships. Deaf people's organizations need to work closely with the academe in the areas of Computer Science, Engineering as well as Linguistics. The Deaf community needs to be constantly giving feedback during the conceptualization and development of research agenda so that the research activity and direction remain relevant. A good example of such collaborations at work is the ongoing "Development on an online Philippine corpus" a joint undertaking between academe, Deaf people's organizations, NGOs and government entities.

To its advantage, the Philippines has a very strong civil society sector. Nongovernment organizations number from 50,000 to 100,000. They serve not only the Filipino people but also cooperate with overseas government agencies and non-governmental organizations. They also have varied scope and expertise in special fields (JICA, n.d.).

4. The Vision

At the initiation of a Sign Language Imaging Group comprised of graduate students from De La Salle University and the University of the Philippines, with the NGO, the Philippine Deaf Resource Center, this research roadmap is proposed for the next two decades:

- By 2013 (5 years hence, or sooner): A good handle on imaging from a phonological perspective; accumulation of 30,000+ (handshapes, NMS, etc.) information

- By 2018 (10 years hence): Grammar of Filipino Sign Language (FSL) documented and in use by imaging researchers

- By 2028 (20 years hence): Real time translation of natural discourse by signer into text (English / Filipino / Philippine language) for nonsigners

5. Potential Challenges and Difficulties

With the current economic crisis, funding for research activity is certainly going to be a primary challenge. The technical challenges shall also depend on the openness of academic administration of Computer Science, Engineering and Linguistics to integrate these applications into its curricular agenda. Coordination across the disciplines shall have to be taken on by leaders who can capably coordinate academe, the Deaf community and government and nongovernment entities. The state of research on sign language linguistics shall also present challenges. The recognition of handshapes, nonmanual signals or segments of sign language discourse shall depend on extensive data and analysis in the linguistics of FSL.

6. Conclusion

The Philippines is poised to make an impact on sign language recognition and computational linguistics in the next 20 years. Partnering of talent in science and technology with strong grassroots deaf empowerment and social responsibility of its other stakeholders shall ensure that this developing democracy shall not drown out the voices of its marginalized minority. Mindful coordination across sectors and disciplines shall hopefully bring about scientific investigations that are not only academically innovative but also concrete, socially relevant and appropriate to the local situation.

References

Abola, J.J.L., M.A.G. Benedicto, L.J. Chiu and I.M. Sarain. 2004. Hand Pose Interpolation. B.S. thesis. De La Salle University - Manila, Philippines.

Aguilos, V.S., C.J.L. Mariano, E.B.G. Mendoza, J.P.D. Orense and C.Y. Ong. 2007. ApoL: A Portable Letter Sign Language Translator. M.S. thesis, De La Salle University - Manila, Philippines.

Aldea, G.M.V., N.G. Guevarra, R.A. Torredondo and S.M.M. Tuvida. 1993. Computer-Assisted Instruction on Elementary English for the Deaf. B.S. thesis. De La Salle University - Manila, Philippines.

Athitsos, V., C. Neidle, S. Sclaroff, J. Nash, A. Stefan, Q. Yuan, A. Thangali. In press. The American Sign Language Video Dataset. Proceedings: IEEE Workshop on Computer Vision and Pattern Recognition for Human Communicative Behavior Analysis.

Basa, T. 2000. Recognition of Static Hand Gestures Using Support Vector Machines. M.S. thesis, University of the Philippines, Diliman, Quezon City, Philippines.

Brosas, J.M.B., L.A.A. Chan, F.C. Escolar and I.T. Lim, Iceal. 2003. A PC-Based Telephone Device for the Deaf using Speech-to-Lip Speaking Animation. B.S. thesis. De La Salle University - Manila, Philippines.

Cadiz, M.M.E. 2003. Sign Language Using Motion Capture Based Animation. M.S. thesis. De La Salle University - Manila, Philippines.

Canono, P. III.T., M.C.G.Leonor, D.O.O. Santos, J.V. Suratos and P.G. Tuason. 2004. Letter Sign Language Translator. B.S. thesis. De La Salle University - Manila, Philippines.

Cebu Sunstar. 2008. ICT Stakeholders Aim to Make Cebu an Innovation Destination.

Chen, Q., N. Geogranas and E.M. Petriu. In press. Hand Gesture Recognition using Haar-like Features and a Stochastic Context-Free Grammar. IEEE Trans. Instrumentation and Measurement.

Cristobal, A. 2006. Unleashing Filipino Creativity and Talent through IP Education, Training and Research. National Symposium on Intellectual Property Education, Training and Research, Jan 30-31, Makati, Philippines.

Damarillo, W. n.d. www.exist.com/blogs/ Funding-software-innovations-Philippines.html.

Florida, R. 2006. Minds on the Move. In: Damarillo, W. n.d.

Garin, V., J.J. Jimenez, J. Miranda and R. Santos. 1992. Word-Image Conversion for Deaf Education (WICONDED). B.S. thesis. De La Salle University - Manila, Philippines.

Huenerfauth, M. 2005. Representing Coordination and Non Coordination in American Sign Language. Proceedings: ASSETS '05, Oct.9-12, 2005. Baltimore, Maryland, U.S.A.

Japan International Coordinating Agency. n.d. http://www.jica-ngodesk.ph/english/Page4.htm.

Mejia, M.M.I., M.J.G. Pantig, N.R.P. Que and J. Velasco. 2002. HandTalk : An Interactive Web-Based Sign Language Modeler. B.S. thesis. De La Salle University - Manila, Philippines.

Nakano, Y., K. Murata, M. Enomoto , Y. Arimoto, Y. Asa and H. Sagawa. 2008. Modeling Human-Agent Interaction Using Bayesian Network Technique. New Frontiers in Artificial Intelligence. Lecture Notes in Computer Science. vol. 4914. Heidelberg: Springer Berlin.

National Sign Language Committee. 2008. Status Report on the Use of Sign Language in the Philippines. Metro Manila: Philippine Federation of the Deaf.

Nolker, C., H. Ritter. 2002. Visual Recognition of Continuous Hand Postures. IEEE Trans. Neural Networks, 13(4), 983-994.

Ong, S. C.W. & S. Ranganath. 2005. Automatic Sign Language Analysis: A Survey and the Future Beyond Lexical Meaning. IEEE Trans. Pattern Analysis & Machine Intelligence, 27(6), 873-891.

Pamparo, D. I. In progress. Extraction of Facial Action Units for Filipino Sign Language.

Pavlovic, V.I. , R. Sharma, & T.S. Huang. 1997. Visual Interpretation of Hand Gestures for Human-Computer Interaction: A Review. IEEE Trans. Pattern Analysis & Machine Intelligence, 19(7), 677-695.

Philippine Deaf Resource Center. 2005. Preliminary Sectoral Position Papers for an Initiative in Language Planning for Sign Language Policy for the Republic of the Philippines: A Compilation. Unpublished manuscript, Quezon City.

Philippine Deaf Resource Center and Philippine Federation of the Deaf. 2004. An Introduction to Filipino Sign Language. Quezon City: Philippine Deaf Resource Center.

Philippine Federation of the Deaf. 2007. A Compilation of Signs from Regions of the Philippines, Part 2. Metro Manila: Philippine Federation of the Deaf.

Philippine Federation of the Deaf. 2005. A Compilation of Signs from Regions of the Philippines, Part 1. Metro Manila: Philippine Federation of the Deaf.

Potamias, M. and V. Athitsos 2008. Nearest Neighbor Search Methods for Handshape Recognition. Petra. 1-8.

Sarmiento, E. In progress. Vision-Based Continuous Filipino Sign Language Recognition.

Thangali, A. and Q. Yuan. 2008. Handshape Recognition for Query-by-Sign ASL Dictionary. 2008 Boston University Computer Science Research Open House. http://www.cs.bu.edu/IAP/ResearchDay2008/IAP08.pdf

Tiongson, P. and L. Martinez. 2007. Full Access: A Compendium on Sign Language Advocacy and Access of the Deaf to the Legal System. Quezon City: Philippine Deaf Resource Center.

Vasilis, A., M. Potamias, P. Papapetrou and G. Kollios. In press. Nearest Neighbor Retrieval Using Distance-Based Hashing. Proceedings: IEEE Conference on Data Engineering, April 2008.

Vogler, C. and S. Goldenstein. In press. Facial Movement Analysis in ASL. Universal Access in the Information Society.

Vogler, C. and D. Metaxas. 2001. A Framework for Recognizing the Simultaneous Aspects of American Sign Language. Computer Vision and Image Understanding, 81, 358-384.

Wang, Q., X. Chen, C. Wang and W. Gao. 2006. A Verification Method for Viewpoint Invariant Sign Language Recognition. International Conference on Pattern Recognition, 1, 456-459.

Wang, Q., X. Chen, C. Wang and W. Gao. 2006. Sign language Recognition from Homography. IEEE International Conference on Multimedia and Expo, pp. 429-432.

Wei, K. 2008. American Sign Language Finger Spelling Recognition System. http://kevinhaptics.blogspot.com/

Wu, Y., J. Lin and T. S. Huang. 2005. Analyzing and Capturing Articulated Hand Motion in Image Sequences. IEEE Trans. Pattern Analysis & Machine Intelligence, 27(12), 1910-1922.

Xu, M., B. Raytchev, K. Sakaue, O.Hasegawa, A.Koizumi , M. Takeuchi and H. Sagawa. 2000. A Vision-Based Method for Recognizing Non-Manual Information in Japanese Sign Language. Advances in Multimodal Interfaces - ICMI 2000. Lecture Notes in Computer Science, 1948. Heidelberg: Springer Berlin.

Yang, M-H, N. Ahuja and M. Tabb. 2002. Extraction of 2D Motion Trajectories and its Application to Hand Gesture Recognition. IEEE Trans. Pattern Analysis & Machine Intelligence, 24(8), 1061-1074.

Unsupervised Approach for Dialogue Act Classification

Kiyonori Ohtake

National Institute of Information and Communications Technology (NICT)/
Advanced Telecommunications Research Institute International (ATR)
2-2-2 Hikaridai, Keihanna Science City 619-0288, JAPAN
kiyonori.ohtake (at) nict go.jp

Abstract. This paper presents an unsupervised approach for dialogue act (DA) classification. We used a latent variable model to compress the dimensions of the feature vector. We introduced a paraphraser to reduce the variety of expressions and to solve the pragmatic problem for DA classification. The paraphraser seemed to work well on some DA classifications in the unsupervised approach. The results obtained by the unsupervised approach were compared with the manually annotated labels. A preliminary experiment for semi-supervised tagging was also carried out, and we discuss these results.

Keywords: Unsupervised, Dialogue Act, Paraphrasing, Latent Variable Model.

1. Introduction

Recognizing the intentions of a user in a dialogue system is very important. So far, many methods have been developed to infer a user's intention in a dialog situation. To infer the user's intention in an utterance, the utterance can be categorized into given classes. Therefore, many studies have designed the classes called dialogue act (DA) labels that approximate a speaker's intention. They annotated the labels on a corpus to analyze the phenomena for DA interaction or to develop a DA tagger in order to infer the DA label from a speech segment (e.g. some utterances, an utterance, or a part of an utterance). Most studies on DA taggers were based on a supervised method (e.g., (Stolcke et al., 2000; Tanaka and Yokoo, 1999)). The labels used in a DA tagger have to be predefined, and supervised methods require a corpus that is manually annotated by the labels.

On the other hand, it is difficult to design a tag set (labels) that can be used to annotate a corpus because the design of a tag set depends on the domain and the task. Therefore, we have to redesign the tag set and construct a corpus annotated with a new tag set if we apply our system to different domains or tasks. In addition, designing a tag set that can be used in any domain or task is very difficult. However, we have to annotate DA tags on a corpus, because many applications require predefined DA tags.

This paper discusses an unsupervised approach to infer the user's intention in a situation by using a dialog system. Unsupervised approach may not achieve highly accurate results when compared to the supervised approach. However, in any domain or task, the unsupervised approach can yield human DA annotators with machine judgments of the DA classification that may be useful to keep the consistency of DA annotation results for a corpus.

In addition, annotating a corpus with given labels is very time-consuming. An unsupervised method is independent of annotation and designing the tag set. In order to achieve an unsupervised method, we need an unsupervised clustering method. So far, many clustering methods have been proposed and discussed for applications in natural language processing (NLP), such as works by Zhao and Karypis (Zhao and Karypis, 2005). However, an utterance is very short against a document that is used in a common NLP application. In addition, the

22nd Pacific Asia Conference on Language, Information and Computation, pages 445–451

feature space that is used to express any natural language expression is extremely large and an utterance is expressed by a very sparse vector in the feature space. Therefore, it is very important to handle a sparse feature vector of an utterance in the huge feature space.

2. DA Annotation

Here, we construct a dialogue system to make an itinerary of one-day sightseeing tour and also develop a dialog corpus for this system. The corpus consists of 100 dialogues between a professional tour guide and a tourist. Each dialog is almost 30-min long. An annotated corpus with DA is needed to construct our dialogue system. Therefore, we have started to design a DA tag set and annotate the DA tags on the corpus.

However, there are several problems that make it difficult for us to maintain consistency in the annotation as follows: (a) segmentation, (b) pragmatics, and (c) multifunctionality.

Sometimes, utterances are fragmental, and it is difficult to recognize an appropriate boundary of an utterance for a DA tag. Hinarejos et al. reported that the correct segmentation for DA is very important for obtaining an accurate result in DA tagging (Hinarejos et al., 2006).

There is a pragmatic problem in the annotation of DA tags. For example, the utterance "Do you know what time it is?" can be recognized as a yes/no **question** from the surface information, but the speaker's intention is a **request** such as "Please tell me the time."

In addition, utterances are generally multifunctional. This problem is closely related to the design of the DA tag set. So far, many DA tag sets have been proposed and used to annotate corpora. Some of them have several layers (e.g., DAMSL (Allen and Core, 1997)) and dimensions.

In this paper, we focus on the pragmatic problem in the DA annotation. We try to resolve the pragmatics problem by paraphrasing. If a euphemism is paraphrased into a straightforward expression, the dialogue system can easily understand the expression.

3. Unsupervised method for DA annotation

In this section, we describe an unsupervised approach to classify an utterance. The overview of the unsupervised approach is as follows:
1. Construct a feature vector from an utterance.
2. Reduce the dimensions of the feature space using a latent variable model.
3. Classify the vector whose dimension was reduced using an unsupervised classification method.

After constructing the feature vector, we use a latent variable model to reduce the dimension of the feature space. Then, we use an unsupervised classification method to classify the vector that produced by using a latent variable model. Finally, we find the class to which the utterance belongs.

We also introduce a rule-based paraphraser to reduce the variety of expressions because a different expression is treated to be completely different in a latent variable model.

3.1. Latent variable models

Several unsupervised text modeling methods, such as PLSI (probabilistic latent semantic indexing (Hofmann, 1999)) and LDA (latent Dirichlet allocation (Blei et al., 2003)), are available to model a text based on the features of words and their frequencies. In general, the latent variables indicate the topics of each segment (some sentences for text or some utterances for speech), and we can use the topic information indicated by the latent variables of the model as a compact surrogate expression for a given feature vector of an utterance. In other words, we can use these models to reduce the dimension of the feature space. Once the model parameters are learned from a corpus, we can infer the topic of a given utterance. If we constructed a latent variable model with k latent variables, we get a k-dimensional vector. This vector is called a topic vector.

We used PLSI—a latent variable model— for general co-occurrence data that associates an unobserved topic variable $z \in Z = \{z_1, \cdots, z_k\}$ with each observation, i.e. with each occurrence of word $w \in W = \{w_1, \cdots, w_M\}$ in document $d \in D = \{d_1, \cdots, d_N\}$.

The probability of a topic under the document ($P(z \mid d)$) is approximated by the following formula:

$$P(z)^2 \prod_{w \in d} P(w \mid z) \sum_{w} n(d, w) P(w \mid z), \quad (1)$$

where $n(d, w)$ indicates the frequency of word w in the document d. The details about how to introduce Equation (1) have been previously shown (Ohtake, 2005). In that paper, Ohtake used PLSI and LDA to evaluate whether a paraphrasing pair is contextually independent or not, as well as if there was not a big difference in the performances between them. Therefore, we use PLSI because it is simpler and faster than LDA.

3.2. Unsupervised clustering method

There are several unsupervised clustering methods. We used the K-means clustering algorithm (e.g., (Duda et al., 2000)) that is very simple because, at the moment, a highly sophisticated method in which analyzing the tendency of the results by an unsupervised approach and manually annotated labels is not necessary. In addition, we have to investigate whether a topic vector reasonably expresses a DA before using a sophisticated clustering method.

3.3. Paraphrasing to reduce variety of expressions

The use of a wide variety of expressions that conveys the same information is natural. However, a different expression is treated to be completely different in a feature space. Therefore, paraphrasing techniques seem to be promising approaches to understand the variety of expressions. In particular, in Japanese, the ending of a sentence or utterance has many expressions even though they convey the same meaning. These expressions are related to the Japanese honorific system, and in most cases the difference in the expression does not affect the DA classification.

We construct a rule-based paraphraser that is very similar to the paraphraser proposed by Ohtake and Yamamoto (Ohtake and Yamamoto, 2001), and most of the rules in the honorific system were derived from their paraphraser. The paraphraser was carefully designed to be free from errors and developed to paraphrase a variety of expressions that convey the same meaning into a standard expression.

The rules of the paraphraser are based on a morphological analysis. We can use regular expressions for pattern matching in a rule and we can conjugate any morphemes that have conjugation to fit in its context. Therefore, a small number of rules cover a large number of targets that need to be paraphrased.

4. Experiments

In this section, we describe our experiments and introduce the data set. We also mention the features that were used in the construction of the PLSI models.

4.1. Data set

We used the ATR Dialogue Database (Morimoto et al., 1994). This database consists of 1,983 dialogues (83,052 utterances) in traveling situations. We used manually transcribed Japanese texts in the database. In the transcribed texts, fillers and disfluencies are tagged with a marker. In order to use precisely analyzed results, we eliminated the fillers and disfluencies in the transcribed texts by a morphological analyzer that was used to obtain morphemes as units like words.

We annotated 13 dialogues (489 utterances) with DA tags used in the paper by Tanaka and Yokoo (Tanaka and Yokoo, 1999) to evaluate the unsupervised classification. The remainder of the data, namely 1,970 dialogues (82,563 utterances), were used to estimate the parameters of the PLSI model.

The original DA tag set that consisted of 26 tags was designed to annotate the dialogue segments that were shorter than an utterance. Therefore, there were multi-labeled utterances in our annotation results because in some cases, a person utters several things in a single utterance. For example, when a person is asked a YES or NO question (YN-QUESTION), the person who answers might say "Yes, I will...(YES, INFORM)." In this case, we treated the last DA tag as the labeled tag of the utterance. In the annotated dialogues, 16 tags were actually used.

4.2. Features for PLSI

We used uni-gram and bi-gram word frequencies. In this paper, a word is considered as a morpheme[1] in Japanese. An element of the feature consists of a pair of morpheme's basic form and POS (part of speech). However, numbers and proper names are generalized by eliminating this basic form. In other words, the features of the numbers and proper names are recognized by only by their POS.

In general, PLSI requires words and their frequencies in order to construct a model from a corpus. However, Serafin et al. showed that adding extra features works well with latent semantic analysis in the DA classification (Serafin et al., 2004). The PLSI model can be regarded as a probabilistic version of a latent semantic analysis. Therefore, we can expect the same effect on PLSI, and we introduced the uni-gram and bi-gram features.

The segment for a unit of a document consists of the utterance and its previous utterance. The dialogues in the database are conversations between two people such as a customer and a clerk.

4.3. Number of variables and performance on differentiation

We constructed PLSI models[2] on the number of latent variables, namely 10, 50, 100, 200, and 300, in order to determine the number of latent variables. The parameter for tempered EM (TEM)—a technique used to ease the over-fitting problem—was set to 0.9 (we use this value in all of the experiments in this study) because this value exhibited the best performance in the preliminary experiments.

We formulated topic vectors from the evaluation dialogue set, and we prepared the average vectors for each DA label from these topic vectors. Finally, we compared each average vector with the others according to their cosine values, and we averaged the cosine values. Therefore, these numbers indicate the distinguishing ability of topic vectors, where a smaller number is better. The average values for each number of latent variables (10, 50, 100, 200, and 300) with all the DA labels are as follows: 0.607, 0.334, 0.288, 0.290 and 0.275, respectively.

4.4. Impact of paraphrasing

We applied the rule-based paraphraser to the data set (83,052 utterances), and all of the 56,027 utterances were paraphrased.

First, we show the result of an unsupervised clustering result with manually annotated labels using a non-paraphrased corpus. We constructed the PLSI model with 100 latent variables from the learning corpus that was not paraphrased. The test set was fed to the PLSI model, yielding the topic vectors. Then, we used the K-means clustering method with 16 clusters because the size of the tag set that was used to annotate the test set is 16. The result is shown in the "without paraphraser" column of Table 1.

Second, we show the result of an unsupervised clustering result with manually annotated labels using a paraphrased corpus. The result is shown in the "with paraphraser" column of

---

[1] We used a morphological analyzer available at `http://mecab.sourceforge.net/`
[2] We used the package available at `http://chasen.org/~taku/software/plsi/`

Table 1. Note that the cluster IDs found in the columns, "with paraphraser" and "without paraphraser" are independent of each other.

Table 1: Unsupervised clustering result with/without paraphrasing and manual labels

manual labels (freq.)	without paraphraser (cluster ID: its frequency)	with paraphraser (cluster ID: its frequency)
ACK (68)	B:7, G:24, H:2, I:1, M:3, N:7, O:8, P:16	a:12, c:14, f:2, g:4, k:3, n:8, p:25
ACT-REQ (44)	B:4, C:3, D:1, F:1, H:6, I:1, J:1, K:1, M:11, N:10, O:5	b:1, c:1, d:1, f:2, g:2, i:7, j:25, k:4, l:1
ALERT (1)	N:1	o:1
APOLOGY (2)	H:1, N:1	n:1, o:1
CONF-Q(29)	B:4, C:1, D:1, H:1, I:3, J:4, K:1, L:1, M:3, N:8, O:2	c:2, d:1, e:6, f:1, g:2, i:2, n:5, o:10
FAREWELL (16)	K:8, M:3, N:5	g:1, i:2, k:2, n:1, o:10
G-WISHES (1)	K:1	o:1
GREET (8)	B:3, M:1, N:4	g:3, o:5
INFORM (198)	B:27, C:11, D:10, E:6, F:2, G:2, H:35, I:7, J:12, K:7, L:14, M:26, N:27, O:12	a:11, b:2, c:1, d:4, e:6, f:16, g:28, h:13, i:10, j:3, k:16, m:18, n:5, o:63, p:2
PERM-REQ (1)	E:1	g:1
SUGGEST (6)	F:3, H:2, M:1	c:2, f:2, m:1, o:1
THANK (20)	A:16, I:2, K:1, N:1	a:1, g:2, i:2, l:10, n:4, o:1
THANK-RES (2)	K:2	o:2
WH-Q (40)	C:1, D:2, F:16, H:4, I:2, K:7, L:2,	a:1, c:19, f:6, g:1, i:10, k:2, n:1
YES (18)	B:6, G:2, H:1, I:5, O:4	a:6, g:9, o:1, p:2
YN-Q (35)	B:2, C:4, F:4, H:6, I:1, M:8, N:7, O:3	a:2, b:4, c:12, f:4, g:2, h:1, i:4, j:1, n:1, o:4

4.5. Semi-supervised approach—preliminary experiment

We carried out a very small experiment for the semi-supervised approach. The experiment is small because the amount of annotated data is very small. We have only 13 annotated dialogues. We used 12 dialogues to construct the average vectors for each label, where a withheld dialogue (32 utterances) was used as the test data.

The method to classify an utterance is very simple. From a learning set, we construct the average vectors for each label. Then, an utterance is given to construct a topic vector using PLSI with 100 latent variables and the average vector closest to the topic vector is calculated. Finally, the label of the average vector is inferred from the utterance's classification. The accuracies of the results are 37.5% (12/32) without paraphrasing and 21.9% (7/32) with paraphrasing.

5. Discussion

When using the latent variable model, the number of latent variables is an issue. In our experiment, there was not a considerable difference between the result using 100 latent variables and the results using more than 100 latent variables; therefore, 100 latent variables seem sufficient for our experiment.

We compared the unsupervised approach and manually annotated labels. It is difficult to conclude whether the unsupervised approach works well or not. There were some cases in which the label and cluster have a strong correlation. For example, the label "THANK" and cluster ID **A** and the label "WH-Q" and ID **F** in the "without paraphraser" column of Table 1 indicate very good cases. On the other hand, the original label "INFORM" indicated a miscellaneous category, and there were so many utterances labeled "INFORM." Thus, utterances labeled "INFORM" were classified into many clusters.

We paraphrased our data set to reduce the variety of expressions. From Table 1, we find a very clear tendency in the result of the label "ACT-REQ (ACTION-REQUEST)" that was used to label utterances asking someone to perform a certain task. In Japanese, there is a large variety of expressions to this end. Without paraphrasing, these expressions are treated differently. On the contrary, we treated them as the same expression when they were paraphrased into a single expression. Therefore, paraphrasing works quite well on utterances labeled "ACT-REQ."

We have to consider the number of variables in a latent variable model and the number of clusters in an unsupervised clustering method. In our experiment, the number of cluster used was the same as the number of labels that were used in the learning corpus. However, if we used more clusters, we might be able to classify a large cluster into proper sub-clusters.

On the other hand, there were some clusters having many elements that correspond to many manually labeled tags. For example, cluster ID **N** in the "without paraphraser" column of Table 1 was related to many labels. From the observation of the test set, the phrase "*onegai shimasu* (please)" seems to be strongly related to this cluster. This phrase is frequently used in Japanese when requesting someone to perform a particular task. Ten utterances labeled "ACT-REQ" were classified in this cluster. However, this phrase is too common to use as a feature. Meanwhile, cluster ID **o** in the "with paraphraser" column of Table 1 was also related to many labels. In these cases, the expressions of number seem to be related to this cluster. We have to consider what feature is effective for DA classification.

We carried out a very small preliminary experiment using a semi-supervised approach. The size of the learning data for the semi-supervised method was too small to evaluate the method. In addition, the accuracies were quite low—37.5% without paraphrasing and 21.9% with paraphrasing. Contrary to our expectations, the result with paraphrasing was worse than that without paraphrasing. The observation results suggested several points. First, some labels did not match their utterances after paraphrasing. The expressions used in the utterances were drastically changed by the paraphraser and the annotated labels had become inappropriate for the paraphrased utterances. Thus, we should control such paraphrasing. When we re-annotated the paraphrased test set, the accuracy increased from 21.9% to 31.3%. Second, paraphrasing caused a side effect. Reducing the variety of expressions constricted the features used by the PLSI. The paraphraser was not designed for DA classification. Some phrases should not be paraphrased and we should retain the original expressions.

6. Conclusion

This paper discussed an unsupervised approach for DA classification using a rule-based paraphraser and a latent semantic model. In the experiments, a PLSI model with 100 latent variables was found to be efficient with respect to its distinguishing ability. At the moment, on the other hand, we are unsure whether the unsupervised approach is promising when comparing the results obtained by the unsupervised approach with the manually labeled results.

The introduction of a paraphraser that reduces the variety of expressions showed good results. In particular, in Japanese, there are many euphemisms for asking someone to perform a particular task. The paraphraser paraphrased such expressions effectively.

Several points remain for our future work as follows:

- A further analysis of the classification results would be useful. In particular, we have to investigate whether the compressed feature space produced by PLSI is really effective for DA classification or not.
- Introducing other features would be effective. We only used uni-gram and bi-gram morphemes. Introducing tri-gram morphemes or other features such as dependency relationships may be effective.
- Tuning the paraphraser is required. The paraphraser was not tuned for DA classification. The paraphraser was designed to be generic.

In addition, we will apply this unsupervised method to the corpus that is now under development for DA annotation.

References

Allen, James and Mark Core. 1997. Draft of DAMSL: Dialog act markup in several layers. *Technical Report, Discourse Research Initiative.*

Blei, David M., Andrew Y. Ng, and Michael I. Jordan. 2003. Latent Dirichlet allocation. *Journal of Machine Learning Research*, 3:993-1022.

Duda, Richard O., Peter E. Hart, and David G. Stork. 2000. Pattern Classification. A Wiley-Interscience Publication.

Hinarejos, Carlos D. Martínez, Ramón Granell, and José Miguel Benedí. 2006. Segmented and unsegmented dialogue-act annotation with statistical dialogue models. In *Proceedings of the COLING/ACL 2006*, pp. 563-570.

Hofmann, Thomas. 1999. Probabilistic Latent Semantic Indexing. In *Proceedings of the 22nd Annual ACM Conference on Research and Development in Information Retrieval*, pp. 50-57.

Morimoto, Tsuyoshi, N. Uratani, T. Takezawa, O. Furuse, Y. Sobashima, H. Iida, A. Nakamura, Y. Sagisaka, N. Higuchi and Y. Yamazaki. 1994. A speech and language database for speech translation research. In *Proceedings of ICSLP '94*, pp. 1791-1794.

Ohtake, Kiyonori and Kazuhide Yamamoto. 2001. Paraphrasing honorifics. In *Workshop Proceedings of Automatic Paraphrasing: Theories and Applications (NLPRS2001 Post-conference Workshop)*, pp. 13-20.

Ohtake, Kiyonori. 2005. Evaluating contextual dependency of paraphrases using a latent variable model. In *Proceedings of the Third International Workshop on Paraphrasing (IWP2005) conjunct with IJCNLP 2005*, pp. 65-72.

Serafin, Riccardo and Brbara Di Eugenio. 2004. FLSA: Extending latent semantic analysis with features for dialogue act classification. In *Proceedings of the 42nd Meeting of the Association for Computational Linguistics (ACL'04)*, pp. 692-699.

Stolcke, Andreas, K. ries, N. Coccaro, E. Shriberg, R. Bates, D. Jurafsky, P. Taylor, R. Martin, C. Van Ess-Dykema, and M. Meteer. 2000. Dialogue act modeling for automatic tagging and recognition of conversational speech. *Computational Linguistics*, 26(3):339-373.

Tanaka, Hideki and Akio Yokoo. 1999. An efficient statistical speech act type tagging system for speech translation systems. In *Proceedings of the Thirty Seventh Annual Meeting of the Association for Computational Linguistics (ACL'99)*, pp. 381-388.

Zhao, Ying and George Karypis. 2005. Hierarchical clustering algorithms for document datasets. *Data Mining and Knowledge Discovery*, 10: 141-168.

Automatically Extracting Templates from Examples for NLP Tasks [*]

Ethel Ong, Bryan Anthony Hong, Vince Andrew Nuñez
College of Computer Studies, De La Salle University, Manila, Philippines
onge@dlsu.edu.ph, bashx5@yahoo.com, link7488933@yahoo.com

Abstract. In this paper, we present the approaches used by our NLP systems to automatically extract templates for example-based machine translation and pun generation. Our translation system is able to extract an average of 73.25% correct translation templates, resulting in a translation quality that has a low word error rate of 18% when the test document contains sentence patterns matching the training set, to a high 85% when the test document is different from the training corpus. Our pun generator is able to extract 69.2% usable templates, resulting in computer-generated puns that received an average score of 2.13 as compared to 2.7 for human-generated puns from user feedback.

Keywords: Template Extraction, Machine Translation, Joke Generation.

1. Introduction

Templates have been used in IE as extraction patterns to retrieve relevant information from documents (Muslea, 1999), and in NLG as forms that can be filled in to generate syntactically correct and coherent text for human readers. They have also been used in machine translation (Cicekli and Guvenir, 2003) and (McTait, 2001), and in pun generation (Ritchie et al, 2006).

In this paper, we present two NLP systems. TExt (Go et al, 2006 and Nunez, 2008), a bi-directional English-Filipino machine translator, extracts translation templates from a bilingual corpus, and together with a bilingual lexicon, uses these templates to translate an input text to another language. T-Peg (Hong, 2008) utilizes semantic and phonetic knowledge to capture the wordplay used in a training set of human jokes, resulting in templates that contain variables, tags, and word relationships that are used to generate punning riddles.

Because manually creating templates can be tedious and time consuming, several researches have worked on automatically extracting templates from training examples that have been preprocessed. In our previous example-based MT, SalinWika (Bautista et al, 2005), templates are extracted from a bilingual corpus that has been pre-tagged and manually annotated with word features, resulting in a long training process. Its successor, TExt (Go et al, 2006), did away with a tagger and instead requires a parallel bilingual corpus and an English-Filipino lexicon to align pairs of untagged sentences to extract translation templates.

Our pun generator, T-Peg (Hong, 2008), on the other hand, subjects the training examples through a pre-processing stage to identify nouns, verbs and adjectives. Instead of manually annotating the example set, the training algorithm relies on existing linguistic resources and tools to perform its task.

---

[*] Acknowledgments: TExt Translation is part of the "Hybrid English-Filipino Machine Translation System" project that is funded by the Department of Science and Technology – Philippine Center for Advanced Science and Technology Research and Development (DOST-PCASTRD). It was developed by Kathleen Go, Manimin Morga, Vince Nunez, and Francis Veto as their undergraduate thesis.

22nd Pacific Asia Conference on Language, Information and Computation, pages 452–459

2. Extracting and Using Templates for Machine Translation

TExt Translation (Go et al, 2006) is an EBMT system that automatically extracts translation templates from a bilingual corpus and uses these to translate English text to Filipino and vice versa. It relies on a bilingual corpus for its training examples, which contains a set of sentences in the source language with a corresponding translation in the target language. Correspondences between the sentences are learned and stored in a database of translation templates.

A translation template is a bilingual pair of patterns where corresponding words and phrases are aligned and replaced with variables. Each template is a sentence preserving the syntactic structure and ordering of words in the source text, regardless of the variance in the sentence structures of the source and target languages. During translation, the input sentence is used to find a matching source template, while the target template is used to generate the translation.

2.1. Translation Templates and Chunks

TExt learns two types of translation templates using the Translation Template Learner heuristic presented in (Cicekli and Güvenir, 2003). A similarity translation template contains a sequence of similar items learned from a pair of input sentences and variables representing the differences. A difference translation template contains a sequence of differing items from the pair of input sentences, and variables representing the similarities. Consider the sentence pairs S1 and S2, and the learned similarity (T1) and difference templates (T2 and T3).

```
S1: The boy is walking. ↔ Naglalakad ang batang lalaki.
S2: The teacher is walking. ↔ Naglalakad ang guro.
T1: The [1] is walking. ↔ Naglalakad ang [1].
T2: [2] boy [3]. ↔ [3] [2] batang lalaki.
T3: [2] teacher [3]. ↔ [3] [2] guro.
```

Using the lexicon to align the corresponding English and Filipino words in the input sentences, the tokens "The", "is walking", and "Naglalakad ang" are retained as constants of T1, while "boy/batang lalaki", and "teacher/guro" are retained as constants of T2 and T3, respectively. [1], [2], and [3] are variables in the template.

A template variable, called chunk, is represented by a numeric value, e.g., [1], to refer to its domain. The domain allows chunks to have a reference from their source template. Specific chunks are labelled as [X.n], where X is its domain and n is its sequence number in the domain. Only the domain is needed to identify if a chunk can be used in translation. For example, if the domain in a template is [X], then any chunk with a domain "X" can be used to fill the variables in the template. From S1 and S2, chunks [1.1] and [1.2] are learned. If another chunk [1.3] is learned from a different set of input sentence pairs in a later training session, then all these chunks can be used during translation to fill variable [1] in T1.

```
[1.1]: boy ↔ batang lalaki          [1.2]: teacher ↔ guro
[1.3]: carpenter ↔ karpentero
```

2.2. Learning Translation Templates

Aligned sentence pairs are analyzed and translation templates are extracted following three steps, namely template refinement (TR), deriving templates from sentences (DTS), and deriving templates from chunks (DTC). TR compares an aligned sentence pair against existing templates in the database. An aligned sentence pair is said to match a given template if it contains a token that matches exactly with a corresponding token in the template itself. There must be a corresponding match in both the source and target languages for the template to be considered. Through these similarities, a candidate refinement is identified. Consider the input sentence pair S3, and the existing template T4 and chunks [4], [5] and [6].

```
S3:    The boy is hopping in the park. ↔
       Nagkakandirit ang lalaki sa parke.
T4:    The [4] is [5] in the [6]. ↔  [5] ang [4] sa [6].
[4.1]: girl ↔ babae          [5.1]: walking ↔ naglalakad
[6.1]: street ↔ kalsada
```

TR considers S3 as a candidate refinement for T4 because of their matching tokens (in *italics*). The identified differences are used to create new chunks, namely [4.2], [5.2] and [6.2].

```
[4.2]:  boy ↔ lalaki            [5.2]:  hopping ↔ nagkakandirit
[6.2]:  park ↔ parke
```

If refinement cannot be performed, DTS is performed to compare the new sentences pair with other aligned sentence pairs. Both Similarity Template Learning (STL) and Difference Template Learning (DTL), as presented in Cicekli and Guvenir (2003), are performed. The differing elements in the input are created as chunks for the similarity templates, while the similar elements are created as chunks for the difference templates. DTL always generates two difference templates for each matching input sentence pairs. Consider sentence pairs S4 and S5.

```
S4: My favorite pet is a dog. ↔ Aso ang aking paboritong alaga.
S5: My favorite color is red. ↔ Pula ang aking paboritong kulay.
```

All similar tokens between S4 and S5 (in *italics*) are preserved as constants in the new similarity template T5 while the differing elements are created as chunks [7] and [8]. On the other hand, all differing tokens are preserved as constants in the new difference templates T6 and T7 while the similar element is created as a new chunk [9].

```
T5:      My favorite [7] is [8] ↔ [8] ang aking paboritong [7]
[7.1]:   pet ↔ alaga                [7.2]: color ↔ kulay
[8.1]:   a dog ↔ aso                [8.2]: red ↔ pula
T6:      [9] pet is a dog ↔ Aso ang [9] alaga.
T7:      [9] color is red ↔ Pula ang [9] kulay.
[9.1]:   My favorite ↔ aking paboritong
```

Templates can also be derived from chunks using DTC. Consider the new sentence pair S6 and existing chunks [10] and [11]. DTC simply takes matching chunks from the knowledge base and uses them as variables to replace parts of S6, resulting in template T8.

```
S6:      Filipinos are known to be cheerful and hospitable. ↔
         Kilala ang mga Pilipino sa pagiging masayahin at mapanauhin.
[10.3]:  Filipinos ↔ mga Pilipino
[11.2]:  hospitable ↔ mapanauhin
T8:      [10.3] are known to be cheerful and [11.2] ↔
         Kilala ang [10.3] sa pagiging masayahin at [11.2]
```

2.3. Using the Learned Templates in Translation

Input sentence tokens are analyzed to collect candidate templates and chunks, which must have at least one word used in the input sentence. The candidates are assigned scores according to the structure of the template or chunk, the presence or absence of chunk variables in templates, and the presence of word matches in templates. The translation output that produces the highest total score is used. In case of a tie, the first candidate with the highest score is selected.

3. Extracting and Using Templates for Pun Generation

T-Peg (Hong, 2008) generates punning riddles using templates learned from training examples of human-generated puns. Punning riddles are jokes that use wordplay and covers pronunciation, spelling, and possible semantic similarities and differences. Various resources are utilized by the learning algorithm, namely the Unisyn phonetic lexicon (Fitt, 2002) that provides the phonological information of words, the MontyTagger (Liu, 2003) for POS tagging, the Electronic Lexical Knowledge Base (Jarmasz and Szpakowicz, 2006) to get the base form of words, the WordNet (2006) for synonym lookup, and the ConceptNet (Liu, et. al. 2004) for semantic analysis to describe the relations between objects.

3.1. Extracting Punning Templates

A T-Peg template contains the source pun (in question-answer format) with variables replacing keywords in the pun. Variables are of three types. Similar-sounding variables represent words with the same pronunciation as the regular variable, for example, *waist* and *waste*. Compound word variables are two variables that combine to form a word, for example *sun* and *burn*.

A template is annotated with word relationships, represented as `<varName1> <relationship type> <varName2>`, to show how one variable is related to another. *Synonym relationships* denote that the first variable is synonymous with the second variable. *Is-a-word relationships* denote that the first variable combined with the second variable should form a word. *Sounds-like relationships* denote that the first variable should have the same pronunciation with the second variable. *Semantic relationships* show how the first variable is related to the second variable.

The training corpus is preprocessed by the tagger, stemmer, and synonym finder. The tagged corpus undergoes valid word selection to identify which of the nouns, verbs, and adjectives in the punning riddle are candidate variables. Word relationships between these variables are then determined by the phonetic checker, synonym checker, and semantic analyzer.

Consider the pun `P1` and its corresponding template `T1`, where "Xn" represents question-side variables, and "Yn" represents answer side variables. "`<var>-0`" represents the similar sounding word of `<var>` from Unisyn, for example, `Y1-0` represents the word "*sun*" which has the same pronunciation as the keyword "*son*" (variable `Y1`). Table 1 lists the semantic word relationships derived from ConceptNet for the variables of `P1`.

```
P1: What kind of boy burns? A son-burn. (Binsted, 1996)
T1: What kind of <X3> <X4>? A <Y1>-<Y2>.
```

Table 1: Word relationships extracted from `P1` using ConceptNet

Word Relationship	For Readability
X3 ConceptuallyRelatedTo Y1	boy ConceptuallyRelatedTo son
X4 ConceptuallyRelatedTo Y1-0	burn ConceptuallyRelatedTo sun
Y1-0 CapableOf Y2	sun CapableOf burn

A compound word (word with a dash "-") is also checked and marked if at least one of its parts has an existing word relationship. From `P1`, the compound word relationship extracted is `Y1-0 IsAWord Y2` (sun IsAWord burn).

The extracted templates are then validated for usability. A template is usable if all of the word relationships form a complete chain. If the chain is incomplete, the template cannot be used in the generation phase since not all of the variables will be filled with possible values.

3.2. Using the Learned Templates in Generation

Generation of puns starts with a keyword input, which is tried with all of the available templates, by substituting it on each variable that has the same POS tag. Word relationship grouping is then performed. Given two variables, say `X1` and `Y4`, there may be more than one word relationship connecting these two variables, e.g., `X1 IsA Y4` and `X1 ConceptuallyRelatedTo Y4`. A word relationship group is satisfied if at least one of the word relationships in the group is satisfied. Consider the pun `P3` and its word relationship groupings shown in Table 2.

```
P3: How is a window like a headache? They are both panes. (Binsted, 1996)
T3: How is a <X3> like a <X5>? They are both <Y4>.
```

The possible word generator checks if the variables can be populated with values to satisfy the word relationships starting with the keyword, while the possible word connector connects the possible words together to form groups of variables to be used for a sentence. The surface form generator takes the groups of variables and substitutes them to the slots in the template to form the punning riddle, before passing to the surface realizer for output to the user.

Table 2: Word relationship groupings for `P3`

Word Relationship	For Readability
X3 ConceptuallyRelatedTo Y4 Y4 ConceptuallyRelatedTo X3 Y4 PartOf X3	window ConceptuallyRelatedTo pane pane ConceptuallyRelatedTo window pane PartOf window
X5 ConceptuallyRelatedTo Y4-0 X5 IsA Y4-0 Y4-0 ConceptuallyRelatedTo X5	headache ConceptuallyRelatedTo pain headache IsA pain pain ConceptuallyRelatedTo headache
Y4-0 SoundsLike Y4	pain SoundsLike panes

Given the keyword "garbage", the possible values for the variables of template **T3** and the sequence of their derivation from the linguistic resources are as follows:

```
X5        ==>  Y4-0   ==>  Y4     ==>  X3
Garbage ==>  waste  ==>  waist  ==>  trunk
```

The word relationships that were satisfied and the filled template are shown in Table 3, resulting in the T-Peg generated pun *"How is a trunk like a garbage? They are both waists."*

Table 3: Filled template `T3` for keyword "garbage"

Word Relationship	Filled Template
X3 ConceptuallyRelatedTo Y4 Y4 ConceptuallyRelatedTo X3 Y4 PartOf X3	waist PartOf trunk
X5 ConceptuallyRelatedTo Y4-0 X5 IsA Y4-0 Y4-0 ConceptuallyRelatedTo X5	garbage IsA waste
Y4-0 SoundsLike Y4	waste SoundsLike waist

4. Translation Quality using Extracted Templates

TExt was trained with four sets of bilingual corpora containing a total of 163 sentence pairs. Corpora#1-3, containing 49, 15 and 41 sentences, respectively, were created by the proponents and verified by a linguist; they contain sentences that have similar structures so that templates can be learned. Corpus #4, containing 58 sentences, was adapted from an essay given by the Filipino Department of De La Salle University - Manila.

Using a Strict Chunk Alignment with Splitting (SCAS) approach in deriving templates from sentences requires all tokens to be aligned and the number of chunks in the source to be equal to that in the target. This resulted in learning more templates that are of good quality, as shown in Table 4 (for Corpus #4), compared to the Loose Chunk Alignment approach (LCA). Correctness refers to the actual templates and chunks learned as well as the proper alignment of tokens in the source and target template or chunk. Notice that LCA has a high error rate, and learning is not bi-directional as it did not learn the same number of templates and chunks.

Table 4: Test results for chunk alignment algorithms applied on Corpus #4

	LCA	SCAS
English to Filipino		
Total # of template pairs learned	5	13
# (%) of correct template pairs	3 (60%)	13 (100%)
Total # of chunk pairs learned	110	29
# (%) of correct chunk pairs	49 (44.5%)	29 (100%)
Filipino to English		
Total # of template pairs learned	6	13
# (%) of correct template pairs	2 (33.3%)	13 (100%)
Total # of chunk pairs learned	131	29
# (%) of correct chunk pairs	64 (48.9%)	29 (100%)

The extracted templates also contained too many frequently occurring words which were filtered to prevent learning templates that have small coverage during translation since they contain only common words as constants. Table 5 shows the results of performing common words filtering combined with SCAS for all four corpora. NCWF (no common words filtering) generated fewer templates and more chunks. CWF (common words filtering) generated more templates and fewer chunks which is preferable because templates are able to capture proper sentence structures that preserve word order in the resulting translation. More templates would also mean more candidates for refinement in subsequent training.

Table 5: Test results for common words filtering with strict chunk alignment algorithm

SCAS with Template Learning Algorithm	NCWF STL	CWF STL	CWF STL + DTL
Total # of template pairs learned	59	73	119
Total # of chunk pairs learned	237	210	218

The last column in Table 5 shows the number of templates learned from Corpora #1-4 when both similarity and difference template learning algorithms are used. The additional templates were mostly derived from existing chunks (Nunez, 2007).

To determine the translation quality using the learned templates and chunks, Corpus #5 containing 30 sentences was derived from Corpora #1-4. Table 6 shows the number of sentences that were translated using templates alone, chunks alone, word-for-word translation, and combination of all three. The STL approach was able to match more templates to the input text while the DTL approach utilizes more chunks. These results correspond to the training results, where STL learned more templates and DTL learned more chunks.

Table 6: Using templates in the translation of Corpus #5

	Templates	Chunks	Word-For-Word	Combination
English to Filipino Translation of Corpus #5				
STL + DTL	15	3	0	12
STL	18	2	0	10
DTL	5	0	8	17
Filipino to English Translation of Corpus #5				
STL + DTL	14	3	0	13
STL	19	1	0	10
DTL	3	12	2	13

Table 7: Error rates in the translation of Corpora #5 and #6

Approach	Corpus #5 WER (%)	Corpus #5 SER (%)	Corpus #5 BLEU	Corpus #6 WER (%)	Corpus #6 SER (%)	Corpus #6 BLEU
English to Filipino Translation						
STL + DTL	15.17	73.33	0.7126	89.90	100.00	0.0523
STL	13.49	60.00	0.7470	89.96	100.00	0.0517
DTL	43.25	86.67	0.4531	91.69	100.00	0.0299
Filipino to English Translation						
STL + DTL	21.85	63.33	0.6771	80.78	100.00	0.0334
STL	18.12	56.67	0.6990	83.19	100.00	0.0322
DTL	55.49	83.33	0.3455	85.46	100.00	0.0337

Table 7 shows the evaluated translation output of Corpora #5 and #6 (containing 126 sentence pairs whose patterns and words do not match the training set). The automatic evaluation methods used were *word error rate* (WER), *sentence error rate* (SER), and *bilingual evaluation understudy* (BLEU). For Corpus #5, since STL was able to match more templates to the input text, the translation is of better quality with lower error rates. In the translation of Corpus #6, cases arise when no matching templates can be found for an input sentence. Chunks are then used, resulting in poorer quality translation with 100% sentence error rate.

5. Quality of Puns Generated from Learned Templates

T-Peg was trained with a corpus of 39 punning riddles derived from JAPE (Binsted, 1996) and The Crack-a-Joke Book (Webb, 1978). Each riddle generates one template, and of these, only 27 (69.2%) are usable. The unusable templates contain missing relationships due to two factors. The phonetic lexicon (Unisyn) contains entries only for valid words and not for syllables. Thus, in P4, the "house-wall" relationship is missing because "wal" is not found in Unisyn to produce the word "wall". The semantic analyzer (ConceptNet) is also unable to determine the relationship between two words, for example, in P5, the "infantry-army" relationship.

```
P4: What nuts can you use to build a house? Wal-nuts. (Binsted, 1996)
P5: What part of the army could a baby join? The infant-ry. (Webb, 1978)
```

The usable templates were manually verified if they contain sufficient information in capturing the wordplay. The rating used is based on the word relationships in the pun. 10 templates were chosen based on their completeness and correctness in capturing the most crucial word relationships. The 10 templates received an average score of 4.0 out of 5, with missing word relationships due to limitations of Unisyn and ConceptNet, for example, in P6, between "heaviest" and "weight"; while in P7, between "tap" and "plumber" and the syllable "ber" that was incorrectly classified as a valid word.

```
P6: Which bird can lift the heaviest weights? The crane. (Webb, 1978)
T6: Which <X1> can <X3> the heaviest <X6>? The <Y1>.

P7: What kind of fruit fixes taps? The plum-ber. (Binsted, 1996)
T7: What kind of <X3> <X4> taps? A <Y1>-<Y2>.
```

Table 8 lists sample puns in the training set and the corresponding generated puns. User feedback gave an average score of 2.7 to the original puns, while the generated puns received an average score of 2.13, showing that computer puns are almost at par with human-made puns.

Table 8: Examples of generated punning riddles

Training Examples	Generated Punning Riddle by T-Peg
What do you call a lizard on the wall? A rep-tile. (Binsted, 1996)	What do you call a movie on the floor? A holly-wood..
What part of a fish weighs the most? The scales. (Webb, 1978)	What part of a man lengthens the most? The shadow.
What keys are furry? Mon-keys. (Webb, 1978)	What verses are endless? Uni - verses .

6. Conclusion

The works presented here explored the use of learning algorithms to automatically extract templates from training examples provided by the user. TExt demonstrated that similarity and difference bilingual translation templates can be extracted from an unannotated and untagged corpus. The learning algorithm also performs template refinement and extracts chunks to supplement the limited lexicon and for deriving additional templates. Further work on TExt may involve semantic analysis of the words in the input sentences in order to select the most appropriate translation for a given word that has different meanings depending on its context in the sentence. The addition of a morphological analyzer for English and Filipino can also help the alignment process of the system.

T-peg demonstrated that computers can be trained to be as humorous as humans by automatically extracting patterns of human-created jokes and using these as templates for the system to create its own jokes, utilizing various linguistic resources. Computer-generated jokes can find application in human-computer dialog systems, to make the conversation and interaction between the human and the computer sound more natural. Future work for T-Peg involves exploring template refinement or merging, which could improve the quality of the learned templates. Some form of manual intervention may also be added to increase the number of usable templates by addressing the missing word relationships caused by limitations of the external linguistic resources.

We are planning to explore automatic extraction of story patterns for use by our children story generation system, Picture Books (Hong et al, 2008). The templates pair approach of TExt can be used to present a basic story structure in different forms suitable for various reading age groups. The approach of T-Peg in extracting and storing word relationships can be explored further as a means of teaching vocabulary and related concepts to young readers.

References

Bautista, M., Fule, M., Gaw, K., and K.L Hernandez. 2004. *SalinWika: An Example-Based Machine Translation System Using Templates*. Undergraduate Thesis. De La Salle University, Manila.

Binsted, K. 1996. *Machine Humour: An Implemented Model of Puns*. Ph.D. Thesis. University of Edinburgh.

Cicekli, I. and H.A. Güvenir. 2003. Learning Translation Templates from Bilingual Translation Examples. *Recent Advances in Example-Based Machine Translation*, pp. 255-286. Kluwer Publishers.

Dale, R. 1995. *An Introduction to Natural Language Generation*. Technical Report, Microsoft Research Institute (MRI). Macquarie University, Australia.

Fitt, S. 2002. *Unisyn Lexicon Release*. http://www.cstr.ed.ac.uk/projects/unisyn/.

Go, K., Morga, M., Nunez, V. and F. Veto. 2006. TExt *Translation: Template Extraction for a Bidirectional English-Filipino Example-Based Machine Translation*. Undergraduate Thesis. De La Salle University, Manila.

Hong, B. 2008. *Template-Based Pun Extractor and Generator*. MSCS Thesis. De La Salle University, Manila.

Hong, A., Siy, J.T., Solis, C. and E. Tabirao. 2008. *Picture Books: An Automated Story Generator*. Ongoing Undergraduate Thesis. De La Salle University, Manila.

Jarmasz, M. and S. Szpakowicz. 2006. *Roget's Thesaurus – Electronic Lexical Knowledge Base ELKB*. http://www.nzdl.org/ELKB/.

Liu, H., P. Singh and I. Eslick. 2004. *ConceptNet*. http://web.media.mit.edu/~hugo/ conceptnet/.

Liu, H. 2003. *MontyTagger*. http://web.media.mit.edu/~hugo/montytagger/.

McTait, K. 2001. Linguistic Knowledge and Complexity in an EBMT System Based on Translation Patterns. In *MT Summit VIII*, September 2001, Spain.

Muslea, I. 1999. Extraction Patterns for Information Extraction Tasks: A Survey. *Proceedings AAAI-99 Workshop on Machine Learning for Information Extraction*.

Nunez, V. 2007. *Combining Similarity and Difference Templates for a Bidirectional Example-Based Machine Translation*. MSCS Thesis. De La Salle University, Manila.

Ong E., Go, K., Morga, M., Nunez, V. and F. Veto. 2007. Extracting and Using Translation Templates in an Example-Based Machine Translation System. *Journal of Research in Science, Computing, and Engineering,* 4(3), 81-98. De La Salle University, Manila.

Ritchie, G., Manurung, R., Pain, H., Waller, A., and O'Mara, D. (2006). The STANDUP Interactive Riddle Builder. In *IEEE Intelligent Systems*, 21(2), 67-69, March/April 2006.

Webb, K. 1978. *The Crack-a-Joke Book*. Puffin Books. London, England.

WordNet, 2006. *WordNet: A Lexical Database for the English Language*. Princeton University.

Recognizing Coordinate Structures for Machine Translation of English Patent Documents[*]

Yoon-Hyung Roh, Ki-Young Lee, Sung-Kwon Choi,
Oh-Woog Kwon, and Young-Gil Kim

Natural Language Processing Research Team, Electronics and Telecommunications Research Institute,
161 Gajeong-dong, Yuseong-gu, Daejeon, 305-350, Korea
{yhroh, leeky, choisk, ohwoog, kimyk}@etri.re.kr

Abstract. Patent machine translation is one of main target areas of current practical MT systems. Patent documents have their own peculiar description style. Especially, abstracts or claims in patent documents are characterized by their long and complex syntactic structures, which are often caused by coordination. So, syntactic analysis of patent documents requires special treatment for coordination. This paper describes a method to deal with long sentences in patent documents by recognizing coordinate structures. Coordinate structures are recognized using a similarity table which reflects parallelism between conjuncts. Our method is applied to a practical MT system and improves its quality and efficiency.

Keywords: Machine Translation, Patent Document, Coordinate Structure, Syntactic Analysis

1. Introduction

Patent machine translation is one of main target areas of current practical MT systems such as the English-Korean patent machine translation system (Kwon, 2007). Patent documents have their own description style and there have been some studies on the analysis of patent documents (Sheremetyeva, 2003; Shinmori and Okumura, 2003; Shinmori and Okumura, 2002). Especially, abstracts or claims in the patent documents are notorious for their long and complex syntactic structures, which are usually caused by coordination or relative clauses. Long sentences formed by relative clauses can be handled by segmentation (Kim et al, 2001). On the other hand, in case of long sentences formed by coordination, segmentation can cause syntactic analysis errors, because a segment resulting from segmentation can be dependent on the other constituents in the parse tree. Also, coordinate structures in patent documents have usually a large number of coordinate conjuncts (which we will call nodes) and can cause syntactic ambiguity explosion and parsing failure at the worst case in practical MT systems. So, syntactic analysis of patent documents requires special treatment for coordination.

There have been many computational researches about coordinate structures (Kaplan and Maxwell, 1988; Kosy, 1986). But, it is unrealistic to apply most of them to large-scale MT systems as mentioned in (Okumura and Muraki, 1994; Kurohashi and Nagao,. 1994). The more practical approaches about analyzing coordinate structures such as (Okumura and Muraki, 1994;

---

[*] This work was funded by the Ministry of Information and Communication of Korean government.

Kurohashi and Nagao, 1994; Agarwal and Boggess, 1992) all analyze coordinate structures using parallelism between conjuncts, but they are mainly targeted to recognizing two conjuncts (i.e., pre-conjuct and post-conjuct). Out of them, (Kurohashi and Nagao,. 1994) is one of the most practical approaches. They recognize coordinate structures in a Japanese sentence by constructing a similarity matrix between bunsetsus and searching a path with the highest parallelism in the similarity matrix using a dynamic programming method. However, that method is inadequate to apply to patent documents which have usually a large number of coordinate nodes and sometimes complex modification such as an inserted clause. We devised an appropriate method to recognize coordinate structures for patent documents using a similarity table. Although our method seems similar to that method in appearance, it is considerably different from that in the manner of constructing a similarity table and finding coordinate structures. Our method is simpler but more effective in patent documents.

In the next section, we outline the characteristics of coordinate structures in patent documents. And in the section 3, we present a method to recognize coordinate structures. In the section 4, we show experimental results and some analysis of the erroneous results, and then conclude our paper with some future works.

2. Coordination in Patent Documents

Figure1 shows a typical sentence in an abstract of a patent document. This sentence belongs to enumeration in the patent description style, and describes elements of a product. By analyzing many example sentences in patent abstracts, we can outline the characteristics of the enumeration sentences of the patent abstracts as follows:

1) They often have some keywords such as "include, comprising, having, step_of, unit, means"
2) In case of enumeration of noun phrase (NP), the definite article such as "the, each, said" is not used in the head node of NP. The definite article is usually used as elaboration.
3) They generally follows the normal form " X (, X)* (,) and X", where "()" means optional, and "*" means any number of repetition.

In this paper, on the basis of above features, we describe a method to recognize coordinate structures especially corresponding to enumeration in patent abstracts.

A machine translation and telecommunications system includes a machine translation engine for translation of input text from a source language to a target language, a dictionary database including a core dictionary and a plurality of sublanguage (domain) dictionaries usable for translation from a source to a target language, a receiving interface for receiving text input from any of a plurality of users, each text input being accompanied by control information including user ID data indicative of one or more sublanguages preferred by a particular user, an output interface, and a dictionary control module coupled to the receiving interface responsive to the user ID data indicative of a sublanguage preference of a particular user for selecting a corresponding sublanguage dictionary of the dictionary database to be used by the machine translation engine along with the core dictionary for performing translation of the particular user's text input.

Figure 1: An example sentence of patent abstract

3. Recognizing Coordinate Structures by Similarity Table

As mentioned above, an enumeration sentence usually enumerates many elements or procedures and each element or procedure can have modifiers and nested coordination. So, overall sentence structure can be excessively complicated and the process of recognizing coordinate structures can be difficult. For this, we simplify the analysis target by recognizing all possible coordinate nodes and construct a similarity table for using parallelism between the coordinate nodes.

3.1.Recognizing Possible Starting Points of Parallel Nodes

Recognizing coordinate structures is carried out after mophological analysis, tagging and base NP(BNP) chunking. The figure 2 represents the result of BNP chunking of the example sentence. Assuming that all of coordinate structures follow the normal form "Xs (, Xm)* (,) and Xe", there are three types of nodes, which are a starting node(Xs), a middle node(Xm), and an ending node(Xe). The starting points of coordinate nodes are recognized by some syntactic cues. By corpus analysis, we find that the syntactic tags of coordinate structures are mainly a noun phrase(NP), a verbal phrase(VP), and a that-clause(SBAR). The syntactic cues for recognizing starting points of coordinate nodes are shown in the table 1.

Table 1: The syntactic cues for recognizing the starting points of coordinate nodes.

Node Tag	Starting Node	Middle Node	Ending Node
NP	PREP|VERB /BNP	, /BNP	(,) and /BNP
VP	PREP|VERB /(ADV) VBG	, /VBG	(,) and /VBG
SBAR	PREP|VERB /that	, /that	(,) and /that

In the table 1, "VBG", "VERB", "PREP", and "ADV" repesents a verb with ing-form, a verb, a preposition, and an adverb respectivey. And '|' means "or" and '/' means the starting point of a coordinate node. In the figure 2, the mark '/' represents the candidate starting points of the coordinate nodes recongnized by the given syntactic cue.[1]

In case that there comes a main verb before a comma or the end of the sentence after the ending node of a NP coordinate structure, we exclude that point from the starting points of the candidate coordinate nodes, regarding it as a starting point of a new clause.

[A machine translation] and [telecommunications system] includes /[a machine translation engine] for [translation] of [input text] from /[a source language] to /[a target language], /[a dictionary database] /including /[a core dictionary] and /[a plurality of sublanguage (domain) dictionaries] usable for [translation] from /[a source] to /[a target language], /[a receiving interface] for /receiving [text input] from /[any of a plurality of users], [each text input] /being accompanied by [control information] /including [user ID data] indicative of /[one or more sublanguages] preferred by /[a particular user], /[an output interface], and /[a dictionary control module] coupled to [the receiving interface] responsive to [the user ID data] indicative of /[a sublanguage preference] of /[a particular user] for /selecting /[a corresponding sublanguage dictionary] of [the dictionary database] to be used by [the machine translation engine] along with [the core dictionary] for /performing [translation] of [the particular user]'s [text input]

Figure 2: The result of BNP chunking and recognition of starting points of coordinate nodes

3.2. Constructing Similarity Table

We construct a similarity table between the recognized nodes in order to use parallelism between the coordinate nodes. In the similarity table, the value of i-th row and j-th column($S_{i,j}$) means the similarity between the i-th candidate node and the j-th candidate node. The similarity between nodes is composed of the head node simiraity($s0$), the head word similarity($s1, s3$), and the structural similarity($s2$). Then, $S_{i,j}$ is calculated as follows:

$$S_{i,j} = s0*(s1 + s2 + s3) \quad (1)$$

s0: tag similarity of the node (e.g., 1 if their tags are the same and are not NP, otherwise 1 if both of their tags are NP and their determiner types are compatible, otherwise 0, the determiner type will be explained later)

---

[1] For simplicity, we omit some starting points of NP nodes, which have no effect on the result.

s1: lexical or tag similarity of the head word (e.g., 6 if their lexicals are the same, otherwise 4 if their tags are the same and their node is not NP and 2 if their tags are the same and their node is NP, otherwise 0).
s2: lexical or tag similarity of the next word of the head word (e.g., 4 if their lexicals are the same, otherwise 2 if their tags are the same, otherwise 0)
s3: determiner similarity in case of NP (e.g., 5 if the determiner type is the same, otherwise 0)

There are four determiner types according to the determiner and the plurality of the head word. The determiner type 1 is the case where there is a indefinite article like "a machine translation engine", the determiner type 2 is the case where there is no determiner and the head word is plural like "one or more sublanguages", the determiner type 3 is the case where there is no determiner and the head word is singular like "translation", and the determiner type 4 is the case where there is a definite determiner like "the receiving interface". The quantifier such as "a plurality of" is considered as the case having no determiner. The determiner type 1 and 2 are compatible with each other. The determiner type 2, 3, and 4 are compatible with one another. We exclude the nodes with the determiner type 3 and 4 as the final coordinate nodes because the element of a product is a common noun and they don't have a definite article as described in the second characteristics of enumeration sentences in the section 2.

The simiarity values assigned above just reflect the rough priority between features with the order of the node tag similarity, the head word similarity, and the structural similarity. Also, the lexical similariy has precedence over the tag similarity. The specific values need to be decided by exeriment.

The figure 3 shows the similarity table of the example sentence. The node number is the sequential number of the recognized coordinate nodes, and the chunk number is the sequential numer of the chunks resulted from the base NP chunkng. The symbols ' <', ' ,', ' >' in the i-th row and the i-th column represent a starting node, a middle node, and an ending node repectively.

For example, S6,4 is the similarity between the node starting with "a receiving interface for" and the node starting with "a core dictionary and", and the similarity value is as follows:
 s0 = 1, s1 = 2, s2 = 0, s3 = 5 → S6,4 = 2 + 0 + 5 = 7
S6,1 is the similarity between the node starting with "a receiving interface for" and the node starting with "a machine translation engine for", and the similarity value is as follows:
 s1 = 2, s2 = 4, s3 = 5 → S6,1 = 2 + 4 + 5 = 11

3.3. Recognizing all Possible Coordinate Structures

All possible coordinate structures are recognized based on the similarity table. A coordinate structure is composed of one starting node, zero or more number of middle nodes, and one ending node. So, for a given ending node, we can generate a coordinate structure by first selecting a starting node having more than zero value of similarity with the ending node, and adding middle nodes having more than zero value of similarity with the ending node between the the starting node and the ending node.

Once a coordinate structure is identified, the scopes of all coordinate nodes are determined except the ending node. The scope of the ending node is not obvious in an English sentence, so temporarily we decide as its scope the minimum scope which can make any coordinate node. For example, in case of NP, its ending position of ending node is the ending position of first BNP and in case of VP, it is first VBG. Once all the scopes of the coodinate nodes are determined, then we make some simple checks whether the scopes of each nodes can be parsed to the correspoding node. The representative checking method is to check how many main verbs exist in a node. In case of NP, VP, and PP, there must be no main verb. Conversely, in case of SBAR, there must be a main verb. A main verb is a verb which have tense and so can form a clause. In case that there is relative clause, we subtract the number of relatives from the number of main verbs. If there is any node which doesn't satisfy that constraint in a coordinate structure, that coordinate structure is excluded.

node No.	chunk No.	head word	1	2	3	4	5	6	7	8	9	10	11	12	13	14	15
1	8	engine	<	7	0	7	7	11	0	0	0	7	11	7	0	9	0
2	26	database		,	0	7	7	7	0	0	0	7	7	7	0	7	0
3	29	including			<	0	0	0	4	4	11	0	0	0	8	0	4
4	30	dictionary				<	11	7	0	0	0	7	7	7	0	11	0
5	34	dictionaries					>	7	0	0	0	7	7	7	0	11	0
6	53	interface						,	0	0	0	7	11	7	0	9	0
7	57	receiving							<	4	6	0	0	0	4	0	6
8	71	being								<	4	0	0	0	4	0	4
9	76	including									<	0	0	0	4	0	6
10	77	user										<	7	7	0	2	0
11	77	interface											,	7	0	2	0
12	97	module												>	0	7	0
13	122	selecting													<	0	4
14	123	dictionary														<	0
15	145	performing															<

Figure 3: Similarity table of the example sentence

3.4.Selecting the Final Coordinate Structure

Since it is assumed that all the coordinate structures follow the normal form "X (, X)* (,) and X", there are as many coordinate structures as the number of the ending nodes in a sentence. The scopes of those coordinate structures should not be crossed. In other words, one coordinae structure either have exclusive scope with the other coordinate structures or is entirely included in the other coordinate structures. We will call such a coordinate structure set a consistent coordinate structure set(CCS). All CCSs can be obtained by checking the no-crossing condition with all possible coordinate structure combinations. In nested coordinate structures, we constrain the inner-most coordinate structure to have the narrowest scope, e.g. have the nearest starting node out of possible starting nodes as its starting node. The inner coordinate structure is considered as one node represented by the starting node when we count the coordinate nodes of the outer coordinate structure. So, we exclude the middle nodes in the outer coordinate structure overlapping with the middle nodes in the inner coordinate structure. As a result, there are 4 CCSs in the example sentence as shown in the figure 4.

The score of a CCS is calculated by the sum of the score of each coordinate structure in the CCS. The score of a coordinate structure is basically calculated by the sum of similarity values between the ending node and the other nodes. In addition to that, some weights according to context are added. Such weights can be given as follows:

1) 7, when the words prior to the starting node is "include | comprise | comprised_of"
2) 7, when the words prior to the starting node is "including | comprising | step_of | means_for"
3) 3, when the word prior to the starting node is "having"
4) 1, when the word prior to the starting node is a verb
5) 3, when the head word of NP is " unit | means"

The scores of the CCSs in the example setence is as follows:
CCS 1: (S5,1 + S5,2 + 7) + (S12,11+S12,10) = 7 + 7 + 7 + 7 + 7 = 35
CCS 2: (S5,4 + 5) + (S12,10 + S12,11) = 7 + 5 + 7 + 7 = 26
CCS 3: (S5,4 + 5) + (S12,1 + S12,2 + S12,6 + S12,11 + 7) = 7 + 5 + 7 + 7 + 7 + 7 + 7 = 47
CCS 4: (S5,4 + 5) + (S12,4 + S12,6 + S12,11) = 7 + 5 + 7 + 7 + 7 = 33

Then we select the outer-most coordinate structures in the CCS with the highest score as the final coordinate structure. In case of the example sentence, the CCS 3 is selected as the CCS having the highest score, and the coordinate structure (1,2,6,11,12) is selected as the final result. In the real cases, we eliminate the final coordinate structure with very small scope corresponding to a very local coordinate structure.

Then, all the nodes of the recognized coordinate structure are parsed, and the whole coordinate structure is reduced to one node. The final parsing result is produced by parsing the whole sentence, with the recognized coordinate structure substitued by that node.

However, there is a problem that the ending point of the ending node is ambiguous, because it is not guranteed that the ending point of the ending node be always the end of the sentence. For this, the scope excluding the ending node is recognized as the scope of the coodinate structure, and reduced to one node, thus leaving the decision of the adequate scope made by parsing.

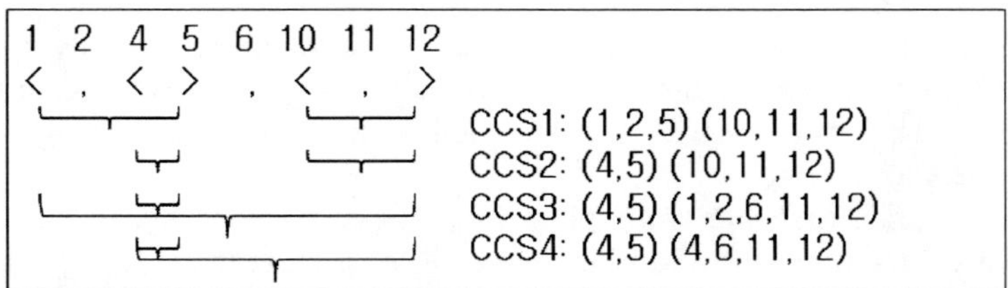

Figure 4: All Possible CCSs in the example sentence

4. Experimental Results

For experiment, we extracted 840 patent abstracts from computer/electronics fields and applied our method to them. Out of 840 abstracts, the number of sentences which has actually coordinate structures is 94 sentences. The average sentence length is 107.1 words/sentence. The table 2 shows the precision and the coverage of our method. It shows relatively high precision but low coverage. Although the ratio of coordinate structures in the entire sentences of abstracts is not so high, considering the importance of an abstract in a patent document and the excessively long sentence length more than 100 words, the correct analysis of coordinate structures has important effect on the overall machine translation quality.

Table 2: Experimental result for recognizing coordinate structures.

Correct	Incorrect	precision	recall	F-measure
70	8	89.7%	74.5%	81.4%

The incorrect results are categorized as follows:
1) The input sentence itself is an erroneous sentence.
2) There is a coordinate structure, but it is not recognized because of low coverage of our method.
3) Incorrect recognition of starting nodes or middle nodes.
4) There is not a coordinate structure, but a coordinate structure is recognized.

The main causes of the errors are shown in the table 3. In many cases, the errors are caused by our assumption about coordination structures such as the form of a coordinate structure or the constraint by the determiner type. From the result, we need to extend the coverage by considering more various cases.

Table 3: Main causes of the errors.

Cause of Errors	Example	Frequency
Comma, PP, etc. are inserted	"determines, for each translation example, a similarity", "comprises, a semiconductor chip"	4
Errors by determiners	"the laminating a sacrificial layer", ", syntax analyzer for"	5
Ambiguous Starting Nodes	"A dictionary retrieval device is constructed by a conversion character definition form for providing group IDs for character subsets, a character-group ..."	3
Uncovered Case	PP, VP(declarative), INFP, "NP VP , ..., and VP" form, SBAR(which-clause)	6

5. Conclusion and Future Works

We presented a method to recognize coordinate structures occurring typically in patent abstracts. The coordinate structures are recognized by searching all CCSs and scoring all CCSs using the similarity table. The experiment shows our method is effective for recognizing coordinate structures in patent abstracts.

  For the future works, first, the target node for recognizing coordinate structures have to be extend to other case such as PP, to-infinitive, or all other relative clauses. Second, we have to consider the case that is out of our assumption such as the form of coordinate structures or the constraint by the determiner type. Lastly, we think that more robust treatment about inserted phrases or clauses is needed.

References

Agarwal, R., and L. Boggess. 1992. A simple but useful approach to conjunct identification. *In Proceedings, 30th Annual Meeting of Association for Computational Linguistics*, pp. 15-21.

Kaplan, R. M., and J. T. Maxwell. 1988. Constituent coordination in Lexical-Functional Grammar. *In Proceedings, Eighth International Conference on Computational Linguistics*, pp. 303-305.

Kim, S.-D., B.-T. Zhang, and Y. T. Kim. 2001. Learning-based Intrasentence Segmentation for Efficient Translation of Long Sentences. *Machine Translation*, 16(3):151-174.

Kosy, D. 1986. Parsing conjunctions deterministically. *In Proceedings of the 24th ACL Conference*.

Kurohashi, S., and M. Nagao. 1994. A syntactic analysis method of long Japanese sentences based on the detection of conjunctive structures. *Computational Linguistics*, 20(4), pp. 507-534.

Kwon, O.-W., S.-K. Choi, K.-Y. Lee, Y.-H. Roh, Y.-G. Kim. 2007. English-Korean Patent Translation System: FromTo-EK/PAT. *MT Summit XI Workshop on Patent Translation*.

Okumura, A., and K. Muraki. 1994. Symmetric pattern matching analysis for English coordinate structures. *Proceedings of the fourth conference on Applied natural language processing*, pp. 41-46.

Sheremetyeva, S. 2003. Natural Language Analysis of Patent Claims. *Proceedings of ACL 2003 Workshop on Patent Corpus Processing Workshop*.

Shinmori, A., M. Okumura, Y. Marukawa, and M. Iwayama. 2003. Patent Claim Processing for Readability. *Proceedings of ACL 2003 Workshop on Patent Corpus Processing Workshop*.

Shnimori, A., M. Okumura,Y. Marukawa, and M. IwaYama. 2002. Rhetorical Structure Analysis of Japanese Patent Claims Using Cue Phrases. *Proceedings of the Third NTRCIR Workshop*.

A Morphological Analyzer for Filipino Verbs[*]

Robert R. Roxas[a] and Gersam T. Mula[a]

[a]University of the Philippines Visayas – Cebu College
Cebu City, Philippines
rrroxas@upv.edu.ph and gersammula@gmail.com

Abstract. This paper presents a morphological analyzer that accepts Filipino verbs conjugated in different forms as inputs and analyzes them to produce the affixes used, the infinitive forms, and the tenses of the original input verbs. A prototype system was implemented and was fed with a file containing 1,050 Filipino verbs conjugated in various tenses using different types of affixes. The preliminary result showed that the accuracy rate was high in three expected outputs, i.e., tenses, infinitive forms, and affixes used.

Keywords: morphological analyzer, context-driven machine translation system, Filipino verbs

1. Introduction

Filipino is a language whose verb conjugations are very complex because it uses different affix (prefix, infix, and suffix) combinations and even duplication of syllables or words. When looking up a word in Filipino dictionary, one needs to know the infinitive form of the verb to be able to find it. This is a difficult task for someone who is not familiar with the way Filipino verbs are conjugated into any of the three tenses: Pangnagdaan (Past), Pangkasalukuyan (Present), and Panghinaharap (Future). These three are commonly known today as Aspektong Perpektibo, Aspektong Imperpektibo, and Aspektong Kontemplatibo, respectively (Dizon, 2006).

Because of the complexity of the language, automated morphological analyzers will be difficult to construct. So researches should be focused on how to capture all possible forms so that a machine translation system can produce accurate translation. One approach is to use a lexicon that stores the context-words that help determine the appropriate equivalent word(s) in the target language. The lexicon must use the infinitive forms of the verbs to facilitate the look up of verbs and use headwords for non-verbs. So with this kind of lexicon in mind, a morphological analyzer that returns the infinitive form of a verb, its tense, and its affix(es) used is necessary.

2. Review of Related Works

When someone attempts to create any machine translation system for natural languages, it is not possible to do away with morphological analyzers. One area of focus for morphological analyzers is the analysis of verbs. Verbs are usually conjugated according to tense, number, voice, and mode while nouns and adjectives are usually declined according to person, number, case, and degree. Some languages have simple forms of verb inflection or conjugation while other languages have complex forms of inflection. Japanese was originally thought to have simple verb inflection, thus it was not the central subject on Natural Language Processing

---

22nd Pacific Asia Conference on Language, Information and Computation, pages 467–473

(NLP). But in recent past, it had become an important subject (Hisamitsu and Nitta, 1994). For other languages, verbs are also given much attention in research. These languages include Chinese (Kim, et. al, 2002), Japanese (Nakamura, 2007), and Korean (Hong, et. al., 2004; Jun, 2007) to name a few.

For languages that have complex ways of adding affixes and duplication of syllables or words, an excellent morphological analyzer is highly necessary. Filipino or Tagalog is one the most complex languages in the world. So several researches have been conducted in the area of morphological analysis for the Filipino language. One is the TagSA (Tagalog Stemmer Algorithm), which tackles on the extraction of the stem of any Tagalog word (Bonus, 2003). Another morphological analyzer, called TagMA (Tagalog Morphological Analyzer), is devoted to extracting the root word both for concatenative and non-concatenative formation (Fortes, 2002). A system called T2CMT (Tagalog-to-Cebuano Machine Translation) was developed (Fat, 2004) that used TagMA and TagSA for its morphological analyzer. Even before the TagMA and TagSA, there was already a morphological analyzer that was created and used in a prototype system that supported English-Filipino and Filipino-English machine translation system (Roxas, 1998).

TagMA (Fortes, 2002) produces three morphological structures (morpheme, CV, and syllabication) to represent an input verb. To do this, it needs to scan the entire word in several stages. It starts by assigning the symbols "C" for consonants or "V" for vowels to the morpheme structure character by character to get the CV structure. Then it scans the CV structure character by character to assign some codes (0-2) to a "C" or "V" to get the syllabification structure. Then the input representation is fed to the GEN function in order to produce a candidate set. It then scans the input string syllable by syllable until the last syllable is encountered. Then the result is subjected to the EVAL function, where the output of the GEN function is checked against the two lexicons (root and affixes) and subjected to some constraints to be able to get the right root of the verb.

Although TagMA was able to morphologically analyze 96% of the sample verbs accurately (Fortes, 2002), the process of analyzing an input verb is quite long and tedious. It only outputs the root, tense, and its affix for a particular input verb. It does not produce the infinitive or dictionary form of the original input verb. The infinitive form is also useful because that is what one usually uses to lookup a word in a dictionary. In fact, T2CMT (Fat, 2004) that used TagMA wrongly translated the Tagalog word "namatay" (to die) to "pinaagi" (by means of or through) in Cebuano, when in fact, the Cebuano translation should be "namatay" also. If a morphological analyzer produces the infinitive form, the translation would be correct. Our proposed system uses the morphological analyzer developed in (Roxas, 1989), which is being extended to cover more possible verb conjugations. If you pass "namatay" to our morphological analyzer, it will give the infinitive form "mamatay" and tense is past or perpektibo. If you consult a dictionary, you will find that its English translation is "to die," which is the intended meaning. Therefore, we believe that there is still a need to develop a morphological analyzer that uses the infinitive forms when checking a word in a dictionary.

3.The Proposed Morphological Analyzer

The morphological analyzer presented in this paper is just one of the components of our Context-driven Filipino-English Machine Translation System. The analyzer will be used during the translation process. This morphological analyzer examines any Filipino verb in various possible inflections and produces the affix(es), the infinitive form, and the tense of the input verb. It should be pointed out that we have no data as to how many infinitive forms are there in Tagalog. We don't know of any study trying to count the infinitive forms of a certain language. Natural languages are evolving. So it is difficult to categorically say that a particular language has that number of infinitive forms. The lexicon will have to be updated from time to time as the language evolves.

In this research, we don't bother so much on generating the root word because the entries in our lexicon will contain the infinitive or dictionary forms of the verbs and will be accessed using that form. We do, however, recognize the value of getting the root of a word, as being done in TagSA and TagMA, but extracting the root of the word is more useful in Information Retrieval System (IRS) than in a machine translation system. We also understand that the root of a word is used in some systems to get the right semantics of compound words in order to come up with a better translation. This is not necessary in our proposed Context-driven Filipino-English Machine Translation System, of which the morphological analyzer being presented here is just a subsystem. We choose the right English equivalent of a Filipino word by checking the neighboring words in a sentence and even in a paragraph. These neighboring words serve as context of the word being translated. So our lexicon must be a different one than the usual dictionary.

The affixes are important because they help in determining the structure of the sentence, the meaning of the entire sentence, etc. The subject of the sentence as well as the object will be easily recognized once the affix has been determined already. For example, if the affix used in the main verb is "UM," the subject of the sentence starts with the word "ang," "si" for personal subject, or uses the nominative case of pronoun. The object starts with the word "ng," "ni" for personal object, or uses the objective case of pronoun. This will be very helpful in the translation itself. As for the tense of the verb that will be output by the analyzer, it is also very useful for the translation process.

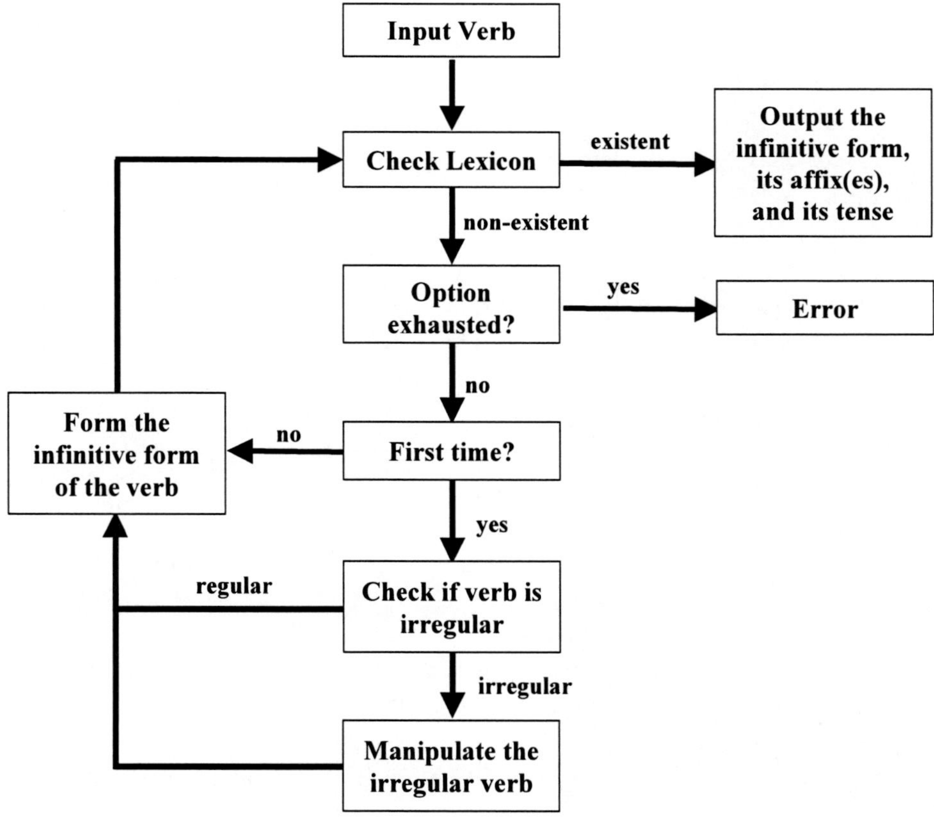

Figure 1: The flow of the morphological analyzer's activities.

4.Extracting Affixes, Infinitive Forms, and Tenses

In getting the infinitive form, the tense, and affix(es) of a Filipino verb, it first consults the lexicon if the word is there. If not, it checks whether or not all possible options were exhausted, in which case, it reports an error. If there are still options, it checks whether or not it is the first time to process the verb. If it is, it has to check whether or not the verb is irregular. If it is, it performs some manipulation and prepares for the formation of the possible infinitive form of the verb. If the verb is regular, the analyzer immediately tries to form the possible infinitive form. Figure 1 shows the flow of actions to take as the input verb is being analyzed.

```
Tense = past           /* default tense, will be changed depending on
                           the input */
If (starting with a double vowel)
   Tense = future
   Replace 1st vowel with "um"       /* iinom -> uminom (inf.) */
Else if (duplicated 1st two chars)
   Tense = future
   Replace 2nd and 3rd chars with "um"/* susulat -> sumulat (inf.)*/
Else if (1st char = 'd' & 3rd char = 'r') and (2nd char = 4th char)
   Tense = future
   Replace 2nd and 3rd chars with "um" /* darating -> dumating (inf.) */
Else if (duplicated 1st 3 letters) and (1st two chars = "ng")
   Replace 3rd to 5th chars with "um"    /* ngingiti -> ngumiti (inf.) */
Else if (1st two chars) = "um"
   If (3rd char <> 4th char)    /* do nothing, uminom = uminom (inf.) */
   If (3rd char = 4th char)
      Tense = present
      Remove the 3rd char             /* umiinom -> uminom (inf.) */
Else if (2nd & 3rd char) = "um"
   If (1st & 4th chars) <> (5th and 6th chars)
      /* do nothing, kumain = kumain (inf.) */
   If (1st & 4th chars) = (5th and 6th chars)
      Tense = present
      Remove 5th & 6th chars           /* kumakain -> kumain (inf.) */
   If (1st char = "d" & 5th char = "r") and (4th char = 6th char)
      Tense = present
      Remove 5th & 6th chars     /* dumarating -> dumating (inf.) */
Else if (3rd & 4th chars = "um")
   If (1st two chars & 5th char) <> (6th to 8th chars)
      /* do nothing, ngumiti = ngumiti (inf.)*/
   If (1st 2 chars & 5th char) = (6th to 8th chars)
      Tense = present
      Remove 6th to 8th chars      /* ngumingiti -> ngumiti (inf.) */
```

Figure 2: The pseudo-code for analyzing "UM–" verbs.

The analyzer performs a certain number of passes until it finds the correct infinitive form of the input verb. If all options have been tried but still the generated infinitive is not found in the lexicon, it reports an error. For each pass, it tries to generate the infinitive form of the input verb. If the generated infinitive form does not exist in the lexicon, it is possible that the option used was not the correct one. So it tries another option. Eventually, it will generate the correct infinitive form. Then it reports the infinitive form, the tense, and the affix(es) used. Filipino verbs use one or more affixes. So it is possible that more than 1 affix is reported.

```
Tense = past            /* default tense, will be changed depending on
                           the input */
If (1st two chars = "in")
   If  (last syllable contains "o")
      Change "o" to "u"
   If (3rd char <> 4th char)
      Move "in" to the end             /* inalis -> alisin (inf.) */
   If (3rd char = 4th char)
      Tense = present
      Remove 1st 3 chars and suffix "in" /* inaalis -> alisin (inf.) */
Else if (2nd & 3rd chars = "in")
   If  (last syllable contains "o")
      Change "o" to "u"
   If (1st & 4th chars) <> (5th  & 6th chars)
      Remove 2nd & 3rd chars & suffix "in"   /* sinulat ->
                                       sulatin (inf.) */
   If (1st & 4th chars) = (5th and 6th chars)
      Tense = present
      Remove 1st 4 chars & suffix "in" /* sinusulat -> sulatin (inf.) */
   If(1st char = 5th char) & (4th char <> 6th char) &
      (4th char = 7th char)
      Tense = present
      Remove 1st 4 chars & suffix "in"   /* tinatrabaho ->
                                       trabahuhin (inf.) */
Else if (last syllable ends with "in")
   Tense = future
   If (1st 2 chars) = (3rd & 4th char)
      Remove 1st two chars               /* susulatin -> sulatin (inf.) */
   If (starting with a double vowel)
      Remove 1st char              /* aalisin -> alisin (inf.) */
   If(1st char = 3rd char) & (2nd char <> 4th char) &
      (2nd char = 5th char)
      Remove 1st two chars          /* tatrabahuhin -> trabahuhin (inf.) */
```

Figure 3: The pseudo-code for analyzing "-IN" verbs.

It should be pointed out that matching a possible infinitive form, derived from the input verb, with one in the lexicon, is no better than generating the infinitive form from the derived root word and the affix used in the input verb. This is true if the correct root word is used. But if the system has to guess for the correct root word, it is possible that an incorrect root is used, which will make the translation fail. This is the case of the word "namatay" as reported in T2CMT (Fat, 2004).

For irregular verbs, they need to be modified a bit so that when they are passed to the section that generates the infinitive forms, it will generate the correct infinitive forms. For instance, in getting the infinitive form of an irregular verb "**binibili**," the analyzer consults Table 1 first. Since the verb "**binibili**" exists in the table, it changes the last "**i**" to "**h**." The verb "**binibili**" becomes "**binibilh**." This word is used to get the infinitive form "**bilhin**." Figure 1 shows the flow of activities as the analyzer executes.

Table 1: Example of some irregular verbs and their corresponding actions to take.

Irregular Verb	Action
binili, binibili	**Change the last "i" to "h"**
dinala, dinadala	**Change the last "a" to "h"**
kinain, kinakain	**Remove the last "i"**
sinunod, sinusunod	**Remove the "o"**
dinakip, dinadakip	**Remove the last "i"**
nilunod, nilulunod	**Change "od" to "ur"**
tinrabaho, tinatrabaho	**Change "o" to "uh"**
binasa, binabasa	**Add "h"**
binago, binabago	**Change "u" and add "h"**
ginawa, ginagawa	**Remove the last "a"**

There are several verb forms or categories in Filipino: UM-, MAG-, -IN, MA-, MAGKA-, PAKI-, I-, -AN, MAGPA-, and PA-IN (Aspillera, 1981). Each category has a corresponding algorithm, which serves as an option mentioned above. When using the analyzer, the verb is passed to any of the algorithms for determining the category that the verb belongs and until the right infinitive form is found. This is done because some words seemingly belong to a certain category but actually belong to different category. If the generated infinitive form is not in the lexicon, most likely it belongs to different category. When all options have been tried and the generated infinitive form does not exist, then it must be a misspelled word or an invalid Filipino verb. Figure 2 shows the pseudo-code for analyzing "UM-" verbs (active) and Figure 3 shows the pseudo-code for analyzing "-IN" verbs (passive).

5.Results and Discussion

The prototype morphological analyzer was fed with 1,050 Filipino verbs conjugated in three different tenses taken from (Aspillera, 1981) plus some verbs used in everyday life. The verbs belong to the UM-, -IN, -AN, I-, MA-, and MAG- categories only. Table 2 shows the preliminary results. In determining the tense of the input verbs, it returned 98.76% accurately, which is very promising. The 1.14% error for determining the tense was primary caused by the irregular verb forms. The undetermined tense, which is 0.095%, was caused by the wrong input word.

Table 2: The result of the initial testing.

Expected Output	Correct	Error	Undetermined
Tense	1,037 (98.76%)	12 (1.14%)	1 (0.095%)
Infinitive form	1,007 (95.90%)	42 (4.00%)	1 (0.095%)
Affix	1,032 (98.28%)	17 (1.62%)	1 (0.095%)

In determining the infinitive forms of the verbs, it got a 95.90% accuracy rate, which is also good as initial results. The error rate was 4.00% and almost all of them resulted from irregular verb forms. Out of the 42 errors, 14 are caused by failing to change the "o" to "u" of the penultimate syllable and 4 are caused by failing to insert "h" on the last syllable for vowel-ending roots without a glottal stop. The undetermined infinitive form, which is 0.095%, is purely caused by the wrong input word. As for determining the affixes of the verbs, the accuracy rate is only 98.28%. The error rate of 1.62% was caused partly by irregular verb formation but a large part of it was caused by the presence of "in" or "ni" that are always found any "I-" verbs in their past and present tenses. The undetermined affix was also caused by the wrong input word.

Many of the errors will be greatly reduced by refining the algorithm. It should be noted that the testing was just a single-pass because the lexicon is not yet fully functional. We can expect a higher accuracy rate than what is presented here, if the multi-pass approach will be used because some errors above will be solved by the multi-pass approach.

6.Conclusion and Future Works

A morphological analyzer that analyzes the Filipino verbs and produces their affixes, infinitive forms, and tenses has been presented. The prototype was tested with 1,050 verbs (regular and irregular) conjugated in three different tenses and the initial results showed high accuracy rate for determining the tense, the infinitive form, and the affix used. The higher accuracy rate is expected to even improve once the lexicon is in place and the multi-pass approach is already implemented.

Future work includes the implementation of the lexicon that employs an innovative way of getting the appropriate meaning to support context-driven machine translation system. We will also add other verb forms that were not yet included in the current prototype and perform further tests when all different forms have been taken into consideration. We will also increase the data set in the next testing.

References

Aspillera, P.S. 1981. *Basic Tagalog.* 8th revised ed. Manila: M&L Licudine Enterprises.

Bonus, D.E.J. 2003. *A Stemming Algorithm for Tagalog Words.* Master's Thesis, De La Salle University.

Dizon, C.B. 2006. *Buklod 2 – Batayang Aklat sa Filipino.* Quezon City: Book Craft Publishing Co., Inc.

Fat, J.G. 2004. *T2CMT: Tagalog-to-Cebuano Machine Translation.* Master's Thesis, De La Salle University.

Fortes, F.C.L. 2002. *A Constraint-based Morphological Analyzer for Concatenative and Non-concatenative Morphology of Tagalog Verbs.* Master's Thesis, De La Salle University.

Hisamitsu, T. and Y. Nitta. 1994. An Efficient Treatment of Japanese Verb Inflection for Morphological Analysis. *Proceedings of the 15th International Conference on Computational Linguistics*, pp. 194-200.

Hong, M., Y.-K. Kim, S.-K. Park, and Y.-J. Lee. 2004. Semi-Automatic Construction of Korean-Chinese Verb Patterns Based on Translation Equivalency. *Proceedings of the Workshop on Multilingual Linguistic Resource*, pp. 87-92.

Jun, J.S. 2007. Co-Event Conflation for Compound Verbs in Korean. *Proceedings of the 21st Pacific Asia Conference on Languages, Information, and Computation*, pp. 202-209.

Kim, D., Z. Cui, J. Li, and J.-H Lee. 2002. A Knowledge Based Approach to Identification of Serial Verb Construction in Chinese-to-Korean Machine Translation System. *Proceedings of the First SIGHAN Workshop on Chinese Language Processing.*

Nakamura, H. 2007. Two Types of Complex Predicate Formation: Japanese Passive and Potential Verbs. *Proceedings of the Pacific Asia Conference on Languages, Information, and Computation, pp. 340-348.*

Roxas, R.R. 1998. *A Prototype Machine Translator of Simple English or Filipino Sentences Using Interlingua.* Master's Thesis, University of the Philippines at Los Baños.

Chunking with Max-Margin Markov Networks[*]

Tang Buzhou, Wang Xuan , and Wang Xiaolong

Department of Computer Science and Technology, Harbin Institute of Technology Shenzhen Graduate School, Shenzhen, 518055,China

{tangbuzhou5125@gmail.com, wangxuan@insun.hit.edu.cn, xiaolongwang@insun.hit.edu.cn}

Abstract. In this paper, we apply Max-Margin Markov Networks (M3Ns) to English base phrases chunking, which is a large margin approach combining both the advantages of graphical models(such as Conditional Random Fields, CRFs) and kernel-based approaches (such as Support Vector Machines, SVMs) to solve the problems of multi-label multi-class supervised classification. To show the efficiency of M3Ns, we compare it with CRFs and other relative systems on the data set of CoNLL-2000 comprehensively. The experiment results show that M3Ns achieves state-of-the-art performance with strong generalization ability, which is better than CRFs.

Keywords: max-margin markov networks; graphical models; conditional random fields; support vector machines; generalization ability

1. Introduction

Text chunking is an intermediate step towards full parsing, which consists of dividing a text in syntactically correlated parts of words. Tasks of chunking are extracting the non-overlapping segments from a stream of data and identifying them with non-recursive cores of various types of phrases. It can be solved as sequential labeling.

Many probabilistic graphical models such as Hidden Markov Models (HMMs) (Zhou et al.,2000; Sang and Buchholz, 2000), Maximum Entropy Models (MEs) (Koeling, 2000), Conditional Random Fields (CRFs) (Lafferty et al., 2001), Semi-Markov Random Fields (Collins, 2002a) have been applied to chunking for their abilities to deal with structured data by taking advantages of the potential of interactions in a factored way (Jordan al., 1998). However, the condition of the probabilistic infinite samples assumption cannot be satisfied in practice and over fitting problem cannot be avoided.

On the other hand, the tasks of chunking can be recognized as a classifying problem, statistic machine learning techniques are also often applied to chunking and various machine learning approaches have been proposed for chunking such as SVMs (Cortes and Vapnik, 1995; Vapnik, 1999) and Boosting (Freund and Schapire, 1996). Compared with probabilistic graphical models, statistic machine learning approaches have no flaw of infinite samples assumption and have strong generalization guarantees theoretically, but they assume that the classification of each object (word or phrase) is independent and ignore some precious correlation information in structured data.

---

[*] This research has been partially supported by the National Natural Science Foundation of China (No.60435020 and No.90612005) and the Goal-oriented Lessons from the National 863 Program of China (No.2006AA01Z197).

22nd Pacific Asia Conference on Language, Information and Computation, pages 474–480

M3Ns is a new framework combining SVMs with graphical models. It is a SVM-like approach that could also deal with structured data efficiently like graphical models do (Taskar, 2003). In practice, M3Ns can not only make use of correlations in structured data, including sequential data, like CRFs, but also efficiently deal with high-dimensional features with high generalization performance like SVMs.

In this paper, we apply M3Ns to the CoNLL-2000 text chunking shared task using distinct chunk representations. In addition, in order to investigate the generalization ability, we compare the performance of M3Ns and CRFs on data sets of different sizes.

2. Max-Margin Markov Networks

In statistical machine learning theory, the task is to learn a function h: X→Y from a training set

$$S = \left\{ (x^i, y^i = t^i = t(x^i)) \in X \times Y \mid i = 1,.., m \right\}$$

of m i.i.d. samples , drawn from a fixed distribution Dx×y. The determinative function h is usual a linear function of features fj with coefficients w_j such that:

$$h_w(x) = \arg\max_y \sum_{j=1}^{n} w_j f_j(x, y) = \arg\max_y w^T f(x, y)$$

(1)

where n is feature space size.

For the sequence labeling problem, the data comes from a domain X×Y where X is a set and $Y = Y_1 \times Y_2 \times \ldots Y_k$ is a Cartesian product of the set of $Y_j = \{1,2,\ldots n_c\}, j=1,\ldots,k$. Be different from most common classification setting, Y is not a single label, but a joint label for an whole sequence.

According to basis SVMs framework, the formal representation of the sequence label problem is provided as follows:

$$\min_w \frac{1}{2}\|w\|^2 + C\sum_{i=1}^{m} \xi_i$$

(2)

$$s.t. \quad w^T \Delta f_i(y) \geq l(y_i) - \varepsilon_i, \forall i, y.$$

Where $\Delta f_i(y) = f(x^i, y^i) - f(x^i, y)$ and $l_i(y)$ (called loss function), and the equivalent dual problem is:

$$\max_\alpha \sum_{i,y} \alpha_i(y) l_i(y) - \frac{1}{2}C\left\|\sum_{i,y} \alpha_i(y)\Delta f_i(y)\right\|^2$$

(3)

$$s.t. \quad \sum_{i,y} \alpha_i(y) = C, \forall i; \quad \alpha_i(y) \geq 0, \forall i, y.$$

In sequence labeling problems, the loss function can be various, such as per-label loss and the proportion of incorrect labels predicted. Here, per-label loss function is used in experiments.

Both the number of constraints in the primal QP in (2) and the number of variables in the dual QP (3) are exponential in the number of labels n_c. They can not be solved by general approaches. In M3Ns, the marginal dual variables are introduced as follows:

$$\mu_i(y_t, y_{t+1}) = \sum_{y \sim y_t y_{t+1}} \alpha_i(y), \forall i, y; \quad \mu_i(y_t) = \sum_{y \sim y_t} \alpha_i(y), \forall i, y. \tag{4}$$

Where $y \sim y_t y_{t+1}$ denotes the full assignment y consistent with partial assignment: $y_t y_{t+1}$. In addition, the marginal dual variables must keep consistent between the pairs and singleton marginal:

$$\mu_i(y_{t+1}) = \sum_{y_t} \mu_i(y_t, y_{t+1}), \forall i, y.$$

(5)

Now, we can reformulate QP (3) in terms of these dual variables, and the original dual can be factored as follows:

$$\max_{\alpha} \sum_{i,y_t,y_{t+1}} \mu_i(y_t,y_{t+1})\ell_i(y_t,y_{t+1}) - \frac{1}{2}C\left\|\sum_{i,y_t}\mu_i(y_t)\Delta f_i(y_t)\right\|^2$$

$$\sum_{i,y_t,y_{t+1}}\mu_i(y_t,y_{t+1})=C;\ \mu_i(y_t,y_{t+1})>0\ \forall i,y.\quad \mu_i(y_{t+1})=\sum_{y_t}\mu_i(y_t,y_{t+1}),\forall i,y. \tag{6}$$

Where the number of variables $\mu_i(y_t,y_{t+1})$ is O(mn_c^2).

To solve the problem (6), Taskar supplied a new SMO and ES algorithms and showed a generalization bound for the task of sequential labeling (Taskar, 2003). In our experiments, we adopt SMO and linear kernel.

3.　Chunking

3.1.Chunking Representation

There is commonly one type of representation for text chunking — Inside/Outside representation. In order to describe the chunking more precisely, Uchimotoetal proposes a new representation for Japanese named entity extraction task (Uchimotoetal., 2000), and Xue introduces another new representation for Chinese segmentation task (Xue, 2003). We called them as Start/End representation. These two types are mentioned in (Taku Kudo and Yuji Matsumoto, 2000). In this paper, a new Start/End presentation will be introduced into chunking.

1、 Inside/Outside

This representation uses the following set of three tags for representing proper chunks (Ramshaw and Marcus, 1995).

I　Current token is inside of a chunk.

O　Current token is outside of any chunk.

B　Current token is the beginning of a chunk which immediately follows another chunk.

Tjong Kim Sang calls this method as IOB1 representation, and introduces three alternative versions — IOB2, IOE1and IOE2 (Tjong Kim Sang and Veenstra, 1999).

IOB2 A B tag is given for every token at the beginning of a chunk. Other tokens are the same as IOB1.

IOE1 An E tag is used to mark the last token of a chunk immediately preceding another chunk.

IOE2　An E tag is given for every token at the end of a chunk.

2、 Start/End

This representation was first introduced in (Uchimotoetal., 2000), and is used for the Japanese named entity extraction task. It requires the following five tags for representing proper chunks.

B　Current token is the start of a chunk consisting of more than one token.

E　Current token is the end of a chunk consisting of more than one token.

I　Current token is a middle of a chunk consisting of more than two tokens.

S　Current token is a chunk consisting of only one token.

O　Current token is outside of any chunk.

We called this representation as IOBES1 for convenience. Another representation was introduced in (Xue, 2003), and is used for the Chinese segmentation task. This method, called IOBES2, introduces two additional tags (B2 and B3) based on IOBES1 for chunks consisting of more than three tokens.

B2　A B2 tag is used to mark the first token immediately following B of a chunk consisting of more than three tokens.

B3　A B3 tag is used to mark the first token immediately following B2 of a chunk consisting of more than four tokens.

Similarly, we introduce another two tags (E2, E3) for chunks consisting more than three tokens.

E2   A E2 tag is used to mark the first token immediately preceding E of a chunk consisting of more than three tokens.

E3 A E3 tag is used to mark the first token immediately preceding E2 of a chunk consisting of more than four tokens.

We called this representation as IOBES3. In the CONLL-2000 text chunking shared task, the grammatical class of each chunk should be identified as a grammatical class label, and we represent them by a pair of an {I, O, B, E, S} label and a grammatical label. Examples of these representations of each phrase are shown in Table 1.

Table 1: Example for each chunk representation

	Inside/Outside				Start/End		
	IOB1	IOB2	IOE1	IOE2	IOBES1	IOBES2	IOBES3
He PRP	I-NP	B-NP	E-NP	E-NP	S-NP	S-NP	S-NP
reckons BZ	B-VP	B-VP	E-VP	E-VP	S-VP	S-VP	S-VP
the DT	B-NP	B-NP	I-NP	I-NP	B-VP	B-VP	B-VP
current JJ	I-NP	I-NP	I-NP	I-NP	I-VP	B2-VP	E3-VP
account NN	I-NP	I-NP	I-NP	I-NP	I-VP	B3-VP	E2-VP
deficit NN	I-NP	I-NP	E-NP	E-NP	E-VP	E-VP	E-VP
will MD	B-VP	B-VP	I-VP	I-VP	B-VP	B-VP	B-VP
narrow VB	I-VP	I-VP	E-VP	E-VP	E-VP	E-VP	E-VP
to TO	B-PP	B-PP	E-PP	E-PP	S-PP	S-PP	S-PP
only RB	B-NP	B-NP	I-NP	I-NP	B-NP	B-NP	B-NP
# #	I-NP	I-NP	I-NP	I-NP	I-NP	B2-NP	E2-NP
1.8 CD	I-NP	I-NP	E-NP	E-NP	E-NP	E-NP	E-NP
billion CD	B-PP	B-PP	E-PP	E-PP	S-PP	S-PP	S-PP
in IN	B-NP	B-NP	I-NP	I-NP	B-NP	B-NP	B-NP
September NNP	I-NP	I-NP	I-NP	E-NP	E-NP	E-NP	E-NP
. .	O	O	O	O	O	O	O

3.2. Feature template

Graphical models (MEMM and CRFs) are highly dependent on feature templates. For the sake of comparing the effectiveness of different types of features, four different templates are selected for experiments. Context predictions of the current token are sources for feature selection. We firstly introduce atomic features in Table 2 (Ratnaparkhi 1996; Koeling 2000), and four templates are shown in Table 3, Table 4, Table 5 and Table 6. Table 3 and Table 4 shows the templates based on pure lexical and POS information, while Table 5 and Table 6 shows the templates based on mix lexical and POS information. We called them tmpt-1, tmpt-2, tmpt-3 and tmpt-4 in turn.

Table 2: Atomic features

Feature tag	Feature remark	Feature tag	Feature remark
W0	Current word	P0	POS tag of the current word
W-1	The previous word	P-1	POS tag of W-1
W-2	The previous word of W-1	P-2	POS tag of W-2
W1	The next word	P1	POS tag of W1
W2	The next word of W1	P2	POS tag of W2

4. Experiments

We will firstly describe the text chunking data set in detail, then present the chunking performance and discuss it.

Table 3: Features based on pure lexical and POS information

Feature type	Features
Atomic features	W0,W-1,W-2,W1,W2,P0,P-1,P-2,P1,P2
pure features	W-2W-1,W-1W0,W0W1,W1W2,P-2P-1,P-1P0,P0P1,P1P2, P-2P-1P0,P-1P0P1,P0P1P2

Table 4: Features based on pure lexical and POS information

Feature type	Features
Atomic features	W0,W-1,W-2,W1,W2,P0,P-1,P-2,P1,P2
Pure features	W-2W-1,W-1W0,W0W1,W1W2,*W-2W-1W0, W-1W0W1,W0W1W2* P-2P-1,P-1P0,P0P1,P1P2,P-2P-1P0,P-1P0P1,P0P1P2

Table 5: Features based on mix lexical and POS information

Feature type	Features
Atomic features	W0,W-1,W-2,W1,W2,P0,P-1,P-2,P1,P2
combined features	W-2W-1,W-1W0,W0W1,W1W2, P-2P-1,P-1P0,P0P1,P1P2,P-2P-1P0,P-1P0P1,P0P1P2, P-1W-1,P0W0,P-1P0W-1,P-1P0W0,P-1W-1W0,P0W-1W0,P-1P0P1W0

Table 6: Features based on mix lexical and POS information

Feature type	Features
Atomic features	W0,W-1,W-2,W1,W2,P0,P-1,P-2,P1,P2
combined features	W-2W-1,W-1W0,W0W1,W1W2,*W-2W-1W0, W-1W0W1,W0W1W2* P-2P-1,P-1P0,P0P1,P1P2,P-2P-1P0,P-1P0P1,P0P1P2, P-1W-1,P0W0,P-1P0W-1,P-1P0W0,P-1W-1W0,P0W-1W0, P-1P0P1W0

4.1. Experimental Setting

Our data set comes from CoNLL-2000 shared task (Tjong Kim Sang and Buchholz, 20001). In this data set, the total of 10 base phrase classes (NP, VP, PP, ADJP, ADVP, CONJP, INITJ, LST, PTR, SBAR) are annotated. This data set consists of 4 sections (15-18) of the WSJ part of the Penn Tree bank for the training data and one section (20) for the test data. I In order to show the relationship between M3Ns and the data set size, we split the CoNLL-2000 training data set into parts with different size: 20%, 40%, 60%, 80% and 100%. For the kernel function, we use the linear kernel function with margin parameter C=1.

In the text chunking task, three rates are usually used to measure the performance of the systems. They are precision P, recall R and F_β.

$$P = \frac{\text{\# of correct proposed chunk}}{\text{\# of proposed chunk}} \quad R = \frac{\text{\# of correct proposed chunk}}{\text{\# of corect chunk}} \quad F_\beta = \frac{(\beta^2 + 1)RP}{\beta^2 R + P}(\beta = 1)$$

4.2. Experimental Results

In the experiment, we compare the performance of different representations and different templates. We also investigate the affects of different sizes of training data to validate the generalization ability of M3Ns.

Firstly, we use tmpt-3 with different **Inside/Outside** templates. Table 7 shows the results of M3Ns on the whole data set. We can see that there is no great difference between them. Secondly, we compared the performance of different templates with representation IOB2. Table 8 shows the experiment result that templates based on mixed lexical and POS information (tmp-3 and tmpt-4) are more suitable than templates based purely on lexical or POS information (tmpt-1 and tmpt-4). Besides, the second-order lexical features such as W-2W-1W0 are not always good. At last, in order to validate the high generalization ability of M3Ns, we compared

---

[1] http://www.cnts.ua.ac.be/conll2000/chunking/

the performance of M3Ns and CRFs[2] on the same training data sets of different sizes. Figure 1 shows the experiment result that the M3Ns achieve better performance and the curve of M3Ns goes more smoothly.

Table 7: Results of different chunk representations on whole data set

	Inside/Outside(tmpt-3)			
	IOB1	IOB2	IOE1	IOE2
precise	93.57	**93.72**	93.42	93.56
recall	93.38	**93.54**	93.40	93.54
F1	93.48	**93.63**	93.45	93.55

Table 8: Results of different templates on whole data set

	IOB2			
	tmpt-1	tmpt-2	tmpt-3	tmpt-4
precise	93.60	93.67	93.72	**93.74**
recall	93.21	93.30	**93.54**	93.41
F1	93.40	93.48	**93.63**	93.58

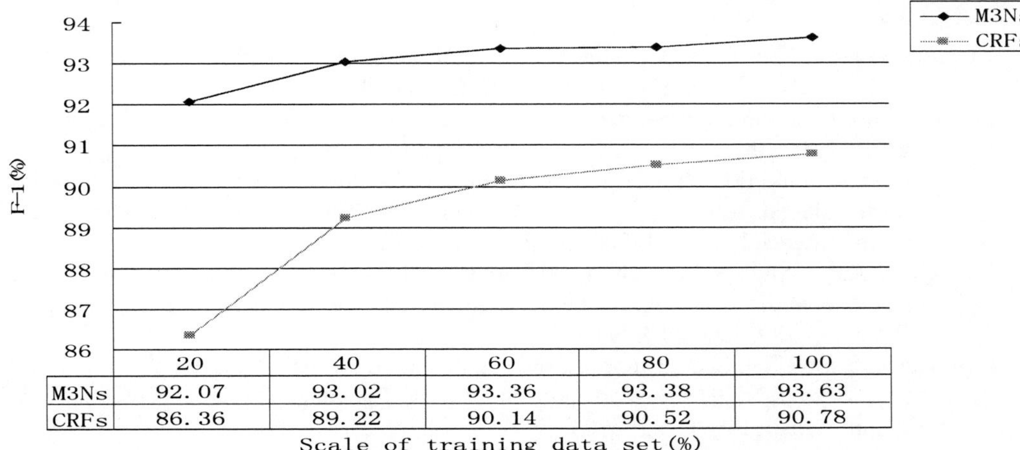

	20	40	60	80	100
M3Ns	92. 07	93. 02	93. 36	93. 38	93. 63
CRFs	86. 36	89. 22	90. 14	90. 52	90. 78

Figure 1: results for CoNLL-2000 training data sets of different size using IOB2 representation

4.3. Comparison with Related Works

In this section, we compare our results with eleven systems in CONLL-2000 (Tjong Kim Sang et al., 2000). Table 9 shows the performance of our system and systems in CONLL-2000.

Table 9: Comparison with systems in CONLL-2000

systems	precision	recall	F	systems	precision	recall	F
Our	**93.74%**	**93.54%**	**93.63**	Koe00	92.08%	91.86%	91.97%
KM00	93.13%	93.51%	93.48%	Osb00	91.65%	92.23%	91.94%
Hal00	93.13%	93.51%	93.32%	VB00	91.05%	92.03%	91.54%
TKS00	94.04%	91.00%	92.50%	PMP00	90.63%	89.65%	90.14%
ZST00	91.99%	92.25%	92.12%	John00	96.24%	88.25%	87.23%
Dej00	91.87%	92.31%	92.09%	VD00	88.82%	82.91%	85.76%

    Clearly, M3Ns performed better than all systems in CONLL-2000. Especially, better than single-algorithm systems: Rule-based systems by Villain and Day, Johansson, and Dejeanbetter; Memory-based systems by Veenstra and Vanden Bosch; and Statistical systems by Pla, Molina and Prieto, Osborne, Koeling, Zhou, and Tey and Su.

    Here, we should mention that some successful systems combined (Taku Kudoh and Yuji Matsumoto, 2001) or features (Zhang et al., 02) enhanced have been better than ours. However,

---

[2] http://crfpp.sourceforge.net/

it is not a fair comparison to our system since it is reasonable to believe that we can achieve appreciable improvement in the similar approaches.

5. Summary

In this paper, we introduce a text chunking system based on Max-Margin Markov Networks. Since M3Ns make full use of correlations in data like CRFs, they can achieve good performance using the same features of CRFs. Furthermore, due to the theoretical generalization guarantee, M3Ns also have special error toleration ability. In our experiments, we have shown that M3Ns perform better than CRFs with high generalization ability. The success of M3Ns in text chunking suggests that the approach might be applicable to other NLP problems such as Part Of Speech (POS) and Named Entity Recognition (NER).

Reference

GuoDong Zhou, Jian Su and TongGuan Tey, Hybrid Text Chunking. In: Proceedings of CoNLL-2000 and LLL-2000, Lisbon, Portugal, 2000.

Erik F. Tjong Kim Sang and Sabine Buchholz, Introduction to the CoNLL-2000 Shared Task: Chunking. In: Proceedings of CoNLL-2000 and LLL-2000, Lisbon, Portugal, 2000.

Rob Koeling, Chunking with maximum entropy models, Proceedings of the 2nd workshop on Learning language in logic and the 4th conference on Computational natural language learning, September 13-14, 2000, Lisbon, Portugal.

John D. Lafferty, Andrew McCallum and Fernando C. N. Pereira. 2001. Conditional Random Field: Probabilistic models for segmenting and labeling sequence data [A]. In: ICML-18 [C], pp.282-289. June 28-July 01, 2001.

Nianwen Xue and Libin Shen. Chinese word segmentation as LMR tagging [A]. In: Proceedings of the Second SIGHAN Workshop on Chinese Language Processing [C], pp.176-179, Sapporo, Japan: July 11-12, 2003.

Lance A. Ramshaw and Mitchell P. Marcus. 1995. Text chunking using transformation -based learning. In Proceedings of the 3rd Workshop on Very Large Corpora,pages 88–94.

Kiyotaka Uchimoto, Qing Ma, Masaki Murata, Hiromi Ozaku, and Hitoshi Isahara. 2000. Named Entity Extraction Basedon AMaximum Entropy Model and Transformation Rules. In Processing of the ACL2000.

Collins, M. (2002a). Discriminative Training Methods for Hidden Markov Models: Theory and Experiments with Perceptron Algorithms. In Proceedings of EMNLP 2002.

Michael I. Jordan, editor. Learning in Graphical Models. MIT press, Cambridge, MA, 1998.

Corinna Cortes and Vladimir Vapnik. Support-vector networks. Machine Learning, 20(3):273–297, 1995.

V. Vapnik. The Nature of Statistical Learning Theory. Statistics for Engineering and Information Science. Springer, New York, NY, 1999.

Yoav Freund and Robert E.Schapire. 1996. Experiments with a new boosting algorithm. In International Conference on Machine Learning(ICML), pages 148–146.

Ratnaparkhi, A.,"A Maximum Entropy Model for Part-Of-Speech Tagging," In Proceedings of EMNLP'1996, New Brunswick, New Jersey, USA, 1996, pp. 133-142.

Tong Zhang, Fred Damerau and David Johnson, Text Chunking based on a Generalization of Winnow. In Journal of Machine Learning Research, volume 2 (March), 2002, pp. 615-637.

Taku Kudoh and Yuji Matsumoto, Chunking with Support Vector Machines, In: "Proceedings of NAACL 2001", Pittsburgh, PA, USA, 2001.